Package Bodi

Package Body	Data Type	Implements Specification	Page
1.1	Stack	1.2	20
3.1	Stack	3.1	125
3.2	Dynamic Stack	3.2	127
3.3	Generic Stack	3.3	133
3.4	Queue	3.4	144
4.1	List	4.1	165
4.2	Linked List	4.2	171
4.3	Indexed List	4.3	177
4.4	Sorted List	4.4	185
5.1	Binary Search Tree	5.1	239
5.3	Heap	5.3	264
5.4	Priority Queue	5.4	268
	Radix Sort	6.2	347
7.1	Set of Discrete Objects	7.1	360
	String Hashing		371
7.2	Hash Table	7.2	383
	Variable Length String	8.1	413
9.1	Adjacency Matrix Graph	9.1	449

Rd : 1.8
2.4, 4.2
4.3 .

3.1 - 3.3, 3.4
4.4 - 4.7
6.1

1.3, 1.4

345 : 7.3
ch. 4 (esp 4.4 - .6)
ch. 5
ch. 9
7.4 d ch. 8

Daniel F. Stubbs

Neil W. Webre

California Polytechnic Institute

Data Structures with Abstract Data Types and Ada

PWS Publishing Company

Boston

PWS PUBLISHING COMPANY
20 Park Plaza, Boston, MA 02116-4324

I⟨T⟩P ™

International Thomson Publishing
The trademark ITP is used under license

PWS Publishing Company is a division of Wadsworth, Inc.

Printed in the United States of America.

2 3 4 5 6 7 8 9—97 96 95 94 93

Library of Congress Cataloging-in-Publication Data
Stubbs, Daniel F., [date]
    Data structures with abstract data types and Ada / Daniel F. Stubbs and Neil W. Webre.
        p.   cm.
    Includes bibliographical references and index.
    ISBN 0-534-14448-9
    1. Data structures (Computer science) 2. Abstract data types (Computer science) 3. Ada (Computer program language) I. Webre, Neil W., [date]. II. Title.
QA76.9.D35S75   1993
005.7'3—dc20

92-43791
CIP

Sponsoring Editor: MICHAEL J. SUGARMAN
Editorial Assistant: CAROL ANN BENEDICT
Production Editors: JOAN MARSH AND KIRK BOMONT
Manuscript Editor: HARRIET SERENKIN
Interior and Cover Design: VERNON T. BOES
Cover Photo: LEE HOCKER
Art Coordinator: LISA TORRI
Interior Illustration: ALEXANDER TESHIN ASSOCIATES
Typesetting: GRAPHIC WORLD INC.
Cover Printing: PHOENIX COLOR CORPORATION
Printing and Binding: ARCATA GRAPHICS, FAIRFIELD, PENNSYLVANIA
Apple ImageWriter is a registered trademark of Apple Computer, Inc.

The central topics of this text are the classical data structures of computer science and the basic algorithms for manipulating those data structures. While covering the topics included in most data structures textbooks, we enhance traditional approaches in a number of ways calculated to strengthen students' understanding and skills in design, analysis, and software engineering. Key features are detailed below.

The programming language Ada is used in the text to both specify and implement the data structures. However, as important as an appropriate language is in studying the subject, the core material is about the data structures, not about the language.

It would be very helpful for students to have some experience with Ada prior to using this book. Ada is an industrial level language designed to solve real problems in application areas. Many of the more advanced features of Ada relate to extensions of and changes in the way programs are engineered. Consequently, Ada is not as easy to "pick up" as FORTRAN or Pascal after programming in another language. The "Pascal subset" of Ada (the Ada constructs that accomplish roughly the same thing as the corresponding Pascal constructs) is easily learned. However, the real elegance and power of Ada come in extending beyond this subset using such constructs as packages, generics, and private types.

The book is organized around the basic structures of computer science: sets, lists, trees, and networks or graphs, with Chapter 1 introducing important concepts and techniques that form the basis of our approach throughout the remainder of the book. In addition, Chapter 6 centers on a set of sorting algorithms rather than on a particular data structure. Chapter 8 focuses on a special category—strings—of the linear data structures discussed in Chapter 4. Chapter 10 can be read at any time after Chapter 2. It discusses a number of design and implementation issues common to many of the data structures presented in the book, some of which are relatively subtle.

Key Supporting Features

ALGORITHM ANALYSIS

The algorithms presented are systematically analyzed using order-of-magnitude estimates of their performance. Sections 1.8.1 and 1.8.2 introduce the approach used.

ALGORITHM COMPLEXITY

Several complexity measures are used throughout the book to measure and record algorithm complexity. The most important of these is McCabe's cyclomatic complexity. The complexity and length are included as a comment for almost all procedure and function implementations in the text. This may be the first time these important analytical concepts are systematically included in an introductory text. Section 1.8.3 describes these measures and how they are used.

TIMING STUDIES

Timing studies are frequently presented comparing the measured performances of several data structures (e.g., comparing the performance of lists and trees), and variations in performance within a single data structure or algorithm (e.g., to reflect changes in performance caused by changing sizes of the objects in the data structure). Although the results of measuring actual run times of algorithms will vary by programming language, compiler, and computer system, the differences can usually be explained. In fact, explaining the differences gives insights into the algorithms and systems involved. Timing studies tend not only to reinforce the conclusions from order-of-magnitude estimates, but also to illuminate other factors not captured by those estimates (e.g., performance on small sets of data, relative performance of operations with the same order of magnitude). Section 6.2.5, for example, contains the results of timing studies for sort algorithms.

USE OF ADA

Ada was designed at a time when data abstraction research was maturing rapidly. It has a consistent syntax and powerful, easy-to-use facilities for data abstraction (packages), error handling (exceptions), generalization (generics), bit manipulation (representation clauses), and parallel computing (tasks). All but the last are used extensively in this text. Some less-complex features such as array slices and discriminant records turned out to be both useful and efficient for implementing a wide variety of data structures. We found Ada to be an excellent language both for introductory computer science courses and for the study of data structures.

ABSTRACT DATA TYPES

Data abstraction is the basis of object-oriented programming, which is the rapidly emerging standard paradigm for programming today. Each data structure that we study in this book is first specified as an abstract data type using an Ada package specification. In some cases, a small client program is then presented to demonstrate the use of the data abstraction. Then one or more implementations in the form of Ada package bodies presents code that meets and implements the specifications. Section 1.4 discusses the approach used.

GENERALIZATION

Ada's generic construct is a powerful and easy-to-use tool for generalizing the usefulness of the data structures that we design and study. Thus, for instance, we can design a generic list abstract data type that can be easily instantiated to handle any type of data object within the list. We consistently design our data abstractions as generic packages. Section 1.5.2 describes this approach to abstract data types.

ABSTRACTION SPECIFICATION

Ada's facilities for tightly specifying the syntax of a data abstraction are good, but there are no facilities for specifying semantics through the use, for instance, of assertions, preconditions, and postconditions. We have developed a systematic method for writing semantic specifications using a template and Ada comments. At the heart of the technique is the statement of pre- and postconditions

The authors of this book found designing and programming data structures in Ada a pleasure compared to other languages we have used—FORTRAN, COBOL, Pascal, Modula-2, C++, and C. There was only one small instance in which Ada let us down and forced us to find a workaround (sliding semantics; due for correction in Ada 9X). Workarounds were the rule rather than the exception in other languages. In Ada, there was a way, often elegant, to accomplish everything we wanted to do. Not only are the features of the language comprehensive, but the combination of features result in some extraordinarily concise and powerful specifications and code.

included in the specification of every procedure and function in the book. Section 1.4 describes the approach used throughout the text.

BIT MANIPULATION

In many high-level languages, there is no way to access and manipulate individual bits. Ada's representation clauses provide an easily used vehicle for doing so. We present data structure implementations—such as bit-map representations of sets, and radix sorting using a bitwise examination of sort keys—that make use of the inherent efficiency of bitwise accessible data. Section 7.2 presents an example of the use of bit manipulation techniques.

RECURSION

The use of recursion is introduced and used with increasing frequency as the book progresses. Appendix B presents a discussion of the basic principles of recursion and can be covered anytime after the study of stacks in Chapter 3. However, the importance of recursion is perhaps best demonstrated by its use in implementing important operations throughout the text.

Acknowledgments

When we began development of this book we received valuable suggestions, including complete units of code, from Hoyt Warner. Additional helpful comments were provided by Lois Brady and Jim Etheredge, our colleagues at Cal Poly. Several reviewers provided excellent suggestions for improving the book. They include Alan Cutting, Roger Williams College; Joseph E. Lang, University of Dayton; James Ludwig, University of Washington at Seattle; Dewey Rundus, University of South Florida; and Curt White, Indiana–Purdue University.

We'd like to extend our appreciation to Mike Sugarman, our editor at PWS-Kent, who provided a great deal of assistance throughout the development of the book. Our thanks also to Harriett Serenkin, who did her usual outstanding job of editing the manuscript.

We appreciate the professional guidance and support from many individuals who have been involved in the production of this text. We feel they have produced the most attractive data structures text available. We would like particularly to thank production editors Kirk Bomont and Joan Marsh. We would also like to thank editorial assistant Carol Ann Benedict, designer Vernon Boes, and art coordinator Lisa Torri.

Source Code

The source code for all packages in this text is available on the internet by anonymous ftp. Details regarding how to acquire the code are provided at the following address: COMPSCI.PWS@APPLELINK.APPLE.COM

We plan to extend the code provided by including, for example, additional operations in existing packages and perhaps additional packages. Procedures to test the abstract data type may also be provided.

A list of modifications and additions will be readily accessible.

Dan Stubbs & Neil Webre

*To skiing
and sailing*

Brief Contents

Contents

1

Introduction

We believe that the bulk of the problems with contemporary software flow from the fact that it is too complex. Complexity per se is not the culprit, of course; rather it is our human limitations in dealing with it. Dijkstra said it extremely well when he wrote of "our human inability to do much." It is our human limitations, our inability to deal with all the relations and ramifications of a complex situation simultaneously, which lies at the root of our software problems. In other contexts we (humans) have developed an exceptionally powerful technique for dealing with complexity. We abstract from it. Unable to master the entirety of a complex object, we choose to ignore its inessential details, dealing instead with a generalized, idealized model of the object—we consider its "essence." (Shaw, 1980)

Abstraction permeates the whole of programming. (Gries, 1979)

1.1 Introduction

In this chapter we will introduce the basic notions, approach, and terminology used throughout the book. Note that all sections do not have to be covered in detail before proceeding to the following chapters. Sections 1.1 to 1.5 should be covered. Sections 1.6 and 1.7 can be covered lightly or covered with material from later chapters. Section 1.8 is important and should be covered in detail.

Section 1.2 begins with the crucial ideas of data type and data structures. Section 1.3 follows with an introduction to the equally important concept of abstraction. Section 1.4 puts these concepts together to introduce abstract data types, which form the basis of the approach we apply to all the data structures in this book. Section 1.4 provides an example of the specification, use, and body (implementation) of a common abstract data type—stacks.

Section 1.5 discusses component objects that make up data structures, and Section 1.6 discusses the structures most often used to organize them— linear, set, tree, and network. Special attention is paid to the notion of linearity.

Section 1.7 discusses the effects of computer memories and processors on the storage and operation of data types. Section 1.8 addresses algorithm complexity and performance. It introduces several easy to calculate measures of algorithm complexity that we use throughout the book. The important order-of-magnitude method of estimating and predicting algorithm performance is also introduced.

1.2 Data Types and Data Structures

da-ta: Factual information (as measurements or statistics) used as a basis for reasoning.
struc-ture: Arrangement or relationship of elements (as particles, parts, or organs) in a substance, body, or system.

—The New Merriam-Webster Pocket Dictionary

Computers store and operate upon data. These data can normally be categorized into *types.* A typical computer or computer language has certain types that are *predefined*—that is, exist as part of the computer or language.

The language Ada, for instance, has the following types, among others, pre-defined:

boolean	float	integer
character	array	record

predefined types

Variables and constants of these types take values that allow computer programs to reason, calculate, search, display, and so on.

Each type has an associated set of values. These values constitute the type's *domain.* Three examples from Ada are the following:

Type	*Domain*	
boolean	false, true	
character	128 ASCII characters	
integer	integer'first .. integer'last	*-- Depends on the implementation.*

(*Integer'first* and *integer'last* are **attributes** of type *integer*—smallest and largest integer values, respectively, for the Ada implementation you are using. This varies from system to system.)

Each type has a defined set of operations on the values of the type:

Type	*Operators*	*-- Partial list only.*
boolean	and, or, not, xor, := , . . .	
character	&, >, <, =, := , . . .	
integer	+, −, *, /, mod, rem, := , =, . . .	

The domain and operations together form the essence of a data type.

The Ada data types shown above all have the property that they are somehow elementary or simple. In fact, the term for them in Ada is *scalar.*

Notice that for each, we normally consider their values to be *atomic;* that is, we consider each to have values that have no parts. Take the boolean values *false* and *true*. They are analogous to the bit values 0 and 1, respectively. They are not decomposable. They have no parts. The same is true for the character value *a* and the integer value 8. We treat each as a whole, single entity.

Integer values might be viewed differently. Take the value 154. Normally, we consider 154 to be a single, atomic quantity. We choose not to worry about its composition. We could, if we wished, decompose 154 into a sequence of base 10 digits in the following form:

$$154 = 1 \times 10^2 + 5 \times 10^1 + 4 \times 10^0$$

The same is true of real values. We normally consider 154.68 to be a single atomic value, but we could consider its base 10 parts:

$$154.68 = 1 \times 10^2 + 5 \times 10^1 + 4 \times 10^0 + 6 \times 10^{-1} + 8 \times 10^{-2}$$

For each of these types, we can decompose its values, but we normally choose not to do so. This will be true of many of the data types we study.

Atomic or scalar types are those whose values we consider to have no component parts. Notice that for each of the types, Ada provides no operators that directly allow us to access a component part of the values.

A **data type** is
1. A **set** of values called the type's *domain*
2. A set of **operations** on those values

Ada's predefined types *array* and *record* differ fundamentally from the simple types. They are *aggregates*. As an example, an array can be declared as follows:

type sample **is array**(1 .. 3) **of** boolean;

Sample is a data type exactly like the scalar types. It has a set of allowable values and a set of operations on the values. The domain of *sample* is small enough that it can be displayed in its entirety. It consists of the eight values shown in Figure 1.1.

(1) true	(1) true	(1) true	(1) true
(2) true	(2) true	(2) false	(2) false
(3) true	(3) false	(3) true	(3) false
(1) false	(1) false	(1) false	(1) false
(2) true	(2) true	(2) false	(2) false
(3) true	(3) false	(3) true	(3) false

FIGURE 1.1 Domain of the eight values of type *sample*.

These eight values are different from the values of scalar types in that each value has component parts. Take, for instance, the array value

(1) true   -- *An aggregate data value can be decomposed into*
(2) false   -- *component parts; we call each part a component*
(3) true   -- *object.*

which is a single value, taken as a whole, of type *sample*. Alternatively, the value can be viewed as having three component parts, with each part a value taken from the domain of type *boolean*. There is a boolean value associated with index value (1), another with index value (2), and a third with index value (3). These three component values are related to each other by the index value with which they are associated.

Aggregate type *sample* is a **structured type**. Each of its values is an aggregate of simpler objects, and these objects are arranged in a pattern with respect to each other; that is, with some **structure**.

In this case, the structure is provided by the array indexes. We will see in Chapter 2 that an array is successive values of a linear type (the index type) coupled one to one with values of a **component object type**. In Figure 1.1, the index type is a subrange of integers, and the component type is boolean. The template for the array, whatever the component object type, is

(1) component value
(2) component value
(3) component value

A **data structure** is a **data type** whose values
1. Can be decomposed into a set of **component objects**, each of which is either simple (atomic) or another data structure
2. Include a set of associations or relationships (**structure**) involving the component objects

A data structure is a special kind of data type. Since it is a data type, it must, like any other data type, have a domain of allowable values and a set of operations. To see what those operations for the Ada array type *sample* are, first, consider the operations that act upon objects of type *sample* as a single, whole entity. One such operation is assignment. If we have two variables declared in Ada:

a, b : sample;

we could assign a value to *a* and assign *a*'s value to *b* with the following Ada statement:

a := sample'(true, false, false);
b := a;

This takes the three boolean values comprising the value of *a* and copies them as a whole into *b*. The copy operation preserves the order of the components.

A second kind of operation for structured types is one that acts not on the array as a whole, but on one of the component pieces of it. If we had the boolean variable

c : boolean;

the Ada assignment statement

c := a(2);

copies into *c* the boolean value associated with the index 2, while

a(2) := c;

replaces the boolean value associated with index 2 with the value stored in *c*. The same kind of demonstration can be made for Ada records, which are also data structures as opposed to scalar data types. We will see that we can also build our own data structures using Ada's predefined data types and data structures as building blocks. Each will have domains, operations, component objects, and structure. Our emphasis in this book will be on data structures rather than on scalar data types.

EXERCISES 1.2

1. Explain the following terms in your own words:

data value	data structure
scalar data type	atomic data type
aggregate type	component object
data type	

2. What is the domain of Ada's type character? Is it scalar or an aggregate?

3. What is the domain of the enumerated type *day*:

   type day **is** (sun, mon, tue, wed, thu, fri, sat);

4. What is the domain of type *x*:

   subtype value **is** integer **range** −1 .. 1;
   type x **is array** (0 .. 2) **of** value;

■ 1.3 Abstraction

ab-stract: That which comprises or concentrates in itself the essential qualities of a larger thing or of several things.
—The New Merriam-Webster Pocket Dictionary

An *abstraction* of a thing has two qualities: It suppresses irrelevant detail, and it seeks to isolate the essence of the thing being abstracted. Section 1.2 illustrated how we could, in our minds, switch off and on an awareness of the details of an integer. We could treat the integer value as a whole, or we could view it as a sequence of base 10 digits multiplying powers of 10. Similarly, the array assignment statement

b := a;

treats the array values as single objects, whereas the statement

c := a(i);

requires an awareness that any array value is composed of component values organized in a structure.

The abstraction of an object or idea depends on the use we wish to make of it. The United States of America is a single entity from the view point of the United Nations. It is a collection of states from the president's viewpoint. A national weather forecaster has a completely different view of it, and so on. The abstraction we use depends on its intended use. Political boundaries are not an issue with a weather forecaster, but environmental and physical ones are. To a President, political boundaries are of paramount importance.

The process of abstracting is used endlessly and frequently by people. If we had to worry about every detail of every object with which we deal, we would not get far. We ignore details that are not necessary to accomplish what we are trying to do.

For instance, we can read data from a file or a terminal using Ada's procedure

text_io.get(x);

without knowing the details of how *get* functions internally.

The apparently simple *get* action may cause a whole host of complex actions by the underlying system. How this is done is usually of no concern to us because we simply wish to input some data. If we had to write all the code to implement the conceptually simple *get(x)* each time we used it, we would not get programs written very quickly and we would lose much of our productivity. That is one of the reasons high-level languages such as Ada are so important. They provide us with abstractions that hide details that are important but that would obscure the process. We lose some direct control over the computing system, but our productive effect is greater.

The use of ***procedural abstractions*** (subprograms) is a well-known technique that spares the programmer concern over details. Take the function *sqrt,* which returns the square root of its argument. It is supplied as part of a library of standard functions in many programming languages. It is actually an algorithm whose details normally don't concern us. All that matters is that it accurately computes and returns its result. If we want to take the square root of a variable *x,* we say *sqrt(x)* rather than programming the algorithm.

There is a second kind of abstraction common in programming, called ***data abstraction,*** which is the object of study in this book. We begin our study of it in Section 1.4.

Thus in programming, we try to deal at a level of detail that is close to the problem at hand in order to relieve ourselves of excessive work. This is true when we deal with both data and procedures. We deal with abstractions and not with the reality of the underlying implementation details. We deal at an appropriate ***level of abstraction.***

EXERCISES 1.3

1. List three real-life abstractions outside of computing that you deal with. Explain how each is an abstraction and how the process of abstracting helps you.

1.4 Abstract Data Types

How can we apply the notion of abstraction to data types? Consider the example of Ada integers. They are positive and negative whole numbers, including zero, that fall in a range *integer'first .. integer'last,* where the limits are constants that depend on the particular Ada implementation and computer system being used. We would like to be able to say that they are whole numbers in the range $-\infty .. +\infty$. Computers, however, no matter how large, have finite components. They cannot represent objects of arbitrary size. For a typical computer that allots 32 bits to hold integer objects, *integer'first* might be -2^{31} and *integer'last* might be $2^{31} - 1$. ($-2{,}185{,}232{,}348$ and $2{,}185{,}232{,}347$, respectively). These whole numbers form the domain of Ada's type *integer*.

Integers are whole numbers, and we usually treat them as having no component parts. Therefore, they form a scalar data type. Since they are a data type, they must have operations. We will write the entire description of Ada integers in a form called a ***specification.*** A specification is an exact statement of our abstraction written in a systematic way. Of particular importance is the fact that it has little, if any, reference to how integers are actually stored in the digital computer. This is an example of the principle of ***information hiding.*** Only the details necessary for the user to make use of integers effectively are presented. Specifications, therefore, provide an interface with the outside world.

■ SPECIFICATION 1.1 Integers*

-- *Domain:* *All whole numbers* k *such that integer'first* ≤ k ≤ *integer'last, where*
-- *integer'first and integer'last are determined by the implementation of Ada.*

-- *Exceptions:* *Each of the integer operations below either produces a correct result or*
-- *cause a numeric_error exception to occur.*

-- *Operations:* *In the specification below, assume an integer variable* k *and two expressions*
-- f *and* g *whose resulting values are of type* integer.

Unary Operators

+	**results**	$+f$: The same as f.
−	**results**	$-f$: Changes the sign of f.
abs	**results**	**abs** f: Absolute value of f.

Assignment

:=	**results**	$k := f$: f's value is copied into k.

Binary Arithmetic Operators (all return an integer result)

+	**results**	$f + g$: Adds f to g.
−	**results**	$f - g$: Subtracts g from f.
*	**results**	$f * g$: Multiplies f by g.
/	**results**	f/g: Divides f by g and truncates the result. $(g/ = 0)$
mod	**results**	f **mod** g: f modulo g. $(g/ = 0)$
rem	**results**	f **rem** g: f remainder g. $(g/ = 0)$

Binary Relational Operators

=	**results**	$f = g$: True if f and g evaluate to the same integer value.
/=	**results**	$f /= g$: True if $f = g$ is not true.
< (>)	**results**	$f < g$ $(f > g)$: True if f evaluates to an integer that is less than (greater than) g's value.
<= (>=)	**results**	$f \le g$ $(f \ge g)$: True if $(f < g)$ or $(f = g)$ is true $((f > g)$ or $(f = g)$ is true).

Range Operator

in	**results**	k **in** integer **range** $f .. g$: True if $k \ge f$ and $k \le g$.

Attributes

integer'first (integer'last)		
integer'pred(k)	**results**	Returns the smallest (largest) integer value.
(integer'succ(k))	**results**	Returns $k + 1$ $(k - 1)$.
	exceptions	Constraint_error if $k + 1$ $(k - 1)$ is outside of the integer domain.
integer'pos(k)	**results**	Returns k. -- *Although defined for integers, these are not useful.*
integer'val(k)		-- *They exist only because they are defined for all*
		-- *scalar types.*
integer'image(k)	**results**	Returns a string image of k with a leading space or "$-$".
integer'value(S)	**results**	Returns the integer whose string image is in string. -- S *is a string.*
	exceptions	constraint_error if S is not a proper image of an integer literal with an optional space or $-$ leading it.

(continued)

Specification 1.1 (continued)

Other attributes

Integers inherit other attributes because they are a subclass of other types. For instance, integer is a type and as such inherits attributes that are applicable to all types. Integer is a discrete type and inherits the attributes that are applicable to all discrete types, and so on. See Appendix D.

---

*Note the use of the results clause in specifying what each operation does. These are discussed in more detail in Section 1.4.1.

The one reference to details of how integers are implemented in the digital computer is in the domain statement. The lower and upper limits of the integer's domain are determined by the number of bits used to store each integer and by the technique used to represent integers using those bits.

Type *integer* is provided by most programming languages. Several other scalar types are in Ada. We can write a specification similar to Specification 1.1 for each.

There is a section in Specification 1.1 labeled Attributes. Ada provides a facility called ***attributes*** that can be applied to data types and data objects. Attributes are analogous to subprogram function calls but with a somewhat different syntax. They are predefined in Ada and are mainly interrogatory in nature. They are usually used to extract information about a data type or object.

In a few instances, attributes are used to set characteristics of a type or object. For instance, suppose we declare a type *count* that has a range 0 .. 255 and we want it to be represented in 8 bits (1 byte) in the computer's memory. First, we declare type *count;* then, we set its size by using the Ada attribute *size:*

type count **is range** 0 .. 255;
for count'size **use** 8;   -- *8 bits.*

Any variable of type *count* will be 1 byte in length.

Attributes are introduced in Section 4.1.4 of the *Ada Language Reference Manual* (1983) *(Ada LRM),* and a complete list of Ada's predefined attributes is given in Appendix A of the *Ada LRM.* Individual attributes are introduced throughout the *Ada LRM* as the objects that have the attributes are encountered in the text. An overview of Ada's type and attributes is given in Appendix A.

1.4.1 A Structured Data Abstraction—Stacks

We have seen how scalar data type *integer* was specified. It had the characteristic that it was one of the types predefined by Ada. To see how to design and specify data types that are (1) data structures rather than scalar data types and (2) are not predefined, we will use an example.

A common and simple data structure is a ***stack.*** It has a last-in first-out characteristic. We can consider it to be a list or linear arrangement of elements

```
6    2    7    8        4
                        ^
                       top
```

The right end is marked as the top of the stack. New items can be added only at the top, and items can be removed only from the top. The operations of adding and removing are called *push* and *pop,* respectively. If, for example, we push 5 then 1 onto the stack, we have

```
6    2    7    8    4    5       1
                              ^
                             top
```

If we pop the stack once, we remove 1 and get

```
6    2    7    8    4    5
                         ^
                        top
```

Thus by pushing and popping, the stack grows and shrinks.

Stacks are not predefined in Ada or, for that matter, in most programming languages. If we need to use a stack, we have to build our own or find one in a library. If we decide to build our own stack type, we must first decide what its abstraction is, then write it down in a systematic way as we did for integers in Specification 1.1. Here is a list of questions that present the characteristics of structured types we should write down:

1. What is the data type of its component parts?
2. In what sort of structure are the components arranged?
3. What are the constraints on its allowed values (domain)?
4. What operations are defined for values of the type?

Let's start by applying these characteristics to the stack type we want to design.

1. What is the data type of its component parts?

To make things simple, suppose the objects in the stack are natural numbers. (We will see later how to use Ada *generics* to broaden considerably the kinds of objects that can be in the stack.)

Component objects: Natural numbers.

2. In what sort of structure are the components arranged?

A stack can be conceptualized in a number of ways, but the simple idea of a linear arrangement of natural numbers with its right end marked as *top* is sufficient for our purposes. In addition, the objects in the list are in order of when they were placed (pushed) into the list. The most recently pushed object (newest) is on the right end, and the least recently pushed (oldest) object is at the left end.

Structure: The objects are arranged linearly in order of their arrival in the stack; the latest arrival is called the top object.

We have specified the type of the component objects and the structure. We now move to the third requirement in writing our specification.

3. What are the constraints on its allowed values (domain)?

How many objects can our stack hold at its maximum? Computers are finite, so there is some upper bound on the size of the stack. Let us arbitrarily say that our stack can hold no more than 100 natural numbers. (Later we will see several ways for allowing more flexibility in specifying the maximum size of the stack.)

In specifying abstract data types, we follow the statements of the kind of object in the data structure and the specification of the structuring of those objects with a description of their combined effect on the domain of the stack's possible values. We call this the **_constraint_** statement.

Constraints: $0 <=$ number_of_objects $<= 100$.

As you will see, _number_of_objects_ is a function and one of the operations we specify shortly.

Figure 1.2 summarizes the relationships among component objects, structure, constraints, and domains. At this point, we have limited the composite values that are allowed stack values. The domain is vast (any sequence of 100 or fewer natural numbers forms the domain), primarily because the domain of the natural numbers is so large.

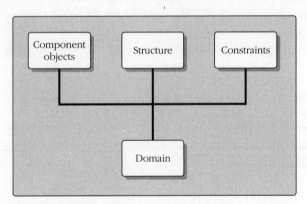

FIGURE 1.2 Determination of a domain of allowed values.

Finally, we are ready to address the last of our data structure characteristics.

4. What operations are defined for values of the type?

We need operators that allow us to do things with our stack values. We mentioned two operations—_push_ and _pop;_ there are others. Let's consider them one at a time, starting with _push_, the operation that adds new objects to the stack.

First, we write the *syntax* of *push* as an Ada procedure:

procedure push (the_object : natural);

Recall that Ada has two subtypes of integers that are useful:

subtype natural **is** integer **range** 0 .. integer'last
subtype positive **is** integer **range** 1 .. integer'last

The syntax of a procedure or function is a *protocol*—a form for activating the procedure and exchanging information with it.

We have the syntax of how *push* is to be used, but we have not specified exactly what *push* is to do or how the case of appending to a stack that has already reached its maximum length is to be handled. These issues address the *semantics* of the operation. There is no formal way in Ada to specify an operation's semantics. We have to create one.

First, we must specify the normal results of executing the operation when there are no errors. We do so by attaching a **results** clause to the procedure syntax specification in the form of an Ada comment:

procedure push (the_object : natural);
-- *results:*   *The object is appended to the stack as its top object.**

We have to address one possible difficulty. If the stack already held 100 objects, appending an extra natural number would result in a stack of length 101. The result would not be in the domain of stack values, and thus *push* could not be allowed. We, therefore, need some mechanism to handle failure of an operation to complete its execution successfully. We consider two means of dealing with the problem.

The first is to warn users not to try to *push* onto a stack that is already at its maximum size. The consequences of doing so will be undefined and the statement in the *results* clause will be invalidated. We make this warning by another clause in the semantic specification, which we call the **assumes** clause. It is a *precondition;* that is, a condition that the client or user must assure is met for the procedure to operate successfully:

procedure push (the_object : natural);
-- **assumes:**   *The number of objects in the stack is less than 100.*
-- **results:**   *The object is appended to the stack as its top object.*

The result of an attempt to execute a procedure whose precondition is violated is undefined.

What happens if a user disregards the notice and tries to *push* a new natural number onto a stack that has 100 objects? The answer is anything! The procedure may do nothing, or it may append a 101st character, or it may terminate execution of the program, or it may perform any of a number of other actions.

*All Ada comments begin with the two-character sequence "--".

We can view the **assumes** clause as part of a contract between the user and the implementor of the stack data structure. The results are guaranteed only if the stated conditions are met.

Notice that in the **assumes** clause we did not have to specify that *the_object* is a valid natural number. This is an inherent precondition that is stated in the procedure statement—in the syntax specification.

If the stack designer wanted the stack to contain only natural numbers whose values were in the range 0..30 but the syntax specifying the *push* procedure was

procedure push (the_object : natural);
-- ***assumes:***   *The number of objects in the stack is less than 100.*
-- ***results:***   *The object is appended to the stack as its top object.*

the **assumes** clause would have to include the additional constraint:

procedure push (the_object : natural);
-- ***assumes:***   *0 <= _the object<= 30 and the number of objects in the stack is less than 100.*
-- ***results:***   *The object is appended to the stack as its top object.*

On the other hand, if there were a type

subtype count **is** integer **range** 0..30;

and the procedure statement were written as

procedure push (the_object : count);
-- ***assumes:***   *The number of objects in the stack is less than 100.*
-- ***results:***   *The object is appended to the stack as its top object.*

then the extra constraint is accounted for in the typing of *the_object* as being of type *count,* and the **assumes** clause can remain as before.

In using the *push* operation, a user must ensure that the precondition is met, possibly by guarding calls to *push* as in the following **if** statement:

```
if number_of_objects < max_size then
    push(x);
    else ...;                              -- Take some other action.
end if;
```

A second approach to the error problem is to let the user attempt to *push,* then if *number_of_objects = max_size* report an error and failure of the operation. Ada's ***exception*** feature provides an excellent mechanism for doing this. Suppose we declare an exception *stack_full*. We can then write our specification using the exception by adding an **exceptions** clause:

procedure push (the_object : count);
-- ***results:***   *The object is appended to the stack as its top object.*
-- ***exceptions:***   *A stack_full exception is raised if number_of_objects = max_size.*

We write the **exceptions** clause of the specification in this brief way. It means that if *number_of_objects = max_size* when the *push* is called, that is, before *push* has done its work, nothing is done as a result of executing *push* except that a *stack_full* exception is raised and propagated back to the calling Ada unit and execution of *push* is abandoned.

Now, a user need not test a precondition in advance (although he or she is still free to do so) but must write an exception handler for the exception:

    push(x);
        .
        .
        .

exception when stack_full => ... ;   *-- Take corrective actions.*
        .
        .
        .

A third method to solve the problem follows the philosophy of the exception and can be used when the language has no exception mechanism; for instance, Pascal, C, or Modula-2. In this case, an explicit flag is provided that indicates whether execution of *push* has been successful:

procedure push (the_object : natural; done : **out** boolean);
-- results: *If number_of_objects < max_size when push is executed, the_object is appended*
--   *to the stack as its top object and done is true; otherwise done is false.*

Note the addition of another variable, *done,* the absence of both **assumes** and **exception** clauses, and the more complex **results** clause. Users now write the following sort of code:

    push(x, success);
    if not success
        then ... ;   *-- Take corrective actions.*
    end if;

In this book, we normally use **Ada exceptions to report error conditions in subprogram units.**

In the data structures designed and specified in this book, we normally use exceptions rather than preconditions since Ada has an exception mechanism, and explicit guards and tests using *if* statements can be avoided. This results in cleaner, more uniform, more concise code.

Now that we provided the methods for specifying operations, we move to other operations of the natural stack. From the preceding discussion we saw that an operation that tells the user the length of the stack is useful, even if exceptions are used. An example of such an operation as an Ada function is as follows:

function number_of_objects **return** natural;
-- results: *Returns the number of natural numbers currently in the stack.*

There is no need for an **exception** clause since there is no possibility of an exception.

We need some way of reading the top number on the stack. We therefore design a function *top* that allows us to see the top object without changing the stack:

function top **return** natural;
-- **results:**   *A copy of the top object of the stack is returned.*
-- **exceptions:**   *A stack_empty exception is raised if number_of_objects = 0.*
-- **notes:**   *The stack is unchanged.*

Here we see the use of the **note** clause to add extra comments that clarify the specification. Thus, the full range of clauses we use for a semantic specification is

Specification of Procedures and Functions

procedure   <name> (argument list . . .);

or

function   <name> (argument list . . .) **return** <type>;
-- **assumes:**   *Preconditions.*
-- **results:**   *Results of execution when the preconditions are true.*
-- **exceptions:**   *Exceptions that may be generated and the conditions that cause them.*
-- **notes:**   *Clarifying and additional comments.*

We continue in this vein. As it stands at this point, the stack can only grow. Now consider the *pop* operation that removes an object—specifically the top one—from the stack:

We specify a function ***top*** that returns the top number on the stack without removing it from the stack.

procedure top **return** natural;
-- **results:**   *Returns a copy of the stack's top number.*
-- **exceptions:**   *A stack_empty exception is raised if number_of_objects = 0.*

With stacks it is also common to combine the effects of the *top* and *pop* operations as we defined them above. Since we can ***overload*** the names of functions and procedures in Ada, we can design an alternate *pop* function:

function pop **return** natural;
-- **results:**   *The top object is removed from the stack and returned.*
-- **exceptions:**   *A stack_empty exception is raised if number_of_objects = 0.*

We now have all of the pieces of our specification, which we gather into Specification 1.2, which is an Ada *package*. A package consists of objects collected together into a compilation unit. Typically, a package has constants, types, variables, procedure, and functions. As we develop this text, we will see why these collections are useful and make sense for use with abstract data types.

There are two parts to packages—a *specification* and a *body*. The specification describes the view of the package the user or client sees. It has all a programmer needs to write code that uses the package. The body is the actual code and data structures that implement the package. Rather than try to understand all of this in the abstract, we will follow the development of a stack and see how it is used.

■ SPECIFICATION 1.2   Stack of Natural Numbers

-- *Component objects:*   *Natural numbers.*

-- *Structure:*   *The objects are arranged linearly in order of their arrival in the stack;*
--   *the latest arrival is called the top object.*

-- *Constraints:* $0 <= number\_of\_objects <= max\_size.$ -- *Number_of_objects and max_size appear below.*

package natural_stack_package **is**

    max_size   : **constant** natural := 100;   -- *Maximum stack size.*

    stack_full   : **exception**;
    stack_empty : **exception**;

    procedure push (the_object : natural);
    -- *results:*   *The object is appended to the stack as its top object.*
    -- *exceptions:*   *A stack_full exception is raised if number_of_objects = max_size.*

    function number_of_objects **return** natural;
    -- *results:*   *Returns the number of natural numbers in the stack.*

    function top **return** natural;
    -- *results:*   *A copy of the top object of the stack is returned.*
    -- *exceptions:*   *A stack_empty exception is raised if number_of_objects = 0.*
    -- *notes:*   *The stack is unchanged.*

    procedure pop;
    -- *results:*   *The top object is removed from the stack.*
    -- *exceptions:*   *A stack_empty exception is raised if number_of_objects = 0.*

(continued)

Specification 1.2 (continued)

> **function** pop **return** natural;
> -- **results:** *The top object is removed from the stack and returned.*
> -- **exceptions:** *A stack_empty exception is raised if number_of_objects = 0.*

end natural_stack_package;

Bear in mind that the specification is somewhat arbitrary. Many of its elements involve design decisions, and we are constrained by the general abstraction we are trying to achieve—in this case a stack. If we are designing a building, the specifications—blueprints—we produce are generally constrained by the type of building we are designing—a medium size library, a small branch bank office, a single family home, and so on. We would still be free to make many decisions on the design, but we are guided by the overall abstraction. It orients our design and both rules in and rules out certain features.

We have specified a data abstraction, *natural_stack_package,* that we invented. We have a concise, complete specification of the data type. What we have done is to write *functional specifications.* We have specified **what** the data abstraction is and what it does. We have enough for a user to use the abstraction in programming. What we have not addressed is **how** the abstraction is to be implemented in code. What we have written is an *interface specification* that is the meeting point for the user and the coder. The coder must write code that meets the specifications. If that is done, a user can use the package with confidence.

1.4.2 Using an Abstraction—
The Parentheses-Matching Program

Before looking at the code that implements the abstractions, let's look at an example of a user program that makes use of the abstraction without knowing how it will be implemented. In fact, that is the sign of a well-specified interface. It should be concise, precise, and complete.

To illustrate the point, we will write a program called *paren_match* that attempts to write open and close parens in expressions. An *expression* is a combination of operators and operands that combine to calculate a result. (See *Ada LRM,* 1983, Section 4.4 for a complete discussion.) In expressions, paired parentheses are used to indicate computation groups. The most common expressions produce a numeric or boolean result. Figure 1.3 shows some examples.

> If the user **needs to see the code** used to implement a data type in order to use the data type, then the **specification of the data type is deficient.**

$(((a + b)*d)/((e + f)*(a*c)))$ -- *Numeric result.*
$((x \text{ and } y) \text{ or } (z \text{ and } q))$ -- *Boolean result.*

FIGURE 1.3 Sample expressions.

One of the most common difficulties in writing expressions is assuring that the parentheses match; that is, that there is the same number of open and close parentheses. For our example, we will write an Ada program that counts the number of parentheses, finds the right-most open parenthesis or the left-most close parenthesis in the expression that is unmatched, and indicates its position. If we encounter three closed parentheses, we match them in the inverse order in which the open parentheses were encountered.

The key to implementing the program is to use a stack to store the positions of open parentheses as they are encountered. As each close parenthesis is encountered, the top open parenthesis can be removed from the stack since it has been matched. A pseudocode outline of the algorithm is given in Figure 1.4.

```
procedure match (expression : string) is
begin
    for i in 1 .. number of characters in the expression loop
        case (ith character of the expression) is
            when '(' => push i onto the stack;
            when ')' => if the stack is empty then
                            i is the position of the left-most unmatched ')';
                            exit the procedure;
                        else pop the position of the latest '(' from the stack;
                        end if;
            when others => do nothing;
        end case;
    end loop;
    if the stack is not empty then
        the top position on the stack is the position of the right-most unmatched '(';
    end if;
end match;
```

FIGURE 1.4 Pseudocode for the parentheses-matching procedure.

The program is shown in Figure 1.5; Figure 1.6 gives sample results.

```
with text_io, natural_stack_package;
use text_io;

procedure paren_match is

    expression    : string (1 .. 80);
    size          : natural;

    procedure clear_stack is separate;
    -- results:  Clears the natural_stack to empty.

    procedure match(expression: string) is separate;
    -- results:  Checks that the parentheses in the expression match. If not,
    --           points (with a '∧') to the first parenthesis not matched.
```

FIGURE 1.5 Parentheses-matching program using a stack of naturals.

(continued)

Figure 1.5 (continued)

begin

> put_line("Test the matching of parentheses in expressions.");
> put_line("Enter an empty line to quit.");

> **loop**
> > put_line("Enter an expression:");
> > get_line(expression, size);
> > **exit when** size = 0;
> > match(expression(1 .. size));
> **end loop**;

end paren_match;

```
    separate (paren_match)
    procedure match(expression : string) is
    begin
      clear_stack;                          -- Clear the stack if necessary.
      for i in natural range expression'range loop
        case expression(i) is               -- Treat kth character of e.
          when '(' => natural_stack_package.push(i);
          when ')' => if natural_stack_package.number_of_objects = 0 then
                        set_col(positive_count(i));
                        put_line("∧ mismatched");
                        return;
                      else natural_stack_package.pop;
                      end if;
          when others => null;              -- Ignore other characters.
        end case;
      end loop;
      if natural_stack_package.number_of_objects = 0 then
            put_line("All parentheses have a match.");
      else  set_col(positive_count(natural_stack_package.top));
            put_line("∧ mismatched");
      end if;
    exception
      when stack_full => put("This expression has more parentheses ");
                         put_line("than the program can handle.");
    end match;

    separate(check_parens)
    procedure clear_stack is
    begin
      while natural_stack_package.number_of_objects /= 0 loop
        natural_stack_package.pop;
      end loop;
    end clear_stack;
```

FIGURE 1.5 (continued)

$$(((a+b)*c/d)*(e+f)*(g/b)))$$
$$\wedge \text{ mismatch}$$

$$(((a+b)*c/d)*((e+f)*(g/b))$$
$$\wedge \text{ mismatch}$$

$$(((a+b)*c/d)*((e+f)*(g/b)))$$
All parentheses match

FIGURE 1.6 Sample output from program *paren_match*.

We constructed a procedure *clear_stack* that emptied the stack. The question of whether the procedure should have been provided as one of the procedures of the *natural_stack_package* is a design issue that has no clear answer. We provided enough information to make the operation possible using the specified procedures and functions but did not provide the operation directly as part of the package. Each procedure and function that we specify as part of the data abstraction makes the interface larger and more complex. Where we draw the line is the kind of question that makes design interesting.

The program shows that we can use the abstract data type without knowing any of its implementation details. All we knew was its specification. Languages like Ada have the ability to separate specifications from implementation code, thus hiding the actual details and code from the user.

We have broken our program into subprograms, but we have done it in a way that is centered on the data rather than on the steps the program must take in order to perform its task. Data decomposition, and its descendents **object-oriented** and **class-oriented** design, are powerful new tools in software engineering.

1.4.3 Implementation of the Specifications— *natural_stacks*

The specification is a form of contract between a user and an implementor of a data type. The method of constructing programs using specifications is therefore sometimes called programming by contract. A user can assume that the actual performance of the package will conform to the specification. An implementor—the person who codes the body of the package—must write code that also conforms to the specification.

Package Body 1.1 is an implementation of the abstract data type. The implementation is straightforward and meets the specification.

■ **PACKAGE BODY 1.1   Stack of Naturals—**
                          Implements Specification 1.2

package body natural_stack_package **is**

    type array_of_objects **is array** (positive **range** <>) **of** natural;
    subtype count **is** integer **range** 0 .. max_size;

(continued)

Package Body 1.1 (continued)

```
size       : count := 0;                          -- Number of objects stacked.
objects    : array_of_objects (1 .. max_size);    -- Array holding the stack objects.

procedure push (the_object : natural) is
begin
    size := size + 1;                             -- Raises an exception if size = max_size.
    objects(size) := the_object;
exception
    when constraint_error | numeric_error => raise stack_full;
end push;

function number_of_objects return natural is
begin
    return size;
end number_of_objects;

function top return natural is
begin
    return objects(size);                         -- Raises an exception if size = 0.
exception
    when constraint_error => raise stack_empty;
end top;

procedure pop is
begin
    size := size - 1;                             -- Raises an exception if size = 0.
exception
    when constraint_error | numeric_error => raise stack_empty;
end pop;

function pop return natural is
begin
    size := size - 1;                             -- Raises an exception if size = 0.
    return objects(size + 1);
exception
    when constraint_error | numeric_error => raise stack_empty;
end push;

end natural_stack_package;
```

Variables *size* and *objects* together form a ***representation*** of the stack. They are the lower level data structures—in this case, predefined data types—used to store the stack's contents and state.

The process we have followed is summarized in Figure 1.7. First, we choose data types, constants, and variables that will be used to represent the data structure we are designing. Then we code the functions and procedures that are specified. The figure shows the central role of the specification, which is the meeting point for users and implementors of the data type. The large box above the specification summarizes all of the pieces that go into a specification. The box below the specification summarizes the two parts of an implementation.

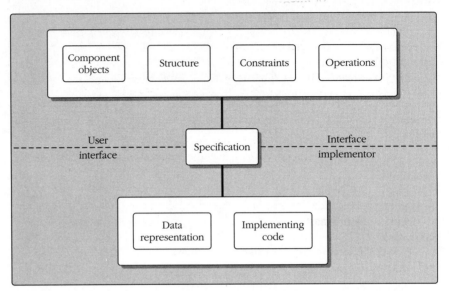

FIGURE 1.7 Summary of the data abstraction components.

This is the approach we shall take throughout the remainder of the book. That is, we will take an idea for a data abstraction, create a design, and write a specification for it as we did for Specification 1.2. We often write a small program that demonstrates the use of the data abstraction. Then we develop one or more implementations that meet the specification. No matter what implementation we choose, it must always meet the specification.

1.4.4 Advantages of Abstract Data Types

There are several advantages to approaching the study of data structures from the point of view of abstract data types. In Section 1.4.3 we saw several of them—precise, complete specifications, modularity, and information hiding. We will now look at four others—simplicity, integrity, reusability, and implementation independence.

Simplicity

An initial problem with the abstract data type approach is the use of the word "abstract." Unfortunately, many people infer that an abstraction is theoretical, abstruse, and therefore difficult to understand. In computer science, the process of abstraction is intended to have just the opposite effect. The goal is to simplify by separating the essential qualities from the inessential detail. With abstract data types, <u>we separate the abstraction of a data type from the code used to implement it</u>. Users do not need to know the coding details. In fact, those details may interfere with the use of the data type. Users do not need to know how type *integer* is actually stored in a digital computer in order to make effective use of integers. In Section 1.4.3 we just saw, for example, that we did not have to know the details of the representation and code that implements natural stacks in order to write a program that uses natural stacks.

The problem is that the amount of complexity with which our minds can cope at any instant is considerably less than what is often in the software being constructed. This is even true of the data structures we study in an introductory data structures text such as this one. Our approach is therefore to begin the study of each data structure by considering only the specification of its abstract data type, independent of its representation and implementation. This has the effect of simplifying the study of data structures.

It would be incorrect to infer that the study of representation and implementation is ignored or even given secondary consideration. After the specification of each data abstraction, we carefully consider, usually from more than one point of view, representations, implementations, and associated complexity and performance issues.

Integrity

The natural stack data type as specified in Specification 1.2 had some constraints associated with it. One constraint was that the stack could hold no more than 100 natural numbers. This constraint was enforced by the specifications. Look again at the representation of the stack as stored (and hidden from the user) in the package body:

```
type array_of_objects is array (positive range <>) of natural;
subtype count is integer range 0 .. max_size;
size     : count := 0;                    -- Number of objects stacked.
objects  : array_of_objects (1 .. max_size);   -- Array holding the stack objects.
```

Why were these types and variables placed in the package body and not in the package specification? If they had been placed in the specification, they would be visible to the user and available to him or her to manipulate. Suppose that the user's program had the statement

```
natural_stack_package.size := natural_stack_package.size + 1;
```

but had no associated storing of a new natural number in *objects(size)*. The stack would apparently hold *size* natural numbers, but only *size* − 1 have been placed in it. The stack would have lost its <u>***integrity***</u>.

We avoid these possibilities by hiding the representation of the data from users. The only way they can manipulate the variables in the package body is through the operations we designed and specified. Our approach is to implement data structures using Ada package bodies. They act as black boxes with push buttons and data lines. For each procedure and function there is a push button and data lines that carry their arguments in and out. The user cannot see the interior but can use the box by pushing the appropriate buttons and providing and receiving data on the data lines. The data structures and algorithms that implement the operations are *encapsulated* within the package body. The integrity of the data structures hidden within the box are protected. If the operations are implemented correctly, the integrity of the data can be guaranteed. Figure 1.8 presents a stylized view of the natural stack data type modeled after the commonly used schematic of a VLSI hardware chip.

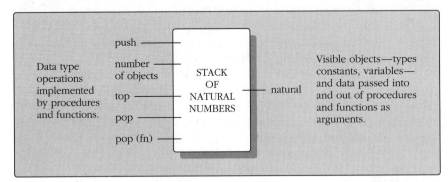

FIGURE 1.8 Encapsulation and information hiding in an abstract data type.

Note that the abstract data type approach lends itself to separating the specification of a data type from its implementation. The specification defines an interface that is done first (ideally) with no attention to the way in which the representation and implementation will be carried out. The implementation is then done carefully and in such a way as to assure preservation of the integrity of the data structure. Users of the data structure whose only access to it is through the defined operations can never compromise its integrity.

Ada provides another important mechanism for information hiding—the **private** clause. We will explain **private** clauses and make extensive use of them later.

Reusability

Understanding the specifications of a well-designed package, then linking and using a thoroughly tested and reliable package body requires a fraction of the effort required to design, specify, code, and test the package. Thus, reuse of existing packages can greatly increase the productivity of software developers. It is one of the potentially greatest productivity enhancers available. A problem is to determine which generally useful packages are needed.

Data abstractions are key components of any library of reusable packages. Programs are built on data types, and there is a fair degree of consensus on what constitutes the set of common data types. Several commercial and public domain libraries are available to developers. There is a parallel between these libraries of software modules and the catalogs of VLSI chips available to hardware designers.

Implementation Independence

Let us return to the natural stack data type. Suppose there are several users who are performing operations on stacks of natural numbers. We may not know what they are doing, but we do know that each user is permitted to perform only those operations in the specifications.

Suppose that it is desirable, or necessary (perhaps to improve performance), for us to change the way in which we implemented the abstract data type. Perhaps we have discovered a more efficient algorithm for one or more of the operations. What effect would changes in the body of the natural stacks package have on users who are already using it? We would expect no change except possibly in the performance (speed or use of memory) of the operations. The operations should act just as they did before the changes, assuming, of course, that the specifications do not change. Generally, changes to and recompilation of the body of a package require nothing more than rebinding (relinking the components) the system so the new package body is included. Most importantly, recompilation of the user units is not required.

Users are not dependent on how implementations are actually done, except possibly a change of performance (speed of execution, amount of memory used, etc.), as long as the implementation meets the specifications.

EXERCISES 1.4

1. Explain the following terms in your own words:

precondition	data type specification
component object	simplicity
package body	implementation independence
implementation	domain
exceptions	package
postcondition	information hiding
representation	data integrity

2. We said that the result of executing an operation when its precondition is not met is undefined. It is the duty of the user to assure this before execution. Users can, however, make mistakes. Discuss the extent to which the code implementing a procedure or function should check the validity of its preconditions. Should it check? If so, what should it do when it detects that the precondition is not met. What is the effect on the user?

3. We saw that for structured abstract data types, the datatype of the component objects and the structure specification join together to define the domain. What other factors enter into the determination of the domain? Give an example.

4. Modify the parentheses-checking program in Figure 1.5 to point to all unmatched parentheses in an expression rather than to point only to the first one encountered.

5. Explain in your own words the differences between a procedural abstraction and a data abstraction.

■ 1.5 Component Objects, Generic Types, and Mappings

We defined a data structure as a data type possessing component objects arranged according to some structure.

1.5.1 Component Objects

Some data structures manipulate their component objects in such a way that there is no need for them to be aware of the internal composition of the objects. Consider an array, which is a **generic** data type, in that we can declare, or **instantiate**, a specific array to have any one of a wide range of component object types. We can have, for instance,

type rec **is record**
    x : float;
    k : integer;
end record;
type day **is** (sun, mon, tue, wed, thu, fri, sat);

type i_array **is array**(1 .. 20) **of** integer;
type r_array **is array**(1 .. 20) **of** rec;
type d_array **is array**(1 .. 20) **of** day;

a, b   : i_array;
s, t   : r_array;
c, d   : d_array;
r   : rec;

Any array type treats its component objects as atomic objects. The array type operations above have no need to know about any structure in the component objects. We can write statements such as

a := b;
c(i) := d(i);

We could also say

r.x := s(i).x;

which makes use of the fact that type *rec* itself has component parts. The righthand side refers to the *x* field of the *i*th record of the array *s*. It is the reference to *s(i)* that fetches the record from the array. The addition of .*x* happens only after the array reference has been resolved.

We will see many data structures such as arrays, stacks, queues, and many kinds of lists that treat their component objects as atomic objects. These kinds of data structures manipulate their component objects as indivisible wholes.

1.5.2 Generic Types

Ada has a very powerful generic feature that allows us to build our own generic data types. Let us take the example of stacks again. The stack we designed in Specification 1.2 was constrained to a single stack of natural numbers. We could have more than one such stack by making the stack generic, then instantiating the stack more than once. Taking the *natural_stack* package specification, we add the word **generic** to the package statement, which becomes

generic
package natural_stack **is**   -- *The rest of the specification is the same.*
:
:

Suppose our program needed three different stacks of natural numbers, say *ns*1, *ns*2, and *ns*3. In the client program or unit that uses the stacks we include the three instantiation statements

with natural_stack;

package ns1 **is new** natural_stack;
package ns2 **is new** natural_stack;
package ns3 **is new** natural_stack;

Then, using the stacks in the same program requires that the stack being operated upon be explicitly identified. For example, the statement

push(x);

is ambiguous. Which stack is being pushed? If it were *ns*2, we must qualify the call to *push* as follows:

ns2.push(x);

Similarly,

if ns3.stack_size > 0
    then x := ns3.pop;
:
:

ns1.pop

and so on.

Now suppose that we needed—either in the same program or in different programs—stacks that will stack arbitrary types of objects in the same way we can have arrays with different component types. We can use Ada's generic facility to do this too. Suppose we want stacks in which both the type of object stored and the maximum stack size are generic. Again using the analogy with arrays, it is much the same as being able to instantiate an array not only with

All of the data types in this book will be specified as **generic types** since our interest is in the **structure and operation**, not in the kind of objects in the structure. This is possible because the logic of the operations is largely independent of the type of object being manipulated.

a chosen component type but also with an index range (which indirectly determines the size of the array). Suppose we want the maximum stack size to default to 100 if the user gives no directive to set it otherwise. Specification 1.3 is then the generic version of our stack. The syntax changes are slight and are confined to the new **generic** section that precedes the package statement.

■ SPECIFICATION 1.3   Generic Stack

-- *Elements:*   *Generic objects.*
-- *Structure:*   *The objects are arranged linearly in order of their arrival in the stack;*
--   *the latest arrival is called the top object.*
-- *Constraints:*   *0 <= number_of_objects <= max_size.*   -- *Number_of_objects and*
                                                                    -- *max_size appear below.*

generic

    type object_type **is private**;   -- *Type of object to be stacked.*
    max_size : natural := 100;   -- *Maximum stack size; defaults to 100.*

package generic_stack_package **is**

    stack_full   : **exception**;
    stack_empty   : **exception**;

    procedure push (the_object : object_type);
    -- *results:*   *The object is appended to the stack as its top object.*
    -- *exceptions:*   *A stack_full exception is raised if number_of_objects = max_size.*

    function number-of_objects **return** natural;
    -- *results:*   *Returns the number of objects in the stack.*

    function top **return** object_type;
    -- *results:*   *A copy of the top object of the stack is returned.*
    -- *exceptions:*   *A stack_empty exception is raised if number_of_objects = 0.*
    -- *notes:*   *The stack is unchanged.*

    procedure pop;
    -- *results:*   *The top object is removed from the stack.*
    -- *exceptions:*   *A stack_empty exception is raised if number_of_objects = 0.*

    function pop **return** object_type;
    -- *results:*   *The top object is removed from the stack and returned.*
    -- *exceptions:*   *A stack_empty exception is raised if number_of_objects = 0.*

end generic_stack_package;

Now the program *paren_match* in Figure 1.4 is changed slightly. The first few lines of the program become

with text_io, generic_stack_package;
                 -- Note change here to import generic_stack_package not natural_stack_package.
use text_io;

procedure paren_match **is**

    package natural_stack **is new** generic_stack_package(natural);
                   -- Instantiation of a natural stack with default maximum size = 100.
    use natural_stack;
    .
    .
    .

The rest of the program is exactly as before.

We could have made the maximum stack size different, say 50, by the statement

package natural_stack **is new** generic_stack_package(natural, 50);

or, alternatively, by

package natural_stack **is new** generic_stack_package (object_type => natural,
                                            max_size => 50);

We now have a general type of stack. The essence of the stack type remains, but the kind of object being stacked and the maximum stack size wait to be determined by the user at the time of use. We could instantiate a stack of objects of predefined type *float* and another of user-defined type *rec,* where

type rec **is record**
    x : string(1 .. 20);
    y : float;
    z : integer;
end record;

by the statements

package float_stack **is new** generic_stack_package(float);
package rec_stack **is new** generic_stack_package(rec, 50);

    Assuming

f : float;
r : rec;

the stacks are manipulated, as follows:

r := rec_stack.top;

float_stack.push(f);

rec_stack.pop;

and so on.

1.5.3 Keys and Maps

A central problem in computer science is that of finding the objects in a data structure whose values meet some condition or criterion. It is similar to the notion of assigning a unique identifier to an object. Examples include unique driver's license numbers assigned to people, unique bank account numbers assigned to accounts, unique Social Security numbers held by U.S. citizens, and unique identifying numbers assigned passports. In the case of each of these identifiers, only one object in the class of objects has a specific identifier value. Such unique-valued items associated with and perhaps part of objects are often called **keys**. Often we have data types that store their component objects in two parts—a key part and an associated data part.

A **map** associates data with keys. A bank teller, when supplied with a bank account number, retrieves all of the data on the account uniquely identified by the account number. Figure 1.9 shows the notion of a map from unique key values to data values. The mapping is one-to-one. Each key value is associated with at most one data object, and each data object is associated with exactly one key value.

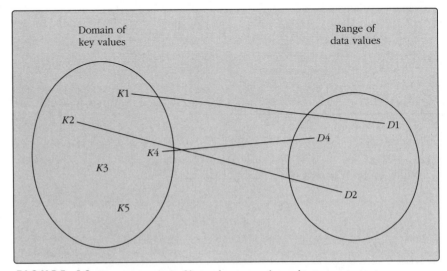

FIGURE 1.9 One-to-one map of key values onto data values.

A second type of mapping we might be concerned with is one-to-many. That is, each domain (key) value can be associated with more than one data object. Figure 1.10 illustrates the concept. An example is the selection of all students at a university who have a specific major, say computer science. A major value does not determine a specific data object (student) but rather a set of zero or more students. In the case of unique keys and a one-to-one mapping, each key value determined either zero or one student. We are going to be less concerned with one-to-many mappings in this book than with unique key value (one-to-one) mappings. Many of the data types we will discuss can be modified to include one-to-many mappings. These changes are often left as exercises.

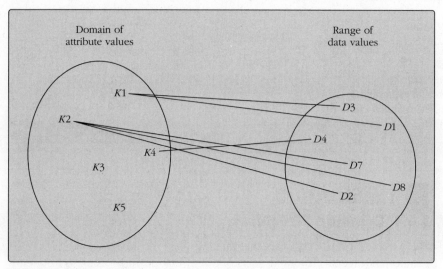

FIGURE 1.10 One-to-many map of key values onto data values.

In data structures that include mapping operations, the keys are considered to be embedded within the objects. We will see in Chapter 4 how this is handled generically.

As an example of a mapping operation, let us look at procedure *find* from the *mapped_list_package* data type of Chapter 4. Its specifications are given in Figure 1.11. This procedure provides a mapping operation between keys and data and tells the user whether zero or one data object has been

```
procedure find   (the_list      : mapped_list;
                  target_key     : key_type;
                  target_object  : out object_type;
                  found          : out boolean);
-- results:  The list is searched for a list object for which the object's key = target_key; if found,
--           the object is copied into target_object and found is true; otherwise found is false.
```

FIGURE 1.11 A procedure that uses maps.

found to match a given key. This sort of mapping operation will be found in a number of data types that we discuss in this book.

Most of the data structures we specify and implement have all of their component objects of the same data type. Thus, we'll see a stack of component objects all of which are the same type, a binary tree holding component objects all of the same type, and so on. Ada provides only one data type that has the property that it can hold components of different data types—records. A given record type can, and almost always does, have component objects that are of a variety of data types.

EXERCISES 1.5

1. Write a program using the generic stack package of Specification 1.3 that will
   a. Read in 10 integers entered in ascending order and print them in descending order.
   b. Read in 10 strings, one per line, that hold up to 20 characters each and are entered in ascending alphabetical order. Then print them in descending alphabetical order.

In the program, use two instantiations of the generic stack package.

2. Write three examples of mappings between keys and data that occur in everyday life. In each case, identify the key and the data. What is done with the data?

1.6 Structure
1.6.1 Common Structures

The specification of a data type includes the relationship among the data type's component objects. Several aspects of these relationships occur so frequently and are of such general applicability that we introduce them at this point. Most of this book is organized around them.

There are four basic structural relationships—set, linear, tree, and network; they are illustrated in Figure 1.12. A structure in which there is no relationship among the component objects other than common membership, such as the members of a university class, has a *set* structure. A structure in which each object, except the last, has a unique following (or successor) object, as in a character string, has a *linear* structure. A structure in which the relationship is hierarchical, as in a genealogy tree, has a *tree* structure. Finally, a structure in which each object is related to an arbitrary number of other objects, such as a network of cities and roads connecting them, has a *network,* or *graph,* structure.

In addition to these basic relationships, component objects of a data structure may be *totally ordered.* To understand the concept of totally ordered, consider the following.

In many cases of practical interest, relationships among objects will be determined by the relationships among the key values of the objects. Therefore, throughout this book we assume that the relationship among any collection of objects is the same as that among the key components of those objects.

If a, b, and c are any members of a set S, $<op>$ is a binary boolean operator, and

1. $a <op> a$
2. If $a <op> b$ and $b <op> c$, then $a <op> c$
3. If $a <op> b$ and $b <op> a$, then $a = b$

then set S is **partially ordered** by $<op>$.

If, in addition,

4. either $a <op> b$ or $b <op> a$ for any a and b in S

then S is **totally ordered** by $<op>$.

We know and are comfortable with the fact that the integers, when combined with the comparison operator ≤, form an ordered set. If a, b, and c are integers, the following are true:

1. $a \leq a$
2. If $a \leq b$ and $b \leq c$, then $a \leq c$
3. If $a \leq b$ and $b \leq a$, then $a = b$

Since items (1), (2), and (3) are true, we say that the integers are **partially ordered** with respect to the operator ≤. In addition, we know that any two integers can be compared in the sense that

4. either $a \leq b$ or $b \leq a$.

Adding (4) allows us to say that the integers are totally ordered by the operator ≤. We generalize this example to any set of objects (say S) and any relationship (say <op>) defined for pairs of objects from S. If a, b, and c are any objects from S and <op> is a binary boolean operator, then if (1)–(4) are true, S is said to be totally ordered by <op>.

What does this mean for the objects that are the basis of the data structures we will study? In an intuitive sense, a set of objects is ordered if any two of the objects can be compared and if, as a result of the comparison, we can establish that one object is larger than or follows the other or that the two objects are the same.

In many cases the key component of an object is either an integer or a real number. In such cases, the operator ≤ provides a useful ordering of the set of elements. It is also frequently the case that the key component of an object is a character string such as a name. In this case, the operator that orders the strings is different. As an example, let S_1 and S_2 be two such strings. We say that $S_1 \leq S_2$ if S_1 is the same as or "alphabetically" precedes S_2. The more formal word for alphabetical ordering is **lexicographic** ordering. More generally, if the strings have characters other than letters, the order is defined by the order of the characters in the character set being used. Ada uses the ASCII character set as a standard (see the *Ada LRM,* Appendix C, type character).

Finally, we need to consider the difference between an **ordered set** of objects and a **linear set** of objects. Our intuition about ordered sets is likely to be based on attributes of the integers (together with the operator ≤) since integers are so familiar. This is unfortunate in the present setting because the integers make up a set that is both ordered and linear, whereas an ordered set does not always have linear structure. Consider two examples. The first is the set of elements $S = \{a, b, c, d\}$, which are shown in Figure 1.13 linked together by directed arcs. Let x and y be any pair of these elements. We will say that $x \leq y$ if there is a directed arc or sequence of directed arcs that originates at x and terminates at y. We will also say that $x \leq x$. S, together with the operator ≤, forms an ordered set.

Now we define y to be the *successor* of x if there is a directed arc from x to y. The essence of linearity is that successors are unique. That is, each element but one (called the last element) has a single successor element, and that successor element is not the successor of any other element. In our

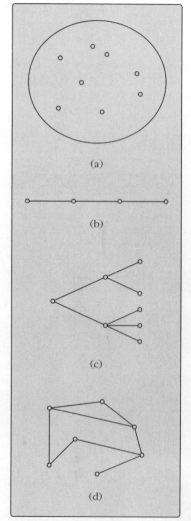

FIGURE 1.12 Common structures. (a) set; (b) linear; (c) tree; (d) network.

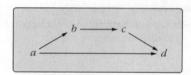

FIGURE 1.13 A directed graph (network).

example, *a* has two successors and therefore the relationship among the elements of *S* is not a linear one.

A second example of a set in which the elements are ordered but not linear is the set of real numbers together with the operator ≤. We are tempted to say that if *r* is any real number (Ada's predefined type *float* is a common example), the successor of *r* is the smallest real value greater than *r*. The problem is that such a number does not exist since between any two real numbers is an infinite number of other real numbers.

1.6.2 Linear and Ordered Structures

We just described two relationships that can exist among the elements of a data type or the component objects of a data structure. Each of these structures gives rise to a set of operations. Many data types are so common that we frequently use the operations without thinking about the fact that they are tied to an underlying structure.

If a set of elements is ordered, we can specify and implement a collection of relational operators (=, <, ≤, >, ≥, ≠) for them. Most data types that are predefined for high-level programming languages are ordered, and most of them include the relational operators in their specifications.

If a collection of elements has a linear structure, we can specify *find_the_successor, find_the_predecessor,* and *find_the_position* operations. These operations are possible because the elements to which they are applied have a linear structure. For instance, for Ada's predefined type *character,* the attributes

character'succ(ch)

character'pred(ch)

and

character'pos(ch)

are predefined. Type *character* is a predefined enumeration data type (the *Ada LRM,* Appendix C). All enumeration types are linear, with the successor of each element being the one immediately to its right in the type declaration.

There is a natural one-to-one correspondence between the elements of a set with linear structure and a subset of the natural numbers (see Figure 1.14). The first element is associated with 1 (or sometimes 0), the second with 2 (1), and so on, until the last element is associated with *n* (*n* − 1), the number of elements in the set. We frequently refer to the *k*th number of the set. This correspondence adds an implicit ordered structure to the elements. We call an element's associated natural number its *position.*

There is an annoying discrepancy in whether to start at 0 or 1 in the association. The problem exists within a single language. For instance, in Ada we can have two types with the following linear structure:

```
e—e—e—e—      Linear list
1  2  3  4  ···  Positions
```

FIGURE 1.14 Correspondence between linearly arranged objects and their positions in the list.

type day **is** (sun, mon, tue, wed, thu, fri, sat);
type line **is** string(1 .. 80);

d : day;
s : line;

The position of the first element of type *day* is *day'pos(sun),* which is 0. The first element of *s* is *s*(1). Although this is not a major problem, it requires being clear about the position of the first element.

1.6.3 Representing Abstract Structures

In this section we introduce the basic, most frequently used, terms for discussing the implementations of data structures. We base our discussion on a linear list of names. We want to store these names in a random access memory in such a way that we can represent the list's linear structures. Assuming the positions of the elements in the list are 0, 1, 2, . . . , there are several ways we can do this. We give three examples, Scheme 1, 2, and 3, and assume that each name occupies 8 bytes of memory.

Scheme 1

Scheme 1 implements the abstract linear structure by placing each name's successor immediately after the name in memory. It assumes 8 characters per name, padded with blanks if necessary.

Scheme 1

	Address	Name
Names stored in	1000	Milton
successive memory	1008	Dickens
locations without	1016	Eliot
regard to order.	1024	Arnold
	1032	Conrad

In order to retrieve an element, we must know its memory address. Given a position *k* of an element we want to retrieve, we can compute its memory address as follows:

address of element k = 1000 + k * 8

If an element is at memory address *addr,* we locate its successor by the computation

successor (addr) = addr + 8

Generally, in order to access an element of the list, we **calculate** its address.

We can do this because of the way in which we have **positioned** the elements in memory.

Scheme 2

Suppose we want to find a given name. If we use Scheme 1, we have to step iteratively through the names of the list using the calculation for successors. Suppose, however, that we arrange the names according to the value of their first letters.

Scheme 2

	Address	Name
Each name is positioned	1000	Arnold
in memory according to	1008	—
the value of its first letter.	1016	Conrad
	1024	Dickens
	1032	Eliot
	1040	—
	.	.
	.	.
	.	.
	1104	Milton

With Scheme 2, we can calculate the position of the name directly (assuming that each name begins with a different letter). Assume that each name is in

name : string(1 .. 8). :

Then

address (name) = 1000 + 8 * (character'pos(name(1)) − character'pos('A'))

Again, because of the way in which we positioned the names in the memory, a simple calculation does the job.

Thus, in Scheme 1 and in Scheme 2, we are able to *access* (find the address of) our data by *positioning* it carefully and systematically in the memory, then computing memory addresses by *calculation.*

Scheme 3

Each element in Scheme 3 contains both a name and an address. The address is that of the successor of the name. The address is not part of the data but is part of a technique for relating the data and preserving the linear structure. Assume that Scheme 3 takes an additional 4 bytes per address; the composite (name, successor address) therefore requires 12 bytes.

Scheme 3

	Address	Name	Successor address
The address of the	0988	—	1000
first name is in	1000	Dickens	1048
0988. From there	1012	—	—
the others can be	1024	Milton	1072
found by following	1036	Conrad	—
the links.	1048	Eliot	1024
	1060	—	—
	1072	Arnold	1036

The successor operation can be implemented, when positioned at the address of an element, by going to the address in the successor address field. The data can then be held in random locations in the memory but still be threaded together logically by the successor addresses. These addresses are often called *pointers.* Thus Eliot points to Milton, and so on. (Ada calls pointer types *access types,* although Ada's access types are more general and are not necessarily memory addresses.)

Dickens → Eliot → Milton → Arnold → Conrad → X

We have implemented the abstract list structure by *linking* related elements using pointers. Scheme 3, like scheme 1, provides sequential access only. We cannot calculate the address of a given name. We can only go to the first name, Dickens, then follow the pointers through the list until we encounter the target name.

Scheme 1 provides access by a name's position. Scheme 2 provides access by a name's first letter. Scheme 3 provides sequential access to the names.

We have illustrated the two ways in which we will implement the abstract structure of our data structures in the linear memories available to us in most computer systems. They are by positioning and calculation or by linking with pointers.

Implementing abstract structures in computer memories is done by

1. **Positioning and calculation**
2. **Linking** with pointers

EXERCISES 1.6

1. Explain the following terms in your own words:

   linear relationship   partially ordered
   set relationship   totally ordered
   tree relationship   lexicographic order
   network structure   ordered set
   positioning and calculation   linking with pointers

2. Which attributes (or combination of attributes) of commonly available data on the following entities have the unique identification property?

   a. Persons
   b. Universities
   c. Corporations
   d. Dogs

3. List two real-world objects or organizations that are organized according to each of the following structures:

   a. Set
   b. Linear
   c. Tree
   d. Network

4. Is the structure of the ASCII character set linear? Ordered? Totally ordered? Explain your answer.
5. Here is the Ada array type *sample:*

   type sample **array**(1 .. 10) **of** float;

   Are the elements ordered? Linear? If so, in what way?

6. Refer to the list of names in Section 1.6.2. Which of the implementation schemes is most efficient for each of the following operations? Why?
   a. Find a given name.
   b. Print all the names (in any order).
   c. Find the fifth name in the list in alphabetical order.
   d. Delete a given name. Assume you know the name's address.

■ 1.7 Memories and Processors

If an abstract data structure is to be useful, that is, used for computation, it must be implemented in code using a programming language, and that code must be translated into the machine code of a computer using a memory. A user can work with abstractions such as files, stacks, queues, and binary trees, but each of them must be implemented. The implementor must make the abstraction appear real to the user. For instance, in Ada we can use a string abstraction using Ada's predefined *string* data type. How strings are actually represented in the memory of the computer and how operations such as taking a slice of a string is actually carried out on the computer being used are the concerns of the compiler designer and writer.

Implementors should design implementations that are concise and that execute rapidly. Sometimes an implementor can make certain operations efficient at the expense of others. It therefore helps to know with what frequency each operation is used. Tradeoffs can often be made between the amount of memory used and the speed of execution of the code. These issues and others are part of the design of a solution to the implementation problem.

Implementors must also be familiar with the tools available for implementation—programming languages, memories, processors, and techniques for implementing structures—and must have a good knowledge of common data structures and their performance characteristics.

The remainder of this section reviews some aspects of computer memories and processors. Section 1.8 then looks at performance issues and how performance is measured.

1.7.1 Memories

Computers can remember. Like people, their memory systems are composed of different types of memories that come in many forms—fast (random access memory or cache) and slow (magnetic tape); large (optical disk) and small (registers); volatile (random access memory—needing constant power to remember) and nonvolatile (magnetic disk); random access memory (RAM), direct access (disk), and sequential access (tape); portable (floppy disk) and not portable (internal hard disk).

Most systems use a mixture of memory types. A typical microcomputer may have registers, RAM, read only memory (ROM), and disks (hard and floppy). Larger systems have a wider mix. Generally, the faster the memory, the higher the cost. We can think of our programs and data as being divided into pages (with several thousand bytes per page) and these pages migrating among the memories as they are used or become unused. Files migrate from disk into RAM, from there to cache, pieces from there to registers to be actively worked on. If data were changed, the page might migrate back out from cache to RAM, then to disk. Often, these migrations are invisible to the user, who is dealing with convenient abstractions such as arrays, records, and commands in a high-level language.

Sets of data stored on disks and tapes (among other long-term storage media) are called *files*. Most often, data in files are preserved after programs using them terminate. Some files are created by a program, then erased before the program terminates. These are *temporary* files.

The term *random access* refers to the timing and manner of access to data in memory. Random access memories have the ability to access all data in them by a memory address in a more or less constant amount of time. That is, the speed with which a piece of data is accessed is independent of where in the memory it resides. Typically, the times range from nanoseconds (10^{-9} seconds) to microseconds (10^{-6} seconds). For the remainder of this book, we assume a random access memory that behaves as if it were defined as the following type:

type RAM **is array** (0 .. memory_size − 1) **of** byte;

The type of memory being used has a definite effect on the performance of the data structures implemented on it. Some data structures and some algorithms exhibit excellent performance with random access memories but poor performance when direct or sequential access memories. The reverse is also true.

This book is primarily concerned with **data structures and algorithms** that are to be **implemented in random access memories**. The implementations chosen and their performance characteristics are dependent on this assumption.

1.7.2 Processors

A second important aspect of implementing data structures is the processor. In general, a *processor* is a device, either abstract or real, that allows a variety of data types and data structures and has a specified set of operations it can execute. Some processors are physical, such as an Intel™ i/486 chip or an IBM™ 3090 mainframe computer. Some are virtual, such as the C shell of a UNIX™ system or a compiler/run-time system such as Ada. Certain data structures and commands are available for the programming language BASIC and others for the language Ada.

High-level languages are most often designed to hide lower level details from users. In some cases, it is difficult. For instance, Ada's type *integer* might have a range of −32,768 .. 32,767 for an Ada compiler that compiled code to be run on a 16-bit microcomputer, but the range might be −2,185,232,348 .. 2,185,232,347 if the same code were compiled to be run on a 32-bit mainframe.

1. Milton
2. Dickens
3. Eliot
4. Arnold
5. Conrad

. . . .
. . . .

FIGURE 1.15 List of names in random order.

type array_of_names **is array**
(1 .. n) **of** name;
list : array_of_names;
test : name;

. . .
. . .

loop
    i := i + 1;
    test := list (i);
    exit when test = "Eliot";
    exit when i = n;
end loop;

FIGURE 1.16 Search in a random access memory.

test : name;

. . .
. . .

loop
    i := i + 1;
    get (names, test);
    exit when test = "Eliot";
    exit when 1 = n;
end loop;

FIGURE 1.17 Search in a sequential file.

At every level—hardware, operating system, and programming language—the processors must be chosen wisely to fit the task at hand. The processors used for the space shuttle are probably quite different from the processors used at your local bank. In this book, our primary concern is with the specification and implementation of data structures. We will generally not be concerned with low-level details such as exist at the hardware or operating system levels, although many of the data structures we study are used at these levels. We will be more interested in concepts and principles. We specify and implement the data structures we study in a high-level programming language in order to avoid distraction by irrelevant details. The language we have chosen is Ada. It is powerful, standard, and widely used; it also has excellent facilities for building a wide range of data structures.

1.7.3 Effects of Memory and Processors

Many of the conclusions that we will draw regarding performance will be based on a fact whose importance is easy to overlook. We have assumed that the data types we will consider are stored in a random access memory. Consider the operation we demonstrated earlier: Find the position in a list of names of the name "Eliot." Assume the names are stored consecutively but in no particular order, as shown in Figure 1.15.

If the list were stored in an array, *list*, the code segment might be as shown in Figure 1.16.

We can estimate that the time to fetch a name from the array [test := list (i)] is comparable to the time to test whether the name fetched is the one for which we are searching (**exit when** test = "Eliot").

Now suppose that the list of names is stored in a sequential file *names* on a magnetic tape. The equivalent search becomes that shown in Figure 1.17.

In this case, the time to fetch the name [get (names, test)] can be expected to be much longer than the time for the comparison—100–10,000 times longer is not uncommon. The speed with which the search is made is completely determined by the time to fetch each list name from its memory; in this case, a magnetic tape.

The logic of the two code segments is essentially the same, but the determinants of performance are quite different because of the characteristics of the memories. This is an example of a situation that occurs often. We will find that different algorithms may be needed to solve the same problem if the memories storing the data have different characteristics.

■ 1.8 Complexity, Metrics, and Performance

When we implement an abstract data type, we want to know the performance characteristics of our implementation. That's because we can write an implementation that meets the specification perfectly but is impossibly slow when executed. As an analogy, suppose we want an automobile for local errands

... would be efficient and would ... meet our needs, but it would be ...

... use of system resources? Does ... ? Does it require an inordinate ... ? Is it rigid in its use of memory, ... the amount of data? Can it handle ... ents be the same length? Are the ... nly some of the factors that must ... entation.

1.8.1 Metrics

Certain operations occur often when executing operations on data structures. ... list of names in Section 1.6.3 and perform the following ... position of the name "Eliot" in the list. In order to do so ... e list, starting with the first name and comparing each with Eliot. The time taken to accomplish the search is determined by the number of names in the list, the position of the name being sought, and the time to examine each name and step to the next. More simply, the time taken will be proportional to the number of names in the list. Over all permutations of the ordering of the list, we expect the name being sought to be halfway down the list. If the list is of size n names, the expected number of comparisons made would be approximately $n/2$. The time taken for the search would be

$$\text{time}_{\text{search}} \sim n/2$$

We often find, especially when searching, that performance of an algorithm is proportional to the number of comparisons, which in turn is some function of the size of the data structure. Thus, we use the number of comparisons as a *metric.*

Another commonly used metric for performance is the number of data object moves that must be made. For example, if we wish to reverse the order of the names in the list, we can write

```
for i in 1 .. n/2 loop
    swap(list(i), list(n − i + 1));
end loop;
```

where *swap* is a procedure that exchanges the values of two variables. *Swap* is called $n/2$ times, and each call takes three moves to swap the data. The time taken by the whole process is proportional to n, the size of the list. The number of data element moves is another common metric that we will use.

Time itself is a primary metric; comparisons and moves are used to predict times of execution of algorithms. The performance of algorithms is discussed in Section 1.8.2.

There are other characteristics of algorithms that are important; for instance, the size of the source code and its complexity. The size of the code

The two most **common metrics** we use for predicting performance are

1. The number of **data element comparisons**
2. The number of **data element moves**

will have an effect on the resources that have to be used to execute the algorithm; in this case, the resource would likely be bytes of random access and mass storage memory.

Complexity is more difficult to define. Complex code might be expected to be difficult to understand, to debug, to modify, and to maintain. The study of complexity has been an active field of investigation in computer science for many years. One of its primary objectives has been to define complexity and to find metrics we can use to measure it. This is discussed in Section 1.8.3.

1.8.2 Performance Estimation

We often use the mathematical notion of ***orders of magnitude*** to predict performance characteristics of algorithms and data structures. It is rough but effective. As an example, let's look again at Figure 1.15. If we assume that the name for which we are searching is in the list and every element is equally likely to be the target of the search, we can estimate that the expected number of comparisons that will be done in a search is

$$E_{compares} \sim (n + 1)/2$$

A certain amount of time is taken to do a compare, increment the index, and test for indexing to the end of the list. Call that time C_1. In addition, some time is taken outside of the loop to start and to finish. Call that time C_2. The expected time to do the search can be approximated as

$$E_{search\ time} \sim C_1 * (n + 1)/2 + C_2$$
$$= C_1 * n + (C_1/2 + C_2)$$
$$= C_1 * n + C_3$$

where

$$C_3 = C_1/2 + C_2$$

The values of the constants depend on many factors—the computer system being used and the language being used, among others. In general, we are not interested in the actual values of the constants but rather in the fact that the expression is a linear function of n, the number of names in the list. Doubling the list will double the time of execution. In fact, we do not care that the expression is strictly linear in n, only that the leading or dominant term for large n will come from the $C_1 * n$ component. We say that the order of magnitude of the expression is n, and we write it as $O(n)$; thus,

$$E_{search\ time} \sim O(n)$$

Now suppose that the expression that we determined was

$$C_1 * n + C_2/n + C_3$$

The order of magnitude of this expression is also $O(n)$. The reason is that as n becomes large, the second term becomes vanishingly small, the third term remains constant, and the first term grows linearly in magnitude.

More generally, if we have two functions $f(n)$ and $g(n)$ for n a positive integer, we can say that

$$f(n) \sim O\,[g(n)]$$

if we can find some constants C and N such that

$$f(n) \le C*g(n) \text{ for all positive integers } n \ge N$$

As an example, suppose $f(n) = 5n^2 + 2n$. Choose $g(n) = n^2$. Can we find constants C and N such that

$$5*n^2 + 2*n \le C*n^2$$

Dividing by n^2, we have

$$5 + 2/n \le C$$

When $n = 1$, the left side of the equation is at its maximum—7. As n increases, the left side decreases and approaches 5. Therefore, if we choose $C = 7$ and $N = 1$, the inequality is true for all positive n. We can then say that $5*n^2 + 2*n$ is $O(n^2)$.

For any $g(n)$ that has the property of having $f(n) \le C*g(n)$ for positive integers $n \ge N$, we can say that $f(n) \sim O[g(n)]$. Thus, we can say that

$$5*n^2 + 2*n \sim O(n^3), \text{ and } O(\sqrt{n}*n^2), \text{ and } O(n^2*\log n), \text{ and so on}$$

We are most interested in functions $g(n)$ that often occur in the study of data structures. They are shown in Figure 1.19.

One practical way to determine the order of magnitude of an expression is to set all constants to 1, then let n be large and see which term is the largest. In the example above,

$$10.3*n + 0.061/n + 13.7 => n + 1/n + 1$$

For $n = 1000$, setting all constants to 1, we get

$$n + 1/n + 1 = 1000 + 0.001 + 1$$

The dominant term is the first n, so we conclude that

$$10.3*n + 0.061/n + 13.7 \sim O(n)$$

Figure 1.18 is a series of expressions and their orders of magnitude.

$n*(n+1)/2$	$=> O(n^2)$
$15*n*\log n + 0.1*n^2 + 5$	$=> O(n^2)$
$1/n$	$=> O(1/n) = O(n^{-1})$
20 (or any constant)	$=> O(1)$
$(6*\log n + 3*n + 7)/(2*n - 5)$	$=> O(1)$

FIGURE 1.18 Examples of expressions and their orders of magnitude.

Expressions in more than one variable are slightly more complex. Suppose we have an expression in variables x and y:

$$2.3*x*y + 1.2*\log x + 3.3*x^2 + 6.3*x*\log y$$

As x and y both become large, the terms $2.3 * x * y$ and $3.3 * x^2$ will dominate. As x becomes large and y is fixed, the term x^2 dominates, whereas if y becomes large and x is fixed, the term $x * y$ dominates. If both x and y grow large, then both are comparable. Thus, we can say that the expression is $O(x*y + x^2)$.

If the amount of time expected for execution of an algorithm is $O(1)$, then its execution time is constant and is not affected by the number of data elements. If it is $O(n^2)$, then the time to execute grows as the square of the number of data elements. Doubling the amount of data results in the algorithm taking four times longer. Figures 1.19 and 1.20 give some idea of the relative magnitudes for common orders of magnitude. As you can see, for large n some orders of magnitude are dramatic improvements over others.

Order of magnitude	n = 8	n = 128	n = 1024	n = 1,000,000
$O(1)$	1	1	1	1
$O(\log_2 n)$	3	7	10	~20
$O(\sqrt{n})$	3	11	32	1,000
$O(n)$	8	128	1024	1,000,000
$O(n * \log_2 n)$	24	896	10,240	~20,000,000
$O(n^2)$	64	16,192	1,048,576	1,000,000,000,000

FIGURE 1.19 Orders of magnitude for sample values of n.

Smaller ⟵————————————————————————⟶ **Larger**

$$(\ldots \quad \bullet \quad 1 \quad \bullet \quad \log n \quad \bullet \quad \sqrt{n} \quad \bullet \quad n \quad \bullet \quad n \log n \quad \bullet \quad n^2 \quad \ldots)$$

FIGURE 1.20 Ranking of common orders of magnitude.

We will find that some sort methods execute in $O(n^2)$ time, whereas more advanced, efficient methods execute in $O(n * \log_2 n)$ time. To see how much better the latter is than the former, suppose $n = 1024$. Then,

$$n^2 = 1024^2 = 1,048,576$$

while

$$n * \log_2 n = 10,240$$

The $O(n * \log_2 n)$ method can be expected to execute in about 1/100 of the time required by the $O(n^2)$. It would seem that if the advanced sort took 1 minute, the simple sort would take about 100 minutes. That may not be the case. We have temporarily ignored the constant multipliers of the terms. The simple sort does simple things for each of its 1,048,576 operations, whereas the advanced sort does more complex things for each of its 10,240. This translates into the fact that the constant multiplying the $n * \log n$ term is likely to be larger than the one multiplying the n^2 term. There is often some transition value of n below which the $O(n^2)$ methods perform better than the $O(n * \log n)$ method. Stated another way, complex methods are often not efficient if the problem is too small. The point of transition can be determined by experiment.

Be cautious in concluding too much from order-of-magnitude estimates. If two sort methods, for instance, sort in times that are both $O(n^2)$, it does not mean they are equally fast. One may be three time faster than the other, a difference of great practical importance. Doubling the amount of data can be expected to quadruple the time each method takes to sort. The faster sort will still be three times faster than the slower.

We suggest you do the Exercises 1.8 relating to orders of magnitude to assure that you understand the concept because it will be used heavily throughout this book.

The use of orders of magnitude to estimate the execution times (expected, best, worst) of algorithms can easily be abused. Execution times are used because they are quantitative, are important to minimize, and produce numbers or orders-of-magnitude estimates that are easy to compare. Other less quantifiable aspects of algorithms may be at least as important. It is a well-documented fact that over the life of a software product, more time and money are spent maintaining and enhancing it than was spent developing it. Within the development activity itself, more time and money are spent on testing than on designing and programming. In addition, computer time is cheap compared to the cost of people time. Given these facts, choosing the "best" algorithms and data structures is not as clear as considering time to be the primary factor. Clear, simple, but less-efficient algorithms have the virtues that are important for efficient testing, maintenance, and modification. They may result in a lower cost overall for the software, even if they do use more machine resources.

> Since we learn a great deal from our efforts to construct more efficient algorithms, it is **tempting to focus too heavily on the execution times of algorithms as the sole measure of their relative merits.** Execution times are only one measure of an algorithm's worth. Other qualities may be at least as important and are often less quantitative and less well understood.

> Fast algorithms dramatically decrease run time for certain tasks. Designing them offers not only the promise of better performance but also a better understanding of the problems underlying all computational tasks. (Bentley, 1979)

1.8.3 Algorithm Complexity

Numerous schemes have been proposed for measuring the complexity of a program. The variety of proposals reflects the fact that there are many dimensions to the problem of measuring complexity. For example, we might consider a long algorithm more complex than a short one, or an algorithm with a large number of test-and-branch (e.g., if, case, loop, . . .) statements more complex than one with few such statements. We might also consider a program with nested test-and-branch statements more complex than a program with all such statements occurring sequentially. There are algorithms with long, complicated arithmetic expressions, algorithms with many subprograms and many arguments passed among them thereby creating complex interfaces, and so on.

After choosing any attribute as a complexity metric, we still need to determine a quantitative measure for that attribute. For instance, if we pick algorithm length, we are faced with determining how to measure that length. Is it the number of lines of code? the number of statements? How are comments (which many regard as a necessity for well-written code) included in the count, and so on?

A wide variety of complexity measures has been proposed. Some are complex and difficult to compute—especially without special software to do

> We use three measures of **algorithm complexity**:
> 1. **Unit length** as measured by the number of Ada statements and declarations
> 2. **Unit control flow complexity** as measured by the number of basic control flow paths
> 3. The **number of recursive subprogram calls**

the analysis. We have adopted several metrics to use in analyzing the software units in this book. Our criteria for metrics are

1. There should be only a few metrics.
2. The metrics should intuitively relate to our normal perception of complexity.
3. The metrics should be easy to compute—no special software should be required.

Requirement (3) does not rule out complexity analysis software. It simply means that in the absence of such software, we can, with reasonable effort, compute the metrics by hand.

Figure 1.21 presents four example blocks of code that we will use to illustrate the discussion of complexity. Our measures of complexity are in-

```
-- Length 4   Complexity 1
begin
    a := b;
    b := c;
    c := d;
    d := 3;
end;
```
           (a)

```
-- Length 4   Complexity 3
begin
    if a = b and c <= d/3 then
        if a < d+c/12 then a := 0;
        else a := 1;
        end if;
    end if;
end;
```
           (b)

```
-- Length 5   Complexity 4
begin
    case a is
        when c1 => result := s1;
        when c1 => result := s2;
        when c1 => result := s3;
        when others => result := s4;
    end case;
end;
```
           (c)

```
-- Length 2   Complexity 1              -- Notice that our complexity measure does not reflect the
begin                                    -- computational complexity of the block of code.
    a := ((t_rec + hav)**d)/sqrt(a ** 2 − float((beta * (del mod d));
    x := ((del − hav − 2 * gamma) ** par_del − 12.0/pi);
end;
```
           (d)

FIGURE 1.21 Blocks of code of differing complexity. (a) Four sequential statements; (b) nested if statements; (c) case statement; (d) two statements with complex numeric expressions.

cluded with most Ada implementations (bodies) as comments. How we compute them is the subject of the remainder of this section.

Unit Length

The number of lines of source code is a widely used and often disparaged measure of complexity. It measures, in a sense, the length of the program. Since programmers have some probability of introducing an error with each line of code they write, a long program is more prone to error than a short one. Lines of source code (often abbreviated as SLOC) is a crude measure of complexity since complexity also depends on what kind of code makes up the statements.

We will use the following measure of **length** for Ada units. (In this text, an Ada unit is normally a procedure or function.) We essentially count statements and declarations:

> The **length** of a program unit is the **number of semicolons** in the code of the unit, **minus one**. Semicolons in subprogram argument lists are included, but those in comments and literals are not.

One is subtracted from the number of semicolons so that a procedure or function with a single statement has length 1. Figure 1.22 shows an example.

```
function even (test_value : integer) return boolean is
-- Length 1   Complexity 1
begin
     return (test_value rem 2 = 0);
end even;
```

FIGURE 1.22 A function with two semicolons (;) and hence a length of 1.

This definition is debatable, as is most everything associated with length measures, but we will consistently use it throughout the text. Every semicolon associated with a unit outside of those in comments and literals is counted—including those in the argument list and in **with** and **use** statements. For

```
with random;
procedure sample (arg_1 : type_1; arg_2 : type_2; arg_3 : type_3) is
-- Length 9   Complexity 1
     temp_1 : type_1;
     temp_2 : type_2;
     temp_3 : type_3;
begin
     temp_1 := random;
     temp_2 := arg_1 + arg_2;
     temp_3 := arg_3;
end sample;
```

FIGURE 1.23 A function with ten semicolons (;) and hence a length of 9.

example, the procedure in Figure 1.23 has length 9 because it contains 10 semicolons: One semicolon appears in the **with** statement, two appear as separators for the formal parameters, three terminate the declarations of the local variables, three terminate the assignment statements, and one terminates the procedure block.

We can argue the fine points of how to count Ada statements, but since using lines of code, or statements, is a rough metric at best, the measure we have adopted seems adequate—and it is easy to determine. The use of various length and size measures to aid in the design of software is described in Halstead (1977).

Control Flow Complexity

The second complexity measure we will use was proposed by McCabe (1976) as the *cyclomatic complexity* or *cyclomatic number* of a program. McCabe's original paper is worth reading for further details. A discussion of applications of cyclomatic complexity measures appears in McCabe (1989). An interesting discussion of basic properties of complexity measures and an assessment of several specific complexity measures in terms of these properties is given in Lakshmanan (1991). Here we informally introduce cyclomatic complexity and describe how to compute it for Ada program units.

Control flow complexity attempts to measure the complexity of the flow of control in program units. In Figure 1.21(a) the flow is sequential from top to bottom. In Figures 1.21(b) and 1.21(c) there are optional paths through the code, and the path chosen by the executing program depends on the truth value of the expressions (predicates) in the **if** statements [Figure 1.21(b)] and on the value of *a* in the **case** statement [Figure 1.21(c)].

A field of mathematics called *graph theory* forms the basis for McCabe's work. It would be too much of a digression at this point to develop the graph theory necessary to give a full formal development of cyclomatic program complexity. Refer instead to McCabe (1976) for a formal discussion.

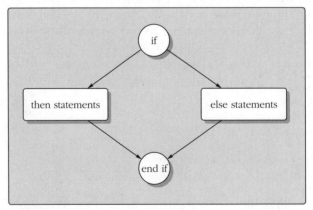

FIGURE 1.24 if statement control flow. Cyclomatic complexity is 2.

Algorithms execute their statements in sequential order until a ***control statement*** is encountered. An **if** statement is an example of a control statement. Figure 1.24 shows the flow of execution for an **if** statement. One of the two branches is chosen each time it is executed.

The cyclomatic complexity of a structured code segment with one entry node and one exit node is the number of **independent**, or **basic paths**, in the code segment. These basic paths have the property that they are independent of each other, and all paths through the code can be constructed as combinations of them. Thus, we are not determining all paths, but a basic set of independent paths that can be used to construct all paths.

McCabe showed that the cyclomatic complexity of structured code is the number of binary branches in the code plus 1. Since an **if** statement branches two ways, we count it as one binary branch and conclude that its cyclomatic complexity is 2.

It is this result, that the complexity of a structured program unit is the number of binary control branch points plus 1, that leads to simple techniques for computing complexity. We will, in this section, continue to tie our examples to the related control flow graphs, but we will soon see that the complexity of structured code can easily be determined without reference to the associated graph.

The control flow of a **for** loop without an **exit when** or **exit** statement within the loop is shown in Figure 1.25. It has one branch point (at the **for ... loop**) node. Its complexity is also 2.

Binary branches are seen in the flow graph as the nodes that have two outgoing directed lines. Flow graphs such as those in Figures 1.24 and 1.25 can be drawn for each Ada construct. We represent a group of sequential statements with no flow control statements as a node or box with the entire group of sequential statements in it. A statement calling a procedure or function is treated as a sequential statement.

Case statements deserve special mention. A **case** statement with n **when** clauses can be replaced by $n - 1$ nested **if** statements. Thus, the number of binary branches in a **case** statement with n **when** clauses is $n - 1$.

We can apply the computation of complexity to the examples in Figure 1.21. The results are summarized in Figure 1.26.

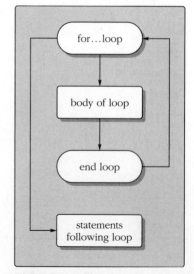

FIGURE 1.25 Flow graph for a **for** loop. Cyclomatic complexity is 2.

Figure	Binary branches	Cyclomatic complexity
1.21(a)	0	1
1.21(b)	2	3
1.21(c)	3	4
1.21(d)	0	1

FIGURE 1.26 Complexity computations for Figure 1.21.

We can apply the technique to a larger unit such as a procedure or function. Figure 1.27 shows procedure *match* that was copied from Figure 1.5

```
(1)    separate (paren_match)
(2)    procedure match(expression : string) is
(3)
(4)    -- Length 16    Complexity 7
(5)
(6)    begin
(7)        clear_stack;                              -- Clear the stack if necessary.
(8)        for i in natural range expression'range loop
(9)          case expression(i) is                   -- Treat kth character of e.
(10)            when '(' => push(i);
(11)            when ')' => if number_of_objects = 0 then
(12)                               set_col(positive_count(i));
(13)                               put_line("∧ mismatched");
(14)                               return;
(15)                        else pop;
(16)                        end if;
(17)            when others => null;                 -- Ignore other characters.
(18)          end case;
(19)        end loop;
(20)        if number_of_objects = 0 then
(21)               put_line("All parentheses have a match.");
(22)        else   set_col(positive_count(top));
(23)               put_line("∧ mismatched");
(24)        end if;
(25)    exception
(26)        when stack_full => put("This expression has more parentheses");
(27)        when stack_full => put_line("than the program can handle.");
(28)    end match;
```

FIGURE 1.27 Copy of the *match* procedure from Figure 1.5.

of this chapter. It is a subprogram of the parentheses-matching example of the use of stacks in Section 1.4.2. Line numbers are added for later reference.

An Ada unit such as a procedure or function has a control flow graph consisting of the Ada construct flow graphs fitted together to form a flow graph for the whole unit. Figure 1.28 shows the flow graph for *match*. The flow graph of the **exception** section of the procedure is shown as a disconnected component of the overall flow graph.

Execution can flow in any allowable path through the flow graph from the **begin** to the **end** statements of the procedure. In the case of unusual or error conditions, execution can be aborted at any point and switched to the **exception** section. There are many paths possible between the **begin** and **end** statements. Any of these paths can be constructed from combinations of the procedure's basic paths. The number of those basic paths is, as demonstrated for the individual **if**, **for**, and **case** statements, the number of binary branches plus 1.

For Ada, the rules for counting binary branches are given in Figure 1.29.

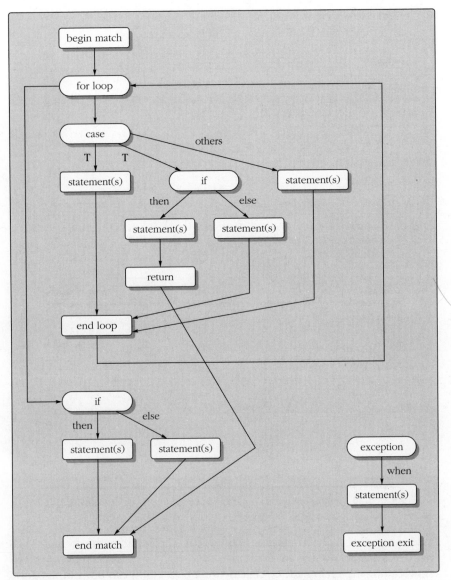

FIGURE 1.28 Flow graph for procedure *match* shown in Figure 1.27.

Using these rules, the complexity of procedure *match* is computed as shown in Figure 1.30.

Thus, in applying the rules of Figure 1.29 to procedure *match*, we find that its cyclomatic complexity is 7. Note that we did not have to refer to the flow graph to compute the complexity. We worked directly from the source code using the counting rules.

We could work directly from the flow graphs and compute the cyclomatic complexity in another way. The flow graph is composed of nodes and edges

The **binary branch count** for an Ada unit is as follows:

Add 1 for each

1. **if** statement
2. **elsif** clause of an **if** statement
3. **while ... loop** statement
4. **for ... loop** statement
5. **when** clause of a **case** statement
6. **exit when** clause of a **loop**
7. **when** clause of an **exception** section

Subtract 1 for each

1. **case** statement

The ***cyclomatic complexity*** of an Ada unit is the ***Ada binary branch count plus 1.***

FIGURE 1.29 Rules for computing the complexity of an Ada unit. (These rules do not take Ada ***tasks*** into consideration.)

Construct	Line number	Contribution
for ... loop	8	+1
case	9	−1
when	10	+1
when	11	+1
if	11	+1
when	17	+1
if	20	+1
when	26	+1
Total		6
Plus 1		+1
Complexity		7

FIGURE 1.30 Computing the complexity of procedure *match* of Figure 1.27.

(the directional lines connecting the nodes). The flow graph of Figure 1.28 has two components that are unconnected to each other by any edge. McCabe showed that the cyclomatic complexity of a flow graph can be computed as

$$complexity = e - n + 2*p$$

where e is the number of edges, n the number of nodes, and p the number of disconnected components. For the flow graph of procedure *match,* we have $n = 17$, $e = 20$, and $p = 2$. Therefore,

$$complexity = 20 - 17 + 2*2 = 7$$

As a practical matter, programmers have source code, not flow graphs, at their disposal. Since the two methods give the same result, the binary branch count is almost always the most useful method, and it is the one we adopt.

McCabe also determined a method for dealing with units that are broken down into subprograms:

> The **overall complexity** of a parent unit and its subprograms is the **sum** of the **complexity of the parent unit** and the **complexities of the individual subprograms.**

An **exception** section can be treated in the same way as a subprogram— that is, as a disconnected portion of the flow graph. When computing the complexity of a unit that has an **exception** section, however, we include a count of the **when**'s in the **exception** clause into the overall binary branch count of the unit. This gives the same result as computing the complexities of the main body and **exception** section separately, then adding them.

McCabe noted that program units with a cyclomatic complexity greater than approximately 10 tend to be more error prone. This has subsequently been verified by experiments. If the complexity is above 10, the programmer should consider introducing further modularity by the creation of more procedures and/or functions. From now on, for the sake of brevity, we will shorten the term "cyclomatic complexity" to "complexity."

Program units with **cyclomatic complexity greater than 10** are more error prone and should be decomposed into subprograms.

Recursive Subprogram Calls

The third measure of the complexity of a subprogram is a measure of its degree of recursiveness. We call a subprogram *recursive* if there are one or more places in its code at which the subprogram calls itself or if it calls another subprogram or sequence of subprograms that eventually results in another call to the original subprogram before it is finished with the original activation. Appendix B is concerned with recursion.

We will include in our complexity measures of an algorithm the number of recursive calls, whether direct or indirect recursion, in the unit's code.

Indicating the Complexity and Performance of Subprograms

We will indicate the complexity and performance of each procedure or function that we present in this book by including an Ada comment in the body of the unit directly following the procedure or function statement. We use a template with components as follows:

-- *Length ??   Complexity ??   Recursion ??   Performance O(??)*

When the subprogram is not recursive, we will omit the *recursion* measure since it is zero. Thus, for procedure *match* of Figure 1.27, we have

```
separate (paren_match)
procedure match(expression : string) is
-- Length 16   Complexity 7   Performance O(n), where n is the number of characters in expression
begin
    clear_stack;                                    -- Clear the stack if necessary.
    for i in natural range expression'range loop
        case expression(i) is                       -- Treat ith character of expression.
            ⋮
            ⋮
```

At times, we will expand the *performance* measure to show the best, worst, and/or expected performance of an algorithm.

When a parent procedure or function has one or more other procedures or functions embedded in it (i.e., internal subprograms), we will list the metrics for each individually. If you wish to compute the overall length, complexity, and recursiveness of the collection, you can add the individual measures for each subprogram to form totals for the composite.

1.8.4 Timing Studies

Although it is not common—at least in data structures books—to make specific comparisons of measured times required to perform operations for different data types and algorithms, we include timing studies in which we timed the executions of algorithms. We have, more often than not, been surprised by the results. Often they did not agree with our theoretical predictions, usually because there were subtle factors that we overlooked. We include the timing studies precisely because of this fact. They augment the coarser order-of-magnitude estimates.

There is a pitfall associated with timing studies. The results depend not only on the data structures being used, but also on the compiler and underlying hardware and operating system. Sometimes odd effects that are observed are the results of decisions made by the compiler writers. Although such effects cannot be entirely eliminated, the examples we have chosen generally illustrate the effects of data structure selection and algorithms implementation issues.

EXERCISES 1.8

1. Explain the following terms in your own words:

memory	direct access
cache	random access
order of magnitude	sequential access
file	metric
processor	

2. What are the order-of-magnitude estimates for the following expressions?

   a. $4 * n^2 + 10 * n + 120$

   b. $6.1 * \log n + n_{1/2} + 5.5$

   c. $7 * n * [(\log n)/(5 * n^2)] + 3 * n_{1/2}$

   d. $(5/n) + 0.33 * n_{1/4}$

   e. $2.1 * n * m + 16 * n^2 + 4 * m + 3.2 * m \log n$

3. Show that the expressions below are the orders of magnitude shown by finding constants C in each case such that $f(b) \leq C * g(n)$ for $n \geq N$, where $f(n) \sim O[g(n)]$.

   a. $1.3 * n + 3.22 * n * \log n \sim O(n * \log n)$

   b. $1.3 * n + 3.22 * n * \log n \sim O(n^2)$

c. $0.17/(n + 3.0) \sim O(1/n)$

4. Choose a programming language other than Ada, such as Pascal or C, and lay out the rules for determining that construct count and cyclometric complexity for procedures and functions written in the language.

5. Verify the length and complexity of the algorithms in figures
    a. 4.21
    b. 6.56
    c. 8.45

■ 1.9 Summary

In Chapter 1 we introduced concepts that are fundamental to our study of data structures. Some of these, which set the stage for the remainder of the book, are as follows:

Data types
    Predefined types
Categories of data types
    Atomic (scalar)
    Data structures
    Predefined data types
Abstract data types
    Specification
    Representation
    Implementation
Specification process
    Objects ⎫
    Structure ⎬ Domains
    Constraints ⎭
    Operations
Advantages of abstract data types
    Modularity
    Information hiding
    Precision of specification
    Simplicity
    Integrity
    Implementation independence
Generic data types
Indexes, keys, and maps
Representation of structure
    Positioning and calculation
    Linking with pointers
Memories and their effects on data types
Computational complexity, performance, and metrics
    Unit length
    Cyclomatic complexity
    Recursiveness
    Order-of-magnitude bounds

2

Arrays, Records, and Simple Linked Structures

■ 2.1 Introduction

This chapter deals with three data types that are used for representing and implementing almost all of the complex data structures we will study. One is an access type, frequently called a pointer, and the other two are structured types—arrays and records. Their occurrence as predefined data types in most general-purpose programming languages attests to their fundamental nature.

This chapter also introduces linked lists. Linked lists are among the simplest of linked data structures and provide a good introduction to the use of pointers.

Arrays and records are among the most widely used data structures. Historically, arrays appeared as the primary data structure in programming languages intended for scientific computation. Records evolved from the application of computers to problems involving business data processing. A more integrated view of computing prevails today, and we realize that both of these data structures are necessary for a wide variety of computation.

Both arrays and records are data structures and hence are made up of individual objects, which can be atomic or other data structures. The differences between them stem from the fact that all objects of an array must be of the same data type, whereas those of a record can be (and usually are) a variety of types. Figure 2.1(a) shows an array whose component objects are all of type *float;* Figure 2.1(b) shows a record whose components are of four different data types.

Array			Record			
Memory address	Data value	Index value	Memory address	Data value	Object name	Object length (bytes)
500	10.4	1	1000	2351	r.idno	4
504	−13.5	2	1004	83	r.grade	2
508	112.74	3	1006	true	r.married	1
512	8.2	4	1007	500.75	r.salary	8

a : **array** (1 .. 4) **of** float;

```
subtype score is natural range 0 .. 100;
r : record
      idno    : natural;
      grade   : score;
      married : boolean;
      salary  : float;
   end record;
```

(a)   (b)

FIGURE 2.1 Typical memory layouts for an array and a record. (a) Memory layout and declaration of an array. (b) Memory layout and declaration of a record.

The ability of records to group and handle (e.g., move, copy, input, output) a collection of data of differing types as a single entity is a distinct advantage. It also, however, results in a disadvantage that we now discuss. A component object of an array is selected by specifying the value of its index. For instance, referring to the array in Figure 2.1(a),

a(i) := 0.0;

assigns the value 0.0 to a single object of the array and the value stored in the index variable *i* unambiguously determines which object. The value of *i* can be set at any time by the executing program. Figure 2.2(a) shows an example.

for i **in** a'range **loop**	r.idno := 0;
a(i) := 0.0;	r.grade := 0;
end loop;	r.married := false;
	r.salary := 0.0;
or	or
a := (a'range => 0.0)	r := (0, 0, false, 0.0);
(a)	(b)

FIGURE 2.2 Storing values in (a) an array and (b) a record.

A component of a record is identified by specifying its name. Referring to the record *r* in Figure 2.1(b),

r.married := true;

assigns the value *true* to a single object (field) of the record, and the name *r.married* unambiguously selects which field. The selection must be done at the time the program is written. That is, the programmer must write *r.married*. In the case of arrays, the programmer might write *a(i)*, but the fact that the value of *i* can be changed at run time means that the selection of the specific object of *a* is not fixed until the program executes. In short, although the programmer must commit to a specific field of a record at the time of writing the program, a commitment to a specific object of an array can be avoided until the program is executing.

Data structures are stored in random access memory in a way that allows their components to be identified and used. Figure 2.1 shows typical arrangements for arrays and records. Later in this chapter we shall see the role that positioning the component objects plays in the subsequent accessing of the objects.

There is an alternative to this orderly arrangement of objects in memory: The objects may be scattered about memory. Since the abstract relationship (structure) among objects must be retained, we must then have a way of retaining the relationships among the scattered data. For example, consider the integers 3, 5, 7, and 9 ordered by magnitude. Thus 5 follows (is greater than) 3; 7 follows 5; and 9 follows 7. We can store them (on the page) in a left-to-right order that mirrors the logical order of whole numbers; see Figure 2.3(a). If they are stored in a scattered fashion as in Figure 2.3(b), their physical order no longer indicates their logical order.

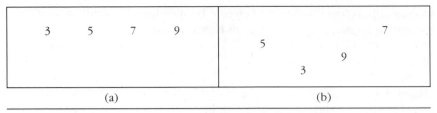

FIGURE 2.3 Orderly (a) and scattered (b) arrangements of objects.

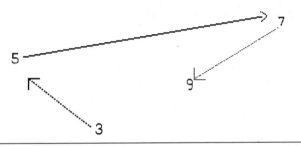

FIGURE 2.4 Linked structure among scattered objects.

FIGURE 2.5 Normal way of depicting linked structure. The objects may not be in the same physical order.

For convenience we will use the term "pointer" to refer to objects whose types are Ada access types.

The logical order can be regained by associating a directed line with each object that links the object with its successor in size (see Figure 2.4). Data structures implemented in this way are called ***linked data structures***. Figure 2.5 shows the way in which the linked structure of Figure 2.4 is usually drawn. The objects appear to be orderly, but in fact they may be scattered about the memory.

A primary characteristic of linked structures is that each object is placed in a **node**, and the node contains not only the object but also the position(s) in some storage medium of logically related object(s). We will call these position fields pointers. Their values are shown as directed lines and are memory addresses in whatever type of storage medium is being used to store the data. They might be addresses in a random access memory, relative record positions on a magnetic tape, or disk addresses (surface, track, sector, byte) on a magnetic disk. In this text, we are primarily concerned with data stored in random access memories, so our pointers will normally be addresses in random access memory. Ada terminology for these locator types is access types. The concept is more general in Ada, where an access type may be a memory or storage address, but it also may be implemented quite differently.

The rest of this chapter is organized as follows. Section 2.2 deals with arrays. Each array has a number of parameters associated with it, such as the type and bounds of its index(es) and the type of its component data. These parameters are identified and discussed in Section 2.2.1. Array mapping functions—that is, functions that transform an index value into an actual memory address—are derived in Section 2.2.2. Section 2.2.3 deals with array descriptors—data structures that hold information about arrays.

Not every array fits the normal mold, and two special cases are discussed as examples in Section 2.2.4—triangular arrays and sparse arrays. In Section

2.2.5, issues such as dynamic array memory binding and unconstrained arrays are discussed.

Section 2.3 deals with records. The record abstraction is formalized in Section 2.3.1, and record type parameters are identified and discussed in Section 2.3.2. The mapping of record components onto random access memories is also covered in Section 2.3.2.

Variant record types are records that have components that appear to be different in different contexts. A certain portion of the record may seem to have certain fields or be a certain size at one time and appear different at another time. These ideas are introduced in Section 2.3.3. That section also introduces a related, useful feature of Ada, record discriminants.

Section 2.4 covers pointers, dynamic allocation of memory, and an elementary linked structure—linked lists. Recursion is introduced through recursive operation on linked lists. Section 2.5 is a summary.

■ 2.2 Arrays

Because arrays are such useful data structures and are predefined for most programming languages, you are probably familiar with their use. Therefore, here we would like to specify the array abstraction; we would like to present the essence of an array. First, let's look at an example. Suppose we have an array type *sample* declared in Ada, with an array variable *a* of that type:

subtype index **is** positive **range** 1..3;
type sample **is array** (index) **of** integer;

a : sample;

The three things we specified when declaring the array type were

1. Its name
2. Its index type
3. The type of its component objects

By our definition of a type, stating that the index and component object types are specified implies that the set of values that each allows is also specified. In the case of the index, which must be linear, the set of values is {1, 2, 3}.

Suppose that we assigned a value to the array variable *a*:

a := (19, 48, 11);

so equivalently

a := (1 => 19, 2 => 48, 3 => 11);

There is a one-to-one correspondence between the index values of the array and the data values. These are shown in Figure 2.6.

Index value	One-to-one correspondence	Data value
1	↔	19
2	↔	48
3	↔	11

FIGURE 2.6 Correspondence between index and data values in an array.

It is the two data types—the index type and its range, and the component object type—and the one-to-one relationship between their values that play the central role in the array abstraction that we specify in Specification 2.1.

■ SPECIFICATION 2.1   Array

-- *Objects:* *Generic, but all component objects must be the same data type.*

-- *Structure:* *An index type is specified, which must be linear. There is a one-to-one*
--   *correspondence between the values of the index type and the component object*
--   *values represented in the array.*

-- *Operations:* *There are six operations specified. Only the first two are necessary since the*
--   *others can be programmed using them. Ada provides four array attribute*
--   *functions, and those too are listed. Assume* c *is a variable and* e *is an*
--   *expression of the component type of the array;* i, j, *and* k *are expressions of*
--   *the index type of the array;* a *and* b *are both arrays of the same type.*

   c := a(i)   -- *Array object copy.*
-- *results:* *The component object associated with index* i *is copied into* c.
-- *exceptions:* *Constraint_error if* i *is outside the range of index values for* a.

   a(i) := e   -- *Array object update.*
-- *results:* *The value of* e *is copied into the component of* a *associated with index value* i.
-- *exceptions:* *Constraint_error if* i *is outside the range of index values for* a.

   a := b   -- *Array copy.*
-- *results:* *The entire array* a *is copied into* b.

   a = b   -- *Array equality. Since "=" is provided, so is "/=."*
-- *results:* *True if* a(i) = b(i) *for all* i *in the index range of* a *and* b; *false otherwise.*

  a(j .. k)   -- *Array slice.*
-- *results:* *An array that is the subset of* a *extending from index* j *through index* k.
-- *exceptions:* *Constraint_error if* j *or* k *is outside the range of index values for* a.

  a & b   -- *Array concatenation.*
-- *results:* *The concatenation of* a *and* b. *The length of* a & b *is* a'length + b'length.

-- *Attributes**

  a'last
  (a'first)
-- *results:* *Returns the high (low) bound of the index range of* a.

  a'range
-- *results:* *Returns the range* a'first .. a'last.

(continued)

Specification 2.1 (continued)

a'length
-- ***results:*** *Returns the number of index values in a'range.*

---

*Some other attributes are inherited, since arrays are a subclass of other Ada objects. See Appendix A.

In cases in which the component type of the array is a discrete type [any enumeration type (includes type *character*) or integer type], the other relational operators are also included—"<," "<=," ">," ">=." If we have two arrays

type discrete_array **is array** (integer **range** <>) **of** integer;

a, b : discrete_array (1..10);

a := (2, 3, 4, 2, 1, 5, 6, 7, 8, 9);
b := (2, 3, 4, 2, 6, 5, 6, 7, 8, 9);

if b > a **then** . . .   -- *True; the first four objects are equal, so the comparison is determined*
-- *by the fifth objects, 1 and 6, respectively. 6 > 1 => b > a.*

The comparisons are done from the first toward the last object. The comparison continues as long as the objects are equal. The first unequal objects encountered determine the relationship. Objects following the first unequal ones don't contribute to the comparison. If the objects are characters and *a* and *b* are strings, we get the familiar comparison by alphabetical (**lexicographic**) order.

You see in the above example an assignment of a composite value to an array:

a := (2, 3, 4, 2, 1, 5, 6, 7, 8, 9);

The value is called an ***array aggregate***. It can take a number of other forms. Suppose that we wanted the first five objects of the array *a* to have a value 0, and the remainder have a value 1. This can be done in a number of aggregate forms:

a := discrete_array'(1..5 => 0, 6..10 => 1);
a := discrete_array'(1..5 => 0, others => 1);
a := discrete_array'(6..10 => 1, others => 0);
a := (0, 0, 0, 0, 0, 1, 1, 1, 1, 1);

If we wanted objects 1, 3, and 7 to be 1 and the rest 0, we could form the aggregate

a := discrete_array'(1 | 3 | 7 => 1, others => 0);

See the *Ada LRM,* 1983, Section 4.3.2, for a discussion.

Given an index value, the memory address of the component object associated with that index value can be determined. In fact it is determined by a simple calculation performed using the ***array mapping function.*** We will see that the form of this function is

$$addr(a(i)) = C_0 + C_1 * i$$

a linear function of *i,* where C_0 and C_1 are constants. One multiplication and one addition are required to find the memory address for a given value of *i.* Thus the time required to determine the memory address of the array object associated with any of its index values is the same. The amount of time does not depend on the value of the index or on the size of the array. Because of this fact, arrays are said to have ***random access*** to their component objects. This is also the source of the term ***random access memory*** since, as noted in Chapter 1, memory can be described as an array of bytes.

The index type must be linear. Because of the one-to-one correspondence between the values of the index and the component data objects of the array, the array components inherit the linear structure of the index type by association.

The component object type of an array can be another array (it cannot be the same array); thus,

type inner **is array** (1 .. 3) **of** integer;
type sample **is array** (1 .. 2) **of** inner;

a : sample;

Using Ada syntax, a reference to the *j*th component of the inner array in the *i*th component of the outer array is

a(i)(j)

An alternative is a two-dimensional array:

type sample **is array** (1 .. 2, 1 .. 3) **of** integer;

a : sample;

and a reference to the *j*th component of the inner array in the *i*th component of the outer array is

a(i, j)

In Ada, an array of arrays with two indexes is a different data type from a two-dimensional array with two indexes. In some programming languages (e.g., Pascal) they are synonymous.

This idea can be extended to any level of nesting of arrays. The result is *multidimensional arrays.* Figure 2.7 shows an example.

```
type page is range 1 .. 500;
type line is range 1 .. 60;
type column is range 1 .. 80;

type book is array (page, line, column) of character;

b : book;

    .
    .
    .

b(35, 17, 28) := 'd';           -- Set the 28th character of the 17th line on the 35th page to 'd'.

for k in 1 .. 80 loop
    put (b(34, 16, i));                    -- Write the 16th line of the 34th page.
end loop;
```

FIGURE 2.7 Example of a three-dimensional array.

In a two-dimensional array, there is a one-to-one correspondence between index pairs and component data objects. That is, an object is uniquely determined by one value of each of the two indexes. The situation is similar with three or more indexes. In Figure 2.7, the reference to

b(35, 17, 28)

is to a single character of the book, and the triplet of index values (35, 17, 28) determines the character position of the $500 * 60 * 80 = 2,400,000$ possible character positions exactly.

A two-dimensional array is given in Specification 2.2.

■ SPECIFICATION 2.2   Two-Dimensional Array

-- *Objects:*   *Generic, but all component objects must be the same data type.*

-- *Structure:*   *Two index types are specified, each of which must be linear. There is a one-*
--   *to-one correspondence between the values of the Cartesian product of the index*
--   *types and the component object values.*

-- *Operations:*   *Three operations are specified. Only the first two are necessary as the others*
--   *can be programmed using those two. Assume c is a variable, e is an*
--   *expression of the component type of the array, and i and j are expressions of*
--   *the first and second index types, respectively, of the array. a and b are both of*
--   *the same array type.*

```
    c := a(i, j)                                    -- Array object copy.
```
-- *results:*   *The component object associated with index pair (i, j) is copied into c.*
-- *exceptions:*   *Constraint_error if i or j is outside the range of index values for a.*

(continued)

Specification 2.2 (continued)

a(i, j) := e   -- *Array object update.*
-- **results:**   *The value of* e *is copied into* a *and is associated with index pair* (i, j).
-- **exceptions:**   *Constraint_error if* i *or* j *is outside the range of index values for* a.

a := b   -- *Array copy.*
-- **results:**   *The entire array* a *is copied into* b.

-- **Attributes***

a'last(k)
(a'first(k))
-- **results:**   *Returns the high (low) bound of the range of the kth index of* a; k = *1 or 2.*

a'range(k)
-- **results:**   *Returns the range a'first(k) .. a'last(k).*

a'length(k)
-- **results:**   *Returns the number of index values in a'range(k).*

---

*Some other attributes are inherited, since arrays are a subclass of other Ada objects. See Appendix A.

Note that the slice operation is not specified because in Ada we cannot take a slice of a multidimensional array.

We will show in Section 2.2.2 that the array mapping function (the function that computes the memory address of a component object given its index values) for an array of d dimensions is of the form

$$\text{addr}(a(i_1, i_2, i_3, \ldots, i_d)) = C_0 + C_1 * i_1 + C_2 * i_2 + C_3 * i_3 + \cdots + C_d * i_d$$

where $C_0, C_1, C_2, \ldots, C_d$ are constants whose values are determined before the array is used by the program, and $i_1, i_2, i_3, \ldots, i_d$ are the values of the d indexes. For the moment, accept that the array mapping functions are of this form. In that case, we can make four observations:

1. The memory address of an array component can be calculated from its index values.
2. For an array of d dimensions, the calculation requires d multiplications and d additions.
3. The amount of calculation is not dependent on the size of the array or on the size of the range of any of its indexes, but rather on the number of indexes (dimension of the array).
4. The amount of computation is the same for all components of the array (random access).

The amount of calculation necessary to access an object of an array given its index values is small in comparison with that required by many other data structures. In particular, there is no searching, only a calculation.

Arrays provide us with a form of *positional access* in which we specify which object of the array we want by its position in the range of index(es) values. They do not, however, provide us directly with an *associative access;* that is, access to an object that holds a particular value such as some target key value. For instance, using Figure 2.7, in order to find the first instance in the book of character '*', we have to search using code like the following:

```
found := false;
outer_loop:
for i in page'range loop
    for j in line'range loop
        for k in column'range loop
            if b(i,j,k) = '*' then
                page_no   := i;                    -- Record the position found.
                line_no   := j;
                col_no    := k;
                found     := true;
                exit outer_loop;
            end if;
        end loop;
    end loop;
end loop;
```

Access to the character '*' is not by a simple calculation but is a search whose execution time is a function of how long the book is and where '*' first occurs, if it occurs.

2.2.1 Array Parameters

Several parameters are associated with an array: the base address at which the array is stored in memory, its component object type, its index type(s), its (their) lower and upper bounds, and the number of indexes—its number of dimensions.

The memory address of the first byte of the first array object is called the **base address** of the array. The time at which the array is assigned a position in memory is called its **binding time.** Binding the array to a memory space can occur at a variety of times during the compilation, linking, loading, and execution of the program. We assume that the binding of the arrays discussed in the following sections is done some time before the array is first used by the executing program. We use the identifier b to designate the base address.

Each index type of the array must be of an ordered linear type (Section 1.5). Each index value therefore corresponds to a natural number that is its ordinal position. For our discussion, therefore, we can assume that each index is a subrange of the integers. Each index type can thus be considered to have a smallest and a largest value, called the lower bound and upper bound, respectively. We use the notation lo_k for the low bound of the kth index and hi_k for the high bound of the kth index. An array with d indexes can be assumed to be declared as

type example **is array** $(lo_1 .. hi_1, lo_2 .. hi_2, \ldots, lo_d .. hi_d)$ **of** component_type;

To illustrate the relationship between general linear index types and their positions, consider the following example:

type day **is** (sun, mon, tue, wed, thu, fri, sat);

type sample **is array** (day) **of** float;

The values of type *day* have ordinal position $0 .. 6$. The array can be considered to have been declared as

type sample **is array** (natural range $0 .. 6$) **of** float;

The integer (natural) subrange form can be used internally for computation of the array mapping function that requires integer indexes, whereas the programmer can use the more convenient index form of type *day*. The compiler can produce the code that makes the correspondence. The programmer is thus relieved of the tedium of matching index type values to integer values as is required in older programming languages that do not have enumerated types. The possibility of error is also reduced. For these reasons, we confine the discussion of array mapping functions in the following sections to arrays whose indexes are subranges of the integers.

We will often further simplify the array index bounds by making the lower bounds 1 and designating the upper bounds as u_i; thus,

type example **is array** $(1 .. u_1, 1 .. u_2, \ldots, 1 .. u_d)$ **of** component_type;

Take care in using **multidimensional arrays** since the **memory space** they require **grows** in proportion to the **product of the index range sizes** and can become quite large.

The memory space needed to store an array is a function of the number of indexes, the bounds of the indexes, and the component type of the array. If the component type requires L bytes of memory for a single value of the type, then an array of

type example **is array** $(1 .. u_1, 1 .. u_2, \ldots, 1 .. u_d)$ **of** component_type;

requires a minimum of

$$L * u_1 * u_2 * u_3 * \cdots * u_d \text{ bytes}$$

Recall the book example in Figure 2.7, reproduced here:

type page **is range** $1 .. 500$;
type line **is range** $1 .. 60$;
type column **is range** $1 .. 80$;

type book **is array** (page, line, column) **of** character;

Since the component type is *character,* we can reasonably assume each character takes 1 byte and the parameters of the array type are

$$L = 1$$
$$d = 3$$
$$u_1 = 500$$
$$u_2 = 60$$
$$u_3 = 80$$

Memory space required = $1 * 500 * 60 * 80 = 2,400,000$ bytes, or approximately 2.4 megabytes.

In summary, we have the following array parameters:

b	The base address of the array in memory.
L	The number of bytes in a single value of the component type.
d	The dimensionality (number of indexes) of the array.
$lo_k .. hi_k$	The lower and upper bounds of the kth index's range.

or

$1 .. u_k$	Simplified lower and upper bounds of the kth index's range to clarify the discussion.

We turn now to a discussion of how array mapping functions are used to transform index values into the memory address of the specified component object.

2.2.2 Array Mapping Functions

The simplest case of an array mapping function (AMF) is an AMF for an array of one dimension. Figure 2.8 shows an example of an array a stored in the normal way in which arrays are stored in a memory—the component objects immediately following each other in order of their index values.

The question is how, given a specific index value, to determine the position in memory of the corresponding component object. To find the first address of the ith object of an array, we must skip the first $(i - 1)$ objects, each of which is L bytes—a total of $(i - 1) * L$ bytes. This number of bytes added to the base address b will give the address of the first byte of the ith array object. The expression for the address of $a(i)$ is then

$$\text{addr}[a(i)] = b + (i - 1) * L$$
$$= (b - L) + i * L$$
$$= C_0 + C_1 * i$$

so that

$$C_1 = L$$
$$C_0 = b - L$$

C_1 and C_0 are introduced because they are constants. Their values can be calculated once before the array is used and they don't change. They are simple in the one-dimensional case; they become more complex with more dimensions. What changes is the specific value of i as the user varies it in using the array.

For the array   **type** one_dimen **array** (1 .. 5) **of** integer;
                 a : one_dimen;

we have $L = 4$ -- Assume integers require 4 bytes.
                 $d = 1$
                 $u_1 = 5$

Also assume $b = 500$ -- Array stored starting at memory address 500.

Memory address	Index value	Sample component object value
500	1	−12
504	2	7
508	3	47
512	4	26
516	5	−52

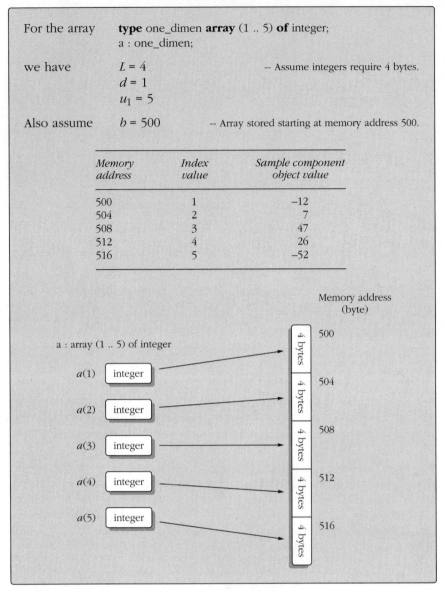

FIGURE 2.8 Sample array of one dimension stored in memory.

Applying this general form to the array in Figure 2.8, we find that

$C_1 = L = 4$
$C_0 = b - L = 500 - 4 = 496$

The array mapping function for that array is

$\text{addr}[a(i)] = 496 + 4 * i$

and the memory address of $a(4)$ is found as

$$\text{addr}[a(4)] = C_0 + C_1 * i = 496 + 4 * 4 = 512$$

The parameters b and L enter into the calculation of C_0 and C_1, whereas u_1 does not.

Let us derive a similar AMF for the case of a two-dimensional array. A question immediately arises as to how such arrays are stored in the memory. The two natural storage schemes are ***row-major order*** and ***column-major order***. The terms "row" and "column" come from the fact that two-dimensional arrays are often shown in a tabular form:

type two_dimen **is array** $(1 .. 3, 1 .. 2)$ **of** integer;

Col	1	2
Row		
1	54	39
2	72	13
3	17	45

The two natural ways of storing this array in the one-dimensional array of bytes that make up random access memory is to store them one row (horizontal slice) at a time (row-major order) or one column (vertical slice) at a time (column-major order). Figure 2.9 shows the array stored in row-major order.

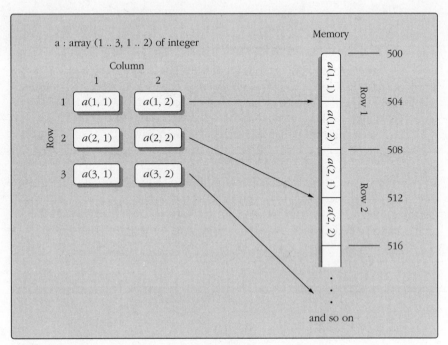

FIGURE 2.9 Sample array of two dimensions stored in memory.

Most programming languages use row-major order. The important exception is FORTRAN. The difficulty comes when subroutines written in FORTRAN are called from another language. This is often done with Ada, which has a pragma that allows interfacing Ada programs with subprograms written in other languages. Since there is so much existing code in FORTRAN, an interface is frequently used with it. If an array of two or more dimensions is passed between the two languages, an adjustment must be made to ensure the languages exchange the array correctly.

For the two-dimensional array

type two_dimen **is array** (1 .. 3, 1 .. 2) **of** integer;
a : two_dimen;

we have

$L = 4$ -- *Assume integers require 4 bytes.*

$d = 2$ $u_1 = 3$ $u_2 = 2$

Also assume arbitrarily that

$b = 500$ -- *Array stored starting at memory address 500.*

Memory address	Index values	Component object value	
500	1, 1	54	row 1
504	1, 2	39	
508	2, 1	72	row 2
512	2, 2	13	
516	3, 1	17	row 3
520	3, 2	45	

We can write the AMF as follows. If we want to know the address of the array object $a(i, j)$, since the array is stored in row-major order, we must skip the first $(i - 1)$ rows. Each row has 2 (u_2) objects, each of which is 4 (L) bytes in length. Once we have arrived at the first byte of the ith row, we must skip $(j - 1)$ objects, each of which is L bytes. We then have

$$\text{addr}[a(i, j)] = b + (i - 1) * u_2 * L + (j - 1) * L$$

In this form, there are three multiplications and four additions and subtractions. Since the terms b, u_2, and L and the constant 1 are all known in advance, we rearrange the expression in order to minimize the amount of computation needed once the AMF is evaluated for a given i and j:

$$\text{addr}[a(i, j)] = b - (u_2 + 1) * L + u_2 * L * i + L * j$$
$$= C_0 + C_1 * i + C_2 * j$$

where

$C_2 = L$
$C_1 = u_2 * L$
$C_0 = b - (u_2 + 1) * L$

These constants can be computed in advance, leaving only i and j as variables.

Taking the example in Figure 2.9, we have

$C_2 = L = 4$
$C_1 = u_2 * L = 2 * 4 = 8$
$C_0 = b - (u_2 + 1) * L = 500 - 3 * 4 = 488$

The AMF is then

$\text{addr}[a(i, j)] = 488 + 8 * i + 4 * j$

As an example, the address of the component with index values (3, 1) is

$\text{addr}[a(3, 1)] = 488 + 8 * 3 + 4 * 1 = 516$

We can continue with arrays of more dimensions. If we have an array of three dimensions,

type three_dimen **is array** $(1 .. u_1, 1 .. u_2, 1 .. u_3)$ **of** integer;   *-- The lower bounds are 1 for simplicity.*

we can view the array as pages, where each page holds a two-dimensional array. The first (left-most) index indicates the page number, the middle index indicates the row, and the last (right-most) indicates the column. Figure 2.10 is a visualization.

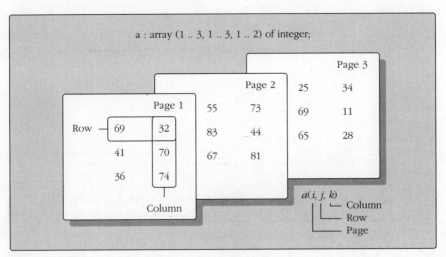

FIGURE 2.10 Visualization of a three-dimensional array.

Each page holds $u_2 * u_3$ objects and, since each object is L bytes in size, takes a total of $u_2 * u_3 * L$ bytes. We know that each row takes $u_3 * L$ bytes. To get to the object $a(i, j, k)$, we must skip $(i - 1)$ pages, $(j - 1)$ rows, then $(k - 1)$ individual objects. The array mapping function is

$$addr[a(i, j, k)] = b + u_2 * u_3 * L * (i - 1) + u_3 * L * (j - 1) + L * (k - 1)$$
skip (i − 1) pages   skip (j − 1) rows   skip (k − 1) objects

As we have done before, we can rearrange the expression into a more efficient computational form by using the fact that all terms but i, j, and k are known in advance:

$$addr[a(i, j, k)] = b - (u_2 * u_3 + u_3 + 1) * L + u_2 * u_3 * L * i + u_3 * L * j + L * k$$
$$= C_0 + C_1 * i + C_2 * j + C_3 * k$$

where

$$C_3 = L$$
$$C_2 = u_3 * L = u_3 * C_3$$
$$C_1 = u_2 * u_3 * L = u_2 * C_2$$
$$C_0 = b - (u_2 * u_3 + u_3 + 1) * L = b - (C_1 + C_2 + C_3)$$

From the right-most forms of the expressions, to determine the constants, we can find expressions for the general case of d dimensions (Figure 2.11).

AMF for Arrays with d Indexes

type d_dimen **is array** $(1 .. u_1, 1 .. u_2, \ldots, 1 .. u_d)$ **of** component_type;
a : three_dimen;

$$AMF: addr[a(i_1, i_2, \ldots, i_d)] = C_0 + C_1 * i_1 + C_2 * i_2 + \cdots + C_d * i_d$$

where

$$C_d = L$$

$$C_{d-1} = u_d * C_d$$

$$C_{d-2} = u_{d-1} * C_{d-1}$$

$$\vdots$$

$$C_1 = u_2 * C_2$$

$$C_0 = b - (C_1 + C_2 + \cdots + C_d)$$

FIGURE 2.11 General array mapping function for any number of dimensions.

It becomes more difficult to construct a visualization as the number of dimensions grows to more than three. Probably it is best not to try to visualize in those cases.

The form of the array mapping function is not changed if the lower bounds of the indexes are other than 1. The expression that determines the value of the C's becomes a bit more complex, however.

As an example of an application of an AMF, suppose we had an array of four dimensions

type four_dimen **is array** $(1 .. 12, 1 .. 6, 1 .. 10, 1 .. 3)$ **of** float;
a : four_dimen;

type *float* takes 8 bytes, and the first byte of the array is at 1000.

We have

$$L = 8 \qquad b = 1000 \qquad d = 4$$
$$u_1 = 12 \qquad u_2 = 6 \qquad u_3 = 10 \qquad u_4 = 3$$

Then

$$C_4 = L = 8$$
$$C_3 = u_4 * C_4 = 3 * 8 = 24$$
$$C_2 = u_3 * C_3 = 10 * 24 = 240$$
$$C_1 = u_2 * C_2 = 6 * 240 = 1440$$

$$C_0 = b - (C_1 + C_2 + C_3 + C_4)$$
$$= 1000 - (1440 + 240 + 24 + 8) = -712$$

and the AMF is

$$\text{addr}[a(i_1, i_2, i_3, i_4)] = -712 + 1440 * i_1 + 240 * i_2 + 24 * i_3 + 8 * i_4$$

To illustrate the concepts more clearly, we used the simplified form of multidimensional arrays

type example **is array** $(1 .. u_1, 1 .. u_2, \dots, 1 .. u_d)$ **of** component_type;

rather than the more general form

type example **is array** $(lo_1 .. hi_1, lo_2 .. hi_2, \dots, lo_d .. hi_d)$ **of** component_type;

in which the lower bound of each index range is not necessarily one. Derivation of the array mapping functions for the more general form is an extension of the simplified form and is left as Exercises 2.2, 5.

It is the homogeneity and regularity of arrays that allow us to derive concise AMF's that give rapid, random access to array components. In the cases treated so far, we used the fact that each component object is the same size and each row holds the same number of components. If this were not the case, we might have difficulty finding a concise AMF. We will see in Section 2.2.4 that in certain cases we can relax these restrictions somewhat and still obtain an AMF.

2.2.3 Array Descriptors

The parameters of an array are gathered into a single data structure called an *array descriptor.* Since the various pieces of information vary in type, the logical data structure to hold the information is a record. The descriptor record might look like the following*:

*This record is for demonstration; it will not actually compile in Ada.

```
type bounds is record
    low, high : integer;                        -- Assume integer indexes for this example.
end record;
type bounds_list is array (1 .. dim) of bounds;
type constants is array (0 .. d) of integer;
type array_descriptor (name_size : positive; dim : positive) is record
    name            : string(1 .. name_size);   -- Name of the array or array type.
    object_size     : positive;                  -- Component object size, in bytes.
    base_address    : system.address;            -- Address of first byte of array.
    bound           : bounds_list;               -- Bounds on each index.
    C               : constants;                 -- Constants of the AMF.
end record;
```

When an array or array type is declared, some of these quantities such as the name are fixed. Others such as the base address must wait until the array is assigned a position in the memory. In an unconstrained array type, the number of dimensions and the type of each index are known, but the bounds are not known until a variable constrains the type. Thus, when type *string* is declared, it is an unconstrained array type with character components and one dimension. The name of the type is *string,* and its name length is 6. So *name_size, dim, name, object_size,* and the constants $C_1 .. C_d$ are known. The other parameters must wait until the type is constrained—to determine *bounds*—and until the array is assigned to memory—for *base_address* and C_0—to be determined.

Array descriptors provide information about the array. For instance, here a type *matrix* is declared:

```
type matrix is array (integer range <>, integer range <>) of float;
```

and a function *mean* is written to determine the mean of all of the values in the array:

```
function mean (M : matrix) return float is
-- Length 5   Complexity 3   Performance O(n * m), where n is M'length(1) and m is M'length(2).
    sum : float := 0.0;
begin
    for i in M'range(1) loop
        for j in M'range(2) loop
            sum := sum + M(i, j);
        end loop;
    end loop;
    return (sum/float(M'length(1) * M'length(2)));
end mean;
```

The code is written using array attributes. The values of these attributes are found in the array descriptor of the actual argument passed for *M.* For a call

```
X : matrix (1 .. 12, 1 .. 20);

mn := mean(X);
```

the attributes of X are from X's descriptor:

X'range(1) = X_descriptor.bound(1).low .. X_descriptor.bound(1).high

X'range(2) = X_descriptor.bound(2).low .. X_descriptor.bound(2).high

X'length(1) = X_descriptor.bound(1).high − X_descriptor.bound(1).low + 1

X'length(2) = X_descriptor.bound(2).high − X_descriptor.bound(1).low + 1

For this reason, in some programming languages when an array is passed as an argument in a function or procedure call, it is the array descriptor or a pointer to the descriptor that is passed.

2.2.4 Special Arrays

Some arrays have special properties that allow considerable savings in the memory required to store them. If we take advantage of this, the generalized AMF's derived in Section 2.2.2 do not apply and we must derive AMF's on a case-by-case basis. We will examine two special cases to illustrate the techniques.

Lower Triangular Matrices

A lower triangular matrix is a two-dimensional array that is square (i.e., has the same number of rows and columns). To simplify the discussion, we assume the standard case

$$lo_1 = lo_2 = 1 \quad hi_1 = hi_2 = n$$

In addition,

$$a(i, j) = 0 \quad \text{for } j > i$$

An example is shown in Figure 2.12.

$a_{1,1}$	0	0	...	0
$a_{2,1}$	$a_{2,2}$	0	...	0
$a_{3,1}$	$a_{3,2}$	$a_{3,3}$	...	0
...	...	...	...	...
$a_{n,1}$	$a_{n,2}$	$a_{n,3}$	...	$a_{n,n}$

FIGURE 2.12 A lower triangular matrix.

The number of objects on or below the diagonal (the line from $a_{1,1}$ through $a_{n,n}$) is

$$N = n * (n − 1)/2$$

Since we know that the objects above the diagonal are zero, we do not have to store them. In that case, we would save

$$(n^2 − N) * L = [n * (n + 1)/2] * L \text{ bytes}$$

or roughly 50% of the space required to store the array in the normal fashion. To see that we can still derive an AMF if we store only the lower triangle, Figure 2.13 shows an arrangement in memory.

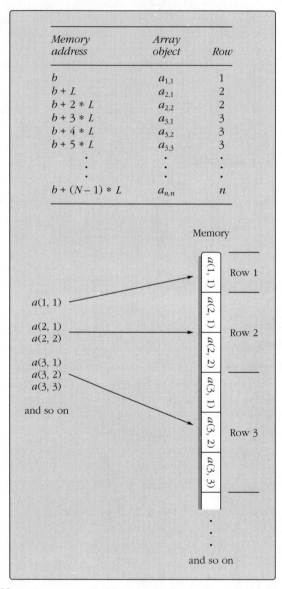

FIGURE 2.13 Dense storage of a lower triangular matrix.

Note that in Figure 2.13 row i is i objects in length. In order to reach the ith row, we must skip over $(i - 1)$ rows. In order to reach the jth object of a row, we must skip over $(j - 1)$ objects. These observations are the key to writing an AMF, which follows:

$$\text{addr}[a(i, j)] \quad \text{for } i \geq j$$
$$= b + [1 + 2 + 3 + \dots + (i - 1)] * L \qquad \text{-- Skip (i - 1) rows.}$$
$$+ (j - 1) * L \qquad \text{-- Skip (j - 1) columns.}$$

$$= b + L * \sum_{k=1}^{i-1} (k * L) + (j - 1) * L$$

Using the well-known identity

$$\sum_{k=1}^{n} k = n * (n + 1)/2$$

we reduce the sum in the AMF

$$\sum_{k=1}^{i-1} (k * L) = i * (i - 1)/2$$

then find the AMF to be

$$\text{addr}[a(i, j)] = C_0 + C_1 * i * (i - 1) + C_2 * j$$

where

$$C_1 = L/2 \quad C_2 = L \quad C_0 = b - L$$

Evaluation of the AMF for a particular (i, j) value takes three multiplications and three additions (one is actually a subtraction, or the addition of -1). If we had stored the matrix as a normal two-dimensional array, evaluation of the AMF would have taken two multiplications and two additions. In effect, we traded increased access time for decreased memory space. This is one example of the many times this tradeoff appears in computing.

There are a number of common cases in which a similar approach can be taken. Examples are an upper triangular matrix in which the objects below the diagonal are zero and a tridiagonal matrix in which all the objects not on the diagonal or immediately on either side of it are zero. Both cases have regularities that allow derivation of a special AMF (see Exercises 2.2).

Sparse Arrays

Some arrays, called *sparse arrays,* have the property that most of their objects are the same value (say 0 for purposes of the discussion). The few values that are different (nonzero) are sprinkled about the array in an irregular fashion. Take for instance a satellite scan of a section of ocean in attempting to spot ships on the surface. If a two-dimensional grid is superimposed on the surface, all readings will be that of the ocean surface except at the few positions at which there are ships. In our discussion, we will use a two-dimensional array, but the arguments and conclusions generalize to any number of dimensions. Figure 2.14 is an example of a sparse array.

If we stored the array in the usual fashion for a two-dimensional array, most of the array space would be taken up storing the background, or zero, value.

Col	1	2	3	4	5	6
Row						
1	0	0	5	0	0	0
2	8	0	0	0	2	0
3	0	7	0	0	0	0
4	0	0	0	8	0	0

FIGURE 2.14 A sparse array.

Condensed index	Sparse matrix indexes	Component value
1	(1, 3)	5
2	(2, 1)	8
3	(2, 5)	2
4	(3, 2)	7
5	(4, 4)	8

FIGURE 2.15 Condensed array for a sparse array.

One approach to using less memory is to form a condensed array that contains not only the component values, but for each component that is nonzero, the value of its two indexes. Such a condensed array is shown in Figure 2.15.

The condensed array might be the following type:

type condensed_object **is record**
    i   : index_type_1;
    j   : index_type_2;
    value : object_type;
end record;

type condensed_array **is array** (1 .. max) **of** condensed_object;

where *max* is the greatest number of nonzero objects that are expected. The condensed objects could alternatively be placed in a linked list (see Sections 2.4 and 4.3).

What we have lost in this approach is random access. If we want to find the data value at position (i, j), we no longer have an AMF that is a concise calculation. We must search the condensed array for a matching value of (i, j) in its record. If none is found, the value of the object is 0. If found, it is the data value stored along with the (i, j) value in the condensed table.

In addition, storage space is required not only for each object, but also for its index pair (i, j). The total space used is at least

max * (index_type_1'size + index_type_2'size + component_type'size)/8

where *T'size* is the number of bits required to store an object of that type. The divisor is 8, the number of bits in a byte. (See *Ada LRM,* 1983, Section 13.7.2.) This must be compared with the space used for normal storage assuming the entire array has *m* rows and *n* columns:

$$n * m * \text{object\_type'size}/8$$

If the maximum number of nonzero objects is neither known nor easily estimated in advance, the value of *max* may be difficult to determine. This is a common problem when using arrays. Space is allocated to them without regard to whether data are actually stored in all positions. Thus, we need a data structure that will expand and contract to fit the amount of data present at the time. This leads to pointers, dynamic memory allocation, and linked structures—subjects we take up in Section 2.4.

2.2.5 Dynamic Arrays and Unconstrained Arrays

We assumed that the parameters of arrays are fixed at some time before we begin the use of the array. This ensures that the constants of the AMF are determined before the AMF is used for access to array objects. In this section, we examine two ways in which the setting of the parameters is delayed until the execution of the program.

Dynamic Arrays

Suppose we write a program that computes the means and standard deviations of the objects in arrays of floating-point numbers. Assume the arrays are in a data file and each array is preceded by the size of the array. Data may look like those in Figure 2.16.

8	2.3	0.1	9.34	2.2	1.0	−0.34	3.9	−1.2	-- Array has 8 objects.
4	3.3	−2.1	8.8	−1.3					-- Array has 4 objects.

FIGURE 2.16 Sample data for the mean value program.

Since we don't know how large the largest array might be but we do know just before reading the array how large it will be, it would be advantageous to make each array exactly the size necessary to hold its data. We accomplish this with Ada's **declare** . . . **begin** . . . **end** construct. Entry to a **declare** . . . **begin** . . . **end** construct causes a frame to be placed on the stack as if there had been a procedure call. The program is shown in Figure 2.17.

```
with text_io, float_math_functions;
use text_io, float_math_functions;
procedure stats is
-- Length 28   Complexity 4
-- Performance O(n * m), where n is the number of arrays and m is the average array size.
    package nio is new integer_io(natural); use nio;
    package fio is new float_io(float); use fio;
    size : natural;                          -- The number of objects in the array.
begin
    loop
        get(size);
        exit when size = 0;
        declare                              -- Begin the declare . . . begin . . . end block.
            a : array (1 .. size) of float;  -- The array is dynamically sized and
            sum : float := 0.0;              -- bound to memory.
            mean, st_dev := float;
        begin

            for i in 1..size loop            -- Read the array and compute the sum of its objects.
                get(a(i));
                sum := sum + a(i);
            end loop;
            mean := sum / float(size);

            sum := 0.0;
            for i in 1 .. size loop          -- Compute the standard deviation.
                sum := sum + (a(i) − mean)**2;
            end loop;
            st_dev := sqrt(sum / float(size − 1));
```

FIGURE 2.17 Program demonstrating dynamic array creation.

(continued)

Figure 2.17 (continued)

```
            put("Mean is "); put(mean, fore => 5, aft => 3, exp => 0); new_line;
            put("Standard deviation is "); put(st_dev, fore => 5, aft => 3, exp => 0);
            new_line;
         end;
      end loop;
end stats;
```

FIGURE 2.17 *(continued)*

Unconstrained Arrays

There are many instances in which we wish to declare an array data type but leave the fixing of bounds of the array index(es) until later. Suppose we wish to declare a type of two-dimensional array we shall call *matrix* and later declare matrices of different sizes. Figure 2.18 has examples of the declaration and its use. Suppose also that we have a procedure *counts* that will print the number

```
type matrix is array (integer range <>,
   integer range <>) of boolean;                    -- An unconstrained array type.
   .
   .
   .
procedure counts (x : matrix) is separate;
   .
   .
   .
A : matrix(1 .. 20, -10 .. 10);                     -- A is constrained.
B : matrix (3 .. 12, 1 .. 30);                      -- B is constrained.
   .
   .
   .
counts(A);
counts(B);
```

FIGURE 2.18 Unconstrained array.

```
procedure counts (X : matrix) is
-- Length 9   Complexity 4   Performance O(n * m), where n is X'length(1) and m is X'length(2).
   num_true : natural := 0;
   total_objects : natural := X'length(1) * X'length(2);   -- Uses length of each index.
begin
   for i in X'range(1) loop                          -- Uses range of first index.
      for j in X'range(2) loop                       -- Uses range of second index.
         if X(i, j) then
            num_true := num_true + 1;
         end if;
      end loop;
   end loop;
   put("Total objects = ");   put(total_objects); new_line;
   put("Number true = ");     put(num_true); new_line;
   put("Number false = ");    put(total_objects - num_true); new_line;
end counts;
```

FIGURE 2.19 Use of unconstrained arrays in subprograms.

of objects in the array, the number that are true, and the number that are false. Type *matrix* is said to be unconstrained, while objects A and B are constrained.

We can write *counts* in a general way making use of Ada's array attributes to determine parameters of the array at the time the program runs, even though we don't know them at the time of writing the program. The procedure *counts* is shown in Figure 2.19.

In this program, we make use of the Ada array attributes *length* and *range* to write the code that uses the array (matrix) in a general way without knowing the specific values of the array parameters. Features such as these greatly increase the ability of the programmer to write reusable code without knowing specifics at the time of writing the code.

There is another method for dynamic array allocation using dynamic memory allocation and pointers. It is discussed in Section 2.4.

EXERCISES 2.2

1. Explain (a) why an array is said to have random access to its component objects, and (b) in what sense an array is a linear data type.

2. Suppose we have an unconstrained array type *vector* declared as follows:

   type vector **is array** (integer **range** <>) **of** float;

   Write an Ada function " + " that allows the addition of two vectors of the same length and index ranges such that the *i*th object of the result is the sum of the *i*th objects of the two vectors being added.

3. What is an array mapping function?

4. Applying the general expressions for array mapping functions given in Figure 2.11, determine the array mapping functions of an array A of each of the following array types:

   a. **type** one_d **array** (1 .. 20) **of** object;

      $L = 8, b = 1000$

   b. **type** two_d **array** (1 .. 10, 1 .. 20) **of** object;

      $L = 16, b = 500$

   c. **type** three_d **array** (1 .. 10, 1 .. 20, 1 .. 12) **of** object;

      $L = 16, b = 500$

   d. **type** four_d **array** (1 .. 20, 1 .. 12, 1 .. 13, 1 .. 5) **of** object;

      $L = 4, b = 2000$

5. Derive array mapping functions for arrays of 1, 2, 3, and the *d* dimensions in the case in which the arrays

are declared with arbitrary lower bounds on the index ranges:

type example **is array** $(lo_1 .. hi_1, lo_2 .. hi_2, \ldots, lo_d .. hi_d)$ **of** component_type;

Model the results after those shown in Figure 2.11.

6. Applying the general expressions for array mapping functions that you derived in Exercise 5, determine the array mapping functions of an array A of each of the following array types:

   a. **type** one_d **array** (1 .. 20) **of** object;

      $L = 8, b = 1000$

   b. **type** one_d **array** (integer **range** −20 .. 20) **of** object;

      $L = 8, b = 1000$

   c. **type** two_d **array** (1 .. 10, 15 .. 20) **of** object;

      $L = 16, b = 500$

   d. **type** three_d **array** (1 .. 10, 15 .. 20, −3 .. 12) **of** object;

      $L = 16, b = 500$

   e. **type** four_d **array** (−15 .. 20, 3 .. 12, 1 .. 13, integer **range** −10 .. 5) **of** object;

      $L = 4, b = 2000$

7. Determine an array mapping function for the arrays in Exercises 4(b) and 4(c) assuming that the arrays are in column-major order rather than row-major order.

8. Determine a general AMF analogous to the one in Figure 2.11 for arrays of any number of dimensions that are stored in column-major order.
9. Find array mapping functions for the following:
   a. An upper-triangular matrix in which all objects below the diagonal are zero and in which only the diagonal and upper triangle are stored in memory (see Section 2.2.4 and the lower-triangular case).
   b. A tridiagonal matrix in which $a_{i,j} = 0$ for $|i - j| > 1$.
   c. A band matrix in which $a_{i,j} = 0$ for $|i - j| > k$ for some fixed value of k.
10. Speculate about how you might represent an array whose index values change while the array holds data. Read Standish (1980) and modify your speculations based on what you read.

■ 2.3 Records

The most important characteristic of records is their ability to group individual components of a variety of types and treat the collection as a single unit. For example, a record describing a person can include a name (string), social_security_number (natural), address (another string of a different length), and date_of_birth (a record with three integers). The information can be treated either as a single whole and manipulated—stored, copied, written to a file, retrieved, and so on—or any field can be accessed and manipulated separately. The components themselves are often not atomic types but are other data structures. The record type contributes greatly to logical conciseness and ease of programming. Figure 2.20 has an example of record types.

```
type date is record
      month   : range 1 .. 12;
      day     : range 1 .. 31;
      year    : range 1880 .. 2100;
end record;

type employee is record
      name                    : string(1 .. 25);
      social_security_number  : natural;
      address                 : string(1 .. 80);
      date_of_birth           : date;
end record;

E : employee;
```

FIGURE 2.20 Examples of records.

The components of records are traditionally referred to as *fields*. If the name of a component is *date_of_birth*, we speak of the *date_of_birth* field. We will use this terminology.

The fact that records are able to group data of disparate types leads to a drawback in dealing with them. Component values of the record are identified by their *field names*. These names must be set when the programmer writes the program. They cannot be varied when the program is executing. For arrays, a programmer could, for instance, write

type vector **is array** (positive **range** <>) **of** float;

A : vector(1 .. 50);

get(i);

A(i) := 0.0;

thereby leaving the determination of which component of *A* is to be set to 0.0 until the program is executing and the value of *i* is determined. Or all components of *A* could be set to the value 1.0 with the concise loop

for i **in** A'range **loop**
    A(i) := 1.0;
end loop;

No analogous actions exist for records. Referring to the records in Figure 2.20, if we set the *social_security_number* field to 0, we must write

E.social_security_number := 0;

or, to change *date_of_birth,*

E.date_of_birth := (5, 21, 1960);

In the latter example, we see the use of a ***record aggregate,*** which consists of a list of expressions (literals in this example) whose values correspond to the order of the declaration of the fields of the record. Alternatively, we could name the fields and permute the order in any way:

(year => 1960, month => 5, day => 21)

Ada provides a substantial number of facilities to access and manipulate records and their components. We will discuss these in following sections and see many examples of the use of records, but first we will specify the record data abstraction.

2.3.1 Record Abstract Data Type

Consider again the record types declared in Figure 2.20. A record of this type has four fields. The name and data type of each field is given as part of the specification of the record type. If we have a record variable *E* declared

E : employee;

and we make the assignment (using a record aggregate literal)

E := ("Smith, Joan ...", 236_52_7364, "123 Peach, ...", (5, 21, 1960));

then we have a one-to-one correspondence between the fields (as identified by the field names) and the values of the fields as shown in Figure 2.21.

E.name	↔	"Smith, Joan . . ."
E.social_security_number	↔	236_52_7364
E.address	↔	"123 Peach, . . ."
E.date_of_birth	↔	(5, 21, 1960)

FIGURE 2.21 One-to-one correspondence between field names and field values.

The internal structure of the fields of a record is that of a set. The fields are declared in a certain order, but that is only because we must write them down in some order. We cannot say that *E.social_security_number* is the successor to *E.name*. That is, *E.name* does not logically follow *E.social_security_number*. If we permute the list in Figure 2.21, the correspondences are the same:

E.date_of_birth	↔	(5, 21, 1960)
E.address	↔	"123 Peach, . . ."
E.name	↔	"Smith, Joan . . ."
E.social_security_number	↔	236_52_7364

We can now generalize these notions and write the specification of the record type.

■ **SPECIFICATION 2.3   Record***

-- **Objects:** *Component objects can be any Ada type (although there are some restrictions)*
-- *and are specified when the record type is declared..*

-- **Structure:** *A set of identifiers is given, one for each field, together with a data type for*
-- *each field. The record is a set of <identifier, value> pairs, where the identifier*
-- *of each field is paired with a value of the data type of the field.*

```
type R is record
    identifier 1 : type 1;
    identifier 2 : type 2;
    identifier 3 : type 3;

            .
            .
            .

    identifier n : type n;
end record;
```

-- **Operations:** *Four operations are specified. Only the first two are necessary as the third*
-- *can be programmed using them. Assume c is a variable, e is an expression of*
-- *one of the component types of the array, and A and B are records of type R.*

c := A.identifier   -- *Record field copy.*
-- **results:** *The component object associated with the field identified*
-- *by identifier is copied into c.*

(continued)

Specification 2.3 (continued)

A.identifier := e   -- *Record field update.*
-- **results:** *The value of* e *is copied into the field of record* A *identified by identifier.*

A := B   -- *Record copy.*
-- **results:** *All fields of record* B *are copied into the corresponding fields of record* A.

A = B   -- *Record equality.*
-- **results:** *True if* A.*field* i = B.*field for all corresponding fields of* A *and* B;
--   *false otherwise.*

---

*Some attributes are inherited, since records are a subclass of other Ada objects. See Appendix A.

The operation $A := B$ retrieves and changes entire records in a single, concise operation. The first two operations retrieve and change individual record components. The power of these operations is enhanced by the fact that the data type of the fields can be nearly any predefined type or user-defined type, including complex abstract data type. The ability to create valuable data structures with various combinations of field types within records is practically limitless.

An important aspect of records is that although the fields are listed in the declaration in a specific order, the combination of identifiers and values forms a set. Some compilers take the liberty of rearranging the order in physical memory in order to economize on memory usage. Figure 2.22 is a record type with several levels.

type name **is new** string(1 .. 25);

type system **is record**
        word_size   : range 8 .. 128;
        manufacturer   : name;
        serial_ports   : range 0 .. 16;
        parallel_ports : range 0 .. 4;
end record;

type system_record **is record**
        model   : name;
        info   : system;
end record;

type computer_list **is array** (1 .. 1000) **of** system_record;

computer : computer_list;

FIGURE 2.22 Data structures of combined arrays and records.

We can retrieve or update any component at any level in the structure. *computer* is an array of records that has component records, which in turn have arrays in them. The word size of the *j*th computer is computer(j).info.word_size

Setting the first character of the *j*th computer's model name to 'X' is done by

computer(j).model(1) := 'X'

Doing the same for the first character of its manufacturer's name gives us

computer(j).info.manufacturer(1) := 'X'

Array indexing in combination with record field identifiers is typical of record use in practice.

Identifiers in themselves need not be unique names, as long as the full name of the identifier is unique. The full name of an identifier is the name fully qualified with names of higher-level records. Figure 2.23 is an example of nested records, which are records with fields that are also records.

type date **is record**
    month   : range 1 .. 12;
    day   : range 1 .. 31;
    year   : range 1880 .. 2100;
end record;

type action **is record**
    action_code   : range 0 .. 20;
    action_date   : date;
end record;

type employee **is record**
    name   : string(1 .. 25);
    social_security_number   : natural;
    address   : string(1 .. 80);
    start   : action;
    stop   : action;
end record;

E : employee;

FIGURE 2.23 Nested records.

There are two fields in the record with the name *month*. Each has a different full name:

E.start.action_date.month

and

E.stop.action_date.month

2.3.2 Record Parameters and Memory Mappings

Records are normally stored in memory beginning at some memory address we will call the record's **base address**, designated by *b*. More often than not the fields follow each other in consecutive memory locations. Consider the record in Figure 2.24 and assume the number of bytes for each object as given.

```
type month_type   : range 1 .. 12;
type day_type     : range 1 .. 31;
type year_type    : range 1880 .. 2100;

type date is record
    mon    : month_type;                              -- 2 bytes.
    day    : day_type;                                -- 2 bytes.
    yr     : year_type;                               -- 2 bytes.
end record;

type employee is record
    name    : string(1 .. 23);                        -- 23 bytes.
    b_date  : date;                                   -- 6 bytes.
    id      : natural;                                -- 4 bytes.
    addr    : string(1 .. 80);                        -- 80 bytes.
end record;
```

FIGURE 2.24 A nested record.

We might expect to find the fields arranged out in memory (assuming a base address of 0) as shown in Figure 2.25. Many computer architectures, however, require that numeric quantities of a given length in bytes start on a memory address that is divisible by that length. Thus, 2-byte numeric data must start on an even byte, 4-byte numeric data must start on a byte whose address is divisible by 4, and so on. On such an architecture, the memory layout of the employee record would more likely be that shown in Figure 2.26.

b_date is aligned on an even address since its first field (and all others) is a 2-byte numeric, and *id* is aligned on an address divisible by 4 since it is a 4-byte numeric. Consequently, the record takes three more bytes, which is called *padding*.

Ada has a pragma called *pack* that instructs the compiler to remove all padding from the record:

pragma pack(employee);

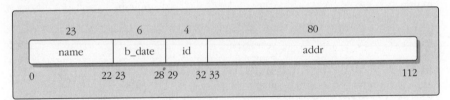

FIGURE 2.25 Memory layout for a record—packed, fields as listed.

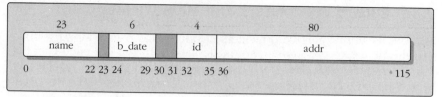

FIGURE 2.26 Memory layout for a record—aligned, fields as listed.

The compiler might revert back to the form of Figure 2.25 at the expense of extra code that moves numeric fields to temporary memory spaces that are aligned properly each time the field is used. A more intelligent solution is to make use of the fact that the fields of a record form a set. Any order of the fields is permissible. In fact, a user may not be aware of the physical ordering in the memory. That being the case, the fields could be rearranged for storage as shown in Figure 2.27.

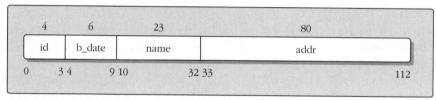

FIGURE 2.27 Memory layout for a record—aligned, packed, fields permuted.

Caution: Pragma *pack* can be applied to any data type. Although it is part of the Ada specification, it is not required and may not be supported by some Ada compilers. Also, its use will probably make the program run slower.

When a field is referenced in a program, at least three things about it must be known by the compiler:

1. Its data type
2. Its length (in bytes or in other suitable measures)
3. Its distance, or **offset**, from the base of the record

Identifier	Data type	Length	Offset
Name	string	23	10
b_date	date	6	4
b_date.mon	month_type	2	4
b_date.day	day_type	2	6
b_date.yr	year_type	2	8
id	natural	4	0
addr	string	80	33
<whole record>	employee	119	0

FIGURE 2.28 Record descriptor.

The compiler might construct a ***record descriptor,*** which is a table of these items and the name of the identifier for each field. Referring to Figure 2.24 and assuming the record memory layout of Figure 2.27, we might have a record descriptor for a record *E* of type *employee,* as shown in Figure 2.28.

The mapping function that allows access to a named field is accomplished by looking up the field name in the record descriptor, adding the field's offset to the record's base address in memory, then manipulating the data according to their data types and lengths.

2.3.3 Variant Record Schemes and Record Discriminants

Some languages provide for the declaration and creation of records that allow a number of variants under the umbrella of a single record data type. Ada's facilities for these kinds of records, which we shall call ***variant records,*** are reasonably extensive.

The idea of a variant record is that the size or structure of a part of the record depends on the value of some other field or fields of the record. In Ada, the fields are called ***discriminants.*** A discriminant is declared in a special way, and there may be constraints on what can be done with it. For instance, in certain cases, the value of a discriminant field may not be changed after it is initially assigned a value.

As an example, suppose we want to create a record to describe a person and have as one of its fields an array that holds the names of the person's children. One approach is to have the array of children's names be as large as the maximum number of children any employee has. This is shown in Figure 2.29(a).

In Figure 2.29(b), the field *child* is said to **depend on the discriminant.** If we were to declare a variable for a person with four children, we could declare

P : person(4);

The declaration sets the value of the discriminant to 4 and the *child* array appears to be

child : kid_list(1 .. 4);

In this context, *P* is a **constrained** record. The value of its discriminant cannot be changed by assignment of a new value. Thus,

P.num_children := 5;   *-- Illegal.*

or

P.num_children := P.num_children + 1;   *-- Illegal.*

```
type name is new string(1 .. 25);
type date is record ...                          -- Same as in Figure 2.24.
max_kids : constant := 15;                       -- Maximum number of children.
type kid_list is array (natural range <>) of name;

type person is record
     full_name      : name;
     b_date         : date;
     num_children   : natural;
     child          : kid_list(1 .. max_kids);
end record;
```
                              (a)

```
subtype name is string(1 .. 25);
type date is record ...                          -- Same as in Figure 2.24.
type kid_list is array (natural range <>) of name;

type person(num_children : natural) is record    -- num_children is the discriminant.
     full_name   : name;
     b_date      : date;
     child       : kid_list(1 .. num_children);
end record;
```
                              (b)

FIGURE 2.29 Record with and without discriminant. (a) Without discriminant; (b) with discriminant.

are illegal statements. *P.num_children* can be used as a constant. We could say

```
num := P.num_children + 1;                       -- Valid.
```

as a valid statement. At first, the constraint on discriminants seems to be quite restrictive. It is, but there are variations on the discriminant theme that greatly increase its utility.

Suppose the *person* record type declaration had been modified slightly to be

```
subtype count is natural range 0 .. 12;
type person(num_children : natural := 0) is record   -- num_children is
     full_name   : name;                             -- the discriminant.
     b_date      : date;
     child       : kid_list(1 .. num_children);
end record;
```

The only difference from the original is that the discriminant has a default value of 0. Now if we declare two variables *P* and *Q*

```
P : person(4);
Q : person;
```

P is **constrained** and acts just as it did in the previous case. The value of *P.num_children* may not be changed. *Q,* on the other hand, is **unconstrained**. Its discriminant variable, *P.num_children,* may be changed during execution but only by assigning a new value to the whole record. If person *Q* had a new child (named "Susan," with the name stored in a string *new_child*), we could change the record to reflect the new child as follows:

```
Q := ( num_children    => Q.num_children + 1,        -- The discriminant.
       full_name       => Q.full_name,
       b_date          => Q.b_date,
       child           => Q.child & new_child);      -- A dependent field.
```

Ada forces the assignment of the entire record to avoid the integrity problem that would be caused, for instance, by incrementing the number of children without adding the name of the new child.

The power of discriminanted records takes an extra dimension when combined with dynamic memory allocation, as we shall see in Section 2.4.

Before we proceed, we will point out some characteristics of Ada discriminants:

1. A discriminant can be any discrete type.
2. There can be more than one discriminant in a single record type.
3. A discriminant's value can be changed only if a default value is declared for the discriminant.
4. If a discriminant's value can be changed, it can only be changed as a result of a complete record assignment.

Variant Records

A second use of discriminants is in designing records that have variant parts or substructures. Suppose we wish to declare a record type that will hold information about various substances. The kind of information stored varies with the category of the substances. Suppose we have three categories— solid, liquid, and gas. We declare a variant record using a discriminant in Figure 2.30.

```
type state is (solid, liquid, gas);
type substance(kind : state := solid) is record
    name      : string(1 .. 20);
    number    : positive;
    case kind is
       when solid   =>   hardness   : float;
       when liquid  =>   boil       : float;
                         freeze     : float;
       when gas     =>   null;
    end case;
end record;
```

FIGURE 2.30 Variant record with three variants.

If we have a variable

S : substance;

and assigned a record for a solid to *S*

S := (state => solid, name => "iron ", number => 123, hardness => 2.45)

then *S* would appear, until changed, to be a record with

kind   = solid
name   = "iron "
number   = 123
hardness = 2.45

The other fields would not exist. If *S* were subsequently changed by the assignment

S := (state => liquid, name => "water ", number => 456,
      boil => 100.0, freeze => 0.0);

S would change to

kind   = liquid
name   = "water "
number   = 456
boil   = 100.0
freeze   = 0.0

The internal structure of *S* appears to vary as the value of the discriminant changes. Some fields appear and disappear; others remain for all variations.

The other variant of *S*, gases, has the property that it has no fields in the variant part of the record:

S := (state => gas, name => "nitrogen ", number => 789);

EXERCISES 2.3

1. Write the type statements for an Ada record that holds information about an object with which you are familiar.

2. Each field of an Ada record has a data type. What restrictions are placed on the data types?

3. Is the following record specification valid for Ada? Explain.

```
type a is record
    a : record
        a : integer;
        b : float;
    end record;
end record;
```

4. Consider the following data type *A*:

        type B **is record**
            key   : integer;
            data   : string(1 .. 15);
        end record;
        type C **is array** (integer **range** <>) **of** B;
        type season **is** (winter, spring, summer, fall);

        type A **is record**
            E : C(5 .. 10);
            D : season;
        end record;

    a. Draw a diagram that shows the relationship among the components of *A*.
    b. Describe how the address of the character *A.E(7).data(5)* might be determined.

5. For the record type *A* in Exercise 3, assume that integers take 4 bytes, characters take 1 byte, and the values of the enumerated type *season* take 2 bytes each. Assume also that a data object that takes *n* bytes must be stored in a memory address that starts on a byte divisible by the length of the object (2-byte objects must start on an even byte address; 4-byte objects must start on a byte address that is divisible by 4, etc.). Suppose we have a variable

    sample : A;

    and *sample* is stored in memory starting at byte 500 of the memory. Show the layout of a single record of type *A* in memory, including padding. What percentage of the space occupied by *sample* is padding?

6. Give a type statement using Ada variant records that holds information about an object with which you are familiar.

7. Compare the Ada data types *array* and *record*. Organize your discussion into three parts— component objects, structure, and operations—and describe how a component identifier of each is converted into a memory address.

■ 2.4 Pointers and Simple Linked Lists

Arrays and records both use calculations to locate their component objects. Arrays use an array mapping function with the indexes of the array as independent variables. Records add the offsets of fields designated by the field identifier to the base address of the record. With ***linked structures***, a different approach is taken. Each data structure component holds not only the component object of the structure, but also one or more addresses (pointers) to related objects. Rather than being implicit in the way the objects are placed in the memory, as with arrays and records, the structure is explicit through the pointers.

A ***linked list*** is a linked structure that is linear. In its simplest form—a singly linked list—each component (**node**) of the list holds a data object and a pointer to the object's successor. An illustration is given in Figure 2.31.

In this section, we will first study pointers and the closely related concept of dynamic memory allocation. We will see how both concepts are used in the construction of simple linked lists. Then, we will look at the characteristics and uses of linked lists in more detail. A full specification of a linked list abstract data type is given in Chapter 4, Specification 4.2.

2.4.1 Pointers

A ***pointer*** is a data type whose values are the locations of objects. (Pointer types are called ***access types*** in Ada; we will use the term "pointer.") If you

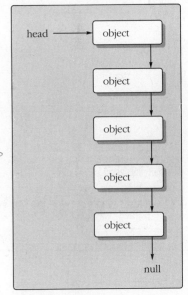

FIGURE 2.31 Conceptual view of a singly linked list.

wrote your home address on a slip of paper and gave it to a friend, the piece of paper holds a pointer to you. Telephone books hold lists of pointers, one to your physical address and one to your telephone address (number).

In computer systems there are many ways of specifying the locations of objects, and there are many kinds of objects. The data we are seeking might be in one of the 16 fast registers of a computer's CPU, and the register designator would be its address. The data might be in the (i, j)th position of a two-dimensional array, in which case (i, j) could be considered to be the pointer. (It would, of course, have to be transformed into a memory address by the array's AMF.) The data object might be in the 15th byte of sector 37, track 183, surface 3 of a large hard disk. The four-tuple <15, 37, 183, 3> would be its address in that medium and, consequently, a pointer value. Any location, whether it is at the abstract, virtual, or physical level, can be the value of a pointer.

In the following discussion, we assume pointers whose values are memory addresses in the computer system's random access memory. Some languages, Ada included, are intentionally vague about what constitutes a pointer value. They like to have the user consider a pointer to be something that, in the abstract, provides access to objects. We will take a more concrete approach. Our pointers are random access memory addresses. The arguments made, the data structures considered, and the conclusions drawn will be valid for any form of pointer or access type.

In practice, RAM addresses take forms that are dependent on the architecture of the computer system and the modes of addressing of that system. For simplicity, we will assume that, as stated in Chapter 1,

type RAM **is array** (0 .. memory_size − 1) **of** byte;

A pointer is therefore an index into the RAM array. The AMF is trivial. The memory address of the object is the value of the pointer:

address(object) = pointer's value

There is one special value needed for pointer types. It is called the ***null value***. It is the pointer that points nowhere. It is often the value 0 or *memory_size-1*. The value used is of little concern since the programming language chooses a value to represent null; the programmer uses the reserved word *null* to designate the value.

Although Ada does not normally place values into variables when the variables are declared unless the programmer appends ":= *value*" to the declaration, Ada places an initial value of *null* in all pointer variables. Thus, if we declared a pointer variable (we'll shortly show how to do this)

Ada assigns the initial value null to every pointer variable.

p : rec_ptr;

then *p* has the value *null* initially.

Suppose we have a record type

```
type rec is record
    key    : integer;
    data   : string(1 .. 5);
end record;
```

and a pointer type and pointer variable

```
type rec_ptr is access rec;
p : rec_ptr;
```

Variables of type *rec_ptr* have as values the memory addresses of objects of type *rec*. Note that *p* is such a variable. It is located someplace in RAM, and its value is a RAM address. Figure 2.32 has two views of the idea: Figure 2.32(a) is conceptual; Figure 2.32(b) is physical.

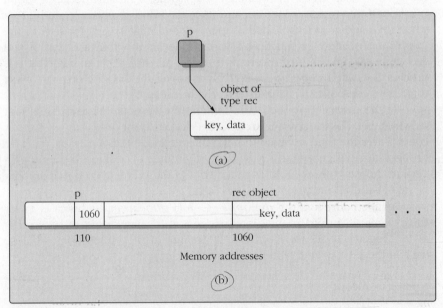

FIGURE 2.32 Pointing at an object. (a) Conceptual view; (b) physical view.

The components of the *rec* object pointed at by *p* are *p.key* and *p.data*, respectively, and the entire record is *p.all*. The following statements are illustrations of the use of *p.rec:*

```
p.key := 20;
p.data := "three";

p.all := (20, "three");
```

Access types can be declared for many objects in Ada. Access types in Ada are, however, restricted to accessing (pointing to) objects of the type they are declared to access.

One note about the conceptual view as given in Figure 2.32 is in order. The arrow is shown going from the pointer variable and ending someplace on the box that stands for the node. An arrow ending anywhere on the node is meant to indicate that the pointer has in it the address of the first byte of the node. It introduces too much clutter to have the pointer arrow always go to the left end of the box.

How might the address of a record of type *rec* be placed in *p?* This is normally done by dynamic memory allocation, which is discussed in the next section.

2.4.2 Dynamic Memory Allocation

Ordinary variables come into existence when the unit in which they are declared and its data area is elaborated. For a package, a variable declared within it is bound to a memory location and its initial value, if any, is loaded into it when the package is established in memory and made ready for use. In the case of a procedure or function, a variable declared within it is established each time the function or procedure is called. Ada has a special name for this process: It is called ***elaboration.*** Roughly speaking, the elaboration of an object establishes the object and makes it ready for use.

In the cases above, the establishment of objects is tied to the Ada unit in which the objects are declared. Once declared, the user has no further control over the time at which the objects are elaborated. A variable can't be brought into existence in this way at any other time. In addition, the user must declare the variables to hold as much data as there are, even if that amount is unknown until the program is executing.

reasons for DMA

An alternative to this is ***dynamic memory allocation.*** In this case, a user can dynamically bring variables into existence at any time during the execution of the program. To see the mechanics of dynamic memory allocations, suppose we had these types and variables declared:

```
type rec is record
    key  : integer;
    data : string(1 .. 5);
end record;
```

and a pointer type and pointer variable:

```
type rec_ptr is access rec;
p : rec_ptr;
```

initial value of null (pointing to nothing)

Dynamic memory allocation is used to create an instance of an object with a pointer pointing to it. In this example, we have the record type *rec* and pointer (access) type *rec_ptr;* a pointer variable *p.* The *p* initially has the value *null,* so it points at nothing. In order to create a record of type *rec* and have *p* point to it, we place the following command in our code:

p := **new** rec;

When the program executes that statement, it allocates as much space as needed for an object of type *rec* from a pool of space (usually called the *heap*) available for this purpose. In this case, assuming that integers take 4 bytes of space, the amount of space allocated would be at least 4 + 5 = 9 bytes.

The value now in *p* is the address in memory of the first byte of the record. The names of the *key* field, the *data* field, and the entire record are, respectively,

p.key   p.data   p.all

and we can use them as we would any variable.

If the heap space is exhausted when the allocation statement is executed and there is no more space in the pool, a *storage_error* exception is generated at the point of the allocation statement.

If the statement that declared *p* had instead declared three pointers, say *p, q,* and *r*

p, q, r : rec_ptr;

we could allocate three instances of records of type *rec:*

```
p   := new rec;
q   := new rec;
r   := new rec;
```

Alternatively, we could have an array of three pointers:

type node_pointer_array **is array** (integer **range** <>) **of** node_ptr;

p : node_pointer_array (1 .. 3);

Allocating the three instances of the record type can be accomplished by

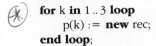

```
for k in 1 .. 3 loop
    p(k) := new rec;
end loop;
```

The second record and its fields, for instance, are *p(2).all, p(2).key,* and *p(2).data.* Each pointer would point to a different area of the memory where its instance type *rec* resides.

Section 3.2.5 of Chapter 3 will discuss the pool of memory (heap) from which the run-time system obtains space for the instances.

There is an additional feature of the dynamic allocation that is quite useful. We can specify a value to be assigned to the object at the time of allocation so we don't have to write separate lines of code to do so. Suppose we want to allocate an instance of *rec* with *p* pointing to it, then load data into the fields of the record. We could do this with the statement sequence

```
p := new rec;
p.key = 12
p.data = "datum"
```

Ada has a feature that allows all of this to happen in a single statement:

```
p := new rec'(12, "datum");
```

The instance of *rec* is established, a pointer to it is placed into *p,* and the values of the fields are loaded into them as the record is created. The material

```
(12, "datum")
```

is a record aggregate value.

Dynamic memory allocation is important in a broad variety of data structures and programs. It provides them with the ability to request space for data only at the time needed and in the exact amounts needed. The program could be run many times with differing amounts of data, and each time it would use only the space required. You will see many examples of the use of these techniques in this book.

Now, we look at the reverse process, dynamic deallocation.

Dynamic Deallocation

If space for program objects can be allocated dynamically, then it seems reasonable that it can be *deallocated*—that is, returned to the heap. There is a feature of Ada that allows this to be done—*unchecked_deallocation* (see the *Ada LRM,* Section 13.10). Let us return to the example that we used to introduce allocation:

```
type rec is record
    key   : integer;
    data  : string(1 .. 5);
end record;

type rec_ptr is access rec;
p: rec_ptr;
        .
        .
        .
p := new rec;
```

Suppose the instance of *rec* pointed at by *p* is used, then is no longer needed. How do we release its memory? The specification of Ada's generic storage deallocation procedure is

```
generic
    type object_type is limited private;
    type pointer_type is access object_type;
procedure unchecked_deallocation (a_pointer : in out pointer_type);
```

Without going into the mysteries of why the procedure is declared like this, let us look at an example of how it is used to return the memory used by the object of type *rec* pointed at by the pointer *p*. We must import the procedure into our program, then instantiate it in the declaration section of our program for the specific types we have in place of *object* and *name*:

```
with unchecked_deallocation;

procedure my_program is

    type rec is record
        key    : integer;
        data   : string(1 .. 5);
    end record;

    type rec_ptr is access rec;

    procedure free is new unchecked_deallocation(rec, rec_ptr);
```

and so on.

Now, to deallocate the instance of the *rec* object pointed at by *p*, we can write the statement

```
free(p);
```

This statement, when executed, has the effect of releasing the memory space used by the instance of *rec* that *p* points at, and *p* is set to *null*. The space is, in theory, available to be reused again for later allocations.

The name *unchecked_deallocation* stems from a chronic problem in the use of pointers. Suppose there were two pointer variables, *p* and *q*, declared

```
p, q : rec_ptr;
```

Look at the following code segment:

```
p := new rec;

q := p;                    -- Make q point to the same instance as p. They hold the same address.
```

```
free(p);                  -- Sets p to null and releases the space occupied by rec back to the heap.

q.all := (1, "CRASH");              -- But the space q is pointing to has been released!
```

At the time of the last statement of this sequence, the space pointed to by *p*—the same as pointed to by *q*—was deallocated. *q,* however, still has a pointer to it. The statement would execute in Ada with no run-time error, but what would be happening? The new record value,

(1, "CRASH")

would dutifully be stored. Suppose the deallocated space has been reallocated to another instance of *rec* or to another variable. It would be overwritten. An entire universe of pathological, hard-to-find bugs is possible as a result.

The name *unchecked_deallocation* comes from Ada's inability to check for this kind of error. The question to a pointer, What are you pointing at? has a simple answer. The question to an instance of *rec,* What points at you? is a difficult one.

We now make use of these concepts in linked data structures, taking one of the simplest structures first—linked lists.

2.4.3 Simple Linked Lists

One of the reoccurring problems in programming how to deal with a set of data when you do not know how much data there will be. Suppose we wanted to read a set of floating-point numbers into the program, hold the numbers internally in a data structure, and make use of them in several places later in the program. One approach would be to declare an array of *float* and place the data into the successive objects of the array as we read each data item from the file. The problem is in declaring the array:

x : **array** (1 .. ??) **of** float;

What should be the upper bound on the range of index values? If we make it too high, we tie up all the unfilled array space, since *x* will go unused if there isn't enough data to fill it. On the other hand, if we make it too low, the array will fill and there will still be more data arriving. Let us make a guess, say *max,* then look at a loop that loads the data into *x:*

```
max : constant integer := 1000;

type data_array is array (1 .. max) of float;
x   : data_array;
n   : natural := 0;
while not end_of_file loop
    n := n + 1;
    get(x(n));
end loop;
```

If the size of floating-point numbers is 4 bytes, we tie up at least 4 * 1000 bytes for *x*. If only 200 numbers are entered, we use 800 bytes and waste 3200.

A question is how can we construct a data structure that starts at size zero, grows in small increments as each data item is read, then stops growing at a size just large enough to hold the amount of data entered. One answer is with the linked list.

A linked list consists of nodes. Each node has a data object, as well as a pointer to another node. The pointers thread the nodes together in some order. Figure 2.33 shows the concept.

Let's look at how these nodes are declared and created. You will see that the technique uses records, pointers, and dynamic allocation. A node is a record declared as follows (assuming that the data are single numbers of type *float*):

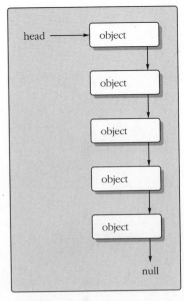

FIGURE 2.33 Conceptual view of a linked list.

```
type node is record
    data : float;
    next : node_ptr;        -- Linking pointer to another node.
end record;
```

The node holds a single datum and a pointer. There has to be an associated pointer type

```
type node_ptr is access node;
```

There is a small problem—the declaration of type *node* needs to know what type *node_ptr* is and vice versa. The problem is solved in Ada by an incomplete declaration, that can be done as follows:

```
type node;
type node_ptr is access node;
type node is record
    data : float;
    next : node_ptr;
end record;
```

A linked list needs one pointer that always points to the first node in the list. In that way the list can be entered, then the pointers threading the nodes can be followed to traverse through the individual nodes of the list. We'll use near-standard terminology for the head pointer and name it *head*. If a separate pointer is also kept that points to the last node of the list, it is often named *tail*:

```
head  : node_ptr;
tail  : node_ptr;
```

Let us now write a small program that reads in a set of numbers of unknown length, then prints the numbers in the reverse order in which they were read. It is shown in Figure 2.34 and combines dynamic memory allocation with pointers and operations on a simple linked list.

```
with text_io; use text_io;
procedure main is
-- Length 18   Complexity 3   Performance O(n), where n is the number of data objects.
    type node;
    type node_ptr is access node;
    type node is record
      data : string(1 .. 10);
      next : node_ptr;
    end record;

    head   : node_ptr;                          -- Remember, these start with the value null.
    p      : node_ptr;

begin
    while not end_of_file loop                  -- Read the data and build a linked list.
      p := new node;                                     -- Allocate a new node.
      get(p.data);                            -- Read the next number into its "data" field.
      p.next := head;              -- Make its "next" field point to the current head node.
      head := p;                             -- Make the head pointer point to the new node.
    end loop;

    p := head;                                      -- Traverse the list printing the data.
    while p /= null loop
      put(p.data); new_line;
      p := p.next;                                  -- Link to the next node in the list.
    end loop;
end main;
```

FIGURE 2.34 A program to place data in a linked list and print the data in reverse order.

Figure 2.35(a) shows the list just before insertion of the new node at its head, and Figure 2.35(b) shows the list just after the insertion.

The first loop in the program repeatedly inserts new nodes into the list. In this instance, it links them so that each new node becomes the new first, or head, node. This is a particularly simple form of insertion.

Suppose q is pointing to some node of the list and we wanted to insert a new node, pointed to by p, between the node pointed to by q and the one that follows it. Figure 2.36 shows the situation before the insertion.

After the following code is executed, the nodes appear as shown in Figure 2.37:

```
p.next := q.next;
q.next := p;
```

The order in which the above statements are executed is critical. If the order is reversed, the insert fails and the tail of the list is permanently lost. Study Figure 2.36 to see why this is so.

The new node is threaded between the others. Remember that it is not physically there. It can be anyplace in the memory. Following the linking

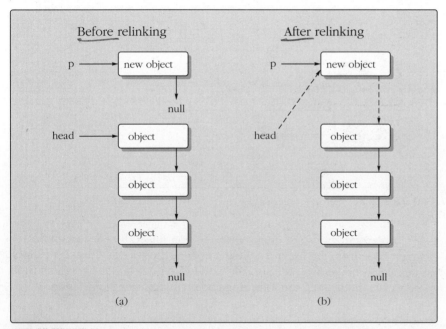

F I G U R E   2.35 Linked list of nodes before and after a new node is added.

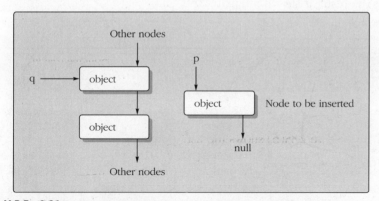

F I G U R E   2.36 Before insertion of a new node between others in the list.

pointers will cause the nodes to be visited in the order shown, regardless of where they physically reside.

The second loop in the program in Figure 2.34 is an example of *traversing* the linked list. Each node is visited in turn and something (in this case printing the data) is done with each node. The loop is repeated here:

```
p := head;                                  -- Traverse the list printing the data.
while p /= null loop
    put(p.data); new_line;
    p := p.next;                            -- Link to the next node in the list.
end loop;
```

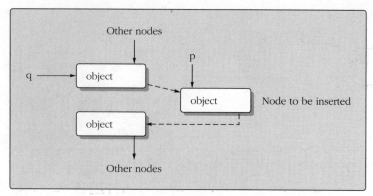

FIGURE 2.37 After insertion of a new node between others in the list.

Other operations are often performed on linked lists; for example, deleting a node from the list and adding a node at the tail of the list. Let us look at deleting a node. If *p* points to the node to be deleted and *q* points to its predecessor node, then the following code will perform the deletion:

```
q.next := p.next;
free(p);
```

The result is shown in Figure 2.38.

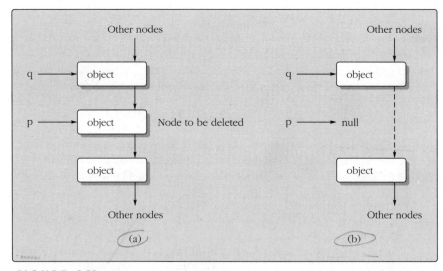

FIGURE 2.38 Deletion of a node of the list. (a) Before deletion. (b) After deletion.

2.4.4 Dynamic Allocation of Variable Size Objects

There is one further aspect of dynamic allocation in Ada that can be very useful. In the case we have seen of records of type *rec,*

```
type rec is record
    key   : integer;
    data  : string(1 .. 5);
end record;
```

```
type rec_ptr is access rec;
p : rec_ptr;
```

each instance of the record is the same length—probably 9 bytes.

Suppose our data objects are of different lengths. Take, for instance, strings read from the terminal as lines of text. The user might enter lines from 0 to 80 characters in length. It is possible using Ada to allocate space for the lines dynamically so the exact number of bytes needed for each line is allocated to it. It is done by using records with discriminants.

Consider the declarations

```
subtype line_length is positive range 1 .. 80;      -- Number of characters in a line.
```

```
type line_text(len : line_length) is record      -- Lines; notice the discriminant.
    text : string(1 .. len);
end record;                 discriminant
```

```
type line_ptr is access line_text;
```

```
p           : line_ptr;
input_line  : string(line_length);
```

Type *line_text* is a discriminanted record type, and *p* is a pointer to instances of a record of that type. Suppose we read a line with a *get_line* procedure from package *text_io*. Recall that *get_line* reads the characters of the input line and returns them in a string, together with a second variable that holds number of characters read. Now we put this all together to read a line, allocate a *line_text* record just long enough to hold it, and place the characters and length into the allocated record:

```
get_line(input_line, n);
```

```
p := new line_text(n)'(n, input_line(1..n));
```

The second statement allocates a *line_text* record with its discriminant equal to *n* and loads the *len* field with *n* and the *text* field with a string, *input_line(1 .. n)*, that is exactly *n* bytes in length (Figure 2.39). Another line read that has a different length would have a different amount of memory allocated.

2.4.5 Application of Pointers and Lists

Next, we will consider a problem and solve it in three ways, making use of the features we studied in this section. The problem is to read lines of text that are of varying size, store them, sort them into alphabetical order, and print

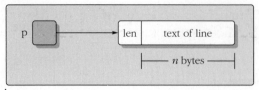

FIGURE 2.39 Result of allocating a line of text with *len* characters.

the results. We do not know in advance how many lines there will be or how long any single line will be until we read it. We do know that any line can hold at most 80 characters. An empty line signals the end of data.

The three solutions we will show are

1. Using a fixed size array of fixed size lines, with 80 characters of space for each line
2. Using a fixed size array of pointers to instances of lines of different lengths
3. Using a linked list of lines of differing lengths

Assume that, although we don't know it in advance, there is a test set of data with 200 lines and an average of 40 characters per line.

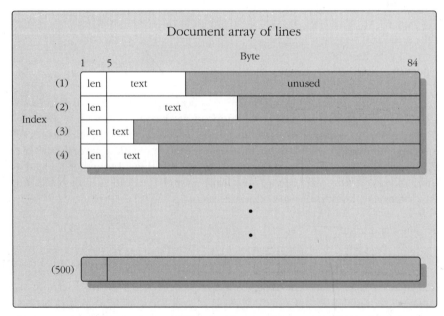

```
Subtype line_length is positive range 1 .. 80;
type line_data is record
    length  : line_length;
    text    : string(line_length);
end record;
type lines is array (natural range <>) of line_data;

document : lines(1 .. 500);
```

FIGURE 2.40 The document as a static array of fixed size line space.

Solution 1 *Fixed Size Array of Fixed Size Lines, with 80 Characters of Space for Each Line*

For the first solution, we take a straightforward approach and use a fixed size array of lines. We have to guess at the maximum number of lines because we can't delay specifying the size of the line array beyond the point where we start placing lines into it. We choose 500, and use the same approach for each line. We save space for 80 characters, even though fewer may be read. The data structures are declared as shown in Figure 2.40.

If fewer than 500 lines arrive, we waste space. It is tied up by our program, but it is unused. Since each character takes 1 byte of memory and we assume that the line length stored with it takes 4 bytes, we can estimate that the array *document* takes $84 * 500 = 42,000$ bytes. Since we read only 200 lines of average size 40 bytes plus a 4-byte length field, the number of bytes actually filled with data is only $44 * 200 = 8800$ bytes. So we waste $42,000 - 8800 = 33,200$ bytes. The program is shown in Figure 2.41.

```
with text_io; use text_io;

procedure sort_lines is
-- assumes:  The lines are 80 characters or less, and there are no more than 500 lines.
-- results:  Reads document up to 500 lines, sorts it in ascending order, and prints it.
--           Implementation is a static array of 80 character strings.
-- Length 22   Complexity 2   Performance—Determined by the sort chosen.
    subtype line_range is natural range 0 .. 500;
    subtype line_length is positive range 1 .. 80;
    type line_data is record
      length   : line_length;
      text     : string(line_length);
    end record;
    type lines is array (natural range <>) of line_data;

    document    : lines(1 .. line_range'last);     -- Space for all document lines.
    num_lines   : line_range := 0;                 -- Number of lines in document.
    len         : natural range 0 .. line_length'last;    -- Length of the line.
    new_line    : string(line_length);

    procedure sort(doc : in out lines) is separate;
    -- results:  Sorts document in ascending order of lines.
    procedure print(doc : lines) is separate;
    -- results:  Prints document.

begin
-- Read all input lines to a maximum of 500.
    loop
        get_line(new_line, len);
        exit when (len = 0) or (num_lines = 500);
        num_lines := num_lines + 1;
```

FIGURE 2.41 Line sorting program using static memory.

(continued)

Figure 2.41 (continued)

```
        document(num_lines).length := len;
        document(num_lines).text(1 .. len) := new_line(1 .. len);
    end loop;

    sort(document(1 .. num_lines));
    print(document(1 .. num_lines));

end sort_lines;
```

FIGURE 2.41 *(continued)*

Solution 2   Fixed Size Array of Pointers to Instances of Lines of Different Lengths

In the second solution, we use dynamic memory allocation of varying size records, as we illustrated in Section 2.4.4, combined with an array of pointers.

Rather than have the 42,000 byte array of strings, *document,* we use an array of 500 pointers pointing to dynamically allocated lines of text. Allocated space for each line varies since the *line_text* record has a discriminant and is allocated the required space as the data arrive. A conceptual view is shown in Figure 2.42.

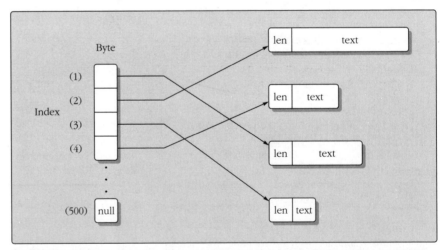

FIGURE 2.42 The document using variable sized dynamic memory allocation and an array of pointers to the allocated line nodes.

As each line is read, its length is determined and an instance allocated that is matched in size with the length of the line. A pointer to it is placed in the next available position in the array (Figure 2.43).

If we assume, as is typical, that a pointer takes 4 bytes of memory, then the array *doc,* which is now an array of pointers, requires 500 * 4 = 2000 bytes. Each line is allocated storage as needed. On the authors' system, the number of bytes needed for a *line_text* record is 5 bytes plus the number of characters in the line. If we read 200 lines that were on average 40 characters in length,

```ada
with text_io; use text_io;

procedure sort_lines is
-- assumes:  The lines are 80 characters or less, and there are at most 500 lines.
-- results:  Reads document, sorts lines in ascending order, and prints them.
-- Length 21   Complexity 2   Performance—Determined by the sort chosen.
      subtype line_range is natural range 0 .. 500;            -- Number of lines.
      subtype line_length is positive range 1 .. 80;   -- Number of characters in a line.
      type line_text(length : line_length) is record       -- Lines; note the discriminant.
        text : string(1 .. length);
      end record;
      type line_ptr is access line_text;                      -- Pointers to lines.
      type lines is array (positive range <>) of line_ptr;   -- Arrays of line pointers.

      document   : lines(1 .. line_range'last);        -- Pointers to document lines.
      num_lines  : line_range := 0;                      -- Number of lines found.
      len        : natural range 0 .. line_length'last;       -- Length of a line.
      new_line   : string(line_length);

      procedure sort(doc : in out lines) is separate;
      -- results:  Sorts document in ascending order.
      procedure print(doc : lines) is separate;
      -- results:  Prints document.

begin
-- Read all input lines up to a maximum of 500.
      loop
        get_line(new_line, len);
        exit when (len = 0) or (num_lines = 500);
        num_lines := num_lines + 1;      -- Allocate a new line and store the pointer to it.
        document(num_lines) := new line_text'(len, new_line(1 .. len));
      end loop;

      sort(document(1 .. num_lines));
      print(document(1 .. num_lines));

end sort_lines;
```

FIGURE 2.43 Line-sorting program using dynamic memory allocation and an array of pointers.

$200 * 45 = 9000$ bytes would be required for the lines for a total of $2000 + 9000 = 11,000$ instead of the 42,000 bytes needed in the program of Figure 2.41 (Solution 1). We now have a program that, with some fixed overhead for a pointer array, is the same length and complexity but will adjust in two ways the space it requires to conform to the amount of data arriving:

1. It allocates space only for the lines read.
2. It allocates for each line space for only the number of characters in the line plus 5 bytes.

We saved considerable space by this approach, but we still have the problem of having a maximum of 500 lines.

Solution 3   Linked List of Varying Size Nodes

Refer back to Figure 2.33, a conceptual view of a singly linked list. If the objects were lines of text, we could apply the linked list to a solution of the problem of reading, sorting, and printing the lines of a document. We would like a linked list of lines, and the space allocated for each line should be matched to the length of the line. The conceptual view of our data would be as shown in Figure 2.44.

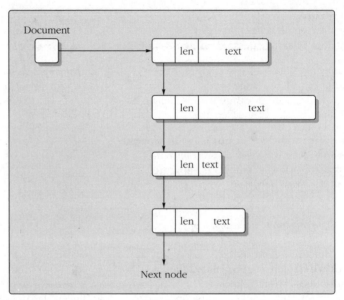

FIGURE 2.44 The document as a linked list of varying size lines.

Since the list is to be sorted after being constructed, we could add new lines at any place in the list. The head of the list turns out to be a particularly simple place to add new lines, so we add them there. A linked list solution to the line-sorting problem is given in Figure 2.45. Notice that we are using a discriminant on the nodes of the list which, consequently, vary in size.

The number of bytes required by this solution can be estimated as follows. Each node must hold a discriminant value, the characters of the line, and a pointer to the next line. Lines are on average 40 characters in length, we assume 4 bytes for a pointer, and the discriminant on the authors' system takes 5 bytes. Each node then takes 40 + 4 + 5 = 49 bytes. There are 200 nodes, so the total required for the data is 49 * 200 = 9800 bytes. Contrast this with the 11,000 bytes required by solution 2, and the 42,000 bytes of solution 1. It is not much better than solution 2 for the amount of data assumed, but this solution has a second advantage. It can potentially handle more than 500 lines. The total number is dependent on the size of the heap. In addition, it is no more complex than the other two solutions.

Note that an exception handler for *storage_error* exceptions is included.

```
with text_io; use text_io;

procedure sort_lines is
-- assumes:  The lines are 80 characters or less in length.
-- results:  Reads document, sorts lines in ascending order, and prints them.
-- Length 22   Complexity 2   Performance—Determined by the sort chosen.
    subtype line_length is positive range 1 .. 80;

    type list_node(length : line_length);        -- Necessary for the next type declaration.
    type node_ptr is access list_node;                    -- Pointers to list nodes.
    type list_node(length : line_length) is record      -- Full declaration of a list node.
      next : node_ptr;
      text: string(1 .. length);            discriminant
    end record;

    document, p   : node_ptr;                    -- Head of the list and working pointer.
    len           : natural range 0 .. line_length'last;      -- Length of the line.
    new_line      : string(line_length);

    procedure sort(document : in out node_ptr) is separate;
    -- results:  Sorts document in ascending order of lines.
    procedure print(document : node_ptr) is separate;
    -- results:  Prints document.

begin
    -- Read all input lines.
    loop
      get_line(new_line, len);
      exit when (len = 0);                    -- Note that the check for 500 lines is gone.

      -- Allocate a new list node, store length and text in it, and have its link point to head of
      -- document.
      p := new list_node'(len, new_line(1 .. len), document);
      document := p;                    -- Make doc point to new node as new list head.
    end loop;

    sort(document);
    print(document);
exception
    when storage_error => put_line("Exhausted memory—too many lines.");
                          put_line("Sorting and printing what was read.");
                          sort(document);        -- Note: sort and print may not
                          print(document);       -- execute successfully because of
end sort_lines;                                  -- memory problems.
```

FIGURE 2.45 Line-sorting program using a linked list.

We have been able to remove the fixed 500 line limit we had in our nonlinked list solutions to this problem, but the allocation heap is finite. A document may exhaust the heap space and the p := **new** *line* statement would cause a *storage_error* exception to be generated. Our exception handler notes what happened, then processes the lines it has been able to read and link into the list.

We will leave the *sort* procedure to a general discussion of linked list sorts in Chapter 6. The *print* procedure is shown in Figure 2.46 and is an example of a traversal through a linked list.

```
separate (sort_lines)
procedure print(doc : node_ptr) is
-- Length 4   Complexity 2   Performance O(n), where n is the number of lines.
      p : node_ptr := doc;                              -- Start at the head of the list.
begin
      while p /= null loop                              -- next = null in the tail node.
         put_line(p.text);
         p := p.next;                                   -- Link to next node of the list.
      end loop;
end print;
```

FIGURE 2.46 Linked list traversal—printing list.

2.4.6 Recursion and Linked Lists

A recursive operation is one that is defined in terms of itself. The factorial of an integer *n* is written as *n*!; it is the product of all of the integers between 1 and *n* inclusive:

$$n! := n*(n-1)*(n-2)*\cdots*1$$

We could define the factorial recursively:

$$1! = 1$$
$$n! = n*(n-1)!$$

There is a special case (1!) and a general case ($n! = n*(n-1)!$). Procedures can be written recursively. A procedure to compute the factorial of a positive number in Ada might look as shown in Figure 2.47.

```
function factorial (n : positive) return positive is
-- Length 3   Complexity 2   Recursion 1   Performance O(n)
begin
      if n = 1 then
         return 1;
      else return (n * factorial(n-1));
      end if;
end factorial;
```

FIGURE 2.47 A recursive factorial function.

In the **else** clause, the function calls itself with a different argument. The return is delayed until the second call to factorial is completed. This second call, assuming $n > 2$, also makes a call to factorial and can't return until it is completed. This continues until there is finally a call with 1 as the argument.

The **then** branch of the **if** statement is taken, and the pending returns are resolved cascading back to the original recursive call. Finally it is resolved, and a return is made from the original call. Appendix B has a more complete discussion of recursion.

We now introduce the use of recursion with linked lists. Suppose we had the linked list of lines built while running the program in Figure 2.45. The procedure *print* was specified to print the lines in the linked list:

procedure print(doc : line_list.linked_list) **is separate;**

We could write the procedure *print* by traversing through the list as shown in Figure 2.48.

```
separate(sort_lines)
procedure print(doc : node_ptr) is
-- Length 3   Complexity 2   Recursion 1   Performance O(n)
begin
    if p /= null then                          -- next = null in the tail node.
        print (p.next);              -- Print the remainder of the list in inverse order.
        put_line(p.text);                              -- Print this node.
    end loop;
end print;
```

F I G U R E 2.48 Print lines in reverse using recursion.

Suppose we wished *print* to print the list in the reverse order from which it is stored in the list—from the tail to the head. In the case of the problem of lines of text we have been considering, the lines would print in inverse alphabetical order. This could be awkward since we would have to traverse the list against the pointers, not an easy task. The job is simple with recursion. The idea is, when sitting at a node, to print in reverse the remainder of the list, then to print the node. It is easier to understand the code than to try to explain what happens. Figure 2.48 gives the print procedure for reverse printing.

All executions of the statement *put_line(p.text);* are deferred until the recursive calls by the statement *print (p.next);* step through the list to the tail node. At that point *p.next* is *null,* that call to *print* returns, and the statements *print (p.next);* execute on the nodes of the list in reverse order.

While we are considering the inverse order print, let us see how the list might be printed by replacing the recursion with a stack. In fact, recursion is accomplished using a stack, but the details are hidden. We will explicitly show the stacking.

What we will do is create a stack of node pointers. As we traverse the list from head to tail, we will place the pointers to the nodes of the list onto the stack. When we have reached the end of the list, we will *pop* the stack until it is empty, printing the *text* field of each node popped. The stack package we will use is the generic stack of Specification 1.3. Figure 2.49 is the print procedure.

```
with stack_package;
procedure print(doc : node_ptr) is
-- Length 10   Complexity 3   Performance O(n)
     package ptr_stack is new stack_package (node_ptr);

     the_stack : ptr_stack.stack (1000);
     p : node_ptr := doc;

begin

     while p /= null loop                              -- Traverse the list.
       ptr_stack.push(the_stack, p);                   -- Stacking pointers.
       p := p.next;
     end loop;

     while stack_size /= 0 loop                         -- Pop the stack.
       put_line(ptr_stack.top (the_stack).text);        -- Printing nodes.
       ptr_stack.pop (the_stack);
     end loop;

end print;
```

FIGURE 2.49 Print lines in reverse using a stack. Note the increase in length and complexity over the recursive version of Figure 2.48.

2.4.7 Linked List Variations

There are a number of variations on the linked list theme. We will discuss circular lists and multiply linked lists.

Circular Lists

The idea of a *circular list* is to make the tail node's pointer point back to the head node instead of to *null*. In fact, in many instances, there is no conceptual head or tail to the list. There has to be at least one pointer outside the list that provides access to one node. From there, all others can be reached by chaining along the links. Figure 2.50 shows the idea.

Multiply Linked Lists

Lists can be multiply linked. The linked lists we have seen thus far have had one set of linkages. A doubly linked list is one in which each node points to its successor node as well as to its predecessor node. Figure 2.51 illustrates the idea for both the noncircular and circular versions.

The declaration of nodes with two pointers is simple and is illustrated as follows:

```
type   node;
type   node_access is access node;                     -- Pointer to list nodes.
```

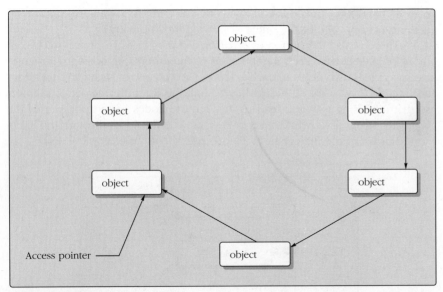

FIGURE 2.50 Circular linked list.

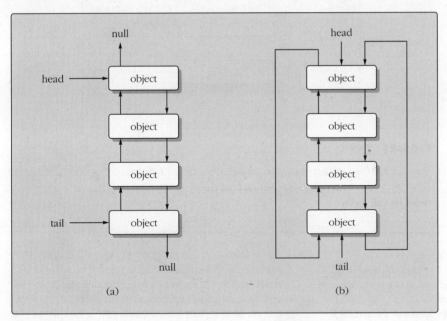

FIGURE 2.51 Doubly linked lists. (a) Noncircular; (b) circular.

```
type   node is record                              -- List nodes.
          obj    : object;                         -- User objects.
          next   : node_access;                     -- List links.
          prior  : node_access;                     -- List links.
       end record;
```

nodes w/ 2 pointers

In the doubly linked lists shown, one link path (following *prior* pointers) is the exact opposite of the other (following *next* pointers).

There is also the notion of **_multilinked lists_** in which there are two or more pointer chains, each independent of the others. Suppose, for instance, we had at least two fields in each node—one a character string and the other an integer. Now suppose we wished to link the list with one set of pointers so that traversing it would lead us through the nodes in sorted order of the character string field, while another linkage would lead us through the list in sorted order of the integer field. Figure 2.52 shows an example.

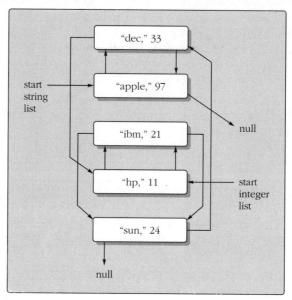

FIGURE 2.52 Multilist linked two ways.

EXERCISES 2.4

1. Describe in your own words Ada's access types.
2. Explain the difference between a pointer illustrated as a line with an arrowhead on the end and a pointer implemented as an address in RAM.
3. Write a sort procedure for the program in Figure 2.43. Test the program with your procedure in it.
4. Rewrite the program in Figure 2.45 to eliminate the *sort* subprogram. Insert each new line (not at the head of the list) but in the list in such a way that the list, at any point in the processing of the lines, is sorted. This involves searching the linked list for the insertion point, then inserting the new node at that point.

5. Add a feature to the program in Figure 2.45 that, after reading all of the lines and placing them in the list, reads prefix strings from the terminal. Prefix strings are short strings. Have the program delete any line in the list with its first letters equal to a prefix string. Then have it print the resulting list.
6. Using the linked list that follows, track by hand the sequence of calls and the argument pointer in the recursive version of the print procedure that prints a list of lines in reverse order:

head→ "line 1" → "line 2" → "line 3" → "line 4" → null

■ 2.5 Summary

We have discussed three data types—arrays, records, and pointers—that are predefined in most programming languages, and one user-defined data type—linked lists. The former three are used in various combinations to construct most user-defined data structures.

The component objects of arrays are normally all of the same data type, which implies that they are normally the same size. This, together with systematic, sequential placement of the objects in memory, makes it possible to specify uniquely which component object is wanted and to use a simple array mapping function to map the array's index(es) to a memory address. An important attribute of arrays is that the index can be a variable whose value varies or is set at execution time.

The component fields of records are identified by their names, and their memory addresses are computed by adding the known offsets of the identifiers to the base address of the record. In contrast to arrays, the identifiers of fields must be known at the time the program is written. Records fields can be, and most often are, a variety of data types.

Arrays and records provide random access to their component objects. Once the identifier of a component is known, access to it is rapid. In order to achieve this rapid access, a price must be paid. The identifiers are restricted to an index in the case of arrays and to a name in the case of records. Objects can be accessed using other attributes, such as the content of one or more of their subcomponents being equal to a given value. Such access, however, almost certainly means a search is needed through all or some subset of the components. Searching is inherently slower and less efficient than the simple calculations required if an index or name is known.

Access to the component objects of linked structures is carried out by following chains of pointers. If, for example, a singly linked list holds the data, we start at the head and traverse down the linking pointers. There is no efficient access by index, position, or name. However, if a traverse is required—as would be the case if every object had to be examined during a search—then pointers are particularly efficient. It is normal to find that the list traverse

```
while p /= null loop
    process(p.all);
    p := p.next;
end loop;
```

is faster than an equivalent array traverse

```
for i in A'range loop
    process(A(i));
end loop;
```

The hidden factor is the array mapping function that must be computed for each cycle of the **for** loop. The statement $p := p.next$ is inherently simpler and faster.

One of the most important attributes of linked structures is their ability to grow and shrink as the amount of data being processed changes. We saw that we could have a linked list not only adjust its length to equal the number of objects in it, but also, by using discriminated records, the nodes themselves could be varied in size to accommodate the amount of data in varying-sized component objects. These effects were achieved through the use of a combination of features, including pointers and dynamic memory allocation. We will see much of these techniques in the remainder of this book.

Often we will find that abstract data types that we design and specify have a number of reasonable implementations. Package bodies that use different methods, some linked, some not, can be written to meet the same specification. Often these different implementations have different performance characteristics. For instance, to find the ith component of an array involves a simple calculation. A linked list must be partially traversed to reach its ith component. On the other hand, traversing a linked list is faster than traversing an array.

3

Stacks and Queues

■ 3.1 Introduction

In Chapter 2, we looked at three data types—arrays, records, and pointers—that are at what might be called a *low level of abstraction*. They are predefined types in most programming languages and are used to build almost all other data types. In this chapter we take up two classes of data types that are generally not predefined but are relatively simple and normally written by users or obtained from existing libraries of packages. They are *stacks* and *queues.* Both are extremely important to computing.

We saw an example of a stack in Chapter 1, which was used to illustrate how to design, specify, and build an abstract data type. The major attribute of a stack is that the component that is removed is the one that was most recently added to it. It is said to have a *last-in/first-out (LIFO)* behavior.

The simplicity of stacks belies their importance in computing. Many computer architectures have stacks built in and have machine level instructions that operate a hardware stack. The sequencing of calls to and returns from subprograms exhibits a stack behavior (the latest subprogram entered is the first one that must be exited). Arithmetic expressions are often evaluated by a sequence of stack operations, and many handheld calculators operate on a stack principle. Stacks are the subject of Section 3.2.

Queues are data types whose major feature is that the object in the queue that arrived earliest is the one removed. Queues exhibit a *first-in/first-out (FIFO)* behavior. They are frequently found in everyday life: Lines at the bank, grocery store, and cinema are examples of queues. Many queues are also being used in computing. I/O requests are queued for service on a disk in a multiuser time-shared system; tasks are queued for access to a processor to run them; characters input from a terminal are queued in a buffer as they are processed by the system, and so on. FIFO queues are the subject of Section 3.3.

One important variation of queues is the priority queue. These are queues in which the queue order is not on the order of arrival of the objects into the queue but rather the "importance" of the objects. The importance of an object is measured by some attribute of the object called its *priority*. Several objects in a priority queue can have the same priority value. Within a given priority, we might specify that the objects are to be taken from the priority queue in first-in/first-out order, we might specify random order within a priority, or we might choose some other scheme. Section 3.4 examines priority queues.

A common example of a priority queue is found in the emergency room of hospitals. During large emergencies, a procedure called triage is followed to order treatment of the patients: first priority—all patients with the worst injuries who are likely to survive if given treatment; second priority—patients who are not likely to survive; third priority—patients with severe but not life-threatening injuries; fourth priority—patients who have more minor injuries. Section 3.5 gives an example of the use of FIFO and priority queues in scheduling I/O operations on a magnetic disk. Section 3.6 summarizes the chapter.

EXERCISES 3.1

1. In your own words, explain the following terms:
    a. Stack
    b. Queue

c. Priority queue

2. Give two examples from everyday life of a stack, a queue, and a priority queue.

■ 3.2 Stacks   *LIFO*

We saw an example of a stack in Chapter 1, Specification 1.2. Here, we consider the use of stacks and the stack abstraction. The following is an example of the use of a stack to evaluate an arithmetic expression.

Using a stack to evaluate the expression $(5 + 7) * 10$

Operation	Stack contents
push (5)	5
push (7)	7 5
"+"	12
push (10)	10 12
"*"	120

The result, 120, is the element on top of the stack.

The operations "+" and "*" combine the top two numbers on the stack, popping both off, then pushing the result of the operation onto the stack. Thus "+" in the table pops 7 then 5 from the stack, adds them, and pushes the result 12 back onto the stack. Each such operation uses two stack objects and produces one. The final result, 120, is on the top of the stack. This simple mechanism can be used to evaluate arithmetic expressions, no matter how complex.

We can imagine a stack in a number of ways. We can think of the stack as a linear arrangement of the stack objects, with the order of arrival into the stack as the ordering of the objects. The top object is the latest arrival, and the bottom is the earliest. Figure 3.1(a) shows this view. Or we think of the stack as an unordered collection of objects, each object tagged with its time of arrival into the stack. Figure 3.1(b) shows this view. The imagined process of popping the stack is different in the two views. In the linear case [Figure 3.1(a)], we remove the top object. In the tagged collection view [Figure 3.1(b)], we search for the object with the latest time on its tag then remove it. Each is a perfectly valid conceptualization of a stack. It does not mean we have to write our code following one scheme or the other. What we have is an abstraction. In practice, stack implementations are almost always done like the conceptualization in Figure 3.1(a). But if we imagined the stack as in Figure 3.1(b), nothing that the stack package does as seen from the outside (i.e., not looking at the code, but only at the specification) violates our conceptual view.

Pascal	← top (latest) object	Shannon, 1315
Shannon		Hopper, 1155
Hopper		Babbage, 0931
Codd		Pascal, 1430
Babbage		Codd, 1015
	(a)	(b)

FIGURE 3.1 Two conceptual views of a stack structure. (a) Linear arrangement; (b) set of time-stamped objects.

The point is not to confuse the conceptualization and the implementation of the data type. We shall see in Section 3.4 that the most efficient implementation of a priority queue, which can be conceptualized as a linear list of objects ordered by priority values, is a data structure that is quite different and is not even linear—it is a form of binary tree.

3.2.1 Static and Dynamic Stacks

The specification of the generic stack in Chapter 1, Specification 1.2, is reproduced here as Specification 3.1. A package body using an array of objects for implementation is given in Package Body 3.1.

■ SPECIFICATION 3.1   Generic Stack

-- Same as Specification 1.2,
-- with the addition of
-- procedure clear.

-- Structure: *The objects are arranged linearly in order of their arrival in the stack;*
--   *the latest arrival is called the top object.*

-- Constraints: $0 <= number\_of\_objects <= max\_size.$
--   *Number_of_objects and max_size appear below.*

generic

    type object_type **is private**;   *-- Type of object to be stacked.*
    max_size : natural := 100;   *-- Maximum stack size; defaults to 100.*

package stack_package **is**

    stack_full   : **exception**;
    stack_empty   : **exception**;

    procedure push (the_object : object_type);
    -- results: *The_object is appended to the stack as its top object.*
    -- exceptions: *Stack_full is raised if number_of_objects = max_size.*

(continued)

Specification 3.1 (continued)

function top **return** object_type;
-- **results:**   *A copy of the top object of the stack is returned.*
-- **exceptions:**   *Stack_empty is raised if number_of_objects = 0.*
-- **notes:**   *The stack is not changed.*

procedure pop;
-- **results:**   *The top object is deleted from the stack.*
-- **exceptions:**   *Stack_empty is raised if number_of_objects = 0.*

function pop **return** object_type;
-- **results:**   *The top object is deleted from the stack and returned.*
-- **exceptions:**   *Stack_empty is raised if number_of_objects = 0.*

function number_of_objects **return** natural;
-- **results:**   *Returns the number of objects currently in the stack.*

procedure clear;
-- **results:**   *The number of objects in the stack is set to 0; the stack is empty.*

end stack_package;

■ **PACKAGE BODY 3.1   Generic Stack—Implements Specification 3.1**

package body stack_package **is**

    subtype count **is** natural **range** 0 .. max_size;
    subtype index **is** positive **range** 1 .. max_size;
    type array_of_objects **is array** (index) **of** object_type;

    latest   : count := 0;   -- *Number of objects stacked; also the index of latest arrival.*
    objects : array_of_objects;   -- *Array holding the stack objects.*

    procedure push (the_object : object_type) **is**
    -- *Length 3   Complexity 2   Performance O(1)*
    begin
      latest := latest + 1;   -- *Raises an exception if latest = max_size.*
      objects(latest) := the_object;
    exception
      when constraint_error | numeric_error => **raise** stack_full;
    end push;

    function top **return** object_type **is**
    -- *Length 2   Complexity 2   Performance O(1)*
    begin
      return objects(latest);   -- *Raises an exception if latest = 0.*
    exception
      when constraint_error => **raise** stack_empty;
    end top;

(continued)

Package Body 3.1 (continued)

```
procedure pop is
-- Length 2   Complexity 2   Performance O(1)
begin
   latest := latest − 1;                         -- Raises an exception if latest = 0.
exception
   when constraint_error | numeric_error => raise stack_empty;
end pop;

function pop return object_type is
-- Length 3   Complexity 2   Performance O(1)
begin
   latest := latest − 1;                         -- Raises an exception if latest = 0.
   return objects(latest + 1);   _____
exception
   when constraint_error | numeric_error => raise stack_empty;
end pop;

function number_of_objects return natural is
-- Length 1   Complexity 1   Performance O(1)
begin
   return latest;
end number_of_objects;

procedure clear is
-- Length 1   Complexity 1   Performance O(1)
begin
   latest := 0;
end clear;

end stack_package;
```

If we wish to have a <u>linked implementation</u> of the stack specified in Specification 3.1, we can do so. We will, however, change the specification slightly to take advantage of one of the benefits of using a linked structure. Specification 3.1 has a generic parameter

```
max_size : natural := 100;                       -- Maximum stack size; defaults to 100.
```

If we delete this item, we have no stated bound on the stack. The stack can continue to grow until the heap space is exhausted. We can then rewrite the stack specification by rewriting the first few lines. The result is Specification 3.2.

■ **SPECIFICATION 3.2   Generic Dynamic Stack**

-- **Structure:** *The objects are arranged linearly in order of their arrival in the stack;*
--   *the latest arrival is called the top object.*

(continued)

Specification 3.2 (continued)

-- *Constraints:*   *The maximum stack size is implementation*   -- *The* **Constraint** *statement*
--   *dependent and is unknown.*   -- *is different from that in*
                                                                          -- *Specification 3.1.*

generic
    type object_type **is private**;   -- *Type of object to be stacked.*
    NO max-size   -- *The max_size parameter was removed from here.*   →*cannot test : do NOT do (not a*
    package dynamic_stack_package **is**   *good constraint)*

    -- *The rest of the specification is the same as Specification 3.1.*

end dynamic_stack_package;

    Package Body 3.2 is a straightforward implementation using a linked list. Each object pushed onto the stack is placed in a new node that is inserted at the head of the linked list of nodes. When the stack is popped, the head node of the list is removed from the list.

■ **PACKAGE BODY 3.2** **Generic Dynamic Stack—Implements Specification 3.2**

with unchecked_deallocation;

package body dynamic_stack_package **is**

    type node;   -- *The nodes of the linked list that holds the stack objects.*
    type node_pointer **is access** node;
    type node **is record**
      object   : object_type;
      next   : node_pointer;
    end record;

    type list_type **is record**
      head   : node_pointer;   -- *Head points to list node that holds the stack's top object.*
      size   : natural := 0;   -- *The number of nodes (objects) in the list (stack).*
    end record;

    procedure free **is new** unchecked_deallocation(node, node_pointer);
    the_list : list_type;

    procedure push (the_object : object_type) **is**
    -- *Length 3   Complexity 2   Performance O(1)*
    begin
      the_list.head   := new node'(the_object, the_list.head);   -- *Put the_object at*
      the_list.size   := the_list.size + 1;   -- *the list's head.*
    exception
      when storage_error => **raise** stack_full;   -- *Raised if no space is left to allocate.*
    end push;

(continued)

Package Body 3.2 (continued)

```
function top return object_type is
-- Length 2   Complexity 2   Performance O(1)
begin
  return the_list.head.object;
exception
  when constraint_error => raise stack_empty;
end top;


procedure pop is
-- Length 5   Complexity 2   Performance O(1)
  hold : node_pointer := the_list.head;
begin
  the_list.head   := the_list.head.next;
  the_list.size   := the_list.size − 1;
  free(hold);
exception
  when constraint_error => raise stack_empty;
end pop;


function pop return object_type is
-- Length 3   Complexity 1   Performance O(1)
  hold : object_type := top;
begin
  pop;
  return hold;
end pop;


function number_of_objects return natural is
-- Length 1   Complexity 1   Performance O(1)
begin
  return the_list.size;
end size;


procedure clear is
-- Length 2   Complexity 2   Performance O(n)
begin
  while the_list.size > 0 loop
    pop;
  end loop;
end clear;


end dynamic_stack_package;
```

We could make one simple modification to Package Body 3.2 so as to implement Specification 3.1, the generic stack with a specified upper bound on its size. The modification is in the push procedure. A test must be added to see if the stack is at its maximum size:

```
procedure push (the_object : object_type) is
begin
    if the_list.size = max_size then                  -- Test for user-specified limit.
      raise stack_full;
      else ... ;                                      -- Insert at the head of the list.
    end if;
exception
    when storage_error => raise stack_empty;
end push;
```

Thus we can see that more than one implementation of a single specification is possible, and the implementations can be based on totally different data representations. We should keep this in mind when designing specifications, and try to avoid any specification that leans toward one implementation method. In this way, we can substitute different implementations in order to meet certain objectives, such as efficiency of time or space and dynamic sizing.

3.2.2 Multiple Stacks

Specifications 3.1 and 3.2 can provide for multiple stacks in the same program by instantiating the generic packages for as many object types and as many of the same object types as needed. If we wished to have three stacks, two whose objects are integers and another whose objects are strings of five characters each, we would instantiate the three as follows:

```
with stack;

type string_5 is string(1 .. 5);

package is_1 is new stack_package(integer, 50);
package is_2 is new stack_package(integer, 100);
package ss_1 is new stack_package(string_5, 200);
```

The operations on the stack would be differentiated from each other by prefixing each operation call with the package name:

```
is_1.push(6);

is_2.push(9);

ss_1.push("hello");
```

In this manner, we can instantiate as many stacks as needed. The objects' types and the maximum sizes of each instantiation could be specified at the time of instantiation.

The specifications and implementations we have developed to this point are examples of ***abstract data objects***, a form of ***abstract state machine***. Each instance of the package manipulates an instance of the data structure, and the data structure is hidden within the package body.

There is an alternative method that allows for a single instantiation, and then declaration of multiple stacks having the same type of object. We show this now as a variant that is easily done in Ada. It is the form we will use in the rest of the book. It is an ***abstract data type*** approach.

Specification 3.3 is a stack specification that declares a type *stack* that users can use to create multiple stacks that hold the same type of objects. Note that type *stack* did not appear in either Specification 3.1 or 3.2. Instead the user had to instantiate a stack package for each stack he or she required, even though there could have been several stacks whose objects were of the same type. Specification 3.3 remedies that problem by declaring a *stack* type with its representation given in the <u>private</u> clause of the specification. A detailed discussion and an example follow the specification.

■ SPECIFICATION 3.3   Generic Stack (Abstract Data Type)

```
-- Structure:  A set of objects of a user-specified type that are ordered by time
--             of insertion into the stack; the latest arrival is called the top object.

-- Constraints:  0 <= number_of_objects <= max_size.
--               Number_of_objects and max_size appear below.

generic

    type object_type is private;                        -- Type of objects to be stacked.

package stack_package is

    type stack (max_size : positive) is limited private;   -- See private section below.

    stack_full     : exception;
    stack_empty    : exception;

    procedure push (the_stack : in out stack; the _object : object_type);
    -- results:   the_object is added to the_stack as its top object.
    -- exceptions:   stack_full is raised if the number of objects on the stack = max_size.

    procedure pop (the_stack : in out stack);
    -- results:   The top object is deleted from the stack.
    -- exceptions:   stack_empty is raised if the number of objects on the stack = 0.

    function top (the_stack : stack) return object_type;
    -- results:   A copy of the top object of the stack is returned.
    -- exceptions:   stack_empty is raised if the number of objects on the stack = 0.

    function number_of_objects (the_stack : stack) return natural;
    -- results:   Returns the number of objects on the stack.
```

(continued)

Specification 3.3 (continued)

procedure clear(the_stack : **in out** stack);
-- *results:*   *The stack size is set to zero; the stack is empty.*

private

    type array_of_objects **is array**(positive **range** <>) **of** object_type;

    -- *Type stack is represented by a constrained discriminant record.*
    type stack(max_size : positive) **is record**
      latest   : natural := 0; -- *Number of objects stacked and the index of latest arrival.*
      objects   : array_of_objects(1 .. max_size);
    end record;

end stack_package;

Before discussing the details of the specification, we will show how the stacks are created and manipulated. Taking the same example we used before—two stacks of integers and one stack of strings of five characters—the equivalent instantiations using the multiple stack package are as follows:

with stack_package;   -- *As specified in Specification 3.3.*

subtype string_5 **is** string(1..5);

package int_stack **is new** stack_package(integer);
package str_stack **is new** stack_package(string_5);

To create the stacks, we have to declare three variables of type *stack* and specify for each its maximum size (number of objects that it can hold). Thus,

int_stack_1, int_stack_2 : int_stack.stack(100);
str_stack_1   : str_stack.stack(100);

Since the stack size is specified at the time the stacks are declared, we could have declared the stacks to be of three different maximum sizes; that is,

int_stack_1 : int_stack.stack(50);
int_stack_2 : int_stack.stack(100);
str_stack_1 : str_stack.stack(200);

The operations on the stack are differentiated from each other by pre-fixing each operation call with the package name and the stack variable being passed. Note that there is now an extra argument in each call to the stack operations—the specific stack being operated upon:

```
int_stack.push(int_stack_1, 6);
int_stack.push(int_stack_2, 9);
str_stack.push(str_stack_1, "hello");
```

There are times when multiple instances of the same type of abstract data type are needed, and, in those cases, this approach is necessary. Such a case is discussed in Section 4.2—Simple Lists—where multiple list variables are needed because of the necessity to concatenate two lists of the same type.

The **private** section of the specification holds the data types and data structures that will be used to represent the stack data type. Information in **private** sections can be seen by clients who are using the package but can't be used in any code written by them. For instance, a data type **array_of_objects** is declared in the **private** section of Specification 3.3. That type is visible to a user but is not usable by him or her; that's because although it appears in the specification, it appears only in the **private** section. If the user were to declare a variable

x : int_stack.array_of_objects(1 .. 20);   -- *Illegal.*

the compiler would reject the declaration.

If, however, a user declared a variable of type *stack,*

my_stack : int_stack.stack (20);   *Legal*

the declaration is perfectly correct since type *stack* is declared outside the **private** section in an incomplete declaration. If the user then decided to reference a field of the stack record

my_stack.latest := my_stack.latest + 1;   -- *Illegal.*

the reference would be incorrect since the field *latest* appears only in the **private** section and is thus not accessible by the user. In addition, the Ada language specifies that since *stack* is a ***limited private*** type, a user can only use a variable of type *stack* as a procedure parameter or as a value returned by a function. Thus, for example, the assignment (":=") and tests for equality ("=") are not allowed between two stacks.

The **private** section is used to make the Ada compiler aware of what type *stack* actually is but shields those details from use by the client. If the client were allowed to manipulate the field values, as in the illegal statement above, the client could compromise the integrity of the stack. In this case, the user might add one to *latest* without placing a new object onto the stack. The next *pop* or *top* execution, among others, would be in error.

The user can manipulate the value in the field *latest* but only by using *push* or *pop*. In this way, the integrity of the stack record is retained. Only the package body directly manipulates the values in the **private** section.

The representation chosen for type *stack* in Specification 3.3 uses a record that has a discriminant. The representation is arbitrary. A record with a dis-

The **private section of a package** specification is used to declare items that the **compiler needs at the time of compilation** of the specification but the designer wants to make **unusable directly by the user**.

criminant is used to illustrate some of the ramifications of its being chosen and to show some of the variety available with Ada. In this case, it permits a user to declare different sized stacks for the same instantiation of the stack package.

The discriminant has no default value. The user must specify a maximum stack size when declaring a variable of type *stack*.

The code implementing Specification 3.3 is given in Package Body 3.3. The major difference from Package Body 3.1 is the need to prefix all references to the fields of the record comprising the stack type—*max_size, latest,* and *objects*—with the name of the stack variable.

■ PACKAGE BODY 3.3 Generic Stack—Implements Specification 3.3

```
package body stack_package is

    procedure push (the_stack : in out stack; the_object : object_type) is
    -- Length 4   Complexity 2   Performance O(1)
    begin
        the_stack.objects(the_stack.latest + 1) := the_object;      -- May raise a
        the_stack.latest := the_stack.latest + 1;          -- constraint_error exception.
    exception
        when constraint_error => raise stack_full;
    end push;

    procedure pop (the_stack : in out stack) is
    -- Length 2   Complexity 2   Performance O(1)
    begin
        the_stack.latest := the_stack.latest - 1;       -- May raise a constraint_error or
    exception                                             -- numeric_error exception.
        when constraint_error | numeric_error => raise stack_empty;
    end pop;

    function top (the_stack : stack) return object_type is
    -- Length 2   Complexity 2   Performance O(1)
    begin
        return the_stack.objects(the_stack.latest);              -- May raise a
    exception                                         -- constraint_error exception.
        when constraint_error => raise stack_empty;
    end top;

    function number_of_objects (the_stack : stack) return natural is
    -- Length 1   Complexity 1   Performance O(1)
    begin
        return the_stack.latest;
    end number_of_objects;

    procedure clear(the_stack : in out stack) is
    -- Length 1   Complexity 1   Performance O(1)
```

(continued)

Package Body 3.3 (continued)

```
    begin
       the_stack.latest := 0;
    end clear;

end stack_package;
```

3.2.3 Holding Variable-Sized Objects in a Data Structure

How might we have the stack include **objects of variable size?** For instance, in Chapter 2 (Figures 2.37, etc.) we wanted to hold variable length lines read from a file. We were able, using records with discriminants and dynamic memory allocation, to allocate varying lengths of storage spaces matched to the size of the lines. Suppose we wanted to retain this feature in another program that reads the lines and prints them in the reverse order from which they were read. (For instance, suppose the lines of the input file were sorted in ascending order and we wanted to print them in descending order.) We can do this by pushing the lines onto a stack as they are read, then repeatedly popping the stack and printing the lines until the stack is empty. The pseudocode for the program is as follows:

```
loop
      read a line;
      exit when the line is of zero length;
      push the line onto the stack;
end loop;
while the stack size is not zero loop
      pop the stack and print the line popped;
end loop;
```

Variable length objects can be included in any data structure by placing **pointers to the objects rather than the objects themselves** in the data structure.

Our stack abstractions (Specifications 3.1, 3.2, and 3.3) are not able to take varying length objects in a single stack instance. We can create multiple stacks, each with different type objects, but we cannot create one stack whose objects can vary in size. There is a way around the restriction. It is to create the variable length objects ourselves, then stack pointers to the objects. That is the approach used in Figure 3.2, the program that inverts the order of variable length lines.

The statement in the first loop that pushes a new line's pointer onto the stack is especially interesting and powerful. The comment attached to it summarizes what tasks are accomplished by this one statement.

We have shown an example of placing variable length objects on a stack by placing pointers to the objects rather than the objects themselves onto the stack. This technique is generally applicable for almost any data type.

```
with text_io, stack_package; use text_io;

procedure invert_lines is
-- assumes:   The lines are 80 or less characters, and there are 500 or less lines.
-- results:   Reads lines and prints them in the reverse of the order in which they were read.
-- Length 14   Complexity 3   Performance O(n), where n is the number of lines.

        subtype line_length is positive range 1 .. 80;          -- Number of characters in a line.
        type line_text(length : line_length) is record           -- Varying length lines.
          the_text : string(1 .. length);
        end record;
        type line_pointer is access line_text;                    -- Pointers to lines.

        package line_stacks is new stack_package(line_pointer);   -- Stack of pointers to lines.
        the_stack  : line_stack.stack(500);
        new_line   : string (line_length);
        len        : natural range 0 .. line_length'last;          -- Length of the new line.

begin
    loop                                                           -- Read the lines.
       get_line(new_line, len);
       exit when len = 0;

       line_stacks.push(the_stack, new line_text'(len, new_line(1 .. len)));  -- Allocate new line space of the correct size to hold
                                                                              the line, load the line data into it, and push the
                                                                              -- pointer to it onto the stack.

    end loop;
    while line_stacks.number_of_objects (the_stack) > 0 loop       -- Print the lines.
       put_line(line_stacks.top (the_stack).the_text);
       line_stacks.pop (the_stack);
    end loop;
end invert_lines;
```

F I G U R E **3.2** Program that demonstrates a method of placing varying length objects onto a stack by stacking pointers rather than objects themselves.

3.2.4 Stack Frames and Heaps in Memory Management

Many operating systems manage the memory of the computer system using a memory layout as shown in Figure 3.3. We are interested in the portion of memory labeled "Available user space." The portion of the memory labeled "Stack" has the memory allocated implicitly to variables locally declared in procedures and functions. Each time a procedure is executed, one of the first actions of the system is to create a *frame* that holds the variables and constants local to that procedure, as well as other data internally used by the system in executing the procedure. The frame is pushed onto the stack. The frames are inherently variable in length since different procedures have different numbers and types of variables and constants, and the local variables may hold objects such as unconstrained arrays whose bounds, and hence sizes, are fixed only when the procedure is called.

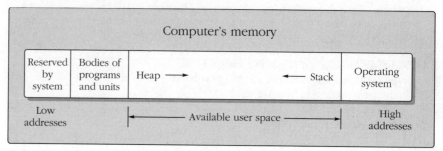

FIGURE 3.3 Typical memory layout (simplified) in a computer system.

The *heap* shown in Figure 3.3 is the pool of space used by the system for dynamic memory allocation. Pointers to dynamically allocated data point into this area. The stack uses space working downward in the memory, while heap space is consumed working upward. As an example, Figure 3.4 shows a program that has nested procedures *A* and *B*.

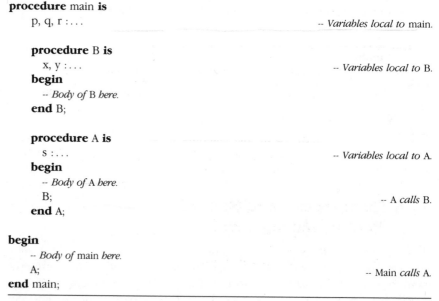

```
procedure main is
    p, q, r : ...                           -- Variables local to main.

    procedure B is
        x, y : ...                          -- Variables local to B.
    begin
        -- Body of B here.
    end B;

    procedure A is
        s : ...                             -- Variables local to A.
    begin
        -- Body of A here.
        B;                                  -- A calls B.
    end A;

begin
    -- Body of main here.
    A;                                      -- Main calls A.
end main;
```

FIGURE 3.4 Nested procedures.

The flow of execution among the procedures is based on the stack principle. When the main procedure is executing, but before *A* is called, the stack looks as shown in Figure 3.5.

After the main procedure has called procedure *A* and *A* has subsequently called procedure *B,* which is executing in the body of its code, the stack looks

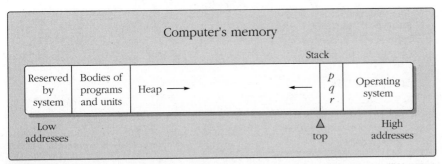

FIGURE 3.5 Stack and memory while in body of *main* before calling *A*.

as shown in Figure 3.6. There are three frames on the stack—one each for *main*, *A*, and *B*.

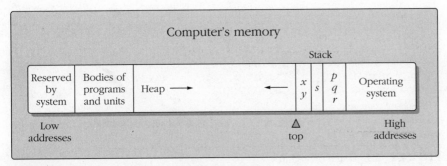

FIGURE 3.6 *Main* has called *A*, and *A* has called *B*.

The variables declared in this example in effect come into existence when the procedure in which they are declared activates and begins to execute. As each procedure completes its execution and returns to the calling unit, its variables are popped from the stack and cease to exist. Each time a procedure is called, the execution of the procedure is called an ***activation*** of the procedure. The case shown in Figures 3.4–3.6 is a simplification, although one that demonstrates the critical notions. A stack frame might also have saved registers and machine states, arguments if any, and so on. The frames are inherently variable in size. A detailed discussion is outside the scope of this book.

The heap in Figure 3.6 is not a stack. As mentioned, it is the pool of space used for dynamic memory allocation. Suppose we look at a modified version of the nested procedures we just used for demonstrating stack frames. This version, shown in Figure 3.7, has dynamic memory allocation.

When the program is in procedure *B* and after its dynamic memory allocation of *M* has been done, the memory looks as shown in Figure 3.8.

After returning from *B* to *A*, then returning from *A* to *main*, but before deallocating any instances of *M*, the memory is in a state shown in Figure 3.9.

```
procedure main is
    subtype M is string(1 .. 20);
    type M_ptr is access M;
    p, q, r : M_ptr;                          -- Variables local to main; pointers to M's.

    procedure B is
    x, y : . . .                               -- Variables local to B.
    begin
        -- Body of B here.
        r := new M;                            -- Allocate a new instance of type M.
    end B;

    procedure A is
    s : . . .                                  -- Variables local to A.
    begin
        -- Body of A here.
        q := new M;                            -- Allocate a new instance of type M.
        B;                                     -- A calls B.
    end A;

begin
    -- Body of main here.
    p := new M;                                -- Allocate a new instance of type M.
    A;                                         -- Main calls A.
    -- More code here.
    free(q);                                   -- Deallocate the instance pointed at by q.
end main;
```

FIGURE 3.7 Nested procedures.

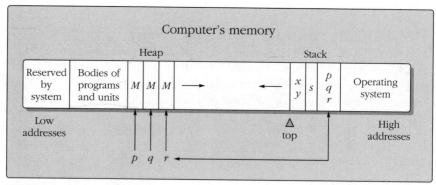

FIGURE 3.8 Executing *B*'s body, and after three dynamic allocations of *M*'s.

The stack has been popped, freeing the frames for *B* then *A*, but the allocations of *M* persist.

After the execution of *main* proceeds and executes the statement *free(q)*, the allocation of *M* that *q* points to is returned to the pool of available space (Figure 3.10).

The heap and the stack in this example work into the same overall pool

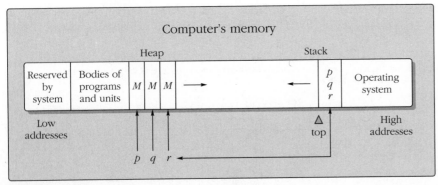

FIGURE 3.9 Executing *main*'s body, but before any deallocation.

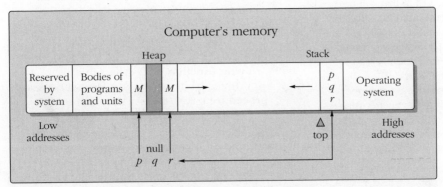

FIGURE 3.10 Executing *main*'s body, deallocation by *free(q)*.

of space that lies between the user programs and units and the operating system. They work against each other. Many dynamic allocations will cause the heap space to grow to the point where another procedure activation may not be possible because there is no space for its stack frame.

This simplified example gives you insights into the mechanisms for dynamic memory allocation and procedure (and function) activation and makes you more aware of the circumstances when experiencing a *storage_error* exception due to heap or stack exhaustion. It is not the only possible configuration of stacks and heaps (Aho, 1977).

EXERCISES 3.2

1. Using the example evaluation of the expression $10 * (5 + 7)$ as a guide, show how the stacking mechanism might be used to evaluate the following expressions:
   a. $(3 - 5)/(2 - 7)$
   b. $(a * b)^3 + 20$

2. Integers are input into a stack in order 1, 2, 3, ... By interleaving *push* and *pop* operations, various permutations of the integers can be obtained. For example, *push*(10), *push*(2), *put*(*pop*), *push*(3), *put*(*pop*), *put*(*pop*) puts out the integers in the order 2, 3, 1.

a. If the first three integers are input in order, what outputs are possible?

b. Of the six distinct permutations of {1, 2, 3}, one cannot be produced by (a). Explain why.

c. Extend your explanation of (b) to describe the output permutations that cannot be achieved if the first *n* integers are input in order.

3. Specifications 3.1 and 3.2 both had *pop* functions (as well as *pop* procedures). Function *pop* (but not procedure *pop*) was removed in Specification 3.3 and Package Body 3.3. Why? Try to add a *pop* function to the multiple stacks specification and body and determine what difficulty arises.

4. Referring to the program in Figure 1.6 of Section 1.4.2, write a program using one of the generic stack packages developed in this section (3.2) that will take expressions read from the standard input file, find and remove any unmatched parentheses, and write the expression with the unmatched parentheses removed. The program ends when a null expression is read.

5. Write a program using the dynamic stack of Specification 3.2 to determine how deep a dynamic stack of integers can get on the system you are using for Ada. In order to do this, you will have to write an exception handler to handle the *stack_full* exception that will be generated by the *push* procedure when storage is exhausted.

6. Modify Specification 3.3. and Package Body 3.3 to add the following operations to the stack package:

a. Include a generic procedure called traverse that will walk through each object on the stack calling a procedure *process* for each object. Code and test the modified stack. The following specification for the procedure should be used. Add the usual comments to complete the specifications.

```
generic
    with procedure process (the_object : object_type);
procedure traverse (the_stack : in out stack);
```

Show an example of using *traverse* on a stack in two separate instantiations to do two separate processes on the stack objects—one is to print the objects, and the other is your choice.

b. Include a generic procedure called *purge* that will delete all objects from the stack for which *to_be_purged* is true:

```
generic
    with function to_be_purged
        (the_object : object_type) return boolean;
procedure purge (the_stack : in out stack);
```

7. An operation *clear* is often provided with stack abstractions. It clears the stack by setting the size to zero, effectively erasing all the stack objects. Is it a necessary operation? If not, what operation(s) can be used in its place? What are the performance implications?

■ 3.3 **FIFO Queues**

A queue is a data type that exhibits a first-in/first-out behavior. Objects can be added to the queue at any time. The only object that can be removed is the one in the queue that was entered earliest. After the earliest entry is removed, the second earliest entry assumes the role of earliest. The operation of entering new objects is called ***enqueueing***. Removing the earliest arrival is called ***serving, or dequeueing,*** the object.

Consider the queue abstraction in some concrete examples. The queues of people waiting for service at a bank, to board a bus, and to enter the cinema are common, everyday examples. The people arrange themselves linearly in order of their arrival. The first to be served is the one at the head (earliest arrival) of the queue. The linear physical arrangement determines the relative position for service.

Another example of a queue is found in some stores. When entering, the customer takes a number from a sequence of numbers on tickets or tags.

Customers are then free to wander about until their number is called. The numbers are called in order of increasing value. The customer who steps forward when a number is called is the one who will be served next. In this example, the waiting customers also form a queue, but the time order is not determined by physical position; it is determined by the values on the tickets or tags. As we discussed in Section 3.2 (Stacks), there is more than one way to build an abstraction. In these examples we showed two implementations of the same basic queue abstraction.

The queue abstraction is given in Specification 3.4. This specification is similar to stack Specification 3.3. Note that we could have patterned the queue specification after either Specification 3.1 or 3.2.

■ SPECIFICATION 3.4 Generic FIFO Queue

```
-- Structure:   The objects are arranged linearly in order of their arrival in the stack;
--              the earliest (first) arrival is at the head of the queue, and the latest (last) arrival
--              is at the tail.

-- Constraints:  0 <= number_of_objects <= max_size.      -- Number_of_objects and
                                                          -- max_size appear below.

generic

    type object_type is private;                -- Type of objects to be queued.

package queue_package is

    type queue(max_size : positive) is limited private;

    queue_full    : exception;
    queue_empty   : exception;

    procedure enqueue(the_queue : in out queue; the_object : object_type);
    -- results:   The_object is added to the queue.
    -- exceptions:  A queue_full exception is raised if
    --              the_queue.number_of_objects = max_size.

    procedure dequeue(the_queue : in out queue);
    -- results:   The object that has been in the queue longest is removed from the queue.
    -- exceptions:  A queue_empty exception is raised if the_queue.number_of_objects = 0.

    function head (the_queue : queue) return object_type;
    -- results:   A copy of the object that has been in the queue longest is returned.
    -- exceptions:  A queue_empty exception is raised if the_queue.number_of_objects = 0.

    function number_of_objects(the_queue : queue) return natural;
    -- results:   Returns the number of objects in the queue.
```

(continued)

Specification 3.4 (continued)

procedure clear (the_queue : **in out** queue);
-- **results:**   *The number of objects in the queue is set to zero; the queue is empty.*

private

type array_of_objects **is array**(positive **range** <>) **of** object_type;

type queue(max_size : positive) **is record**
first   : natural := 0;   *-- Index of the object added to the queue earliest.*
last   : natural := max_size;   *-- Index of the object added to the queue latest.*
size   : natural := 0;   *-- Number of objects in the queue.*
objects   : array_of_objects(1 .. max_size);   *-- Array of queued objects.*
end record;

end queue_package;

Note the similarity between queues and stacks. The stack operation *push* corresponds to the queue operation *enqueue,* and the stack *pop* (procedure) corresponds to the queue operation *dequeue.* (We added a *pop* function in the stack specification as a convenience; it is a combination of *top* and procedure *pop.*) The difference is that in stacks the latest arrival is removed (popped), whereas in queues the earliest arrival is removed (dequeued).

3.3.1 Queue Implementation

We will consider an array implementation of a queue. An array implementation of a stack has the advantage that only one end (the top) is involved in operations *push* and *pop.* A queue has to deal with two ends. Arrivals go on one end, whereas departures come from the other end. Figure 3.11 shows a queue stored in an array. It is a snapshot of one instant in time.

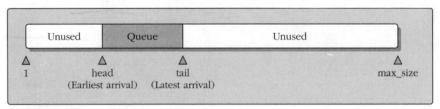

FIGURE 3.11 A queue in an array.

After some transactions on the queue—dequeueing from the head and enqueueing at the tail—the queue might look as shown in Figure 3.12.

The queue crawls forward in the array, expanding and contracting according to the relative numbers of enqueues and dequeues. The interesting case occurs when the queue reaches the end of the array as shown in Figure 3.13.

FIGURE 3.12 The queue at a later time.

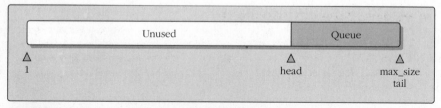

FIGURE 3.13 The queue at the right end of the array.

Something will have to be done to handle the next enqueue operation. One approach is to slide the queue back to the beginning of the array. The amount of work to do so is $O(n)$, so that is an unattractive solution. A more efficient solution to the problem is to "wrap" the queue to the beginning of the array. In effect, the array becomes circular. Figure 3.14(a) shows a linear view of the array, and Figure 3.14(b) shows the array as a circular structure.

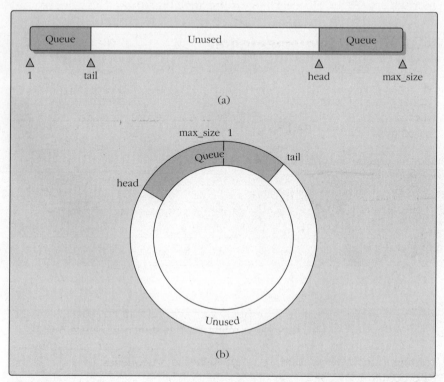

FIGURE 3.14 The queue in wrapped state. (a) As a linear array; (b) as a circular array.

Package Body 3.4 has the code that implements the circular queue notion. As you can see, the initial choices of values for *first* and *last* and the use of modulo arithmetic result in simple, concise code.

■ **PACKAGE BODY 3.4 Generic Queue—Implements Specification 3.4**

package body queue_package **is**

```
    procedure enqueue(the_queue : in out queue; the_object : object_type) is
    -- Length 5   Complexity 2   Performance O(1)
    begin
      the_queue.size := the_queue.size + 1;                              -- Raises an exception if size = max_size.
      the_queue.last := (the_queue.last mod the_queue.max_size) + 1;     -- Wraps when the_queue.last = max_size.
      the_queue.objects(the_queue.last) := the_object;
    exception
      when constraint_error | numeric_error => raise queue_full;
    end enqueue;

    procedure dequeue(the_queue : in out queue) is
    -- Length 3   Complexity 2   Performance O(1)
    begin
      the_queue.size := the_queue.size - 1;                              -- Raises an exception if size = 0.
      the_queue.first := (the_queue.first mod the_queue.max_size) + 1;   -- Wraps when the_queue.first = max_size.
    exception
      when constraint_error | numeric_error => raise queue_empty;
    end dequeue;

    function head(the_queue : queue) return object is
    -- Length 3   Complexity 2   Performance O(1)
    begin
      if the_queue.size = 0 then raise queue_empty;
        else return the_queue.objects(the_queue.first);
      end if;
    end head;

    function number_of_objects(the_queue : queue) return natural is
    -- Length 1   Complexity 1   Performance O(1)
    begin
      return the_queue.size;
    end number_of_objects;

    procedure clear(the_queue : in out queue) is
    begin
      the_queue.size := 0;
      the_queue.first := 0;
      the_queue.last : = max_size;
    end clear;

end queue_package;
```

Section 3.5 gives an example of an application of queues and priority queues to accessing data on a magnetic disk. Before proceeding to this example, we will consider priority queues in Section 3.4.

EXERCISES 3.3

1. Write and test a linked implementation of queues as specified in Specification 3.4. What performance drawbacks does this have? What would the benefits be of using a doubly linked list (see Exercises 2.4, 6)? Compare the lengths, complexities, and performances of the linked implementation of the operations with those of Package Body 3.4.

2. Queues are often specified with another operation—*purge*. The idea is to be able to remove arbitrary nodes within the queue, that is to abort the normal queue order for these nodes. The specification of the *purge* procedure is

    generic
        with function to_be_purged (an_object :
            object_type) **return** boolean;
    procedure purge (the_stack : **in out** stack);

    Rewrite Specification 3.4 to add the new generic procedure. Modify Package Body 3.4 to meet the new specification, and write a program to test the results.

3. Modify Specification 3.4 to add a new operation—*copy*—that will copy one queue into another. As a result, the two queues will have exactly the same objects in the same order—they will be equal. Rewrite Package Body 3.4 according to your specification and write a program to test it.

4. A *deque* (pronounced "deck") is a form of list that has both stack-like and queue-like operations. There are push-like and enqueue-like operations to add new objects at either end, and dequeue-like and pop-like operations to retrieve objects and delete them from the other end. A client can execute these operations in any mix. Design and write specifications in the form of an Ada specification package for a deque. Write a package body using either an array or a linked implementation that meets your specification. Write a program that tests your package and demonstrates that it is correct.

■ 3.4 Priority Queues

The queues we discussed in Section 3.3 follow a first-in/first-out pattern. The queues we discussed here are an important variation of the queue idea—*highest-priority-in/first-out queue*. We mentioned a few examples of this kind of queue in Section 3.1. We will call these queues *priority queues*.

Each object that arrives for enqueueing into a priority queue has an associated priority. The object, including its priority, is placed into the priority queue. The object dequeued is one of those in the queue that is associated with the highest priority among all objects in the queue. There may be more than one object in the queue associated with the same priority value. We may have three objects of priority 2, five with priority 4, and so on, assuming the priorities are integers.

An FIFO queue is a priority queue in which the object's priority is determined by the length of time the object has been in the queue. The longer time corresponds to higher priority, and no two objects can have the same priority. It is similar with a stack, in which case the shorter time corresponds to higher priority.

The priorities must be of some ordered data type, although the type need not be linear (see Section 1.6.1). Therefore, any type that allows a comparison to determine that one of its values is larger than or equal to another is allowed for priorities.

We consider the entries in a priority queue to have their priorities attached to them in any way the user chooses. One way is to have each queue object be a record with two fields—one the priority associated with the object to be queued and the other the object itself. You can see in Specification 3.5 that there are two generic functions in the generic parameters—*priority_of* and "< =". The first allows the priority queue package to determine the priority of a queue object, and the second allows the comparison of two priorities. We can then write the priority queue specification—Specification 3.5.

■ SPECIFICATION 3.5   Generic Priority Queue

-- *Elements:*   *A generic object with an associated priority.*

-- *Structure:*   *The objects are arranged linearly in order of priorities, with the highest*
--   *(largest) priority at the head of the priority queue.*

-- *Constraints:* $0 <= number\_of\_objects <= max\_size.$ -- *Number_of_objects and max_size appear below.*

generic

    type object_type **is private**;   -- *Type of objects to be queued.*
    type priority **is limited private**;   -- *Type of the priorities.*
    with function priority_of(the_object : object_type) **return** priority;
    -- *results:*   *Returns the priority of the object.*
    with function "< =" (left, right : priority) **return** boolean **is** <>;
    -- *results:*   *Returns true if left has a lower or equal priority than right; otherwise returns false.*

package priority_queue_package **is**

    type priority_queue (max_size : positive) **is limited private**;
    queue_full   : **exception**;
    queue_empty   : **exception**;

    procedure enqueue (the_queue : **in out** priority_queue; the_object : object_type);
    -- *results:*   *The object is added to the queue.*
    -- *exceptions:*   *A queue_full exception is raised if the number of objects = max_size.*

    procedure dequeue (the_queue: **in out** priority_queue);
    -- *results:*   *An object in the queue associated with the highest priority in the queue is removed*
    --   *from the queue and returned.*

(continued)

Specification 3.5 (continued)

-- ***exceptions:*** *A queue_empty exception is raised if the number of objects is zero.*
-- ***notes:*** *If there is more than one object with the highest priority, dequeue arbitrarily chooses*
--   *which to dequeue; however, the object dequeued is the same one that would be*
--   *returned by function* head *if it had been called.*

function head (the_queue : priority_queue) **return** object_type;
-- ***results:*** *Returns a copy of an object of the queue associated with the highest priority in the*
--   *queue.*

function number_of_objects (the_queue : priority_queue) **return** natural;
-- ***results:*** *Returns the number of objects in the queue.*

procedure clear (the_queue : **in out** priority_queue);
-- ***results:*** *Sets the number of objects in the queue to zero; the queue is empty.*

private

   type array_of_objects **is array**(positive **range** <>) **of** object_type;

   type priority_queue (max_size : positive) **is record**
      last   : natural := 0;
      objects : array_of_objects(1 .. max_size);
   end record;

end priority_queue_package;

In order to make the manner in which the priority queue is used more concrete, Figure 3.15 presents a partial example of a program that uses a priority queue.

The package instantiation could have been shortened since the function names of the fourth generic parameter, "<=", are identical and we declared our generic parameter as

with function "<=" (p, q : priority) **return** boolean **is** <>;

Since we included the trailing phrase "is <>" and the function "<=" is predefined for type *natural,* we can omit the fourth generic parameter. The meaning of the phrase is that if a function with the name "<=" for two arguments of type *natural* can be found within the scope of the instantiation, it will be used if the fourth generic parameter is omitted:

package item_queue **is new** priority_queue_package (object_type => queue_object,
                                                    priority   => natural,
                                                    priority_of => get_priority);

with priority_queue_package, ... ;

procedure main **is**

    subtype item_to_queue **is** string (1 .. 80);

    type queue_object **is record**
      item_priority   : positive;
      item   : item_to_queue;
    end record;

    function get_priority (the_object : queue_object) **return** natural;

    package item_queue **is new** priority_queue_package (object_type   => queue_object,
                                         priority   => natural,
                                         priority_of => get_priority,
                                         "<="   => "<=");

    function get_priority (the_object : queue_object) **return** natural **is**
    begin
      return the_object.item_priority;
    end get_priority;

    .
    .
    .

FIGURE 3.15 Example of an instantiation of a priority queue.

3.4.1 Queue Implementations

Suppose we chose to represent the priority queue as a singly linked list. We could use the *linked_lists* abstraction of Specification 2.4. Each node would contain a queue object (see type *queue_object* in Specification 3.5) and a linking pointer. Our objective would be to keep the list in order of priority with the highest priorities at the list head. Figure 3.16 shows such a list ordered on priorities, with larger integers being higher priorities. The arrows indicate possible points of insertion (enqueueing) of a new object whose priority is 7.

    The *enqueue* procedure must sequentially search for an insertion point before doing the actual insertion. Assuming there are n objects in the queue whose priorities are uniformly distributed, we can expect to search through $(n + 1)/2$ nodes before the proper position is found. The insertion is then done with the *insert_node* procedure of *linked_lists*. The search operation is $O(n)$, and the insertion is $O(1)$. We conclude that the *enqueue* operation is $O(n)$.

    If an array implementation rather than a linked implementation were used along with a sequential search for the position of a new object being inserted with a given priority and with the queue objects in the array in sorted order of priority, the search is still $O(n)$. The actual insertion is also $O(n)$

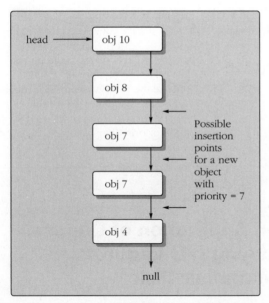

FIGURE 3.16 Linked list implementation of a priority queue.

since on average half of the list must be moved to make a place for the new entry. [We shall see in Sections 4.4 and 4.5 that moving sections of lists can be accomplished by the use of Ada slice moves. Moving a slice, while still $O(n)$, may be much faster than moving the objects of the list one at a time within a loop.]

We shall also see (in Chapter 4) that it is possible to search for the point of insertion in an array using a binary search, an $O(\log_2 n)$ operation, a considerable improvement over $O(n)$. We must still, however, move half the array on average to do the actual insertion.

There is a nonlinear data structure that results in considerably improved performance for large priority queues. It is called a *heap* (a form of binary tree implemented in an array; not to be confused with the dynamic memory allocation heap). Section 5.9 is about heaps and their use for implementing priority queues. With this implementation, both *enqueue* and *dequeue* execute in a time that is $O(\log_2 n)$. We leave the implementation to Chapter 5, Section 5.9. Figure 3.17 summarizes the performance of the proposed priority queue implementations.

	Array	Linked list	Heap
Enqueue	$O(n)$	$O(n)$	$O(\log_2 n)$
Dequeue	$O(1)$	$O(1)$	$O(\log_2 n)$

FIGURE 3.17 Performance estimates of priority queue implementations.

EXERCISES 3.4

1. Design, code, and test a package body using an array implementation of the priority queue (Specification 3.5). Make a table of the lengths, complexities, and orders of magnitude of the performance of the procedures and functions of the priority queue for your implementation.

2. Design, code, and test a package body using a linked implementation of the priority queue (Specification 3.5). You may have to modify the package specification in order to do this. Try to make the minimum changes

outside of the **private** section of the specification. Make a table of the lengths, complexities, and orders of magnitude of the performance of the procedures and functions of the priority queue for your implementation, and compare those measures with the same measures for the array implementation of Exercise 1.

3. Discuss the relative advantages and disadvantages of the array and linked implementations of priority queues.

4. Explain the following:
   a. How a stack could be considered to be a special case of a priority queue.
   b. How an FIFO queue could be considered to be a special case of a priority queue.

5. Suppose the priority of a priority queue object is to be a key value that uniquely identifies the object. Explain how a priority queue can be used for sorting the data on the priority (key) value.

■ 3.5 An Application of Queues: Scheduling I/O Requests on a Magnetic Disk

Interactive time-shared computer systems often encounter a problem in scheduling input/output (I/O) tasks for a magnetic disk. It is common to find such systems serving many users logged on simultaneously but having one, or perhaps a few, large magnetic disk drives. For example, such a system might serve 50 users but have only one magnetic disk of several hundred megabytes capacity. At any instant in time, the users could be running programs, reading electronic mail, compiling programs, editing text, and so on. These activities generate a stew of I/O requests to read and write on the magnetic disk(s). The servicing of these I/O requests can create a bottleneck that substantially affects system performance. The disk, whose activities are partly mechanical, is far slower than the electronic components in the system's CPU and memory. Since the disk is a relatively slow device and the completion of the users' tasks often depends on some disk I/O, it is important that disks be used as efficiently as possible. Therefore, the *throughput* (I/O actions per second) should be as high as we can make it.

The I/O requests generated by the users are intermixed, and at any time the disk can expect to have a group of I/O requests waiting to be serviced. The ordering of this servicing so as to maximize throughput, and the varieties of queues used to do so, is the subject of this section.

We can consider a disk to be a single platter (*surface*) with a *read/write* head mounted on an arm that can move radially across the disk. Figure 3.18 shows a view of the disk. Most disks have multiple surfaces, often by having multiple platters stacked above each other, but we will use a single surface to illustrate the use of queues. The results are easily generalized to multiple surfaces.

The disk, which is rotating at a constant velocity (3600 rpm is typical), is divided into a set of concentric circles called *tracks*. Tracks are normally numbered $0 .. hi\_track$. Each track is divided into segments called *sectors*. Sectors are also usually numbered $0 .. hi\_sector$.

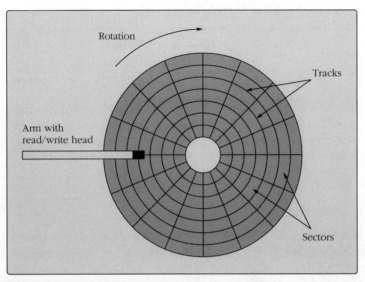

FIGURE 3.18 Sectored magnetic disk.

By the time an I/O request arrives at the disk, it is simply a request to either read or write a specific sector on a specific track. An address in memory is also given. It is the base address of the data that are to be written to the sector in the case of a write or the base address of the space in memory that is to receive the sector's data in the case of a read. Thus an I/O request takes the form

<action, track, sector, memory address>

where *action* is *read* or *write*. No matter how complex the action generating the I/O request, it is distilled down to this simple form by the time it reaches the disk.

The time that it takes a disk to satisfy an I/O request is the sum of the times taken for three component actions that must happen in a sequence. First, the arm is moved until the read/write head is positioned over the target track. The time taken is called the **seek time**. Second, there is a wait (called the *latency time*) until the target sector arrives by rotation under the read/write head. Third, the data in the sector are transmitted to or from the memory in a time (called the **transmission time**) that is dependent on the density of the bits on the disk and the speed of the rotation. We then have

$$time_{I/O} = time_{seek} + time_{latency} + time_{transmission}$$

We simplify the expression by assuming that the transmission time and the latency time are constant since we cannot do much about either of them. We will concentrate on minimizing the seek time, which is, in fact, the major contributor to the total time. We will further simplify the expression by assuming that the seek time is a linear function of the number of tracks that must be crossed to arrive at a target track. Moving from track 0 to track 100 takes 10 times longer than moving from track 0 to track 10. We call the track at which the head sits when the seek starts the start track (T_{start}) and the track to which it is moving the target track (T_{target}). Our expression for the time to accomplish the I/O request can be written with these assumptions as

$$time_{I/O} = time_{seek} + C_2$$
$$= C_1 * abs(T_{target} - T_{start}) + C_2$$

The collection of requests waiting for services changes with time. During a time period, some requests are serviced and are removed from the group, while new requests arrive to be added to it. The mix of tracks and sectors awaiting service is continually changing.

3.5.1 Disk-Scheduling Policies

What should the policy be for scheduling the waiting I/O requests? The first approach might be to argue that the I/O requests should be serviced on a first-come/first-served basis—an FIFO queue. The requests should, when they arrive, be placed in an FIFO queue. Such a policy seems fair. When the disk has completed an I/O request, the I/O scheduler interrupts the CPU and control is given to the I/O scheduler. It dequeues the next request from the I/O request queue and passes it to the disk, which begins to serve the request. Control is turned back to the program that was executing when the interrupt happened.

Is this "fair" strategy really fair? Why not have the disk go to the nearest request as measured by the distance from the track it is on to the track with a new request? It would seem that such a policy would result in a smaller average seek time and thus keep the disk transmitting data a higher proportion of the time. The disk head will always move the shortest distance to the next request. This strategy is called a ***shortest-seektime-first (SSTF)*** strategy. The FIFO strategy, in attempting to be fair to everyone, would in fact be unfair to everyone because it would take a longer time on the average to satisfy I/O requests. The system would appear to the users to be running more slowly since the disk would spend more of its time in head movement.

What data abstraction can be used to represent the set of I/O requests waiting service under an SSTF disk-scheduling policy? A priority queue fits the requirements. The priority of an I/O request *req* is determined by the distance between the target track of the request and the track on which the head is currently positioned; that is,

$$priority_r = abs(T_r - T_{current})$$

When the disk completes serving its current I/O request, the I/O scheduler dequeues the highest priority item as determined by this expression and passes it to the disk for service.

One problem with this scheme is that the priorities of the requests are continually shifting. Refer to the example in Figure 3.19(a). Initially, the read/write head is positioned at some track, call it the current track T_C. Three I/O

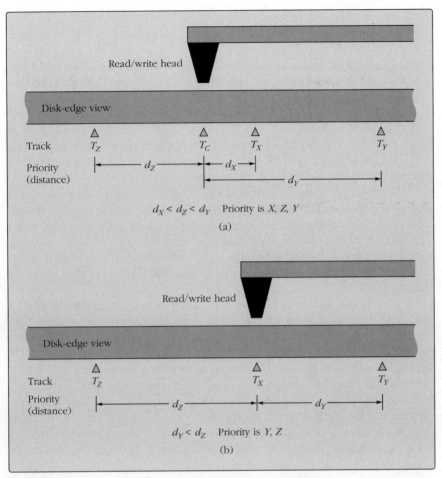

FIGURE 3.19 Serving requests and shifting priorities: (a) Before serving X; (b) after serving X.

requests, X, Y, and Z, located at tracks T_X, T_Y, and T_Z, respectively, are waiting for service. The priorities are the distances (d) of the three requests from T_C and are shown with X having the highest priority, Z the next highest, and Y the lowest. The head is consequently moved to request X, which is then served [Figure 3.19(b)]. At that point, note that the priorities of the other two requests have interchanged in order. Y now assumes a higher priority than Z. The priorities are not static. Servicing the highest priority request may change the relative priorities of the others.

Nonetheless, the abstraction to be used is that of a priority queue, but one in which the priorities might shift any time the queue's highest priority request is dequeued and served.

The implementation issues are interesting, as you will see when you do Exercises 3.5, 1, 2, and 4.

To see what sort of improvement we get over an FIFO strategy by using an SSTF strategy, we use as a metric the throughput of the disk. A complete answer is complex, and we suggest you refer to Hofri (1980) and Coffman (1982). A number of factors can affect the results—the rate of arrival of new requests, the distribution of the requests on the surface of the disk, and the characteristics of the disk drive. Hofri (1980) demonstrates that with a uniform random distribution of the I/O requests on the disk surface and parameter settings that approximate an IBM 3330 disk, SSTF is superior to FIFO in the mean time the requests have to wait for service. Similar results were obtained for requests distributed nonuniformly on the disk surface, although the superiority of SSTF over FIFO was not as great.

We have chosen a strategy that will increase the disk's throughput and reduce the time that requests have to wait for service. Increasing the amount of productive work that the disk does per unit of time should speed up overall system operation and give users a shorter response time to commands and running programs. Is keeping the disk as busy as possible the right thing to do? We shall see that the answer may be yes, but there are other considerations.

Look at the situation in Figure 3.20. Again we see the disk from an edge view. The symbol Δ points to the tracks in the request queue. There is one cluster of requests in the vicinity of the current head position and a second cluster at some distance from the head. Assume that requests are continually arriving, some for the near cluster and some for the far one. If we use an SSTF strategy, the head will remain in the near cluster for some time, especially as new requests in the cluster are arriving. Only when the near cluster is reduced to zero will the head move to the far cluster and begin servicing its requests. The disk is being used efficiently, but some users are having to wait inordinately long times before their I/O requests are satisfied. They therefore have the impression the system is performing poorly.

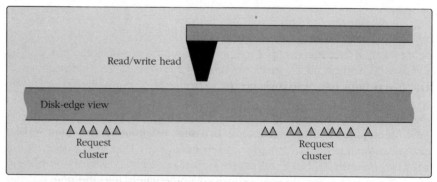

FIGURE 3.20 Nonuniform request distribution in two clusters.

The problem is one of human engineering. The system hums along for one group of users and appears to crawl for another. Would it not be better to have a moderately slower average response time while assuring that no one experiences an unacceptably long wait? We could do so by returning to an FIFO strategy. But there is another approach that would give a low expected response time while avoiding abnormally slow response times for some users. Consider the following approach.

Suppose we temporarily restrict the movement of the disk arm to one direction, say right to left as shown in Figure 3.21. Any requests that are in front of the read/write head (in its direction of travel) will be serviced with an SSTF strategy. The head sweeps across the disk in one direction, stopping at each track with a pending I/O request to service the request. It ignores any requests that fall behind it. When it has traveled to a point where there are no more requests in front of it, it switches direction and begins to sweep in the opposite direction using the same strategy. The cycle repeats endlessly. We call this a *sweep/SSTF* strategy. In this way, we can attempt to strike some balance between minimizing average seek time and avoiding inordinately long request waits.

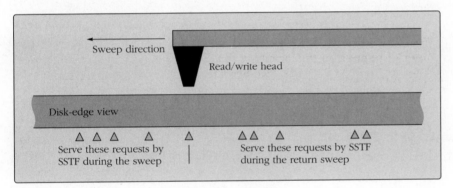

FIGURE 3.21 Sweep/SSTF disk-scheduling strategy.

What are the implications of the strategy on the data abstraction chosen to implement the strategy? The set of requests ahead of the read/write head in the direction of the sweep is a priority queue based on track number. The set of requests behind the head is also a priority queue, but one that will not be served until the head switches its sweep direction. The priorities of the second queue are inverted on track number. Regardless of the details, conceptually we have two priority queues.

Remember that the situation is dynamic. As requests are being served, new requests are arriving and are being enqueued. Those on tracks behind the head are enqueued in the return queue. A question arises about those in front of the head. Should they be placed immediately into the queue being processed or into the return queue? We leave these questions to you in Exercises 3.5, 3 and 4.

Coffman (1982) discusses the performance of the sweep/SSTF strategy. Again we emphasize that it is a complex problem. Our primary purpose here is to study the data structures involved, not to do an in-depth study of disk-scheduling strategies. (For a review of the literature on the disk-scheduling problem, see Wiederhold, 1983, page 341.)

3.5.2 Disk Schedule Abstraction

The topics discussed in Section 3.5.1 are implementation details. They are concerned with techniques for carrying out the scheduling strategy. Clients using the schedule should, however, be shielded from the scheduling details. We can design a disk schedule abstract data type that does so.

The essence of a disk scheduler lies in two operations: (1) presenting a new request to be scheduled and (2) obtaining from the scheduler the next request to be scheduled for the disk. Specification 3.6 is the specification for a disk scheduler.

■ SPECIFICATION 3.6   Disk Scheduler

-- *Objects:*   *Disk I/O requests (see type* io_request *below).*

-- *Structure:*   *Some priority ordering of the requests in the schedule*
--   *(FIFO, SSTF, sweep/SSTF, or other).*

-- *Constraints:*   *0 <= number_of_requests <= max_requests.*

generic

    low_sector, high_sector, low_track, high_track : natural;   -- *Disk parameters.*
    max_requests : positive;   -- *The maximum number of requests that can be in a schedule.*

package disk_schedule **is**

    type io_action   **is** (read, write);
    subtype sector_range   **is** natural **range** low_sector .. high_sector;
    subtype track_range   **is** natural **range** low_track .. high_track;

    type io_request **is record**
      request_id : integer;   -- *Need not be a unique key.*
      action   : io_action;
      track   : track_range;
      sector   : sector_range;
    end record;

    type schedule **is limited private**;

    schedule_full   : **exception**;
    schedule_empty   : **exception**;

    procedure enter_request (the_schedule : **in out** schedule; the_request : io_request);
    -- *results:*   *The request is entered into the schedule.*
    -- *exceptions:*   *A schedule_full exception is raised if number_of_requests(the_schedule) = max_requests.*

(continued)

Specification 3.6 (continued)

procedure get_next_request (the_schedule : **in out** schedule; the_request : **out** io_request);
-- **results:** *The highest priority request according to the scheduling strategy being used is deleted*
-- *from the schedule and is returned in the_request.*
-- **exceptions:** *A schedule_empty exception is raised if number_of_requests(the_schedule) = 0.*

generic
   with function to_be_purged (the_io_request : io_request) **return** boolean;
-- **results:** *Returns true if the_io_request is one that is to be purged; otherwise returns false.*
procedure purge_requests (the_schedule : **in out** schedule);
-- **results:** *Delete all requests in the schedule for which to_be_purged (the_io_request) is true.*

function number_of_requests (the_schedule : schedule) **return** natural;
-- **results:** *Returns the number of I/O requests in the schedule.*

generic
   with procedure process_a_request (the_io_request : **in out** io_request);
-- **results:** *"Processes" the_io_request in a manner chosen by the client.*
procedure traverse (the_schedule : **in out** schedule);
-- **results:** *Walks through all I/O requests in the schedule calling procedure process_a_request for each.*

private

   type a_schedule;   *-- The actual type of the schedule is hidden in the package body.*
   type schedule **is access** a_schedule;   *-- Points to a schedule.*

end disk_schedule;

Clients using the disk schedule need not know which disk-scheduling strategy is being used in the body of the package. Thus, various strategies can be tried to determine an optimal approach with no change at all in the client code. The only changes would be in the body of the disk-scheduling package. Making such changes would involve only a recompilation of the disk schedule body and a relinking (rebinding) of the program.

EXERCISES 3.5

1. Design, write, and test an FIFO queue implementation of the disk schedule in Specification 3.6.
2. Design, write, and test an SSTF priority queue implementation of the disk schedule in Specification 3.6.
3. Design, write, and test a sweep/SSTF priority queue implementation of the disk schedule in Specification 3.6. Hint: Consider a single doubly linked list.
4. Could the queue abstraction (Specification 3.4) or the priority queue abstraction (Specification 3.5) be used in the solution to the above exercises:
    a. Exercise 1. Explain why or why not or with what modification.
    b. Exercise 2. Explain why or why not or with what modification.
    c. Exercise 3. Explain why or why not or with what modification.

■ 3.6 Summary

In Chapter 3 we discussed data structures that have the property that retrieval and removal of objects from them are restricted to a single object determined by some ordering. With stacks, the client has access only to the most recently added object; with queues, to the object added earliest; with priority queues, to an object with the highest priority. It is the implementor's job to use appropriate data structures to make these operations efficient.

Different implementations of stacks and queues generally are very efficient, with all operations executing in time $O(1)$. We might expect to find some differences in the timing of the operations if linked and array implementations were compared.

We have seen Ada implementations with the data structure representation in the package body (Package Bodies 3.1 and 3.2) and the representation in a **private** clause of the specification (Specifications 3.3., 3.4, and 3.5). It is a combination of Ada's **limited** and **private** types together with private declarations in the specification that are used to support information hiding. The data can only be manipulated and accessed through the operations specified in the packages.

Priority queues implemented as arrays or linked lists of objects and priorities inherently have $O(n)$ performance for one of the two operations (*enqueue* and *dequeue*). We referenced an implementation using binary tree heaps that exhibits $O(\log_2 n)$ performance and that will be considered in detail in Chapter 5.

4

Linear Structures

■ 4.1 Introduction

In this chapter we will study several abstract data types that have a common property—they have linear structure. The simplest example of this sort of structure is a *list*. We already saw one example of a list—the linked list of Section 2.4.3—and several other data types that are, or could be considered, linear—arrays, stacks, and queues.

Linear structures are important because they are so natural and occur so often, both alone and as components of more complex structures. They are found both in computing and in everyday life. A line (queue) of customers at a bank, autos waiting at a traffic light, records stored on a magnetic tape, the statements of a computer program, the pages of a book, the characters on a line of text, and the batting order of a baseball team are all linear. In each case, there are first and last objects, and every object but those two has both a unique predecessor and successor.

We begin the chapter with a study of simple lists (Section 4.2). First, we consider lists that are unordered except for their positions in the list. The order of the objects is determined by the user by placing objects in the list in whatever order is desired:

object—object—object—object   List

Section 4.3 covers a topic we discussed in Chapter 2—**linked lists**. Here, a linked list abstraction is designed and a corresponding package is specified and implemented. Many of the operations on linked lists are already built into Ada, so the design presents a dilemma for the designer. Too much design can easily make existing operations that are simple and elegant in Ada become clumsy. For this reason, the design of the linked list data type differs radically from most of the other data types in this book. Objects that are encapsulated and hidden in most other data types are made visible to the user. It might be classed as an open, minimalist design:

object → object → object → object   Linked List

Section 4.4 presents lists that are indexed and mapped. Lists whose objects can be accessed by position are called indexed lists. Certain actions on the list objects specify which object to operate upon by specifying the position of the target object. For instance, an operation is provided that allows retrieval of the ith list object, where i is the position of the object in the list. An index can be overlaid onto any list type. Thus we can have an unordered list that is indexed, a sorted list that is indexed, a frequency-ordered list that is indexed, and so on.

The essence of linearity lies in the uniqueness of each object's preceding and succeeding object. An important consequence of linearity is our ability to assign an integer value to each list object. Suppose we assign the integer 1 to the first object, then assign to each of the remaining objects the integer value one higher than the integer assigned to its predecessor. Moving through the objects successively from the list head, the integers 1, 2, 3, . . . , are assigned up to n, the number of objects in the list. We call these integers the *positions* (or *indexes*) of the objects. Indexed lists, as mentioned previously, have the ability to access list objects by position:

#1 #2 #3 #4
object—object—object—object | Indexed List |

Lists whose objects can be accessed by their key values are called mapped lists. For instance, an operation *find* is provided in which a key value is given and the object, if any, with that key value is returned. As with indexing, this property can be overlaid onto any type of list. Some types of list orders, such as sorted lists, are particularly efficient at implementing *find*. Others require a sequential search to implement *find*. A mapped list is represented as follows:

<key, data>—<key, data>—<key, data> | Mapped List |

Section 4.5 is concerned with lists in which some ordering of the list objects is specified. Chronological lists have their objects ordered by the order of insertion of the objects into the list. The earliest arrival is first, the next earliest arrival is second, and so on, to the last object, which is the latest object to have been inserted:

object—object—object—object | Chronological List |
earliest ——————————→ latest inserted

A second type of ordered list is one that orders the list objects by key values. We will call these sorted lists. The objects in the list have an embedded key; the first list object has the smallest key, the next the second smallest key, and so on. We will show that such lists can be particularly effective at providing a map between keys and data. Operation *find*, which attempts to locate an object of the list with a given key value, is particularly efficient for such lists. Sorted lists are as follows:

<key_1, data>—<key_2, data>—<key_3, data> | Sorted List |

$key_1 < key_2 < key_3 < \cdots$

Another type of list that is effective at providing a map between keys and data is a frequency-ordered list. In such lists, the list objects are ordered by the frequency with which the objects are the subject of *find* operations. In the simplest case, the object with the key that is most frequently the target of *find* is placed at the head of the list. The second most frequent target of *find* searches is placed second, and so on. We can show that such an arrangement minimizes the expected number of probes in a sequential search:

<key, data>—<key, data>—<key, data> | Frequency-Ordered List |
most frequent ——————————→ least frequent

There are several variants of the basic frequency-ordered scheme. One we shall consider has the list "learn" as it is subjected to *find* operations. That is, the list continually reorders itself in an attempt to approximate the optimal ordering. Elements that are the subject of *find_key* operations are moved to or toward the head of the list. These lists are called self-organizing lists.

Rings are circular structures that are not, strictly speaking, linear. Although each object has a unique predecessor and successor, there are no first and last objects. The structure is circular. In all other ways the data type is linear like, so we include it in this chapter and study it in Section 4.6:

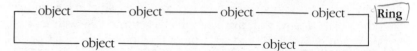

Sequences are lists that have a more primitive set of operations than most list types. They have neither access by position nor access by key. Accessing operations are limited to advancing sequentially through the list starting at the head. A common manifestation of sequences is the sequential file, including Ada's *text_io* and *sequential_io* file types. Sequences and these two Ada file types are examined in Section 4.7. A sequence is as follows:

object—object—object—object   Sequence
cursor→

object—object—object—object
    cursor→

We will pay close attention to performance characteristics of the implementations of each of the linear types that we study in this chapter. We provide order-of-magnitude estimates of expected performance and, in some cases, measured times of execution. Figure 4.1 presents a summary of the list types in this chapter.

List type	Characteristics
• Simple list	Basic list operations.
• Linked list	Nodes with objects and linking pointers.
• Indexed list	Each list object has an associated position and can be accessed by its position.
• Mapped list	Each list object has an embedded key and can be accessed by key value.
• Sorted list	A mapped list in which the list objects are ordered by their keys.
• Frequency-ordered list	A mapped list in which the list objects are ordered by the frequencies with which each object is accessed.
• Ring	A simple list in which there is no first or last object. Every object has a predecessor and successor. Strictly speaking, a ring is not linear.
• Sequence	A list that is accessed via a cursor that moves sequentially through the list. Sequential files are common examples.

FIGURE 4.1 Summary of the list types in this chapter.

If you have written computer programs, you undoubtedly used a software package that operates on at least two levels of lists. One is a text editor or word processor. The lines of the program form one kind of list, whereas the characters of each line form another. The program is in effect a list of lists. You might be able to send the cursor to the *i*th line of the program (indexed access) or to a line that holds a specified text string (a form of mapped access). You can certainly move the cursor from one line to the previous or next line or from one character to the previous or next character (sequential access). There is a strong resemblance between the list operations we shall study and the operations provided by the text editor because both operate upon lists.

■ 4.2 Simple Lists

Here we will design a simple list abstraction. Only a few operations will be provided. There will be no mapping of keys to data nor will there be indexed access. There are no ordering constraints—the user is free to insert and remove list objects in any order. We will provide for multiple lists. Specification 4.1 is the specification.

There are six operations. "&," *head, tail, clear,* and *number_of_objects* provide operations on a single list. A second version of "&" provides an operation for two lists. Note that type *list* is private. The data structures that will be used to implement the list type are given in the **private** section of the specification. The client can see them but not use them.

■ SPECIFICATION 4.1 List

-- **Structure:** *A set of objects of a user-specified type that is ordered linearly.*

-- **Constraints:** $0 <= number\_of\_objects <= max\_size.$ -- *list_size and max_size*
                                                                  -- *appear below.*

generic

    type object_type **is private**;   -- *Type of objects in the list.*
    max_size : **in** positive;   -- *Maximum size of the lists.*

package list_package **is**

    type count **is** natural **range** 0 .. max_size;
    type list(size : count := 0) **is private**;
    list_full   : **exception**;
    list_empty   : **exception**;
            discriminant
function "&" (the_list : list; the_object : object_type) **return** list;
-- **results:** *Returns the list with the_object appended to its end.*
-- **exceptions:** *A list_full exception is raised when number_of_objects(the_list) = max size.*

(continued)

Specification 4.1 (continued)

function "&" (left, right : list) **return** list;
-- *results:* *Returns left and right* <u>concatenated</u> *in that order.*
-- *exceptions:* *A list_full exception is raised when number_of_objects(left) +*
-- *number_of_objects(right) > max_size.*

function empty_list **return** list;
-- *results:* *Returns the list that has zero objects.*

function head (the_list : list) **return** object_type;
-- *results:* *Returns the first object on the list.*
-- *exceptions:* *A list_empty exception is raised when number_of_objects(the_list) = 0.*

function tail (the_list : list) **return** list;
-- *results:* *Returns a list consisting of all of the list except its head object.*
-- *exceptions:* *A list_empty exception is raised when number_of_objects(the_list) = 0.*

function number_of_objects(the_list : list) **return** natural;
-- *results:* *Returns the number of objects in the list.*

private

```
    type array_of_objects is array(positive range <>) of object_type;
    type list(size : count := 0) is record
      objects : array_of_objects(1 .. size);
    end record;
```

end list_package;

Note that the <u>function "&"</u> is overloaded (in this case, there are two functions named "&"). Suppose we have two lists, *list_1* and *list_2,* and a variable *an_object* of type *object_type.* To append a new object to list *list_1,* we would say

list_1 := list_1 & an_object;

To <u>concatenate the lists *list_1* and *list_2*</u> and place the result into list *list_1,* we say

list_1 := list_1 & list_2;

<u>Ada determines which "&"</u> to use by examining the arguments (operands). In the first case, the arguments are a list and an object; in the second case they are two lists. These facts are sufficient for Ada to make a determination.

Note that type *list* is **private**, not **limited private**. This means that assignment and test for equality are available to the user. To test whether *list_1* and *list_2* hold the same objects in the same order, we can say

if list_1 = list_2 . . .

    Similarly, list assignment is

list_1 := list_2;

    If type *list* had been declared **limited private,** neither of these would be available to a client. The only way for the client to assign one list value to another or to test for the equality of two lists would be to call some procedure or function of the package *list_package* that would do each. Consequently, such functions or procedures would have to be provided as part of the package. In this case, it is sufficient to let the predefined ":=" and "=" operations do the job.

    head returns a copy of the first (head) object of the list:

an_object := head (list_1);

and *tail* returns a list consisting of all list objects except for the head object. Thus,

list_1 := tail (list_1);

effectively removes the first list object from *list_1*.

    Package Body 4.1 demonstrates how powerful Ada is for this application. By using records with discriminants, record aggregates, array concatenation, and slices, we get a set of procedures, with each procedure one executable statement in length, excluding the exception handlers.

■ **PACKAGE BODY 4.1** **Lists—Implements Specification 4.1**

```
package body list_package is

    function "&" (the_list : list; the_object : object_type) return list is
    -- Length 3   Complexity 2   Performance O(n)
    begin
        return list'(the_list.size + 1, (the_list.objects & (the_object)));
    exception
        when constraint_error | numeric_error => raise list_full;
    end "&";

    function "&" (left, right : list) return list is
    -- Length 2   Complexity 2   Performance O(n)
    begin
        return list'(left.size + right.size, (left.objects & right.objects ));
    exception
        when constraint_error | numeric_error => raise list_full;
    end "&";
```

(continued)

Package Body 4.1 (continued)

```
function head (the_list : list) return object_type is
-- Length 2   Complexity 2   Performance O(1)
begin
   return the_list.objects (1);
exception
   when constraint_error => raise list_empty;
end head;

function tail (the_list : list) return list is
-- Length 3   Complexity 2   Performance O(n)
   subtype tail_array is array_of_objects(1 .. the_list.size − 1);
begin
   return list'(the_list.size − 1, tail_array(the_list.objects (2 .. the_list.size)));
exception
   when constraint_error => raise list_empty;
end tail;

function empty_list return list is
-- Length 2   Complexity 1   Performance O(1)
   null_list : list(0);
begin
   return null_list;
end empty_list;

function number_of_objects (the_list : list) return natural is
-- Length 1   Complexity 1   Performance O(1)
begin
   return the_list.size;
end number_of_objects;
end list_package;
```

The implementations of the operations in Package Body 4.1 are simple due to the nature of the discriminant record type chosen to represent a list. Each operation is a single line of code. The order-of-magnitude estimates of performance are straightforward, but a bit of explanation is required. Let us take the first "&" function as an example. The single line of code in the procedure (aside from the exception handler) is

return list'(the_list.size + 1, (the_list.objects & (the_object)));

What is returned is a record with a discriminant value of *the_list.size + 1* and an array of objects [*the_list.objects & (the_object)*], that holds *the_list.size + 1* objects. If the size of the result is a list of *n* (= *the_list.size + 1*) objects, then the work involved is $O(n)$. Timing studies show that to be the case on the authors' system.

The complication is that slice operations can be very efficient on some computer architectures. Timing studies on one of the primary Ada compilers available to the authors show that a slice movement is more than 20 times

The movement of a slice of an array can be much faster than the movement of the array object by object using a loop.

faster than object-by-object assignment. Thus, although function "$\&$" is $O(n)$, it is a very fast $O(n)$.

With that proviso, we can summarize the performance estimates of the list operations as shown in Figure 4.2.

Operation	Performance
"$\&$" (append object)	$O(n)$
"$\&$" (concatenate lists)	$O(n)$
head	$O(1)$
tail	$O(n)$
empty_list	$O(1)$
list_size	$O(1)$

FIGURE 4.2 Performance estimates of the list data type (Package Body 4.1). The estimates are the same for array and linked implementations.

4.2.1 Linked Lists

We implemented the list abstraction specified in Specification 4.1 as an array embedded in a discriminant record. You saw in Specification 3.2 and Package Body 3.2 how a stack abstraction previously implemented with an array (Specification 3.1 and Package Body 3.1) could be alternatively implemented as a linked list.

EXERCISES 4.2

1. Write a program that will take as input two strings that are polynomials and will add the polynomials. For example, if the two polynomials are

   $3.5*x**3 + 2.1*x - 12.3$
   $1.8*x**3 + 4.2*x**2 - 2.7*x + 1.0$

   the result is

   $5.3*x**3 + 4.2*x**2 - 0.6*x - 11.3$

   You can assume that the operators "$+$" and "$-$" are always surrounded by spaces. You can also assume that the polynomials are entered from the highest power of x to the lowest. Solve the problem by instantiating a list package, declaring two lists, and placing the coefficients and powers of x into the lists. The lists are then to be "added" in the polynomial sense.

2. Expand the list package in Specification 4.1 to include the operations below. Specify, implement, and test your changes.
   a. Append new objects to the head of the list.
   b. Return a "head" list; that is, the list minus its tail object.
   c. Traverse the list applying some generic procedure supplied by the user to each list object.

3. Package Body 4.1 has the disadvantage that the "$\&$" function that concatenates a single object to the list involves moving the entire list. The operation is $O(n)$ (although probably fast since a slice is moved) rather than $O(1)$, which would be the case if the single object being appended were the only thing moved. Can you modify Specification 4.1 and Package Body 4.1 to eliminate the list copy. If so, how? Implement your ideas.

4. Modify the **private** section of Specification 4.1 to represent lists without using a record discriminant. Rewrite Package Body 4.1 to reflect the changes you made.

5. Modify the **private** section of Specification 4.1 to represent lists as linked lists. Rewrite Package Body 4.1 to reflect the changes you made. Fill in a third column of Figure 4.2 with the performance estimates of your implementation.

6. Discuss the appropriateness of the list abstraction for solving the problem in Exercise 1.

▮ 4.3 Linked List Abstraction

A major goal with a linked list abstraction is to avoid making it clumsy. The linked structure is concise, simple, and efficient and is partially built into the Ada language. Normally in data abstractions, we will hide the internals and allow the user to deal with the data abstraction only through the specified operations (procedures and functions). All of the data abstractions to this point have done so. We will take a different tack with the linked list abstraction. In order to make it efficient and simple, we will make much of the structure visible to the user. This means that a careless user could change parts of the list in a way that would make the list lose its integrity. For instance, if the user had p pointing to a node in the middle of the list and executed the statement

p.next := null;

the linkage of that node to the next one would be lost with no way to recover the lost tail portion of the list since nothing points to it (see Figure 4.3).

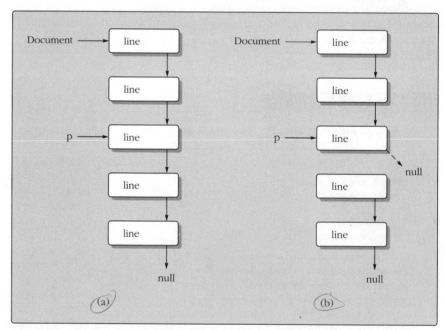

FIGURE 4.3 Breaking the linkage of a linked list. (a) Original list; (b) after "p.next := null;".

We will make the nodes of the list visible to the user and allow the user to change and manipulate the user objects as well as the linking pointers. We will provide operations that are a bit lengthy and/or complex. In going from one node to the next, the user would deal directly with the node saying, for instance, p := p.next;

Because the operation is so simple in Ada, instead of providing some *find_next* procedure we allow the user to write it using Ada's predefined facilities. We do not hide the nodes and pointers in the package body but let the user manipulate them directly.

Insertion and deletion of nodes, as well as concatenation of two lists, take more thought and coding. We will provide these operations as services. Specification 4.2 is the specification for linked lists.

■ SPECIFICATION 4.2 Linked Lists

```
-- Elements:    Generic type object_type within linked list nodes of type node
--                  (see types object_type and node below).

-- Structure:   A linear arrangement of nodes; each node points to its successor. The
--                  pointer in the last node is null.

-- Constraints: The number of nodes in the list is bounded at some unknown value
--                  dependent on the implementation.

generic

    type object_type is private;

package linked_list_package is

    type    node;
    type    node_access is access node;                         -- Pointer to list nodes.
    type    node is record                                      -- List nodes.
      object  : object_type;                                    -- User objects.
      next    : node_access;                                    -- List links.
    end record;

    type    linked_list is record          -- Notice that the linked_list type is not private.
      head, tail  : node_access;                 -- Pointers to the first and last nodes.
      size        : natural := 0;                         -- The number of list nodes.
    end record;                              -- Note: Ada initializes pointers to null.

    type insert_place is (at_head, after_node);

    procedure insert_node (the_list     : in out linked_list;
                           the_object   : object_type;
                           place        : insert_place := after_node;
                           after        : node_access := null);
    -- assumes:   after is either null or points to a node of the list.
    -- results:   A new node is created with the_object in it and is linked into the linked list
    --                 (a) if place = after_node, then after the list node pointed at by after or
    --                 (b) if place = at_head, then as the list's new head node.
```

(continued)

Specification 4.2 (continued)

```
-- exceptions:   A storage_error exception is raised if a new node cannot be created.
--               A constraint_error exception is raised if after = null when place = after_node.

procedure delete_node (the_list : in out linked_list; pointer : in out node_access);
-- assumes:   pointer points to a node of the linked list.
-- results:   The node accessed by pointer is removed from the list and the memory
--            it occupies is deallocated; pointer is set to null.
-- exceptions:   A constraint_error exception is raised if pointer is null.
-- notes:   (...pred.node → pointer.node → succ.node...) becomes
--          (...pred.node → succ.node...) after the deletion.

procedure concatenate (left, right : in out linked_list);
-- results:   The right list is concatenated to the tail of the left list; left becomes
--            the concatenation of the two lists; right becomes an empty list.

end linked_list_package;
```

There is no private section, so everything declared in the specification can be accessed by the user. The specification is generic in the kind of object to be placed in the nodes, so a user can instantiate the package for any kind of user data. If we had the *line_data* record used in the line-sorting program of Figure 2.43

```
subtype line_length is positive range 1 .. 80;
type line_data(length : line_length := 1) is record
    text   : string(1 .. length);
end record;
```

we could instantiate a linked list of these records with the statement

```
package line_list is new linked_list_package(line_data);
```

Figure 4.4 is another solution to the line-sorting program of Section 2.4.5 (reading, sorting, and printing lines of text), this time using the *linked_list_package*.

The version of the line-sorting program in Figure 4.4 loses the feature of having the nodes be of varying lengths as was the case for the solutions in Figures 2.43 and 2.45. This is due to the interaction between the discriminanted record that is the list object and the generic nature of the linked list objects. The linked list package cannot be instantiated with an object type that is unconstrained. Its size must be fixed, and hence we choose to fix it at a size of 80 characters.

If you are uncomfortable using pointers and linked structures, we suggest you read and understand the body of the linked list package (Package Body 4.2) thoroughly before proceeding.

```
with text_io; use text_io;
with linked_list_package;
procedure sort_lines is
```
-- **assumes:**   *The lines are 80 characters or less in length.*
-- **results:**   *Reads document, sorts lines in ascending order, and prints lines.*
-- *Length 23   Complexity 3   Performance* O(n), *where* n *is the number of lines.*

```
      subtype line_length is positive range 1 .. 80;
      type line_data(length : line_length := 1) is record
        text   : string(1 .. length);
      end record;
```

-- *Instantiate a linked list of lines using the linked_lists generic package (Specification 2.4).*
```
      package line_list is new linked_list_package(line_data); use line_list;

      document  : linked_list;                          -- The linked list of lines.
      new_line  : string(line_length);
      len       : natural range 0 .. line_length'last;

      procedure sort(doc : in out line_list.linked_list) is separate;
      procedure print(doc : line_list.linked_list) is separate;

begin
```
      -- *Read all input lines.*
```
      loop
        get_line(new_line, len);
        exit when len = 0;
        line_list.insert_node(document, (len, new_line(1 .. len)), at_head);
      end loop;
      sort(document);
      print(document);
exception
      when storage_error => put_line("Exhausted memory − too many lines.");
                            put_line("Sorting and printing what was read.");
                            sort(document);          -- Note: Sort and print
                            print(document);         -- might not execute if
end sort_lines;                                      -- memory is exhausted.
```

F I G U R E 4.4 Line-sorting program using the linked list abstract data type.

■ **PACKAGE BODY** 4.2 **Linked Lists—Implements Specification 4.2**

with cpu_clock;
```
with unchecked_deallocation;
package body linked_list_package is

      procedure free is new unchecked_deallocation(node, node_access);

      procedure insert_node (the_list   : in out linked_list;
                             the_object : object_type;
```

Package Body 4.2 (continued)

```
                                 place      : insert_place := after_node;
                                 after      :node_access := null) is
-- Length 13   Complexity 3   Performance O(1)
    p : node_access := new node;                                        -- Working pointer to the new node.
  begin
    p.object := the_object;                                             -- Place the object into new node.
    case place is
      when after_node => p.next := after.next;   -- Arrange linkages appropriately, depending on the value of argument place.
                         after.next := p;
      when at_head    => p.next := the_list.head;
                         the_list.head := p;
    end case;
    if after = the_list.tail then                                       -- Adjust tail pointer if necessary.
      the_list.tail := p;
    end if;
    the_list.size := the_list.size + 1;
  end insert_node;


  procedure delete_node (the_list : in out linked_list; pointer: in out node_access) is
  -- Length 12   Complexity 4   Performance O(n)
    pred : node_access;
  begin
    if pointer = the_list.head
      then   the_list.head := the_list.head.next;                       -- Head node to be deleted.
      else   pred := the_list.head;
             while pred.next /= pointer loop                            -- Find predecessor to ptr.node.
               pred := pred.next;
             end loop;                              -- pred points to predecessor of pointer.node, the node to be deleted.
             pred.next := pointer.next;                                 -- Link predecessor around node to be deleted.
    end if;
    if pointer = the_list.tail then
      the_list.tail := pred;                                            -- Adjust tail if necessary.
    end if;

    free(pointer);                                                      -- Deallocate pointer.node.
    the_list.size := the_list.size - 1;
  end delete_node;


  procedure concatenate(left, right : in out linked_list) is
  -- Length 4   Complexity 2   Performance O(1)
  begin
    if right.size > 0 then
      left.tail.next  := right.head;
      left.tail       := right.tail;
      left.size       := left.size + right.size;
      right           := linked_list'(null, null, 0);
    end if;
  end concatenate;


end linked_list_package;
```

Figure 4.5 shows the state of the list just after entering and just before leaving the *delete_node* procedure. The arrows that change from solid to dashed lines are those whose values have been changed by the deletion process.

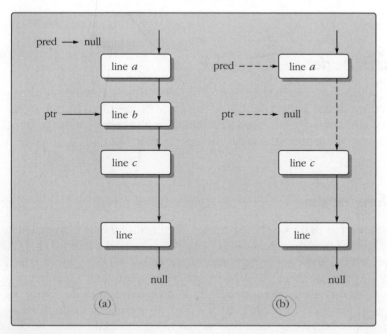

FIGURE 4.5 Linked list segment before and after deletion of ptr.node. (a) Before deletion; (b) after deletion.

Since the nodes of the list can be directly accessed by a user, there are several operations implicitly provided to the user in addition to the three explicitly provided by the three procedures of *linked_list_package*. Some of these are given in Figure 4.6 (*p* is a node pointer, *an_object* is type *object_type,* and *the_list* is a list).

Operation	Example
Point to the first node of the list	p := the_list.head
Point to the successor of a node	p := p.next
Retrieve the object from a node	x := p.an_object
Change the value of the node's object	p.an_object := x
Determine how many objects (nodes) are in the list	n := the_list.size

FIGURE 4.6 Examples of linked list operations executed by a user.

4.3.1 Length, Complexity, and Performance

There are only three linked list procedures provided in the linked list package, but they are relatively more lengthy and more complex than the average procedure or function we encountered in the other packages we studied.

To see how efficient the linked list operations are, we'll look at each one and determine an order-of-magnitude estimate of its performance. Refer to Package Body 4.2 for this discussion.

insert_node

With any insertion, each statement of the algorithm is executed at most once, regardless of the size of the list or the place of insertion. In fact, either five or six statements are executed, depending on the results of the test in the **if** statement. Therefore, we can say the operation is $O(1)$.

delete_node

If the head node is the one being deleted, then again either five or six statements are executed, and the operation is $O(1)$. If a node in the interior of the list is to be deleted, the **else** branch of the **if** statement is taken, and it contains a loop in which the statement *pred := pred.next* is executed a number of times depending on how far along in the list the node to be deleted is. Since *pointer* points to the node to be deleted, the loop is attempting to find that node's predecessor because its *next* pointer has to be changed during the deletion process. If we were trying to delete the *k*th node, the loop would iterate $k - 1$ times to reach its predecessor. If we assume that every node in the list is equally probable as the target of the deletion, excluding the head node since it is a special case, the expected number of times the loop iterates (with n nodes in the list) is

$$E_{\text{iterations}} = [1 + 2 + 3 + \cdots + (n - 1)]/(n - 1)$$
$$= (\sum_{k=1}^{n-1} k)/(n - 1) = n*(n - 1)/[2*(n - 1)] = n/2$$

As our intuition suggests, we must, on average, traverse half the list. Outside the loop all other statements are executed at most once. We can then conclude that the *delete_node* operation is $O(n)$.

concatenate

Each of the four statements inside the **if** statement is executed at most once. The *concatenate* operation is $O(1)$.

The results of the linked list operations are summarized in Figure 4.7.

Operation	Linked list
insert_node	$O(1)$
delete_node	$O(1)$ or $O(n)$
concatenate	$O(1)$

FIGURE 4.7 Performance estimates for linked list operations.

Body 4.3 (continued)

```
dure delete (the_list : in out indexed_list; at_index : positive) is
 b 5   Complexity 2   Performance O(n)

 _index > the_list.size
en raise faulty_position;
se    the_list.objects(at_index .. the_list.size − 1)
                   := the_list.objects(at_index + 1 .. the_list.size);
      the_list.size := the_list.size − 1;

 if;
lete;

dure change (the_list       : in out indexed_list;
             at_index       : positive;
             the_object     : object_type) is
 b 5   Complexity 2   Performance O(1)

 _index > the_list.size
en raise faulty_position;
se the_list.objects(at_index) := the_object;
 if;
aange;

dure clear (the_list : in out indexed_list) is
 b 1   Complexity 1   Performance O(1)

list. size := 0;
ear;

on number_of_objects (the_list : indexed_list) return natural is
 b 1   Complexity 1   Performance O(1)

rn the_list.size;
umber_of_objects;

·d_list_package;
```

The list is held in an array *objects* [Figure 4.8(a)]. Figure 4.8 shows the sequence of actions necessary to insert a new object into the interior of the list. If the insertion is at position *i*, then the list objects in the range *i* .. *n* (*n* = list size) have to be shifted to make room for the new object. The new object is subsequently inserted into the vacated space at position *i*. Assuming each position is an equally likely target for an insertion, the expected number of objects to be moved is

$$[n + (n − 1) + (n − 2) + \cdots + 1 + 0]/(n + 1) = n/2 \sim O(n)$$

Therefore, we can conclude that the *insert* operation has an expected performance of $O(n)$.

1. Redesign the linked list specification to hide the *linked_list*, *node*, and *node_access* types, and provide the operations on the list (Figure 4.6) as functions and procedures.
2. Use the linked list package (Specification 4.2) to build an implementation of the simple list package (Package Body 4.1).
3. Add operations to the linked list abstraction (Specification 4.2 and Package Body 4.2) that

   a. Exchange a node with its predecessor in the list by relinking the nodes.
   b. Exchange a node with its successor in the list by relinking the nodes.

4. Design, implement, and test a doubly linked list data type analogous to Specification 4.2 and Package Body 4.2 for singly linked lists.

4.4 Indexed and Mapped Lists

This section concerns lists whose objects have an associated or embedded value that allows the objects to be accessed efficiently by specifying the value. The objects in indexed lists have associated positions in the list, whereas the objects in mapped lists have embedded keys. Specifying the position or key uniquely determines which object of the list is being referenced. Sections 4.4.1 and 4.4.2 discuss these two list types.

4.4.1 Indexed Lists

A list is an ***indexed list*** if some of its operations allow actions on the list that are based on positions in the list. Recall that one of the aspects of linearity is that we can pair the objects of the list one to one with integers starting with, for example, 1 for the head or first object, and pairing successive integers with successive objects of the list until the last list object is paired with *n*, the number of objects in the list. We call the integer with which an object is paired the object's ***position***.

Suppose we have an operation

procedure delete (the_list : **in out** indexed_list; at_index : positive);

that removes (deletes) the *i*th object from a list, where *i* = *at_index*. The operation is based on position since that is the way the object to be removed is identified.

Specification 4.3 is the specification of a list that has the property of being indexed. It has operations that are somewhat different from the operations of the basic list given in Specification 4.1. The intent is to show not only the indexing property but also some of the possible variations in operating on linear structures. We'll see even more variety in other types of lists.

One significant operation that was added is the *change* function, which allows changes to specified objects that are in the list. An object is denoted by its position. The same is true with the other operations of the type.

■ SPECIFICATION 4.3   Indexed Lists

-- **Structure:**   *A set of objects of a user-specified type where the objects are ordered linearly.*
--   *Each list object is associated with an integer; the first (head) list object is associated*
--   *with 1. Each other list object is associated with an integer that is one greater than the*
--   *integer associated with its predecessor in the list.*
-- **Constraints:**   *0 <= number_of_objects <= max_size.*   -- *list_size and max_size appear below.*

generic

    type object_type **is private**;   -- *Type of objects in the list.*

package indexed_list_package **is**

    type indexed_list (max_size : positive) **is limited private**;

    list_full   : **exception**;
    list_empty   : **exception**;
    faulty_position : **exception**;

    procedure insert (the_list   . : **in out** indexed_list;
                at_index   : positive;
                the_object : object_type);
-- **results:**   *The object is inserted into the_list at position at_index; all list objects following the*
--   *object are at positions one greater than before the insertion.*
-- **exceptions:**   *A faulty_position exception is raised if at_index > number_of_objects(the_list) + 1.*
--   *A list_full exception is raised if number_of_objects(the_list) = max_size.*
-- **notes:**   *At_index can be one greater than number_of_objects(the_list) to allow appending new objects to the end of the list.*

    function list_object (the_list : indexed_list; at_index : positive) **return** object_type;
-- **results:**   *Returns a copy of the object of the list at position at_index.*
-- **exceptions:**   *A faulty_position exception is raised if at_index > number_of_objects(the_list).*

    procedure delete (the_list : **in out** indexed_list; at_index : positive);
-- **results:**   *The object at position at_index is deleted from the list; all objects following it*
--   *take positions one less than before the deletion.*
-- **exceptions:**   *A faulty_position exception is raised if at_index > number_of_objects(the_list).*

    procedure change (the_list   : **in out** indexed_list;
                at_index   : positive;
                the_object : object_type);
-- **results:**   *The object in the list at position at_index is changed to the new value the_object.*
-- **exceptions:**   *A faulty_position exception is raised if at_index > number_of_objects(the_list).*

    procedure clear (the_list : **in out** indexed_list);
-- **results:**   *number_of_objects(the_list) is 0.*

    function number_of_objects (the_list : indexed_list) **return** natural;
-- **results:**   *Returns the number of objects in the list.*

(continued)

Specification 4.3 (continued)

private

    type array_of_objects **is array** (positive **range** <>) **of** object_type;

    type indexed_list (max_size : positive) **is record**
     size   : natural;
     objects : array_of_objects (1 .. max_size);
    end record;

end indexed_list_package;

    Implementation of the specification is straightforward. An array of objects is ideal for storing the list since arrays have the property of being efficiently indexed.

    Package Body 4.3 is an implementation of Specification 4.3. It uses discriminent records and arrays.

■ PACKAGE BODY 4.3   Indexed Lists—Implements Specification 4.3

package body indexed_list_package **is**

    procedure insert (the_list   : **in out** indexed_list;
                at_index   : positive;
                the_object : object_type) **is**
-- *Length 9   Complexity 4   Performance O(n)*
    begin
      if   the_list.size = 0   **then**   the_list.size := 1;
                                      the_list.objects(1) := the_object;
      elsif at_index > the_list.size + 1   **then raise** faulty_position;
      elsif the_list.size = the_list.max_size   **then raise** list_full;
      else   the_list.objects(at_index + 1 .. the_list.size + 1)
                                   := the_list.objects(at_index .. the_list.size);
          the_list.objects(at_index) := the_object;
          the_list.size := the_list.size + 1;
      end if;
    end insert;

    function list_object (the_list : indexed_list; at_index : positive) **return** object_type **is**
-- *Length 4   Complexity 2   Perfomance O(1)*
    begin
      if at_index > the_list.size
        then raise faulty_position;
        else return the_list.objects(at_index);
      end if;
    end list_object;

Package

  proc
-- *Len*
  begi
    if

     en
  end

  proc
-- *Len*
  begi
    if

     en
  end

  proc
-- *Len*
  begi
    the
  end

  func
-- *Len,*
  begi
    re
  end

end inde

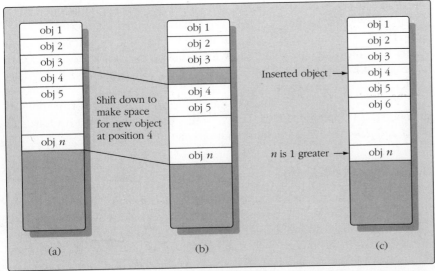

FIGURE 4.8 Insertion into an indexed list at position 4. Performance is $O(n)$. (a) List in the array *object*; (b) shifted for insertion; (c) after insertion.

Similarly, removal of an object using the *delete* procedure causes a shift in the other direction and also has an expected performance of $O(n)$. The other operations execute in a time that is $O(1)$.

There is an alternative insert operation that is faster. Suppose we take the object at the position at which the insertion is to be made and just move it to the end of the list. In doing so, we create a gap into which we can place the object being inserted. Figure 4.9 shows the process. The advantage is that

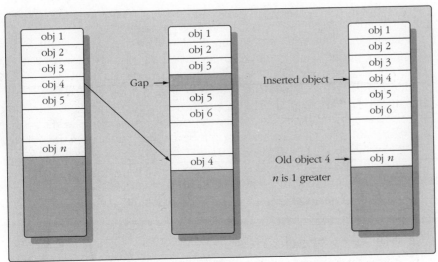

FIGURE 4.9 Insertion into an indexed list at position 4 (alternative method). Performance is $O(1)$.

Operation	Performance
insert	$O(1)$ or $O(n)$
list object	$O(1)$
delete	$O(1)$ or $O(n)$
change	$O(1)$
make_list_empty	$O(1)$
list_size	$O(1)$

FIGURE 4.10 Performance estimates of the indexed list data type (Package Body 4.3).

insertion takes $O(1)$ effort instead of $O(n)$. The disadvantage is that one object, the one moved, changes its position relative to the others in the list.

The *delete* operation has a similar implementation to the insert operation. Rather than move up the slice below the point of removal to cover the gap, we could move the nth (tail) object into the gap, then reduce n by 1. That implementation is also $O(1)$.

Figure 4.10 shows a summary of the performance estimates of the indexed list operations implemented as arrays. Notice that, if the alternative forms of *insert* and *delete* are chosen, all operations can be $O(1)$.

4.4.2 Mapped Lists

In Section 1.5.2 we discussed mappings. Briefly, a mapping allows us to access the objects of a data structure by specifying their key values. We now consider a list object to have an embedded part of itself called its **key**. The key values in the list are to be unique—that is, no two list objects have the same key value. We can now design operations such as retrieval of the object that has a given (target) key value. Specification 4.3 has a retrieval operation that we name *find* that is specified as follows:

procedure find (the_list   : sorted_list;
                target_key : key_type;
                the_object : **out** object_type;
                found   : **out** boolean);
-- **results:** *If the list holds a list object for which key_of(list_object) = target_key, then*
--   *the_object = that list_object; and* found *is true; otherwise* found *is false.*

The idea of identifying objects by their keys is the crux of mapping: There is a mapping between a key and its associated object. This idea is common in practice. For instance, a bank identifies your account for a transaction by the specification of a target key—your bank account number.

Rather than immediately designing a mapped list data type, we will delay writing a specification until we have discussed sorted lists in Section 4.5.2. The sorted list data type we will design will be a mapped list. There is a close relationship between the two since the reason for having the list sorted on key values is to make mappings of (in fact, searching for) target keys efficient.

EXERCISES 4.4

1. Design, implement, and test a list data type that has the property of being both indexed and mapped.

4.5 Ordered Lists

Ordered lists have the property that there is some ordering relationship that the list objects must satisfy. The lists we have discussed had no statement about list ordering in their specifications. The list objects could be in whatever order the user placed them. In the following sections, we discuss three list orderings. There are others, but these three are typical, and the first two, chronological order and sorted order, are common in practice.

4.5.1 Chronological Lists

A *chronological list* is one in which the objects in the list are in order of their insertion into the list. The list of Specification 4.1, coincidentally, would be a chronological list if it were not for the "&" that concatenates two lists. Insertions of single objects are always at the tail end of the list, and there is no way to rearrange the list objects without removing them from the list and reinserting them.

The linked list (Specification 4.2) is not a chronological list. The *insert* operation allows insertion of new list objects at any place in the list. Thus, the order of the objects does not necessarily correspond to the insertion order.

We will not develop a separate specification for chronological list but merely note that some types of lists have this characteristic.

4.5.2 Sorted Lists

A *sorted list* is an ordered list in which the order of the list objects is determined by their key values. For purposes of our discussion, we define the objects to be arranged in the list such that the keys are in ascending order. Each list object's key is greater than the key of its predecessor and less than the key of its successor.

As we have mentioned, the reason for sorting is to make searching efficient. An everyday example is the telephone directory. We can think of the directory as a list. Each object in the list consists of three parts—name, address, and telephone number. We consider names to be the keys and address and phone number to be the data. The typical operation is to find the phone number of someone with a given name. If the book were arranged randomly by name, the only way to find the name for which we are searching would be to start comparing at the beginning (or anywhere) and search sequentially through the book matching each name with the one for which we are searching.

Luckily, phone books are sorted on the name field. If we are searching for someone whose name begins with the letter "S," we are likely to open the book two-thirds to three-fourths of the way through. We do not begin the search on page 1. What we are doing is eliminating a large section of the book that we don't need to examine. We are able to do this because of the sorted order of the entries. With a sequential search of unsorted data, we are able to eliminate only one entry at a time.

The search continues as we cast away increasingly smaller groups of pages until we turn a few single pages. We then skip about until we find the region of the name we are seeking, and only then do we search sequentially through individual names.

An important reason for sorting data is to make searches, either by people or computers, efficient. Computer searches use somewhat different techniques than those used by people, but all searches rely on casting out large groups of data that we are certain cannot include the object for which we are searching. The gain in efficiency over a sequential search can be enormous. A **_binary search_** (which we examine in detail shortly) executes in a time of $O(\log_2 n)$. A **_sequential search_** executes in $O(n)$ time. The search of a telephone book that we just described corresponds roughly to a binary search. If you want to know how painful an $O(n)$ search is, search a telephone book for a given telephone number rather than for a given name.

Before discussing these and other search techniques, we will write the specification for a sorted list abstract data type. The specification is given as Specification 4.4. Four of the seven operations require a key value as one of the arguments. The data type has the property of providing a mapping between keys and data of the list objects.

■ SPECIFICATION 4.4   Sorted Lists

-- **Structure:**   *The list objects are objects of type "object_type." The objects are arranged linearly in the list. The key values in the list are unique, which means that no two list objects have the same key values. For all list objects, the key of an object is greater than its predecessor's key and less than its successor's key.*

-- **Constraints:** $0 <= number\_of\_objects <= max\_size.$ *-- List_size and max_size appear below.*

generic

    type key_type **is private**;
    type object_type **is private**;

    with function key_of (the_object : object_type) **return** key_type;
    -- **results:**   *Return the key associated with the object.*

    with function ">" (left, right : key_type) **return** boolean **is** <>;
    -- **results:**   *True if the left key > the right key; false otherwise.*

package sorted_list_package **is**

    type sorted_list (max_size : positive) **is limited private**;

    list_full   : **exception**;
    list_empty : **exception**;

    procedure insert (the_list : **in out** sorted_list; the_object : object_type);
    -- **assumes:**   *No list object has a key value equal to key_of(the_object).*
    -- **results:**   *The object is inserted into the list in its proper position so that the list remains sorted on the keys of the list objects.*
    -- **exceptions:**   *A list_full exception is raised if number_of_objects(the_list) = the_list.max_size.*

    procedure delete (the_list : **in out** sorted_list; target_key : key_type);
    -- **results:**   *Removes the list object for which key_of(list_object) = target_key from the list; does nothing if no list object has that key value.*

(continued)

Specification 4.4 (continued)

procedure change (the_list : **in out** sorted_list; the_object : object_type);
-- **results:** *Replaces the list object for which key_of(list_object) = key_of(the_object) with the_object; does nothing if no list object*
--   *has that key value.*

procedure clear (the_list : **in out** sorted_list);
-- **results:** *The number of objects in the list is 0 and the list is empty.*

procedure find (the_list   : sorted_list;
                    target_key   : key_type;
                    the_object   : **out** object_type;
                    found   : **out** boolean);
-- **results:** *If the list holds a list object for which key_of(list_object) = target_key, the_object returns that list_object and found is*
--   *true; otherwise found is false.*

function number_of_objects (the_list : sorted_list) **return** natural;
-- **results:** *Returns the number of objects in the list.*

generic
   with procedure process(the_object : object_type);
   -- **results:** *"processes" a list object.*
procedure traverse (the_list : **in out** sorted_list);
-- **results:** *Procedure process is called for each list object, from the first to the last, progressing through the list in sorted order by key.*

private

   type array_of_objects **is array** (positive **range** <>) **of** object_type;

   type sorted_list (max_size : positive) **is record**
      size   : natural;
      objects : array_of_objects (1 .. max_size);
   end record;

end sorted_list_package;

The package is, as usual, generic. An object type and a key type must be specified. Two functions are required from a user: The first extracts the key from an object; the second determines whether one key is greater than the other. Within the generic package is a generic procedure, *traverse*. It is used to progress through the list one list object at a time, from the first object to the last, calling a procedure *process* for each list object. The procedure *process* is supplied by the user and does whatever is necessary to each list object. *traverse* is provided because there is no set of the other operations that allows visiting each and every list object. The only other way to access objects is by specifying their key values. If the universe of possible keys is large and we don't know what key values are represented in the list, it may be prohibitively expensive in time to execute a *find* operation for each possible value, then to process only those that are found as a result of the search.

Since this is our first encounter with functions and procedures as generic parameters, we will give an example of their use for the case at hand—sorted lists. Suppose we wish to build a sorted list whose keys are integers and whose data are a 25-character string. Assume that the maximum list size is 1000 objects. Suppose further that we need to traverse the list for two reasons: The first is to print the list; the second is to find the alphabetically first character string. We will instantiate two versions of *traverse*—one for each chore. The code fragment in Figure 4.11 shows all three instantiations.

The body of the sorted list package is given as Package Body 4.4. The critical subunit of the package is an internal function *search*. It is invisible to

```
with sorted_list_package, text_io; use text_io;
procedure my_program is

    subtype string_25 is string (1 .. 25);

    type list_record is record
       key    : integer;
       data   : string_25;
    end record;

    function extract_key (the_record : list_record) return key_type;

    package my_list is new sorted_lists(key_type      => integer,
                                        object_type   => list_record;
                                        key_of        => extract_key);

    smallest : string_25 := (1 .. 25 => character'val(127));      -- The largest character
                                                                  -- value.

    procedure print (a_record : list_record);
    procedure smallest_data (the_record : list_record);

    procedure print_traverse is new my_list.traverse(print);
    procedure smallest_traverse is new my_list.traverse(smallest_data);

    procedure print(a_record : list_record) is
    begin
       put(a_record.key); put_line("   " & a_record.data);
    end print;

    procedure smallest_data (the_record : list_record) is
    begin
       if the_record.data < smallest then
          smallest := the_record.data;
       end if;
    end smallest_data;

    and so on
```

FIGURE 4.11 Instantiating the sorted list package and two instantiations of the *traverse* procedure.

the user but is used in the bodies of four of the seven operations of the list. This is due to the fact that the sorted list is basically a mapped list, and the four operations to which we refer base their actions on a target key value. The list object (if it exists) having the target key value must be located before completing its task. *search* is a function that locates the target list object. Its specification is given as part of Package Body 4.4. Otherwise, the code for the operations of sorted lists is not complex.

■ PACKAGE BODY 4.4 Sorted Lists—Implements Specification 4.4

```
package body sorted_list_package is

        function search(the_list : sorted_list; target_key : key_type) return natural is separate;
        -- results:   If there is an object in the list with key_of(list_object) = target_key, search returns
        --                 the position of the object; if not, search returns the position
        --                 that the target object would have occupied had it been in the list.
        -- notes:   This is an internal function not visible to the user.


    procedure insert (the_list : in out sorted_list; the_object : object_type) is
    -- Length 8   Complexity 2   Performance O(n)
        pos : natural;
    begin
        if the_list.size = the_list.max_size then raise list_full; end if;
        pos := search(the_list, key_of(the_object));
        the_list.size := the_list.size + 1;
        -- Make room for new object by moving a slice to make a gap at pos.
        the_list.objects(pos + 1 .. the_list.size) := the_list.objects(pos .. the_list.size − 1);
        the_list.objects(pos) := the_object;
    end insert;


    procedure delete (the_list : in out sorted_list; target_key : key_type) is
    -- Length 5   Complexity 3   Performance O(n)
        pos : natural;
    begin
        pos := search(the_list, target_key);
        if pos in 1 .. the_list.size and then key_of(the_list.objects(pos)) = target_key then
        -- Eliminate the list object to be deleted.
        the_list.objects(pos .. the_list.size − 1) := the_list.objects(pos + 1 .. the_list.size);
        the_list.size := the_list.size − 1;
        end if;
    end delete;


    procedure change (the_list : in out sorted_list; the_object : object_type) is
    -- Length 5   Complexity 3   Performance O(search)
        pos : natural;
    begin
        pos := search(the_list, key_of(the_object));
        if pos in 1 .. the_list.size and then key_of(the_list.objects(pos)) = key_of(the_object) then
            the_list.objects(pos) := the_object;                                               -- Replace target object.
        end if;
    end change;
```

(continued)

Package Body 4.4 (continued)

```
procedure clear (the_list : in out sorted_list) is
-- Length 1   Complexity 1   Performance O(1)
begin
   the_list.size := 0;
end clear;


procedure find (the_list    : sorted_list;
                target_key  : key_type;
                the_object: out object_type;
                found       : out boolean) is
-- Length 9   Complexity 3   Performance O(search)
   pos : natural;
begin
   found := false;
   pos := search(the_list, target_key);
   if pos in 1 .. the_list.size and then key_of(the_list.objects(pos)) = target_key then
      found := true;
      the_object := the_list.objects(pos);
   end if;
   -- notes:  If found returns false, then no value is assigned to the_object. Some Ada compilers require that values be assigned to
   --         all out mode parameters. The authors' compiler did not. Test your compiler for this feature.
end find;


function number_of_objects (the_list : sorted_list) return natural is
-- Length 1   Complexity 1   Performance O(1)
begin
   return the_list.size;
end number_of_objects;


procedure traverse (the_list : in out sorted_list) is
-- Length 2   Complexity 2   Performance O(n)
begin
   for i in 1 .. the_list.size loop
      process(the_list.objects(i));
   end loop;
end traverse;

end sorted_list_package;
```

The performances of *change* and *find* depend almost entirely on the performance of *search*. We see that, aside from *search*'s execution, *insert* and *delete* have $O(n)$ performances due to the movement of a slice. Assuming random insertion and deletion points, we expect to have to move approximately $n/2$ objects. The move should be efficient since it is a slice rather than an object-by-object move; but it is still $O(n)$. Since a search should, in the worst case, also be $O(n)$, we can say that *insert* and *remove* exhibit $O(n)$ performance (Figure 4.12).

Change and *find,* on the other hand, have O(1) performance aside from the performance of *search*. The performance of *search* will determine their performance.

Operation	Performance
insert	O(*n*)
delete	O(*n*)
change	O(search)
find	O(search)
make_list_empty	O(1)
list_size	O(1)
traverse	O(*n*)

FIGURE 4.12 Performance bounds for the sorted list data type (Package Body 4.3).

4.5.3 Searching in Lists

We have left the critical *search* function's body as a separate function. We now discuss a number of search strategies that might be used.

Sequential Search, Disregarding the Sorted Order

The first search we design is one that ignores the sorted order of the objects in the list. It is really unsuitable for sorted lists, but it could be used to search unordered lists. It simply starts at the head of the list and progresses through the list one object at a time, testing each object to see if its key is equal to the target key. It must also test each pass through the loop to determine whether the loop index has progressed beyond the end of the list.

```
separate (sorted_list_package)
function search(the_list : sorted_list; target_key : key_type) return natural is
-- Length 5  Complexity 3  Performance O(n)
    k : natural := 1;
begin
    while k <= the_list.size and then key_of(the_list.objects(k)) /= target_key loop
      k := k + 1;
    end loop;
    return k;
end search;
```

FIGURE 4.13 Sequential search of a sorted list, ignoring the sorted order.

A sticky point is the matter of what position should be returned if the end of the list is encountered without the target object being found. The algorithm in Figure 4.13 returns the position *size* + 1. Since its specification states that it is to return the position the target object would have occupied had it been in the list, the position returned may be (or is likely to be) in error. This search strategy, which is fine for unordered lists, is not suitable for sorted lists because of this problem.

If the target object is in the list, we would expect the search to proceed on the average halfway through the list—~ *n*/2 comparisons. If it is not in the list, there would be *n* comparisons. In both cases, its performance is O(*n*).

Sequential Search Using a Sentinel, Disregarding the Sorted Order

In the algorithm in Figure 4.13, each pass through the loop involved two different comparisons—one to see if the end of the list had been reached and another to see whether the target object had been reached. It is possible using a simple action to remove one of these tests from the loop and replace it with a single test after the completion of the loop.

The idea is to place the target key into the object just past the end of the list; that is, to create a dummy object at position *the_list.size + 1*. Then the search can proceed without testing for the end of the list, knowing that a key matching the target key will eventually be found. The principle is the same regardless of whether the list is sorted, as long as a sequential search is being made. Note that this approach fails unnecessarily if *the_list.size = max_size*.

The speed of execution gained by using a sentinel depends on the programming language, the compiler, and the architecture of the host system.

Sequential Search of a Sorted List

If a search is done on a sorted list and the sorted order is taken into account, there are two gains. First, an unsuccessful search can stop as soon as it encounters the point in the list where the target object should have been. There is no need to search through the entire list. Thus the amount of work done, and hence the execution time, is reduced. Second, the position of the missing object can be indicated accurately; therefore, if an insertion of a new object follows, it can be done at the appropriate list position.

The idea is to compare the target key to the key of the list objects starting at the first object. As long as the keys of the list are less than that of the target key, we proceed with the search by progressing to the next object. As soon as a key is encountered that is equal to or larger than the target key, we know there is no need to search further since all list keys beyond that point are even larger. The position at which the first larger key is encountered is the position the target object would have occupied had it been in the list. The algorithm is shown in Figure 4.14. It meets the specifications of function *search*. Since the expected number of probes in both the cases of successful and unsuccessful searches is $n/2$, the performance of the search is $O(n)$.

```
separate(sorted_list_package)
function search(the_list : sorted_list; target_key : key_type) return natural is
-- Length 5   Complexity 3   Performance O(n)
    k : positive := 1;
begin
    while k <= the_list.size and then (target_key > key_of(the_list.objects(k))) loop
        k := k + 1;
    end loop;
    return k;
end search;
```

FIGURE 4.14 Sequential search of a sorted list, using the sorted order.

Binary Search of a Sorted List

The search algorithms we discussed have $O(n)$ performance. One of the great benefits of a sorted list stored in an array is that it makes nonlinear searching possible. The type of nonlinear search that we consider first is a binary search. We shall see that its performance is $O(\log_2 n)$. It provides a vast improvement in search time, especially for large lists.

Suppose in searching the list we compare the target key to the key of the object at the midpoint of the list. The midpoint position can be calculated as

$$mid = (size + 1)/2$$

The list object at the midpoint position is the median object. Since the list is sorted, if the target key is less than the key of the object at position *mid,* we know for certain that the target object cannot be in the half of the list with positions *mid .. size.* Figure 4.15 is a pseudocode description of the process.

if key_of(the_list.objects(mid)) > target_key
    then reduce the search to the range 1 .. *mid* − 1
elsif key_of(the_list.objects(mid)) < target_key
    then reduce the search to the range *mid* + 1 .. *size*
else the target object is at position *mid*

FIGURE 4.15 A binary search probe of a sorted list.

The payoff of this approach is that with one, or perhaps two, compares we can rule out fully half of the list as being certain not to hold the target object. We have replaced the $n/2$ compares of the sequential search with one or two compares. It is this ability to rule out large portions of the list without having to search them in detail that gives binary searches their superb performance.

Having ruled out half the list, we concentrate on the other half and are faced with the same problem. Is the target object in the now-reduced list? We can take the same approach with the sublist as we took with the original list and continue the process until we have found the target object during the search or until the sublist size is reduced to one object.

If we assume that the lower half of the original list was discarded, then we are dealing with the sublist in the position range $(mid + 1) .. size$. The midpoint of this list is at

$$mid = [(mid + 1) + size]/2$$

where the *mid* on the right side is the middle position of the original list. Figure 4.16 shows an example of the process.

The performance of binary searches is demonstrated by noting that with each probe approximately half of the list is discarded. To see how many times a list of size n can be halved before the resulting list holds only one object, let k be the smallest integer such that

$$n/2^k = 1$$

Solving for k, we get

$$k = ceiling(\log_2 n)$$

where *ceiling*(x) returns the smallest integer that is larger than or equal to x.

target_key = "Knuth"

Probe 1

low →		1 Aitken	
		2 Babbage	
		3 Backus	
mid →		4 Hopper	mid = (1 + 7)/2 = 4
		5 Knuth	
		6 Lovelace	
high →		7 Shannon	

Probe 2

low →		5 Knuth	
mid →		6 Lovelace	mid = (5 + 7)/2 = 6
high →		7 Shannon	

Probe 3

low, high →	5 Knuth

FIGURE 4.16 Probe sequence in a binary search for *target_key* = *"Knuth"*.

We ignored the possibility of finding the target object during the process of halving the list (see Figure 4.16). Taking this into account, it can be shown that an upper bound on the number of probes required to search the list is

$$\text{floor}(\log_2 n) + 1$$

where *floor*(x) returns the largest integer that is less than or equal to x. The average number of probes for a successful search is approximately

$$\log_2(n) - 1$$

We can now conclude that a binary search requires $O(\log_2 n)$ comparisons, or probes. How good is this compared with a sequential search? Perhaps the gain is best demonstrated by the following example.

If one probe takes 1 microsecond, then, on average, in 1 second a sequential search could find an object in a list of

$$n = 2,000,000$$

objects. In the same time, a binary search could find an object in a list of size:

$$n = 2^{1,000,000} \sim 10^{300} = 1,000,000,000,000,000,000,000,000,000,000,$$
$$000,000,000,000,000,000,000,000,000,000,$$
$$000,000,000,000,000,000,000,000,000,000,$$
$$000,000,000,000,000,000,000,000,000,000,$$
$$000,000,000,000,000,000,000,000,000,000,$$
$$000,000,000,000,000,000,000,000,000,000,$$
$$000,000,000,000,000,000,000,000,000,000,$$
$$000,000,000,000,000,000,000,000,000,000,$$
$$000,000,000,000,000,000,000,000,000,000,$$
$$000,000,000,000,000,000,000,000,000,000$$

Although it is easy to understand how a binary search works, it is somewhat tricky to write a correct algorithm. The *search* function we are trying to implement has the additional requirement that if the search doesn't find the target object, the position it would have held is returned. Building this into the binary search further complicates it, although it does not necessarily make the algorithm less efficient.

A pseudocode version of the binary search algorithm we discussed is given in Figure 4.17. This algorithm can be improved somewhat in a number of ways. Bentley (1983b) and Standish (1980) discuss a number of methods for doing so. We will look at one variation.

```
low := 1; high := size;

while low <= high loop
      mid := (low + high)/2;
(1)   if target_key < key_of(the_list.objects(mid))
          then discard the upper sublist by setting high to mid − 1;
(2)   elsif target_key > key_of(the_list.objects(mid))
          then discard the lower sublist by setting low to mid + 1;
(3)   else the target object is at position mid; search successful;
      end if;
end loop;
```

FIGURE 4.17 Binary search pseudocode, method 1.

Notice that two tests are done within the loop in the algorithm of Figure 4.17 in order to determine which of three conditions hold:

1. $target\_key < key\_of(the\_list.objects(mid))$
2. $target\_key > key\_of(the\_list.objects(mid))$
3. $target\_key = key\_of(the\_list.objects(mid))$

The equality is tested in case the probe lands exactly on the target object in the process of halving the lists. The probability of that happening (assuming all objects are equally likely to be the target of the search) is

$$p \leq 1/(high - low + 1)$$

p is small until the sublist size becomes quite small. Thus, the third condition is unlikely until the last stages of the search.

If we did not test for the equality, we could reduce the number of tests in the loop from two to one. We could then test for equality once, when the sublist is reduced to a single object and the search is completed. We could avoid wasting the effort of testing for an improbable event, even though on occasion we will probe on the target object and not be aware of the fact that we have encountered it until the decomposition to one object. The new algorithm is given in Figure 4.18.

We conducted some timing studies using lists of integers for both suc-

separate(sorted_list_package)
function search(the_list : sorted_list; target_key : key_type) **return** natural **is**
-- *Length 12   Complexity 5   Performance O(log₂n)*

```
      low    : natural := 1;
      high   : natural := the_list.size;
      mid    : natural;
begin

      if the_list.size = 0 or else target_key > key_of(the_list.objects(the_list.size)) then
         return the_list.size + 1;
      end if;

      while high > low loop
         mid := (low + high)/2;
         if target_key > key_of(the_list.objects(mid))
           then low := mid + 1;
           else high := mid;
         end if;
      end loop;

      return high;
end search;
```

FIGURE 4.18 Binary search, method 2.

cessful and unsuccessful searches. Method 1 is faster for successful searches on average, and the differences are larger for smaller lists. This is because method 1 sometimes probes directly onto the target object and the search can terminate even though the sublist size hasn't been reduced to a single object. The smaller the list being searched, the greater the probability of that happening. Method 2 always continues to probe until that sublist consists of just one object. The differences in times were in all cases less than 15%.

The situation is reversed for unsuccessful searches. Method 1 loses time by testing for an event (probing at the target object) that will never occur. Method 2 only tests for equality once—outside the loop. Again, the time differences are less than 15%. What we did in our attempt to improve the search in method 2 was the same sort of thing we did when using a sentinel— remove tests from the loop.

A binary search is ideal for a sorted list that is static—that is, has no insertions and deletions. A problem arises when the list is not static and objects are being added and removed from the list. Since the list must be kept sorted, new objects cannot be added at any position. They must be placed into the list at a position that keeps the sorted order. Doing so involves moving, on average, half the list. That is an $O(n)$ operation. If the list weren't sorted, we could add new objects at the end of the list with no movement of the existing objects. Adding in that way is an $O(1)$ operation. The drawback is that since the list is not sorted, searches must be sequential searches, which are $O(n)$.

Figure 4.19 shows the order-of-magnitude estimates of four list operations on mapped lists—sorted and unsorted, linked and array representations. A linked sorted list is in column 1 of the table. Even though the list is sorted, a binary search cannot be used because the list is linked and there is no efficient way to compute where the middle object is.

Operation	List Linked sorted	List Linked chronological	List Array sorted	List Array chronological
Find (by key)				
Expected	$O(n)$	$O(n)$	$O(\log_2 n)$	$O(n)$
Maximum	$O(n)$	$O(n)$	$O(\log_2 n)$	$O(n)$
Insert				
Expected	$O(n)$	$O(1)$	$O(n)$	$O(1)$
Maximum	$O(n)$	$O(1)$	$O(n)$	$O(1)$
Delete				
Expected	$O(n)$	$O(1)$	$O(n)$	$O(n)$
Maximum	$O(n)$	$O(1)$	$O(n)$	$O(n)$
Traverse				
Any order	$O(n)$	$O(n)$	$O(n)$	$O(n)$
Sorted order	$O(n)$	$O(n \log_2 n)$	$O(n)$	$O(n \log_2 n)$

FIGURE 4.19 Estimates of list performance (assuming the place of insertion or deletion is known).

4.5.4 Frequency-Ordered Lists

If a list is to be searched sequentially in order to provide a mapping between keys and data and if the order of the objects in the list is not of importance to the user, then it may be advantageous to arrange the objects so that the object that is most often the target of a *find* operation given a target key is placed at the head of the list, the second most often at the second list position, and so on. We call this a *frequency-ordered list*. Each object has an associated probability that it will be the target of the search. We denote the probability that the ith list object will be the target of the search by p_i. In searching sequentially, the probability that one probe is needed is p_1, the probability that two probes are needed is p_2, and so on. The expected number of probes is

$$E_{probes} = 1 \times p_1 + 2 \times p_2 + 3 \times p_3 + \cdots + n \times p_n$$

Each term is the probability of an object being the target times the number of probes it will take to determine if that object is the target.

E_{probes} can be minimized by arranging the objects so that

$$p_1 >= p_2 >= p_3 >= \cdots >= p_n$$

If the probabilities are all equal ($p_i = 1/n$), then the ordering is immaterial, and E_{probes} reduces to the familiar

$$E_{\text{probes}} = 1 + 2 + 3 + \cdots + n) \times 1/n = (n + 1)/2$$

We are assuming that the probabilities are known in advance and the list is built by the user so that the objects are correctly ordered.

A distribution that often occurs in real systems is the so-called 80–20 distribution. For instance, a bank may find that 80% of its daily account transactions happen on 20% of its accounts, and 20% of that 20%—the most active 4% of the accounts—account for 80% of the 80%, or 64% of the transactions, and so on. The distribution can be approximated mathematically, and the result is that the expected number of probes is

$$E_{\text{probes}} = 0.122 \times n$$

which is a factor of 4 improvement over the $n/2$ probes that would be expected for random permutations of the list objects.

Regardless of the distribution, we can always expect the best performance by arranging the objects so they are ordered by decreasing probability, or frequency, of access by key.

4.5.5 Self-Organizing Lists

If the probabilities are not known in advance or if they vary with time, then the order in which the objects should be placed is not clear. An algorithm can, however, be designed that makes the objects adjust their positions in the list to approximate the optimal arrangement. Such lists are called ***self-organizing lists.*** We will consider three methods.

The first method uses recorded frequencies as approximations of the unknown or changing probabilities. An additional field, say *freq,* is attached to the list objects. Each time the *find* operation locates a list object, the *freq* field is incremented by 1. The list is kept sorted in decreasing order on the *freq* field.

Since the list is sorted on the frequencies, new list objects inserted into the list will always start with frequency 0 and can thus be added at the end (tail) of the list. An *insert* procedure would have to do this.

The second self-organizing list method avoids the overhead of an additional field in the list object. This method "rewards" a list object each time it is the target of a *find* operation by moving it forward (toward the head) in the list by one position. That is, the found object swaps places with its predecessor. In this way, objects frequently found move toward the head of the list, whereas objects not often found drift toward the tail.

The third method is similar to the second. It "rewards" found objects by moving them to the list head. We will not discuss it in detail.

All three methods have a learning characteristic. If the frequencies change over time, the list follows by readjusting its ordering to approximate the optimal order that will give the minimum expected search time. Bentley (1985) gives an analysis of the performance of self-organizing lists.

EXERCISES 4.5

1. Stacks and queues can be implemented as lists that are ordered chronologically. Write an implementation of the *queue* abstraction by using and instantiating the list package specified in Specification 4.1.
2. Can priority queues be implemented using the same sort of chronologically ordered list as was done in Exercise 1? If so, how?
3. What is the order-of-magnitude estimate of the time it would take to build a list of n objects by appending each to the end of the list (Specification 4.1)?
4. What is the maximum number of probes made by a binary search that searches a table of n objects, where n is
   a. 128 objects
   b. 1024 objects
   c. 1,000,000 objects
   What is the expected number of probes in each case?
5. Conduct timing studies in a system available to you using Ada to find out how large a list of integers must be before a binary search becomes more efficient than a sequential search. Remember, for a small list, a sequential search is probably faster. The question is, What is "small"?
6. Conduct timing studies to determine the relative performance of the binary search of method 1 (Figure 4.17) and of method 2 (Figure 4.18). Do the experiment for both successful and unsuccessful searches.
7. An interpolation search is one in which rather than dividing the list in half, we estimate where to probe. If we know the target and smallest keys of the list being searched, we can compute at what fraction of the interval the target key is:

   fraction = (target − smallest)/(largest − smallest)

   We then probe at that fraction of the range of indexes:

   probe = smallest + fraction * (largest − smallest)

   Depending on the value of the key at the probe position, we reduce the range by adjusting the lower or upper bound in the same way we did for a binary search. Implement and test the *search* procedure specified in Package Body 4.4 using an interpolation search.
8. Conduct timing studies to see how the search times for an interpolation search compare with those of a binary search.
9. Design, implement, and test a self-organizing list data type for which the object that is searched for moves forward in the list by one position. Remember that a self-organizing list is a mapped list—the objects are accessed by their keys.
10. Give some examples of applications in which frequency-ordered and self-organizing lists might be used.
11. Construct a table showing the orders-of-magnitude estimates for array and linked implementations of self-organizing lists.
12. Implement the function *search* of Package Body 4.4 using the binary search whose pseudocode is outlined in Figure 4.17. Be sure to meet the specifications exactly.

■ 4.6 Rings

Time-sharing computer systems allow a single computer system to be shared among many interactive users. Each user has the impression that he or she is the only one on the system. Assume that each user is sitting at an interactive terminal and that the system has associated a packet of data (which we will call the terminal data packet) with that terminal.

Imagine that each terminal data packet contains communications data and work space. Suppose that the packets are held in a circular structure, or ring, such as that in Figure 4.20. A cursor indicates the terminal that is currently receiving the service of the computer system (T_8 in Figure 4.20). After some interval of time, usually some number of microseconds or milliseconds, the cursor is moved forward in the ring by one packet and the next terminal (T_6

in Figure 4.20) begins to receive service. Service to the terminals continues in this fashion with the cursor moving endlessly around the ring and each terminal receiving a slice of service. Computer systems are fast enough so users are normally unaware that the interleaving process is taking place.

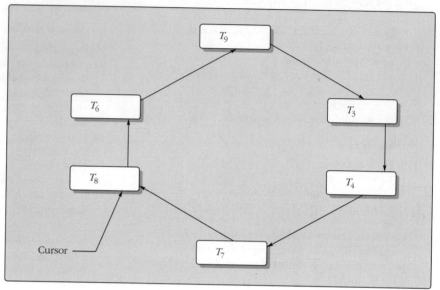

FIGURE 4.20 A ring.

Users log onto and off of the system. Data packets for new users must be placed into the ring, and those of users logging off must be removed. Since the only access into the ring is through the cursor, terminals logging off must wait until the cursor reaches them before they are removed. Terminal packets of new users can be inserted into the ring at any point. Insertion just after the point of the cursor is often a convenient spot. Since the position of the cursor is random when there is a new arrival, the placement of terminals in the ring is random.

This is an example of a data abstraction we will call a ***ring***. Each object in the ring, without exception, has an object that follows it. In the case of a single object, the object follows itself. There are no head, tail, or ends. There is just a cursor and the ring. The structure is like a linear structure with its ends tied together. Although the structure has linear-like characteristics, there is no notion of position since there is no head object from which to start the position count. Each object has a successor object.

We again call your attention to the fact that the specifications given in this book are, at least in part, arbitrary. Specification 4.5 is the specification of a ring.

Although it is possible to represent a ring as an array, such a representation is not very efficient. We suggest a linked list representation, which is nearly ideal, and we leave the package body for you as an exercise.

■ SPECIFICATION 4.5 Rings

-- *Structure:* *The structure of a ring is circular. Each ring object has a unique successor. In*
-- *the case of a ring with one object, that object is its own successor.*

-- *Constraints:* *0 <= number_of_objects <= unknown upper bound* -- *See function*
  -- *number_of_objects.*

generic

    type object_type **is private**;

package ring_package **is**

    type ring **is limited private**;

    ring_full   : **exception**;
    ring_empty : **exception**;

procedure move_cursor_forward (the_ring : **in out** ring);
-- *results:* *The cursor is moved forward to the successor of the current object.*
-- *exceptions:* *ring_empty exception is raised if number_of_objects(the_ring) = 0.*

function current_object(the_ring : ring) **return** object_type;
-- *results:* *A copy of the current object is returned.*
-- *exceptions:* *ring_empty exception is raised if number_of_objects(the_ring) = 0.*

procedure change_current_object(the_ring : **in out** ring; the_object : object_type);
-- *results:* *The current object's value is changed to the_object.*
-- *exceptions:* *ring_empty exception is raised if number_of_objects(the_ring) = 0.*

procedure insert_an_object(the_ring : **in out** ring; the_object : object_type);
-- *results:* *The_object is inserted into the ring at an arbitrary point.*
-- *exceptions:* *A ring_full exception is raised if an additional object cannot be added.*

procedure delete_current_object(the_ring : **in out** ring);
-- *results:* *The current ring object is removed from the ring.*
-- *exceptions:* *ring_empty exception is raised if number_of_objects(the_ring) = 0.*

function number_of_objects (the_ring : ring) **return** natural;
-- *results:* *The number of objects in the ring is returned.*

private

    type ring_node;
    type ring_pointer **is access** ring_node;
    type ring_node **is record**
      object : object_type;
      next   : ring_pointer;
    end record;

(continued)

Specification 4.5 (continued)

```
type ring is record
    current_node   : ring_pointer;
    size           : natural := 0;
end record;

end ring_package;
```

EXERCISES 4.6

1. Implement rings (Specification 4.5) using the linked list package (Package Body 4.2).
2. Implement rings (Specification 4.5) using an array.

3. Design, implement, and test a ring abstraction in which it is possible to move the ring cursor in both directions. Use a doubly linked list for your implementation.

■ 4.7 Sequential Files

Another common linear type is the ***sequential file***. A sequential file's objects have no explicit positions, keys, or predecessors. They differ in their operations from the other linear types we have studied. The user can start at the head of the sequence of objects and step through the objects one at a time until the last object is reached.

Many programming languages include ***sequences*** as predefined data types in the form of sequential files. Pascal's standard file type is an example. Ada provides files as packages. In that form, *text_io* and *sequential_io* are files that have strong sequential characteristics.

The notion of the sequential data type we specify is one that contains a finite number of component objects arranged linearly. Regardless of the number of objects in the sequence, another object can be appended to the end to form a sequence one larger. The effect is that there is no specified upper bound on the size of the sequence—the sequence is ***unbounded***. As an abstraction, this causes no problem since we need not concern ourselves with implementation details. The abstraction is useful, and certain variations of it can be used for data types such as strings and files.

We must, however, keep in mind that computers are finite. We cannot truly implement an unbounded data type. Take the example of files. Files often have no explicit upper bound on the number of objects they can hold, but an attempt to add one more object when the disk holding the file is out of space causes an error. Ada causes an exception to be raised that we could, if we chose, handle. In other languages, the effect of writing when out of space is the abnormal termination of the program.

Probably the most widely used kind of sequential list is the sequential file. Ada has two predefined file types that can be viewed as forms of sequential files. They are specified by packages *sequential_io* and *text_io*. You are undoubtedly familiar with *text_io*. Package *sequential_io* is more concise and probably not as familiar to you, so we will examine it briefly. The observations we make will apply to either.

The specifications of the *sequential_io* package are copied directly from the *Ada LRM* (1983) and are shown as Specification 4.6. We have not followed our usual form for writing specifications of procedures and functions, except for the specification of procedure *read,* which is included as an example. Refer to the *Ada LRM* (1983) for the full specifications.

Once the file is open, say for reading (*in_file* mode), the cursor is initially positioned under the first object in the file. Successive reads cause it to move forward one position in the file for each read. It eventually moves beyond the last object in the file. The end of file is said to have been reached, and function *end_of_file* would return true. There is no way to go backward, except to execute procedure *reset,* which resets the cursor back to the first object. Thus,

---

■ **SPECIFICATION 4.6** **Sequential Input/Output**

-- *Refer to the* Ada LRM, *Chapter 14.*

with io_exceptions;
generic
    type object_type **is private**;
package sequential_io **is**

    type file_type **is limited private**;
    type file_mode **is** (in_file, out_file);

    -- *File management.*

    procedure create (file   : **in out** file_type;
                 mode : **in** file_mode := out_file;
                 name : **in** string := "";
                 form   : **in** string := "");

    procedure open (file   : **in out** file_type;
                mode : **in** file_mode;
                name : **in** string;
                form   : **in** string := "");

    procedure close (file   : **in out** file_type);
    procedure delete (file   : **in out** file_type);

(continued)

Specification 4.6 (continued)

```
procedure reset   (file      : in out file_type;
                   mode       : in file_mode);
procedure reset   (file      : in out file_type);

function mode     (file      : in file_type) return file_mode;
function name     (file      : in file_type) return string;
function form     (file      : in file_type) return string;

function is_open (file       : in file_type) return boolean;
```

-- *Input and output operations.*

```
procedure read    (file      : in file_type; item : out object_type);
```
-- **results:** *The object that is at the file cursor is returned in item, and the cursor is moved forward one position in the file.*
-- **exceptions:** *Mode_error is raised if the file is not open in in_file mode.*
--   *End_error is raised if the cursor is beyond the last object in the file.*
--   *Data_error is raised if the object read cannot be interpreted as a value of type object_type.*

```
procedure write   (file      : in file_type; item : in object_type);

function end_of_file (file   : in file_type) return boolean;
```

-- *Exceptions.*

```
status_error  : exception renames io_exceptions.status_error;
mode_error    : exception renames io_exceptions.mode_error;
name_error    : exception renames io_exceptions.name_error;
use_error     : exception renames io_exceptions.use_error;
device_error  : exception renames io_exceptions.device_error;
end_error     : exception renames io_exceptions.end_error;
data_error    : exception renames io_exceptions.data_error;
```

private   -- *Implementation dependent.*

end sequential_io;

---

the only way to move among the objects of the file is to reset the file and execute zero or more reads.

The package provides the notion of a ***file state*** or, as Ada calls it, ***file_mode.*** The file can be in an input mode, in which case data (in the form of objects) can be read from it. Or it can be in an output mode, in which case objects can be written to it. It cannot be in both modes at the same time.

An object written to the file is placed at (appended to) the end of the file and becomes the new last object in the file. Thus, repetitive writes place the objects into the file in the order in which they were written. Prior to writing, the file must be placed in output mode. This can done by calling the procedure *reset* with a file identifier and the *mode* parameter set to *out_file.* It has the effect of placing the cursor at the beginning of the file and erasing the contents of the file, if any. There is no way to open an existing file as a sequential file and append new objects to the existing set. This problem may be remedied in revisions of the Ada language. If an object is written to the file and there is no more storage space on the device holding the file, a *use_error* exception is raised.

The procedures *create, open, close,* and *delete* are concerned with the connection of the internal file identifier to the external file name as it exists in the operating system of the computer system on which the program is running.

Consider a small example of the use of the *sequential_io* package. The program in Figure 4.21 will do the following:

1. Create an external file named "my_data.data"
2. Read text data using *text_io*
3. Form the data into records
4. Write the records to the "my_data.data" sequential file of records
5. Reset the file for input
6. Read and process all the records of the file
7. Close the file

```
with text_io, sequential_io;
use text_io;
procedure files is

    type object_type is record
       key     : integer;
       name    : string(1 .. 12);
       salary  : float;
    end record;

    package my_file is new sequential_io(object_type);
    package iio is new integer_io(integer);
    package fio is new float_io(float);

    the_file : my_file.file_type;
    the_object : object_type;

    procedure process (an_object : object_type) is separate;      -- Process a record.

begin
    my_file.create(the_file, my_file.out_file, "my_file.data");
    loop
       exit when text_io.end_of_file(standard_input);
       iio.get (the_object.key);    skip_line;              -- Get the data from the terminal.
       get (the_object.name);       skip_line;
       fio.get (the_object.salary); skip_line;
       my_file.write(the_file, the_object);                 -- Write the record to my_file.
    end loop;
```

FIGURE 4.21 A program illustrating the use of a sequential file.

(continued)

Figure 4.21 (continued)

```
        my_file.reset(the_file, my_file.in_file);        -- Reset for input to beginning of file.
        loop
           exit when my_file.end_of_file(the_file);
           my_file.read(the_file, the_object);
           process(the_object);
        end loop;
        my_file.close(the_file);        -- Allow any exceptions to be handled by the run-time system
end files;                              -- and abort the program; that is, provide no exception handlers.
```

FIGURE 4.21 *(continued)*

EXERCISES 4.7

1. Is it possible to use Ada sequential files (Specification 4.6) to create a file of varying length strings that are stored as records with discriminants (as, e.g., type *line_text* of Figure 2.43)? If so, write a program that will create such a file. Many systems store some additional bytes for their own use with each object written. How many are stored per object in the file on a system available to you? Tip: You can use the attribute *X'size*, where *X* is a variable, to determine the size of each record before you write it to the file. *size* returns, the number of bits, not bytes.

2. Write a program that will read words (a word is, for this application, a contiguous string of letters only) from an input text file (not the terminal), place each word in a sorted list (Specification 4.4), count the number of times each word has occurred by looking up the word in the sorted list each time it occurs and incrementing its count by 1, and, once the input data are exhausted, write the words together with their counts onto a sequential file. The <word, count> pair should be formed into a record, and the output file should be a file of those records. Write and test a companion program that will read the <word, count> file and print a list of the words and counts.

4.8 Timing Studies of List Operations

We discussed performance estimates using order-of-magnitude methods for the operations on the various list types we studied. To see how good those estimates are, in this section, we present the results of some timing studies concerning lists.

Figure 4.22 shows the times to insert objects into a list. The legends attached to the timing curves in Figure 4.22 are interpreted as follows:

Array (append)	The list is implemented as an array. New objects are appended to the end of the list.
Linked (append)	The list is implemented as a linked list. New objects are appended to the end of the list.
Linked (sorted)	The list is implemented as a linked list and the objects in it are sorted. New objects must be placed in a position so that the list remains sorted
Linked (no duplicates)	The list is implemented as a linked list. Insertion requires searching the list to assure that it does not contain a duplicate key. If it doesn't, the new object is appended to the end of the list.

Time to insert one element

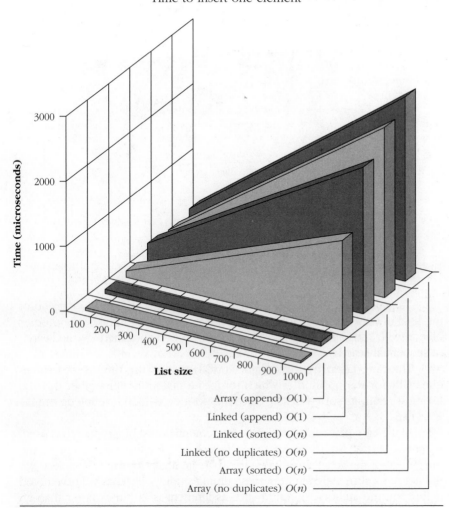

FIGURE 4.22 Times to insert objects into lists.

Array (sorted)	The list is implemented as an array and the objects in it are sorted. New objects must be placed in a position so that the list remains sorted. A <u>binary search</u> is used.
Array (no duplicates)	The list is implemented as an array. Upon insertion of a new object, the list is searched for an object with the same key. If none is found, the new object is appended to the end of the list.

Appending to the end of the list with no search is very fast, as can be seen in the two curves labeled (append). They are shown using an expanded scale in Figure 4.23. The time taken by the linked list append is more than twice as long as that for the array case. That is due to the dynamic storage allocation necessary to allocate a node for the new object.

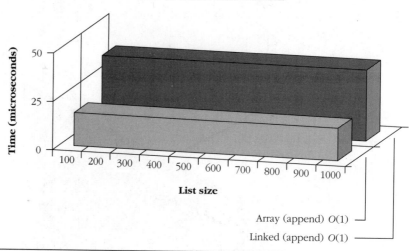

Time to insert one element

FIGURE 4.23 Blowup of the two (append) curves of Figure 4.22.

The curves in Figure 4.22 labeled (no duplicates) append to the end of the list but do a search before the append to assure that there are no other objects with the same key. The time they take is determined by the search (a sequential search).

The time taken by the linked (sorted) case is the time to search sequentially for the position at which to do the insertion. Remember that the list must retain its sorted order. Once the position is found, relinking the list is $O(1)$.

In the case of a sorted list, array implementation, a <u>binary search</u> is used. It should be fast. The time we see in Figure 4.22 for that case is due to the movement of the array slice necessary to create a gap for the new object. We did not use a slice assignment in these timing studies. Since, as we have noted before, on the authors' system a slice assignment is 20 times faster than an object-by-object move in a loop, it is interesting to conjecture what the curve would have been had a slice assignment been used (see Exercises 4.8, 2 and 4.8, 3).

Figure 4.24 shows the times to search a list. The lists are in sorted order by key. In the case of the array implementation, two search methods were used—a sequential search and a binary search. The superiority of a binary search is apparent.

The sequential search of a linked list is faster than the sequential search of an array. The difference is the array mapping function computation. Although it consists of only one multiplication and one addition, finding the memory address of the next array object is slower than finding the next node of a linked list. In the linked case, the next pointer of the node has the address directly, with no calculation required.

Figure 4.25 shows the binary search times using an expanded scale. We can see the log n characteristic of the curve.

Time to retrieve one element

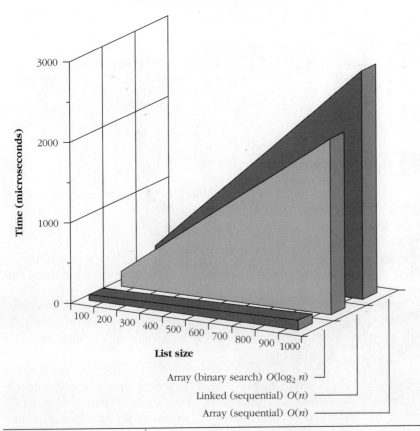

FIGURE 4.24 Times to find (retrieve) an object with a given key value.

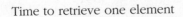

Time to retrieve one element

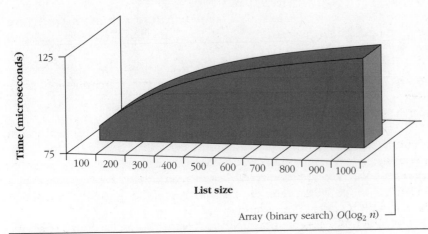

FIGURE 4.25 Binary search of a sorted list.

EXERCISES 4.8

 1. Repeat the time studies done in this section using the computer system and compiler available to you.

 2. In the case of a sorted array with a binary search, a slice of the array must be moved to make a space for objects being added to the list. Do timing studies for (a) the slice being moved one object at a time in a loop and (b) the slice being moved with a single slice assignment statement. Compare the results.

3. Do a timing study to determine how much faster, with your system and compiler, slice moves are compared to loops that move one object of the slice each iteration.

■ 4.9 Summary

We have seen a variety of linear and linear-like structures in this chapter, specifically, lists, rings, and sequences. We saw a number of variations of lists — some included indexes and some included maps. Others varied not in structure but in the operations of the type. In Chapter 8 we shall see another linear type — strings — that is distinguished from the lists in this chapter in that its component objects are always characters and the operations of the string type are distinctive.

Based on the timing studies we presented, it appears that if we wanted a list with a map between keys and data, then the performance of a sorted list with an array implementation, a binary search, and an Ada slice move for insertion and deletion is superior.

Lists tend to have at least one of their operations with $O(n)$ performance. The most effective, a sorted list with a binary search, is an array implementation and suffers from the static declaration of an array space. There is no dynamic storage allocation, and the structure cannot grow and shrink with the number of objects at hand. We turn now to a structure that goes a long way to meeting these two requirements — trees.

5

Trees

...trees, the most important non-linear structure arising in computer algorithms. (Knuth, 1973a)

Trees are a species of nonlinear structure of considerable importance in computer science, partly because they provide natural representations for many sorts of nested data that occur in computer applications, and partly because they are useful in solving a wide variety of algorithmic problems. (Standish, 1980)

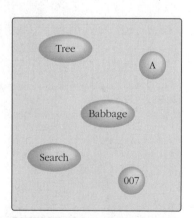

FIGURE 5.1 Each of these nodes contains a single item—the value of the key for the element in that node.

5.1 Introduction

This chapter introduces data structures that have a *hierarchical,* or *nested,* or *one-to-many relationship* among their component elements. One reason we are interested in these *hierarchical data structures* is that they represent, in a natural way, many of the relationships among elements that surround us in our world: the relationship between parent and child is one to many. *One-to-zero* and *one-to-one* relationships are special cases of one-to-many relationships. The relationship between a person and the books the person owns is one to many. The relationship between a person and the books the person has read is one to many. The relationship between a basketball team and the players on that team is one to many. The relationship between a car and the people in the car is one to many. The list of examples is endless. In this chapter we will discuss the use of a computer to represent and manipulate such one-to-many structures.

Most of Chapter 5 (Sections 5.2–5.8) is concerned with binary trees. Binary trees are simple in the sense that the hierarchical relationships are, at most, one to two. They are useful in their own right, but they also exhibit many characteristics of other types of trees. Thus, a study of binary trees prepares you for the study of other hierarchical structures. We will consider several variations of binary trees, including binary search trees, AVL trees, threaded trees, and heaps.

Another type of tree, quite different from a binary tree, is a B-tree. We will introduce this important data structure in Section 5.10 in order to indicate some of the variety in the way computers are used to represent trees, as well as because of the importance of this particular structure in computer science. The discussion of B-trees is introductory. It describes a data structure that is frequently used in conjunction with the storage of large data files on direct access storage devices. The name "B-tree" is unfortunate. It is often inferred that B-tree is a synonym for binary tree or that B-tree refers to a special type of binary tree. A B-tree is, however, quite a different data structure.

5.2 Terminology

We begin our discussion of tree terminology with ordered trees, a type of tree that is naturally represented using digital computers. Ordered trees will provide a perfect jumping off point for our discussion of other types of trees. We begin with several basic notions about trees.

5.2.1 Elements of Trees

A tree can contain any objects we choose. We will assume that the objects are all standard objects as described in Chapter 1; that is, each object contains information divided into two parts: a key part and a data part. The key part has the unique identification property.

When we discuss trees we will rarely refer to their objects but will instead refer to their nodes. Each *node* may contain one or more objects. Reference to a node is therefore an implicit reference to the objects it contains. They will appear as globes, spheres, or capsules in the figures in this chapter.

For the sake of simplifying our discussion, the data each node in a tree will contain are a single object (see Figure 5.1). Such nodes and the information they contain will be illustrated by printing the element inside the globe or sphere that represents the node. If the object in each node has both a key part and a data part, we will normally print the key part (but not the data part) in the globe or sphere representing the node.

In addition to containing data elements, a node can contain information about its relationship with other nodes. Exactly what additional information it contains depends on how the tree is implemented. It is customary to illustrate hierarchical relationships among nodes with arcs connecting pairs of related nodes. These arcs are referred to as edges or branches or links. We will call them *edges*. Note that there are other relationships among nodes besides hierarchical relationships. We will introduce some of them in a later section. In this chapter we will reserve the term "edge" to describe hierarchical relationships. (See Figure 5.2.)

Each edge in an ordered tree (which we have not defined yet) connects two distinct nodes. Each of these edges has an orientation, or direction. In the trees we will discuss, the direction can always be inferred from its illustration. Even so, it is sometimes helpful to show the direction explicitly, and we will use the traditional arrowhead ($\rightarrow$) for this purpose.

The components of a tree we have introduced are nodes and edges. The nodes of a tree have a hierarchical relationship. The edges, from our current perspective, are used to illustrate hierarchical relationships among nodes. In Section 5.2.2 we will describe hierarchical relationships and contrast them with linear relationships.

5.2.2 Structure of Trees—Hierarchical Relationships

The essential requirement of a linear structure, you may recall, is that each object, with two exceptions, has a unique successor and a unique predecessor. A logical view of a linear data structure is shown in Figure 5.3. In a more formal vein, we can characterize a linear structure as being empty, as containing a single element, or as having the relationship among its elements described in Figure 5.4.

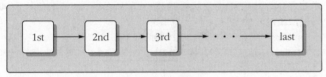

FIGURE 5.3 A logical view of a linear data structure.

The relationship among objects in a linear structure is one to one. Look at the characterization of a linear structure in Figure 5.4 to see that this is the case. The relationship among nodes in a tree is one to many, or hierarchical, or nested, as shown in Figure 5.5. A tree is a natural structure for keeping

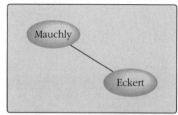

FIGURE 5.2 Two nodes connected by an edge. Each node contains a single element that contains information about a person. The key value, which is shown, is the person's last name.

1. There is a unique first element, which has no predecessors and has a unique successor.
2. There is a unique last element, which has no successors and has a unique predecessor.
3. Each element, other than the first and the last, has a unique predecessor and a unique successor.

FIGURE 5.4 Relationships among elements in a linear structure.

1. There is a unique first node, called the <u>root node</u>, that has no predecessors and that can have many successors.
2. There can be many nodes that have no successors. These nodes are called <u>leaf nodes</u>, and each of them has a unique predecessor.
3. Each node that is neither the root node nor a leaf node has a unique predecessor and at least one successor.

FIGURE 5.5 Relationships among nodes in a hierarchical structure.

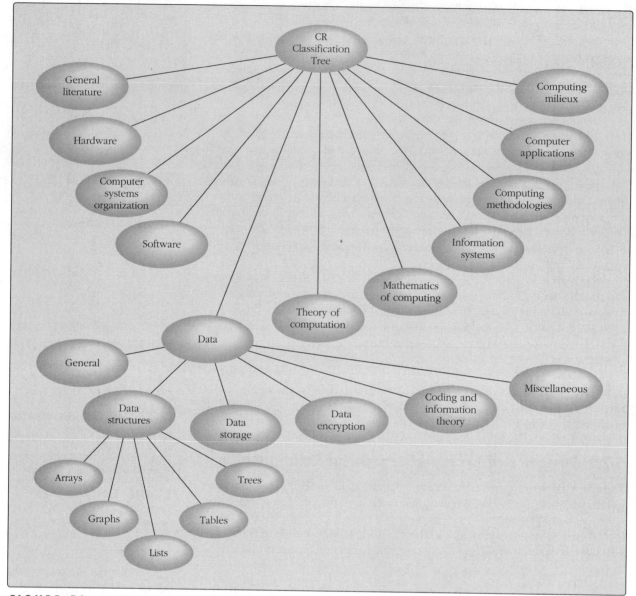

F I G U R E 5.6 A CR Classification Tree of topics in computer science. (*Computing Reviews,* 1982)

track of information that has a one-to-many (or hierarchical, or nested) relationship among its elements.

Another example of the use of trees is the classification of topics that make up a subject. One way the subjects of computer science might be categorized is presented in *Computing Reviews* (1982). It provides an outline of the way computer science subjects can be organized in order to help you locate books and articles by subject; it is called the "CR Classification Tree."

Figure 5.6 is a portion of the tree that shows how data structures and trees fit into the larger scheme of things.

We can contrast the basic relationships among nodes in a tree with the corresponding relationships among elements in a linear data structure. Compare Figures 5.4 and 5.5. Observe that besides terminology, the only basic difference between trees and linear data structures is the number of successors an element (or node) is permitted to have.

The tree described in Figure 5.5 is oriented by its root node. Since it may not be obvious why this is the case, we will discuss the point further. First, we need some terminology.

For each node, let there be an edge between that node and each of its successors. There are no other edges. (There are other relationships among nodes, but we will not represent them with edges.) All the figures above show both nodes and edges.

A *simple path* is a sequence of nodes—$n1, n2, \ldots, nk$—such that the nodes are all distinct and such that there is an edge between each pair of nodes—$(n1,n2), (n2,n3), \ldots, (n[k-1],nk)$. This simple path is said to be from node $n1$ to node nk. The *path length* of any simple path is equal to the number of nodes it contains, which is one greater than the number of edges. (In some texts the path length is the number of edges.)

Each node in an oriented tree is connected to the root node by a unique simple path. In Figure 5.6, "Trees" is connected to "CR Classification Tree" by the following path: CR Classification Tree, Data, Data structures, Trees. In Figure 5.7, node H is connected to the root node by the path A, D, H (whose path length is three). Node I is connected to the root node by the path A, C, G, I (whose path length is four). Every edge in the tree participates in at least one such path. (See Figure 5.8.)

The direction associated with each edge is the direction that is away from the root and toward the leaf node of any path of which it is a member. If an edge participates in several paths, the direction assigned is the same in every case, so the direction of an edge is well defined. Normally these directions are not explicitly shown, since once the root node is identified the directions are easy to determine.

Much of the terminology used to describe trees is borrowed from genealogy. Genealogy describes the hierarchical relationships between a person and his or her ancestors and descendants. Because these relationships are hierarchical, the terms used to describe them can be directly applied to trees.

The relationship between a node and its successors is described as a *parent–child relationship*. The predecessor of a node is said to be that node's *parent*. A successor of a node is said to be that node's *child*. In a tree, every node except the root node has a unique parent. A node that has no children is called a *leaf node*. Every node that is not a leaf node has at least one child. Two nodes that have the same parent are said to be *siblings*.

The tree in Figure 5.9 has six leaf nodes; K is the root node; E is the parent of both B and J; and J is the parent of G. The children of S are P and V, and the child of Z is W. Since N and Q have a common parent, they are siblings.

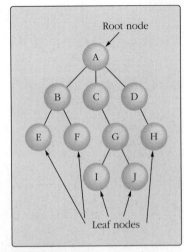

FIGURE 5.7

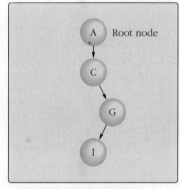

FIGURE 5.8 The unique simple path from the root node to the node containing I, with directions indicated by arrowheads. (From Figure 5.7.)

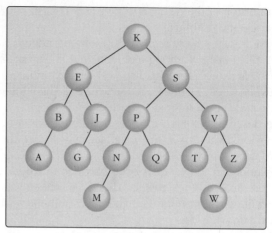

FIGURE 5.9 An example of a binary tree with six leaf nodes. The ancestors of J are K and E. The ancestors of M are K, S, P, and N. The root node is the only node that has no ancestors. The descendants of P are M, N, and Q. The descendants of V are T, W, and Z. The leaf nodes have no descendants.

Our next objective is to generalize the terms "parent" and "child" so as to provide definitions of the terms "ancestor" and "descendant." Our intuition tells us that the ancestors of a node consist of its parent, the parent of its parent, and so on. "And so on," however, is not a very satisfactory phrase to include in a definition. There are several approaches we could take to make the definition more precise, and from them we choose a recursive one. This is done because, as will become more apparent, recursion is an important tool when dealing with trees.

First, we will define *ancestors*. Let A be any node in a tree. If A is the root node, it has no ancestors. Otherwise, the parent of A and all the ancestors of the parent of A are ancestors of A. Node A has no other ancestors. We could also have defined the ancestors of a node as those nodes that lie on the unique simple path between the given node and the root of the tree.

Which are the *descendants* of a node? Try to define this term—both intuitively and formally—before reading on.

Let D be any node in a tree. If D is a leaf node, it has no descendants. Otherwise, each child of D and all the descendants of each child of D are descendants of D. Node D has no other descendants.

Given any node in a tree, that node together with all of its descendants turn out to be a particularly important subset of a tree, called a *subtree*. If T is any tree, a subtree of T is any node in T, say S, together with all the descendants of S.

Let S be any node in a tree. To visualize either the descendants of S or the subtree whose root is S, remove the edge of the tree between S and its parent. All the nodes that are still connected to S are S's descendants. Together with S, this set of descendants forms a subtree of the original tree and has the root node S. Figure 5.10 is an illustration of a subtree of Figure 5.9.

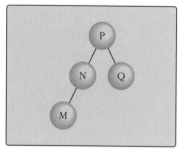

FIGURE 5.10 A subtree whose root node is P. It is formed from Figure 5.9 by disconnecting P from its parent.

We have described trees by using pictures, in terms of the relationships among their nodes, and by using examples. We have yet to specify what we mean by oriented trees and ordered trees. We have deferred doing so because the usual definitions of these terms are recursive. It seems that these definitions are more palatable if the basic idea of a tree has already been introduced.

We will begin with a *recursive definition* of an oriented tree (i.e., a definition in which oriented tree is defined in terms of itself).

An *oriented tree* contains a finite collection of one or more nodes. One of these nodes is called the root node. The remaining nodes, if any, are partitioned into disjoint sets, each of which is an oriented tree.

Recursive definition of an oriented tree.

The selection of a unique root node determines the orientation of each edge in the tree. That is why a tree with a designated root node is called an oriented tree. [See Standish (1980) and Knuth (1973a) for a discussion of the difference between a tree and an oriented tree.]

If we start with an oriented tree and add an ordering among the subtrees of each (and every) node, the result is an ordered tree. An *ordered tree* contains a finite collection of one or more nodes. One of the nodes is called the root node. The remaining nodes, if any, are partitioned into m disjoint sets, T_1, $T_2, \ldots, T_m$, which are ordered by their subscripts, and each of them is an ordered tree. Figure 5.11 shows an example of an ordered tree.

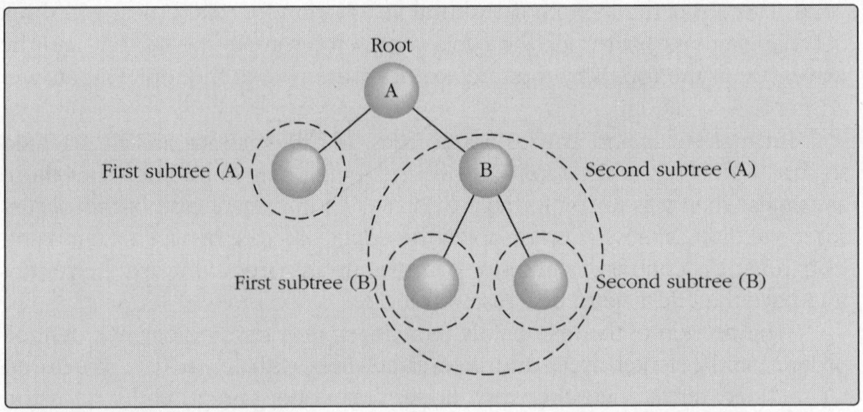

Recursive definition of an ordered tree.

FIGURE 5.11 Illustration of an ordered tree. In this example the first subtree is to the left of its parent, and the second subtree is to the right of its parent.

Observe that each of the sets, $T_1, T_2, \ldots, T_m$, in the above definition not only is an ordered tree in its own right but is also a subtree of the original tree. The term "ordered" is appropriate since the subtrees are ordered by their subscript values; that is, $T_j \leq T_k$ if $j \leq k$. An ordered tree is an oriented tree because it has a unique root node.

Many techniques can be used to order the subtrees of a node. If a node has k subtrees, there are k factorial ($k!$) distinct ways of ordering them. In computer science the subtrees of a node are usually ordered because of the way nodes are represented. It is this implicit ordering, which occurs because the children of a node are usually specified as members of a list, that makes

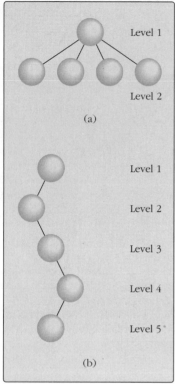

Level 1

Level 2

(a)

Level 1

Level 2

Level 3

Level 4

Level 5

(b)

FIGURE 5.12 Levels of trees: (a) A tree of height 2; (b) a tree of height 5.

ordered trees the natural focus of study in computer science.

Now that we have defined ordered and oriented trees, we will introduce a few more terms that will be used throughout Chapter 5.

A major difference between linear structures and trees exists when we talk about *height*. Let us define the height of a linear data structure containing n elements to be n. What is the *height of a tree*? To determine the height it is helpful to introduce the notion of *level*. Each node in a tree is at a particular level in that tree. The root node is assigned level 1, and each child has a level that is one greater than the level of its parent. Figure 5.12 shows the levels associated with two trees.

The height of a tree is the maximum level associated with any of its nodes. The tree in Figure 5.6 contains many nodes and has a height of 4; the tree in Figure 5.7 contains 10 nodes and has a height of 4; and the tree in Figure 5.9 contains 15 nodes and has a height of 5.

An alternate definition of height can be given in terms of path length. Recall that the length of a path is the number of nodes it contains. The height of an oriented tree is the path length of the longest simple path that begins at its root node.

The final topic of this section is a philosophical one. If you look back at the illustrations of the trees presented so far, you will discover that in each case the root node is at the top of the illustration and the tree "grows" downward. There is certainly no horticultural justification for this (unless you think of a hanging vine); after all, the roots of real trees are at the bottom and the leaves are at the top. Why then do we draw the root at the top? The answer is simple—tradition!

In most texts and articles about trees, the illustrations are all oriented so that the root is at the top. We will usually follow this tradition, but there are times when it is uncomfortable to do so. An important case of this occurs when we discuss moving up or down the edges of a tree between a child and its parent. It is contrary to intuition to move up in a tree—toward the root—and have the effect be to decrease the level.

This section of the text mainly introduced new terminology. We defined ordered and oriented trees and contrasted trees with linear data structures. We defined terms including root node, leaf node, parent, child, ancestor, descendant, simple path, path length, height, and level. We also began to make use of recursion in dealing with trees. All the remaining sections of Chapter 5 will use the ideas and notation you learned in this section.

EXERCISES 5.2

1. Describe the following terms.

ordered tree	oriented tree	descendant
parent	ancestor	child
edge	node	path length
siblings	simple path	tree height

2. What are the similarities between a linear data structure and a hierarchical data structure? What are the differences?

3. Figure 5.13 shows six nodes connected by five edges. The edges have no orientation or direction. Choosing any node as the root node orients the tree in the sense

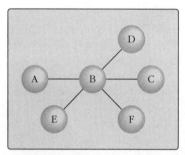

FIGURE 5.13

that it implies a direction or orientation for each edge. Since there are six nodes, there are six possible distinct oriented trees—one for each possible root node. Draw these six oriented trees using arrowheads to show the orientation of each edge.

4. Consider the tree in Figure 5.9. (a) What is its height? (b) What are its leaf nodes? (c) What is the unique simple path from the root node to each of the leaf nodes? (d) What is the path length of each of these paths?

5. The following algorithm finds all the ancestors of a node and pushes a pointer to each of them on a stack. The pointer to the node that is the root of the tree is called *root.* Assume that procedures *push* and *find_parent* are provided. Replace procedure *ancestor* with a recursive procedure that does the same thing.

```
procedure ancestor (the_tree : binary_tree;
  ptr : node_pointer; the_stack : in out stack);
-- assumes:   the_stack is empty.
-- results:   A pointer to each ancestor of the node pointed at by
--            ptr has been pushed onto the_stack.
begin
    while ptr /= the_tree.root loop
        find_parent (the_tree, ptr);      -- ptr is replaced by a
                                          -- pointer to ptr's parent.
        push (the_stack, ptr);            -- ptr is pushed on stack S.
    end loop;
end ancestor;
```

Procedure *ancestor* returns a stack that provides access to a target node's ancestors. If the ancestors are obtained by removing them successively from the top of the stack, then their order starts with the root of the tree and follows tree edges to the target node. How might access to the target node's ancestors be provided in the order that is the reverse of that just described?

5.3 Binary Trees

A binary tree is recursively defined as follows: a **binary tree** either is empty or is a node, called the **root** node, together with two *binary trees.* The two *binary trees* are disjoint from each other and from the root node and are called the left and right subtrees of the root.

Figure 5.14 shows a binary tree with six nodes. Observe that a binary tree has the following characteristics: (1) each node has at most two subtrees, (2) each subtree is identified as being either the left or right subtree of its parent, and (3) a binary tree may be empty.

We draw binary trees with the root at the top growing downward and with left and right children always positioned (respectively) to the left or right of their parent. A leaf node has no children and is thus the parent of two empty subtrees. Likewise, the parent of one child is also the parent of one empty subtree. It is sometimes helpful to show empty subtrees in tree diagrams, and we use the symbol □ for that purpose. Figure 5.14(b) shows the binary tree in Figure 5.14(a) with its empty subtrees added.

Figure 5.15 shows a binary tree each of whose nodes contains a name, a year, and the title of a presentation. The individuals are all recipients of the

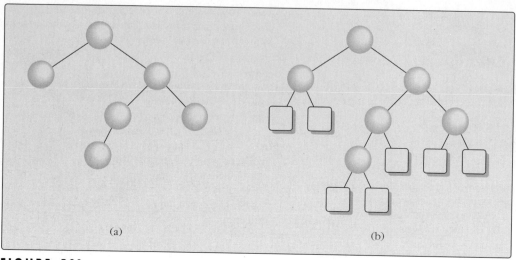

FIGURE 5.14 Two binary trees. In (a) the tree is shown without an indication of its empty subtrees. In (b) the empty subtrees are explicitly shown.

Association for Computing Machinery (ACM) Turing Award for distinguished contributions to computer science. The year is the one in which the award was presented, and the title is the title of the presentation made at the awards ceremony. This example shows that binary tree nodes may contain a large amount of information. Do not be misled by the examples in the remainder of this chapter where the binary tree illustrations show nodes that contain only integer identifiers.

The next example shows the use of binary trees to store nested information. Figure 5.16 shows two simple algebraic expressions. Both expressions are completely grouped in the sense that no precedence rules are needed in order to evaluate them unambiguously. The grouping symbols provide nesting, or hierarchical, information. They prescribe the order in which the terms are to be evaluated.

Figures 5.17 and 5.18 show two alternate ways of presenting the expressions in Figure 5.16. Figure 5.17 emphasizes the nesting of operations. Figure 5.18 shows how this nesting can be represented by binary trees. The point is that if we store the components of these expressions in trees, we can use the tree structure to provide the same information supplied by the grouping symbols or the nesting.

The trees in Figure 5.18 are expression trees. They are closely related to parse trees, which are important to compilers during the evaluation of expressions. We defer further discussion of expression trees to the exercises.

Ada's types and attributes have a nested (or hierarchical) relationship that is shown in Figure 5.19. Each rectangle shows an Ada type and the attributes for that type. Figure 5.19 shows, for example, that Ada's scalar type has subtype *real,* which in turn has subtypes *floating point* and *fixed point.* The attributes are nested as well. Any scalar type, including fixed point, has attributes *first*

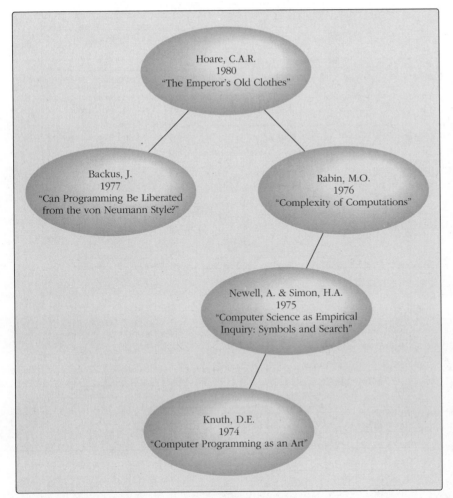

FIGURE 5.15 A binary tree containing information about recipients of the ACM Turing Award. Note that each object in a node contains three items.

$$\{[(a + b) * c] + 7\}$$
(a)

$$(a + b) * (c + 7)$$
(b)

FIGURE 5.16 Two simple nested expressions.

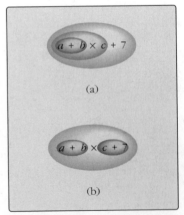

FIGURE 5.17 Nested representations of the expressions in Figure 5.16.

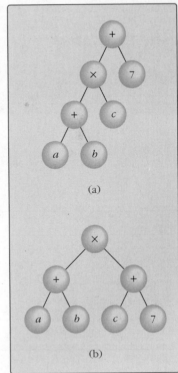

FIGURE 5.18 Binary tree representations of the expressions in Figure 5.16.

and *last*. Any real type, including floating point, has the attributes *large*, *small*, ..., *mantissa*.

A binary tree (that is not empty) *is an oriented tree* because the root node must be identified. A binary tree *is an ordered tree* because we distinguish the subtrees of each node by identifying them as the left and right subtrees.

We close this section with a discussion of the shape of binary trees. A list with n objects can be visualized as lying on a line of length n. A binary tree with n nodes has many possible shapes. It has a maximum height of

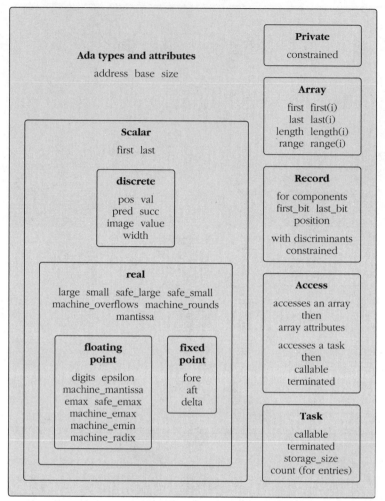

FIGURE 5.19 Ada's types and attributes shown so as to emphasize their nested (or hierarchical) relationships.

n—but what is its minimum height? Figure 5.20 shows binary trees that contain six, seven, and eight nodes—all of minimum height for the nodes they contain.

In Figure 5.21 each row contains information about one level in a binary tree. The first column identifies the level, the second shows the maximum number of nodes on that level, and the third shows the sum of the values in the second column up to that level. That is, for each level, the third column shows the maximum number of nodes in a binary tree of that height.

Figure 5.21 shows that the minimum height, h, of a binary tree with n nodes is given by the relation

$$n = 2^b - 1$$

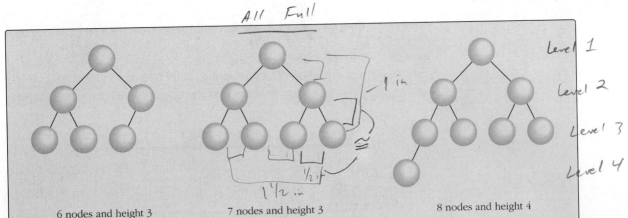

FIGURE 5.20 Three binary trees. Each tree has the minimum possible height for the number of nodes it contains.

or

$$h = \log_2(n + 1)$$

The above result is correct only if $n + 1$ is a power of 2. In other cases, the value of the logarithm must be rounded up to the next integer value. Rounding up corresponds to the case in which the last level of the tree does not contain all possible nodes. A binary tree is said to be **full** if each of its levels, except possibly the last, contains as many nodes as possible. All the trees in Figure 5.20 are full.

We conclude that the height of any binary tree containing n nodes is between ceiling $[\log_2(n + 1)]$ and n and that the height of a full binary tree is ceiling $[\log_2(n + 1)]$.

Look at the trees in Figure 5.20. Note that the vertical distance between nodes on adjacent levels is almost the same as the horizontal distance between nodes on the lowest level. Using that ratio we can calculate the size of a rectangle that is just big enough to contain a binary tree that has the maximum

Binary tree level	Maximum nodes on this level	Cumulative nodes
1	1	1
2	2	3
3	4	7
4	8	15
.	.	.
.	.	.
.	.	.
k	2^{k-1}	$2^k - 1$

FIGURE 5.21 Relationships between tree level and number of nodes. Column 3 is obtained from column 2 by the relation $2^k - 1 = 1 + 2 + 4 + 8 + \cdots + 2^{k-1}$.

number of nodes on each level. We will assume that the vertical distance between levels is one-half inch and the horizontal distance between nodes on the last level of the tree is also one-half inch. Figure 5.22 shows the size of the rectangle needed to contain several trees. A tree that is 9 inches tall and more than 2 miles wide is an impressive horticultural phenomenon!

Tree height	Rectangle height	Rectangle width
3	1 inch	1.5 inches
7	3 inches	31.5 inches
13	6 inches	170.6 feet
19	9 inches	2.06 miles

Handwritten annotations:
3 2·½ = 1 inch
64 nodes — 7 6·½ = 3 inches
4096 nodes – 13 12·½ = 6 inches 31.5 inches — 63 ⊗.5 = 31.5
262,144 nodes @ level 19 18·½ = 9 inches 170.6 feet — 4095 ⊗.5 = 2047.5
                                                          or
                                                    170.625 f

FIGURE 5.22 The height and width of a rectangle just big enough to contain a binary tree.

1. Show how a binary tree might be used to represent the relationship between one person and all of that person's ancestors. Sketch the tree for yourself and your ancestors. What person is in the root node of the tree.

2. What are the possible heights of a binary tree that contains 100 nodes? What are the possible heights of a full binary tree that contains 100 nodes?

3. If a full binary tree contains 10 nodes, how many of its nodes are on the last two levels of the tree? What if it contains 100 nodes? *n* nodes?

4. Show both nested and binary tree representations of these expressions:

   a. $[(a + b) \times (c + d)] + 55$
   b. $\{[(a + b) \times [(c + d) + (e + f)]\} + 55$

5. Suppose that the vertical distance between levels in a binary tree is ½ inch and that the horizontal distance between the centers of nodes on the last level is also ½ inch. What are the dimensions of the smallest rectangle that can contain a full binary tree with 1,000,000 nodes? What if the tree contains 1,000,000,000 nodes?

6. Figure 5.19 shows the nested (hierarchical) relationships among Ada's types. Describe the values of attributes *first* and *last* when applied to the following types: *scalar, discrete, real, floating point, fixed point.*

7. Sketch the tree that corresponds to the nested data in Figure 5.19 that describes Ada's types and attributes.

5.4 Binary Search Trees—Specification

We specify that each node of a binary tree must contain an object of type *object_type* in which a key value of type *key_type* is embedded. There is no restriction on type *object_type*. But, the values of type *key_type* must be ordered so that it is possible to determine when two key values are equal and, if they are not equal, which value is smaller. For discussion, we will take *key_type* to be type *integer,* but keep in mind that any ordered type will do.

A binary search tree imposes additional constraints on a binary tree. If *N* is any node with key value key_N, then (1) all key values in the left subtree of *N* must be less than key_N, and (2) all key values in the right subtree of *N* must be greater than key_N. Figure 5.23 shows a binary search tree. Examine

must be greater than key$_N$. Figure 5.23 shows a binary search tree. Examine each node and its two subtrees to verify that the binary search tree conditions are satisfied.

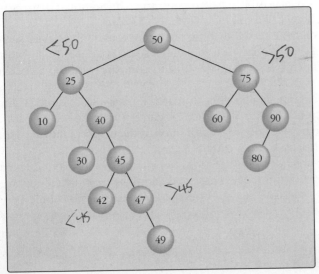

FIGURE 5.23 A binary search tree with 13 nodes and of height 6.

An algorithm to find the node containing a given key value illustrates how the tree's structure makes it easy to search. The search always starts with the tree's root node. A search algorithm is given in Figure 5.24.

```
function find (the_node : binary_search_tree_node; target_key : key_type) return boolean is
begin
    if the_node is the root of an empty subtree then return false;
    elsif target_key equals the_node's key value then return true;
    elsif target_key is less than the_node's key value then
        find (the_node's left child, target_key);          -- Recursive search of the_node's left subtree.
    else find (the_node's right child, target_key);        -- Recursive search of the_node's right subtree.
    end if;
end find;
```

FIGURE 5.24 Algorithm to find a key value in a binary search tree.

For the tree in Figure 5.23 the search path from the root to the node containing 42 is shown in Figure 5.25.

Note the similarity between the binary search of a list (Chapter 4) and the search of a binary search tree. At each step, the binary search of a list compares the target value with a list value and thereby decides to continue by searching the right or left half of the remaining list. At each step, the search of a binary search tree compares the target value with a node's key value and thereby decides to continue by searching the right or left subtree of the node being examined. If a binary tree is balanced in the sense that right and left

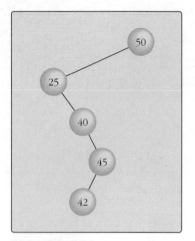

FIGURE 5.25 The search path, Figure 5.23, from the root to 42.

subtrees usually contain equal numbers of nodes, we expect searching a binary search tree will require about the same number of compares as the binary search of a list—$O(\log_2 n)$. → if tree is balanced

In fact, the number of nodes visited when a binary search tree is searched is at most equal to the height of the tree. In Section 5.3 we saw that the maximum height of a full binary tree is $O(\log_2 n)$.

It is valuable to see that the algorithm to search a binary search tree is similar to the algorithm for a sequential search of a list. To show this, Figure 5.26 presents a list search algorithm to compare with the algorithm in Figure 5.24.

We see that an algorithm to search a binary search tree is simple—not much different from an algorithm to search a list. The search path, however, promises to be short because it is limited by the height of the tree. Performance issues are discussed in Section 5.7.

The remainder of this section contains the specification of a binary search tree, Specification 5.1. The basic operations—insert, delete, update, and retrieve—are standard, and the effect of these operations should be clear. The

---

```
function find (the_node : list_node; target_key : key_type) return boolean is
begin
      if the_node is the first node of an empty list then return false;
      elsif target_key equals the_node's key value then return true;
      else find (the_node's successor, target_key);              -- Recursive search of the list that follows the_node.
      end if;
end find;
```

FIGURE 5.26 Algorithm to find a key value in a list using a sequential search.

---

traverse operations (there are four traversal orders specified) may require some explanation. Likewise, the characteristics of a binary tree—size, height, and especially average path length—may need to be explained. These discussions are given in Section 5.5.

■ SPECIFICATION 5.1   Binary Search Tree

-- **Structure:**   *A binary tree either is empty or is a node, called the root node, together with two*
--   *binary trees. These two binary trees are disjoint from each other and from the root node and are designated*
--   *the left and right subtrees of the root node.*

--   *Note that a binary tree has a hierarchical structure. There is (unless the tree is empty) a unique root node.*
--   *Each node (except the root) has a unique parent. Each node has zero, one, or two children. Each child is*
--   *either the left or right child of its parent.*

--   *We assume that each node contains an object that is composed of a key value of type key_type and a*
--   *data value of type data_type. Function equal is used to assure that distinct tree nodes do not contain equal*
--   *key values. The key values must form an ordered set, and function "<" is used to both construct and search*
--   *a binary search tree.*

(continued)

Specification 5.1 (continued)

-- ***Constraints:***   *0 ≤ number_of_objects ≤ unknown upper bound.*

--   *Note that the size of a binary tree increases and decreases dynamically and, at its maximum, uses all available*
--   *memory on its computer system. The implication is that dynamic memory allocation/deallocation is to*
--   *be used.*

generic
     type object_type **is private**;
     type key_type **is private**;

     with function key_of (the_object : object_type) **return** key_type;
     with function equal (left, right : key_type) **return** boolean;
     with function "<" (left, right : key_type) **return** boolean **is** <>;

package binary_tree_package **is**

     type binary_tree **is limited private**;

     type traverse_order **is** (pre_order, in_order, post_order);

     type status **is record**
       size   : natural;
       height   : natural;
       ave_path_length : float;
     end record;

     tree_empty   : **exception**;
     tree_full   : **exception**;
     duplicate_node : **exception**;
     missing_node : **exception**;

     generic
       with procedure process (the_object : object_type);
     procedure traverse (the_tree : binary_tree; the_order : traverse_order);
-- ***results:***   *Procedure process is applied to the_object in each node in the_tree. The order in which the node*
--   *values are processed is specified by the_order as follows:*

--   *case the_order is*
--   *when pre_order => each node is processed before any node in either of its subtrees;*
--   *when in_order => each node is processed after all nodes in its left subtree and before any node in its right subtree;*
--   *when post_order => each node is processed after any node in either of its subtrees;*
--   *end case;*

     generic
       with procedure process (the_object : object_type);
     procedure level_traverse (the_tree : binary_tree);
-- ***results:***   *Procedure process is applied to the_object in each node in the_tree. The order in which the node*
--   *values are processed is as follows: Each node at level k in the_tree is processed after all nodes at level*
--   *k − 1 and before any node at level k + 1.*
-- ***notes:***   *The order in which nodes are processed on any one level is determined by the implementor.*

(continued)

Specification 5.1 (continued)

generic
　key_width : positive := 3;
　with procedure put_key (the_key : key_type);
　-- **results:**　*The value of the_key is written in exactly key_width columns.*
procedure put_tree (the_tree : binary_tree);
-- **results:**　*the_tree is written to standard output as shown in the example below. Horizontal spacing is*
--　　　　　*based on each key value being written in exactly key_size columns. In the example shown, key_width*
--　　　　　*is 3 and the key values are all integers in the range 0..999. The interesting part is writing those*
--　　　　　*vertical connectors! This procedure is handy while verifying that the implementation of other*
--　　　　　*operations is correct.*

```
--                +--[750]--+
--                |         +--[650]
--        [500]--|
--                |                        +--[476]
--                |               +--[450]--|
--                |               |         +--[445]
--                |      +--[400]--|
--                |      |         +--[350]
--        +--[250]--|
--                +--[ 55]
```

procedure insert (the_tree : **in out** binary_tree; the_object : object_type);
-- **results:**　*A node containing the_object is added to the_tree.*
-- **exceptions:**　*duplicate_node is raised if the_tree contains a node with key value key_of(the_object).*
--　　　　　*tree_full is raised if the_tree does not contain a node with key value key_of(the_object), but an*
--　　　　　*additional node cannot be added to the tree.*

procedure delete (the_tree : **in out** binary_tree; target_key : key_type);
-- **results:**　*The node in the_tree with key value target_key is deleted.*
-- **exceptions:**　*missing_node is raised if the_tree does not contain a node with key value target_key.*

procedure update (the_tree : **in out** binary_tree; the_object : object_type);
-- **results:**　*The node in the_tree whose key value is key_of(the_object) has its value replaced by the_object.*
-- **exceptions:**　*missing_node is raised if the_tree does not contain a node with key value the_key.*

function retrieve (the_tree : binary_tree; target_key : key_type) **return** data_type;
-- **results:**　*The node in the_tree whose key value is target_key has its data value returned.*
-- **exceptions:**　*missing_node is raised if the_tree does not contain a node with key value target_key.*

function find (the_tree : binary_tree; target_key : key_type) **return** boolean;
-- **results:**　*Returns true if the_tree contains a node whose key value is target_key; otherwise returns false.*

function empty (the_tree: binary_tree) **return** boolean;
-- **results:**　*Returns true if the_tree is empty; otherwise returns false.*

(continued)

Specification 5.1 (continued)

function characteristics (the_tree : binary_tree) **return** status;
-- ***results:*** *Returns the following values for the_tree:*
--   *status.size*   *Number of nodes in the_tree.*
--   *status.height*   *Height of the_tree.*
--   *status.ave_path_length*   *Average length of a path from the root to a node in the_tree.*

procedure make_tree_empty (the_tree : binary_tree);
-- ***results:*** *the_tree is empty.*

procedure copy (the_tree : binary_tree; the_copy: **in out** binary_tree);
-- ***results:*** *the_copy is a distinct tree that is a duplicate of the_tree.*
-- ***exceptions:*** *tree_full is raised if the_copy cannot be constructed.*

procedure balanced_copy (the_tree : binary_tree; the_copy: **in out** binary_tree);
-- ***results:*** *the_copy contains the same object values as the_tree, but its height is the minimum possible*
--   *for a binary tree with that content. Thus, the height of the_copy is less than or equal to the height of*
--   *the_tree.*
-- ***exceptions:*** *tree_full is raised if the_copy cannot be constructed.*

private

-- *The private clause, which describes one possible representation of a binary tree, is given in Section 5.5.*
-- *Other representations are described in Section 5.6.4.*

end binary_tree_package;

EXERCISES 5.4

1. The number of objects examined during the find operation in Figure 5.24 is at most the height of the binary search tree that is the target of the find. Explain why.

2. Write the specification for a procedure that compares two binary trees to see if they are equal. Be sure to specify precisely what it means for binary trees to be equal.

3. Write the specification for a procedure that returns the mirror image of a binary tree. Let *BT* be a binary tree. Mirror$_{BT}$, the mirror image of *BT*, is related to *BT* as follows. Let *n* be any node in *BT* with left child n_L and right child n_R. Then node *n* is in Mirror$_{BT}$ with left child n_R and right child n_L. Mirror$_{BT}$ contains no other nodes. It may help to draw several binary trees and their mirror images.

4. Write the specification for a procedure that returns an extended copy of a binary tree. Each node in the copy of the tree contains the number of nodes in both its left and right subtrees.

5. Write the specification for a function that searches a binary search tree and returns the node that contains the object in the *k*th position among all objects in the tree. Position here refers to the position an object would occupy if the objects were all in a list sorted with respect to the tree's key values.

6. Write the specification for a generic procedure that copies, to a new tree, all the nodes in a given tree that meet a user-prescribed condition. The nodes to be copied are selected by a function that is a generic parameter for the copy procedure.

7. Write an instantiation of the binary search tree specified in Specification 5.1 for each pair of key and data types shown in the following table.

	object_type	key_type	Comment
a	integer	integer	
b	string(1 .. 10)	string(1 .. 10)	
c	A record type with several components including an integer	integer	Discuss the options available for specifying functions equal and "<".
d	A record type with several components including string(1 .. 10)	string(1 .. 10)	Discuss the options available for specifying functions equal and "<".
e	A record type with two components— an integer and either a stack, a queue, or a list	integer	The object_type is obtained by instantiating the appropriate package as described in Chapter 3 or 4.
f	A stack, a queue, or a list		The object_type is obtained by instantiating the appropriate package as described in Chapter 3 or 4. Discuss the options available for key_type.
g	A tree		The key_type is obtained by instantiating the tree specified in Specification 5.1. Discuss the options available for key_type.

■ 5.5 Binary Search Trees—Basic Operations

Section 5.4 discussed binary search trees and illustrated one of the most important operations on binary search trees—*find*. This section continues with descriptions of other basic operations: *insert, delete,* and *traverse.* In each case the examples and text descriptions are accompanied by pseudocode that is not specific to any representation or implementation—although the structure of the pseudocode is similar to Ada. Representation and implementation of these operations is discussed in Section 5.6.

5.5.1 Insert

When a key value is added to a binary search tree its position is found by searching the tree using the search technique in *find* (Section 5.4). If the key value to insert is not found, then it is added as a child of the node where the search terminated. If the key value to insert is found, the *duplicate_node* exception is raised. Figure 5.27 is a binary search tree that has been annotated to show the positions where some of the possible new key values would be inserted. For example, a new key value between 45 and 50 would be inserted as the right child of 45, and a new key value between 80 and 90 would be added as the right child of 80. What values would be inserted as the right child of 10?

Figure 5.28 gives an algorithm for *insert*. Verify that procedure *insert* is correct for the tree in Figure 5.27.

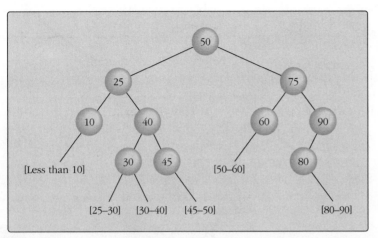

FIGURE 5.27 Some of the insertion positions in a binary search tree. Where would a value between 60 and 75 be inserted?

procedure insert (the_tree : **in out** binary_tree; the_object : object_type) **is**
    the_node is a binary_search_tree_node that is initialized to contain the_key and the_data;
begin
    if the_tree is an empty tree **then** add the_node as the_tree's root node;
    else search the_tree for a node containing the_key as its key value;
      if the search is not successful, **then**
        let the_leaf be the leaf node where the search ended;
        if the_key is less than the_leaf's key value **then**
          add the_node as the_leaf's left child;
        else add the_node as the_leaf's right child;
        end if;
      else the tree already contains a node whose key value is the_key;
        raise the duplicate_node exception;
      end if;
    end if;
end insert;

FIGURE 5.28 An algorithm for procedure *insert*.

5.5.2 Delete

Operation *delete* deletes a specified key, and its associated object, from a binary search tree. In some cases this operation is as simple as deleting an object from a list. There are cases, however, in which this is a more complex operation. The discussion that follows is based on four examples. The first two show cases where the deletion is simple. The final two illustrate more complex possibilities. You are encouraged to refer ahead to the pseudocode in Figure 5.33 or the Ada implementation in Section 5.6 whenever you feel the additional detail will help.

In the following discussion reference to a key, say 80, is a reference to the object whose key is 80. Remember that each tree node contains an object that always has an associated key value.

Figure 5.29 shows a tree before and after deleting 80. This is a simple case because the node containing the key value to delete has no children. The deletion is accomplished by making the left subtree of 90 an empty subtree. The node containing 80 is removed from the tree.

Figure 5.30 shows a tree before and after deleting 110. This is a simple

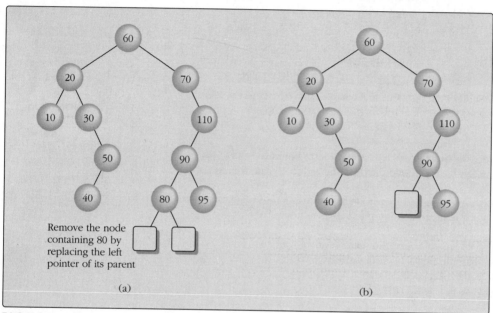

FIGURE 5.29 (a) Before and (b) after removing the node containing 80.

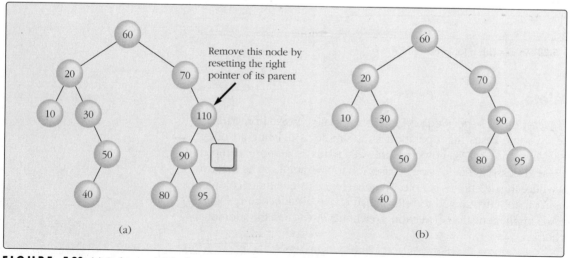

FIGURE 5.30 (a) Before and (b) after removing the node containing 110.

case because the node containing the key value to delete has no right child. The deletion is accomplished by making the node containing 90 the right child of the node containing 70. The node containing 110 is removed from the tree.

The two cases considered so far were simple because the node containing the value to delete had at least one empty subtree. Consider deleting 20 from the tree in Figure 5.30(a). The problem is that deleting 20 by removing the node that contains 20 leaves two subtrees competing to become the left subtree of 60. To resolve this conflict, which is inherent in deleting an object from a multiway tree, we need another approach.

In the following discussion we will distinguish between deleting an object and removing a node from a binary tree. In the two examples above we deleted an object with a specified key value by removing the node that contained that object. In the examples that follow, the node that is removed from the tree will not be the node that contains the object with the target key value.

Remember, remove refers actually to removing a node from the tree. Delete refers to deleting an object with a prescribed key value from the tree—without necessarily removing the node that originally contained that object.

Figure 5.31 shows the deletion of 60 from a binary tree. The key point is that the node containing 60 does not have an empty subtree. The first step is to find the largest key value in 60's left subtree—50 in this case. The object with key value 60 is replaced by the object with key value 50—without changing the nodes that contain these values. Why must the value that replaces 60 be the *largest* value in its left subtree?

The node containing the largest key value must have an empty right subtree because a right child always contains a value larger than its parent. For example, in Figure 5.31(a), if 50 had a right child then that right child's

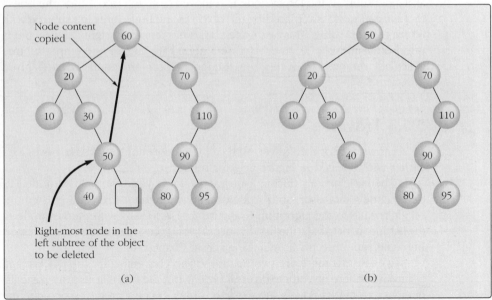

FIGURE 5.31 (a) Before and (b) after deleting 60 by replacing 60 with 50 and removing the node containing 50.

key value would be larger than 50. We complete the deletion by removing the node containing the largest object in the left subtree, which is easy because it does not have a right child.

It may have already occurred to you that instead of using the largest value in the left subtree, as shown in Figure 5.31, we could use the smallest value in the right subtree. The details are shown in Figure 5.32.

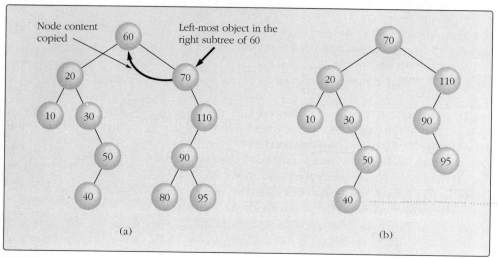

FIGURE 5.32 (a) Before and (b) after deleting 60 by replacing 60 by 70 and removing the node containing 70.

In summary, procedure *delete* searches for the node that contains the key value to be deleted from the tree—the target node. If the target node has an empty subtree, the target node is removed from the tree. If not, the object in the target node is replaced by the object in the node in its left subtree with the largest key value. This last node always has an empty right subtree and is removed from the tree. In every case a node with at least one empty subtree is actually removed from the tree. Pseudocode for procedure *delete* is given in Figure 5.33.

5.5.3 Traverse

To set the stage for tree traversal, recall the algorithm to traverse a list given earlier and repeated in Figure 5.34 for reference.

The basic actions during list traversal are (1) find the first list node, (2) find a node's successor, and (3) determine when the list remaining is empty. An alternative to the algorithm in Figure 5.34 is to start with the last node in the list and work toward the first by successively accessing a node's predecessor. Implementation details in Ada are given in Chapter 4.

We see that there are two natural ways to traverse a list: first to last and last to first. There are other traversal orders, but the two that use the basic list operations—find a node's successor and find a node's predecessor—are the ones almost always used.

procedure delete (the_tree: **in out** binary_tree; target_key : key_type) **is**

begin

    search the_tree for a node containing an object with target_key as its key value;
    if the search is successful **then**
        let the_node be the node that contains target_key as its object's key value;

        if the_node does not have a right child **then**
            the_node's left child replaces the_node in the_tree;
        elsif the_node does not have a left child **then**
            the_node's right child replaces the_node in the_tree;
        else let large_left be the node containing the largest key value in the_node's left subtree;
            replace the_node's object with large_left's object;
            large_left's left child replaces large_left in the_tree;
        end if;

        the_tree.size := the_tree.size − 1;
    else the search was not successful;
        raise the missing_node exception;
    end if;
end delete;

FIGURE 5.33 An algorithm for **procedure** *delete*.

generic
    procedure process (the_object : object_type);
    -- **results:** *Process the_object in a list node.*
procedure traverse (the_list : list) **is**
    the_node is a list_node that is initialized as the first node in the_list;
begin
    while the_node is not the first node in an empty list **loop**
        process (the_node's object value);
        assign the_node's successor to the_node;
    end loop;
end traverse;

FIGURE 5.34 An algorithm to traverse a list.

    Traversal orders for a binary tree are not so apparent, and we will describe four of them in some detail. We begin with a heuristic description of three traversal orders that is intended to set the stage for a more formal presentation.

    Figure 5.35 shows a binary tree, including its empty subtrees, and a dashed line around the tree. The dashed line shows the path of a tree observer as he or she "observes" the nodes of the tree. The arrowheads show the tree observer's direction. The order of observation for each node, relative to its two subtrees, is as follows:

1. The node is observed—for the first time.
2. All the nodes in the node's left subtree are observed.
3. The node is observed—for the second time.
4. All the nodes in the node's right subtree are observed.
5. The node is observed—for the third and final time.

The three traversal algorithms we are now discussing are called preorder, inorder, and postorder. The order in which a binary tree's nodes are processed is the following.

1. During a ***preorder*** traversal each node is processed the first time it is observed.
2. During an ***inorder*** traversal each node is processed the second time it is observed.
3. During a ***postorder*** traversal each node is processed the third time it is observed.

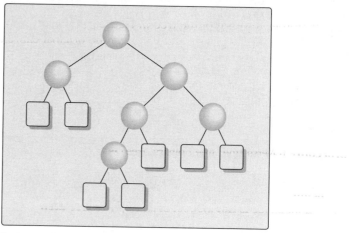

FIGURE 5.35 The path of a tree observer.

Figure 5.36 shows three copies of the binary tree in Figure 5.35. Each node is labeled with an integer that shows the processing order for that node. From left to right, the trees illustrate preorder, inorder, and postorder traversal.

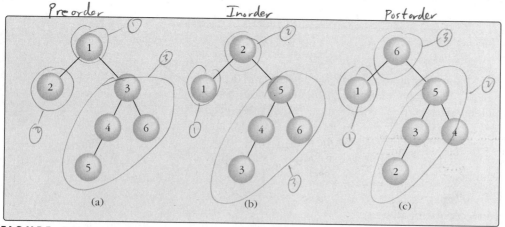

FIGURE 5.36 Traversal orders for the tree in Figure 5.35. (a) Preorder; (b) inorder; (c) postorder.

A review of the tree observer's path around the tree leads to the following, more commonly used, descriptions of tree traversal orders:

1. During a **preorder** traversal each node is processed before any node in either of its subtrees.
2. During an **inorder** traversal each node is processed after all nodes in its left subtree and before any node in its right subtree.
3. During a **postorder** traversal each node is processed after all nodes in both its subtrees.

Figure 5.37 shows an expression tree. Its traversal orders are as follows:

preorder: x, +, a, b, +, c, 7
inorder: a, +, b, x, c, +, 7
postorder: a, b, +, c, 7, +, x

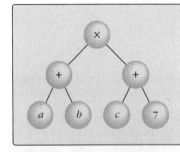

FIGURE 5.37 A binary tree that contains the components of an expression. Three traversal orders for this tree are shown in the text.

Postorder traversal of the tree in Figure 5.37 processes the nodes in an order that is conducive to the evaluation of the original expression.

Figure 5.38 provides pseudocode for inorder traversal. The pseudocode for preorder and postorder traversal is almost identical. Look at Specification 5.1 to see that traverse is a generic procedure. Section 5.6 provides further detail about implementation of this important operation.

procedure traverse (the_tree : binary_tree) **is**   -- *Inorder traversal of a binary tree.*

    procedure inorder (the_node : binary_tree_node) **is**
    begin
      if the_node **is not** the root of an empty subtree **then**

        inorder (the_node's left child);   -- *Recursively process the_node's left subtree.*
        process (the_node.object);
        inorder (the_node's right child);   -- *Recursively process the_node's right subtree.*

      end if;
    end inorder;

begin
    inorder (the_tree.root);
end traverse;

FIGURE 5.38 Inorder traversal of a binary tree.

Please observe that Figure 5.38 contains an elegant algorithm for what might, without recursion, be a rather messy process. Since tree traversal and recursion are topics of major importance, more about traversal, including nonrecursive algorithms, is given in Section 5.6. Then, in Section 5.10, we will see that traversal of B-trees, in which a parent may have many children, is a simple variation of the algorithm in Figure 5.38. A fourth and conceptually simple traversal order is level order traversal.

In a level order traversal the root is processed first, the nodes at level two are processed next, the nodes at level three are processed next, and so on. Or, stated more succinctly, during a level order traversal each node at level k is processed after all nodes at level $k - 1$ and before any node at level $k + 1$.

It is the implementation of level order traversal, Section 5.6, that is interesting. Next, Section 5.6 discusses the representation and implementation of binary tree algorithms.

EXERCISES 5.5

1. Consider the binary search tree in Figure 5.39. Using the notation in Figure 5.27, show the positions at which any possible integer would be inserted into the tree.

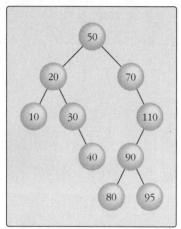

FIGURE 5.39 Example of a binary search tree.

2. Start with the binary tree in Figure 5.39 and show the result of deleting each of the following objects: (a) 80, (b) 30, (c) 90, (d) 70, (e) 20, and (f) 50. Each deletion acts on the original tree.

3. In what order are the nodes in Figure 5.39 processed during (a) a preorder, (b) an inorder, and (c) a postorder traversal?

4. Give examples, if possible, of trees such that the following two traversal orders process all nodes in the same order:
   a. Preorder and inorder
   b. Preorder and postorder
   c. Inorder and postorder
   Note that all traversal orders are the same if the tree is empty or contains a single node. First experiment with trees that contain two or three nodes; then work with larger trees.

5. Consider a binary tree containing n nodes whose key values are $1, 2, \ldots, n$.

Consider all permutations of the first n integers, and in each case attempt to construct a binary tree whose preorder sequence is $1, 2, \ldots, n$ and whose inorder sequence is the permutation.

For $n = 2$, you need to construct two trees: The first tree has both preorder and inorder traversal orders 1, 2, and the second has preorder traversal order 1, 2 and inorder traversal order 2, 1. Both trees can be constructed.

For $n = 3$, attempt to construct six trees—one for each permutation of the first three integers. You will only succeed in constructing trees for five of the six permutations.

Suppose for $n = 5$, the preorder traversal order is 1, 2, 3, 4, 5 and the inorder traversal order is 4, 2, 1, 3, 5. Is there one tree with these two traversal orders? If so, its root contains 1, the left subtree of 1 contains 2 and 4, and the right subtree of 1 contains 3 and 5. Why? This tree cannot be constructed because 3 precedes 4 in the preorder traversal, but 4 is in the left subtree of 1 and 3 is in the right subtree of 1.

Generalize the discussion in the preceding paragraph. If the preorder traversal order is $1, 2, \ldots, n$ and the inorder traversal order is $i_1, i_2, \ldots, i_n$, then describe the circumstances under which the appropriate tree cannot be constructed.

6. For the traversal operations described in this section, there are three basic operations:
   a. Process a node.
   b. Traverse a node's left subtree.
   c. Traverse a node's right subtree.

   These three operations can be preformed in any order so there is a total of three factorial or six traversal orders. For example, preorder traversal occurs when these three operations are applied to each node in the order listed. What order of these operations corresponds to inorder traversal? What order corresponds to postorder traversal?

   Exercises 5.4, 3 describes the mirror image of a binary tree. What order of the three operations above corresponds to preorder, inorder, and postorder traversal of the mirror image of a binary tree?

■ 5.6 Binary Search Trees— Representation and Implementation

This section begins by presenting a dynamic representation for a binary tree. Any representation that works for a binary tree also works for a binary search tree, since the ordering of nodes in a binary search tree is maintained by procedures *insert* and *delete*.

In Section 5.6.1 we present the dynamic representation. Based on that representation we continue, in Section 5.6.2, the study of binary tree traversal algorithms. In particular, we consider in more detail the relationship between traversal and the underlying data structures, stacks or queues, used to store nodes whose processing is deferred.

Section 5.6.3 contains the body for Package 5.1 (given in Section 5.4). Then, Section 5.6.4 discusses alternate representations for a binary tree.

5.6.1 Representation

The private clause for Specification 5.1 is given in Figure 5.40. It shows a common representation for a binary tree. Other possible representations are discussed in 5.6.4.

```
private                                    -- Binary tree representation.

    type binary_tree_node;
    type node_pointer is access binary_tree_node;

    type binary_tree_node is record
       object      : object_type;
       left, right : node_pointer;          null
    end record;
                      → limited private
    type binary_tree is record
       size  : natural := 0;
       root  : node_pointer;
    end record;

end binary_tree_package;
```

FIGURE 5.40 A common representation for a binary tree. If the tree is not empty, it is an oriented tree because the root is specified. Also, this is an ordered tree because each subtree is identified as either the left or right subtree.

Figure 5.41 illustrates a binary tree as represented in Figure 5.40. The intent of Figure 5.41 is to help you visualize the representation we will be using in this section. It is worth recalling that in Ada, pointers are automatically initialized to null. Therefore, when an instance of a binary tree is elaborated, its size is zero and its root pointer is null.

Implementation of Specification 5.1, a binary search tree, based on the representation above is given in Section 5.6.3. Before that, Section 5.6.2 provides further discussion of an important tree operation—traverse.

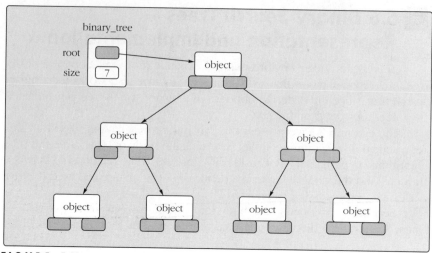

FIGURE 5.41 Illustration of a binary tree as represented in Figure 5.40.

5.6.2 More on Traverse

Study the implementation of procedure *traverse* in Section 5.6.3 and note the importance of recursion to this operation. Remember that a recursive procedure call causes execution of a segment of code to be deferred while the recursive procedure call is executed immediately. Deferred execution is achieved by putting all information needed to resume the interrupted execution on a stack.

One way to study traversal in depth is to write traversal algorithms that do not use recursive procedure calls. Instead, such procedures will manage their own stacks. We begin with a nonrecursive version of preorder traversal.

To assist in describing our nonrecursive traversal algorithm Figure 5.42(a) presents an example of a binary tree. A further aid to the discussion is the notion of the left and right shells of a node. Let N be any node in a binary tree. N's *left shell* is N together with any node that is the left child of a node in the left shell. The left shells of nodes A, C, E, and F and the order that the nodes are processed during a preorder traversal are shown in Figure 5.42(b). A node's right shell has a similar definition.

The preorder traversal algorithm is given in Figure 5.43. In terms of Figure 5.42, this algorithm traverses each of the four left shells. The actions taken during a shell traversal are (1) process a node, (2) save the root of the right subtree—if it exists—on the stack, and (3) continue the traversal, or, if the end of the shell has been reached, pop the stack to get the next left shell to traverse.

Compare the traversal order with the left shells in which they occur in Figure 5.42(b). You will see a simple correlation between the left shells and the preorder traversal order.

The role of the stack in all our traverse algorithms is critical. In the

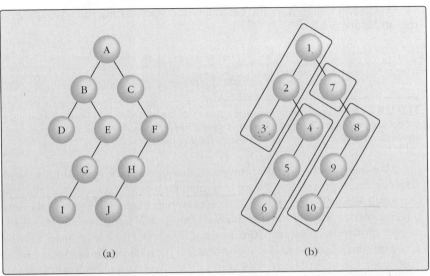

FIGURE **5.42** (a) Example of a binary tree. (b) The order in which nodes are processed during a preorder traversal. Also outlined with rectangles are the left shells of A, C, E, and F.

```
procedure preorder (the_tree : binary_tree) is
-- Length 12   Complexity 4   Performance O(n)
-- The while loop will be executed n times—once for each node in the_tree.
      package stack is new stack_package (node_pointer);
      S    : stack.stack ((the_tree.size + 1)/2);
      ptr  : node_pointer := the_tree.root;
begin
      stack.push (S, null);

      while ptr /= null loop
          process (ptr.object);

          if ptr.right /= null then stack.push (S, ptr.right);
          end if;

          if ptr.left /= null then ptr := ptr.left;
          else ptr := stack.top(S); stack.pop(S);
          end if;

      end loop;
end preorder;
```

-- Nonrecursive preorder traversal.

-- Why is the maximum stack size set to (the_tree.size + 1)/2?

ⓐ programmer manages the stack

-- Procedure process is applied to each object in the_tree.

-- Save right subtrees for future processing.

-- Continue the left shell traversal, or get the next left shell.

FIGURE **5.43** Nonrecursive preorder traversal of a binary tree.

recursive implementations the burden of managing the stack is passed from the programmer to the compiler and the run-time system. In Figure 5.43 the programmer manages the stack. The role of the stack is further emphasized by showing, in Figure 5.44, the content of the stack during the traversal of the tree in Figure 5.42.

FIGURE 5.44 Stack content during traversal of the binary tree in Figure 5.42 using procedure *preorder*. The stack content is shown immediately after each of the four shells has been traversed. The symbol → X stands for a pointer to node X.

We have discussed three traversals that use a stack to hold information about deferred processing. If we use a queue instead of a stack for this purpose, the result is level order traversal. For example, Figure 5.45 shows the level traversal order for a particular binary tree—each node is labeled with an integer showing its position in the traversal. The order for a level order traversal is not unique since the nodes at any one level can be processed in any order. The order shown in Figure 5.45 is the order that corresponds to the implementation in Section 5.6.3. See Section 5.4 for a specification of level order traversal.

Pseudocode for a level order traversal algorithm is given in Figure 5.46.

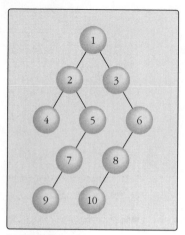

FIGURE 5.45 A level order traversal order for a binary tree.

```
procedure level_traverse (the_tree : binary_tree) is
      the_queue is an empty queue;
      the_node is a binary tree node initialized as the root of the tree.
begin
      if the_node is not the root of an empty tree then enqueue the_node in the_queue;
      end if;

      while the_queue is not empty loop
           Let the_node be the node removed from the head of the_queue;
           process the_node;
           enqueue, in the_queue, the root of each of the_node's subtrees that is not empty;
      end loop;

end level_traverse;
```

FIGURE 5.46 Algorithm for level order traversal of a binary tree.

We have now seen traversal algorithms that depend on both stacks and queues to keep information about tree nodes whose processing has been deferred. The stack-based traversals are simple to write since recursive procedure calls can be used. The queue-based traversal provides an order that is particularly easy to visualize but requires the implementor to manage the queue explicitly.

Traversal algorithms for graphs (Chapter 9) are also based on using stacks or queues to hold information about the graph objects whose processing is deferred. In addition, using stacks or queues is a special case of using priority queues and some important algorithms require the generality of a priority queue.

Section 5.6.3 now gives the package body of the *binary_tree_package*.

5.6.3 Implementation

This section contains the package body that implements Specification 5.1. Notice the frequent use of recursion in these implementations.

■ **PACKAGE BODY 5.1** **Dynamic Binary Search Tree**   *-- Implements Specification 5.1*

with queue_package;   *-- A queue is needed for level order traversal.*
package body binary_tree_package **is**

    procedure traverse (the_tree : binary_tree; the_order : traverse_order) **is**
    -- Length 5   Complexity 3   Performance O(n)
    -- Each of the n *objects in the_tree is processed.*

        procedure preord (p : node_pointer; level : positive) **is**
        -- Length 5   Complexity 2   Recursion 2
        begin
          if p /= null **then**
            process(p.object);   *-- Process an object.*
            preord(p.left);   *-- Recursively process the left subtree.*
            preord(p.right);   *-- Recursively process the right subtree.*
          end if;
        end preord;

        procedure inord (p : node_pointer; level : positive) **is**
        -- Length 5   Complexity 2   Recursion 2
        begin
          if p /= null **then**
            inord(p.left);   *-- Recursively process the left subtree.*
            process(p.object);   *-- Process an object.*
            inord(p.right);   *-- Recursively process the right subtree.*
          end if;
        end inord;

        procedure postord (p : node_pointer; level : positive) **is**
        -- Length 5   Complexity 2   Recursion 2
        begin
          if p /= null **then**
            postord(p.left);   *-- Recursively process the left subtree.*
            postord(p.right);   *-- Recursively process the right subtree.*
            process(p.object);   *-- Process an object.*
          end if;
        end postord;

(continued)

Package Body 5.1 (continued)

```
begin
  case the_order is
    when pre_order => preord(the_tree.root);
    when in_order => inord(the_tree.root);
    when post_order => postord(the_tree.root);
  end case;
end traverse;

procedure level_traverse (the_tree : binary_tree) is
-- Length 13   Complexity 5   Performance O(n)
-- Each of the n objects in the_tree is processed.

  package queue is new queue_package (node_pointer);       -- Instantiate a queue.
  Q   : queue.queue((the_tree.size+1)/2);
  ptr : node_pointer := the_tree.root;
begin
  if ptr /= null then queue.enqueue(Q, ptr);
  end if;

  while queue.number_of_objects (Q) > 0 loop      -- While the queue is not empty,
    ptr := queue.head(Q);                         -- get the object at the head of the queue,
    queue.dequeue(Q);
    process (ptr.object);                                         -- process it, and

    if ptr.left /= null then queue.enqueue(Q, ptr.left);        -- add any children
    end if;
    if ptr.right /= null then queue.enqueue(Q, ptr.right);           -- to the queue.
    end if;
  end loop;

end level_traverse;

function find (the_tree : binary_tree; target_key : key_type) return boolean is
-- Length 8   Complexity 4   Performance   Expected O(log_2 n)   Worst Case O(n)
-- The maximum search length is equal to the height of the tree. The expected height of a binary search tree
-- is O(log_2 n), and its maximum height is O(n).
  ptr : node_pointer := the_tree.root;
begin

  while ptr /= null loop
    if target_key = key_of(ptr.object) then return true;
    elsif target_key < key_of(ptr.object) then ptr := ptr.left;
    else ptr := ptr.right;
    end if;
  end loop;

  return false;
end find;
```

(continued)

Package Body 5.1 (continued)

```
procedure insert (the_tree : in out binary_tree; the_object : object_type) is
-- Length 18   Complexity 7   Performance   Expected O(log₂n)   Worst Case O(n)
-- The point of insertion is found by searching the_tree. The performance of insert is therefore
-- approximately the same as the performance of function find.
   ptr : node_pointer;
   scout, scout_parent : node_pointer := the_tree.root;
   target_key : key_type := key_of(the_object);
begin
   ptr := new binary_tree_node'(the_object, null, null);
   if scout = null then the_tree.root := ptr;
   else

      while scout /= null loop                         -- Search for a node containing key_of(the_object).
         scout_parent := scout;
         if target_key = key_of(scout.object) then
            raise duplicate_node;
         elsif target_key < key_of(scout.object) then
            scout := scout.left;
         else scout := scout.right;
         end if;
      end loop;

      if target_key < key_of(scout_parent.object) then    -- scout_parent now accesses the parent
                                                           -- of the node that will be inserted.
         scout_parent.left := ptr;                   -- Add the new node as the left child of scout_parent.
      else scout_parent.right := ptr;               -- Add the new node as the right child of scout_parent.
      end if;
   end if;
   the_tree.size := the_tree.size + 1;
exception
   when storage_error => raise tree_full;
end insert;
```

the_key : key_type := ——

```
procedure delete (the_tree : in out binary_tree; target_key : key_type) is
- Length 3   Complexity 1   Performance   Expected O(log₂n)   Worst Case O(n)
-- The delete operation is constrained to a single path between the root of the tree and a leaf node.
-- The length of such a path is expected to be O(log₂n) and is at most O(n).
      keep_this_node : node_pointer;

   procedure sub_delete (ptr : in out node_pointer; target_key : key_type) is
   -- Length 10   Complexity 6   Recursion 2
      procedure sub_sub_delete (qtr : in out node_pointer) is
      -- Length 4   Complexity 2   Recursion 1
      begin
         if qtr.right /= null then sub_sub_delete (qtr.right);   -- Find the right-most node.
         else keep_this_node.object := qtr.object;              -- Copy the right-most node's object.
            qtr := qtr.left;                        -- Remove the right-most node in target_key's left subtree.
         end if;
      end sub_sub_delete;
```

(continued)

Package Body 5.1 *(continued)*

```
        begin
            if ptr = null then raise missing_node;                         -- target_key is not in the tree.
            elsif target_key < key_of(ptr.object) then
                sub_delete (ptr.left, target_key);                         -- Search the left subtree.
            elsif not (target_key = key_of(ptr.object)) then
                sub_delete (ptr.right, target_key);                        -- Search the right subtree.
            else keep_this_node := ptr;
                                                                           -- target_key is found, ready to delete it.
                if ptr.right = null then ptr := ptr.left;                  -- target_key's node has an empty right subtree.
                elsif ptr.left = null then ptr := ptr.right;               -- target_key's node has an empty left subtree.
                else sub_sub_delete (ptr.left);    -- target_key is a node with two children, find the largest key value in the left subtree.
                end if;

            end if;
        end sub_delete;


    begin
        sub_delete (the_tree.root, target_key);
        the_tree.size := the_tree.size − 1;
    end delete;

    procedure make_tree_empty (the_tree : binary_tree) is
    begin
        null;                                                              -- Implementation left as an exercise.
    end find;


    procedure update (the_tree : in out binary_tree; the_object : object_type) is
    begin
        null;                                                              -- Implementation is left as an exercise.
    end;


    function retrieve (the_tree : binary_tree; target_key : key_type) return object_type is
    begin
        null;                                                              -- Implementation is left as an exercise.
    end;


    function characteristics (the_tree : binary_tree) return status is
    -- Length 4   Complexity 2   Performance O(n)
        stat: status := (0, 0, 0.0);
        total_path_length : natural := 0;

        procedure in_order (p : node_pointer; level : positive) is
        -- Length 8   Complexity 3   Recursion 2
        begin
            if p /= null then
                in_order (p.left, level + 1);                              -- Process the left subtree.
```

(continued)

Package Body 5.1 (continued)

```
          stat.size := stat.size + 1;                                    -- Gather statistics for the current node.
          if level > stat.height then stat.height := level;
          end if;
          total_path_length := total_path_length + level;
          in_order (p.right, level + 1);                                 -- Process the right subtree.
       end if;
     end in_order;

  begin
     in_order (the_tree.root, 1);
     if stat.size > 0 then
        stat.ave_path_length := float(total_path_length)/float(stat.size);
     end if;
     return stat;
  end characteristics;
```

size/root rec.

```
function empty (the_tree : binary_tree) return boolean is
-- Length 1   Complexity 1   Performance O(1)
begin
  return (the_tree.size = 0);
end empty;

procedure copy (the_tree : binary_tree; the_copy : in out binary_tree) is
-- Length 4   Complexity 2   Performance O(n)
  procedure recursive_copy (ptr : node_pointer; copy_ptr : in out node_pointer) is
  -- Length 5   Complexity 2   Recursion 2
  begin
    if ptr /= null then
       copy_ptr := new binary_tree_node'(ptr.object, null, null);
       recursive_copy (ptr.left, copy_ptr.left);
       recursive_copy (ptr.right, copy_ptr.right);
    end if;
  end recursive_copy;

begin
  the_copy := (the_tree.size, null);
  recursive_copy (the_tree.root, the_copy.root);
exception
  when storage_error => raise tree_full;
end copy;

procedure balanced_copy (the_tree : binary_tree; the_copy : in out binary_tree) is
-- Length 9   Complexity 2   Performance O(n)
-- Each node's content is copied first to sorted_node_list, then to the_copy.
  type array_of_nodes is array (1 .. the_tree.size) of object_type;

  sorted_node_list : array_of_nodes;
  list_index : positive := 1;
```

(continued)

Package Body 5.1 (continued)

```
procedure append_to_list (the_object : object_type) is
-- Length 2   Complexity 1
begin
   sorted_node_list (list_index) := the_object;
   list_index := list_index + 1;
end append_to_list;


procedure tree_to_list is new traverse (append_to_list);


procedure list_to_tree (low, high : natural) is
-- Length 4   Complexity 2   Recursion 2
   mid : natural := (high + low)/2;
begin
   if low <= high then
      insert (the_copy, sorted_node_list(mid));        -- Insert the middle array object into the_copy.
      list_to_tree (low, mid - 1);                     -- Recursively insert the objects in the left half of the array.
      list_to_tree (mid + 1, high);                    -- Recursively insert the objects in the right half of the array.
   end if;
end list_to_tree;


begin
   tree_to_list (the_tree, in_order);                  -- Copy the tree objects to a list in sorted order.
   the_copy := binary_tree'(size => 0, root => null);  -- Make sure the_copy is empty.
   list_to_tree (1, list_index - 1);                   -- Copy objects from the sorted list to the_copy. Choose an
end balanced_copy;                                     -- order that guarantees that the_copy is balanced.


end binary_tree_package;
```

5.6.4 Alternate Representations

Using the representation in Figure 5.40, a binary tree with n nodes will reference $n + 1$ empty subtrees. This is illustrated in Figure 5.47, which shows a binary tree with six nodes and its seven empty subtrees.

The representation of a binary tree in Figure 5.40 contains a null pointer for each empty subtree. The intent of our first alternate binary tree representation is to put the null pointers that identify empty subtrees to work.

Figure 5.48 shows three segments of binary trees. In each case, when a node does not have a right subtree, its right pointer (a dashed arc with an arrowhead in the figure) points to its inorder successor.

Observe that if a node *does not have a right child,* then its inorder successor can be characterized as follows. (1) The inorder successor of a left child is the child's parent. (2) The inorder successor of a right child is the closest ancestor in whose left subtree it is positioned. There is one exception. There is one node (unless the tree is empty) that does not have an inorder successor. That node is found by starting at the root and accessing right children until a node with no right child is found.

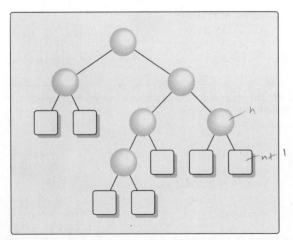

FIGURE 5.47 A binary tree and its empty subtrees. If a binary tree has *n* nodes, then it has *n* + 1 empty subtrees.

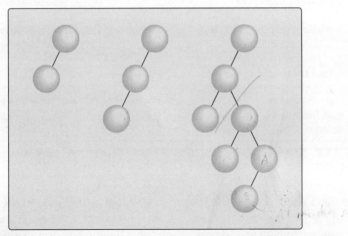

FIGURE 5.48 Three binary trees in which the pointer to a node's empty right subtree is replaced by a pointer to that node's inorder successor.

It is easy to modify the representation in Figure 5.40 to replace right pointers to empty subtrees with pointers to a node's inorder successor. We add a boolean variable that is true if the right pointer accesses an inorder successor and false otherwise. Figure 5.49 shows the addition to the representation given in Figure 5.40. Trees that use pointers in this way are often called *threaded trees.*

Now, we implement inorder traversal assuming that inorder successors are identified as presented in Figure 5.49. The result is shown in Figure 5.50. Left shells are described in Section 5.6.2.

The advantages of the traversal in Figure 5.50 are that (1) it saves memory because a stack is not needed, (2) it runs faster because stack operations have

```
type binary_tree_node is record
    object          : object_type;
    left, right     : node_pointer;
    inorder_succ    : boolean;          -- True if field right accesses the inorder successor.
end record;
```

FIGURE 5.49 The representation of a binary tree node is modified so that the right pointer can be used to point to either a node's right child or, if there is no right child, to the node's inorder successor.

```
procedure inorder (the_tree : binary_tree) is                    -- Inorder traversal.
-- Length 9   Complexity 4   Performance O(n)
    p : node_pointer := the_tree.root;
begin
    while p /= null loop                              -- While there is a left shell to process.

        while p.left /= null loop                          -- Traverse a left shell.
            p := p.left;
        end loop;

        process (p.object);                      -- Process the last object in a left shell.

        while p.inorder_succ loop        -- While there is a pointer to an inorder successor.
            p := p.right;                                  -- Get the inorder successor.
            process (p.object);                                        -- Process it.
        end loop;

        p := p.right;               -- Start at the root of the next left shell—if there is one.
    end loop;
end inorder;
```

FIGURE 5.50 Inorder traversal using access to inorder successors as represented in Figure 5.49.

been eliminated, and (3) the traversal can begin at any node in the tree. Note that an inorder traversal that uses a stack must begin at the tree's root because to continue from an arbitrary node requires the information that would be in the stack based on starting the traversal at the root. Further details about threaded trees are given in Reingold (1986, pages 240–251).

It is also possible to represent a binary tree using any one of several sequential (array) representations. Consider the representation in Figure 5.51.

With the representation in Figure 5.51, information about the location of a node's children must be "hard wired" into the algorithms that operate on the tree. For example, the object at array position k can have its children placed at positions $2k$ and $2k + 1$. This scheme requires some method to determine the absence of an object at a particular location. One approach is to assign an object value to indicate this absence. A better technique is to add a boolean field to *object_type* that would be true if an object is present and false otherwise.

Remember that a tree is full if every position in the tree contains a node—except possibly for the positions in the last level. A binary tree is **complete** if

```
type index is integer range 1 .. max_size;

type array_of_objects is array (index) of object_type;

type binary_tree is record
      size      : natural := 0;
      the_tree  : array_of_objects;
end record;
```

FIGURE 5.51 A binary tree representation using an array without storing information about the location of an object's children. The root is assumed to be in array position 1.

it is full, and all nodes in the last level are "as far to the left as possible." The representation in Figure 5.51 would work well for storing a complete tree, and the indication of the presence or absence of an object is not needed since it can be calculated based on the value of *size*.

The representation in Figure 5.51 would only make sense if most object positions between 1 and the size of the tree actually contained a node. Otherwise, too much memory would be allocated but not used, and algorithms that operate on the tree would spend too much time accessing positions that are empty.

Another possible binary tree representation is to create a record type, call it *binary_tree_object,* that contains the positions of the object's children. The result is shown in Figure 5.52.

```
type count is integer range 0 .. max_size;
type index is integer range 1 .. max_size;

type binary_tree_object is record
      object      : object_type;
      left, right : count;           -- The value 0 indicates an empty subtree.
end record;

type binary_tree_space is array (index) of binary_tree_object;

type binary_tree is record
      size      : natural := 0;
      the_tree  : binary_tree_space;
end record;
```

FIGURE 5.52 A binary tree representation using an array and including the positions of the left and right children. The root is assumed to be in array position 1.

The representation in Figure 5.52 is similar to the representation in Section 5.6.1. The main difference is the replacement of pointers to subtrees with the array indexes of subtrees.

We have seen three alternate representations for binary trees. The first uses pointers that would otherwise be null to access related nodes in the tree.

This makes more effective use of the memory used to store the tree at the cost of slightly more complex *insert* and *delete* operations.

The second representation stores the binary tree in an array by positioning the children of the node in position k at positions $2k$ and $2k + 1$. This is an attractive approach if the tree is full or complete, but it may waste memory and cause basic tree operations to be slow otherwise. This representation is used in Section 5.9.

Finally, in Figure 5.52 an array representation is used that stores the positions of a node's children as fields of each tree object. This approach eliminates the need to allocate memory dynamically each time a node is added to the tree—as required by the dynamic representation discussed in all other sections of this chapter.

EXERCISES 5.6

1. Suppose the representation of a binary tree (Figure 5.41) is changed to the following:

   private   *-- Binary tree representation.*

       type binary_tree_node;
       type binary_tree **is access** binary_tree_node;
                  -- A binary_tree is simply a pointer.
       type binary_tree_node **is record**
         key   : key_type;
         data   : data_type;
         left, right : binary_tree;
       end record;

   end binary_package;

   What are the advantages and disadvantages of this new representation? Discuss the effect of this representation on the size and complexity of the implementations of the binary search tree operations.

2. Implement a procedure that makes a copy of a binary tree. Exercises 5.4, 2 asks for a specification for this operation. Do not use the implementation given in the package body earlier in this section. Instead, proceed as follows:
   a. Use a recursive function in your implementation.
   b. Do not use recursion in your implementation—use a stack.
   c. Do not use recursion in your implementation—use a queue.

3. Implement a procedure that returns the mirror image of a binary tree. Exercises 5.4, 3 defines the mirror image of a binary tree.

   a. Use a recursive function in your implementation.
   b. Do not use recursion in your implementation—use a stack.
   c. Do not use recursion in your implementation—use a queue.

4. Implement a procedure that returns an extended copy of a binary tree. Each node in the copy of the tree contains the number of nodes in both its left and right subtrees. Exercises 5.4, 4 asks for a specification for this operation.

5. Implement a function that searches a binary search tree and returns the object in the kth position among all objects in the tree. Position here refers to the position an object would occupy if the objects were all in a sorted list. Exercises 5.4, 5 asks for a specification for this operation.
   a. Implement this function for a binary search tree.
   b. Implement this function for an extended binary tree. An extended binary tree is described in Exercises 5.6, 4.

6. a. Write a recursive implementation of insert.
   b. Write a recursive implementation of insert that assumes the tree is not empty.

7. Function *find_internal* cannot be specified in package *binary_tree_package* in Section 5.4 because type *node_pointer* is only visible in the package body. Thus, *find_internal,* if implemented in the package body, can only be used by other operations in the package body.

   function find_internal (the_tree : binary_tree;
     the_key : key_type) **return** node_pointer;
   *-- **assumes:** the_tree is not empty.*
   *-- **exceptions:** If the_tree contains a node with key value*

> -- *the_key, then a pointer to that node is*
> -- *returned; otherwise a pointer to the node that*
> -- *is the parent of the node that would contain*
> -- *the_key if it were in the tree is returned.*

a. Write an implementation for function *find_internal.*
b. Discuss how *find_internal* might be used to implement other operations such as *insert, delete,*

and *update.* In particular, show how use of *find_internal* reduces the complexity of these implementations.

8. Implement operation *insert* for the representation in (a) Figure 5.49, (b) Figure 5.51, and (c) Figure 5.52.
9. Implement operation *delete* for the representation in (a) Figure 5.49, (b) Figure 5.51, and (c) Figure 5.52.
10. Implement operation *traverse* for the representation in (a) Figure 5.49, (b) Figure 5.51, and (c) Figure 5.52.

■ 5.7 Performance

Figure 5.53 summarizes the number of moves and/or compares needed to perform basic operations on lists and trees. Since a binary search tree orders the objects it contains, it is compared with lists that order their objects by keeping them in sorted order. We see that the expected performance of a binary search tree is superior if inserts and/or deletes are common. In the worst case, however, a binary search tree performs like a list, that is, $O(n)$ operations are needed for each of the operations shown.

Operation	List Linked sorted	List Array sorted	Binary search tree Linked
Insert			
Expected	$O(n)$	$O(n)$	$O(\log_2 n)$
Maximum	$O(n)$	$O(n)$	$O(n)$
Delete			
Expected	$O(n)$	$O(n)$	$O(\log_2 n)$
Maximum	$O(n)$	$O(n)$	$O(n)$
Retrieve by Value			
Expected	$O(n)$	$O(\log_2 n)$	$O(\log_2 n)$
Maximum	$O(n)$	$O(\log_2 n)$	$O(n)$

FIGURE 5.53 Number of operations (moves and/or compares) for basic manipulations of lists and binary search trees.

Recall that the binary search of a sorted array has a worst case performance of $O(\log_2 n)$. So, retrieving information from a sorted array is, among the operations considered, the only one that is guaranteed to be fast in all cases.

A binary search tree can be constructed so that each node has exactly one child. The height of such a tree is n, and its performance is much like that of a linked list. This explains the $O(n)$ worst case performance for the three binary search tree operations in Figure 5.53.

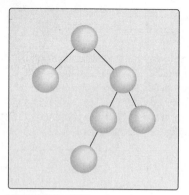

FIGURE 5.54 A binary tree to illustrate expected search length. The expected search length is 15/6.

The expected performance of a binary search tree is more complex. Consider the binary tree in Figure 5.54. The expected search length for that tree is the average of the path lengths to all of its nodes. That is, $(1 + 2 + 2 + 3 + 3 + 4)/6 = 15/6 = 2\frac{2}{3}$.

The expected value in Figure 5.53 for a binary search tree is the average of the expected search lengths for a large collection of trees. The collection is formed by considering all permutations of the first n integers and constructing one tree for each permutation. Given a permutation, a tree is formed by inserting the integers, in order, into the tree.

For example, there are six (three factorial) permutations of the first three integers: (1, 2, 3), (1, 3, 2), (2, 1, 3), (2, 3, 1), (3, 1, 2), and (3, 2, 1). The six trees formed from these permutations are shown in Figure 5.55. The expected search lengths for these trees are (from left to right): 2, 2, 5/3, 5/3, 2, and 2. The expected search length for a binary tree with three nodes is then $(2 + 2 + 5/3 + 5/3 + 2 + 2)/6 = 17/9$. This analysis for a binary tree with n nodes is complex. Details are given in Knuth (1973a), Wirth (1976), and Standish (1980). The result is that the expected search length is 1.4 $\log_2 n$, which yields the $O(\log_2 n)$ entries in Figure 5.53.

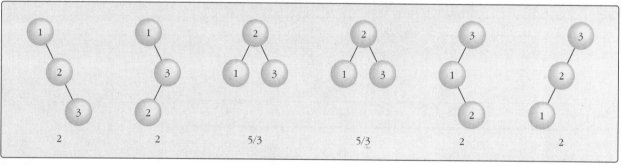

FIGURE 5.55 The six binary search trees that result from constructing trees using the six permutations of the first three integers. Shown below each tree is its expected search length.

Next, Figure 5.56 shows the expected time to retrieve one object from each of five data structures. The slowest performance is for a degenerate binary search tree; that is, a binary tree with n objects and of height n. Somewhat faster is the sequential search of a list stored in either an array or as a linked list. Finally, much faster is the binary search of a sorted array, or retrieval from a binary search tree whose values are inserted in random order. Compare Figure 5.56 with Figure 5.53.

It is clear from Figure 5.56 that the three slowest retrievals have linear, that is $O(n)$, performance. The time scale is too large to tell much about the two faster algorithms. So, Figure 5.57 shows these faster retrieval times with an appropriate time scale. Notice also that the list sizes are a factor of 10 larger in Figure 5.57.

Remember that searching a binary search tree requires about 40% more compares than the binary search of a sorted array. Why, then, does Figure 5.57 show that binary search tree retrievals are faster? One important difference is

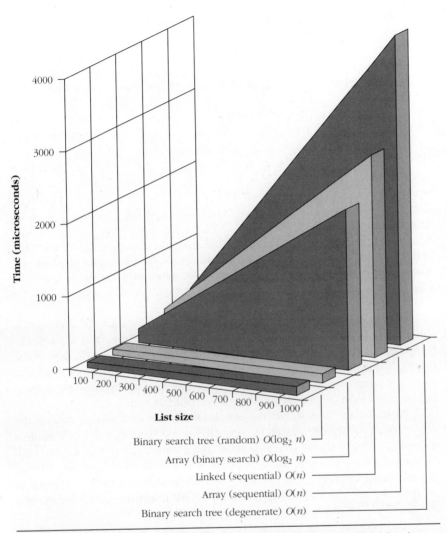

FIGURE 5.56 Observed time needed to retrieve one object from each of five data structures. Each data structure was searched for all objects it contained. The total time for all retrievals was divided by the list size to obtain the time shown. The slowest time is for a degenerate binary search tree. The fastest is for a binary search tree constructed by inserting random key values. For comparison, the time for three list search algorithms is also reported: sequential search of a list stored in an array, sequential search of a linked list, and binary search of a sorted list stored in an array.

that each probe for a binary search requires a calculation to determine the next midpoint and the application of an array mapping function to convert that position into an address. Traversing a binary search tree requires the comparison of two key values then accessing the next node using a pointer whose value must only be read. The major difference is *calculating* the address of the next object to access versus *reading a pointer* to the next object to access.

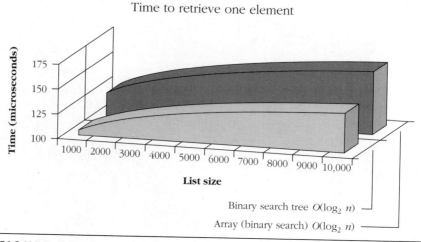

FIGURE 5.57 Observed time needed to retrieve one object from each of two data structures. Refer to Figure 5.56 for a discussion of the results shown.

In addition, remember that the timing data shown are for a particular compiler, a particular implementation of these algorithms, and a particular computer. Changing any of these would alter the results. The shapes of the curves, however, would not change, and the relative performances would be about the same on many systems. You are encouraged to repeat some of these timing studies on one or more systems available to you.

Next, Figure 5.58 shows the average time for an insertion during the construction of a binary search tree containing list size objects. Once again, a degenerate binary search tree is slowest, and a binary search tree constructed by inserting key values in random order is fastest. For comparison, average insertion times during construction of two lists is shown. One list is stored in an array and the other as a singly linked list. A list insertion includes traversing the list to assure that a duplicate value is not added.

The two list times and the degenerate binary search tree time are essentially the time to traverse those structures. The random binary search tree is much faster because it accomplishes the same job (not allowing duplicates) while traversing a path of length $O(\log_2 n)$.

Finally, we compare the time to insert random objects in a binary search tree with the time to insert an object into a list by appending it on the end. These list insertions have a performance that is $O(1)$ and are faster than a binary search tree insertion. But it is important to see that construction of a binary search tree has performance that is much closer to appending an object to a list than to a list insertion that maintains sorted order or that avoids duplicates. This is important because a binary search tree provides both these characteristics: duplicates are avoided, and an inorder traversal accesses tree objects in sorted order.

Figure 5.59 compares the performance of insert for a random binary search tree with the performance of appending an object on the end of a list.

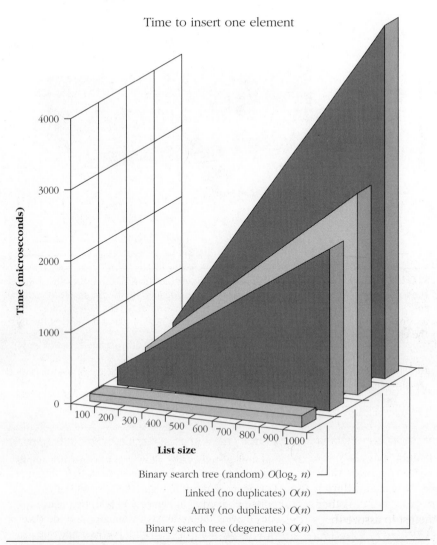

Time to insert one element

FIGURE 5.58 Observed time to insert one object into each of four data structures. The total time to insert list size objects into a list was divided by the list size to obtain the time shown. The slowest time is for a degenerate binary search tree. The fastest is for a binary search tree constructed by inserting random key values. For comparison, the time for insertion into two lists is also reported: a list stored in an array and a singly linked list. The majority of the time shown for the lists is the time to search the list to assure that a duplicate value is not added.

The binary search tree performance is $O(\log_2 n)$, whereas it is $O(1)$ for both list representations.

We have seen that the expected performance of a binary search tree makes it an attractive alternative to list structures if ordering the information based on key values is important. A possible concern is that in its worst case a binary search tree has the $O(n)$ performance characteristics of a list. Possible

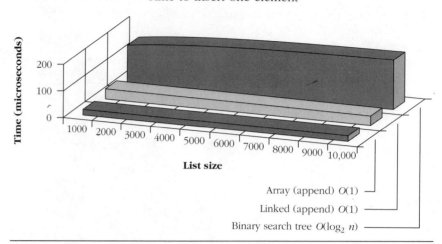

FIGURE 5.59 Observed time to insert one object into each of three data structures. The total time to insert list size objects into a list was divided by the list size to obtain the time shown. The slowest time is for a random binary search tree. The fastest is for constructing a list stored in an array by appending each new object at the end of the list. The effort required for the two list structures is $O(1)$.

adjustments to provide tree structures with $O(\log n)$ worst case performance are described in Sections 5.8 and 5.10.

EXERCISES 5.7

1. Construct a binary search tree by inserting random values. Compute the average number of compares needed to find an object in the tree. Compare the value you compute with $1.4 * \log_2 n$.
Let $P(n)$ be the average number of compares needed to find an object in a binary search tree of size n. Write a program to compute $P(n)$ for a tree constructed by the insertion of random values. Plot the ratio $(1.4 * \log_2 n)/P(n)$ versus n for n in the interval from 0 to 1000.

2. Run timing studies that allow you to construct graphs comparable to those in Figures 5.56–5.59.

3. Provide more detail in Figure 5.53. Specifically, replace each entry in Figure 5.53 with two entries—one showing the number of compares and the other showing the number of moves. For example, the expected number of operations to insert into a list stored in a sorted array is $O(\log_2 n)$ compares and $O(n)$ moves.

■ 5.8 AVL Trees

We have seen that binary trees are likely to have a height that is $O(\log_2 n)$. We have also seen that binary trees may have a height that is $O(n)$ Many operations on a binary search tree are based on traversing all or part of a path from the root to a leaf. A path length of $O(\log_2 n)$ for these operations is desirable, whereas $O(n)$ is a relative disaster. A natural question is the following: Can we insert and delete objects from a binary tree so that (1) the height of the tree is at most $O(\log_2 n)$ and (2) the cost of insertion and deletion is also at most $O(\log_2 n)$? The answer is yes, and we will explore one approach, AVL trees, in this section.

An AVL tree is a special case of a height-balanced tree. A binary tree is a **height-balanced p-tree** if for each node N in the tree, the difference in height of N's two subtrees is at most p. An **AVL tree** is a height-balanced 1-tree. That is, in an AVL tree the difference in height of the two subtrees of any node is at most 1. Figure 5.60 shows three examples.

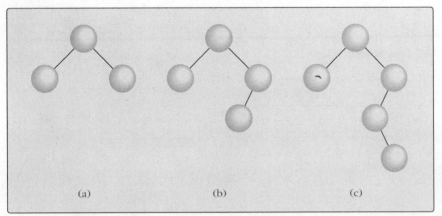

(a)   (b)   (c)

FIGURE 5.60 The example in (a) is a height-balanced p-tree for any p—including $p = 0$. The example in (b) is a height-balanced p-tree for any $p > 0$. The example in (c) is a height-balanced p-tree for any $p > 1$. The examples in (a) and (b) are AVL trees, but the example in (c) is not.

To introduce the discussion of AVL trees, consider the sequence of trees constructed by inserting, in order, the key values $1, 2, 3, \ldots, n$. The resulting binary search tree is shown in Figure 5.61. Two of the AVL trees that result from the same sequence of insertions are shown in Figure 5.62.

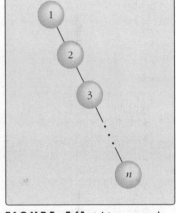

FIGURE 5.61 A binary search tree after inserting $1, 2, 3, \ldots, n$.

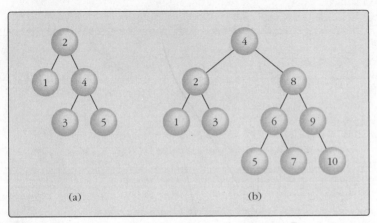

(a)   (b)

FIGURE 5.62 An AVL tree after inserting (a) 1, 2, 3, 4, 5 and (b) $1, 2, 3, \ldots, 10$.

Figure 5.61 shows that the binary search trees produced are essentially lists and therefore have the $O(n)$ performance that characterizes that data structure. Figure 5.62 shows two AVL trees that have the minimum possible height for the number of nodes they contain. AVL trees appear to eliminate the $O(n)$ worst case performance of binary search trees.

We can write the specification for an AVL tree by making simple modifications to the specification for a binary search tree. In particular, we need only add notes to the *insert* and *delete* specifications in Specification 5.1. The result, Specification 5.2, is given next.

■ SPECIFICATION 5.2   AVL Tree Specification*

-- *Structure:*   An AVL tree is a binary search tree with the additional requirement that if N is any
--   node in the tree, the difference in height between N's left and right subtrees is at most 1.

-- *Constraints:* $0 \leq size \leq unknown\ upper\ bound.$
--   Except as noted in the specifications of procedures insert and delete, the specification of an AVL tree is
--   identical to the specification of a binary search tree as given in Specification 5.1. The skeleton of the
--   specification is repeated for ease of reference.

generic
       type object_type **is private**;
       type key_type **is private**;
       with function key_of (the_object : object_type) **return** key_type;
       with function equal (left, right : key_type) **return** boolean;
       with function '<' (left, right : key_type) **return** boolean **is** <>;

package AVL_tree_package **is**

       type AVL_tree **is limited private**;

       generic
              with procedure process (the_object : object_type);
       procedure traverse (the_tree : AVL_tree; the_order : traverse_order);

       generic
              with procedure process (the_object : object_type);
       procedure level_traverse (the_tree : AVL_tree);

       procedure insert (the_tree : **in out** AVL_tree; the_object : object_type);
       -- *results:*   A node containing the_object is added to the_tree.
       -- *exceptions:*   duplicate_node is raised if the_tree contains a node with key value key_of(the_object).
       --   tree_full is raised if the_tree does not contain a node with key value key_of(the_object), but an
       --   additional node cannot be added to the_tree.
       -- *notes:*   An implicit requirement, because formal parameter the_tree is an AVL tree, is that the result of
       --   this operation is an AVL tree.

---

*There is no package body for Specification 5.2. The next package body is therefore Package Body 5.3.

(continued)

Specification 5.2 (continued)

procedure delete (the_tree : **in out** AVL_tree; target_key : key_type);
-- **results:** *The node in the_tree with key value target is deleted.*
-- **exceptions:** *missing_node is raised if the_tree does not contain a node with key value target_key.*
-- **notes:** *An implicit requirement, because formal parameter the_tree is an AVL tree, is that the result of*
--   *this operation is an AVL tree.*

   -- *Specifications for the remaining operations are the same as for these operations*
   -- *in a binary search tree. Several examples are given for ease of reference.*

   procedure update (the_tree : **in out** AVL_tree; the_object : object_type);
   function retrieve (the_tree : AVL_tree; target_key : key_type) **return** object_type;
   function find (the_tree : AVL_tree; target_key : key_type) **return** boolean;
   function empty (the_tree : AVL_tree) **return** boolean;
   function characteristics (the_tree : AVL_tree) **return** status;
   procedure make_tree_empty (the_tree : AVL_tree);

private
-- The **private** clause is discussed in Exercises 5.8, 2.
end AVL_tree;

Without worrying about the details of implementing the *insert* and *delete* operations, we next compare the performance of AVL and binary search trees. Figure 5.63 shows the number of compares needed for the basic operations.

	Binary search tree	AVL tree
Operation	Linked	Linked
Insert		
Expected	$O(\log_2 n)$	$O(\log_2 n)$
Maximum	$O(n)$	$O(\log_2 n)$
Delete		
Expected	$O(\log_2 n)$	$O(\log_2 n)$
Maximum	$O(n)$	$O(\log_2 n)$
Retrieve by value		
Expected	$O(\log_2 n)$	$O(\log_2 n)$
Maximum	$O(n)$	$O(\log_2 n)$

FIGURE 5.63 A comparison of the number of compares needed for basic operations on AVL trees and binary search trees.

Figure 5.63 shows that AVL trees provide the desired upper bound on performance. In general it can be shown (Knuth, 1973a, p. 453) that the height of an AVL tree never exceeds $1.45(\log_2 n)$. Figure 5.63 also provides an overview of relative performance. We will continue to pursue the performance issue in order to develop more concrete results.

Some notation will be useful. Let $\text{AVL}_{\min}(h)$ be the minimum number of nodes necessary to construct an AVL tree of height h. A little thought, and perhaps sketching a few AVL trees, will convince you that $AVL_{min}(1) = 1$, $AVL_{min}(2) = 2$, $AVL_{min}(3) = 4$, and $AVL_{min}(4) = 7$.

Figure 5.64 shows an illustration of an AVL tree. The point of Figure 5.64 is that it shows the relationship between the root and its two subtrees if the tree contains the minimum possible number of nodes for its height. That is, the tree that determines $AVL_{min}(h)$—because it contains the minimum number of nodes for its height—must be composed of subtrees that also contain the minimum number of nodes for their height. These subtrees must differ in height by 1 in order to minimize the number of nodes in the entire tree.

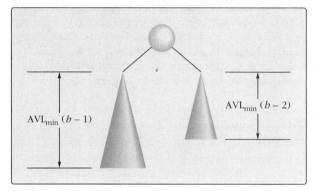

FIGURE 5.64 The root node and its two subtrees if the tree contains the minimum number of nodes of any AVL tree of height h.

Figure 5.64 shows that $AVL_{min}(h)$ satisfies the relation

$$AVL_{min}(h) = AVL_{min}(h - 1) + AVL_{min}(h - 2) + 1$$

Using this relationship we can construct Figure 5.65.

Tree height h	Minimum nodes in an AVL tree of height h	Minimum nodes in a binary search tree of height h	Maximum nodes in either an AVL or a binary search tree of height h
1	1	1	1
2	2	2	3
3	4	3	7
4	7	4	15
5	12	5	31
6	20	6	63
7	33	7	127
8	54	8	255

FIGURE 5.65 The minimum and maximum number of nodes in AVL and binary search trees of a specified height.

Another way to view the data in Figure 5.65 is to determine the possible heights of a tree containing n nodes. This is an important question because the height of a tree determines the number of compares needed to perform all the basic operations.

Figure 5.66 illustrates, in a more graphic way than Figure 5.65, the effectiveness of an AVL tree in maintaining a small height. We are assured, for example, that an AVL tree that contains 1,000,000 nodes will have a maximum height of 28.

Number of nodes in the tree	Possible heights of a binary search tree	Possible heights of an AVL tree
10	4 .. 10	4 .. 4
100	7 .. 100	7 .. 9
1,000	10 .. 1,000	10 .. 13
10,000	14 .. 10,000	14 .. 18
100,000	17 .. 100,000	17 .. 23
1,000,000	20 .. 1,000,000	20 .. 28

FIGURE 5.66 Possible heights of a binary search tree and an AVL tree for a given number of nodes.

It is tempting to now discuss the details of algorithms for inserting and deleting objects in an AVL tree. Our basic objective has, however, been met. Figures 5.63 and 5.66 clearly establish that AVL trees solve the worst case performance problems of binary search trees. Details of insertion and deletion algorithms for AVL trees are given in Stubbs & Webre (1989), pp. 210–216. Section 5.10 will discuss an entirely different type of balanced tree, a B-tree, and will conclude with figures comparable to Figures 5.63 and 5.66.

EXERCISES 5.8

1. Write the specification and the implementation for a function that is passed a binary tree and a positive value p. The function returns true if the tree is a height-balanced p-tree. Consider both recursive and nonrecursive implementations. Consider using function characteristics in Specification 5.1.
2. Refer to the binary tree representation in Figure 5.40. For an AVL tree the representation should be extended to allow each node to record information about the heights of its two subtrees. One way to do this is to add an enumerated type such as

type balance **is** (tall_left, balanced, tall_right)

then add a component of type *balance* to type *binary_tree_node*.
   Replace the **private** clause in Figure 5.40 by the **private** clause described above. How does this change in the **private** clause change Specifications 5.1?
3. Implement procedure *insert* for an AVL tree. Implement procedure *delete* for an AVL tree.
4. Extend Figure 5.65 to include trees of height 9 and 10.
5. Extend Figure 5.66 to include trees of size 10,000,000, 100,000,000, and 1,000,000,000.

▌ 5.9 Heaps and Priority Queues

Priority queues were described in Chapter 3. In this section we introduce heaps and show how a heap can be used to provide an effective implementation of a priority queue. Since a heap can be thought of as a binary tree subject to some specific constraints, a discussion of heaps was deferred until binary trees had been introduced.

5.9.1 Heap Data Structures

Suppose that *the_object(1), the_object(2), ..., the_object(n)* is a sequence of ordered objects. This sequence is a heap if

the_object(i) < the_object(2i) and the_object(i) < the_object(2i + 1)

for all applicable values of *i*. These two inequalities will be referred to as the **heap conditions**. Alternatively, "<" could be replaced by ">=," ">," or "<=" in the heap conditions. Figure 5.67 shows three arrangements of a sequence of integers that form a heap. Each sequence contains the same set of integers. The arrows in Figure 5.67(b) show the elements that are related by the heap conditions.

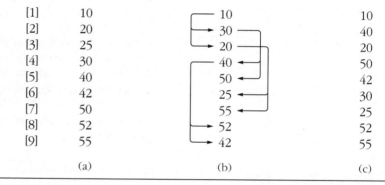

	(a)		(b)		(c)
[1]	10		10		10
[2]	20		30		40
[3]	25		20		20
[4]	30		40		50
[5]	40		50		42
[6]	42		25		30
[7]	50		55		25
[8]	52		52		52
[9]	55		42		55

FIGURE 5.67 Three distinct heaps formed from the same set of integers.

The data in Figure 5.67(a) are sorted. Sorted data always form a heap, but as indicated in Figure 5.67, many other arrangements of the same data also form a heap.

In what sense is a heap a binary tree? Consider the heap in Figure 5.67(b) and construct a binary tree as follows. Insert the elements from the heap into a binary tree filling one level at a time. Start at the tree root and work down toward the leaf nodes. Within each level, the nodes are added from left to right. Applying this technique produces the binary tree shown in Figure 5.68. A digit in brackets, [ ], has been appended to each node to show the order in which it was added to the tree. Recall that the binary tree representation we are now discussing is the same as that presented in Figure 5.51 in Section 5.6.4.

The tree in Figure 5.68 is a complete tree. Recall that a binary tree is complete if (1) each of its levels, except possibly the last, is full, and (2) the nodes on the last level all occur in the left-most positions.

Look at Figures 5.67 and 5.68. The elements related by the heap conditions are precisely the elements that have a parent–child relationship in the binary tree; that is, the elements connected by the arrows in Figure 5.67(b) are

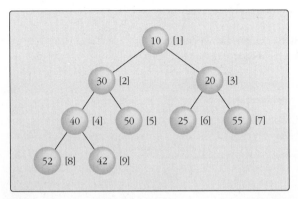

FIGURE 5.68 The binary tree constructed from the tree in Figure 5.67.

precisely the elements connected by the edges of the binary tree. A heap is a complete binary tree in which each parent is less than either of its children.

In Figure 5.68 note that along any path from the root to a leaf, the elements always form an increasing sequence. Since this is true for any path, we conclude that the root element in the heap is the smallest element. This fact makes heaps particularly attractive for implementing priority queues.

We are ready for the specification of a heap. Specification 5.3 follows.

■ SPECIFICATION 5.3 Heap

-- *Structure:*   *An array of objects of user-specified type to which basic heap*
--   *operations are applied.*

generic
    type object_type **is private**;
    type priority **is limited private**;
    with function priority_of (the_object : object_type) **return** priority;
    -- *results:* *Returns the priority value associated with the_object.*
    with function "<" (left, right : priority) **return** boolean;

package heap_package **is**

    type heap **is array** (natural **range** <>) **of** object_type;
    -- *The index type for a heap is unconstrained in order to provide flexibility in the way it is used.*
    -- *For example, refer to the private clause of the specification for a priority queue (Specification*
    -- *5.4). All three heap operations require, however, that heap'first = 1.*

    procedure sift_up (the_heap : **in out** heap; the_target : natural);
    -- *assumes:*   *the_heap'first = 1 and objects in the slice the_heap(1 .. the_target − 1) satisfy*
    --   *the heap conditions.*
    -- *results:*   *The object in position the_target has been "sifted up" so objects in the slice*
    --   *the_heap(1 .. the_target) satisfy the heap conditions.*

(continued)

Specification 5.3 (continued)

procedure sift_down (the_heap : **in out** heap; the_target, last : natural);
-- *assumes:*   *the_heap'first = 1 and objects in the slice the_heap(the_target + 1 .. last)*
--   *satisfy the heap conditions.*
-- *results:*   *The object in position the_target has been "sifted down" so objects in the slice*
--   *the_heap(1 .. the_target) satisfy the heap conditions.*

procedure heap_create (the_heap : **in out** heap; size : positive);
-- *assumes:*   *the_heap'first = 1.*
-- *results:*   *Objects in the slice the_heap(1 .. size) satisfy the heap conditions.*

end heap_package;

We continue with a discussion of the heap operations in Specification 5.3, including, at the end of the discussion, the body for package heap. The generic parameters for Specification 5.3 are identical to those for Specification 3.5—the priority queue package. This makes it easy to use the heap operations in a package body for priority queues. A heap implementation of priority queues, we will see, provides improved performance. Heaps will be seen again in Chapter 6, where they serve as the basis of an effective sort algorithm. Also, in Chapter 9, several important graph algorithms require the use of a priority queue—whose efficient implementation uses a heap.

How can we take an arbitrary sequence of elements and rearrange them to form a heap? To see one approach, consider Figure 5.69. Figure 5.69 shows two views of a complete binary tree. Figure 5.69(b) is a traditional view of a binary tree and its edges. Figure 5.69(a) is a sequential representation of the same tree. The heap conditions are not satisfied. Observe, however, that five of the elements have no children—and therefore satisfy the heap conditions.

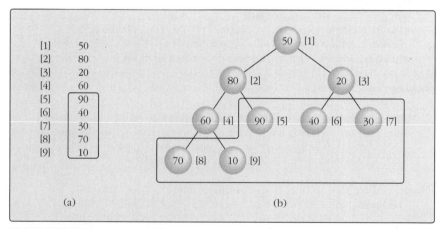

(a)   (b)

FIGURE 5.69 Two logical views of the same data. Boxed elements have no children and therefore satisfy the heap conditions.

The heap construction process is to increase, one element at a time, the set of elements that satisfies the heap conditions. The first step, Figure 5.69(a), is to insert 60 into the sequence below it. Our objective is to add 60 to the elements that satisfy the heap conditions. The technique is easier to visualize using Figure 5.69(b). Since there is only one level of the tree below 60, at most one descendant of 60 will be affected. Observe that if 60 is exchanged with its smaller child, 10 in this case, then the last six elements in the sequence will satisfy the heap conditions. This is the basic operation in constructing a heap—moving small children up one level in the tree.

Next we insert 20 into the sequence of six elements below it. Figure 5.69 is still applicable and shows that there is only one level of the tree below 20. Hence, there is only one element of concern in terms of the heap relationships. This time, since 20 is smaller than its smallest child, no exchange is necessary. The situation at this point is shown in Figure 5.70.

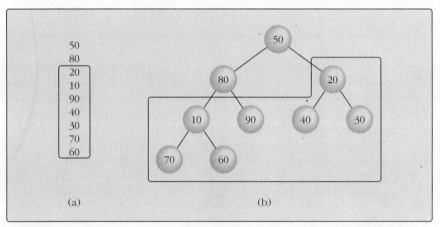

(a)   (b)

FIGURE 5.70 The data after 60 and 20 have been inserted. Boxed elements must, because of the construction, satisfy the heap conditions.

Next we insert 80 among the seven elements below it. The only elements that might be affected by this insertion are elements on a path from 80 to a leaf node. The edges in this path are always between a parent and the parent's smallest child. The path terminates when a node is found that has no child smaller than the element being inserted. For 80, as shown in Figure 5.70(b), the path is from 80 to 10 and from 10 to 60.

If the path length is not zero, the insertion process is to save the element being inserted, move the content of each of the other nodes in the path up one level, and insert the original element into the terminal node of the path.

The final step, Figure 5.71, is to insert 50 into the sequence below it. The insertion path is from 50 to 10, where it terminates because both children of 10 are larger than 50. The final action is to exchange 50 and 10. The result is the heap shown in Figure 5.72.

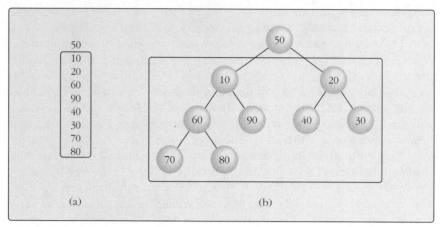

FIGURE 5.71 The data after 80 have been inserted. Boxed elements must, because of the construction, satisfy the heap conditions.

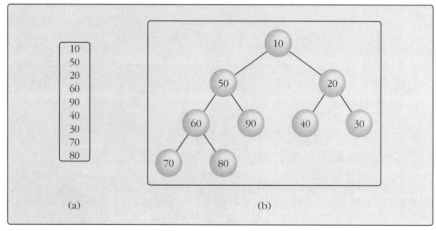

FIGURE 5.72 A heap.

The package body for a heap now provides an Ada implementation of the heap operations.

■ **PACKAGE BODY 5.3**   **Heap—Implements Specification 5.3**

package body heap_package **is**

    procedure sift_up (the_heap : **in out** heap; target : natural) **is**
  -- *Length 9   Complexity 2   Performance* O(log₂n)
     child : natural := target;
     parent : natural := target/2;
     test : object_type := the_heap(target);

(continued)

Package Body 5.3 (continued)

```
  begin
    while parent > 0 and then
        priority_of(test) < priority_of(the_heap(parent)) loop
        the_heap(child) := the_heap(parent);
        child := parent; parent := parent/2;
    end loop;
    the_heap(child) := test;
  end sift_up;


  procedure sift_down (the_heap : in out heap; target, last : natural) is
  -- Length 13   Complexity 5   Performance O(log₂n)
    child : natural := target + target;
    parent : natural := target;
    test : object_type := the_heap(target);
  begin
    while child <= last loop
      if child < last then
        if priority_of(the_heap(child + 1)) < priority_of(the_heap(child)) then
          child := child + 1;
        end if;
      end if;
      exit when priority_of(test) < priority_of(the_heap(child));
      the_heap(parent) := the_heap(child);
      parent := child; child := parent + parent;
    end loop;

    the_heap(parent) := test;
  end sift_down;


  procedure heap_create (the_heap : in out heap; size : positive) is
  -- Length 5   Complexity 2   Performance O(n log₂n)
    next : natural := size − 1;
  begin
    while next > 0 loop
      sift_down (the_heap, next, size);
      next := next − 1;
    end loop;
  end heap_create;


end heap_package;
```

With discussion of the heap data structure complete, we turn to the use of a heap to implement a priority queue. A priority queue specification is given in Specification 3.5. Specification 3.5 is repeated below for reference and because several operations have been added. The only differences between Specification 3.5 and Specification 5.4 are the additional operations *copy* and *iterate*.

■ SPECIFICATION 5.4   Priority Queue

-- **Structure:**   *A set of objects of user-specified type. Access to the objects is based*
--   *on a priority value that the user assigns to each object.*
-- **Constraints:** $0 \leq number\_of\_objects \leq max\_size.$

with heap_package;
generic
    type object_type **is private**;
    type priority **is limited private**;
    with function priority_of (the_object : object_type) **return** priority;
    with function "<" (left, right : priority) **return** boolean **is** <>;

package priority_queue_package **is**

    type queue (max_size : positive) **is limited private**;

    queue_empty : **exception**;
    queue_full   : **exception**;

    procedure enqueue (the_queue : **in out** queue; the_object : object_type);
    -- **results:**   *the_object is added to the_queue.*
    -- **exceptions:**   *queue_full is raised if the_queue contains max_size objects.*

    procedure dequeue (the_queue : **in out** queue);
    -- **results:**   *The highest priority object is deleted from the_queue.*
    -- **exceptions:**   *queue_empty is raised if the_queue is empty.*

    function head (the_queue : queue) **return** object_type;
    -- **results:**   *Returns the object in the_queue with the highest priority.*
    -- **exceptions:**   *queue_empty is raised if the_queue is empty.*

    procedure clear (the_queue : **in out** queue);
    -- **results:**   *Sets the number of objects in the_queue to zero.*

    procedure copy (the_queue : queue; the_copy : **in out** queue);
    -- **results:**   *The_copy is a duplicate of the_queue.*
    -- **exceptions:**   *queue_full is raised if the_copy is too small to contain a duplicate of*
    --   *the_queue.*

    function number_of_objects (the_queue : queue) **return** natural;
    -- **results:**   *Returns the number of objects in the_queue.*

    generic
      with procedure process (the_object : object_type);
    procedure iterate (the_queue : queue);
    -- **results:**   *Procedure process is applied to each object in the_queue until all objects have been*
    --   *processed. The objects are processed in an unspecified order.*

private

    -- *The heap package is instantiated with exactly the same types and functions that are used to instantiate the priority queue package.*
    package heap_pak **is new** heap_package (object_type, priority, priority_of, "<");

(continued)

Specification 5.4 (continued)

```
type queue (max_size : positive) is record
   last      : natural := 0;
   objects   : heap_pak.heap(1 .. max_size);
end record;

end priority_queue_package;
```

We have seen that the objects investigated during either *sift_up* or *sift_down* lie along a path from the root to a leaf of a complete binary tree. A bound on the effort to perform either *sift_up* or *sift_down* is therefore $O(\log_2 n)$. We will use this information to compare three possible representations for a priority queue.

Suppose a priority queue is stored in an array in chronological order. To enqueue an object requires appending the object to the end of the array—so $O(1)$ work is needed. To dequeue an object requires a sequential search of the array to find the object with the highest priority—so $O(n)$ effort is expended.

Suppose a priority queue is stored in an array with the objects sorted according to their priority value. To enqueue an object requires finding its sorted position and moving objects to make a space at that position—so $O(n)$ moves are needed. To dequeue an object requires returning the object at one end of the array, so $O(1)$ effort suffices.

Finally, suppose the priority queue objects are stored in an array so that the heap conditions are satisfied with respect to the priority values. To enqueue an object we place it at the end of the array and execute *sift_up*—so at most $O(\log_2 n)$ effort is needed. To dequeue an object we can (1) return the object in the first position of the array, (2) copy the object from the last position of the array to the first position, (3) reduce the heap size by one, and (4) apply *sift_down* to the object now in the first position. Thus, dequeue requires at most $O(\log_2 n)$ effort.

A comparison of the three approaches just discussed is shown in Figure 5.73. As the priority queue size becomes large, the heap representation will provide substantially better performance. The memory requirement is the same for all three approaches.

Operation	Priority queue Array chronological order	Priority queue Array sorted on priority	Priority queue Array satisfies heap conditions with respect to priority
Enqueue	$O(1)$	$O(n)$	$O(\log_2 n)$
Dequeue	$O(n)$	$O(1)$	$O(\log_2 n)$

FIGURE 5.73 Comparison of the performance of three representations of priority queues.

Based on the performance advantages shown in Figure 5.73, we now present a heap-based implementation of a priority queue.

■ **PACKAGE BODY 5.4** **Priority Queue—Implements Specification 5.4**

```
package body priority_queue_package is

    procedure enqueue (the_queue : in out queue; the_object : object_type) is
    -- Length 6   Complexity 2   Performance O(log₂n)
    -- The performance is essentially that of sift_up.
    begin
        if the_queue.last = the_queue.max_size then raise queue_full;
        else the_queue.last := the_queue.last + 1;
            the_queue.objects(the_queue.last) := the_object;
            heap_pak.sift_up (the_queue.objects, the_queue.last);
        end if;
    end enqueue;

    procedure dequeue (the_queue : in out queue) is
    -- Length 5   Complexity 2   Performance O(log₂n)
    -- The performance is essentially that of sift_down.
    begin
        if the_queue.last = 0 then raise queue_empty;
        else
            the_queue.objects(1) := the_queue.objects(the_queue.last);
            the_queue.last := the_queue.last − 1;
            heap_pak.sift_down (the_queue.objects, 1, the_queue.last);
        end if;
    end dequeue;

    function head (the_queue : queue) return object_type is
    -- Length 3   Complexity 2   Performance O(1)
    begin
        if the_queue.last = 0 then raise queue_empty;
        else return the_queue.objects(1);
        end if;
    end head;

    procedure clear (the_queue : in out queue) is
    -- Length 1   Complexity 1   Performance O(1)
    begin
        the_queue.last := 0;
    end clear;

    procedure copy (the_queue : queue; the_copy : in out queue) is
    -- Length 5   Complexity 2   Performance O(n)
    -- The slice assignment copies all objects in the_queue.
    begin
        if the_queue.last > the_copy.max_size then raise queue_full;
        else
            the_copy.last := the_queue.last;
            the_copy.objects(1 .. the_queue.last) := the_queue.objects(1 .. the_queue.last);
        end if;
    end copy;
```

(continued)

Package Body 5.4 (continued)

```
function number_of_objects (the_queue : queue) return natural is
-- Length 1   Complexity 1   Performance O(1)
begin
   return the_queue.last;
end number_of_objects;

procedure iterate (the_queue : queue) is
-- Length 2   Complexity 2   Performance O(n)
-- All objects in the_queue are processed.
begin
   for index in 1 .. the_queue.last loop
      process (the_queue.objects(index));
   end loop;
end iterate;

end priority_queue_package;
```

This section has presented the basic operations on a heap and has shown the advantages of using a heap to implement a priority queue.

EXERCISES 5.9

1. The figure below shows two views of data arranged as shown in Figure 5.69. Using illustrations similar to those in Figures 5.69 through 5.72, show the construction of a heap for the given data. How many compares and how many moves are needed?

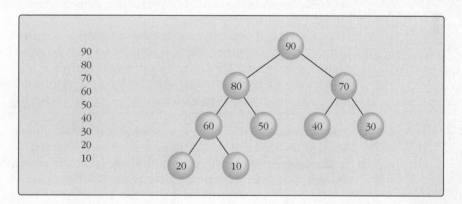

2. How many moves and how many compares are needed to construct a heap using procedure *heap_create* if the initial data are (a) sorted, (b) a heap, (c) in the inverse of sorted order?
3. Procedure *heap_create* constructs a heap with the smallest object in the first position. What changes would be necessary so that the largest element would be in the first array position?
4. Which positions might be occupied by the object with the third largest priority in a priority queue of size 32? Assume the priorities are unique.
5. What are the minimum and maximum numbers of objects that must be moved during operation *dequeue* in Package Body 5.4. Show example priority queues of sizes 7, 15, and 31 that achieve these bounds.

6. Use a random number generator to generate priorities for elements to be inserted into a priority queue. Determine the number of moves and the number of compares required for operations *enqueue* and *dequeue* in Package Body 5.4. Plot these values as a function of the size of the priority queue. Plot the value of $\log_2(number\_of\_objects)$ on the same graph.

7. Replace *heap_create* with an algorithm that uses *sift_up* instead of *sift_down* to construct a heap.

8. Explain why a heap is a good data structure for implementing a priority queue.

9. Consider the following specification.

   function merge_priority_queue (PQ1, PQ2 : heap_type) **return** heap_type;
   -- ***assumes:*** *Type heap_type is an unconstrained array of objects that satisfy the heap conditions.*

   -- ***results:*** *PQ1 and PQ2 are merged together so the objects*
   -- *in the unconstrained array satisfy the heap*
   -- *conditions.*

   One algorithm for *merge_priority_queue* is to insert, using *sift_up*, each of the objects in *PQ2* into a copy of *PQ1*. Another algorithm is to alternate the source of insertions: one from *PQ1*, then one from *PQ2*, then one from *PQ1*, then one from *PQ2*, and so on. Which of these algorithms would require the fewest compares. Refer to Sack and Strothotte (1985) for a discussion of implementing *merge_priority_queue*.

10. If a priority queue is small, might it be preferable to store objects in an array in some order other than a heap—for example, in sorted order or chronological order? Explain your answer.

■ 5.10 B-Trees

A B-tree is a special type of tree that has properties that make it useful for storing and retrieving information. Like a binary search tree, finding an object stored in a B-tree requires searching only a single path between the root and a leaf. Like an AVL tree, the insertion and deletion algorithms guarantee that the longest path between the root and a leaf is $O(\log n)$. The insertion and deletion algorithms are, however, quite different from those used for an AVL tree.

Each B-tree node can contain many elements and can have many children. Because of this, and because it is well balanced (like an AVL tree), a B-tree provides the possibility of very short path lengths for accessing very large collections of objects. Because of this, B-trees are among the most frequently used data structures in computer science—especially for large external files.

We begin our presentation of B-trees with examples that illustrate the insertion and deletion processes. We will include algorithmic descriptions of these operations and specifications for a B-tree. This section concludes with a discussion of the performance of B-trees. Implementation of procedures *traverse,* and *level_traverse* for a B-tree are given in Appendix D.

5.10.1 Insertion Examples

Let m denote the **order** of a B-tree. Each node in a B-tree has between ceiling $\lceil (1/2)\, m \rceil$ and m children, or it has no children. The root node is the only exception to this rule, and it has between 2 and m children, or it has no children. That is, the order of a B-tree gives the maximum number of children of a node in the tree. In a B-tree of order 50 each node either has between 25 and 50 children, or it has no children. The root node of a B-tree of order 50 has between 2 and 50 children. So, the order of a B-tree bounds the growth in the number of nodes between one level and the next. A node with no children is a *leaf node*.

The number of objects in a B-tree node is bounded by ceiling $[(1/2)\,m] - 1$ and $m - 1$. If a B-tree node has children, then the number of children is exactly one more than the number of objects that node contains. If a B-tree node contains 32 objects, then either it is a leaf node (and has no children), or it has 33 children.

Figure 5.74 shows a B-tree of order 5 with the minimum number of objects in each node. The root node has one object, and each of the other nodes has two. (We will not worry about the values of the objects for the moment and simply represent each of them with an x, although they all must have distinct values.) The point of Figure 5.74 is to show the structure of a B-tree in which each node contains the minimum number of objects.

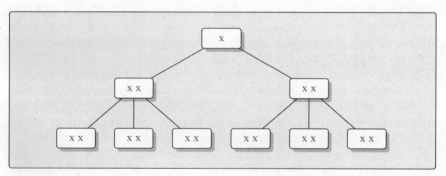

FIGURE 5.74 A B-tree of order 5. Each node contains the minimum number of objects possible.

Figure 5.75 shows a B-tree of order 5 in which each node contains between the minimum (two) and the maximum (four) number of objects. Each node is either a leaf node (with no children) or has exactly one more

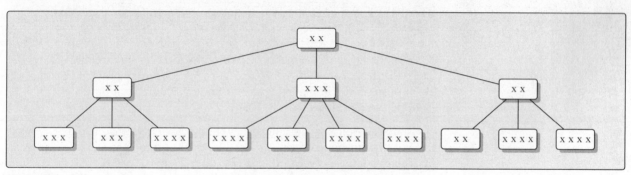

FIGURE 5.75 A B-tree of order 5. Each node contains between two and four objects.

child than the number of objects it contains. All leaf nodes are on the same level. We will see why this is always true shortly.

Binary search trees have an expected search length of $O(\log_2 n)$. The base of the logarithm is 2 because the branching is usually 2-way. During a search we usually take one of two branches, effectively eliminating (1/2) of the data from further searching. If the branching were 10-way, we would take 1 of 10 branches, effectively eliminating (9/10) of the data from further searching. The expected search length would then be $O(\log_{10} n)$.

One motivation for constructing m-way trees is that the expected search length is $O(\log_m n)$. How can we build m-way trees? The most useful and effective such tree in computer science is the B-tree.

We will illustrate B-trees and B-tree insertion using a B-tree of order 5. Order 5 is picked to keep the B-tree illustrations small enough to fit on a page. Each node in our example must contain between two and four objects—except the root node, which must contain between one and four objects. The objects in our example, to keep things simple, will be integers.

Starting with an empty B-tree, insert 10, 20, 30, and 40. The result of these four insertions is a root node containing four objects as shown in Figure 5.76. The objects are stored in each node in sorted order as shown. So, inserting the objects in any order produces the same result. The nodes in this example will be labeled A, B, C, and so on, purely for ease of reference.

If we insert any object into the tree in Figure 5.76, we face the problem of adding an object to a node that is full. The node is said to overflow. This is always handled in the same way in a B-tree—the node that overflows is split into two nodes. For example, if we insert 50 into the B-tree in Figure 5.76, the result is the B-tree in Figure 5.77.

| [A] | 10 20 30 40 |

FIGURE 5.76 The root of a B-tree of order 4 that contains four objects and therefore is full.

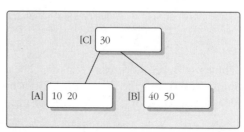

FIGURE 5.77 The B-tree after 50 is inserted into the B-tree in Figure 5.76. Compare Figures 5.76 and 5.77 to see how a B-tree node is split.

Since it lies at the heart of B-tree insertion let us carefully review the steps that lead from Figure 5.76 to Figure 5.77. We attempt to add 50 to node A, the root node, in Figure 5.76. But node A is full, so it must be split. The split occurs as follows:

1. Node A is split by allocating a new node, labeled B, that is initially empty.
2. The two smallest objects, 10 and 20, remain in node A.
3. The two largest objects, 40 and 50, are moved to node B.
4. A new root node, labeled C, is allocated. The median object, 30, is inserted into node C.

The transition from Figure 5.76 to Figure 5.77 illustrates the most important aspect of B-tree insertion: splitting a node. The process, however, needs to be placed in a more general context, as our example will soon illustrate.

If any integer less than 30 is inserted into the tree in Figure 5.77 it will be placed in node A. This is a simple operation since node A is not full. If any integer greater than 30 is inserted into the tree in Figure 5.77 it will be placed in node B. Once again, this is a simple operation since node B is not full. For example, if 25, 42, and 44 are inserted into the B-tree in Figure 5.77 the result is as shown in Figure 5.78. This tree can be searched efficiently because all values less than 30 are in one subtree of the root, and all values greater than 30 are in the other subtree.

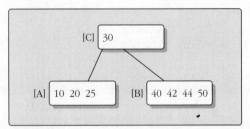

F I G U R E   5.78 The B-tree after 25, 42, and 44 are inserted into the B-tree in Figure 5.77.

Now, starting with Figure 5.78, inserting an integer greater than 30 leads to inserting into node B, a leaf node that is already full. So, inserting an integer greater than 30 requires node B to split. For example, inserting 41 leads to the tree shown in Figure 5.79.

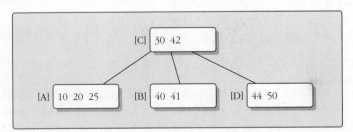

F I G U R E   5.79 The B-tree after 41 is inserted into the B-tree in Figure 5.78.

Here are the steps that lead from Figure 5.78 to Figure 5.79. We attempt to find 41 in the tree in Figure 5.78. The search takes us to node B—the leaf node that would contain 41 if it were in the tree. Node B is full so it must be split to accommodate 41. The node split occurs as follows:

1. Node B is split by allocating a new node, labeled D, that is initially empty.
2. The two smallest objects, 40 and 41, remain in B.
3. The two largest objects, 44 and 50, are moved to D.
4. The median object, 42, is passed up to C, the root node. Since C is not full, it absorbs 42.

We continue by inserting 32, 34, and 55 to the tree in Figure 5.79. No node splits are necessary and the result is shown in Figure 5.80. This tree can be searched efficiently because all values less than 30 are in one subtree, all values between 30 and 42 are in a second subtree, and all values greater than 42 are in the remaining subtree.

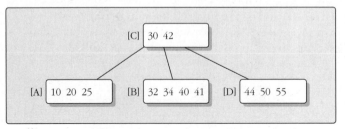

F I G U R E   5.80 The B-tree after 32, 34, and 55 are inserted into the B-tree in Figure 5.79.

Now, inserting any integer between 30 and 42 will cause a node split. For example, insert 36 into the B-tree in Figure 5.80. The result is shown in Figure 5.81.

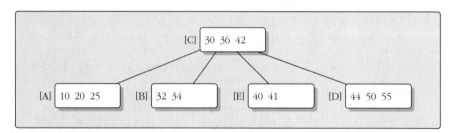

F I G U R E   5.81 The B-tree after 36 is inserted into the B-tree in Figure 5.80.

We continue the example by inserting 14 and 18. A node split occurs when 18 is inserted. We next insert 27 and 29. The result is shown in Figure 5.82. Note how the values in the root node determine the range of possible values in each subtree. In Figure 5.82 the root node has five subtrees, the maximum possible for any node in a B-tree of order 5.

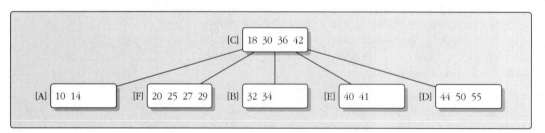

F I G U R E   5.82 The B-tree after 14, 18, 27, and 29 are inserted into the B-tree in Figure 5.81.

Next we insert 22. This causes node F to split. The median value, 25, is passed to C, the root node. But, C is full, so it is split and a new root node is added. The result is shown in Figure 5.83. Examine the transition from Figure 5.82 to Figure 5.83 carefully, as it illustrates the basic mechanism for insertions in a B-tree.

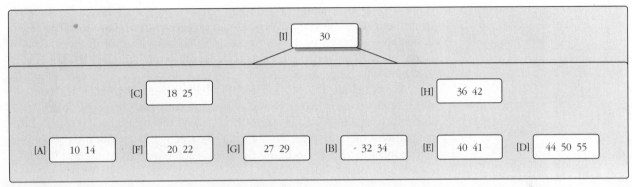

FIGURE 5.83 Inserting 22 into the B-tree in Figure 5.82 causes two nodes to split. The result is shown here.

Based on the example in Figures 5.76 through 5.83 we can write an algorithm for insertion in a B-tree. The result is given in Figure 5.84.

```
procedure insert (the_tree : in out B_tree; the_object : object_type) is
begin
    Search for an object in the_tree with key value key_of (the_object);

    if the search is successful then raise duplicate_object;
    else let leaf_node be the leaf node in the_tree where the search for new_key terminates.

        while leaf_node is full and therefore must be split loop
            Split leaf_node and insert the_object.
            Replace leaf_node with leaf_node's parent, and replace the_object with
                the value of the_object passed up a level as a result of the node split.
        end loop;

        if leaf_node is not an empty node then
            leaf_node is not full and the_object is inserted;
        else add a new root node containing the_object;
        end if;
    end if;

end insert;
```

FIGURE 5.84 An algorithm for B-tree insertion.

Inserting an object begins at a leaf node—the leaf node that would contain the object if it were in the tree. The **while** loop in Figure 5.84 then follows a path from that leaf node back to the root of the tree. As long as nodes on that path are full, a node split occurs and the search continues with the parent of the node just split. But as soon as a node is found that is not full, the insertion is completed by inserting an object into that node. If all nodes on the path to the root are full, then a new root node is added.

Note that the height of a B-tree is increased only by adding a new root node. That is, the height of a B-tree increases only if all nodes on the path from the root to the leaf node where an object is inserted are full. The result is that all leaf nodes in a B-tree occur on the same level of the tree. Thus, a B-tree is well balanced, and the path length from the root to any leaf is guaranteed to be relatively short.

We conclude this section with a final example. To make the example more realistic it involves a B-tree of order 5 with more than 40 objects. It is difficult to fit a tree of this size on the page if the root is at the top and the tree grows down the page. So, the example tree is drawn with the root on the left so that the tree grows to the right. Look at Figure 5.85 to see that it indeed shows a B-tree of order 5.

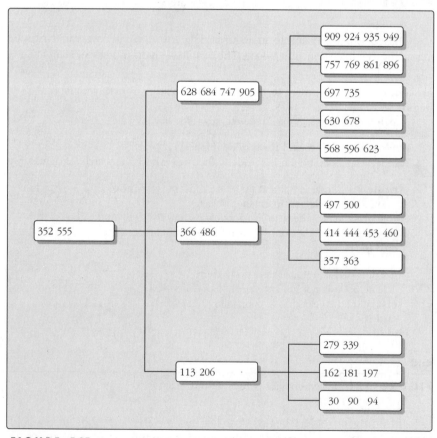

FIGURE 5.85 An example B-tree of order 5.

What values, when inserted into the tree in Figure 5.85, will cause exactly one node split? Study Figure 5.85 to see that the answer is values between 366 and 486.

What values, when inserted into the tree in Figure 5.85, will cause two node splits? Study Figure 5.85 to see that the answer is values larger than 747. Since the root node is not full, inserting a single value cannot cause the height of the tree to increase.

The effect of inserting 800 into the tree in Figure 5.85 can be shown by drawing only the portion of the tree that is changed by the insertion. The result is shown in Figure 5.86.

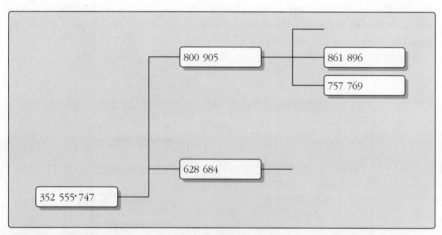

FIGURE 5.86 A portion of the B-tree in Figure 5.85 after inserting 800. Only the nodes whose content is changed by the insertion are shown in this figure.

One of the advantages of a B-tree is that searching for a key value requires traversing only a single path from the root to a leaf. The algorithm for this operation is given in Figure 5.87 and should be compared with the similar algorithm for a binary search tree in Figure 5.24.

```
procedure find (the_node : B_tree_node; target_key : key_type) return boolean is
begin
      if the_node is the root of an empty subtree then return false;
      elsif target_key equals any of the_node's key values then return true;
      elsif target_key is greater than kvₙ then
         find (The node pointed at by pₙ, target_key);          -- Recursive search of the subtree pointed at by pₙ.
      else let kvⱼ be the smallest key value in the_node greater than target_key;
         find (The node pointed at by pⱼ₋₁, target_key);        -- Recursive search of the subtree pointed at by pⱼ₋₁.
      end if;
end find;
```

FIGURE 5.87 Algorithm to find a key value in a B-tree.

In Figure 5.87 let $kv_1, kv_2, \ldots, kv_n$ be the key values in *the_node*. Also, let $p_0, p_1, p_2, \ldots, p_n$ be the pointers that point to *the_node*'s subtrees. Recall that the pointers are either all null, or none of them is null. Note that p_k points to a subtree that contains only key values in the range $kv_{k-1} \ldots kv_k$. What values are in the subtrees pointed at by p_0 and p_n?

Next, using the tree in Figure 5.85 as an example, we will develop an algorithm for deletion.

5.10.2 Deletion Examples

We begin by deleting only objects located in a leaf node of the tree. We will see later that to convert the deletion of any object to the deletion of an object in a leaf node is a simple process—similar to the same process for a binary search tree.

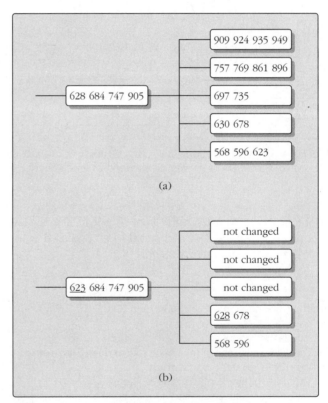

FIGURE 5.88 The B-tree in Figure 5.85 after deleting 630. Only the nodes whose content is changed by the deletion are shown in (b). Objects moved during the deletion are underlined. (a) The subtree of the B-tree in Figure 5.85 that will be affected by deleting 630—before the deletion. (b) The subtree of the B-tree in Figure 5.85 that is affected by deleting 630—after the deletion.

Refer to the tree in Figure 5.85. To delete 935, delete it from the leaf node that contains it. To delete 596, delete it from the leaf node that contains it. In general, to delete an object from a leaf node that contains more than ceiling $[(1/2)m]$ objects, delete the object from the node that contains it.

Next consider deleting 630. For convenience, let N_{630} refer to the node that contains 630. In general, let N_x refer to the node that contains x. Further, if an object is removed from a node that contains exactly ceiling $[(1/2)m]$ objects, then that node is said to underflow.

Taking 630 from N_{630} is not permitted because N_{630} would then underflow. Instead we look at siblings adjacent to N_{630} to see if either of them has an extra object that can be borrowed. In this case one of them does; we can borrow 623 from N_{568}.

However, 623 must be borrowed with care. Note that 628, in N_{568}'s parent node serves as a separator between the values in N_{568} and the values in N_{630}. Simply moving 623 to N_{630} would mean that the separator role played by 628 would be destroyed. To avoid this, 623 is moved to its parent, N_{628}, and 628 is moved to N_{630}. The effect of these changes is shown in Figure 5.88.

A similar example is to delete 500 from the tree in Figure 5.85. To do this we borrow 460 from N_{414}. To do this we move 460 from N_{414} to N_{366}, then move 486 from N_{366} to N_{497}. The result of deleting 500 is shown in Figure 5.89.

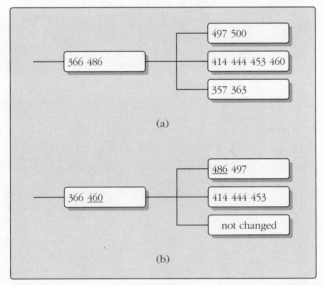

FIGURE 5.89 The B-tree in Figure 5.85 after deleting 500. Only the nodes whose content is changed by the deletion are shown in (b). Objects moved during the deletion are underlined. (a) The subtree of the B-tree in Figure 5.85 that will be affected by deleting 500—before the deletion. (b) The subtree of the B-tree in Figure 5.85 that is affected by deleting 500—after the deletion.

The examples we have seen so far are relatively simple. An object is deleted from a leaf node either by removing it from the node that contains it or by borrowing an object from an adjacent sibling.

The final case arises when there are too few objects to permit a simple removal and there are no extra objects in an adjacent sibling. For example, let us delete 630 from the tree in Figure 5.90.

Node N_{630} does not have an object to spare, and neither do its adjacent siblings N_{568} and N_{697}. We could borrow an object from N_{757}, but the algorithm we will develop here only borrows from an **adjacent** sibling.

We will delete 630 by reversing the node split process used during insertion. We will coalesce N_{630} with one of its adjacent siblings, either N_{568} or N_{697}. First, we show the result of coalescing N_{630} with N_{568}.

In N_{630}'s parent node, the value 628 serves as a separator of N_{568} and N_{630}. If those two nodes coalesce, that separator is no longer needed. So, coalescing

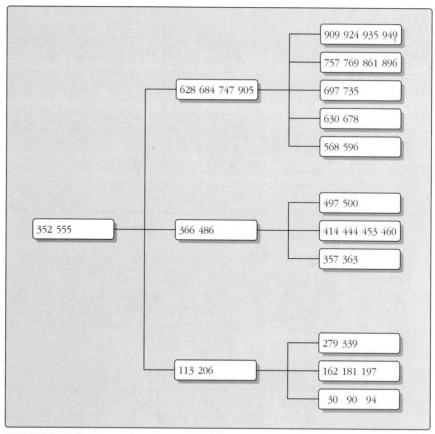

FIGURE 5.90 An example B-tree of order 5.

N_{568} and N_{630} requires that the resulting node also absorbs 628. Since N_{628} contains more than two objects, moving 628 does not cause an underflow. The result of this deletion is shown in Figure 5.91.

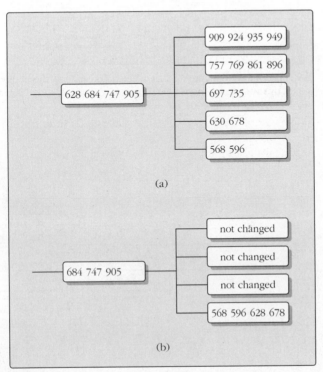

FIGURE 5.91 The B-tree in Figure 5.90 after deleting 630. Only the nodes whose content is changed by the deletion are shown in (b). (a) The subtree of the B-tree in Figure 5.85 that will be affected by deleting 630—before the deletion. (b) The subtree of the B-tree in Figure 5.85 that is affected by deleting 500—after the deletion.

We will delete 630 from the tree in Figure 5.90 again. This time we will coalesce N_{630} and N_{697}. The result is shown in Figure 5.92.

Finally, we will delete 339 from the tree in Figure 5.93. This is more complex because nodes will coalesce at both the third and the second levels of the tree during the deletion.

N_{279} will underflow if 339 is removed so we look to N_{279}'s only sibling, N_{162}. Since N_{162} does not have an object to loan, we must coalesce N_{162} and N_{279}. When these nodes coalesce, their separator, 206, is combined with the remaining objects to produce the tree shown in Figure 5.94.

In Figure 5.94 we see that N_{113} has too few objects, and no object from N_{113}'s only sibling can be borrowed. (If N_{366} contained an additional object, we

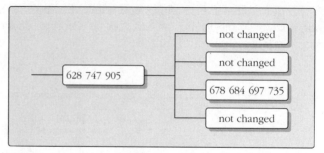

FIGURE 5.92 The B-tree in Figure 5.85 after deleting 630. Only the nodes whose content is changed by the deletion are shown. Compare this result with that shown in Figure 5.91.

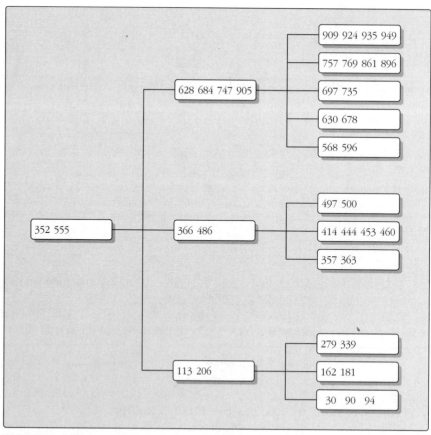

FIGURE 5.93 An example B-tree of order 5.

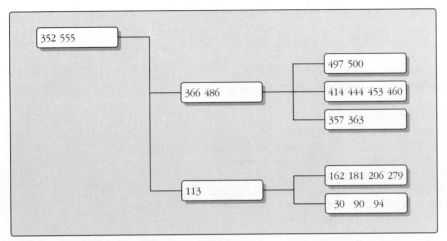

FIGURE 5.94 The first step in deleting 339 in the B-tree in Figure 5.93. Only a portion of the tree is shown. This is not a B-tree because N_{113} has underflowed.

would borrow an object to complete the deletion.) The deletion process continues by coalescing N_{113} and N_{366}. When N_{113} and N_{366} coalesce, they absorb their separator, 352, from the root node. The root node does not underflow because it can survive with only one object. The completed deletion is shown in Figure 5.95.

With these examples completed, the next project is to develop the pseudocode for a deletion algorithm. This algorithm, shown in Figure 5.96, assumes that the object to delete is in a leaf node. We will consider the general case after discussing this special case.

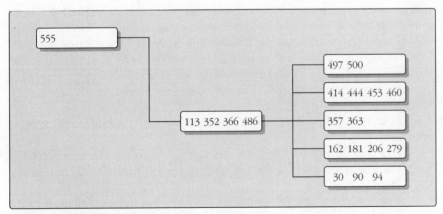

FIGURE 5.95 The deletion of 339 is completed. Only nodes whose content is changed, and their children, are shown.

procedure delete (the_tree : **in out** B_tree; target_key : key_type) **is**   *-- Deletion from a leaf node.*
      finished is a boolean variable initialized to false;
begin
      Search for an object in the_tree with key value target_key;
      if the search is not successful **then raise** missing_object;
      else let leaf_node be the leaf node in the_tree where the target_key value is found.

            while not finished **and** leaf_node is not the root node **loop**
               delete the object whose key value is target_key from leaf_node;
               if leaf_node contains at least ceiling $[(\frac{1}{2})m] - 1$ objects **then** set finished to true;
               elsif leaf_node has a neighbor sibling that contains extra objects **then**
                  borrow the appropriate object from that neighbor sibling and set finished to true;
               else coalesce leaf_node with a neighbor sibling, leaf_node$_{coal}$, assign target_key as the
                  key value of the object in leaf_node's parent that separates leaf_node and
                  leaf_node$_{coal}$, and replace leaf_node with leaf_node's parent.
               end if;
            end loop;

            if not finished **then** delete the object whose key value is target_key from
               leaf_node (which must be the_tree's root node);
               if leaf_node is empty **then** remove leaf_node from the_tree;
               end if;
            end if;
          end if;
end delete;

FIGURE 5.96 An algorithm for B-tree deletion.

What happens if we want to delete an object that is not located in a leaf node? Consider the example in Figure 5.97 (a copy of the B-tree in Figure 5.93). To delete 555 we use a technique similar to the technique we used to delete an element from a binary search tree. We begin by replacing 555 by either the largest value in the subtree that contains values between 352 and 555 or the smallest value in the subtree that contains values larger than 555. Thus, in Figure 5.97, we either replace 555 by 500 or by 568. In either case we are then left with deleting a value from a leaf node.

If 555 is replaced by 500, then the deletion is completed by moving 460 to its parent and 486 to the node containing 497. The result is shown in Figure 5.98. As usual, only nodes whose content changes as a result of the deletion are shown.

If 555 is replaced by 568, the deletion is completed by removing 568 from the leaf node that contains it. This is accomplished as shown in Figure 5.99.

This completes the discussion of insertion and deletion algorithms for B-trees. The next section presents a specification for a B-tree. Its similarity with the specification of a binary search tree is noteworthy. A possible B-tree representation is also given in this chapter.

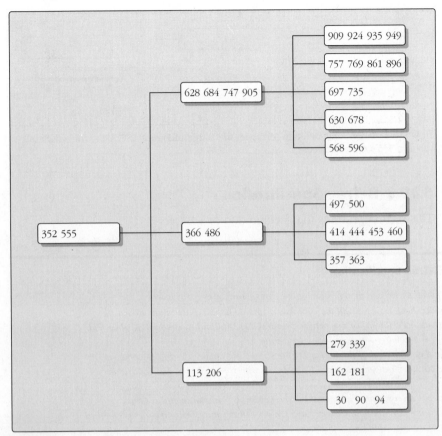

FIGURE 5.97 An example B-tree of order 5.

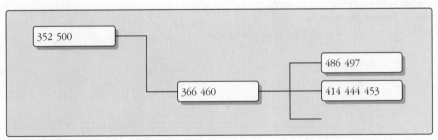

FIGURE 5.98 After deleting 555 from the B-tree in Figure 5.97 using the largest value in 555's left subtree.

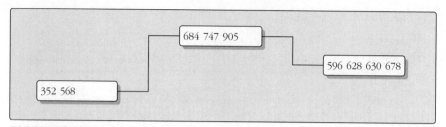

FIGURE 5.99 After deleting 555 from the B-tree in Figure 5.97 using the smallest value in 555's right subtree.

5.10.3 B-Tree Specification

This section presents the specification of a B-tree.

■ SPECIFICATION 5.5   B-Tree Specification

```
-- Structure:  Each B-tree has an order, which we denote m, that determines its structure. A B-tree is a
--             hierarchical structure of nodes. Each node, except the root, has a unique parent. Each node, except the
--             root, is either a leaf node (with no children) or has between ceiling [(1/2)m] and m children. A node with
--             n objects will have exactly n + 1 children—unless it is a leaf node.
--             The leaf nodes all occur on the same level of the B-tree. The root node has between 2 and m children.
--             Each node, except the root, contains between ceiling [(1/2)m] − 1 and m − 1 objects. The root node
--             contains between 1 and m − 1 objects.
--             We assume that each object has an associated key value of type key_type. Function equal is used to
--             assure that distinct objects do not contain equal key values. The key values must form an ordered set, and
--             function "<" is used to both construct and search a B-tree.
-- Constraints:  0 ≤ size ≤ unknown upper bound
-- Notes:  The size of a B-tree increases and decreases dynamically and, at its maximum, uses all available
--         memory on its computer system. The implication is that dynamic memory allocation/deallocation is to
--         be used.

generic
   type object_type is private;
   type key_type is private;
   order : in positive;
   with function key_of (the_object : object_type) return key_type;
   with function '<' (left, right : key_type) return boolean is <>;
   -- results:  Returns true if the value of left is less than the value of right; false otherwise.

package B_tree_package is

   type B_tree is limited private;

   tree_full          : exception;
   tree_empty         : exception;
   duplicate_object   : exception;
   missing_object     : exception;
```

(continued)

Specification 5.5 (continued)

> **generic**
> **with procedure** process (the_object : object_type);
>   -- **results:** *Process the key and data values of an object during traversal.*
> **procedure** traverse (the_tree : B_tree);
> -- **results:** *Each object in the_tree is passed to procedure* process. *The objects in each node are processed*
> -- *after all objects in all nodes in half its subtrees and before all objects in all nodes in the remaining*
> -- *half of its subtrees.*
>
> **generic**
> **with procedure** process (the_object : object_type);
>   -- **results:** *Process the key and data values of an object during traversal.*
> **procedure** level_traverse (the_tree : B_tree);
> -- **results:** *The objects in each node in the_tree are passed to procedure* process. *The order in which objects*
> -- *are processed is determined by a level order traversal. That is, the objects in any node at level* k *are*
> -- *processed after the objects in all nodes at level* k − 1 *and before the objects in any node at level* k + 1.
> -- **notes:** *The order in which nodes are processed on any level is determined by the implementor.*
>
> **procedure** insert (the_tree : **in out** B_tree; the_object : object_type);
> -- **results:** *the_object added to the_tree.*
> -- **exceptions:** *duplicate_object is raised if an object with key value equal to key_of(the_object) is found.*
> -- *tree_full is raised if the_tree does not contain an object with key value equal to key_of(the_object),*
> -- *but it is not possible to add a node to the_tree.*
>
> **procedure** delete (the_tree : **in out** B_tree; target_key : key_type);
> -- **results:** *The object in the_tree with key value target_key is deleted.*
> -- **exceptions:** *missing_object is raised if the_tree does not contain an object with key value equal to*
> -- *target_key.*
>
> **procedure** update (the_tree : **in out** B_tree; the_object : object_type);
> -- **results:** *Let tk be the object in the_tree whose key value equals key_of(the_object). tk is replaced by the_object.*
> -- **exceptions:** *missing_object is raised if the_tree does not contain an object whose key value equals key_of(the_object).*
>
> **function** retrieve (the_tree : B_tree; target_key: key_type) **return** data_type;
> -- **results:** *Returns the_object whose key value is target_key.*
> -- **exceptions:** *missing_object is raised if the_tree does not contain an object whose key value equals target_key.*
>
> **function** find (the_tree : B_tree; target_key : key_type) **return** boolean;
> -- **results:** *Returns true if the_tree contains an object whose key value is target_key; returns false otherwise.*
>
> **function** number_of_objects (the_tree : B_tree) **return** natural;
> -- **results:** *Returns the number of objects in the_tree.*

private

-- *The private clause, which describes one possible representation of a B-tree, is given in the next section.*

end B_tree_package;

Compare the above B-tree specification with the specification of a binary search tree in Specification 5.1. Essentially the only differences in the specifications are those that account for the difference in the number of objects in, and the number of children of, a node. There may be major differences between a binary search tree and a B-tree at the implementation level because insertion and deletion for a B-tree are much more complex. But these differences are not seen at the specification level.

5.10.4 B-Tree Representation

Figure 5.100 shows a **private** clause suitable for representing a B-tree. A B-tree is a record that records the size of the tree and stores a pointer to the root node. Each node contains an array of objects, an array of pointers to children, node size, and a pointer to the node's parent.

Figure 5.101 shows how a B-tree of order 5 might appear if it is represented as described in the private clause in Figure 5.100. Each node contains an array that holds at most four objects and a second array that holds at most five pointers. In Figure 5.101 the root node contains two objects and therefore has three children. In this simple example, the three nodes on the second level are leaf nodes containing three, four, and two objects. Each node on the second level has a pointer to its parent. The root node's parent pointer is null.

```
private
      subtype index is positive range 1 .. order − 1;
      subtype count is natural range 0 .. order − 1;

      type B_tree_node;
      type node_pointer is access B_tree_node;

      type array_of_objects is array (index) of object_type;
      type array_of_pointers is array (count) of node_pointer;

      type B_tree_node is record
         node_size   : count := 0;          -- The number of objects in the node.
         objects     : array_of_objects;    -- The array of objects in a node.
         pointers    : array_of_pointers;   -- The array of pointers in a node.
         parent      : node_pointer;
      end record;

      type B_tree is record
         size    : natural := 0;            -- The number of objects in the tree.
         root    : node_pointer;            -- Initialized to null automatically.
      end record;

end B_trees;
```

FIGURE 5.100 B-tree representation

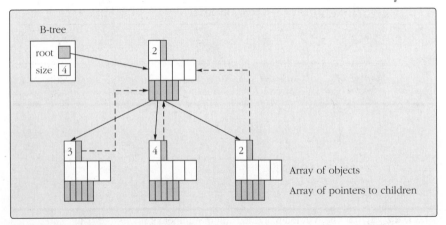

FIGURE 5.101 A pictorial depiction of the representation in Figure 5.100.

Use of this representation to implement several B-tree operations is given in Appendix D. The next section of this chapter discusses the performance of B-trees and compares that performance with the performance of other tree structures.

5.10.5 Performance

The purpose of this section is to get some idea of the performance expected from a B-tree. To do that we will look at upper and lower bounds on the height of a B-tree with a specified order. To warm up to this task we first consider a B-tree of order 7 so that each node of the tree contains between three and six objects.

Figure 5.102 shows both the minimum and maximum number of nodes and objects in each of the first seven levels of a B-tree of order 7. The first level of the tree has one node but may contain between one and six objects. If the first level has one object, then the second level has two nodes—the minimum possible. The minimum number of objects per node is three, so the minimum number of objects on the second level is six.

If there are six objects in the node on the first level, then there must be seven nodes on the second level. If each of the seven nodes contains six objects (the maximum possible) then there will be 42 objects on the second level.

In general, the minimum number of nodes at level $k + 1$ is four times the minimum number of nodes at level k—for all k greater than 2. Similarly, the maximum number of nodes at level $k + 1$ is seven times the maximum number of nodes at level k—for all k greater than 2. Given the number of nodes, multiply by 3 to get the minimum number of objects and by 6 to get the maximum number of objects.

Figure 5.102 also shows the number of nodes possible for each of the first seven levels of a binary search tree. The contrast with a B-tree of order

B-tree of order 7

	Minimum		Maximum		Binary search tree
Level	Number of nodes	Number of objects	Number of nodes	Number of objects	Number of objects
1	1	1	1	6	1 .. 1
2	2	6	7	42	1 .. 2
3	8	24	49	294	1 .. 4
4	32	96	343	2058	1 .. 8
5	128	384	2401	14,406	1 .. 16
6	512	1536	16,807	100,842	1 .. 32
7	1048	3142	117,649	705,894	1 .. 64

FIGURE 5.102 The minimum and maximum number of nodes and objects on each level of a B-tree of order 7.

7 is considerable. On level 7 the B-tree has between 3142 and 705,894 objects, while the binary search tree has between 1 and 64.

Figure 5.102 shows a bound on the number of objects on a particular level. Figure 5.103 shows a similar bound on the number of objects in an entire B-tree of a specified height. The entries in row k of Figure 5.103 can be obtained by adding the corresponding entries in the first k rows of Figure 5.102.

Figure 5.103 shows that a B-tree of order 7 and of height 6 contains between 2047 and 117,648 objects. By contrast, a binary search tree of the same height contains between 6 and 63 objects. The point of Figure 5.103 is not the computations that lead to the values it contains, rather it is to give you

B-tree of order 7—bounds on the number of objects in the tree for a specified height

Height	Minimum objects	Maximum objects	Binary search tree Elements
1	1	6	1 .. 1
2	7	48	2 .. 3
3	31	342	3 .. 7
4	127	2400	4 .. 15
5	511	16,806	5 .. 31
6	2047	117,648	6 .. 63
7	8191	823,542	7 .. 127
8	32,767	5,764,800	8 .. 255

FIGURE 5.103 The minimum and maximum number of objects in a B-tree of order 7 as a function of the height of the B-tree.

some idea of the ability of a B-tree to absorb large numbers of objects with very few levels.

Figure 5.104 presents the inverse of Figure 5.103. In Figure 5.104, given the number of objects in the tree, the heights of all trees capable of storing that number of objects is given. To place these results in perspective, the same results are also shown for binary search trees and AVL trees.

The results in Figure 5.104 can be read from Figure 5.103. Figure 5.104 tells us that if 100,000 objects are stored in a B-tree of order 7, then the height of that B-tree will be 6, or 7, or 8. A binary search tree that holds 100,000 objects will have a height between 17 and 100,000, and the corresponding AVL tree will have a height between 17 and 23.

Objects in B-tree of order 7	Tree height	Binary search tree height	AVL tree height
10	2	4 .. 10	4 .. 5
100	3	7 .. 100	7 .. 9
1,000	4 .. 5	10 .. 1,000	10 .. 14
10,000	5 .. 7	14 .. 10,000	14 .. 19
100,000	6 .. 8	17 .. 100,000	17 .. 23

FIGURE 5.104 The possible heights of a B-tree of order 7, a binary search tree, and an AVL tree that are required to store a specified number of objects.

Figures 5.102, 5.103, 5.104 have been given as a prelude to Figures 5.105, 5.106, and 5.108, which present corresponding information in the general case of a B-tree of order m. These three figures do restrict m (the order of the B-tree) to an odd value. This makes the computations slightly simpler without significantly changing the results.

By adding the columns in Figure 5.105 that report numbers of objects, we obtain Figure 5.106. Figure 5.106 shows bounds on the number of objects in a B-tree with a specified height. When computing the sums for Figure 5.106 it is handy to use the formula for the sum of a geometric series—which is shown below:

$$1 + r + r^2 + r^3 + r^4 + \cdots + r^{k-1} = (r^k - 1)/(r - 1)$$

Let us use the results in Figure 5.106 to look at the expected height of a B-tree of a specific order, say $m = 151$. This is a reasonable value of order for a B-tree stored on disk with each node stored in a page that contains, say, 4096 bytes. Using $m = 151$ in Figure 5.80 leads to Figure 5.81. The last row of Figure 5.107 reports that a B-tree of order 151 and height 6 contains between 5 billion and 11 trillion objects.

The inverse of the table in Figure 5.107 tells us, for a given number of objects, the possible heights of a tree to contain those objects. That inverse is given in Figure 5.108. We see that if a B-tree (of order 151) contains 1 trillion objects, then the height of the tree will be 6 or 7. The height of a binary search

B-tree of order m (if m is odd)

Level	Minimum number of nodes and objects on a specified level		Maximum number of nodes and objects on a specified level	
	Number of nodes	Number of objects	Number of nodes	Number of objects
1	1	1	1	$m-1$
2	2	$(m-1)$	m	$m(m-1)$
3	$2(\frac{1}{2})(m+1)$	$(m-1)(\frac{1}{2})(m+1)$	m^2	$(m-1)\,m^2$
4	$2[(\frac{1}{2})(m+1)]^2$	$(m-1)[(\frac{1}{2})(m+1)]^2$	m^3	$(m-1)\,m^3$
5	$2[(\frac{1}{2})(m+1)]^3$	$(m-1)[(\frac{1}{2})(m+1)]^3$	m^4	$(m-1)\,m^4$
k	$2[(\frac{1}{2})(m+1)]^{k-2}$	$(m-1)[(\frac{1}{2})(m+1)]^{k-2}$	m^{k-1}	$(m-1)\,m^{k-1}$

FIGURE 5.105 The minimum and maximum number of nodes and objects on each level of a B-tree of order m (assumes m is odd). Compare with Figure 5.102.

Number of objects in a B-tree of order m and height h (m odd)

Height	Minimum Number of objects	Maximum Number of objects
1	1	$m-1$
2	$1+(m-1)$	$(m-1)(1+m)$
3	$1+(m-1)\{1+[(\frac{1}{2})(m+1)]\}$	$(m-1)(1+m+m^2)$
h	$1+2\{[(\frac{1}{2})(m+1)]^{h-1}-1\}$	m^h-1

FIGURE 5.106 The minimum and maximum number of objects in a B-tree of order m (m odd) as a function of the height of the B-tree. The values in this figure can be obtained by adding the columns in Figure 5.79 that report the number of objects on each level of the tree.

B-tree of order 151

Height	Minimum elements	Maximum elements
1	1	150
2	151	22,800
3	11,551	3,442,950
4	877,951	519,885,600
5	66,724,351	78,502,725,750
6	5,071,051,000	11,853,910,000,000

FIGURE 5.107 Bounds on the number of objects in a B-tree of order 151 as a function of the height of the tree.

Objects in tree	B-tree height	Binary search tree height	AVL tree height
10	1	4 .. 10	4 .. 5
100	1	7 .. 100	7 .. 9
1,000	2	10 .. 1,000	10 .. 14
10,000	2	14 .. 10,000	14 .. 19
100,000	3	17 .. 100,000	17 .. 23
1,000,000	3 .. 4	20 .. 1,000,000	20 .. 28
10,000,000	4	24 ..	24 .. 33
100,000,000	4 .. 5	27 ..	27 .. 38
1,000,000,000	5	30 ..	30 .. 42
10,000,000,000	5 .. 6	34 ..	34 .. 47
100,000,000,000	6	37 ..	37 .. 52
1,000,000,000,000	6 .. 7	40 ..	40 .. 56

F I G U R E 5.108 Bounds on the height of a tree that contains a specified number of objects. The order of the B-tree is 151.

tree to contain 1 trillion objects is between 40 and 1 trillion, and the height of the required AVL tree is between 40 and 56.

Figure 5.108 intended to give you a feel for representative heights of tree structures. Using the expressions in the last row in Figure 5.106, we can extract expressions for the bounds on the height of a B-tree. A B-tree that contains the maximum number of objects in each node is of minimum height. Thus, the B-tree of minimum height containing n objects is given by,

$$m^h - 1 = n$$

so that,

$$h = \text{ceiling} \left[\log_m(n + 1) \right]$$

A B-tree that contains the minimum number of objects in each node is of maximum height. Thus the B-tree of maximum height containing n objects is given by,

$$1 + 2 \left\{ [(\tfrac{1}{2})(m + 1)]^{h-1} - 1 \right\} = n$$

so that,

$$h = 1 + \text{floor} \left\{ \log_{\lfloor (m+1)/2 \rfloor} [1 + (\tfrac{1}{2})(n - 1)] \right\}$$

So, finally, we see that the height of a B-tree is bounded by $O(\log_m n)$ and $O(\log_{\lceil (m+1)/2 \rceil} n)$. This is a result you might have anticipated without any computation. That is, a tree in which each node has either q children or no children will have a height of $O(\log_q n)$. As Figure 5.108 shows, even with q as small as 2 (which is essentially the case for an AVL tree), a very large set of objects can be stored in a very short tree.

To describe the shape of a B-tree one last time, let us determine reasonable dimensions for a rectangle to surround the diagram of a B-tree (of order 151) that contains 1 trillion objects. Suppose the vertical height is 1 inch per level. The vertical dimension of the illustration is then about 6 inches.

If an object is a nonnegative integer, then the largest integer contains 12 digits (999,999,999,999) and, on the average, an object contains 6 digits. Suppose the integers are displayed using a type style that prints 12 digits per horizontal inch. Then, packing integers in as tightly as possible and ignoring spaces between integers within a node and spaces between nodes, we need 1/2 inch of width per object on the last level of the tree. Figure 5.107 shows that there are 78½ billion objects in the first five levels of the tree. Subtraction shows that the last level will have 921,497,274,250 objects. At 1/2 inch per object that works out to a little over 7 million miles. So, to summarize, the required rectangle is about 6 inches high, and more than 7 million miles wide.

A summary of performance characteristics of three tree structures is shown in Figure 5.109. The performance characterizes two basic types of data structures: lists and trees. Since a binary search tree can degenerate to a list, we see its worst case performance is $O(n)$. In all other cases (except for traverse) the performance is $O(\log_q n)$, where q is the expected number of children of all except the leaf nodes. For binary search trees and AVL trees q is 2. For a B-tree the smallest value of q is $(1/2)\,m$ and this leads to the worst performance. For a B-tree the largest value of q is m and this leads to the best performance. But $q = m$ does not appear in Figure 5.109. Instead, expected performance has $q = (2/3)\,m$. This says that the expected number of children of a node in a B-tree is about two-thirds of the maximum possible. This last result is discussed in Wright (1985), where other expected performance characteristics of B-trees are also given.

Operation	Binary search tree	AVL tree	B-tree of order m
	Linked	Linked	Linked
Insert			
Expected	$O(\log_2 n)$	$O(\log_2 n)$	$O(\log_{(2/3)m} n)$
Maximum	$O(n)$	$O(\log_2 n)$	$O(\log_{(1/2)m} n)$
Delete			
Expected	$O(\log_2 n)$	$O(\log_2 n)$	$O(\log_{(2/3)m} n)$
Maximum	$O(n)$	$O(\log_2 n)$	$O(\log_{(1/2)m} n)$
Retrieve by Value			
Expected	$O(\log_2 n)$	$O(\log_2 n)$	$O(\log_{(2/3)m} n)$
Maximum	$O(n)$	$O(\log_2 n)$	$O(\log_{(1/2)m} n)$
Traverse			
Any Order	$O(n)$	$O(n)$	$O(n)$
Sorted	$O(n)$	$O(n)$	$O(n)$

FIGURE 5.109 Order of magnitude of the effort required to perform basic operations on three basic tree structures.

We conclude this section with the results of two timing studies. Figure 5.110 compares the insertion times for B-trees of three distinct orders with the insertion times for a binary search tree. At first, Figure 5.84 might appear erroneous. B-tree insertions are slower than binary search tree insertions, and the larger the order of a B-tree the longer an insertion takes. But remember that the B-trees in this study are stored in RAM. So the times shown in Figure

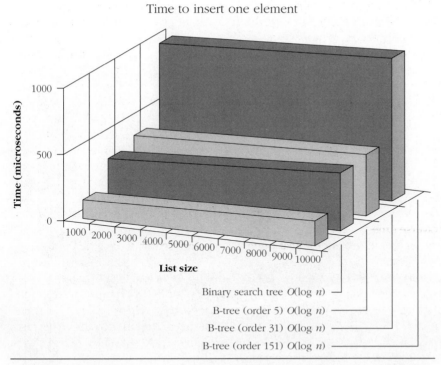

FIGURE 5.110 Average time required to insert one object into four tree structures during the construction of a tree of the size shown.

5.110 are primarily the times needed to insert an object in a node. The data in a node are essentially lists, and the higher the order the longer the lists. From that perspective Figure 5.110 makes sense.

The advantage of a B-tree occurs when it is used to store information on an external disk. Each node can be made into a suitable unit of disk storage such as a sector or block of sectors or track. Accessing a node then involves reading a sector or block. Then performance is dominated by the number of disk seeks, which is essentially the number of nodes that must be accessed. So if we applied the data structures in Figure 5.110 to data stored on an external disk, the relative performances would be the reverse of that shown.

Figure 5.111 compares the average time to retrieve one object from each of five data structures. As is the case in Figure 5.110, the relatively poor performance of B-trees is tied to the fact that the data are all stored in RAM. Thus, the B-tree retrievals are dominated by the time to search the lists of objects in each node. Each node is searched using a binary search, but the overhead associated with a binary search is encountered for each node on the search path. As the path length decreases (due to increasing B-tree order), the overhead associated with initializing and terminating binary searches decreases, and the overall performance improves.

The binary search of an array provides a lower bound for retrieval times for a B-tree stored in RAM. It is a lower bound because the binary search of an array corresponds to the case in which the B-tree order is so large that all

Time to retrieve one element

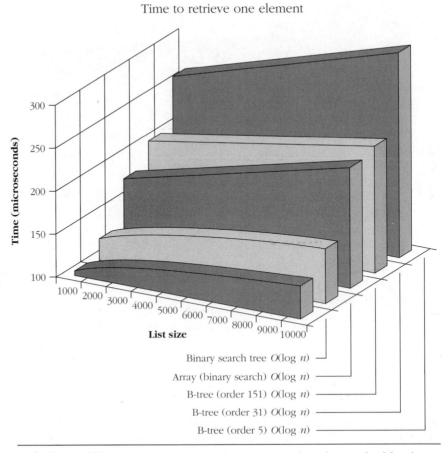

FIGURE 5.111 Average time required to retrieve one object from each of five data structures.

the data fit in the root node. If the data were stored on an external disk, then the time to access one node would be much longer than the time to search a node, and B-tree performance would be clearly the best.

EXERCISES 5.10

1. Start with the tree in Figure 5.97 and insert 510, 520, 530, 540, and 550. Show the tree that results.
2. Start with the tree in Figure 5.97 and insert 502, 504, 506, 508, 510, 512, 514, 516, and 518. Show the tree that results.
3. Start with the tree in Figure 5.97 and insert 930. Show the tree that results.
4. Start with an empty B-tree of order 11. Insert the increasing sequence of values: 1, 2, 3, . . . , n. What is

the smallest value of n such that the tree is of height (a) 2, (b) 3, (c) 4, (d) m.

5. Start with the tree in Figure 5.97 and delete (a) 735, (b) 678, and (c) 279. In each case show the tree that results. Each deletion is applied to the original tree.
6. Start with the tree in Figure 5.97 and show the tree that results after deleting the following sequence of integers: 555, 628, 684, 747, and 905.
7. For a B-tree of order 21, construct a table that shows

the maximum and minimum number of objects in the tree as a function of its height. Using the previous table, construct a second table that shows the possible heights of a tree that contains 10, 100, 1,000, 10,000, 100,000, and 1,000,000 objects.

8. A B-tree of order 3 is referred to as a 2–3 tree because its nodes (except for leaf nodes and the root node) have either two or three children. Discuss the advantages and disadvantages of a 2–3 tree relative to binary search trees and AVL trees. Run timing studies to compare the performance of these three types of trees.

9. The representation of a B-tree in Section 5.10.4 includes a pointer from each node to its parent. A parent pointer can be used during insertion when nodes split and during deletion when nodes coalesce. A parent pointer is, however, not needed for these operations since a stack can be used instead. (a) Explain how a stack might be used to replace parent pointers in an implementation of insert. (b) Explain how a stack might be used to replace parent pointers in an implementation of delete.

■ 5.11 Summary

This chapter introduced several important hierarchical data structures: binary trees, binary search trees, AVL trees, and B-trees. It also described the heap data structure that is convenient to view as a particular type of binary tree. A review of the tree specifications in this chapter: 5.1 binary search tree, 5.2 AVL tree, and 5.5 B-tree, shows that at this level of abstraction they are all very much alike.

The representations of these tree structures are also similar. Space is allocated for each possible object that can be stored in a node, and space is allocated for a pointer to each possible child. In addition, an AVL tree records information about the relative height of its two subtrees, and our B-tree representation includes storage for each node's size and space for a pointer to its parent. The parent pointer is not really necessary (refer to Exercises 5.10, 9), and storing node size is not required but makes several operations easier to implement and improves performance.

The implementation of tree operations shows both the power and elegance of recursion. We showed both recursive and nonrecursive algorithms to emphasize the role of the stack data structure in recursion. We also saw, with level order traversal, the effect on traversal of replacing a stack with a queue. These ideas will be important in Chapter 9 when a more general type of traversal, based on a priority queue, is needed. The similarity between traversal algorithms for binary trees and multiway trees (B-trees) is striking, and you are encouraged to look in Appendix D to view these similarities as well as to enjoy the simplicity and elegance of such implementations.

We saw that keeping a tree balanced in order to assure a short path length from the tree root to the leaf nodes can be important. One balancing approach is provided by AVL trees, and another is given by B-trees. Since B-trees are among the most important data structures in computer science, we carefully introduced the algorithms needed to keep them balanced. (Actually it is B^+-trees that are so important in computer science. However, B^+-trees are a simple variation of B-trees, so you are well prepared to study these intriguing structures.)

Finally, we discussed the performance expected for these balanced hierarchical structures. The performance of basic operations (*retrieve, insert, delete,* and *update*) is excellent because these trees are short and wide, and each operation requires work on only one path between the root and a leaf.

This section concludes with Figure 5.112, which compares the performance of operations on five data structures. In each case (except for a hash table) the data are carefully organized by value—the lists are sorted and the trees are ordered trees. The columns show increasing measures of performance in the range $O(1) \ldots O(n \log n)$.

	Expected number of compares, moves, or objects accessed			
Data structure	*O(1)*	*O(log n)*	*O(n)*	*O(n log n)*
Sorted list (array)		Search	Insert Delete ... Sort	
Sorted list (linked)			Insert Delete Search Sort	
Binary search tree		Insert Delete Search	Sort	
B⁺-tree		Insert Delete Search	Sort	
Hash table	Insert Delete Search			Sort

FIGURE 5.112 Basic operations on five data structures—organized to emphasize visually the close relationship between a data structure and the performance of operations on that data structure.

Basic operations (*insert, delete, . . .*) are placed within the table to show the expected effort to apply the stated operation to the designated data structure. This organization is intended to emphasize visually the close relationship between a data structure and the performance of operations on that data structure. All the basic list operations require $O(n)$ effort—except for searching a sorted list stored in an array (using binary search). All the basic tree operations (except sort) require $O(\log n)$ effort.

The sort operation refers to accessing each stored object in sorted order. Since n objects must be accessed, the minimum effort required is $O(n)$.

Hashing is the subject of Chapter 7—a topic not presented yet. It is included in Figure 5.112 in order to place the other data structures in a broader perspective. Briefly, hashing is the antithesis of ordering data. The order of data in a hash table is random. This explains the $O(n \log n)$ performance of sort for hashed data—accessing data in sorted order requires sorting it first. A valuable exercise is to complete Figure 5.112 for other data structures such as stacks, queues, chronological lists, and binary trees that are not ordered.

6

Internal Sorting

■ 6.1 Introduction

Many different sorting algorithms have been invented, and we will be discussing about 25 of them in this book. This rather alarming number of methods is actually only a fraction of the algorithms that have been devised so far.

Why are there so many sorting methods? ... the answer is that each method has its own advantages and disadvantages so that it outperforms the others on some configurations of data and hardware.

... there are many best methods, depending on what is to be sorted on what machine for what purpose. (Knuth, 1973b)

A good deal of the effort in computing is related to putting data available to users in some particular order. For example, lists of names are frequently printed in alphabetical order, mailing labels are often printed in Zip Code order, and delinquent accounts are often in order according to the length of time the account has been delinquent.

Ordering data has an important impact on searching. Data that are not ordered must normally be searched using a sequential scan of all the data. Ordered data lend themselves to simple search techniques, such as a binary search, which have superior performance characteristics. (See Chapter 4 for a discussion of binary search.)

In this chapter we are concerned with rearranging data so they are in *sorted order*. There are two important and largely disjoint categories related to sorting data—*internal sorting* and *external sorting*. They are illustrated in Figure 6.1.

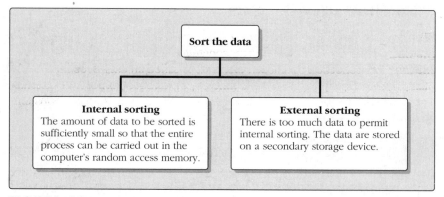

FIGURE 6.1 Sorting data.

Much of the discussion in this chapter assumes that the objects to be sorted are stored in an array. Most of the algorithms can easily be converted to sort objects in a doubly linked list. Only a few of the algorithms work well for singly linked lists, since scanning a list in both directions becomes very expensive. At least one algorithm, radix sort, works well for linked lists, but it does not work for arrays. We will discuss the issues involved in applying sorting algorithms to various list implementations as we proceed.

In this chapter we will be concerned only with internal sorting. There is a large number of internal sorting techniques, and the determination of the best one for a particular problem requires careful analysis of many alternatives.

We will introduce the fundamental principles of internal sorting and suggest references to find out more. There is one internal sort algorithm that is widely regarded as the best general-purpose algorithm available. This algorithm, quicksort, is described in detail in Section 6.3.1.

Internal sorting algorithms are often classified according to the amount of work required to sort a sequence of objects. The amount of work refers to the two basic operations of sorting: comparing two objects and moving an object from one place to another. The major internal sorting techniques fall into one of three categories with respect to the work required to sort a sequence of n objects—simple sort, advanced sort, and radix sort. These categories are shown in Figure 6.2.

Simple sort techniques, discussed in Section 6.2, can be expected to require on the order of n^2 compares and/or moves to sort a list of n objects.

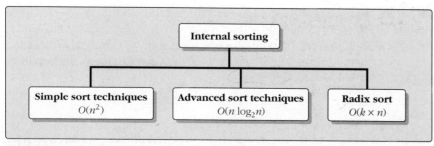

FIGURE 6.2 Internal sorting.

The performance of an algorithm for various representations of the list data structure is important because the user of a sort algorithm will not want to convert the data from one representation to another, sort it, and then convert it back. If the data are in a linked list, the user will want an algorithm that sorts linked lists.

Advanced sort techniques, discussed in Section 6.3, can be expected to require on the order of $n \log_2 n$ compares and/or moves to sort a list of n objects. Radix sort, discussed in Section 6.4, requires on the order of $k \times n$ pointer manipulations to sort a linked list of n objects. (k is the number of characters in the item upon which the sort is based.)

6.1.1 The Sorting Problem

Figure 6.3 shows a list of elements containing information about employees. The information for each employee, contained in one ***element***, is shown on one line. The collection of all such elements is called an employee list. In this example, the employee list contains nine objects and for purposes of internal sorting would probably be stored using either an array or a linked representation.

Element position	Employee number	Name	Department	Salary
1	007	Eckert, John	Hardware	72
2	015	Mauchly, John	Hardware	40
3	021	Backus, John	Language	46
4	036	Turing, Alan	Cryptography	74
5	042	Good, I. J.	Cryptography	40
6	049	von Neumann, John	Language	69
7	077	Hopper, Grace	Language	37
8	098	Babbage, Charles	Hardware	74
9	103	Lovelace, Ada	Language	64

FIGURE 6.3 Employee file sorted into ascending order by employee number.

Each object contains a number of ***fields.*** In our example, each object has four fields and one object position. ***Object position*** refers to the location of the object within the list and is not stored as part of the object. If the list is stored using an array, position is also the ***index, or subscript,*** value of an object.

Any particular copy of a list can be sorted with respect to at most one of its fields (or perhaps a concatenation of several fields). We will call that field the ***sort field, or sort item.*** Sorting a list thus refers to placing the objects in the list in order with respect to the values in the sort item. The sort item can be any item, or combination of items, as long as the values in that item, or combination of items, can be ordered.

For example, if we sort the list in Figure 6.3 using salary as the sort item, we get the list shown in Figure 6.4.

Element position	Employee number	Name	Department	Salary
1	077	Hopper, Grace	Language	37
2	015	Mauchly, John	Hardware	40
3	042	Good, I. J.	Cryptography	40
4	021	Backus, John	Language	46
5	103	Lovelace, Ada	Language	64
6	049	von Neumann, John	Language	69
7	007	Eckert, John	Hardware	72
8	036	Turing, Alan	Cryptography	74
9	103	Babbage, Charles	Language	64

FIGURE 6.4 Employee file sorted into ascending order by salary.

Salary	Element position
37	7
40	2
40	5
46	3
64	9
69	6
72	1
74	4
74	8

FIGURE 6.5 Employee list sorted into ascending order by salary. Element position points to the element as stored in Figure 6.3.

In Figure 6.4 the data in each object have been moved to a new position relative to the other objects. (Note the new values of object position.) If each object contains a lot of data in addition to the value in the sort item, it may be prudent to sort only the sort item without involving the other data in the object. This can result in a substantial performance improvement if the sort technique requires numerous moves of the objects being sorted, as illustrated in Figure 6.5.

Figure 6.5 shows an alternative to Figure 6.4. It is obtained by sorting the salary field (the sort item) of each object, together with the object's position in the list. This permits the list to be sorted without the expense of moving all the data in each object. The object position serves as a pointer to the complete object as it is actually stored (see Figure 6.3). The abbreviated list is often called an ***index array* or *index list.***

Section 6.1.1 establishes an understanding about the basic nature of internal sorting algorithms. To summarize, lists are generally sorted on the value of a particular field. The sort process may involve moving entire objects, or the objects of an index list, or not moving objects at all. The basic sort mechanisms, however, are not affected by how much of each object participates in the sorting operation.

6.1.2 Specification of Sorting Algorithms

Specification 6.1 provides a common interface to the sorting algorithms of this chapter. An interface for all the algorithms is gathered together in one place in order to emphasize the uniformity with which they are accessed. Two exceptions will be discussed: The first will allow sorting a linked list of objects (Section 6.2.4), and the second will provide an interface for a radix sort (Section 6.4).

■ SPECIFICATION 6.1   Sorting Algorithms

-- *The specifications for the sort procedures are collected below for reference and to show their*
-- *uniformity. The implementations, however, are scattered throughout Chapter 6. The*
-- *expected number of compares to execute each sort algorithm is shown as a comment.*

generic
       type object_type **is private**;
       type sort_type **is private**;
       type objects_to_sort **is array** (integer **range** <>) **of** object_type;
       with function sort_on (the_object : object_type) **return** sort_type;
       with function "<" (left, right : sort_type) **return** boolean **is** <>;

package sort_package **is**

       procedure insertion_sort (the_objects : **in out** objects_to_sort);   -- O(n²)
       procedure selection_sort (the_objects : **in out** objects_to_sort);   -- O(n²)
       procedure exchange_sort (the_objects : **in out** objects_to_sort);   -- O(n²)
       procedure quicksort   (the_objects : **in out** objects_to_sort);   -- O(n log_2n)
       procedure mergesort   (the_objects : **in out** objects_to_sort);   -- O(n log_2n)

   -- *results:*   *For each of the five procedures above, the components of the_objects are sorted into ascending order*
   --   *according to the sort_type values of the_objects.*
   -- *notes:*   *Sorting into descending order is accomplished by instantiating "<" with ">".*

       procedure heapsort   (the_objects : **in out** objects_to_sort);   -- O(n log_2n)

   -- *results:*   *The components of the_objects are sorted into descending order according to the*
   --   *sort_type values of the_objects.*
   -- *notes:*   *Sorting into ascending order is accomplished by instantiating "<" with ">".*

end sort_package;

EXERCISES 6.1

1.   Replace Specification 6.1 with a specification to sort a linked list of objects. Use a **private** clause if appropriate.
2.   Replace Specification 6.1 with a specification that includes an array of pointers to the components of the collection of objects to sort. Name the array of pointers PTC. Each sort procedure rearranges the components of PTC so that the *k*th object, in sorted order, is accessed by PTC *(k)*. The advantage of this approach is that it eliminates the need to rearrange the objects that may be large and time consuming to move. Instead, only pointers need to be moved.
3.   Replace Specification 6.1 with a specification that includes an unconstrained array of integers. Name the array of integers *sorted_access*. Each sort procedure rearranges the components of *sorted_access* so that the *k*th object, in sorted order, is accessed by OTS (*sorted_access*(*k*)). The advantage of this approach is that it eliminates the need to rearrange the objects that may be large and time consuming to move. Instead, only integers need to be moved.
4.   a. Instantiate *basic_sorts_package* to sort an array of integers.
     b. Instantiate *basic_sorts_package* to sort an array of objects, each of the following record type.

type days **is** (mon, tues, wed, thurs, fri, sat, sun);

type sort_object **is record**
      int   : integer;
      flt   : float;
      str   : string (1 .. 10);
      bool   : boolean;
      day   : days;
end record;

Give the instantiations needed to sort with respect to each of the five fields and in both ascending and descending order. Give the instantiation needed to sort with respect to two of the five fields.

■ 6.2 Simple Sort Algorithms

In this section we will discuss three simple algorithms that require $O(n^2)$ compares to sort a list of n objects. In each case we will present an implementation of the algorithm, show its application to a sequence of 15 integers, and discuss its performance. The results of some timing trials will conclude this section.

Several of the algorithms in this chapter exchange or swap the values of two objects. We will use procedure *swap*, Figure 6.6, for this purpose. For performance reasons this operation should probably be implemented without the overhead of a procedure call. One way to accomplish this is to use pragma inline *(swap)* as part of the implementation. Because our primary interest is a clear exposition of the basic algorithms, however, we will assume that swap as shown in Figure 6.6 is always available.

procedure swap (first_object, second_object : **in out** object_type) **is**
      temp : object_type := first_object;
begin
      first_object := second_object; second_object := temp;
end swap;
pragma inline (swap)

FIGURE 6.6 An algorithm to exchange the values of two objects.

6.2.1 Selection Sort

Selection sort works by finding the smallest object and placing it first, then finding the smallest object in the remaining list and placing it second, then finding the smallest object in the remaining list and placing it third, and so on. Figure 6.7 summarizes the process.

	Outer loop	Inner loop
Description	Move the jth smallest value into the jth position (its sorted position) in the array.	Find the jth smallest value.

FIGURE 6.7 Description of the roles of the inner and outer loops in selection sort.

Look at the implementation of selection sort in Figure 6.8. Like all simple sort algorithms it has nested loops—an outer loop and an inner loop. The outer loop is executed once for each array position from *the_objects'first* through *the_objects'last* − *1*. Execution of the outer loop moves the *j*th smallest object into its sorted position—the *j*th position in the array.

```
procedure selection_sort (the_objects : in out objects_to_sort) is
-- Length 8   Complexity 5   Performance O(n²)
      smallest : integer;
begin
      for j in the_objects'first .. the_objects'last − 1 loop
        smallest := j;

        for q in j + 1 .. the_objects'last loop
          if sort_on(the_objects(q)) < sort_on(the_objects(smallest)) then
            smallest := q;
          end if;
        end loop;

        if smallest > j then
          swap (the_objects(smallest), the_objects(j));
        end if;
      end loop;
end selection_sort;
```

FIGURE 6.8 An algorithm for selection sort. Note that each execution of the inner loop requires one compare and no moves. The moves all occur in the outer loop.

The inner loop searches for the smallest object in positions *j .. the_objects'last* and records that position as the value of *smallest_index*. After the inner loop finds the index of the smallest object, the outer loop swaps the smallest object with the object in position *j*. The result is that the object in position *j* is sorted and will not be moved again.

When you examine the code in Figure 6.8, refer to Figure 6.7 so you don't lose sight of the basic objectives of the inner and outer loops. Also refer ahead to the example in Figure 6.9 that shows the details of applying *selection_sort* to specific data. Study these three figures in parallel—not individually.

Figure 6.9 shows the effect of applying selection sort to a sequence of integers. The sequence is shown each time execution of the outer loop begins. The integers that have been placed in their sorted positions are underlined. The integers that will be swapped, during the next execution of the outer loop are shown in brackets, [ ]. Rows 2, 8, 11, and 13 do not show any integers in brackets. The reason is that the smallest element is already in its sorted position.

Figure 6.10 summarizes the number of moves and compares during selection sort. The first time the outer loop is executed the inner loop is executed $n − 1$ times. The second time the outer loop is executed the inner loop is executed $n − 2$ times. This continues with the result that the inner loop is executed $(n − 1) + (n − 2) + \cdots + 1$ times. Since the outer loop

[26]	22	48	24	82	86	43	50	72	[20]	72	89	34	54	66
20	22	48	24	82	86	43	50	72	26	72	89	34	54	66
20	22	[48]	[24]	82	86	43	50	72	26	72	89	34	54	66
20	22	24	[48]	82	86	43	50	72	[26]	72	89	34	54	66
20	22	24	26	[82]	86	43	50	72	48	72	89	[34]	54	66
20	22	24	26	34	[86]	[43]	50	72	48	72	89	82	54	66
20	22	24	26	34	43	[86]	50	72	[48]	72	89	82	54	66
20	22	24	26	34	43	48	50	72	86	72	89	82	54	66
20	22	24	26	34	43	48	50	[72]	86	72	89	82	[54]	66
20	22	24	26	34	43	48	50	54	[86]	72	89	82	72	[66]
20	22	24	26	34	43	48	50	54	66	72	89	82	72	86
20	22	24	26	34	43	48	50	54	66	72	[89]	82	[72]	86
20	22	24	26	34	43	48	50	54	66	72	72	82	89	86
20	22	24	26	34	43	48	50	54	66	72	72	82	[89]	[86]
20	22	24	26	34	43	48	50	54	66	72	72	82	86	89

FIGURE 6.9 Application of the selection sort algorithm. Compare Figures 6.7 and 6.9 to make sure you see how selection sort works.

contains no compares and at most one swap and the inner loop contains one compare and no swaps, the results in Figure 6.10 follow.

Note that both loops are **for** loops so the number of times they are executed is not affected by the order of the data that are sorted. Also note that no moves occur in the inner loop.

	Outer loop	Inner loop
Executions	$n - 1$	$1 + 2 + \cdots + (n - 1)$ $= (\frac{1}{2})\, n\, (n - 1)$ $= (\frac{1}{2})\, n^2 + \cdots$
Compares	0	$= (\frac{1}{2})\, n^2 + \cdots$
Swaps	$\leq (n - 1)$	0

FIGURE 6.10 The number of moves and compares required for selection sort of an array.

For random data, the work required for selection sort is $O(n^2)$ compares and $O(n)$ moves. If the initial data are sorted, the **if** statement keeps swap from being executed and there are 0 moves—but the number of compares is the same—$O(n^2)$. If the initial data are in inverse order, the number of compares remains $O(n^2)$, and the number of moves is the maximum, $3\,(n - 1) = O(n)$. Figure 6.10 summarizes these performance results.

Figure 6.11 extends Figure 6.10 to three different initial orders of the data. The number of compares is the same in every case because both the inner and outer loops are **for** loops. The number of swaps in the outer loop is in an **if** statement, so is not executed if the next smallest element is already in position. This is always the case for sorted data; it is never the case for

	Initial data is random	Initial data is sorted	Initial data is inverse
Compares	$(\frac{1}{2}) n^2 + O(n)$	$(\frac{1}{2}) n^2 + O(n)$	$(\frac{1}{2}) n^2 + O(n)$
Swaps	$\leq (n - 1)$	0	$(n - 1)$

FIGURE 6.11 The number of moves and compares required for selection sort of an array assuming three different initial orders of the data to sort.

inverse data, and is occasionally the case for random data. The results are given in Figure 6.11.

6.2.2 Insertion Sort

Insertion sort begins by swapping the last two objects, if necessary, to form a sorted list of length 2. Then the third from last object is placed among the last two to form a sorted list of length 3. Then the fourth from last object is placed among the last three to form a sorted list of length 4. This process continues until the first object is placed in its sorted position and the list is sorted. Figure 6.12 summarizes the process.

	Outer loop	Inner loop
Description	The objects in positions $j + 1$ .. the_objects'last are sorted relative to each other when execution of the loop begins. the_objects(j) is inserted into this sublist so the objects in positions j .. the_objects'last are sorted relative to each other.	Find the position at which to insert the_objects(j).

FIGURE 6.12 Description of the outer and inner loops during insertion sort. Compare these descriptions with the implementation in Figure 6.13.

Figure 6.13 shows an implementation of insertion sort. When the outer loop begins execution, the objects in positions $j + 1$ .. the_objects'last are in sorted order relative to each other. The outer loop takes the object in position j and inserts it among the objects in positions $j + 1$ .. the_objects'last so the objects in positions j .. the_objects'last are sorted. The inner loop determines where the insertion should occur.

When you examine the code in Figure 6.13, refer to Figure 6.12 so you don't lose sight of the basic objectives of the inner and outer loops. Also refer ahead to the example in Figure 6.14 that shows the details of applying insertion_sort to specific data. Study these three figures in parallel.

Figure 6.14 shows the effect of applying insertion sort to a sequence of integers. The sequence is shown each time execution of the outer loop begins. The integers that have been placed in their sorted positions are underlined. The integer that will be moved to its relative sorted position, during the next

```
procedure insertion_sort (the_objects : in out objects_to_sort) is
-- Length 11   Complexity 5   Performance O(n²)
      temp    : object_type;
      k       : integer;
begin
      for j in reverse the_objects'first .. the_objects'last − 1 loop
          k := j + 1;

          while sort_on(the_objects(k)) < sort_on(the_objects(j)) loop
              k := k + 1;
              exit when k > the_objects'last;
          end loop;

          if k > j + 1 then
              temp := the_objects(j);
              the_objects(j .. k − 2) := the_objects(j + 1 .. k − 1);
              the_objects(k − 1) := temp;
          end if;
      end loop;
end insertion_sort;
```

FIGURE 6.13 An algorithm for insertion sort. The inner loop contains one compare. The outer loop contains all the moves.

26	22	48	24	82	86	43	50	72	20	72	89	34	[54]	66
26	22	48	24	82	86	43	50	72	20	72	89	[34]	54	66
26	22	48	24	82	86	43	50	72	20	72	[89]	{34	54	66}
26	22	48	24	82	86	43	50	72	20	[72]	{34	54	66}	89
26	22	48	24	82	86	43	50	72	[20]	34	54	66	72	89
26	22	48	24	82	86	43	50	[72]	{20	34	54	66}	72	89
26	22	48	24	82	86	43	[50]	{20	34}	54	66	72	72	89
26	22	48	24	82	86	[43]	{20	34}	50	54	66	72	72	89
26	22	48	24	82	[86]	{20	34	43	50	54	66	72	72}	89
26	22	48	24	[82]	{20	34	43	50	54	66	72	72}	86	89
26	22	48	[24]	{20}	34	43	50	54	66	72	72	82	86	89
26	22	[48]	{20	24	34	43}	50	54	66	72	72	82	86	89
26	[22]	{20}	24	34	43	48	50	54	66	72	72	82	86	89
[26]	{20	22	24}	34	43	48	50	54	66	72	72	82	86	89
20	22	24	26	34	43	48	50	54	66	72	72	82	86	89

FIGURE 6.14 Application of the insertion sort algorithm. Compare Figures 6.13 and 6.14 to make sure you see how selection sort works.

execution of the outer loop, is shown in brackets, [ ]. The sequence of objects that will be moved one position to the left, by the slice assignment in Figure 6.13, is shown in braces, { }.

Observe that the values in braces on any line appear together on the line below but moved one position to the left. It is the slice assignment that makes that move. If a row does not have any objects in braces, the object in brackets is not moved—it is already sorted relative to the objects that follow it in the list.

Figure 6.15 summarizes the moves and compares required by insertion sort. If the array contains n objects the outer loop is executed $n - 1$ times. The number of executions of the inner loop depends on the data to be sorted. The inner loop searches forward until it finds the target insertion point. On the average the insertion will occur in the middle of the list being searched, so the number of executions is $(\frac{1}{2}) (n - 1 + n - 2 + \cdots + 1)$, which is half the executions of the inner loop during selection sort.

	Outer loop	*Inner loop*
Executions	$n - 1$	$(\frac{1}{2})(1 + 2 + \cdots + (n - 1))$
		$= (\frac{1}{4})\, n\, (n - 1)$
		$= (\frac{1}{4})\, n^2 + \cdots$
Compares	0	$= (\frac{1}{4})\, n^2 + \cdots$
Slice moves	$\leq (n - 1)$	0
Moves	$\leq 2(n - 1)$	0

FIGURE 6.15 The number of moves and compares required for insertion sort of an array.

Again, note that no moves occur in the inner loop. Thus, the work required for insertion sort is $O(n^2)$ compares, $O(n)$ slice assignments, and $O(n)$ moves. The number of components moved by the slice assignment equals the number of executions of the inner loop, however, so the number of components actually moved is $O(n^2)$.

If the data are initially sorted, the inner loop will be executed only once for each execution of the outer loop. The result is that, for sorted data, the effort required for insertion sort is $n - 1$ compares and 0 moves—as contrasted with selection sort, which requires $O(n^2)$ compares no matter how the initial data are ordered.

If the data are initially in inverse order, the inner loop is executed the maximum number of times, $(\frac{1}{2})\, n\, (n - 1)$, which equals the number of compares. The number of slice assignments is $n - 1$, but the total number of objects moved is $3 + 4 + \cdots + (n + 1) = (\frac{1}{2})\, (n + 4)\, (n - 1)$. Figure 6.16 summarizes the performance of insertion sort.

	Initial data are random	*Initial data are sorted*	*Initial data are inverse*
Compares	$(\frac{1}{4})\, n^2 + O(n)$	$n - 1$	$(\frac{1}{2})\, n^2 + O(n)$
Slice moves	$\leq (n - 1)$	0	$(n - 1)$
Moves	$\leq 2\, (n - 1)$	0	$2\, (n - 1)$

FIGURE 6.16 The number of moves and compares required for insertion sort of an array assuming three different initial orders of the data to sort.

It is worth noting the importance of slice assignment to the implementation of insertion sort. Without slice assignment the inner loop in the procedure in Figure 6.13 is replaced by the inner loop in Figure 6.17. Now, as

Figure 6.17 shows, a move appears in the inner loop. The expected number of both moves and compares is $O(n^2)$.

---

while sort_on(the_objects(k)) < sort_on(the_objects(j)) **loop**   *-- Compare.*
   k := k + 1;
   the_objects(k − 1) := the_objects(k);   *-- Move.*
   exit when k > the_objects'last;
end loop;

FIGURE 6.17 The inner loop of an algorithm for insertion sort—implemented without slice assignment.

Timing studies showed that a slice assignment runs 20 times faster than the corresponding individual component assignments on one computer system and 4 times faster on a second computer. You may want to compare the times for slice and individual component assignments on a system available to you.

6.2.3 Exchange Sort

Figure 6.18 shows an implementation of exchange sort—sometimes referred to as "bubble sort." When the outer loop begins execution the objects in positions *the_objects'first .. j − 1* are in their sorted positions. The inner loop swaps pairs of elements in the interval *j .. the_objects'last* so that each pair is placed in the proper order. A boolean variable records the presence of any swaps in the inner loop. If no swaps are made, the data are sorted and an exit from the outer loop is taken.

---

procedure exchange_sort (the_objects: **in out** objects_to_sort) **is**
-- Length 8 Complexity 5 Performance $O(n^2)$
  any_swaps : boolean;
begin
    for j **in** the_objects'first + 1 .. the_objects'last **loop**
      any_swaps := false;

      for q **in reverse** j .. the_objects'last **loop**
        if sort_on(the_objects(q)) < sort_on(the_objects(q − 1)) **then**
          any_swaps := true;
          swap (the_objects(q), the_objects(q − 1));
        end if;
      end loop;

      exit when not any_swaps;
    end loop;
end exchange_sort;

FIGURE 6.18 An algorithm for exchange sort.

The outer loop of exchange sort records the presence or absence of any swaps. Everything else is left for the inner loop. The inner loop examines each pair of elements in the slice *j .. the_objects'last*—in reverse order. Each pair that is out of order is swapped. This has the effect of moving the smallest object in the slice, one position at a time, to the front of the slice—its sorted position. Note that all compares and all moves in *exchange_sort* occur in the inner loop.

Figure 6.19 shows the effect of applying exchange sort to a sequence of integers. The sequence is shown each time execution of the outer loop begins. The integers that have been placed in their sorted positions are underlined. This example shows a case in which the data become sorted before execution of the outer loop is completed.

26	22	48	24	82	86	43	50	72	20	72	89	34	54	66
20	26	22	48	24	82	86	43	50	72	34	72	89	54	66
20	22	26	24	48	34	82	86	43	50	72	54	72	89	66
20	22	24	26	34	48	43	82	86	50	54	72	66	72	89
20	22	24	26	34	43	48	50	82	86	54	66	72	72	89
20	22	24	26	34	43	48	50	54	82	86	66	72	72	89
20	22	24	26	34	43	48	50	54	66	82	86	72	72	89
20	22	24	26	34	43	48	50	54	66	72	82	86	72	89
20	22	24	26	34	43	48	50	54	66	72	72	82	86	89
20	22	24	26	34	43	48	50	54	66	72	72	82	86	89

FIGURE 6.19 Application of the exchange sort algorithm.

Look at the inner loop of *exchange_sort*. The inner loop contains all of this algorithm's compares and moves. The moves that occur are of the worst variety—each time an object is moved it is only moved to its adjacent position. It is easy to see why this algorithm has about the worst performance of any sorting algorithm that has been invented.

Suppose *the_objects* contains n objects and that execution of the outer loop occurs k_{sorted} times before the data are sorted. The number of executions of the inner loop is then

$$(n - 1) + (n - 2) + \cdots + (n - k_{sorted}) = (\tfrac{1}{2}) (2n - k_{sorted} - 1) k_{sorted}$$

These results are summarized in Figure 6.20.

	Outer loop	Inner loop
Executions	k_{sorted}	$(\tfrac{1}{2}) (2n - k_{sorted} - 1) k_{sorted}$
Compares	0	$(\tfrac{1}{2}) (2n - k_{sorted} - 1) k_{sorted}$
Swaps	0	$(\tfrac{1}{2}) (2n - k_{sorted} - 1) k_{sorted}$

FIGURE 6.20 The number of swaps and compares required for exchange sort of an array.

The best performance occurs when k_{sorted} is 1. In this case no moves occur because the data were initially sorted. The number of comparisons to determine this is $n - 1$.

The worst performance occurs when k_{sorted} is $n - 1$. The inner loop is then executed $(\tfrac{1}{2}) (n) (n - 1)$ times. If the initial data are in inverse order, there will be $(\frac{1}{2})(n)(n-1)$ compares and the same number of swaps. Figure 6.21 summarizes the compares and swaps needed to execute exchange sort.

	Initial data are random	Initial data are sorted	Initial data are inverse
Compares	$\leq (\frac{1}{2})\,n^2 + O(n)$	$n - 1$	$(\frac{1}{2})\,n^2 + O(n)$
Swaps	$\leq (\frac{1}{2})\,n^2 + O(n)$	0	$(\frac{1}{2})\,n^2 + O(n)$

FIGURE 6.21 The number of swaps and compares required for exchange sort of an array assuming three different initial orders of the data to sort.

We have seen three algorithms that sort data in an array. The next section provides an algorithm to sort data in a linked list.

6.2.4 Insertion Sort for a Linked List

Insertion sort for a linked list is similar to insertion sort for an array—with the key difference that there are zero moves. Instead of moving the objects to sort, we change the pointers that determine the positions of objects in the list. Figure 6.22 shows an example list to sort. Note that we need only a singly linked list with some mechanism to mark the end of the list for this algorithm. We assume a null terminated list, but a tail pointer or knowing the size of the list would work as well.

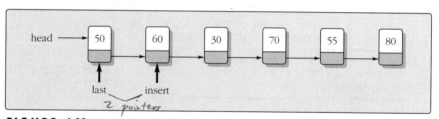

FIGURE 6.22 The singly linked list that will be used to illustrate the insertion sort algorithm.

Figure 6.22 shows two pointers, *last* and *insert,* that will be used during the sort. *insert* is initialized to access the head of the list, and at the beginning of each step of the algorithm, *insert* accesses *last*'s successor.

Suppose the integers shown in the figures are the key components of the objects in the linked list. Then, since *last*.key ≤ *insert*.key (that is 50 ≤ 60), the insertion sort algorithm simply advances *last* and *insert* to their respective successors. The result is shown in Figure 6.23.

In Figure 6.23 observe that *last* points to the last object in a sorted list of length 2. *insert* now points to the object (30 in this case) that is to be inserted into the sorted list of length 2 so it will be a sorted list of length 3. Observe that this is accomplished in Figure 6.24. Also note that *last* was not moved.

Starting with Figure 6.24, we want to insert the object accessed by *insert,* whose key value is 70, into the sorted list whose last object is pointed at by *last.* This is accomplished in Figure 6.25.

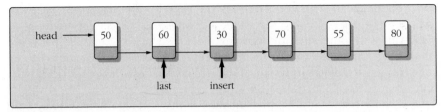

FIGURE 6.23 Now, *last* accesses the last object in a sorted list of length 2.

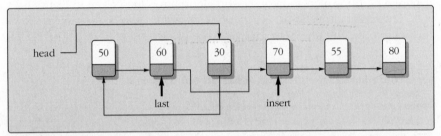

FIGURE 6.24 In this figure, *last* points at the last object in a sorted list of length 3. Note that the transformation from Figure 6.23 to 6.24 required resetting three pointers and changing the object accessed by *insert*.

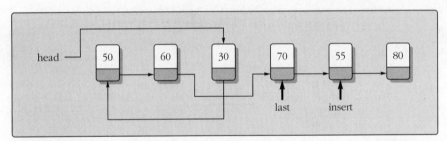

FIGURE 6.25 In this figure, *last* points at the last object in a sorted list of length 4. The transformation from Figure 6.24 to 6.25 required moving *last* and *insert* to their respective successors.

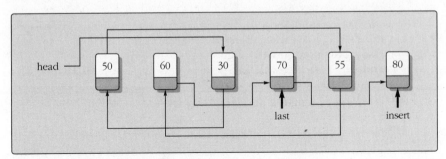

FIGURE 6.26 One final step is needed to complete the sort.

type node;
type pointer **is access** node;
type node **is record**
    key : integer;
    next : pointer;
end record;

FIGURE 6.27 Structure of the linked list for the implementation in Figure 6.28.

Starting with Figure 6.25 we want to insert the object accessed by *insert*, whose key value is 55, into the sorted list whose last object is pointed at by *last*. This is accomplished by scanning the sorted sublist, beginning at *head*, until the sorted position for *insert*'s object is found. Moving an object to its new position requires resetting three pointers. Finally, *insert* is set as the successor of *last*. The result is shown in Figure 6.26.

We are ready for an implementation of this sort algorithm. To keep the presentation simple, assume that each object in the list is a record with two fields: the first with identifier key, and the second—that contains a pointer to another list object—with identifier next. This simple structure is shown in Figure 6.27. Implementation of the sort algorithm is then given in Figure 6.28.

The number of compares for *linked_insertion_sort* is the same as shown in Figure 6.16. The number of moves, slice or otherwise, is zero. The perfor-

```
procedure linked_insertion_sort (head : in out pointer) is
-- Length 9   Complexity 4   Performance O(n²)
-- assumes:   head points to a null terminated linked list.
-- results:   The list pointed at by head is sorted.

     last    : pointer := head;              -- The last node that has been sorted.
     insert  : pointer;                      -- The node to insert in its sorted position.

     procedure move_insert (scout : in out pointer) is
     -- Length 5   Complexity 2   Recursion 1
     -- results:   The node pointed at by insert is moved to its sorted position among the
     --            nodes that precede it in the linked list.

     begin
        if insert.key > scout.key then
           move_insert (scout.next);         -- Recursive search for the insertion position.
        else last.next := insert.next;       -- Move the node pointed at by insert so it is the
           insert.next := scout;             -- predecessor of the node pointed at by scout.
           scout := insert;
        end if;
     end move_insert;

begin
   if head /= null and then head.next /= null then      -- If there are at least two
      insert := head.next;                              -- nodes in the list, start sorting.

      while insert /= null loop
         if last.key <= insert.key then last := last.next;
         else move_insert (head);
         end if;
         insert := last.next;
      end loop;

   end if;
end linked_insertion_sort;
```

FIGURE 6.28 Insertion sort algorithm for a null terminated linked list.

mance of this algorithm is compared to the array sort algorithms in the next section.

6.2.5 Comparison of Simple Sort Algorithms

Figure 6.29 shows the number of compares and moves needed by each of the simple sort algorithms as a function of the initial order of the data. Observe that for random data, exchange sort brings up the rear with $O(n^2)$ compares and $O(n^2)$ moves. Insertion sort is effective for sorted data and data that are almost sorted. Because of this we will combine insertion sort with the quicksort algorithm in Section 6.3 to produce one of the most effective sorting algorithms known.

	Initial data are random	Initial data are sorted	Initial data are inverse
Selection sort array			
Compares	$O(n^2)$	$O(n^2)$	$O(n^2)$
Moves	$O(n)$	0	$O(n)$
Insertion sort array			
Compares	$O(n^2)$	$O(n)$	$O(n^2)$
Moves	$O(n^2)$	0	$O(n^2)$
Insertion sort linked			
Compares	$O(n^2)$	$O(n)$	$O(n^2)$
Moves	0	0	0
Exchange/sort array			
Compares	$O(n^2)$	$O(n)$	$O(n^2)$
Moves	$O(n^2)$	0	$O(n^2)$

FIGURE 6.29 Performance of simple sort algorithms.

To complete the summary, Figure 6.30 shows the size and complexity measures for each of the four sort implementations in this section.

	Size	Complexity
Selection sort		
array	8	5
Insertion sort		
array	11	5
linked	9 + 5 = 14	4 + 2 = 6
Exchange sort		
array	8	5

FIGURE 6.30 Size and complexity measures for the implementations in this section.

We conclude this section with the results of timing studies for the three simple sort algorithms. Figure 6.31 shows the times needed to sort an array of integers that is initially in random order.

The results in Figure 6.31 show the parabolic shape of $O(n^2)$ algorithms. Exchange sort is slow because of the moves in its inner loop and because

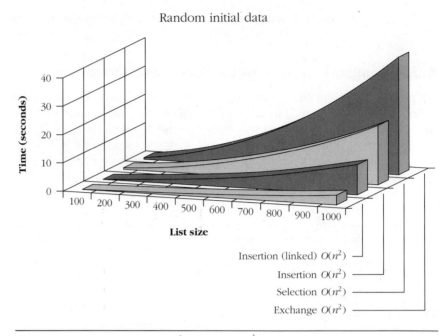

Random initial data

Time (seconds)

List size

Insertion (linked) $O(n^2)$

Insertion $O(n^2)$

Selection $O(n^2)$

Exchange $O(n^2)$

FIGURE 6.31 Time to sort an array of integers that is initially in random order.

array elements are always moved from one position to an adjacent position. Selection sort does twice as many compares as insertion sort and appears to take about twice as long. Recall that slice assignments make the insertion sort algorithm appear faster than it might if implemented in a language without that operation.

Figure 6.32 shows the result of applying the same algorithms to data that are initially sorted.

Exchange sort is fast for sorted data because the algorithm used (Figure 6.18) detects that the data are sorted on the first pass. Insertion sort is fast because only one compare is needed to determine that each object does not need to be moved. Selection sort, however, always makes $O(n^2)$ compares.

Figure 6.33 shows the result of applying the same algorithms to data that are initially in inverse order.

Figure 6.33 shows that exchange sort can become very slow when objects must be moved, one position at a time, through long distances. The performance of selection sort and insertion sort are approximately the same (in the environment in which these timing studies were run) for these initial data.

It was pointed out earlier that Ada's slice assignment makes it possible to keep data move operations out of the inner loop of insertion sort. Different compilers and different computer architectures use this in a variety of ways. If the hardware used includes a block move instruction (a machine level instruction to move a block of bytes from one position to another in memory) with which to implement the slice assignment and the complier uses that block move instruction, then the performance improvement may be substantial. Figure 6.34 compares the slice assignment implementation (Figure 6.13) with an

Basic sorting algorithms
Sorted initial data

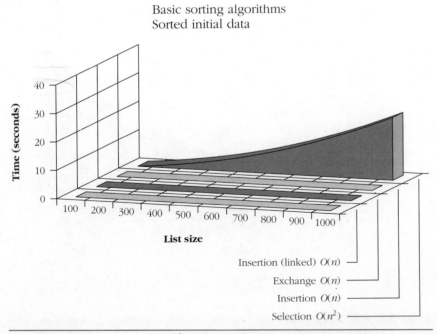

FIGURE 6.32 Time to sort an array of integers that is initially in sorted order.

Basic sorting algorithms
Inverse initial data

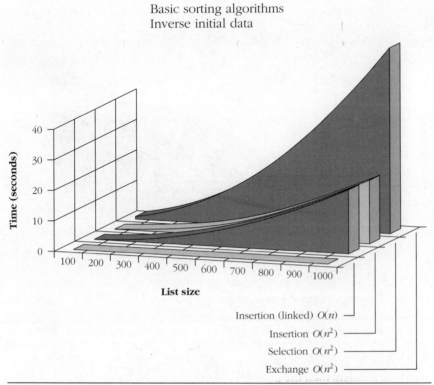

FIGURE 6.33 Time to sort an array of integers that is initially in inverse order.

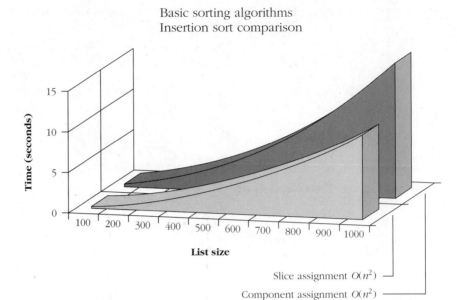

FIGURE 6.34 Time to sort an array of integers that is initially in random order. Compare an implementation using slice assignment (Figure 6.13 in Section 6.2.2) with an implementation without slice assignment.

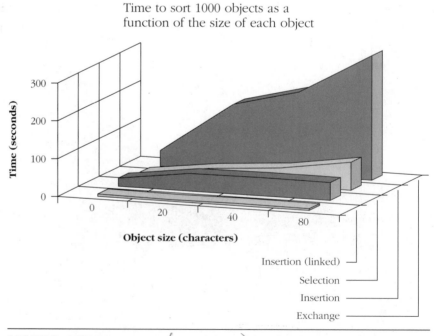

FIGURE 6.35 Time to sort an array of objects that is initially in random order. Each object is an integer and a character string of the length shown in the figure.

implementation that moves objects, one at a time, in the inner loop (Figure 6.17).

Figure 6.34 shows that the slice assignment implementation (in the environment in which these times were determined) ran in about 65% of the time used without slice assignment.

The times reported so far only tell part of the story because the data sorted were simply arrays of integers. Sort algorithms are frequently applied to larger objects where the number of moves has a dominant influence on performance. Figure 6.35 shows the time to sort 1000 items as a function of the size of the items.

Figure 6.35 shows the deteriorating performance, due to the moves in the inner loop, of exchange sort as the objects sorted become large. As the objects become large, selection sort, with a single swap in the outer loop, becomes fastest. As the objects sorted become larger, insertion sort, with a slice assignment in the outer loop, becomes slower relative to selection sort.

Except in rare instances, the algorithms in this section are so dramatically inferior to the algorithms in the next section that they should almost never be used—except on small sets of data. All is not lost, however. We will see that we can combine insertion sort with another algorithm, quicksort, to provide one of the best general-purpose sorting algorithms known.

EXERCISES 6.2

1. Apply the algorithms in Figures 6.8, 6.13, and 6.18 to the following sequence of eight integers:

   56, 27, 22, 95, 79, 45, 45, 96

   In each case keep track of the number of compares and moves required. Compare your results with the estimates in Figure 6.29.

2. Use a random number generator to produce a sequence of n random integers.
   a. Modify each of the algorithms in Figures 6.8, 6.13, and 6.18 to record the number of moves and compares required to sort a list. Plot these values as a function of n. Compare your results with Figure 6.29.
   b. Modify each of the algorithms in Figures 6.8, 6.13, and 6.18 to record, each time an object is moved, the distance it is moved. Plot a histogram of frequency versus distance moved for each algorithm. Discuss your results.

3. A sorting algorithm is stable if it preserves the order of elements with equal key values. Which of the algorithms in Figures 6.8, 6.13, and 6.18 are stable?

4. A sequence of objects is formed by starting with a sorted sequence, then exchanging one pair. For example, starting with the sequence,

   1, 2, 3, 4, 5, 6, 7, 8, 9, 10

   and exchanging the second and fifth elements yields the sequence

   1, 5, 3, 4, 2, 6, 7, 8, 9, 10

   Discuss the effectiveness of the algorithms in Section 6.2 for sorting such a list. Consider both the size of the list and the specific pair of objects exchanged. Fill in Figure 6.29 for this special case.

5. A sequence of n sorted elements has k randomly selected elements appended to its end. Discuss the effectiveness of the algorithms in Section 6.2 for sorting such a list. Fill in Figure 6.29 for this special case.

6. The version of insertion sort in Figure 6.13 uses a sequential search to find the position to insert the element at position j (finding this position is the purpose of the inner loop). Replace the sequential search with a binary search. Modify Figure 6.29 to include the resulting algorithm.

7. Implement the selection sort algorithm for a singly linked list. Modify Figure 6.29 to include the resulting algorithm.

8. Implement the exchange sort algorithm for a singly

linked list. Modify Figure 6.29 to include the resulting algorithm.

9. Figure 6.30 shows that, except for the linked implementation of insertion sort, the complexity of each implementation is 5. Can you provide a linked implementation of insertion sort whose complexity is 5? If so, provide the implementation. If not, explain why.

◼ 6.3 Advanced Sort Techniques

We begin, in Section 6.3.1, with a discussion of quicksort—considered by many to be the best general-purpose internal sorting algorithm known. Figure 6.36 compares the performance of quicksort with the performance of the basic algorithms described in Section 6.2.

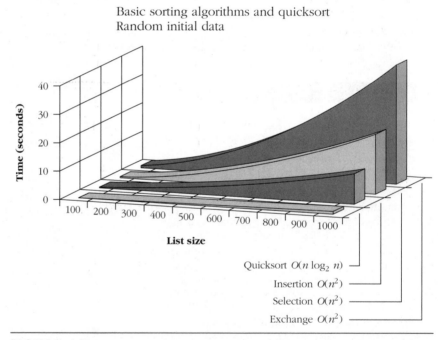

Basic sorting algorithms and quicksort
Random initial data

Quicksort $O(n \log_2 n)$

Insertion $O(n^2)$

Selection $O(n^2)$

Exchange $O(n^2)$

FIGURE 6.36 Time to sort an array of integers initially in random order. Quicksort requires $O(n \log_2 n)$ compares, whereas the three basic sorting algorithms all require $O(n^2)$.

Sections 6.3.2 through 6.3.4 discuss three other algorithms with $O(n \log_2 n)$ expected performance. Following a comparison of algorithm performance in Section 6.3.5, Section 6.4 considers radix sort, an algorithm based on a different underlying process.

6.3.1 Quicksort

Quicksort is a series of steps, each of which takes a list of objects to sort as input. The output from each step is a rearrangement of the objects so that one object is in its sorted position and two sublists remain to be sorted.

If the objects to sort are

$$x(1), x(2), \ldots, x(n)$$

then one step of quicksort rearranges the objects so as to produce the ordering in Figure 6.37.

$$
\underbrace{x(1), x(2), \ldots, x(j-1)}_{\leftarrow \text{ smaller than } x(j) \rightarrow} \quad \underset{\text{(b)}}{x(j)} \quad \underbrace{x(j+1), x(j+2), \ldots, x(n)}_{\longleftarrow \text{ larger than } x(j) \longrightarrow}
$$
$$\text{(a)} \qquad\qquad\qquad\qquad \text{(c)}$$

FIGURE 6.37 Results of applying one step of the quicksort algorithm to the list of objects $x(1), x(2), \ldots, x(n)$. (a) List that remains to be sorted. Each of these objects is smaller than $x(j)$. (b) Object in its sorted position. (c) List that remains to be sorted. Each of these objects is larger than $x(j)$.

Each step of quicksort partitions a list into three disjoint sublists. One of the sublists is a single object that is in its sorted position (Figure 6.37b). The other two sublists share a common property. Each of them contains objects that are all either smaller than (Figure 6.37a) or larger than (Figure 6.37c) the object in its sorted position. This permits each of the two sublists to be sorted without reference to any element in the other two sublists. That is, each step of quicksort replaces the problem of sorting one long list by the problem of sorting two shorter sublists. The sorting problem is said to have been partitioned.

Consider the list of integers in Figure 6.38. Each integer is an object in terms of the discussion above. One way to rearrange these integers so that 53 is in its sorted position is shown in Figure 6.39.

Figure 6.39 shows one of many suitable rearrangements of the integers in Figure 6.38. Any ordering in which the integers less than 53 are to its left and the integers larger than 53 are to its right will suffice.

We will discuss the details of rearranging objects later. At this point we ignore those details and examine the overall structure of quicksort. To begin, we will select the first, or left-most object, as the one to move into its sorted position. Later we will use a selection process that provides better performance.

The complete quicksort process is succinctly described by the recursive algorithm in Figure 6.40.

Suppose that *quicksort1* is applied to the list in Figure 6.41, where *the_objects'first* = 1 and *the_objects'last* = 9. The first execution of *quick1* moves 73 to its sorted position. The result (we describe the process later) is shown in Figure 6.42.

The last two statements in *quicksort1* are recursive calls. In our example, the first pair of calls will be *quicksort1(1,2)* and *quicksort1(4,9)*. The first of these is executed immediately and the second is deferred.

53	59	56	52	55	58	51	57	54

FIGURE 6.38 A list of integers.

$$
\underbrace{52 \quad 51}_{\substack{\longleftarrow \\ \text{Smaller} \\ \text{than } 53}} \quad \underline{53} \quad \underbrace{56 \quad 54 \quad 59 \quad 55 \quad 58 \quad 57}_{\substack{\longleftarrow\qquad\qquad\longrightarrow \\ \text{Larger than } 53}}
$$

FIGURE 6.39 The integers in Figure 6.38 rearranged so that 53 is in its sorted position. Sorted integers are underlined in this and the following figures.

```
procedure quicksort1 (the_objects : in out objects_to_sort) is
    left  : integer := the_objects'first;
    right: integer := the_objects'last;
begin
    if (left < right) then
        Rearrange objects the_objects(left), . . . , the_objects(right) to produce a new
          list such that

        the_objects(left), . . . , the_objects(j − 1) are all smaller than the_objects(j);
        the_objects(j) is in its sorted position;
        the_objects(j + 1), . . . , the_objects(right) are all larger than the_objects(j);

        quicksort1 (the_objects(left .. j − 1));
        quicksort 1(the_objects(j + 1 .. right));
    end if;
end quicksort1;
```

FIGURE 6.40 The first of three versions of quicksort.

73 79 76 72 75 78 71 77 74

FIGURE 6.41 The original list.

72 71 <u>73</u> 76 75 78 79 77 74

FIGURE 6.42 After the first rearrangement in *quicksort1*.

In order to show what recursive calls are made, we will construct a binary tree. Each node in the tree represents a recursive call to *quicksort1*. For each node, the left child shows the first recursive call and the right child shows the second, deferred, recursive call. All the recursive calls that occur while sorting the objects in Figure 6.41 are shown in Figure 6.43.

In Figure 6.43 the leaf nodes are all recursive calls that result in no further execution because the left index value is greater than or equal to the

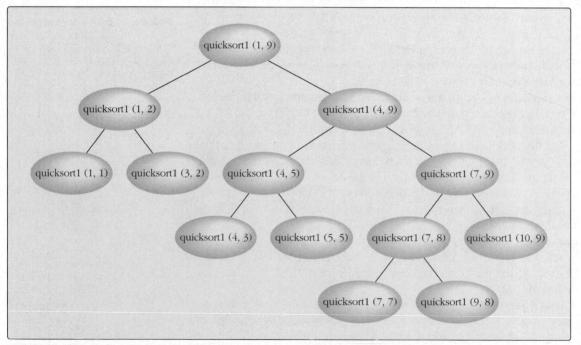

FIGURE 6.43 The initial call and all the recursive calls to *quicksort1* required to sort the sequence in Figure 6.41.

right index value. Some thought will convince you that the recursive calls occur in the order given by a preorder traversal of the tree in Figure 6.43. Figures 6.44, 6.45, and 6.46 show how the integers are rearranged by these calls. Integers known to be sorted are underlined.

Now, with the algorithm introduced, we are ready to discuss the implementation of *quicksort1*. Figure 6.47 shows a complete implementation of the quicksort algorithm.

The discussion of *quicksort2* will focus on the statements labeled 1, 2, 3, and 4 in Figure 6.47. These statements constitute the heart of the rearrangement process that will be described using the integers in Figure 6.48 as an example. Statements 1 and 2 are the inner loop statements for quicksort. Their simplicity is one reason why quicksort is usually fast.

The first time statement 1 is executed it scans to the right, starting with the object whose index is *left* + 1. The scan continues until an object is found that is greater than or equal to *the_objects(left)*. In our example, the scan starts at 15 and ends at 60, as shown in Figure 6.49.

Similarly, statement 2 scans to the left, starting with *the_objects(right)*. This scan ends when an integer less than or equal to *the_objects(left)* is found. Figure 6.50 shows the first two scans.

Since *j < k,* statement 3 has no effect, and statement 4 swaps the two integers where the scans terminated. In our example, 60 and 20 are swapped.

71 <u>72</u> <u>73</u> 76 75 78 79 77 74

FIGURE 6.44 The list after *quicksort1(1,2).*

71 72 73 74 75 <u>76</u> 79 77 78

FIGURE 6.45 The list after *quicksort1(4,9)*

71 72 73 <u>74</u> <u>75</u> <u>76</u> 77 <u>78</u> 79

FIGURE 6.46 The list after *quicksort1(7,8).* The recursive calls *quicksort1(7,7), quicksort1(9,8),* and *quicksort1(10,9)* complete the sort.

```
procedure quicksort2 (the_objects : in out objects_to_sort) is
-- Length 22   Complexity 6   Recursion 2   Performance   Expected O(n log₂n)   Worst Case O(n²)
    j, k : integer;
    pivot : object;
    left : integer := the_objects'first;
    right : integer := the_objects'last;
begin
    if (left < right) then
        if the_objects(right) < the_objects(left) then
            swap (the_objects(left), the_objects(right));          -- Provides a sentinel for the scan to the right.
        end if;
        j := left; k := right; pivot := sort_on(the_objects(left));

        loop
            loop j := j + 1; exit when not (sort_on(the_objects(j)) < pivot); end loop;     -- 1
            loop k := k − 1; exit when not (pivot < sort_on(the_objects(k))); end loop;     -- 2
            exit when (j > k);                                                              -- 3
            swap (the_objects(j), the_objects(k));                                          -- 4
        end loop;

        swap (the_objects(left), the_objects(k));
        quicksort2 (the_objects(left .. k − 1));          -- Recursively sort the left slice.
        quicksort2 (the_objects(k + 1 .. right));         -- Recursively sort the right slice.
    end if;
end quicksort2;
```

FIGURE 6.47 A second version of quicksort.

40 15 30 25 60 10 75 45 65 35 50 20 70 55

FIGURE 6.48 A sequence of integers to sort.

40 15 30 25 60 10 75 45 65 35 50 20 70 55

FIGURE 6.49 Statement 1 scans to the right, searching for an integer greater than or equal to 40.

40 15 30 25 60 10 75 45 65 35 50 20 70 55

FIGURE 6.50 Statement 2 scans to the left, searching for an integer less than or equal to 40.

Note that we will move a large integer to the right and a small integer to the left. The result is shown in Figure 6.51.

40 15 30 25 20 10 75 45 65 35 50 60 70 55

FIGURE 6.51 Values 20 and 60 have been swapped.

Statements 1 and 2 are now repeated, and the scans that result are shown in Figure 6.52.

40 15 30 25 20 10 75 45 65 35 50 60 70 55

FIGURE 6.52 Statements 1 and 2 scan to the right (left) searching for an integer greater than or equal to (less than or equal to) 40.

Again, since $j < k$, statement 3 has no effect, and statement 4 swaps the two integers where the scans terminated. Integers 75 and 35 are swapped and the result is presented in Figure 6.53.

40 15 30 25 20 10 35 45 65 75 50 60 70 55

FIGURE 6.53 After swapping 75 and 35.

Statements 1 and 2 are repeated, once again, and the scans that result are shown in Figure 6.54.

This time (Figure 6.54) the scans have met, $j > k$, so we drop out of the loop. This causes *the_objects(left)* to be swapped with the element that terminated the last left scan. In our example, 40 and 35 are swapped. The result is shown in Figure 6.55.

We now discuss several ways to improve the quicksort algorithm in Figure 6.47. First, look at Figure 6.43 and notice that many of the recursive calls are

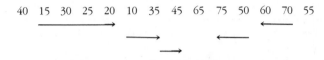

40   15   30   25   20   10   35   45   65   75   50   60   70   55

F I G U R E   6.54 The next pair of scans conducted by statements 1 and 2.

35   15   30   25   20   10   <u>40</u>   45   65   75   50   60   70   55

Less than or equal to 40   Greater than or equal to 40

F I G U R E   6.55 The first partition is complete. 40 is sorted, and two independent sublists are recursively passed to *quicksort2*.

for sublists with only a few objects. It makes sense that quicksort may not be as efficient as a simpler algorithm for short lists because of the overhead associated with quicksort. A study of this issue, in Sedgewick (1978) showed that small sublists, of about length 15 or less depending on the implementation, should be ignored by quicksort and cleaned up at the end using insertion sort. Performance improvements of 12% for large lists and as high as 20% for small lists were obtained.

Next, consider selection of the object used to partition the list. In Figure 6.47 the smaller of *the_objects(left)* and *the_objects(right)* is selected. Ideally, the object selected would be the median value of the sublist to sort. This would mean that quicksort would split the sublist exactly in half. Determining the median of a list is, however, a considerable undertaking by itself, so alternatives have been considered. It was discovered by Sedgewick (1978) that choosing the partitioning element as the median of three sample values works almost as well as using the median value. Our algorithm uses this approach with the details as shown in procedure *median* in Figure 6.56. The size and complexity values in Figure 5.56 include contributions from procedure *median*. Excluding procedure *median* (for comparison with *quicksort2*) those values are size 26, complexity 7, and recursion 2.

Ensuring that *the_objects(left)* is less than *the_objects(right)* is essential in the quicksort algorithm because *the_objects(right)* then serves as a guard to ensure that a scan to the right (statement 1 in Figures 6.47 and 6.56) does not continue past the right end of the array.

Further improvements are possible. Statements 5 and 6 can be ordered so the shortest sublist is processed first and processing the longer sublist is deferred—by putting it on a stack. The advantage is that by placing longer sublists on the stack, the stack depth, and the number of stack operations, is minimized. In particular, it can be shown (Hoare, 1962) that this approach guarantees a maximum stack depth of $O(\log_2 n)$.

A final improvement is to supply your own stack and eliminate the recursive calls. The advantage of this will depend on the efficiency with which the compiler generates executable code for the hardware executing the algorithm.

A good way to visualize the quicksort algorithm is to show the scans associated with sorting data in a way closely related to Figures 6.49 through

```
procedure quicksort3 (the_objects : in out objects_to_sort) is
-- Length 3  Complexity 2  Performance  Expected O(n log₂n)  Worst Case O(n²)
    procedure quick2 (the_objects : in out objects_to_sort) is
    -- Length 23  Complexity 11  Recursion 2
        j, k    : integer;
        pivot   : sort_type;
        left    : integer := the_objects'first;
        right   : integer := the_objects'last;

        procedure median is
        -- Length 10  Complexity 5
        -- results:  Rearrange the elements in positions mid, last, and the smaller of
        --           left and left + 1 as follows:
        --           left          ← median value
        --           left + 1      ← smallest value
        --           right         ← maximum value and sentinel

            mid: integer := (left + right)/2;
        begin
            if sort_on(the_objects(left + 1)) < sort_on(the_objects(left)) then
                swap (the_objects(left + 1), the_objects(left)); end if;
            swap (the_objects(left + 1), the_objects(mid));
            if sort_on(the_objects(right)) < sort_on(the_objects(left + 1)) then
                swap (the_objects(left + 1), the_objects(right)); end if;
            if sort_on(the_objects(right)) < sort_on(the_objects(left)) then
                swap (the_objects(left), the_objects(right)); end if;
            if sort_on(the_objects(left)) < sort_on(the_objects(left + 1)) then
                swap (the_objects(left + 1), the_objects(left)); end if;
        end median;

    begin
        median;
        j := left + 1; k := right; pivot := sort_on(the_objects(left));
        loop
            loop j := j + 1; exit when not (sort_on(the_objects(j)) < pivot); end loop;    -- 1
            loop k := k − 1; exit when not (pivot < sort_on(the_objects(k))); end loop;    -- 2
            exit when (j > k);                                                             -- 3
            swap (the_objects(j), the_objects(k));                                         -- 4
        end loop;
        swap (the_objects(left), the_objects(k));
        if (k − left) > 15 then quick2 (the_objects (left .. k − 1)); end if;              -- 5
        if (right − k) > 15 then quick2 (the_objects (k + 1 .. right)); end if;            -- 6
    end quick2;

begin
    if the_objects'length > 15 then
        quick2 (the_objects(the_objects'first .. the_objects'last));
    end if;
    insertion_sort (the_objects(the_objects'first .. the_objects'last));
end quicksort3;
```

FIGURE 6.56 The final version of quicksort.

6.55. Figure 6.57 shows the scans associated with *quicksort3* applied to an array of 20 random integers. The first row is the initial data. The second row shows the data after median of three modification. Then the scans are shown. From there on each pair of rows shows the data immediately before and immediately after median of three modification. The values in brackets, [ ], identify the sublist that is the target of the next scan. The left value, used to partition the target sublist, is identified as the pivot value. For this illustration the algorithm ignores sublists of length 4 or less (rather than 15 or less as given in Figure 6.56).

Next, we look at some timing studies for two versions of quicksort. Figure 6.58 shows the times for sorting an array of integers initially in random order.

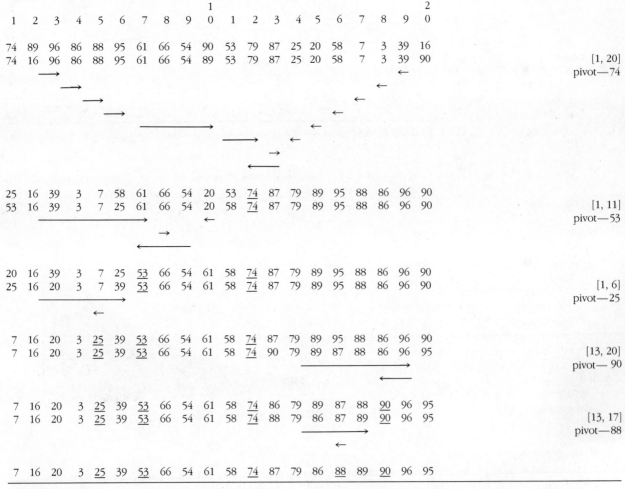

F I G U R E 6.57 A visualization of the *quicksort3* algorithm. The initial data are shown, then the data after median of three modification, then the scans generated by statements 1 and 2 in Figure 6.56, then the data just before execution of statement 5. This process is repeated for each of the recursive calls. Data that are sorted are underlined. Sublists of length 4 or less are ignored.

Quicksort3 is a tad faster, but the difference is too small to see in Figure 6.58.

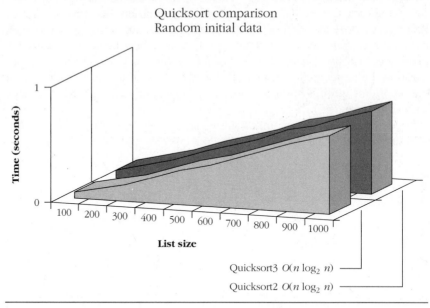

FIGURE 6.58 Compare the times needed by *quicksort2* and *quicksort3* for sorting an array of random integers.

Figure 6.59 compares the times to sort an array of integers originally in sorted order. The result for data originally in inverse order is similar. The

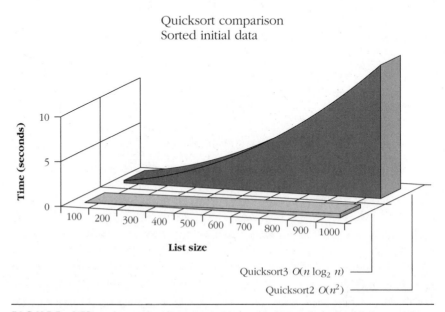

FIGURE 6.59 Compare the times needed by *quicksort2* and *quicksort3* for sorting an array of integers initially in sorted order.

shape of the curve suggests that *quicksort2* has developed $O(n^2)$ performance. In fact it has. What has affected *quicksort2* that has not affected *quicksort3*?

If we repeat the visualization in Figure 6.38, but this time start with sorted data, we will see the problem with *quicksort2*. Figure 6.60 gives the result. Again, the complete sort is not shown, but enough is provided to show the problem.

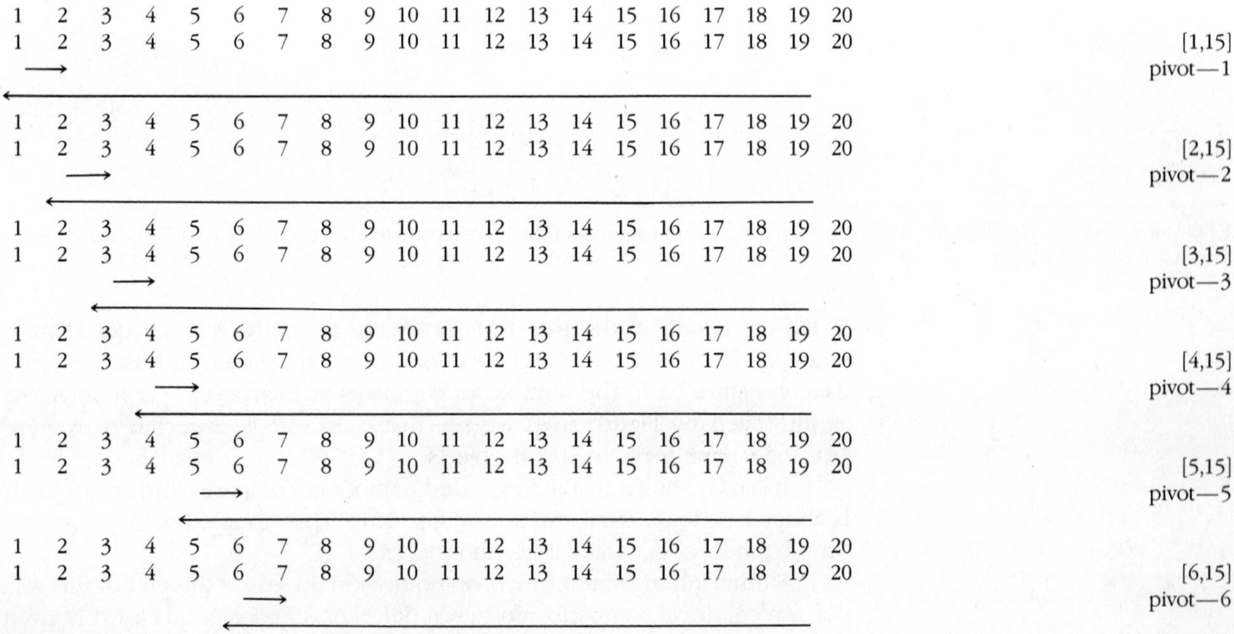

FIGURE 6.60 A visualization of the *quicksort2* algorithm in terms of the scans that are generated by statements 1 and 2 in Figure 6.47. The initial data are sorted.

In Figure 6.60 each step of quicksort confirms that the pivot element is already in its sorted position. Therefore, n steps will be required to sort n objects, and the number of compares will be

$$n + n - 1 + n - 2 + \cdots + 1 = O(n^2)$$

We see *quicksort2* will be slow for data that are initially sorted or nearly sorted. A little reflection will convince you that the same is true if the initial data are inverse or nearly inverse.

We continue by applying *quicksort3* to sorted data. The result is shown in Figure 6.61. We ignore sublists of length 2 or less. In addition, in order to reduce the size of the figure, we combined the scans that correspond to recursive calls on the same level of the tree constructed as shown in Figure 6.43. That is, each set of scans corresponds to one level of the tree constructed as shown in Figure 6.43.

The point we would like to make is that Figure 6.61 shows why quicksort requires $O(n \log_2 n)$ compares to sort a list of length n. We know, from Chapter

1	2	3	4	5	6	7	8	9	10	11	12	13	14	15	16	17	18	19	20
10	1	3	4	5	6	7	8	9	2	11	12	13	14	15	16	17	18	19	20

[1,20]

\# compares = 21

2	1	3	4	5	6	7	8	9	10	11	12	13	14	15	16	17	18	19	20
5	1	3	4	2	6	7	8	9	10	15	11	13	14	12	16	17	18	19	20

[1,9], [11,20]

\# compares = 17

2	1	3	4	5	6	7	8	9	10	11	12	13	14	15	16	17	18	19	20
2	1	3	4	5	7	6	8	9	10	12	11	13	14	15	18	16	17	19	20

[1,4], [6,9]
[11,14], [16,20]
\# compares = 13

1	2	3	4	5	6	7	8	9	10	11	12	13	14	15	17	16	18	19	20

FIGURE 6.61 A visualization of the *quicksort3* algorithm in terms of the scans generated by statements 1 and 2 in Figure 6.56. The initial data are sorted.

5 that the height of the tree that shows the recursive calls by quicksort is $O(\log_2 n)$. The compares at each level of the tree are shown, at least for sorted data, in Figure 6.61. The number of compares at each level is at most n. So, as illustrated by Figure 6.61, we see that quicksort is expected to require $O(n \log_2 n)$ compares to sort n objects.

It can be shown that the expected number of compares during quicksort is about $1.4n \log_2 n$ (Sedgewick, 1988, p. 121). This, coupled with quicksort's simple inner loop, makes it fast in most cases.

Further timing studies involving quicksort appear at the end of this section. An empirical comparison of seven different versions of quicksort is given in Wainwright (1985). An algorithm that uses the mean of a list to be partitioned is discussed in Motzkin (1983). Conspicuous by its absence in this chapter is shellsort, a sort technique with many supporters. Shellsort is outlined and references for it are given in the exercises.

6.3.2 Treesort

Treesort requires two steps: First, the objects are inserted into a binary search tree. Second, the objects are retrieved, in sorted order, using an inorder traversal. Algorithms for both these steps were given in Chapter 5.

Treesort is not an attractive approach to sorting because a heap does the same job with less effort. Instead of putting the objects in a binary search tree, we begin by forming a heap. If, however, the elements are in a binary search tree to begin with, then an inorder traversal accesses them in sorted order with $O(n)$ effort—and requires no compares.

6.3.3 Heapsort

Heapsort is a two-step process. First, the data are arranged into a heap; second, the data are extracted from the heap in sorted order. Heapsort is a cousin of selection sort because both algorithms select then swap into sorted order successively larger (or smaller) objects. Heapsort, however, uses a more efficient data structure (a heap) than selection sort (a list). Note that the algorithm described here sorts in decreasing order.

We construct a heap using the procedures in Specification 5.3. Recall that in a heap the smallest object is in the first position. For example, suppose that the array of objects,

$$x(1), x(2), \ldots, x(n-1), x(n) \qquad \text{-- x(1) is the smallest object.}$$
$$\leftarrow \qquad \text{A heap} \qquad \rightarrow$$

satisfies the heap conditions. We then know that $x(1)$ is the smallest object. The trick is to find the second smallest object. We proceed as follows.

Swap $x(1)$ and $x(n)$ so $x(n)$ is the smallest object. Then apply siftdown (Specification 5.3) to objects $1 .. n - 1$ so $x(1), x(2), \ldots, x(n-1)$ satisfy the heap conditions. The result is shown below:

$$x(1), x(2), \ldots, x(n-1), x(n) \qquad \text{-- x(1) is the second smallest object, and}$$
$$\leftarrow \qquad \text{A heap} \qquad \rightarrow \qquad \text{-- x(n), the smallest object, is sorted.}$$

The next step swaps $x(1)$ with $x(n-2)$, then sifts $x(1)$ down so that $x(1), x(2), \ldots, x(n-2)$ satisfy the heap conditions, and $x(n-1), x(n)$ are sorted. $x(1)$ is now the third smallest element.

The ith step exchanges $x(1)$ with $x[n-(i-1)]$ and shifts down $x(1)$ into the sequence $x(1), \ldots, x[n-(i-1)]$ creating a heap with $n - i$ objects. The sequence $x[n-(i-1)], \ldots, x[n]$ is sorted, and $x(1)$ is the ith largest element.

Figure 6.62 shows how the data are rearranged during heapsort of 15 integers. The first row shows the initial data. The second row shows the data after they are reorganized as a heap. Underlined data are sorted, and data inside brackets, [ ], satisfy the heap conditions.

1	2	3	4	5	6	7	8	9	10	11	12	13	14	15	
26	22	48	24	82	86	43	50	72	20	72	89	34	54	66	-- Initial data.
[20	22	34	24	26	48	43	50	72	82	72	89	86	54	66]	-- Heap constructed.
[22	24	34	50	26	48	43	66	72	82	72	89	86	54]	20	
[24	26	34	50	54	48	43	66	72	82	72	89	86]	22	20	
[26	50	34	66	54	48	43	86	72	82	72	89]	24	22	20	
[34	50	43	66	54	48	89	86	72	82	72]	26	24	22	20	
[43	50	48	66	54	72	89	86	72	82]	34	26	24	22	20	
[48	50	72	66	54	82	89	86	72]	43	34	26	24	22	20	
[50	54	72	66	72	82	89	86]	48	43	34	26	24	22	20	
[54	66	72	86	72	82	89]	50	48	43	34	26	24	22	20	
[66	72	72	86	89	82]	54	50	48	43	34	26	24	22	20	
[72	82	72	86	89]	66	54	50	48	43	34	26	24	22	20	
[72	82	89	86]	72	66	54	50	48	43	34	26	24	22	20	
[82	86	89]	72	72	66	54	50	48	43	34	26	24	22	20	
[86	89]	82	72	72	66	54	50	48	43	34	26	24	22	20	
[89]	86	82	72	72	66	54	50	48	43	34	26	24	22	20	

F I G U R E 6.62 The application of heapsort to a list of 15 integers. Except for the first row, the data are shown as they appear each time the **while** loop is entered in Figure 6.63.

Figure 6.63 provides an Ada implementation of the heapsort algorithm. Compare Figures 6.62 and 6.63 to verify your understanding of the process.

```
procedure heapsort (the_objects : in out objects_to_sort) is
-- Length 8   Complexity 2   Performance O(n log₂n)
      package heap_pak is new heap_package (object_type = > object_type,       -- Instantiates Specification 5.3.
                                            priority    = > sort_type,
                                            priority_of = > sort_on,
                                            "<"         = > "<");

      k : integer := the_objects'last;
begin
      heap_pak.heap_create (heap(the_objects(1 .. the_objects'length)), the_objects'length);
      while k > 1 loop
         swap (the_objects(1), the_objects(k));
         k := k − 1;
         heap_pak.sift_down (heap (the_objects(1 .. the_objects'length)), 1, k);
      end loop;
end heapsort;
```

FIGURE 6.63 An implementation of heapsort.

It is easy to develop an upper bound on the number of compares and moves during heapsort. Constructing a heap requires sifting down ($n/2$) objects with a maximum of $\log_2 n$ compares and moves each. An upper bound on compares and moves to construct the heap is therefore ($n/2$)$\log_2 n$. The **while** loop is executed $n − 1$ times, and each execution results in three moves for the swap and at most $\log_2 n$ compares and moves for siftdown. The total work for heapsort is the sum of these two values and is thus $O(n \log_2 n)$.

Timing studies, comparing heapsort with other sort algorithms, are given at the end of this section.

6.3.4 Mergesort

The underlying idea of mergesort is that it is easy to merge two sorted lists into one (longer) sorted list. Consider the two sorted lists in Figure 6.64a. In Figure 6.64a, integers 10 and 12 are compared, and since 10 is smaller, it is moved to the merged list—as shown in Figure 6.64b. The figure captions are used to describe the first five merges.

Since one compare always adds one object to the sorted list it requires at most $n − 1$ compares to complete such a merge. However, if one of the lists becomes empty, then the remaining objects in the other list can be added to the merged list without any compares.

As Figure 6.64 shows, the simplicity of merging sorted lists occurs because there are only two possibilities for the next object to be added to the merged list. In Figure 6.64f only 30 and 28 must be compared to choose the next merged object. (It is, of course, possible to merge any number of sorted lists— but we will only use two for mergesort.)

```
                             10   20   30   40   50
         Empty               12   24   26   28   44   48   52   54
         ← Merged list →     ←——— Sorted lists to merge ———→
                                        (a)

                             20   30   40   50
         10                  12   24   26   28   44   48   52   54
         ← Merged list →     ←——— Sorted lists to merge ———→
                                        (b)

                             20   30   40   50
         10   12             24   26   28   44   48   52   54
         ← Merged list →     ←——— Sorted lists to merge ———→
                                        (c)

                             30   40   50
         10   12   20        24   26   28   44   48   52   54
         ← Merged list →     ←——— Sorted lists to merge ———→
                                        (d)

                             30   40   50
         10   12   20   24   26   28   44   48   52   54
         ← Merged list →     ←——— Sorted lists to merge ———→
                                        (e)

                             30   40   50
         10   12   20   24   26   28   44   48   52   54
         ← Merged list →     ←——— Sorted lists to merge ———→
                                        (f)
```

FIGURE 6.64 Two sorted lists. (a) Two sorted lists to be merged—compare 10 and 12; (b) compare 12 and 20—move 12 to the merged list; (c) compare 20 and 24—move 20 to the merged list; (d) compare 24 and 30—move 24 to the merged list; (e) compare 26 and 30—move 26 to the merged list; (f) compare 28 and 30—move 28 to the merged list.

The trick is to construct sorted lists that permit the merging process to begin. Our solution will be to begin merging lists of length 1 to form lists of length 2. Then we merge sorted lists of length 2 to form sorted lists of length 4, and so on. Since the lengths of the sorted lists increase by a factor of 2 at each step, we expect the process to be efficient.

The details of one possible implementation of mergesort are shown in the implementation in Figures 6.65 and 6.66. Carefully examine how mergesort works. If a list has length greater than 1 it is split into two pieces and each piece is recursively passed to mergesort. This continues until lists of length 1 are merged. After this happens twice, the algorithm merges the two sorted lists of length 2 to form a sorted list of length 4. Figure 6.65 is not only an interesting sort technique, it is also an excellent application of recursion!

To help explain mergesort, we show two views of the application of mergesort to an array of 15 integers. Figure 6.67 shows the data to sort in the first row. Each subsequent row shows the values as they are merged by *mergesort*. In fact, Figure 6.67 was generated by placing suitable *put* statements immediately after the **for** loop that merges data in Figure 6.65. To help

```
procedure mergesort (the_objects : in out objects_to_sort) is
-- Length 5   Complexity 2   Recursion 2   Performance O(n log₂n)
    mid : integer := (the_objects'first + the_objects'last)/2;
begin
    if the_objects'last > the_objects'first then

        mergesort (the_objects(the_objects'first .. mid));          -- Sort the left half.
        mergesort (the_objects(mid + 1 .. the_objects'last));       -- Sort the right half.

        -- the_objects(the_objects'first .. mid) and
        -- the_objects(mid + 1 .. the_objects'last) are sorted. Merge them!
        merge_lists (the_objects(the_objects'first .. the_objects'last), mid);
    end if;
end mergesort;
```

FIGURE 6.65 An implementation of mergesort.

```
procedure merge_lists (the_objects : in out objects_to_sort; mid : integer) is
-- Length 15   Complexity 5   Performance O(n)
    temp : objects_to_sort (the_objects'range);
    p, q : integer;
begin
    temp (the_objects'first .. mid) := the_objects(the_objects'first .. mid);     -- Copy the first sorted list to temp.
    for j in mid + 1 .. the_objects'last loop                                     -- Copy the second sorted list to temp—reverse
        temp(the_objects'last + mid + 1 − j) := the_objects(j);                   -- the order to create sentinels for both lists.
    end loop;

    p := the_objects'first; q := the_objects'last;
    for k in the_objects'first .. the_objects'last loop                           -- Merge the two sorted sublists from the
        if sort_on(temp(p)) < sort_on(temp(q)) then                              -- temporary array back into the_objects.
            the_objects(k) := temp(p); p := p + 1;
        else the_objects(k) := temp(q); q := q − 1;
        end if;
    end loop;
end merge_lists;
```

FIGURE 6.66 The procedure to merge two sorted lists.

visualize the process, when values are displayed, they are positioned horizontally to appear in the positions into which they are actually merged. Spend some time to make sure you see how mergesort produces the results in Figure 6.67.

Figure 6.67 does not show the recursive calls that are made in the process of merging the list objects. So, Figure 6.68 is Figure 6.67 with additional information—the recursive calls that accompany the merge operations. The positions of the objects targeted by each recursive call are shown in brackets, [ ]. The first recursive call, [1, 8], is applied to the left half of the list. Four more recursive calls, [1, 4], . . . , [2, 2], precede the first merge which sorts 22 and 26.

As you can see, there is a problem showing both merges and recursive calls in one figure. So, while the first half of the list is being sorted, the recursive

26	22	48	24	82	86	43	50	72	20	72	89	34	54	66
22	26													
		24	48											
22	24	26	48											
				82	86									
						43	50							
				43	50	82	86							
22	24	26	43	48	50	82	86							
								20	72					
										72	89			
								20	72	72	89			
												34	54	
												34	54	66
								20	34	54	66	72	72	89
20	22	24	26	34	43	48	50	54	66	72	72	82	86	89

FIGURE 6.67 Application of mergesort to 15 integers. The objects are displayed each time a merge occurs—that is, immediately following the second **for** loop in Figure 6.65.

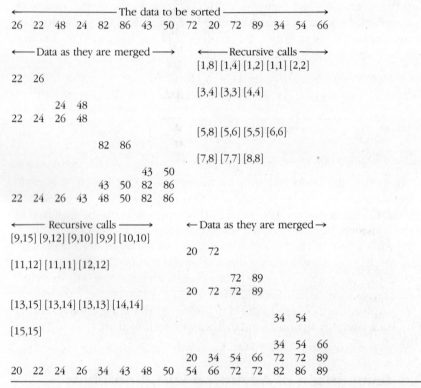

◄──────────── The data to be sorted ──────────►

| 26 | 22 | 48 | 24 | 82 | 86 | 43 | 50 | 72 | 20 | 72 | 89 | 34 | 54 | 66 |

◄──Data as they are merged ──►   ◄──── Recursive calls ────►
[1,8] [1,4] [1,2] [1,1] [2,2]

22 26

[3,4] [3,3] [4,4]

       24 48
22 24 26 48

[5,8] [5,6] [5,5] [6,6]

      82 86

[7,8] [7,7] [8,8]

         43 50
22 24 26 43 48 50 82 86

◄──── Recursive calls ────►   ← Data as they are merged →
[9,15] [9,12] [9,10] [9,9] [10,10]

20 72

[11,12] [11,11] [12,12]

   72 89
20 72 72 89

[13,15] [13,14] [13,13] [14,14]

     34 54

[15,15]

     34 54 66
20 34 54 66 72 72 89
20 22 24 26 34 43 48 50 54 66 72 72 82 86 89

FIGURE 6.68 Application of mergesort to 15 integers. The recursive calls that are made and the data as they are merged.

calls are shown on the right side of the figure. When the right half of the list is being sorted, the recursive calls are shown on the left side of the figure. If you get lost, remember that the merged data shown in Figures 6.67 and 6.68 are identical. Note that as soon as the right half of the list is sorted a final merge completes the sort.

If you study the algorithm in Figure 6.65 you will see that the order in which data is copied into the temporary array is not what you might expect. The order is chosen to make the merge process simple and efficient. See if you can explain how this is done.

How many compares are needed for mergesort? To keep the analysis simple, suppose the number of elements to sort is a power of 2. A little reflection will convince you that we merge two lists of length ($n/2$), four lists of length ($n/4$), eight lists of length ($n/8$), and so on, until we merge ($n/2$) lists of length 1. To merge lists of length 1 requires one compare. To merge lists of length 2 requires two or three compares. To merge lists of length 4 requires between four and seven compares. Generally, to merge two lists of length n requires between ($n/2$) and $n - 1$ compares. So the minimum number of compares needed is

$$1(n/2) + 2(n/4) + 4(n/8) + \cdots + (n/2)\,1 = (n/2) + (n/2) + (n/2) + \cdots + (n/2)$$

The number of terms in this expression is the height of the complete binary tree containing the recursive calls. (Figure 6.43 shows that quicksort uses a similar binary tree of recursive calls.) That height is $\log_2 n$, so the number of compares is ($n/2$) $\log_2 n$. This is the result of applying mergesort to data that are already sorted. The maximum number of compares is

$$[2(n/2) - 1] + 2[2(n/4) - 1] + 4[2(n/8) - 1] + \cdots + (n/2)$$
$$= (n - 1) + (n - 2) + (n - 4) + (n - 8) + \cdots + (n/2)$$
$$= \sum_{k=1}^{\log_2 n} (n - 2^{k-1}) = n \log_2 n - \sum_{k=1}^{\log_2 n} 2^{k-1}$$
$$= n \log_2 n - (n - 1)$$

Therefore, the effort required for mergesort is $O(n \log_2 n)$. It is noteworthy that the worst case performance is $O(n \log_2 n)$, and the worst and best performance differs by only a factor of 2. Thus, mergesort can be expected to provide consistent performance for any set of initial data values.

The algorithm in Figure 6.65 requires an extra array to store temporary values. We have seen an algorithm that uses mergesort for an array of objects. It appears that mergesort will really be at its best for a linked list. The exercises and references explore this issue further.

To explore the mergesort algorithm further, study the algorithm in Huang (1988). For a complex algorithm and mergesort for a linked list, refer to Tanner (1978).

6.3.5 Comparison of Advanced Sort Algorithms

It can be shown that any algorithm that sorts objects by comparing them in pairs requires at least $O(n \log_2 n)$ compares. In fact the lower bound, on average, is $\log_2(n!)$, which is approximated by

$$n \log_2 n - 1.44\,n + O(\log_2 n)$$

Observe that mergesort comes close to this theoretical minimum. The effectiveness of mergesort in reducing the number of compares comes from the fact that it always splits lists to be merged exactly in half. Quicksort would do as well except that reasonable schemes for partitioning lists into pieces do not always split them in half.

Figure 6.69 shows a summary of the number of compares needed by the algorithms of this section. Since the worst case performance of quicksort is considered extremely unlikely, from the point of view of Figure 6.69, these algorithms are, in terms of performance orders of magnitude, essentially all the same.

	Expected	Worst case
Quicksort array compares	$O(n \log_2 n)$	$O(n^2)$
Heapsort array compares	$O(n \log_2 n)$	$O(n \log_2 n)$
Mergesort array compares	$O(n \log_2 n)$	$O(n \log_2 n)$

FIGURE 6.69 The number of compares to sort an array of integers initially in random order.

There are other factors. In terms of extra memory—beyond the memory needed to store the array—heapsort requires none, quicksort requires at most $O(\log_2 n)$ for a stack used by the recursion, and array implementation of mergesort requires an entire extra array. What about implementing these algorithms for a linked list? Surely it can be done, but how efficient will it be? In the case of mergesort, will a linked implementation eliminate the need for extra memory? These are important questions, and suggestions for further study and references are given in the exercises. Clearly, there is much still to

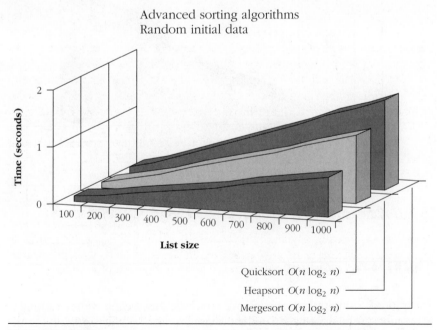

FIGURE 6.70 Times to sort an array of integers initially in random order.

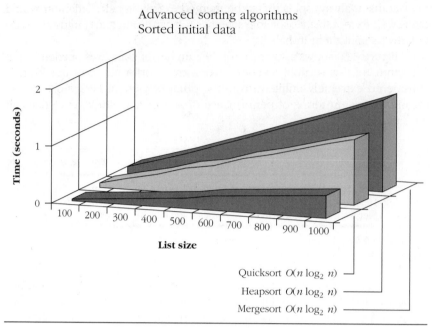

FIGURE 6.71 Times to sort an array of integers initially in sorted order.

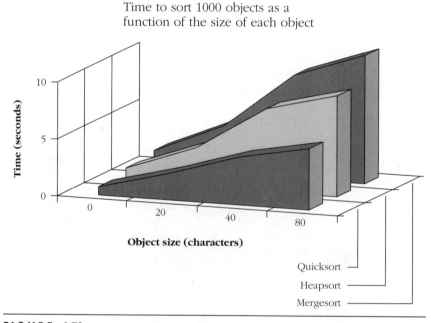

FIGURE 6.72 Time to sort 1000 objects as a function of the size of an object.

be explored about internal sorting. We conclude this section with what might be the most useful information under the circumstances—the results of several timing studies.

Figures 6.70 and 6.71 compare our three advanced sort techniques for sorting an array of integers in random and sorted order. Heapsort and mergesort require about the same time for both initial orderings of the data. Quicksort is faster, by a factor of about 2, for the sorted data. The performance of all three algorithms is $O(n \log_2 n)$, so the similar shape of the curves is no surprise. Look again at statements 1 and 2 in Figures 6.47 and 6.56 to see why quicksort is fast.

Figure 6.72 compares the performance of our three advanced algorithms when the size of the array to sort is fixed (1000 objects) and the size of the array components varies. The major consideration in this case is how many objects are moved. Note that quicksort's moves (Figure 6.56) occur within procedure *median* and as a result of the call to *swap*. There are no other moves.

EXERCISES 6.3

1. Apply the algorithms in Figures 6.47, 6.56, 6.63, and 6.65 to the following sequence of eight integers:

    56, 27, 22, 95, 79, 45, 45, 96

    In each case keep track of the number of compares and moves required. Compare your results with the estimates in Figure 6.69. Also compare the results with those for Exercises 6.2, 1.

2. Use a random number generator to produce a sequence of n random integers.
    a. Modify each of the algorithms in Figures 6.47, 6.56, 6.63, and 6.65 to record the number of moves and compares required to sort a list. Plot these values as a function of n. Compare your results with Figure 6.69. Also compare the results with those for Exercises 6.2, 2.
    b. Modify each of the algorithms in Figures 6.47, 6.56, 6.63, and 6.65 to record each time an object is moved and the distance it is moved. Plot a histogram of frequency versus distance moved for each algorithm. Discuss your results.

3. A sorting algorithm is stable if it preserves the order of objects with equal key values. Which of the algorithms in Figures 6.47, 6.56, 6.63, and 6.65 are stable? Refer to Exercises 6.2, 3 for a comparison.

4. A sequence of objects is formed by starting with a sorted sequence then exchanging one pair. For example, starting with the sequence

    1, 2, 3, 4, 5, 6, 7, 8, 9, 10

    and exchanging the second and fifth elements yields the sequence

    1, 5, 3, 4, 2, 6, 7, 8, 9, 10

    Discuss the effectiveness of the algorithms in Section 6.3 for sorting such a list. Consider both the size of the list and the specific pair of objects exchanged. Discuss the content of Figure 6.69 for this special case. Refer to Exercises 6.2, 4.

5. A sequence of n sorted elements has k randomly selected elements appended to its end. Discuss the effectiveness of the algorithms in Section 6.3 for sorting such a list. Discuss the content of Figure 6.69 for this special case. Refer to Exercises 6.2, 5.

6. Discuss which of the algorithms in Section 6.3 can be effectively implemented for a singly linked list. Provide the implementations for those algorithms that can be effectively implemented.

    The difficulty of implementing quicksort for a singly linked list is that both scans must move in the same direction. To accomplish this, use two pointers to scan the list—call them scan 1 and scan 2. The list is divided into three parts as follows: objects to the left of scan 1 are less than the object used to partition the list, objects between scan 1 and scan 2 are larger than the object used to partition the list, and objects to the right of scan 2 have not been processed. The next paragraph discusses computing a pivot value.

    An alternative to the median of three modification is described in Motzkin (1983). This approach, called meansort, uses the mean value of those objects being partitioned. The mean value for use during partitioning step k is determined during the scan of a previous step. The first partitioning step simply uses the value of the left object.

    To implement mergesort for a singly linked list,

consider beginning by merging whatever sublists happen to be sorted in the original data.

7. Repeat Exercises 6.3, 6 for a doubly linked list.

8. How effective are the methods of Section 6.3 for sorting a list of objects if all the values are the same? Provide the values for Figure 6.69 in this case.

9. Implement a sort algorithm that uses insertion sort to construct sorted sublists of length q, then completes the sort using mergesort. Determine the best value of q (by running experiments) for data that are initially in random order.

10. Implement mergesort using three-way merges instead of two-way merges.

11. An interesting sort technique, with $O(n)$ performance, is distribution sort. For this technique to work the key values must be unique and must all come from a domain small enough that an array can be declared with one component for each possible key value. For example, suppose we want to sort an array of employee records, *random_employee_list,* based on the value of *emp_no* where

type count **is** natural **range** $0 .. max\_emp$;
type index **is** positive **range** $1 .. max\_emp$;

type employee **is record**
    emp_no   : index;
    SSN   : string (1 .. 9);
    data   : string (1 .. 50);
end record;

type employee_list **is array** (index) **of** employee;
type sorted_list **is array** (index) **of** count := (others
  => 0);

number_of_employees : count;
random_employee_list : employee_list;
sorted_employee_list : sorted_list;

The sort algorithm is the simple loop

for k **in** 1 .. number_of_employees **loop**
    sorted_employee_list (random_employee_list
    (k).emp_no) := k;
end loop;

Further information about distribution sort is given in Bentley (1983a) and Sedgewick (1988, pp. 111–113).

12. Implement *retrieve_kth_smallest* using a modification of the algorithm used for quicksort.

function retrieve_kth_smallest (the_array : objects_to_sort; k : positive) **return** object_type;
-- ***results:*** *Returns the kth smallest object contained in*
-- *the_array. If k is 1, then the smallest object is*
-- *returned. If k is the_array'length, then the*
-- *largest object is returned.*
-- ***exceptions:*** *Underflow is raised if* k > *the_array'length.*

Your implementation should be almost the same as that for quicksort. The difference is that continuing to process both subintervals following a quicksort partition is replaced by continuing to process only the subinterval containing the *k*th array component. If the partitioned object is in the *k*th position, processing should stop.

As a simple alternative to the above, use selection sort to sort the first *k* array components for small values of *k* and the modified quicksort algorithm for large values of *k*. Run experiments to determine the values of "small" for the best performance.

13. The speed of quicksort is attributed to three aspects of the algorithm: (a) the simplicity of its inner loop, (b) its ability to move objects long distances, and (c) its use of insertion sort to mop up short sublists.

Insertion sort and exchange sort are particularly deficient with respect to (b). They both move objects from one position to an adjacent position. An effective way to modify either of these algorithms is usually called shellsort. Shellsort attempts to move objects through long distances by a sequence of subsorts that we will call *k*-sorts. For example, if there are the following 10 array components to sort:

$x(1), x(2), x(3), x(4), x(5), x(6), x(7), x(8), x(9), x(10)$

then a 3-sort would be to sort the following three sublists:

$x(1), x(4), x(7), x(10)$
$x(2), x(5), x(8)$
$x(3), x(6), x(9)$

Any technique can be applied to sort the sublists. Shellsort consists of a sequence of *k*-sorts such that the last value of *k* is 1. The intent is that by the time *k* is 1 all objects will be near their sorted position. A sequence of *k* values that appears to work well is

$\dots, 364, 121, 40, 13, 4, 1$

Modify the insertion sort algorithm so that it becomes a shellsort algorithm. Implement your algorithm.

Further information about shellsort is found in Sedgewick (1988, pp. 107–111) and Knuth (1973b).

6.4 Radix Sort

The sort techniques we have discussed so far have been based on comparing the key fields of the items to sort. We know that at least $O(n \log_2 n)$ compares are needed for such sort algorithms. A radix sort is different. In a radix sort objects are positioned based on the individual digit (or radix) values of their key components. For example, sorting the integer 562 would require positioning it with respect to each of its three digits: 5, 6, and 2. Sorting a list of n objects, each of whose key items contains k radix values, thus requires $k * n$ bit radix value comparisons. Since k is fixed, it could be argued that $O(n)$ compares are needed and hence the algorithm is linear in n. But note that if the key values are all distinct, then k must be *at least* $\log_2 n$ and the number of compares, like quicksort, is $O(n \log_2 n)$. Of course, k may be greater than $\log_2 n$.

6.4.1 Radix Sort Example

Figure 6.73 shows a list of integers, each containing three digits, to sort. The sort begins by taking each integer, working from right to left, and moving it to a bin based on the value of its last digit. The result is shown in Figure 6.74.

362 745 885 957 054 786 080 543 012 565

FIGURE 6.73 A list of objects to sort.

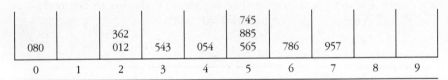

FIGURE 6.74 The integers in Figure 6.73 positioned according to the value of their last digits.

The integers are removed from the bins in Figure 6.74, from left to right, retaining the order from top to bottom in each bin, and a new list is formed as shown in Figure 6.75. Note that the list in Figure 6.75 is sorted with respect to its third digit.

080 362 012 543 054 745 885 565 786 957

FIGURE 6.75 The list formed by collecting the integers, from left to right, based on their positions in Figure 6.74.

Once again each integer is distributed, working from right to left, this time by moving it to a bin based on the value of its second digit. The result is shown in Figure 6.76.

The integers are removed from the bins in Figure 6.76, from left to right, and a new list is formed as shown in Figure 6.77. The list in Figure 6.77 is sorted with respect to its second and third digits.

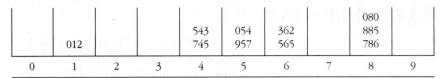

FIGURE 6.76 The integers in Figure 6.75 positioned according to the value of their second digit.

012 543 745 054 957 362 565 080 885 786

FIGURE 6.77 The list formed by collecting the integers, from left to right, based on their positions in Figure 6.76.

Each integer is distributed again, this time by moving it to a bin based on the value of its most significant digit. The result is shown in Figure 6.78.

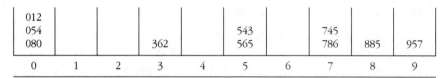

FIGURE 6.78 The integers in Figure 6.77 positioned according to the value of their first digits.

The integers are removed from the bins in Figure 6.76, from left to right, and a new list is formed as shown in Figure 6.77. The list in Figure 6.77 is sorted with respect to its second and third digits.

012 054 080 362 543 565 745 786 885 957

FIGURE 6.79 The integers in Figure 6.78 positioned according to the value of their first digits. The list is sorted.

Before digital computers were widely used for sorting, the radix sort algorithm was the main technique used for sorting large sets of data. To see this, think of each integer as being stored on a card with holes punched in it to record the data. Each of the lists, Figures 6.73, 6.75, 6.77, and 6.79, was a stack of such cards with top-to-bottom order in the stack shown left to right in the figures. A mechanical card sorter could be set to distribute the cards into bins based on the value punched in any one column. Such distributions are shown in Figures 6.74, 6.76, and 6.78. After distributing the cards based on the value in one column, the operator would collect the cards to form a new stack. The process would be repeated for each of the columns on which the sort was to be based. Such cards almost always contained 80 columns of data, and each column was capable of recording any character or digit. Sorting a stack of cards on nine columns (e.g., Social Security numbers) would require the operator to run the stack of cards through the sorter nine times. Census data in the United States was sorted in this way for many years.

6.4.2 Radix Sort Implementation

There are several ways to implement radix sort. Some of these are based on data in a linked list, and others start with data in an array. The implementation in this section sorts data in an array using the principles of radix sort and a simple modification of the quicksort algorithm. The exercises provide suggestions for applying radix sort to a linked list.

Using the radix sort described below requires manipulation of the bits that make up the key field of the data to sort. Ada provides excellent facilities for such bit manipulation, and these are introduced in Section 6.4.3.

Specification of a package that contains radix sort follows. Since the package contains only the sort procedure, it could just as well be a generic procedure. Choose the approach that applies to your situation.

■ **SPECIFICATION 6.2 Radix Sort**

generic
    type object_type **is private**;
    type object_array **is array** (integer **range** <>) **of** object_type;
    key_bits : **in** positive;   *-- Number of bits in the sort key.*

    with function bit_of (the_object : object_type; the_bit : positive) **return** boolean;
    *-- **results:** Returns true if the bit in position the_bit of the_object is 1; otherwise returns false. The least*
    --   significant bit is in position 1. That is, bit positions are: key_bits ⋯ 7 6 5 4 3 2 1

package radix_sort **is**

    procedure radix_exchange_sort (the_objects : **in out** object_array);
    *-- **results:** the_objects are sorted in ascending order.*

end radix_sort;

To see how we will implement *radix_exchange_sort,* consider the data in Figure 6.80.

9	10	11	12	13	14	15	0	1	2
1001	1010	1011	1100	1101	1110	1111	0000	0001	0010

FIGURE 6.80 The data to sort—shown using base 10 and base 2.

The data to sort are shown in two forms—base 10 and base 2. The remainder of the discussion will display the data in base 2. For this example, to keep things simple, each value has only four binary digits. We begin by sorting these objects (using a simple modification of the quicksort algorithm) with respect to their most significant binary digit.

A scan from left to right searches for an object whose high order bit is 1. A scan from right to left searches for an object whose high order bit is 0.

These scans are shown in Figure 6.81. The items where the scans end are exchanged. The result is shown in Figure 6.82.

1001	1010	1011	1100	1101	1110	1111	0000	0001	0010
→									←

FIGURE 6.81 The initial left and right scans for the original data.

0010	1010	1011	1100	1101	1110	1111	0000	0001	1001
	→							←	

FIGURE 6.82 The first and last objects have been exchanged. A second pair of scans occurs next.

The scans continue. As before, the scan to the right searches for a high order bit equal to 1, and the scan to the left searches for a high order bit equal to 0. These scans are shown in Figure 6.82. As before, the items where the scans end are exchanged. The result is shown in Figure 6.83.

0010	0001	1011	1100	1101	1110	1111	0000	1010	1001
		→				←			

FIGURE 6.83 Another pair of values is swapped. Then another pair of scans.

(1)	(2)	(3)	(4)	(5)	(6)	(7)	(8)	(9)	(10)
0010	0001	0000	1100	1101	1110	1111	1011	1010	1001
			→←	—	—	—	—		

FIGURE 6.84 A third pair of values is swapped. Then the scans continue until they meet at the value in the fourth position.

(1)	(2)	(3)	(4)	(5)	(6)	(7)	(8)	(9)	(10)	
1001	1010	1011	1100	1101	1110	1111	0000	0001	0010	[1, 10]—4
0010	0001	0000	1100	1101	1110	1111	1011	1010	1001	[1, 3]—3
0010	0001	0000	1100	1101	1110	1111	1011	1010	1001	[1, 3]—2
0000	0001	0010	1100	1101	1110	1111	1011	1010	1001	[1, 2]—1
0000	0001	0010	1100	1101	1110	1111	1011	1010	1001	[4, 10]—3
0000	0001	0010	1001	1010	1011	1111	1110	1101	1100	[4, 6]—2
0000	0001	0010	1001	1010	1011	1111	1110	1101	1100	[5, 6]—1
0000	0001	0010	1001	1010	1011	1111	1110	1101	1100	[7, 10]—2
0000	0001	0010	1001	1010	1011	1100	1101	1110	1111	[7, 8]—1
0000	0001	0010	1001	1010 .	1011	1100	1101	1110	1111	[9, 10]—1

FIGURE 6.85 Radix sort of sample data using the algorithm in Figure 6.86. A row of data is printed at the beginning of each execution of *sort_recursive*. Study Figures 6.85 and 6.86 in parallel—not sequentially.

The scans continue. As before the scan to the right searches for a high order bit equal to 1, and the scan to the left searches for a high order bit equal to 0. These scans are shown in Figure 6.83. Also as before, the items where the scans end are exchanged. The result is shown in Figure 6.84.

The scans continue. The scan to the left meets the scan to the right before it finds a value whose high order bit is 0. This stops the scan to the left. These scans are shown in Figure 6.84. Now, since the scans have met, the data are

```
package body radix_sort is

procedure radix_exchange_sort (the_objects : in out object_array) is
-- Length 1   Complexity 1   Performance O(n * key_length)

    procedure sort_recursive (left, right : integer; bit : positive) is
    -- Length 17   Complexity 9   Recursion 2
      j, k : integer;
    begin
      if right > left then
        j := left; k := right;

        loop
          while (not bit_of(the_objects(j), bit)) and (j < k) loop
            j := j + 1;
          end loop;

          while (bit_of(the_objects(k), bit)) and (j < k) loop
            k := k - 1;
          end loop;

          exit when (j = k);
          swap (the_objects(j), the_objects(k));
        end loop;

        if not bit_of(the_objects(k), bit) then
          k := k + 1;
        end if;

        if bit > 1 then
          sort_recursive (left, k - 1, bit - 1);
          sort_recursive (k, right, bit - 1);
        end if;

      end if;
    end sort_recursive;

begin
    sort_recursive(the_objects'first, the_objects'last, key_bits);
end radix_exchange_sort;

end radix_sort;
```

F I G U R E   6.86 Implementation of *radix_exchange_sort*.

partitioned. Look at Figure 6.84 and observe that the data are sorted with respect to their most significant bits. Make sure you see why this is the case.

The partitioning is now repeated for the next most significant bit and for the two sublists created by the first partition. In Figure 6.84 the sublists consist of the first three objects and the last seven objects. Unlike quicksort in Section 6.3.1 no object is in its sorted position. But, like quicksort, the problem has been partitioned into two independent smaller pieces.

Figure 6.85 shows the complete details for the data given in Figure 6.80. Each row of data has been annotated to show which sublist is being partitioned and which bit is being used to determine the partition. The code that was executed to produce Figure 6.85 is shown in Figure 6.86. Study Figures 6.85 and 6.86 together.

When studying the algorithm in Figure 6.86 keep in mind that it is a

```
with radix_sort;
with unchecked_conversion;

procedure main is

    type bit is range 0 .. 1;
    for bit'size use 1;                          -- An Ada representation clause.

    type word is array(0 .. 31) of bit;          -- Assume an integer is 32 bits.
    for word'size use 32;                         -- An Ada representation clause.

    function integer_to_word is new unchecked_conversion(integer, word);

    type vector is array (integer range <>) of integer;
    function bit_on (ii : integer; which_bit : positive) return boolean;

    package radix is new radix_sort (integer, vector, 32, bit_on);

    function bit_on (ii : integer; which_bit : positive) return boolean is
      w : word := integer_to_word (ii);
    begin
      return w(32 − which_bit) = 1;
    end bit_on;

begin
    declare
      the_data_to_sort : vector(1 .. 90);
    begin
      ...
      radix.radix_exchange_sort (the_data_to_sort);
      ...
    end;
end main;
```

F I G U R E 6.87 A program that instantiates package *radix_sort*.

simple variation of the quicksort algorithm in Section 6.3.1. Instantiating *radix_sort* is interesting because of the generic function *bit_of* in Specification 6.2. Section 6.4.3 provides an example instantiation. Further information about radix sort is provided in Sedgewick (1988, pp. 135–143).

6.4.3 Instantiation of Radix Sort

Figure 6.87 shows procedure *main* that instantiates *radix_sort*. The interesting part of the instantiation is the implementation of a function that tests whether a particular bit is on or off. To keep the example simple, the field being used for the radix sort is of type integer. In fact, the data to be sorted are simply an array of integers. But the basic idea of how to write an efficient implementation of the generic function *bit_of* in Specification 6.2 is provided.

The first four lines of procedure *main* construct a type, *word,* that is the same size as an integer. Since word is an array of binary values, random access to each of its components should be efficient. To complete the preparation, function *integer_to_word* is instantiated as a function to convert an integer to a value of type word. Recall that the conversion leaves the bit pattern unchanged; it simply gives the converted value a new interpretation.

Now look at the implementation of *bit_on*. The conversion from integer to word, at run time, requires no computation. Checking a bit's value is therefore accomplished by accessing an array component and comparing that component to 1. Further details about Ada's bit manipulation are given in Chapter 7.

EXERCISES 6.4

1. Apply radix sort, as shown in Figures 6.74 through 6.79, to the following list of integers:
482, 213, 928, 204, 145, 428, 659, 379, 235, 47, 577, 992, 66, 131, 22

2. Write the specification for a package that contains a procedure to apply radix sort to objects stored in a linked list.

3. Write the package body for the specification in Exercise 2. Do this (a) by including the list and its needed operations in the package body for radix sort and (b) by instantiating a list that supplies the list operations needed for radix sort.

   One technique for implementing radix sort for linked lists is similar to the distribution into bins approach in Figures 6.74 through 6.79. The bins are replaced by an array of linked lists—one array entry, and hence one linked list, for each possible value of a character in the sort field. With two such arrays, the distribution process alternates between the arrays with no need to collect the objects into a partially sorted list.

4. Instantiate radix sort assuming the objects to sort are records with two fields. The key field, on which the sort is based, is of type *string(1 .. 20)*. You will need to determine the number of bits occupied by a character on the computer used to test your instantiation.

■ 6.5 Summary

We will summarize the sort algorithms discussed in this chapter by presenting, in graphical form, some rules of thumb. Figure 6.88 shows these rules for objects in random order stored in an array. If the list is small, use insertion

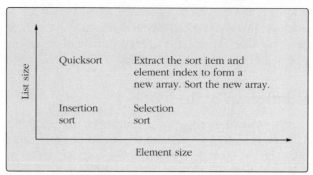

FIGURE 6.88 Rules of thumb for selecting a sort technique for objects stored in an array. The sort item is assumed to be small.

sort for small objects and selection sort for large objects. Both techniques are $O(n^2)$, but for small lists their low overheads make them attractive. Selection sort makes the least moves, so it is faster for large objects. Insertion sort makes fewer compares, so it is faster for smaller objects.

As the number of objects increases, the $O(n \log_2 n)$ effort of quicksort, along with its simple inner loop, makes it a better choice. Finally, as the objects become large, quicksort spends much of its time moving data from one place to another. We suggest that you form a new array in which the data are replaced by the array index of the array component that contains it. The new array, whose components are small, is now sorted using quicksort. The indexes in this sorted array prescribe the sorted order of the original array. If you wish, the original array can be placed in sorted order with $O(n)$ moves.

Figure 6.89 suggests techniques for sorting objects in a doubly linked list. Observe that the horizontal axes in Figures 6.88 and 6.89 have different labels. For arrays it is object size; for linked lists it is sort item size. For a linked list, object size is of little concern since objects are never moved. Sort item size is of interest because if it is small and the list is large, radix sort is attractive.

These rules of thumb apply only to the special cases cited, and even then the figures shown do not prescribe in any quantitative way the location of the boundaries between methods. We can only repeat, "there are many best methods, depending on what is to be sorted on what machine for what purpose" (Knuth, 1973b).

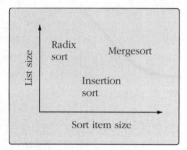

FIGURE 6.89 Suggestions for selecting a sort technique for objects stored in a doubly linked list. Quicksort may be used in place of mergesort; see Exercises 6.3, 9.

7

Sets
and
Hashing

■ 7.1 Introduction

In this chapter we will study data types that share the characteristic that their structure is setlike. Recall from mathematics that a set is a collection of objects. The objects may not have any attributes in common, although most often they do. In Figure 7.1a the members of the collection have no obvious traits in common except that they are members of the collection. We are more likely to find sets like the one in Figure 7.1b in which the members are all people who share some characteristic, such as being enrolled in the same class. In this chapter we are interested in sets of data objects. The members of such sets normally share the characteristic that they are all of the same data type.

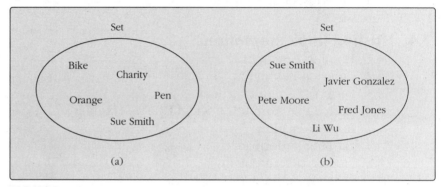

FIGURE 7.1 Two sets.

The study of sets can be divided into two areas. The first is composed of sets of atomic objects—objects of a discrete type. If an object is given, then it can be determined whether it is a member of a given set. It either is or it isn't. If it is, there is nothing more we can learn about it from the set. For instance, let X be a set of characters, then place a set of values into X:

$$X := \{`a` .. `d`, `A` .. `D`\} \qquad \text{-- \textit{This is not an Ada statement.}}$$

If we have a character variable ch and we set $ch = `c`$, the boolean function

is_member $(X, ch) =$ true

Once we determine this, there is nothing more to learn about ch relative to set X. These kinds of sets are discussed in Section 7.3.

The second kind of set is one that has quite different operations and characteristics. Sets of this type provide a map between keys and data (see Section 1.5.2). Objects with embedded keys are placed into the set of such objects. The membership of an object with a given key value can be determined by specifying a key value then executing an *is_member* boolean function. If an object with the given key is present in the set, it can be retrieved or updated. This kind of set is most efficiently implemented by hashing (see below).

We will examine two techniques for implementing sets in Ada. The first, *bit arrays,* uses Ada's ability to manipulate arrays of bits. It is the subject of Section 7.2.

The second is a technique called hashing. It involves using a key value to compute a position in a table called a hash table. Recall from Chapter 2 that, given an index value(s) of an array, we could compute the memory address of the array object by using the array mapping function. The drawback was that we had to know the index of the object we wanted. Often, all we have is the key value of an object. We need a mapping between the keys and their associated data. That is, given a key value, we need to retrieve the associated data from the data structure in which it is stored. We have seen several examples of solving this problem in efficient ways—sorted lists, linked lists, binary trees, and B-trees. Each involved taking the target key and doing some sort of search to find the entry in the data structure with that key value. In each case, the amount of searching increased as the number of entries in the data structure increased—they were all increasing functions of *n,* the number of objects in the data structure.

The position computed by the hashing function might be a location (cylinder, surface, or sector) on a disk drive or an array index in a table that is an array of objects. We restrict the discussion that follows to hash tables that are arrays in random access memory.

Hashing gives us the ability to provide a mapping based on calculations that yield performance similar to array mapping functions. Given a key, say *target,* we apply some function, call it *H,* that returns the memory address of the object with that target key:

$$H(target\_key) := addr(the\_object) \qquad \text{-- } \textit{where key\_of(the\_object)} = \textit{target\_key.}$$

An example of a simple but effective function H is

$$H(the\_key) = the\_key \textbf{ mod } m \qquad \text{-- } \textit{m is some carefully chosen value.}$$

Hashing is the major topic of Section 7.4. Section 7.5 is a summary.

■ 7.2 Bits and Arrays of Bits

Ada has the facility of being able to represent and manipulate arrays of bits. This can provide a particularly compact and efficient way of implementing sets of atomic objects. In Section 7.2.1, we will look at the method representing these bit arrays using Ada. In Section 7.2.2, we'll see a number of the predefined operations available in Ada to manipulate these arrays.

The representation and operations available in Ada are specific to Ada, but they also closely parallel the same representation and operations available at the machine language and hardware architecture level on most computers. Thus, the techniques that you learn will be directly applicable when you are programming in assembly languages and in intermediate level languages such as C.

7.2.1 Representation of Bits and Bit Arrays in Ada

We can represent a single bit in Ada by declaring a type and specifying its representation as follows (*Ada LRM,* 1983, Section 13.2):

```
type bit is new boolean;                    -- A derived type.
for bit'size use 1;          -- Use one machine bit to represent type bit's values.
```

If we have variables *a* and *b,* we can assign them values:

```
a := true;
b := false;
```

a is represented in memory by a single bit whose value is 1 and *b* by a single bit whose value is 0. We can do all of the operations available for boolean types, such as

```
a := a and b;
a := a xor b;
a := a or b;
a := not b;
```

Suppose we wished to have a bit array. We can do so with the following additional declaration:

```
type bit_array is array (1 .. len) of bit;
pragma pack (bit_array);          -- Eliminate padding; pack 1 bit per array element.

a_bit_array : bit_array;
```

The **pragma** attempts to force the compiler to use consecutive bits without padding. While we have stipulated that 1 bit should be used for each value of type *bit,* the array may be implemented by the compiler by using 1 byte per array element but using only 1 bit of the byte. The other 7 bits would hold padding. That **pragma** directs the removal of any padding.

We could make the *bit_array* correspond exactly to the word size of the computer system by making *len* exactly the number of bits in a word. You can verify the number of bits used to store a *bit_array* by using Ada's *size* attribute. Write the value *a_bit_array'size*.

7.2.2 Manipulation of Bit Arrays

Array and boolean operations are now available for the bit arrays. Suppose we have two constants:

```
on  : constant bit := true;                              -- Bit 1.
off : constant bit := false;                             -- Bit 0.
```

and variables *D* and *E:*

```
D, E : bit_array := bit_array'(1 .. len => off);
```

Suppose we have *len* = 7 for demonstration purposes.

We can flip any bit or group of bits on by specifying the index of the bit and setting its value to on:

```
D(3) := on;                                              -- D = 0010000.
D(5 .. 7) := (on, on, on);                               -- D = 0010111.

E := bit_array'(1 | 3 | 5 => on, others => off);         -- E = 1010100.
```

The logical operators are also available:

or   Logical or
and   Logical and
xor   Exclusive or
not   Complement

Starting with the values *D* = 0010111 and *E* = 1010100,

```
D(2)      := not D(2);                                   -- D = 0110111.
E(5 .. 7) := not E(5 .. 7);                              -- E = 1010011.
D         := D xor E;                                    -- D = 1100100.
D(1 .. 3) := D(1 .. 3) and E(5 .. 7);                    -- D = 0100100.
```

and so on. All of the array operations that apply to arrays of discrete type objects are also available:

```
if D = E then ...
```

```
D := E(1 .. 3) & D(3 .. 6);                              -- D = 1010010.
```

and so on.

To shift a *bit_array* left *n* bits and pull 0's in from the right, we might say

```
D := D(n + 1 .. len) & (1 .. n => off);
```

To circular left shift (i.e., have bits shifted off the left side and fill in on the right side),

```
D := D(n + 1 .. len) & D(1 .. n);
```

As you can see, Ada has substantial facilities for bit manipulation. Refer to *Ada LRM,* 1983, Sections 3.5.3, 3.6, 4.5.1, 4.5.2, and 13.2 for background and more information.

We next look at sets of atomic objects and the implementation of these sets using bit arrays.

1. Write a procedure that will take a bit array as input and print its value as a sequence of zeros and ones. For instance, 00101101.

2. Write a program that will allow users to enter the values of 2-bit arrays of known size together with a boolean operator, compute the results of the operation, and print the result using the print procedure developed in Exercise 1. The data will be entered in the form *<value> op <value<*. For instance, 00101101 xor 11010111.

■ 7.3 Sets of Discrete Objects

The techniques of Section 7.2 are ideal for implementation of the abstraction of a set of discrete objects. Such sets might be a set of characters, a set of some objects of some enumerated type such as *day,*

type day **is** (sun, mon, tue, wed, thu, fri, sat);

or a set of the values of some integer subrange,

type month **is range** 1 .. 12;

Section 7.3.1 has the discrete set specification, Section 7.3.2 has an example of its use, and Section 7.3.3 is an implementation.

7.3.1 Discrete Object Set Abstraction

The abstraction is given in Specification 7.1. Note that the private section has bit arrays as the data structure used to represent the sets.

■ SPECIFICATION 7.1 Sets of Discrete Objects

-- *Abstract Structure:* A set of objects of a user-specified discrete type.

-- *Constraints:* There may be implementation-dependent bounds on maximum set size
--   as determined by the number of discrete values in discrete type object, *that is,*
--   object'last − object'first + 1.

generic

    type object_type **is** (<>);   -- *Any discrete type.*

(continued)

Specification 7.1 (continued)

package set_package **is**

    type set **is private**;

    type set_of_objects **is array** (integer **range** <>) **of** object_type;

    function "&" (the_set : set; the_object : object_type) **return** set;
    -- **results:** *Returns the union of the_set and the_object.*

    function "&" (the_set : set; the_objects : set_of_objects) **return** set;
    -- **results:** *Returns the union of the_set and the_objects.*
    -- **notes:** *Allows users a natural notation; for instance, S := S & (e, f, g, . . .), where S is*
    -- *a set and e, f, g, . . . , are objects.*

    function " + " (left, right : set) **return** set;
    -- **results:** *Returns the union of sets left and right.*

    function " − " (left, right : set) **return** set;
    -- **results:** *Returns the set difference left − right.*

    function " − " (the_set : set; the_object : object_type) **return** set;
    -- **results:** *Returns the set difference the_set − {the_object} removing the object from the*
    set.

    function "*" (left, right : set) **return** set;
    -- **results:** *Returns the intersection of sets left and right.*

    function "<" (the_object : object_type; the_set : set;) **return** boolean;
    -- **results:** *Returns true if the_object is a member of the_set; returns false otherwise.*

    function "< =" (left, right : set) **return** boolean;
    -- **results:** *Returns true if left is a subset of right; returns false otherwise.*

    function "<" (left, right : set) **return** boolean;
    -- **results:** *Returns true if left is a proper subset of right; returns false otherwise.*

    function number_of_objects (the_set : set) **return** natural;
    -- **results:** *Returns the number of objects in the_set.*

    function empty_set **return** set;
    -- **results:** *Returns the empty set.*

private

    type bit **is new** boolean;
    for bit'size **use** 1;   -- *Use 1 bit per type bit value.*
    type set **is array** (0 .. object_type'pos(object_type'last)) **of** bit;
    pragma pack (set);   -- *Packs bits in the array.*

end set_package;

The second "&" function is provided to give a handy facility for inclusion of multiple objects into a set. Its declaration is

function "&" (the_set : set; the_objects : set_of_objects) **return** set;

Suppose that *object_type* = *character*. Also suppose that we want to be able to include several characters in the set in one operation:

package char_sets **is new** set_package(character);

ch : character;
the_set : char_sets.set;
function "&" (the_set : set; the_objects : set_of_objects) **return** set
    renames char_sets."&";

        .
        .
        .
ch := 'W';
the_set := the_set & ('d', '#', ch, 'Z');

The last statement computes the characters listed and *the_set*. The **renames** statement is used in place of a **use** clause to illustrate an alternative. If the **renames** and **use** clauses are both absent, the use of the "&" function becomes unwieldy. The last statement in the sequence above would have to be

the_set := char_sets."&" (the_set, ('d', '#', ch, 'Z'));

7.3.2 Application of Discrete Object Sets

As an example of the use of the *set* abstraction, suppose we wish to have a program that will determine which of the printing characters did not appear in some input text file. The objects of the set will be ASCII characters (see Chapter 8). The program is shown in Figure 7.2. It could have been designed more efficiently, but an attempt was made to show a number of different set operations in use.

```
with text_io, set_package; use text_io;
procedure main is
-- Length 30   Complexity 7   Performance (n), where n is the number of characters read.
    package ch_set is new set_package(character); use ch_set;

    printing_chars   : ch_set.set := ch_set.empty_set;
    chars_found      : ch_set.set := ch_set.empty_set;
    chars_not_found  : ch_set.set;
    ch               : character;
```

FIGURE 7.2 Program to print nonoccurring characters. Uses sets.   *(continued)*

Figure 7.2 (continued)

```
begin
    for ch in ' '..'~' loop                                        -- Place printing characters in set printing_chars.
        printing_chars := printing_chars & ch;
    end loop;
    loop
        while end_of_line and not end_of_file loop
            skip_line;
        end loop;
        exit when end_of_file;
        get(ch);
        if ch < printing_chars                                     -- Is ch in the set of printing characters?
            and not (ch < chars_found) then                        -- Has it been found yet?
                chars_found := chars_found & ch;                   -- No; include it in the set of found chars.
            end if;
        end if;
    end loop;

    chars_not_found := printing_chars - chars_found;               -- Compute the set of chars not found using set difference.
    declare
        count : natural := 0;
    begin
        put_line("Printing characters that did not occur:");
        for ch in ' '..'~' loop
            if ch < chars_not_found then                           -- Is x in the set of chars not found?
                put(ch & ' ');                                     -- Yes; print it.
                count := count + 1;                                -- These lines are included to give nice output.
                if count mod 20 = 0 then new_line; end if;
            end if;
        end loop;
    end;
    new_line(2);
end main;
```

F I G U R E   7.2 *(continued)*

Figure 7.3 shows the output produced by the program when its own source code (Figure 7.2 with the comments removed) is used as data.

```
Printing characters that did not occur:
! # $ % & ' * + / 8 9 < ? @ A B C D E F
G H I J K L M N O P Q R S T U V W X Y Z
[ \ ] ^ ' { | } ~
```

F I G U R E   7.3 Output of the program in Figure 7.2 using itself as data.

7.3.3 Bit Array Implementation

Package Body 7.1 puts together the bit array technique with the set of discrete objects abstraction. Note the brevity of the code. Most operations consist of a single executable statement. Bit arrays and the operations that were discussed in Section 7.2 are used throughout.

■ PACKAGE BODY 7.1 Sets of Discrete Objects—Implements Specification 7.1

```
package body set_package is

   on   : constant bit := true;                              -- These are declared for readability of the code below.
   off  : constant bit := false;

   function "&" (the_set : set; the_object : object_type) return set is
      T : set := the_set;
   begin
      T(object_type'pos(the_object)) := on;
      return T;
   end "&";

   function "&" (the_set : set; the_objects : set_of_objects) return set is
      T : set := the_set;
   begin
      for j in the_objects'range loop
         T := T & the_objects(j);                            -- Include each of the objects individually in the set.
      end loop;
      return T;
   end "&";

   function "+" (left, right : set) return set is
   begin
      return left or right;
   end "+";

   function "−" (left, right : set) return set is
   begin
      return (left and right) xor left;
   end "−";

   function "−" (the_set : set; the_object : object_type) return set is
      T : set := the_set;
   begin
      T(object_type'pos(the_object)) := off;
      return T;
   end "−";

   function "*" (left, right : set) return set is
   begin
      return left and right;
   end "*";

   function "<" (the_object : object_type; the_set : set) return boolean is
   begin
      return boolean (the_set (object_type'pos(the_object)));
   end "<";
```

(continued)

Package Body 7.1 (continued)

```
function "<=" (left, right : set) return boolean is
begin
   return boolean ((left and right) = left);
end "<=";

function "<" (left, right : set) return boolean is
begin
   return (left <= right) and (not (left = right));
end "<";

function number_of_objects (the_set : set) return natural is
   count : natural := 0;
begin
   for k in the_set'range loop
      if the_set(k) then count := count + 1; end if;          -- Count the number of bits on.
   end loop;
   return count;
end number_of_objects;

function empty_set return set is
   null_set : constant set := set'(set'range => off);
begin
   return null_set;
end empty_set;

end set_package;
```

EXERCISES 7.3

Read in a set of data consisting of a name and the days of the week that a person is scheduled for an activity. Provide for up to 20 people. The days are represented by a three-letter code that is the first three letters of the day. Use Ada's *enumeration_io* data type for input of the days. Internally the days are declared as an enumerated type

type day **is** (sun, mon, tue, wed, thu, fri, sat);

Use package *sets* (Specification 7.1) with an array of sets, one for each person, to record which days of the week each person works. Then, using set operations, have the program answer the following questions and print the results:

a. Which days of the week, if any, does everyone work?
b. Who, if anyone, works every day?
c. Who works on at least the same days (all of them) as the first person in the list of people?
d. Who, if anyone, does not work Thursdays through Saturdays?

7.4 Hashed Implementations

We studied several methods for the storage and later retrieval of keyed records. Arrays, linked lists, and several kinds of trees provide structures that allow these operations. In each of these structures, the *find* operation is necessarily implemented by some form of search. The key values of records in the structure are compared with the desired, or target, key until either a matching value is found or the data structure is exhausted. The pattern of probes is dependent on the methods of organizing and relating the records of the structure. A sorted list implemented as an array can be probed by a binary search. The same list in linked form can only be searched sequentially.

We might ask if it is possible to create a data structure that does not require a search to implement the *find* operation. Is it possible, for example, to compute the location of the record that has a given key value

memory address of record $= f(\text{key})$

where f is a function that maps each distinct key value into the memory address of the record identified by that key? We shall see that the answer is a qualified yes. Such functions can be found, but they are difficult to determine and can be constructed only if all the keys in the data set are known in advance. They are called **perfect hashing functions** and are further examined in Section 7.4.3.

Normally, there has to be a compromise from a strictly calculated access scheme to a hybrid scheme that involves a calculation followed by some limited searching. The function does not necessarily give the exact memory address of the target record but only gives a **home address** that may contain the desired record:

home address $= H(\text{key})$

Functions such as H are known as **hashing functions**. In contrast to perfect hashing functions, these are relatively easy to determine and can give excellent performance. The home address may not contain the record being sought. In that case, a search of other addresses is required, and this is known as **rehashing**. In Section 7.4.1, we introduce a number of hashing functions, and in Section 7.4.2 we examine several rehashing strategies. In Section 7.4.5 we summarize the performance of hashed implementations.

The fundamental idea behind **hashing** is the antithesis of sorting. A sort arranges the records in a regular pattern that makes the relatively efficient binary search possible. Hashing takes the diametrically opposite approach. The basic idea is to scatter the records completely randomly throughout some memory or storage space—the so-called **hash table**. The hash function can be thought of as a pseudo-random number generator that uses the value of the key as a seed and that outputs the home address of the element containing that key.

One of the drawbacks of hashing is the random locations of stored elements. There is no notion of first, next, root, parent, or child or anything analogous. Thus, hashing is appropriate for implementing a set relationship among elements but not for implementing structures that involve relationships among constituent elements. It is for that reason that hashing is discussed in this chapter on sets. There are, however, other appropriate contexts for a discussion of hashing.

One of the virtues of hashing is that it allows us to find records with $O(1)$ probes. The *FindKey* operation has required a number of probes that depends on n in every implementation of every data structure discussed so far: $O(n)$ for a linked implementation of a list, $O(\log_2 n)$ for an array implementation of a sorted list, and $O(\log_2 n)$ for a binary search tree. Since hashing requires the fewest probes to find something, it is frequently considered to be a particularly effective search technique. Also, since hashing stores elements in a table—the hash table—it is sometimes considered to be a technique for operating on tables. All these views of hashing are correct. We choose to view hashing as a technique for implementing sets. Its other advantages and disadvantages are not changed by this point of view.

It is convenient to consider the hash table to be an array of records and to let the hash function calculate the index value of the home address rather than to calculate its memory address directly. Once the appropriate index value is computed, the array mapping function can complete the transformation into an actual memory address.

Suppose we have a hash table defined with *hash_table_size* = 7 so the table entries are *hash_table(0)*, *hash_table(1)*, . . . , *hash_table(6)*. Further, suppose the key of a standard element is of type *integer*. For illustration, we choose the hash function H as

$H(\text{key}) = \text{key } \textbf{mod } 7$

Notice that the value produced by this function is always an integer between 0 and 6, which is within the range of indexes of the table.

Elaboration of the package will produce the empty table shown in Figure 7.4. If the first record we store has a key value of 374, then the hash function

$H(374) = 374 \textbf{ mod } 7 = 3$

places the record at *hash_table(3)*. This is shown in Figure 7.5. If the next record has a key value of 1091, we get

$H(1091) = 1091 \textbf{ mod } 7 = 6$

and the table becomes that shown in Figure 7.6. A third record with key = 911 gives

$H(911) = 911 \textbf{ mod } 7 = 1$

and the resulting table is shown in Figure 7.7.

Retrieval of any of the records already in the table is a simple matter. The target key is presented to the hash function that reproduces the same table position as it did when the record was stored. If the target key were 740, a value not in the table, the hashing function would produce

Hashing is well suited to data types whose structure is setlike.

Table address	Table contents
(0)	empty
(1)	empty
(2)	empty
(3)	empty
(4)	empty
(5)	empty
(6)	empty

FIGURE 7.4 Empty table.

Table address	Table contents
(0)	empty
(1)	empty
(2)	empty
(3)	374, . . . data
(4)	empty
(5)	empty
(6)	empty

FIGURE 7.5 First record stored at table(3).

Table address	Table contents
(0)	empty
(1)	empty
(2)	empty
(3)	374, . . . data
(4)	empty
(5)	empty
(6)	1091, . . . data

FIGURE 7.6 Second record stored at table(6).

Table address	Table contents
(0)	empty
(1)	911, . . . data
(2)	empty
(3)	374, . . . data
(4)	empty
(5)	empty
(6)	1091, . . . data

FIGURE 7.7 Third record stored at table(1).

$H(740) = 740 \textbf{ mod } 7 = 5$

Interrogating *hash_table(5)*, we find that it is empty, and we conclude that a record with key = 740 is not in the table.

The example we have just seen was constructed to conceal a serious problem. So far, keys with different values have hashed to different locations in the table. That is not generally so and is the case in our current example only because the key values were carefully chosen.

Suppose that insertion of a record with a key value of 227 is attempted. Then,

$H(227) = 227 \textbf{ mod } 7 = 3$

but *hash_table(3)* is already filled with another record. This is called a ***collision***—two different key values hashing to the same location. Why this happens and what to do about it are important considerations because collisions are a fact of life when hashing.

Suppose employee records are hashed on the basis of Social Security number. If a firm has 500 employees, it will not want to reserve a hash table with 1 billion entries (the number of possible Social Security numbers) to guarantee that each of its employee records hashes to a unique location. Even if the firm allocates 1000 slots in its hash table and uses a hash function that is a "perfect" randomizer, the probability that there will be no collisions is essentially zero. This is the ***birthday paradox*** (Feller, 1950), which says that hash functions with no collisions are so rare that it is worth looking for them only in special circumstances. These special circumstances are discussed in Section 7.4.3. In the meantime, we need to consider what to do when a collision does occur.

With careful design, strategies for handling collisions are simple. They are commonly called ***rehashing*** or ***collision-resolution strategies***, and we will discuss them in Section 7.4.2.

We selected the hashing function

$H(\text{key}) = \text{key} \textbf{ mod } n$

in the example we just completed. We will now see why that was a reasonable thing to do and will also look at a number of other hashing functions.

7.4.1 Hashing Functions

Since the advent of the hashing technique, a large and diverse group of hashing functions have been proposed. Some are simple and straightforward; others are complex. Almost all are computationally simple, since the speed of the computation of such functions is an important factor in their use. Lum, Yuen, and Dodd (1971) have a good review of many, including some of the more exotic ones. We will confine our attention to simple but effective hashing functions.

Good hashing functions have two desirable properties:

1. They compute rapidly.
2. They produce a nearly random distribution of index values.

Digit Selection

The first hashing function we will discuss is **_digit selection_**. Suppose the keys of the set of data we are dealing with are strings of digits such as Social Security numbers (nine-digit numbers):

$$\text{key} = d_1 d_2 d_3 d_4 d_5 d_6 d_7 d_8 d_9$$

If the population that makes up the data is randomly chosen, then the choice of the last three digits, $d_7 d_8 d_9$, will give a good random distribution of values. A possible implementation is the following:

hash_table: **array** $(0 .. 999)$ **of** person;

where _person_ is a record type for the key and information we wish to keep. Notice that the hashing function in this case is

$$H(\text{key}) = \text{key } \textbf{mod } 1000$$

which simply strips off the last three digits of the key.

Care must be taken in deciding which digits to select. If the population with which we are dealing is students at a university, for example, the last three digits, $d_7 d_8 d_9$, are probably a good choice, whereas the first three digits, $d_1 d_2 d_3$, are probably not. State universities tend to draw their student bodies from a single state or geographical region. The first three digits of the Social Security number are based on the geographical region in which the number was originally issued. Most students from California, for example, have a first digit of 5 and clustered second and third digits, indicating various subregions of the state; 567, for example, is very common. If the data were for a California university, nearly all the students' records would map into the 500–599 range of the hash table, and a large subgroup would map into position 567. The output of the function would not be uniform and random but would be loaded on certain positions of the table, causing an inordinately high number of collisions. It would not be a good hashing function for that reason.

If the key population is known in advance, it is possible to analyze the distribution of values taken by each digit of the key. The digits participating in the hash address are then easy to select. Such an analysis is called **_digit analysis_**. Instead of choosing the last three digits, we would choose the three digits of the key whose digit analyses showed the most uniform distribution. If d_4, d_7, and d_9 gave the flattest distributions, the hashing function might strip out those digits from a key and put them together to form a number in the range 0–999:

$$H(d_1 d_2 d_3 d_4 d_5 d_6 d_7 d_8 d_9) = d_4 d_7 d_9$$

Caution is advised, since although the digits are apparently random and uniform in value, they might have dependencies among themselves. For example, certain combinations of d_7 and d_9 might tend to occur together. Then if d_9 were always 8 when d_7 is 3, $d_4 38$ would be the only table position mapped to in the range $d_4 30$–$d_4 39$, effectively lowering the table size and increasing the chances of collision. Analysis for interdigit correlations might be necessary to bring such a situation to light.

Division

One of the most effective hashing methods is ***division***, which works as follows:

$$H(\text{key}) = \text{key } \mathbf{mod} \; m = h \quad 0 <= h <= m - 1$$

The bit pattern of the key, regardless of its data type, is treated as an integer, divided in the integer sense by m, and the remainder of the division is used as the table address. h is in the range from 0 to $m - 1$. Such a function is fast on computer systems that have an integer divide, since most generate the quotient in one hardware register and the remainder in another. The content of the remainder register need only be copied into the variable h, and the hash is completed.

In practice, functions of this type give very good results. Lum, Yuen, and Dodd (1971) have an empirical study showing this to be the case. Division can, however, perform poorly in a number of cases. For example, if m were 25, then all keys that were divisible by 5 would map into positions 0, 5, 10, 15, and 20 of the table. A subset of the keys maps into a subset of the table, something that we in general wish to avoid. Of course, using the function $H = \text{key } \mathbf{mod} \; m$ maps all keys for which key $\mathbf{mod} \; m = 0$ into *hash_table(0)*, all keys for which key $\mathbf{mod} \; m = 1$ into *hash-table(1)*, and so on, but that bias is unavoidable. What we do not want to do is to introduce any further ones.

The problem underlying the choice of 25 as the table size is that it has a factor of 5. All keys with 5 as a factor will map into a table position that also has a factor of 5. The cure is to make sure that the key and m have no common factors, and the easiest way to ensure that is to choose m so that it has no factors other than 1 and itself—a prime number. For this reason, most of the time that the division function is used the table size will be a prime number. Lum, Yuen, and Dodd (1971) show, however, that any divisor with no small factors, say less than 20, is suitable.

Multiplication

A simple method based on ***multiplication*** is sometimes used. Suppose the keys in question are five digits in length:

$$\text{key} = d_1 \, d_2 \, d_3 \, d_4 \, d_5$$

The key is squared by

$$
\begin{array}{r}
d_1 \, d_2 \, d_3 \, d_4 \, d_5 \\
\times \; d_1 \, d_2 \, d_3 \, d_4 \, d_5 \\
\hline
r_1 \, r_2 \, r_3 \, r_4 \, r_5 \, r_6 \, r_7 \, r_8 \, r_9 \, r_{10}
\end{array}
$$

The result is a 10-digit product. The function is completed by doing digit selection on the product. In most cases, the middle digits are chosen, for example, $r_4 r_5 r_6$. An example is shown in Figure 7.8.

It is important to choose the middle digits. Consider, for example, choosing the right-most two digits of the product in the example—41. That value comes only from the product of 1×21 and 2×21; that is, only from the right-most two digits of the original key value. All keys ending in 21 will produce the same table location—41. This is the kind of bias we try to avoid introducing. The middle digits, on the other hand, are formed from products involving the left, middle, and right portions of the key. Changing any one digit in the key is likely to change the hash result. Information from all portions of the key is amalgamated in the calculation of the hash table subscript.

Folding

The next hash function we will discuss is *folding*. Suppose we have a five-digit key as we had in the multiplication method:

$$\text{key} = d_1 d_2 d_3 d_4 d_5$$

and the programs are running on a simple microcomputer system that has no hardware divide or multiply but that does have an arithmetic add. One way to form a hash function is to add the individual digits of the key:

$$H(\text{key}) = d_1 + d_2 + d_3 + d_4 + d_5$$

The result would be in the range

$$0 <= b <= 45$$

and could be used as the index in the hash table. If a larger table were needed (there were more than 46 records), the result could be enlarged by adding the numbers as pairs of digits:

$$H(\text{key}) = 0d_1 + d_2 d_3 + d_4 d_5$$

The result would then be between 000 and 207 (09 + 99 + 99). Folding is the name given to a class of methods that involves combining portions of the key to form a smaller result. The methods for combining are usually either arithmetic addition or exclusive or's.

Folding is often used in conjunction with other methods. If the key were a Social Security number of nine digits and the program were implemented on a minicomputer that had 16-bit registers and consequently had a maximum positive integer size of 65535, then the key would be intractable as it stood. It must somehow be reduced to an integer less than 65535 before it can be used. Folding can be used to do this.

Suppose the key in question has a value

$$\text{key} = 987654321$$

key = 54321
(a)

```
     54321
  × 54321
     54321
   108642
  162963
  217284
 271605
2950771041
```
(b)

$b = 077$

(c)

FIGURE 7.8 (a) Key. (b) Results of squaring the key value. (c) Digit selection of the middle digits gives the table position of the record.

We can break the key into four-digit groups, then add them:

$$
\begin{array}{r}
0009 \\
8765 \\
\underline{4321} \\
\end{array}
$$

fold(key) = 13095

This result would be between 0 and 20007. Now apply a second hashing function, say division, to produce a table position within the range $0 \ldots (m-1)$. If the hash table has m positions, the composite function is

$H(\text{key}) = \text{fold(key)} \bmod m$

String Keys

All of the examples in our discussion of hashing functions assumed that the keys were in the form of integers. It is easy to extend the hashing idea to keys of any discrete type (in which integer types are included) since the attribute *pos* is defined for these types. Instead of using the key directly, we substitute *object'pos(key)*. The result is an integer. For instance, the division function would become

object'pos(key) **mod** *hash_table_size*

Another common form of key is a character string. How can we transform strings into an integer so we might operate upon them with the hashing functions we have discussed? One such approach is to use folding.

Although the key string itself is not a numeric or discrete type, its character components are. Each character can have the *pos* attribute applied to it. The idea is to "fold" the positions of the individual characters together by adding them:

```
sum := 0;
for k in key'range loop
    sum := sum + character'pos(key(k));
end loop;
```

The value returned by *character'pos* is between 0 and 127 (see Chapter 8, Strings). The maximum value computed by the loop above is *key'length* * 127. If the key has 20 characters, its folded value is no greater than 2540. If this magnitude is insufficient, it is possible to fold pairs of key characters.

Suppose the key is a character string S of length 2, say the string "ij". We could concatenate the bit patterns used to represent the two strings by multiplying 'i's position by 128, thereby shifting it left 7 bits. Thus for 'i' and 'j', which are represented by bit patterns 1101001 and 1101010, respectively, the result of

character'pos('i') * 128 + character'pos('j') = 13,546 = 11010011101010_2

Pairs of adjacent characters in a string may be combined in this way and the pairs folded by adding their integer equivalents.

Triplets of characters can be handled in the same way, multiplying the positions of the characters of the triplet by 128^2, 128, and 1, respectively.

Figure 7.9 is a function that folds pairs of characters in a key and can be used in place of the hashing function shown in the examples in this section and in the hashing packages later in this chapter.

```
function string_hash(the_string : string; m : positive) return natural is
    sum : integer := 0;
begin
    for k in the_string'range loop
        sum := character'pos(the_string(k)) * 128**(k − 1 mod 2);
    end loop;
    return sum mod m;
end string_hash;
```

FIGURE 7.9 Hashing of a string by folding and division

A second method of hashing strings is given by Pearson (1990). It introduces an array of 1-byte integers with values between 0 and 127 and uses a mixture of exclusive or-ing and indexing into the array. It works as follows.

An array with an index of range 0 .. 127 of 7-bit integers is created, then loaded randomly with the values 0 .. 127, with each unique value in the range appearing in exactly one of the array positions. Each element of the array can be reinterpreted as a bit array of 7-bit elements. We start with a single bit array of 7 bits all set to zeros that we call h. Moving successively through the characters of the string, exclusive-or the 7 bits of the character with the 7 bits of h, reinterpret h as a 7-bit integer, then set h equal to the bit array in the hth position in the array. Repeat the process for all of the characters of the string.

To illustrate the process, suppose we have a set of only 8 characters. Our representation of the characters could be held in 3 bits rather than the 7 required by ASCII characters. Figure 7.10 has the codes for our little character set.

We create a table, say T, of eight elements, each of which is 3 bits, filled randomly with the values 0 .. 7 (Figure 7.11). Start with a variable h with bit pattern 000 = integer 0.

We then proceed down the characters of the string to be hashed, taking 1 character at a time. Using each character and the current value of h, we compute a new value of h with the expression

$$h_{new} := T (ch \textbf{ xor } h_{old})$$

or in pseudocode

```
for k in the_string'range loop                          -- Not valid Ada.
    h := T(the_string(i) xor h);
end loop;
```

Character	Bit code	Integer position
'a'	000	0
'b'	001	1
'c'	010	2
'd'	011	3
'e'	100	4
'f'	101	5
'g'	110	6
'h'	111	7

FIGURE 7.10 An 8-character code using 3 bits.

Index	Bit code in T (index)
0	101
1	001
2	100
3	010
4	111
5	110
6	011
7	000

FIGURE 7.11 Table T of random bit patterns.

The last value of h computed in this way for the string is the hash result. It may seem a bit complex at first glance, but in fact the calculations are fast. The statement in the loop is not valid Ada because some necessary type conversions are left out.

Remember that for exclusive-or,

0 **xor** 0 = 0 1 **xor** 1 = 0
1 **xor** 0 = 1 0 **xor** 1 = 1

As an example, suppose the string to be hashed is "feed." Figure 7.12 shows the development of the final value of h, the hashed position. The value of h that appears in the third column of a row is the value of h computed in the right-most column of the previous row. The value of h that is in the right-most column of the last row, 011 = 3, is the overall result.

Character S(k)	Character's bit code	h_{old}	h xor bit code	$h_{new} = T(h)$
'f'	101	000	101 = 5	110 = T(5)
'e'	100	110	010 = 2	100 = T(2)
'e'	100	100	000 = 0	101 = T(0)
'd'	011	101	110 = 6	011 = T(6)

FIGURE 7.12 Hashing of the word "feed" using Pearson's method.

An Ada implementation of the algorithm is given in package *string_hash_package* of Figure 7.13. It is an excellent example of Ada's bit arrays, as well as its ability to reinterpret any object in several ways by using the generic function *unchecked_conversion. Unchecked_conversion* is instantiated three times, once for each of the reinterpretations needed. There is only one function in the package. A package is used because the table needs to be established and retained throughout the multiple calls to the function.

A drawback of the package as written is that the result is between 0 and 127. If a larger hash table is required, the algorithm must be modified to produce a larger range of values. One way is to make one pass through the characters of the string and produce a value in the range 0 .. 127. Then change any 1 bit in the starting value of h and repeat the process with the changed h starting the process. That will produce a second result between 0 and 127. Multiply one result by 128 and add the product to the second result. The overall result will be between 0 and 127 * 128 + 127; that is, 0 .. 13,546.

If we made a second pass through the string, changing 1 bit of h in our example in Figure 7.12, say the middle of the 3 bits, we would get the result shown in Figure 7.14. As you can see, changing 1 bit in the first letter produces a completely different pattern and answer. The result is 1.

An even larger result can be obtained by changing another bit of the first character and getting a third result, multiplying it by 128^2, and adding it, and so on. Exercises 7.4, 12, asks you to extend the algorithm to do this.

String Hashing Package

package string_hash_package **is**

    function hash(the_string : string) **return** natural;
    -- *results:* *Returns a number between 0 and 127 that is the result of hashing the_string.*

end string_hash_package;

with unique_random, unchecked_conversion;   -- *Package unique_random is in Appendix C.*
package body string_hash_package **is**

```
    type bit is new boolean;          for bit'size use 1;
    type logical is array(0 .. 7) of bit;   pragma pack(logical);
    type count is range 0 .. 127;      for count'size use 7;
    type logical_table is array(count) of logical;

    package rand is new unique_random(127);
```
    -- *results:* *Each call of next_random returns a unique random number chosen from the range 0 .. 127. There is no repetition for*
    --   *the first 128 calls.*

```
    function ch_to_logical is new unchecked_conversion(character, logical);
```
    -- *results:* *Reinterprets an ASCII character as an array of 7 bits.*

```
    function logical_to_count is new unchecked_conversion(logical, count);
```
    -- *results:* *Reinterprets an array of 7 bits as a 7-bit integer.*

```
    function count_to_logical is new unchecked_conversion(count, logical);
```
    -- *results:* *Reinterprets a 7-bit integer as an array of 7 bits.*

```
    zeros : constant logical := (0 .. 7 => false);
    T : array(count) of logical;                          -- Table of random 7-bit integers.

    function hash(the_string : string) return natural is
        h : logical := zeros;
    begin

        for i in the_string'range loop
            h := T (logical_to_count(h xor ch_to_logical(the_string(i))));
        end loop;

        return natural(logical_to_count(h));

    end hash;

begin                                                      -- This executes once when the package is elaborated.
    for i in count loop                                   -- Loads the table with unique random 7-bit integers.
        T(i) := count_to_logical (count (rand.next_random − 1));
    end loop;
end string_hash_package;
```

FIGURE 7.13 String hashing function designed using the method described in Pearson (1990).

Character S(k)	Character's bit code	h_{old}	h *xor* bit code	h_{new} = T(h)
'f' (changed)	101	010	111 = 7	000 = $T(7)$
'e'	100	000	100 = 4	111 = $T(4)$
'e'	100	111	011 = 3	010 = $T(3)$
'd'	011	010	001 = 1	001 = $T(1)$

FIGURE 7.14 Hashing of the word "feed" using Pearson's method with 1 bit changed in the first character.

Remember, once a result has been produced, the division method could be applied to it to produce an overall result that is in the range $0 .. hash\_table\_size$.

7.4.2 Collision-Resolution Strategies

A collision-resolution strategy, or rehashing, determines what happens when two or more elements have a collision, or hash to the same address. We will begin by defining some parameters that will be used to help describe these strategies.

We will call the number of different values that a key can assume R. A 9-digit integer (e.g., a Social Security number) has

$$R = 1,000,000,000$$

The size of the hash table, $hash\_table\_size$, is a second important parameter. It must be large enough to hold the number of elements we wish to store.

The number of records that is actually stored in the table varies with time and is denoted $n = n(t)$. One of the most important parameters is the fraction of the table that contains records at any time. This is called the **load factor** and is written

$$\alpha = \alpha(t) = n/hash\_table\_size$$

In Figure 7.11, $\alpha = 3/7$.

In summary, the keys of our data elements are chosen from R different values, and n elements are stored in the hash table that is of size $hash\_table\_size$ and is $\alpha \times 100\%$ full.

A more general form of hash table is obtained by allowing each hash table position to hold more than a single record. Each of these multirecord cells is called a **bucket** and can hold b records. An array representation of such a hash table is illustrated in Figure 7.15.

The concept of hash tables as collections of buckets is important for tables that are stored on direct access devices such as magnetic disks. For those devices, each bucket can be tied to a physical cell of the device, such as a track or sector. The hashing function produces a bucket number that results in the transfer of the physically related block into the random access memory. Once there, the bucket can be searched or modified at high speed.

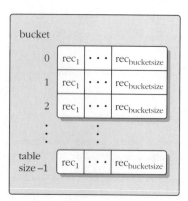

FIGURE 7.15 Hash table of buckets.

Buckets of size greater than 1 are of limited use in hash tables stored in RAM. They tend to slow the average access time to records when searching. We will discuss only buckets of size 1 in this chapter.

The strategies for resolving collisions will be grouped into three approaches. The first approach, *open address methods,* attempts to place a second and subsequent keys that hash to the one table location into some other position in the table that is unoccupied (open). The second approach, *external chaining,* has a linked list associated with each hash table address. Each element is added to the linked list at its home address. The third approach uses pointers to link together different buckets in the hash table. We will discuss *coalesced chaining,* since it is one of the better strategies that uses this technique.

Open Address Methods

For all the open address methods and their algorithms we will use the hash table represented in Figure 7.4. There are several open address methods using varying degrees of sophistication and a variety of techniques. All seek to find an open table position after a collision. Let us return to Figure 7.7, which is repeated for reference as Figure 7.16, and attempt to add the key whose value is 227. Recall that the example hashing function applied to 227 gives

$$H(227) = 227 \bmod 7 = 3$$

so that 227 collides with 374.

Linear Rehashing

A simple resolution to the collision called *linear rehashing* is to start a sequential search through the hash table at the position at which the collision occurred. The search continues until an open position is found or until the table is exhausted. A probe at position 4 reveals an open address, and the new record is stored there. The result is shown in Figure 7.17. A request to find the record with key = 227 generates the same search path used to store it.

To insert an element, we search, beginning at the home address, until an empty address is found or until the table is exhausted. For example, inserting an element whose key is 421 in Figure 7.17 leads to the result in Figure 7.18. We have added a column to our illustration of hash tables—the number of probes required to find each element stored therein. In the case of linear rehashing, it is easy to determine an element's home address from this added information.

We will add a status field to each position in the hash table. Its values are *empty, occupied,* and *deleted.* The use of *empty* is clear. Let us see how we use the values *occupied* and *deleted.*

Figure 7.19 shows the result of adding 624, whose home address is 1, to the hash table in Figure 7.18. The probes needed to find an empty space for 624 are also shown. A subsequent search using linear rehashing to find 624

Table address	Table contents
(0)	empty
(1)	911, . . . data . . .
(2)	empty
(3)	374, . . . data . . .
(4)	empty
(5)	empty
(6)	1091, . . . data . . .

FIGURE 7.16 Three records stored at table(1), table(3), and table(6).

Table address	Table contents
(0)	empty
(1)	911
(2)	empty
(3)	374
(4)	227 ←
(5)	empty
(6)	1091

FIGURE 7.17 Linear rehashing.

Table address	Table contents	Probes
(0)	empty	
(1)	911	1
(2)	421 ←	2
(3)	374	1
(4)	227	2
(5)	empty	
(6)	1091	1

FIGURE 7.18 Hash table and the number of probes required to find an element in the table.

Table address	Table contents	Probes
(0)	empty	
(1)	911	1
(2)	421	2
(3)	374	1
(4)	227	2
(5)	624	5
(6)	1091	1

FIGURE 7.19 The probe sequence when searching for 624 (or any other key value whose home address is 1).

Table address	Table contents	Probes
(0)	empty	
(1)	911	1
(2)	421	2
(3)	374	1
(4)	227	2
(5)	empty	
(6)	1091	1

FIGURE 7.20

will retrace that same path. If any of the three elements, 421, 374, or 227, were deleted and replaced by the value *empty,* subsequent searches for 624 would not work. Upon encountering a location marked *empty,* the search would terminate unsuccessfully. A solution to this problem is to mark with a special value positions from which elements have been deleted.

The drawback to the use of the value *deleted* is that it can clutter up the hash table, thereby increasing the number of probes required to find an element. A partial solution is to reenter all legitimate elements periodically and to mark the remaining locations *empty.*

The performance of a combined hashing/rehashing strategy is measured by the number of probes it makes in searching for target key values. We will examine the performance of linear rehashing in more detail in Section 7.4.5, but we can get a feel for the fact that it may not perform very well by looking at the probe sequence that results when a search of Figure 7.19 is undertaken for a key value of 624. Since 624 **mod** 7 = 1, the search begins at position 1 in the table. The subsequent search is shown. Five probes are required to find 624. There are two problems underlying the linear probe method.

Problem 1. Any key that hashes to a position, say b, will follow the same rehashing pattern as all other keys that hash to b. Any key that hashes to position 1 in Figure 7.19 will follow the probe sequence shown. This guarantees that any key that hashes to 1 will have to collide with all the keys that previously hashed to 1 before it is found or before an empty position is found. We will call this phenomenon ***primary clustering.***

Problem 2. Note in Figure 7.19 that the probe pattern for a rehash from position 1 merged with the probe pattern for a rehash from position 3. The two rehash patterns have merged together, a phenomenon called ***secondary clustering.***

Consider Figure 7.20 (which is a copy of Figure 7.18). There is a substantial difference in the probabilities of positions 0 and 5 receiving the next new key. Only new keys hashing into positions 6 and 0 will rehash (if necessary) to position 0. Keys hashing into any other position will eventually arrive at position 5.

The expected number of probes for any random key not yet in the table can be calculated as shown in Figure 7.21.

The expected number of probes for both ***successful*** (target key in table) and ***unsuccessful*** (target key not in table) ***searches*** will be our measures of performance of rehashing strategies, and we will examine them in a more general way in Section 7.4.5. We will confine our attention here to noting that the performance can be improved by eliminating the problems we noted— primary and secondary clustering.

You may be tempted to resolve the difficulties by introducing a step size other than 1 for linear rehash. Stepping to a new table position in rehashing would become

Original hash position	Number of probes	Empty position found at
0	1	0
1	5	5
2	4	5
3	3	5
4	2	5
5	1	5
6	2	0
Total	18	

FIGURE 7.21 Expected number of probes for an unsuccessful search in the hash table shown in Figure 7.20. Expected number of probes = 18/7 = 2.57.

ReHash := $(p + c)$ **mod** *hash_table_size*

where $1 <= c <= (hash\_table\_size - 1)$. If *hash_table_size* is prime, or at least if c and *hash_table_size* are relatively prime (have no common factors), then the search pattern will cover the entire table, probing at each position exactly once without repetition. This kind of coverage, ***nonrepetitious complete coverage,*** is highly desirable. Obviously, if a table position that was previously probed were again probed during the same rehashing sequence, the duplicate probe would be wasted and would affect performance. If the probe pattern did not cover the entire table, empty spaces that are not included in the pattern would not be discovered.

Although a value of c that is relatively prime to the table size does give a rehash technique that has the properties of nonrepetition and complete coverage, it does not solve nor, in fact, even improve the problems of primary and secondary clustering. An approach that does solve one of these problems is described next.

Quadratic Rehashing

One method of improving the performance of rehashing is to probe at

$k = $ (home address $\pm j^2$) **mod** *hash_table_size*

where j takes on the values $1, 2, 3, \ldots$, until either the target key or an empty position is found or until the table is completely searched. This method, called ***quadratic rehashing,*** is better than linear rehashing because it solves the problem of secondary clustering (it does not solve the problem of primary clustering). Details of this method are given in Radke (1970), where it is shown that rehashing visits all table locations without repetition provided that *hash_table_size* is a prime number of the form $4k + 3$.

Random Rehashing

Envision a rehashing strategy that, when a collision occurs, simply jumps randomly to a new table position. This method is called ***random rehashing***, and the rehash can be considered to be a jump of a random distance from the original hash position or to be a second hash function applied to the same key. If second and subsequent collisions occur, the process is repeated until the target key or an empty position is found or until the table is determined to be full and not to contain the target key. Since each key would have its own random pattern, there would be no fixed rehashing patterns. (The random sequence would have to be determined by the key value, since subsequent accesses with the same key value must follow the same pattern as the original.) Since there would be no common patterns, there would be no primary or secondary clustering. Although this approach is theoretically appealing, it appears difficult to implement. Thus, we turn to schemes that are simpler and whose performances are almost as good.

Double Hashing

Several methods exist that attempt to approximate the random rehashing strategy without the large overhead of calculation required by it. One of these, ***double hashing***, is computationally efficient and simple to apply.

We have seen that the general pattern for linear probing is to probe at

$$(i + c) \quad \textbf{mod } hash\_table\_size$$
$$(i + 2 * c) \textbf{ mod } hash\_table\_size$$
$$(i + 3 * c) \textbf{ mod } hash\_table\_size$$

where c is a constant ($c = 1$ in our original discussion of linear rehashing). The fact that c is a constant is at the root of the inefficiency of linear rehashing, since it causes fixed probe patterns and clustering. Ideally we would like c to be random but subject to constraints on repetition. Although this is possible, such an approach leads to a computational overhead that is too high.

One solution is to compute a random jump size, c, for each key that has collided at position b and needs rehashing. Thus, c would be a function of the key value, so that different keys hashing to the same location are given different values of c. For example, starting with the hashing function

$$H(\text{key}) = \text{key } \textbf{mod } hash\_table\_size$$

we define a related step size function

$$c(\text{key}) = [\text{key } \textbf{mod } (hash\_table\_size - 2)] + 1$$

Suppose 421 is to be stored in Figure 7.22. Then, 421 collides with 911 at position 1. When the collision occurs, c is computed as

Table address	Table contents
(0)	empty
(1)	911
(2)	empty
(3)	374
(4)	227
(5)	empty
(6)	1091

FIGURE 7.22

$c(421) = 421 \textbf{ mod } 5 + 1 = 2$

so the table is probed at

$(1 + 2) \quad \textbf{mod } 7 = 3$ *-- Collision.*
$(1 + 2 * 2) \textbf{ mod } 7 = 5$ *-- Empty.*

If 624 had been the key, it also would have collided with 911 at position 1. Its rehash pattern, however, would have been different; that is,

$c(624) = 624 \textbf{ mod } 5 + 1 = 5$

and the probes would have been at

$(1 + 5) \quad \textbf{mod } 7 = 6$ *-- Collision.*
$(1 + 2 * 5) \textbf{ mod } 7 = 4$ *-- Collision.*
$(1 + 3 * 5) \textbf{ mod } 7 = 2$ *-- Empty.*

The rehash patterns for the two keys, both of which hashed to the same position originally, are different. Although we can find pairs (or groups) of keys that hash to the same position and produce the same step size *c*, the probability of such an event is low for hash tables of reasonable size and a good randomizing step size generator. In fact, the performance of double hashing in terms of the expected number of probes for both successful and unsuccessful accesses is close to that of random rehashing. Since it has essentially the same performance in numbers of probes and a lower overhead in computation per probe, it has a greater overall efficiency.

Any randomizing function that produces a step size that is less than *hash_table_size* − 1 and is not based on the position of the original collision will do. The division algorithm shown is, however, efficient and simple. In order to avoid introducing biases, *hash_table_size* should be a prime number. If we use this method of computing *c* in conjunction with the division method for the original hash, the choice of the two divisors as ***twin primes*** assures an exhaustive search of the table without repetition. If *hash_table_size* is prime, and *k* = *hash_table_size* − 2 is also prime, then an exhaustive search of the table is assured.

External Chaining

A second approach to the problem of collisions, called ***external chaining***, is to let the table position "absorb" all the records that hash to it. Since we do not usually know how many keys will hash into any table position, a linked list is a good data structure to collect the records.

As an example, let *hash_table_size* = 7 and suppose that operation *Create* has initialized the hash table as shown in Figure 7.23.

If a division hash function is chosen, say,

Table address	Table contents
(0)	nil
(1)	nil
(2)	nil
(3)	nil
(4)	nil
(5)	nil
(6)	nil

FIGURE 7.23 Initialized hash table for external chaining.

Table address	Table contents
(0)	nil
(1)	→ 911
(2)	nil
(3)	→ 374
(4)	nil
(5)	nil
(6)	→ 1091

FIGURE 7.24 Hash table after insertion of keys 374, 1091, 911.

Table address	Table contents
(0)	nil
(1)	→ 911 → 421
(2)	nil
(3)	→ 374 → 227
(4)	nil
(5)	nil
(6)	→ 1091

FIGURE 7.25 Hash table after insertion of keys 227 and 421.

Table address	Table contents
(0)	nil
(1)	→ 911 → 421 → 624
(2)	nil
(3)	→ 374 → 227
(4)	nil
(5)	nil
(6)	→ 1091

FIGURE 7.26 Hash table after insertion of key 624.

$H(\text{key}) = \text{key } \textbf{mod } 7$

then insertion of the keys

key = 374	374 **mod** 7 = 3	
key = 1091	1091 **mod** 7 = 6	
key = 911	911 **mod** 7 = 1	

produces the hash table shown in Figure 7.24. Insertion of 227 and 421 produces two collisions (the collisions are not shown in the text):

key = 227	227 **mod** 7 = 3	
key = 421	421 **mod** 7 = 1	

and results in Figure 7.25. Subsequent insertion of 624

key = 624	624 **mod** 7 = 1	

produces the result shown in Figure 7.26.

Each list is a linked list. The designer has all the choices of list characteristics that he or she has for any linked list—method of termination, single or double linkage, other access pointers, and ordering of the list. If the frequencies with which the various records are accessed are quite different, it may be effective to make each list self-organizing.

Observe that the operations in this case are similar to those on lists discussed in Chapter 4. The only differences are that there are many lists instead of one and that the list in which we are interested is determined by the hash function.

External chaining has three advantages over open address methods:

1. Deletions are possible with no resulting problems.
2. The number of elements in the table can be greater than the table size; α can be greater than 1.0. Storage for the elements is dynamically allocated as the lists grow larger.
3. We shall see in Section 7.4.5 that the performance of external chaining in searching for an object with a given key is better than that of open address methods and continues to be excellent as α grows beyond 1.

In the next technique, collisions are resolved, as they are in external chaining, by adding the element to be inserted to the end of a list. The difference is in how the list is constructed.

Coalesced Chaining

To illustrate coalesced chaining, consider the hash table with seven buckets shown in Figure 7.27. The hash table is divided into two parts: the *address region* and the *cellar*. In our example, the first five addresses make up the address region, and the last two make up the cellar.

The hash function must map each record into the address region. The cellar is only used to store records that collided with another record at their home addresses. For our example, we will use the division hash function

$$H(\text{key}) = \text{key } \textbf{mod } 5$$

assuming that each key is an integer.

After inserting key values 27 and 29, we have Figure 7.28. If 32 is inserted next, it collides with 27 and is stored in the empty position with the largest address. In addition, it is added to a list that begins at its home address. The result is shown in Figure 7.29. To assist in visualizing the process, the empty position with the largest address, **epla**, is shown in the figures.

If key value 34 is added, it collides with 29 and is placed in address 5 (the empty position with the largest address) and is added to a list beginning at location 4. The result is shown in Figure 7.30.

Up to this point, coalesced chaining has behaved exactly like external chaining—each new record is added to the end of a list that begins at its home address. The next insertion illustrates how a collision is resolved after the cellar is full.

If 37 is added, it collides with 27, so it is placed in location (3) and added to the end of the list that begins at address (2). The result is shown in Figure 7.31. The point to be made here is that once again the record being inserted was, since its home address was already occupied, placed in the empty position with the largest address. Adding 47 produces the result shown in Figure 7.32.

The term "coalesced" is used to describe this technique because, for example, if 53 were added to the hash table in Figure 7.32, it would cause the list that begins at (2) to coalesce with the list that begins at (3). Note, however, that lists cannot coalesce until after the cellar is full.

The effectiveness of coalesced chaining depends on the choice of cellar size. Selection of cellar size is discussed in Vitter (1982, 1983), where it is shown that a cellar that contains 14% of the hash table works well under a variety of circumstances.

Because overflow records form lists, the deletion problems of open addressing schemes can be solved without resorting to marking records de-

Table address	Table contents	
(0)	empty	↑
(1)	empty	*address*
(2)	empty	*region*
(3)	empty	
(4)	empty	↓
(5)	empty	↑
(6)		*cellar* ↓

FIGURE 7.27 Hash table with seven buckets initialized for coalesced chaining.

Table address	Table contents
(0)	empty
(1)	empty
(2)	27
(3)	empty
(4)	29
(5)	empty
(6)	**epla**

FIGURE 7.28 Hash table after inserting keys 27 and 29. **epla** is the empty position with the largest address.

Table address	Table contents
(0)	empty
(1)	empty
(2)	27
(3)	empty
(4)	29
(5)	**epla**
(6)	32

FIGURE 7.29 Results after inserting key 32.

Table address	Table contents
(0)	empty
(1)	empty
(2)	27
(3)	**epla**
(4)	29
(5)	34
(6)	32

FIGURE 7.30 Results after inserting key 34.

Table address	Table contents
(0)	empty
(1)	**epla**
(2)	27
(3)	37
(4)	29
(5)	34
(6)	32

FIGURE 7.31 Results after inserting key 37.

Table address	Table contents
(0)	epla
(1)	47
(2)	27
(3)	37
(4)	29
(5)	34
(6)	32

FIGURE 7.32 Results after inserting key 47.

Pascal reserved words

and	mod
array	nil
begin	not
case	of
const	or
div	packed
do	procedure
downto	program
else	record
end	repeat
file	set
for	then
forward	to
function	type
goto	until
if	var
in	while
label	with

leted. Any such approach is, however, more complicated than for the external chaining approach since the lists can coalesce. Details of such a deletion scheme, which essentially relinks elements in a list past the element to be deleted, are given in Vitter (1982).

This concludes our introduction to collision-resolution techniques. In Section 7.4.5 we will compare these techniques from the point of view of performance. Before we do so, however, in Section 7.4.3 we will introduce hash functions that guarantee that collisions will not occur—perfect hashing functions.

7.4.3 Perfect Hashing Functions

A perfect hashing function is one that causes no collisions. A ***minimal perfect hashing function*** is a perfect hashing function that operates on a hash table having a load factor of 1.0. Since perfect hashing functions cause no collisions, we are assured that exactly one probe is needed to locate an element that has a given key value. This is, of course, very desirable. The problem is that such functions are not easy to construct.

Perfect hashing functions can be found only under certain conditions. One such condition is that all the key values are known in advance. Certain applications have this quality; for example, the reserved, or key, words of a programming language. In the programming language Pascal there are 36 reserved words: and, array, begin, ... When a compiler is translating a program, as it scans the program's statements it must determine whether it has encountered a reserved word. Suppose the reserved words are stored in a hash table accessible by a perfect hashing function. Determining if a word encountered in the scan is a reserved word requires only one probe. The word is hashed, and the content of the specified table is compared with the word from the scan. If they are the same, a reserved word was found. If not, we can be certain that the word is not a reserved word.

Another condition for perfect hashing functions is a practical one. It concerns the amount of computation necessary to find a perfect hashing function, which can be enormous. The total amount of computation (and therefore time) increases exponentially with the number of keys in the data. The number of possible functions that map the 31 most frequently occurring English words into a hash table of size 41 is approximately 10^{50}, whereas the number of such functions that give unique (perfect) mappings is approximately 10^{43} (Knuth, 1973b). Thus, only one of each of the 10 million functions is suitable. In practice, if the number of keys is greater than a few dozen, the amount of time to find a perfect hashing function is unacceptably long on most computers.

There are several proposals for perfect hashing functions. Sprugnoli (1977) has proposed functions that are perfect but not minimal. Cichelli (1980) has suggested some simple minimal perfect functions and has given examples and the times to compute them. Jaeschke (1981) has proposed other minimal perfect functions that avoid some problems that might arise with Cichelli's method.

Let us look briefly at Cichelli's method. The functions he proposed are for keys that are character strings. Take, for example, the 36 reserved words of Pascal. The hashing function is

$$H(\text{key}) = L + g(\text{key}[1]) + g(\text{key}[L])$$

where

$L = $ length of the key

The function $g(x)$ associates an integer with each character x; thus, $g(\text{key}[1])$ is the integer associated with the first letter of the key, and $g(\text{key}[L])$ is the integer associated with the last letter of the key.

Figure 7.33 shows the value of $g(x)$ for a perfect hashing function for Pascal. Applying those values to *while* gives

$$H(\text{while}) = 5 + g(w) + g(e) = 11$$

Figure 7.34 shows the home addresses of all the Pascal reserved words.

The hashing function is simple, as it should be. There are several problems, however. The first problem is that of looking up the integer associated with the two or more letters, but that can be done with reasonable efficiency. A second and more serious problem is that of determining which integer should be associated with each character. The integers are found by trial and error using a **backtracking algorithm**. (Of course, the associated integer table [see Figure 7.33] need be built only once.) Cichelli (1980) has a good discussion of the backtracking algorithm used for this problem.

In summary, perfect hashing functions are feasible when the keys are known in advance and the number of records is small. In that case, a perfect hashing function is determined in advance of the use of the hash table. Although its determination may be costly, it need be done only once. The resulting access to the records of the hash table requires only one probe.

char	g(char)	char	g(char)
a	11	n	13
b	15	o	0
c	1	p	15
d	0	q	0
e	0	r	14
f	15	s	6
g	3	t	6
h	15	u	14
i	13	v	10
j	0	w	6
k	0	x	0
l	15	y	13
m	15	z	0

FIGURE 7.33 Cichelli's values for function g for Pascal's reserved words.

7.4.4 Hash Table Abstraction and a Double Hashing Implementation

Now that we have studied the ideas and techniques that we will use, we can proceed to develop a hash table abstract data type. The operations are setlike. From the abstract point of view, objects placed in the table have no related objects. An object has no next or prior object, parent or child object, or adjacent object. The object is simply in the table. Once there, we can find it by specifying its key. Its data can then be retrieved or updated. We provide a *traverse* operation so that every member of the table can be visited and processed. Since objects in the table have no related objects, we have no way to progress from one to the next, because there is no "next."

Deletion of objects from the hash table and the reuse of deleted positions is left as an exercise. Specification 7.2 is the specification for hashed tables.

[2]	do	[20]	record
[3]	end	[21]	packed
[4]	else	[22]	not
[5]	case	[23]	then
[6]	downto	[24]	procedure
[7]	goto	[25]	with
[8]	to	[26]	repeat
[9]	otherwise	[27]	var
[10]	type	[28]	in
[11]	while	[29]	array
[12]	const	[30]	if
[13]	div	[31]	nil
[14]	and	[32]	for
[15]	set	[33]	begin
[16]	or	[34]	until
[17]	of	[35]	label
[18]	mod	[36]	function
[19]	file	[37]	program

FIGURE 7.34 The hash table for Pascal reserved words.

■ SPECIFICATION 7.2 Hash Table

-- *Elements:* *Generic objects with associated keys that are of some discrete type.*

-- *Structure:* *The hash table is a set of objects. The objects are not related to each other*
--   *in any way other than being in the table.*

-- *Constraints:* $0 <= number\_of\_objects <= table\_size.$
                        -- *Table_size and number_of_objects appear in the **private** section of this specification.*

generic

    type key_type **is** $(<>)$;   -- *Limited to discrete types.*
    type object_type **is private**;
    with function key_of (the_object : object_type) **return** key_type;
    -- *results:* *Returns the key associated with the_object.*

package hash_table_package **is**

    type hash_table (table_size : positive) **is limited private**;   -- *Table_size should be a prime number.*

    type status **is record**
        number_of_objects : natural;
        load_factor   : float;   -- *Number_of_objects/table_size.*
        expected_probes   : float;   -- *For a key that is in the table.*
    end record;

    duplicate_key   : **exception**;
    hash_table_full   : **exception**;
    missing_object   : **exception**;

    procedure add (the_table : **in out** hash_table; the_object : object_type);
    -- *results:* *Adds the_object to the hash table by hashing/rehashing.*
    -- *exceptions:* *A duplicate_key exception is raised if an object whose key is the same as the key of*
--   *the object being added is already in the table.*
--   *A hash_table_full exception is raised if the hash table is full.*

    procedure find (the_table   : hash_table; target_key   : key_type;
            the_object   : **out** object_type; found   : **out** boolean);
    -- *results:* *If an object in the table has key = target_key, then it is copied into the_object and found is set to true; otherwise found*
--   *is set to false.*

    procedure change (the_table : **in out** hash_table; new_object : object_type);
    -- *results:* *Finds the object in the table whose key = key_of (new_object) and changes its value to new_object.*
    -- *exceptions:* *A missing_object exception is raised if no object whose key = key_of (new_object) is in the table.*

    generic
      with procedure process(the_position : natural; the_object : object_type);   -- *Index of the object in the table.*
    procedure traverse (the_table : hash_table);
    -- *results:* *Visits every object in the hash table in some arbitrary order and calls procedure process for each.*

(continued)

Specification 7.2 (continued)

function table_status (the_table : hash_table) **return** status;
-- *results:* *Returns the status of the hash table.*

private

    type table_object **is record**
      empty : boolean := true;
      object : object_type;
    end record;

    type array_of_objects **is array** (natural **range** <>) **of** table_object;

    type hash_table (table_size : natural) **is record**
      object_count : natural := 0;   -- *Number of objects currently in the table.*
      probe_count : natural := 0;   -- *Total number of probes in adding new objects.*
      objects   : array_of_objects (0 .. table_size); -- *Hash table resides in objects (0 .. table_size − 1).*
    end record;

end hash_table_package;

Specification 7.2, outside of the **private** section, applies to all of the hashing and rehashing methods we have discussed for keys of some discrete type. The generic parameters and the **private** section would have to be changed for keys that are not discrete types, such as *character strings*.

We can now write a number of package bodies, any one of which can be used to implement the specification. We could use any hashing function, any rehashing function, or any method such as open address or chained methods.

Package Body 7.2 is an implementation that uses a division hash function together with double rehashing. The change in a single line of code necessary to use linear hashing is noted in the declaration section of the internal procedure *search*. The critical procedure is the internal procedure *search*. It is not visible to the user. It performs the hashing and rehashing operations.

■ PACKAGE BODY 7.2 Hash Tables—Implements Specification 7.2

-- *notes:* *This implementation is an open address method with a division hashing function and*
--   *double rehashing. The change necessary to use linear rehashing is noted in the declaration*
--   *section of internal procedure* search.

package body hash_table_package **is**

(continued)

Package Body 7.2 (continued)

```
      procedure search(the_table : hash_table; target_key : key_type;
                          position : out natural; number_of_probes : out natural)
      is separate;
      -- results:   Searches for a table entry whose key = target_key. Returns in h the table position of (a) the object, if found,
      --            (b) otherwise, the position of the first position on the search path that is empty, if any; (c) otherwise the table
      --            was searched and neither an empty position nor the target key was found; the position of some arbitrary
      --            object is returned. In all cases, search returns the number of probes taken.
      -- notes:    Procedure search is not visible outside of the package body.


   procedure add (the_table : in out hash_table; the_object : object_type) is
   -- Length 10   Complexity 3   Performance determined by procedure search
      position : natural;
      probes : natural;
   begin
      search (the_table, key_of (the_object), position, probes);
      if the_table.objects(position ).empty
         then                                                              -- Insert the new object at position.
               the_table.objects(position )    := (false, the_object);
               the_table.object_count          := the_table.object_count + 1;
               the_table.probe_count           := the_table.probe_count + probes;
      elsif key_of (the_table.objects(position ).object) = key_of (the_object)
         then raise duplicate_key;
      else raise hash_table_full;
      end if;
   end add;


   procedure change (the_table : in out hash_table; new_object : object_type) is
   begin
      null;                                                               -- Left as an exercise for the reader.
   end change;


   procedure find (the_table : hash_table; target_key : key_type;
                  the_object : out object_type; found : out boolean) is
   begin
      null;                                                               -- Left as an exercise for the reader.
   end find;


   procedure traverse (the_table : hash_table) is
   -- Length 4   Complexity 3   Performance O(n)
   begin
      for k in 0 .. the_table.table_size − 1 loop
         if not the_table.objects(k).empty
            then process( k, the_table.objects(k).object);
         end if;
      end loop;
   end traverse;


   function table_status (the_table : hash_table) return status is
   -- Length 3   Complexity 1   Performance O(1).
```

(continued)

Package Body 7.2 (continued)

begin
    if the_table.object_count = 0 **then**
      return status'(0, 0.0, 0.0)
    else return status'
        (number_of_objects => the_table.object_count,
        load_factor   => float(the_table.object_count)/float(the_table.table_size),
        expected_probes   => float(the_table.probe_count)/float(the_table.object_count));
end table_status;

end hash_table_package;

separate (hash_table_package)
    procedure search (the_table : hash_table; target_key : key_type;
                   position : **out** natural; number_of_probes : **out** natural) **is**
    -- *Length 13   Complexity 3   Performance   Expected* O(1)   *Worst case* O(n)
    -- *The expected performance is* O(1) *when the load factor is sufficiently smaller than 1.*
    -- *(See Figures 7.35 and 7.36.)*
    h, home   : natural: = key_type'pos(target_key) **mod** the_table.table_size;
                      -- *The division hash function.*
    probes_taken : natural := 1;
    step_size   : **constant** positive   -- *Step_size for double hashing.*
               := (key_type'pos(target_key) **mod** (the_table.table_size − 2)) + 1;

    -- *For linear rehashing, replace the declaration of step_size above with*
    -- *step_size : **constant** positive := 1;*

begin
  loop
    exit when the_table.objects(h).empty
      or else key_of (the_table.objects(h).object) = target_key;

    -- *Rehash needed if this position reached.*
    h := (h + step_size) **mod** the_table.table_size;
    probes_taken := probes_taken + 1;
                              -- *Search covered entire table.*
    exit when h = home;
  end loop;

    position := h;
    number_of_probes := probes_taken;

end search;

    The lengths and complexities of the operations are low. Those of procedure *search* are a bit higher. *Search* is called by three of the package's operations and is the determinant of their performance. It searches for the target key and returns a table position *h* as indicated in its specification. It is then up to the calling procedures to interpret the result. Notice that there is no explicit indicator of the case in which the table is full and the rehashing was used to probe at every table position without finding the target key. In that case, the table position of some arbitrary nonempty object is returned. Its key will not be equal to the target key.

Chained hashing is easily implemented, as is coalesced chaining. Both of these implementations are left as exercises.

7.4.5 Hashing Performance

Explicit expressions that give the expected number of compares required for successful and unsuccessful searches can be developed. Results for three different collision-resolution policies are shown in Figures 7.35 and 7.36. Figure 7.35 shows the algebraic expressions [see Knuth (1973b) for their development], and Figure 7.36 shows the results of graphing the algebraic expressions.

Collision-resolution strategy	Unsuccessful	Successful
Linear rehashing	$\frac{1}{2}\left(1 + \frac{1}{(1-\alpha)^2}\right)$	$\frac{1}{2}\left(1 + \frac{1}{(1-\alpha)}\right)$
Double hashing	$\frac{1}{1-\alpha}$	$-\left(\frac{1}{\alpha}\right) \times \log(1-\alpha)$
External chaining	$\alpha + e^{\alpha}$	$1 + \frac{1}{2}\alpha$

FIGURE 7.35 Algebraic expressions for the number of probes expected for successful and unsuccessful searches in a hash table, where α is the load factor.

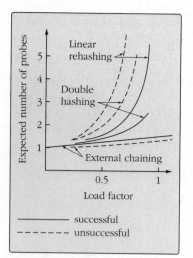

FIGURE 7.36 Number of probes required for successful and unsuccessful searches in a hash table.

Expressions for coalesced chaining are given in Vitter (1982). Note that if the cellar is not full, the result for coalesced chaining is the same as for external chaining. In general, the search effort of coalesced chaining is approximately the same as that of external chaining. See Vitter (1982), in which the performance of coalesced chaining is compared with all the hashing techniques discussed in this chapter. Coalesced chaining is shown to give the best performance for the circumstances we considered.

Notice in Figures 7.35 and 7.36 that the performance curves for hashing methods are monotonically increasing functions of α, the load factor. The performance curves for lists and trees are monotonically increasing functions of n, the number of elements in the data structure. The number of elements, n, is not under the implementor's control. For hashing, however, the load factor, α, may be made arbitrarily small by increasing the table size. For a given value of n, we can reduce the load factor and improve the performance of hashing. The price is more memory.

Data structure	Expected number of compares, moves, or objects accessed			
	$O(1)$	$O(\log n)$	$O(n)$	$O(n \log n)$
Sorted list (Array)		Search	Insert Delete Sort	
Sorted list (Linked)			Insert Delete Search Sort	
Binary search tree		Insert Delete Search	Sort	
B^+-tree		Insert Delete Search	Sort	
Hash table	Insert Delete Search			Sort

FIGURE 7.37 Comparison of the performance of basic operations for several data structures.

Figure 7.37 shows a comparison of the orders-of-magnitude performance expected of five of the data structures we discussed, including hashing. Included are four basic operations that each one performs. All are concerned with mapping keys to objects.

The *sort* operation refers to traversing the objects in the data structure in sorted order by key values. All of the data structures in Figure 7.37 except for hash tables have some aspects of sorting built into their basic structure. Because of that, traversing the objects in sorted order is $O(n)$ for all of them. Hashing is the antithesis of sorting. It randomizes the positions of the objects. Thus, in order to traverse the data in sorted order, they must first be copied from the table and sorted. (See Exercises 7.4, 10.)

Hashing performs well for the three operations *insert, delete,* and *search.* Searching is $O(1)$, and insertions and deletions involve no movement of objects. Hashing is an excellent choice for mapping keys to objects if sorted data are not required. The major impediment to its use is that the keys must be a discrete type or easily transformable into a discrete type.

A timing study of the performance of hashing compared to lists and binary trees was given in Figure 5.2. In it, you can see the superior performance of hashing for accessing objects by their key values.

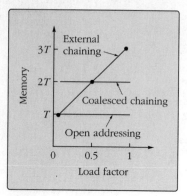

FIGURE 7.38 Memory requirements when an element occupies the same amount of memory as a pointer.

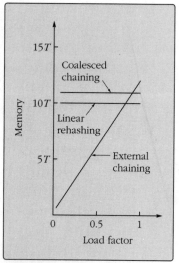

FIGURE 7.39 Memory requirements when an element occupies 10 times the amount of memory of a pointer.

7.4.6 Memory Requirements

In addition to performance, it is important to compare the memory requirements of various hashing techniques. Let T be the number of buckets in the hash table; assume that a pointer occupies one word of memory and that an element occupies w words of memory. The memory requirements for a hash table containing n elements are then

$T \times w$ for any open addressing method

$T \times (w + 1)$ for coalesced chaining

$T + n(w + 1)$ for external chaining

These expressions are based on the following assumptions: Each position in a hash table for open addressing contains room for one element. For coalesced chaining, the hash table contains one pointer and one element in each position. For external chaining, the hash table contains one pointer in each position and one pointer and one element for each element in the table. We will now use the expressions to consider two cases.

If w is 1 (perhaps we store a pointer to an element rather than the element itself), then the memory required as a function of load factor is that shown in Figure 7.38. Open addressing always requires the least memory. When the table is nearly full, open addressing requires only one-third as much memory as external chaining. When the table is nearly full (see Figure 7.36), the performance of open addressing is poor. In that case, coalesced chaining provides good performance with a substantial saving in memory requirements.

If w is 10, then the memory requirements are as shown in Figure 7.39. External chaining is attractive over a wider range of load factors and extracts less of a penalty when the table is nearly full. This analysis leads to the following rules of thumb for constructing hash tables to be stored in RAM:

- For small elements and load factors, open addressing provides competitive performance and saves memory.
- For small elements and large load factors, coalesced chaining provides good performance with reasonable memory requirements.
- If elements are large, external chaining provides good performance with minimum, or nearly minimum, memory requirements.

These rules are based on the assumption that the maximum number of elements in the table can be estimated. Often that is not the case. Take, for example, the symbol table of a compiler that is used to store data about the user-defined identifiers in programs. The compiler must be able to process both large and small programs with a wide range in the numbers of identifiers. It may be possible for the table to overfill; that is, have a load factor greater than 1. The compiler should continue to operate smoothly. Such situations are often handled by the use of external chaining, which continues to function for load factors greater than 1.

7.4.7 Deletion of Hash Table Objects

We will conclude this section with a few comments about deletion. As discussed earlier, hash tables constructed using open addressing techniques pose problems when subjected to frequent deletions. The space previously occupied by a deleted record cannot simply be marked *empty* but must be marked *deleted*. This clutters up the hash table and hurts performance. No such problem arises if external chaining is used for collision resolution. Deletion is handled just as it is for any linked list. For coalesced chaining, deletion is no problem as long as the cellar has never been full, since deletion can be handled essentially as it is for external chaining. Once the cellar is full and the possibility of coalesced lists exists, then deletion must be handled carefully. An algorithm is given in Vitter (1982). It is (slightly) more complicated and would extract a small performance penalty. When designing a hashing strategy, the frequency of deletion must be considered along with performance and memory requirements.

EXERCISES 7.4

1. Explain the following terms in your own words:

hash function	collision resolution
collision	linear rehash
load factor	coalesced chaining
external chaining	perfect hashing function
home address	double hashing

2. The division hash function

   $$H(\text{key}) = \text{key } \textbf{mod } m$$

   is usually a good hash function if m has no small divisors. Explain why this restriction is placed on m.

3. Develop a hash function to convert nine-digit integers (Social Security numbers) into integers in the range $0..999$. Test your hash function by applying it to 800 randomly generated keys. Determine how many of the addresses received 0, 1, 2, ... of the hashed keys.

   Compare your experimental results with the results that would be obtained using a "perfect randomizer." The number of addresses receiving exactly k hashed values if the hash function is a perfect randomizer is approximated by

   $$e^{-\alpha} \frac{\alpha^k}{k!}$$

   where α is the load factor.

4. Develop a hash function to convert keys of the type

   KeyType = **array**[1 .. 15] **of** char;

   into integers in the range $0..999$. Implement your hash function and determine its execution time. Do the same for the hash function in Exercise 3 and compare their execution times.

5. Implement the perfect hashing function described in Section 7.4.3. Determine its execution time and compare it with the results obtained in Exercise 3.

6. Use the hash function $H(key) = key \textbf{ mod } 11$ to store the sequence of integers

   82, 31, 28, 4, 45, 27, 59, 79, 35

   in the hash table

   var table : **array**[0 .. 10] **of** integer;

   a. Use linear rehashing.
   b. Use double hashing.
   c. Use external chaining.
   d. Use coalesced chaining with a cellar size of 4 and the hash function

   $$H(\text{key}) = \text{key } \textbf{mod } 7$$

   For each of the above collision-handling strategies, determine (after all values have been placed in the table) the following:

e. The load factor

f. The average number of probes needed to find a value in the table

g. The average number of probes needed to find a value not in the table

7. Implement a collection of procedures that forms a hashing package according to Specification 7.2. Use

a. External chaining

b. Coalesced chaining with a cellar size of 70

Define a hash function by $H(key) = key \bmod 501$. [The hash function for coalesced chaining will be $H(key) = key \bmod 431$.] Use a random number generator to produce a sequence of integers to store in the hash table. Determine, as a function of the load factor, the average number of probes needed to find an integer in the table.

8. Write a program that will read words (a word is, for this application, a contiguous string of letters only) from an input text file (not the terminal). As words are read from the input file, look up each word in the hash table (Specification 7.2). If the word is there, add 1 to its count. If not, add it to the table with a count of 1. After all of the words are read, create a dynamic array of <word, count> pairs that is exactly the right size to hold the number of words you have (see Section 2.2.5). Sort the array alphabetically by word using Quicksort and print it. Then resort by count and print the list in descending order of the frequency with which the words occurred.

9. Complete Package Body 7.2, procedures *change* and *find*.

10. Modify Specification 7.2 and Package Body 7.2 to include an operation *sort* that will extract copies of the objects in the hash table, place them in the array provided, and sort them by key value. The sorted array is returned. The *sort* procedure is to have a single argument in addition to *the_table*—an array whose index range is

1 .. the_table.table_status.number_of_objects

11. Conduct timing studies patterned after those in Section 5.7 to include the times for hashing. Include in your studies a sorted list with a binary search, a binary search tree, and a hash table. Plot as a function of the list size, and using random keys, the expected time to

a. Insert new objects into the data structure

b. Find objects that are in the table

12. Modify the string hashing algorithm given in Figure 7.13 to produce a hash table position in the range $0 .. 128^2 - 1$.

13. Modify Specification 7.2 and Package Body 7.2 to include an operation *delete*:

procedure delete (the_table : **in out** hash_table;
target_key : key_type);

If an object with a key of *target_key* is in the hash table, it is to be deleted. If not, no action is to be taken by the procedure.

Caution: Adding *delete* requires another boolean field to be added to type *table_object*. Some of the other procedures of the package are also affected. The problem is that objects being deleted cannot be simply erased since they may be on the rehashing path of other objects.

■ 7.5 Summary

In this chapter, we studied data structures with setlike structural characteristics. We covered sets of atomic objects and sets of keyed objects. We used bit maps to implement the former and suggested that hash tables are a natural way of implementing the latter.

The performance gains of using hashing are great. When properly used, accessing objects in a hash table by their key value is an $O(1)$ operation.

We showed that bit maps, which are very economical in their use of memory, are easily and straightforwardly available in Ada.

8

Strings

■ 8.1 Introduction

Much of the information in the world is stored as strings of characters. A book can be thought of as a string of characters. A program can be viewed as a string of characters. A record describing a person's tax return (stored on a disk or tape by the IRS) can be thought of as a string of characters. Since computers are frequently used to store, edit, extract information from, and ultimately output character strings, it is important to have data structures that can be used to carry out these tasks efficiently and effectively.

A number of questions comes to mind. What data structures can be used to store character strings? What operations on character strings are useful? How can they be implemented? What are the performance considerations relating operations to string data structures? In this chapter we will consider these questions and explore some of the answers to them.

Section 8.2 describes individual characters, or character strings of length 1. This is a natural beginning, since character strings are sequences of individual characters. The atomic data type character is supported by many programming languages and forms an important data type in its own right.

Section 8.3.1 begins with the specification of a string data type that permits strings of variable lengths. Section 8.3.2 discusses Ada's predefined data type string—which does not support variable length strings. Section 8.3.3 considers several possibilities for representing a variable length string, and Section 8.3.4 presents a string implementation with emphasis on the algorithm to search one string for occurrences of a second string. Section 8.3.5 outlines two implementation alternatives for the string search algorithms. Section 8.4 is the chapter summary.

■ 8.2 Characters

Most programming languages include a predefined type character. The values of type character usually include Latin letters, numerals, special characters such as "[," "]," "{," "+," and nonprintable control characters. Two popular sets of characters are American Standard Code for Information Interchange (ASCII) and Extended Binary Coded Decimal Interchange Code (EBCDIC). ASCII is used on almost all micro- and minicomputers; EBCDIC is used on IBM mainframes.

The values of type character have a linear relationship that preserves the natural ordering of letters of the alphabet and of the numerals. Other relationships, however, are seemingly arbitrary. In ASCII, numerals precede capital letters, which precede lowercase letters. In the EBCDIC system, lowercase letters precede uppercase letters, which precede the numerals.

Ada supports the ASCII set of characters as described in package Standard. Recall that package Standard is automatically included in the context of every Ada compilation unit. More will be said about Ada's support for data type character shortly.

8.2.1 Fixed Length Representations

The usual technique for representing characters is to store each character using a fixed number of bits in memory. As shown in Figure 8.1, ASCII stores each character in 7 bits, and EBCDIC stores each character in 8 bits. Recall that the maximum number of distinct patterns that can be produced with n bits is 2^n. For easy reference this value is included in Figure 8.1.

Storage scheme	Number of bits to store each character (n)	Maximum number of distinct bit patterns (2^n)
ASCII	7	128
EBCDIC	8	256

FIGURE 8.1 ASCII and EBCDIC use a fixed number of bits to store each character. The ASCII scheme represents 128 distinct characters. The EBCDIC scheme can represent as many as 256 distinct characters.

A common technique is to store each character in 1 byte. A byte is (usually) a sequence of 8 bits. In many computers a byte is the smallest unit of information that can be directly accessed in random access memory. Figure 8.1 shows that an ASCII character does not fill a byte, whereas an EBCDIC character does. If ASCII is used to represent characters and each character is stored in a byte, the extra bit might be used to provide information about how the character is to be displayed—such as a flashing character or in an inverse mode.

8.2.2 Ada's Predefined Data Type Character

Ada provides an enumeration type that supports the 128 values of the ASCII character set. Of these 128 values, 95 are graphic or printable and the remaining 33 are control characters. A way to visualize these values is shown in Figure 8.2, where each control character is indicated by the symbol "[]" and each printable character represents itself.

Since data type character is an enumeration type, every value has an ordinal position. These ordinal positions are shown in Figure 8.2 by placing the 1's digit across the top of the table and the 10's value down the left side. For example, the ordinal position of "!" is 33, the ordinal position of "?" is 63, and the ordinal position of "z" is 122.

Figure 8.2 shows that the control characters are located in positions 0 through 31 and 127. With this information we can write a procedure, *write_ASCII*, that will produce Figure 8.2. The procedure is shown in Figure 8.3.

Procedure *write_ASCII* uses the *pos* attribute that applies to any enumeration type and therefore applies to data type *character*. If *ch* is of type *character*, then *character'pos(ch)* returns the corresponding ordinal value.

Procedure *write_ASCII* contains several *put* statements such as *put* ("[]"). Borrowing from material discussed later in this chapter, note that

	0	1	2	3	4	5	6	7	8	9
0	[]	[]	[]	[]	[]	[]	[]	[]	[]	[]
1	[]	[]	[]	[]	[]	[]	[]	[]	[]	[]
2	[]	[]	[]	[]	[]	[]	[]	[]	[]	[]
3	[]	[]		!	"	#	$	%	&	'
4	(	)	*	+	,	-	.	/	0	1
5	2	3	4	5	6	7	8	9	:	;
6	<	=	>	?	@	A	B	C	D	E
7	F	G	H	I	J	K	L	M	N	O
8	P	Q	R	S	T	U	V	W	X	Y
9	Z	[	\	]	^	_	`	a	b	c
10	d	e	f	g	h	i	j	k	l	m
11	n	o	p	q	r	s	t	u	v	w
12	x	y	z	{	|	}	~	[]		

FIGURE 8.2 The 128 values in the predefined Ada type character. Each control character is shown using the symbol "[]".

```
with text_io; use text_io;
procedure write_ASCII is
begin
    put_line("    0  1  2  3  4  5  6  7  8  9");
    for ch in character loop
      if character'pos(ch) mod 10 = 0 then
        new_line;
        put(character'pos(ch)/10, 2);
        set_col(5);
      end if;
      case ch is
        when ' '..'~' => put (" " & ch);
        when others   => put ("[]");
      end case;
    end loop;
    new_line(2);
end write_ASCII;
```

FIGURE 8.3 A procedure to write Figure 8.2.

a string literal is declared in an Ada program by enclosing it in double quotes. So in an Ada program, "a big salt shaker" is interpreted literally as the character string—a big salt shaker. Now we need to see how to express character literals in Ada.

For the 95 printable characters, the Ada literal is formed by enclosing the character in single quotes. Thus, '5', 'a', 'G', and '?' are Ada literals for the characters shown. Note that the literal for a single quote is formed in the same way as any other character, namely '''.

To refer to the control characters, the direct way is to use the constants shown in Figure 8.4, which are provided in package ASCII. Recall that package ASCII is part of the Standard package.

An Ada program may reference the character with ordinal position 0 as ASCII.NUL, *character'first, character'val(0),* or *character'pred(ASCII.SOH).* The

Constant	Ordinal	Constant	Ordinal	Constant	Ordinal
NUL	0	LF	10	DC4	20
SOH	1	VT	11	NAK	21
STX	2	FF	12	SYN	22
ETX	3	CR	13	ETB	23
EOT	4	SO	14	CAN	24
ENQ	5	SI	15	EM	25
ACK	6	DLE	16	SUB	26
BEL	7	DC1	17	ESC	27
BS	8	DC2	18	FS	28
HT	9	DC3	19	GS	29
				RS	30
				US	31
				DEL	127

FIGURE 8.4 The nonprinting constants in Ada's Standard package ASCII. The ordinal position of the character associated with each constant is also given.

character in ordinal position 127 may be referenced as ASCII.DEL, *character'last, character'val(127),* or *character'succ('~')*.

Special characters are also specified as constants in package ASCII. For example, ASCII.EXLAM is the same as '!', ASCII.SHARP is the same as '#', and ASCII.PERCENT is the same as '%'. The complete list is shown in package Standard, *Ada LRM* (1983, Appendix C). Finally, the lowercase letters are included in package ASCII as the constants *LC_A, LC_B, . . . , LC_Z*. Providing constants for special symbols and lowercase letters allows these characters to be accessed on systems that do not directly support them.

Another view of the printable portion of the ASCII character set is given in Figure 8.5. Each of the 95 rows of Figure 8.5 shows a character followed by the ordinal position of that character expressed using the number bases decimal, octal, and binary.

Figure 8.6 shows an Ada procedure that produces Figure 8.5. Variable *ch* contains the character to be printed, and the loop begins with the first printable character, space. Each time through the loop, information about one character is written. The ordinal position of each character is obtained with the *pos* attribute with the assignment *position := character'pos(ch)*. Writing the value of position in octal and binary is accomplished using the base parameter of procedure *put*. Blank lines are added to Figure 8.5 in strategic places to make the table easier to read.

Ada also specifies a minimal set of 56 characters, the basic character set, that is sufficient to write any Ada program. This allows the full range of Ada capabilities to be reached using a system with a limited character set. The basic character set is shown in Figure 8.7.

In addition to the basic character set, Ada allows use of three replacement characters. For instance, the sharp character, '#', is used to write integer literals in any number base from 2 to 16. The literal 3#2112# is interpreted as 2112 in base 3, and the literal 16#ABCDEF# is interpreted as ABCDEF in base 16.

ASCII	Decimal	Octal	Binary	ASCII	Decimal	Octal	Binary
	32	8#40#	2#100000#	P	80	8#120#	2#1010000#
!	33	8#41#	2#100001#	Q	81	8#121#	2#1010001#
"	34	8#42#	2#100010#	R	82	8#122#	2#1010010#
#	35	8#43#	2#100011#	S	83	8#123#	2#1010011#
$	36	8#44#	2#100100#	T	84	8#124#	2#1010100#
%	37	8#45#	2#100101#	U	85	8#125#	2#1010101#
&	38	8#46#	2#100110#	V	86	8#126#	2#1010110#
'	39	8#47#	2#100111#	W	87	8#127#	2#1010111#
(	40	8#50#	2#101000#	X	88	8#130#	2#1011000#
)	41	8#51#	2#101001#	Y	89	8#131#	2#1011001#
*	42	8#52#	2#101010#	Z	90	8#132#	2#1011010#
+	43	8#53#	2#101011#				
,	44	8#54#	2#101100#	[	91	8#133#	2#1011011#
−	45	8#55#	2#101101#	\	92	8#134#	2#1011100#
.	46	8#56#	2#101110#	]	93	8#135#	2#1011101#
/	47	8#57#	2#101111#	^	94	8#136#	2#1011110#
				_	95	8#137#	2#1011111#
0	48	8#60#	2#110000#	`	96	8#140#	2#1100000#
1	49	8#61#	2#110001#				
2	50	8#62#	2#110010#	a	97	8#141#	2#1100001#
3	51	8#63#	2#110011#	b	98	8#142#	2#1100010#
4	52	8#64#	2#110100#	c	99	8#143#	2#1100011#
5	53	8#65#	2#110101#	d	100	8#144#	2#1100100#
6	54	8#66#	2#110110#	e	101	8#145#	2#1100101#
7	55	8#67#	2#110111#	f	102	8#146#	2#1100110#
8	56	8#70#	2#111000#	g	103	8#147#	2#1100111#
9	57	8#71#	2#111001#	h	104	8#150#	2#1101000#
				i	105	8#151#	2#1101001#
:	58	8#72#	2#111010#	j	106	8#152#	2#1101010#
;	59	8#73#	2#111011#	k	107	8#153#	2#1101011#
<	60	8#74#	2#111100#	l	108	8#154#	2#1101100#
=	61	8#75#	2#111101#	m	109	8#155#	2#1101101#
>	62	8#76#	2#111110#	n	110	8#156#	2#1101110#
?	63	8#77#	2#111111#	o	111	8#157#	2#1101111#
@	64	8#100#	2#1000000#	p	112	8#160#	2#1110000#
				q	113	8#161#	2#1110001#
A	65	8#101#	2#1000001#	r	114	8#162#	2#1110010#
B	66	8#102#	2#1000010#	s	115	8#163#	2#1110011#
C	67	8#103#	2#1000011#	t	116	8#164#	2#1110100#
D	68	8#104#	2#1000100#	u	117	8#165#	2#1110101#
E	69	8#105#	2#1000101#	v	118	8#166#	2#1110110#
F	70	8#106#	2#1000110#	w	119	8#167#	2#1110111#
G	71	8#107#	2#1000111#	x	120	8#170#	2#1111000#
H	72	8#110#	2#1001000#	y	121	8#171#	2#1111001#
I	73	8#111#	2#1001001#	z	122	8#172#	2#1111010#
J	74	8#112#	2#1001010#				
K	75	8#113#	2#1001011#	{	123	8#173#	2#1111011#
L	76	8#114#	2#1001100#	|	124	8#174#	2#1111100#
M	77	8#115#	2#1001101#	}	125	8#175#	2#1111101#
N	78	8#116#	2#1001110#	~	126	8#176#	2#1111110#
O	79	8#117#	2#1001111#				

FIGURE 8.5 Each of the 95 printable ASCII characters followed by the ordinal position of that character expressed using the number bases decimal, octal, and binary.

```
with text_io; use text_io;
procedure values_ASCII is
begin
    for ch in ' '..'~' loop
      put ("   " & ch);
      put (character'pos(ch), width => 9, base => 10);
      put (character'pos(ch), width => 11, base => 8);
      put (character'pos(ch), width => 14, base => 2);
      case ch is
        when '/' | '9' | '@' | 'Z' | '‘' | 'z' => new_line(2);
        when others => new_line;
      end case;
    end loop;
end values_ASCII;
```

FIGURE 8.6 An Ada procedure that produces Figure 8.5.

Letters	All 26 uppercase letters (the 26 lowercase letters are not included)
Digits	0 1 2 3 4 5 6 7 8 9
Special characters	" # & ‘ ( ) * + , − . / : ; < = > _ |
Space character	

FIGURE 8.7 Ada's basic character set.

If a user's system does not include character '#', it can be replaced by ':'. The literals earlier in this paragraph can alternatively be expressed as 3:322: and 16:23:. A summary of the replacement characters is provided in Figure 8.8. A summary of Ada's data type character is shown in Figure 8.9.

Character	Replacement character	Use
#	:	Writing integer literals in bases other than 10
"	%	Writing character string literals
|	!	As a delimiter

FIGURE 8.8 Replacement characters in Ada. Use of these replacement characters is described in *Ada LRM* (1983, Section 2.10).

Data type   **character**

Values	The 128 ASCII characters	-- *95 printable characters and 33 control characters.*
Exceptions	constraint_error	-- *Raised when an attempt is made to assign a value outside the declared range.*
Operations		
Assignment	:=	-- *Assign a character value to a character variable.*
Relational	=, /=, <, >, <=, >=, in, not in	-- *The result is of type boolean.*
Attributes		
Any Ada type	address, base, size	
Any scalar type	first, last	
Any discrete type	pos, val, pred, succ, image, value, width	

FIGURE 8.9 Ada's data type character. Since data type character is discrete, all 12 attributes shown apply.

There are important alternatives to storing each character as a particular pattern using a fixed number of bits. One approach, discussed next, uses a fixed number of bits for each character but interprets each pattern in different ways. How a bit pattern is interpreted is specified by inserting special patterns reserved for that purpose.

8.2.3 Embedded Shift Mode Instructions

Karlgren's (1963) idea for representing more than 2^n distinct characters with n bits closely parallels the use of a shift key, which switches from lowercase to uppercase letters on a standard typewriter or computer terminal. In terms of stored data, the shift key is a bit pattern that is not data but that signals a shift between lowercase and uppercase.

Suppose we want to store the three words

ABSTRACT DATA TYPES

with the first letter of each word uppercase and the remainder of the letters lowercase. We can accomplish this by embedding a shift pattern as follows:

A#BSTRACT #D#ATA #T#YPES

where # signals a shift from lowercase to uppercase or from uppercase to lowercase, as appropriate.

Suppose we have 256 distinct bit patterns and one of them is used to signal a shift in mode, say, between lowercase and uppercase. The number of distinct ways of interpreting the bit patterns is

$$2 * (256 - 1) = 510$$

Further, suppose we use a second bit pattern to signal a shift between italic and Roman type. The number of distinct ways of interpreting the 256 bit patterns is then

$$4 * (256 - 2) = 1016$$

Finally, suppose we use a third bit pattern to signal a shift between bold and not bold type. The number of distinct ways of interpreting the 256 bit patterns is then

$$8 * (256 - 3) = 2024$$

Each character, other than the three mode shift patterns, will be interpreted in one of eight distinct modes made up of uppercase/lowercase, italic/Roman, and bold/not bold.

A problem with embedding mode shift patterns is the storage such patterns occupy. A character string that contains many such shifts requires extra memory to store the mode shift information. The combined effect on storage requirements depends on the frequency of mode shifts and the number of distinct modes.

8.2.4 Character Display Techniques—Some Examples

An IBM PC is designed to be used with either a monochrome or a color graphics terminal. An important component of the display is a section of memory that determines what is displayed on the terminal. The content of this memory is continually read and the result is displayed. This process is called *memory mapping*. Note that this memory can be used in two ways. Anything written to this memory is displayed on the terminal. In addition, the display memory can be read to determine what is being displayed.

In addition to the memory mapping facilities, an IBM PC also has commands that affect the display. These commands do such things as set the size and position of the cursor and clear the display. We will discuss only a subset of the memory mapping facilities.

Suppose we want to display characters on a terminal that permits 25 rows and 80 columns. Each character occupies 2 bytes. The memory needed for memory mapping is therefore,

$2 * 80 * 25 = 4000$ bytes

A monochrome adapter actually contains 4K (4096) bytes. The extra 96 bytes are not used. A color graphics adapter contains 16K bytes. Our interest here is how 2 bytes are used to display each character. Broadly speaking, the first byte tells which character to display and the second tells how to display it, as shown in Figure 8.10.

Character to display	How to display it
First byte	Second byte

FIGURE 8.10 Each character to be displayed is stored in 2 bytes of the memory that is mapped to the terminal. Memory mapped display for an IBM PC.

The character to display is determined by an extended ASCII character set. If the first bit is 0, the character to display is the ASCII character shown in Figure 8.1. The remaining 128 bit patterns, all with first bit 1, produce special effects such as lines and rectangles.

The second byte is interpreted one way for a monochrome monitor and another for a color monitor. We consider only a color monitor. The meaning of each bit is shown in Figure 8.11.

So, for example, to display the character 'A' with a red background, a blue foreground, normal intensity, and not blinking requires the pair of bytes in Figure 8.12.

We have only introduced the display possibilities for IBM PC color graphics terminals. For example, recall that 16K bytes are available for describing characters to be displayed but that only 4k are needed to describe the screen content completely. Actually, the 16K are divided into four screen descriptors, and the user can select which of the four is used to determine what is displayed. So, for instance, four screens can be written to memory, and the user can

Bit position	Effect on the display	
1	Blinking	
2	Red component	
3	Green component	Background color
4	Blue component	
5	Intensity	
6	Red component	
7	Green component	Foreground color
8	Blue component	

FIGURE 8.11 The effect on character display of each bit in the second byte associated with each character. IBM PC color graphics display.

01110101	01000001
First byte	Second byte

FIGURE 8.12 The pair of bytes that are memory mapped into the character 'A' with a red background, a blue foreground, normal intensity, and not blinking on an IBM PC color graphics monitor.

switch among them to change the terminal display. This capability might be used, for example, to produce animation.

In addition, and this is where the 16K of memory applies, the user can deal with individual pixels on the display instead of with characters. The two common screen dimensions are 320 columns and 200 rows per screen (medium resolution) and 640 columns and 200 rows per screen (high resolution). In high resolution the number of pixels is 200 * 640 or 128,000. Since 128,000 divided by 8 (bits per byte) is 16,000 bytes, we see that 16K of memory is needed just to determine on or off for each high-resolution pixel. How such a pixel display can be used to display characters and graphics is fascinating—but far beyond the scope of this discussion.

The second example in this brief section is the Apple ImageWriter dot matrix printer. We will mention only a few of its capabilities.

Characters to be printed are sent to the printer using ASCII. Note however that switches on the printer (not under software control) can be set to provide different versions of the ASCII characters: British, German, French, Swedish, Italian, Spanish, and American.

To cause the ImageWriter to switch between different printing modes, control characters are sent. Several of these are shown in Figure 8.13. Note that in each case the first byte is the ASCII escape character, whose ordinal position is 27. In each case shown, the first byte following the escape character is not a character to be printed but is an instruction to change the printer's mode of operation.

The ImageWriter can also accept variable length commands. For example, horizontal tabs are set by transmitting escape '(' and a sequence of tab settings separated by commas and terminated by a period. To set tabs at columns 5, 10, 15, and 20 would require the following sequence of bytes:

Escape '(' 5 ',' 10 ',' 15 ',' 20 '.'

The bit stream to accomplish this is

00010111 01000000 00000101 01000100 00001010 01000100 00001111 01000110

This illustrates one way to embed a variable length set of instructions in a stream of bytes that are otherwise interpreted as ASCII characters. The first

Bit patterns	Effect on the Imagewriter
00010111 01011000	Start underlining text
00010111 01011001	Stop underlining text
00010111 00100001	Start boldface text
00010111 00100010	Stop boldface text
00010111 00111110	Left-to-right printing only
00010111 00111100	Bidirectional printing

FIGURE 8.13 Pairs of bytes sent to the ImageWriter to change the way it prints characters.

byte is a graphic character that identifies the next byte as a command, the second byte identifies all subsequent bytes—until a terminator is found—as additional commands. Another alternative is illustrated by the next example.

The following command causes the ImageWriter to print bit images according to a specified number of subsequent bytes. The command is

Escape 'G' dd dd <the data to print goes here>

Each d in the line above is a decimal value stored in 4 bits. The possible values for dd dd in this command are the integers from 0 to 9999. Thus, this command tells the printer to treat a specified number of bytes (between 0 and 9999) in a special way. Each data byte causes one vertical column of up to 8 dots to be printed. The leftmost bit causes the bottom dot to be printed, and the rightmost bit causes the top dot to be printed. The following byte, 01101011, causes the dots in Figure 8.14 to be printed.

Exercises 8.2, 1 illustrates another way to embed a variable length set of instructions in a stream of bytes that are otherwise interpreted as ASCII characters. The first byte is a graphic character that identifies the next byte as a command; the second byte identifies its two successors as specifying the number of bytes to interpret in a special way. The data to be printed follows.

This section has shown several possible uses of embedding command characters and command sequences for particular display devices. We introduced only a few of the possibilities. This ends our discussion of using a fixed number of bits to record information about each character. There are also many interesting ways to use a variable number of bits to store characters. But we will skip this important topic and proceed to the discussion of character strings.

Bit	Dot
0	·
1	·
2	
3	·
4	
5	·
6	·
7	

FIGURE 8.14 The column of dots that correspond to the byte 01101011 on Apple's ImageWriter.

EXERCISES 8.2

1. Show what is printed when the ImageWriter receives the following data sequence:

00010111 01000111 00000000 00001111 00000001
00000011 00000111 00001111 00011111 00111111

01111111 11111111 11111111 11111111 11111111
01111111 00111111 00011111 00001111

2. Explain why the maximum number of bit patterns that can be represented with n bits is 2^n.

3. What are the advantages and disadvantages of embedded mode shift characters?

4. Specify and implement an Ada function that converts any uppercase alphabetic character to lowercase.

5. How many distinct ways can you think of to write the character 'A' using Ada?

■ 8.3 Strings

Strings are important in computer science because many fundamental elements are strings. A program is a string, the data read by a program is a string, and the manuals describing computers and languages are composed of strings. Many programs, for example text editors, have the manipulation of strings as their primary focus, and most programming languages provide a predefined data type string.

This sentence, including spaces and the period at the end, is a string. This paragraph is a string. A ***string*** is simply a sequence of characters. A ***string data type*** is a set of strings together with operations on those strings.

In this section we are interested in both general issues about string data types and the support Ada provides for strings. In Section 8.3.1 we begin with the specification of a string data type and a discussion of the operations in that specification. In Section 8.3.2, we describe Ada's predefined data type string—noting that Ada's predefined string type is limited to fixed length strings. Section 8.3.3 discusses several ways to represent variable length strings. One representation (based on an unconstrained discriminant record) is chosen and an implementation of the specification in Section 8.3.1 is given in Section 8.3.4. An important problem in computer science applications is the string-matching problem—which is to find occurrences of a string of characters (or pattern) in a generally much longer character string. Section 8.3.5 is devoted to a discussion of algorithms to solve the string-matching problem.

8.3.1 Specification of a Variable Length Data Type String

We begin with some notation used to describe strings. We can refer to the characters of a string in terms of their position in the string. If S is a string, then $S(1)$ is its first character, $S(2)$ [the successor of $S(1)$] is its second character, and $S(k)$ [the successor of $S(k-1)$] is its kth character. Integer k is the ***position*** of character $S(k)$ in string S. If S contains n characters, then it is said to have ***length*** n. If S is a string of length n and if $1 \leq j \leq k \leq n$, then the sequence of characters

$$S(j), S(j+1), \ldots, S(k)$$

is a ***substring*** of S. A string that contains no characters is called the ***empty string*** and has length 0.

Observe that a string is an indexed list (in the sense of a list in Chapter 4) of characters. Each nonempty string has first and last characters, each character (except the last) has a unique successor, each character (except the first) has a unique predecessor, and each character has a unique position in its string. Thus, in terms of the positional relations between elements, lists and strings are the same. As we are about to see, however, operations on strings are quite different from operations on lists. To that end, Specification 8.1 for strings is given next.

■ **SPECIFICATION 8.1 Variable Length Strings**

```
-- Abstract Structure:   A string is a sequence of characters. The characters in a string have a linear
--                       relationship. That is, each nonempty string has first and last characters, each character (except the last) has
--                       a unique successor, each character (except the first) has a unique predecessor, and each character has a
--                       unique position in its string.
-- Constraints:   Representation issues are discussed in Section 8.3.3.
```

generic
    max_length : **in** natural := 80;   -- *The maximum number of characters in a string.*
package string_package **is**

    subtype string_length **is** natural **range** 0 .. max_length;
    type var_string **is** ... ;   -- *Representation and implementation issues are described in Sections 8.3.3 and 8.3.4.*

    function convert_from_ada (ada_string : string) **return** var_string;
    -- *results:* *Converts from Ada's predefined type string to type var_string and returns the result.*

    function convert_to_ada (the_string : var_string) **return** string;
    -- *results:* *Converts the_string from type var_string to type string and returns the result.*

    function length (the_string : var_string) **return** string_length;
    -- *results:* *Returns the number of characters in the_string.*

    function "&" (the_string : var_string; the_char : character) **return** var_string;
    -- *assumes:* *length(the_string) <= max_length − 1.*
    -- *results:* *Returns the string formed by appending the_char to the end of the_string.*

    function "&" (left, right : var_string) **return** var_string;
    -- *assumes:* *length(left) + length(right) <= max_length.*
    -- *results:* *Returns the string obtained by appending right to the end of left.*

    function insert (sub_string : var_string; target_string : var_string; the_place : string_index) **return** var_string;
    -- *assumes:* *length(sub_string) + length(target_string) <= max_length.*
    -- *results:* *Insert sub_string into target_string so that the position of the first character of sub_string is*
    --   *the_place.*

    function delete (the_string : var_string; the_place : string_index; the_length : string_length) **return** var_string;
    -- *assumes:* *the_place + the_length − 1 ≤ length(the_string)*
    -- *results:* *Returns the string obtained by deleting from the_string the substring beginning*
    --   *at position the_place containing the_length characters.*

(continued)

Specification 8.1 (continued)

function sub_string (the_string : var_string; the_place : string_index; the_length : string_length) **return** var_string;
-- **assumes:** *length(the_string) >= the_place + the_length − 1.*
-- **results:** *Return the substring of the_string that contains the_length characters and begins at position*
-- *the_place.*

function "<" (left, right : var_string) **return** boolean;
-- **results:** *Returns true if left alphabetically precedes right. The examples below illustrate the results when*
-- *strings left and right are not the same length.*
-- *value of left*	*value of right*	*value returned by left < right*
-- *abc*	*abcdef*	*true*
-- *abcdef*	*abc*	*false*
-- *aaa*	*abcdef*	*true*

-- *The empty string is "<" any string—except the empty string.*

function ">" (left, right : var_string) **return** boolean;
function "<=" (left, right : var_string) **return** boolean;
function ">=" (left, right : var_string) **return** boolean;
-- **results:** *The specification for each of these functions is analogous to that for function "<".*

function find_char (the_string : var_string; the_char : character; start_search : string_index) **return** string_length;
-- **results:** *Search the_string for the first occurrence of the_char. The search begins at position start_search. If*
-- *the_char is found, its position is returned; otherwise 0 is returned. The search is from start_search to the*
-- *end of the_string only. Characters preceding start_search are not searched.*

function find_string (the_string : var_string; the_pattern : var_string; start_search : string_index) **return** string_length;
-- **assumes:** *length (the_pattern) > 0.*
-- **results:** *Search the_string for the first occurrence of the_pattern. The search begins at position start_search.*
-- *If the_pattern is found its position is returned; otherwise 0 is returned. The search is from start_search to*
-- *the end of the_string only. Characters preceding start_search are not searched for occurrences of*
-- *the_pattern.*

private

    type var_string **is** ...   -- *Representation and implementation issues are described in Sections 8.3.3 and 8.3.4.*

end string_package;

Figures 8.15 and 8.16 illustrate the use of many of the operations specified in the *var_strings* package. In both figures the first column numbers the examples, the second column shows the string(s) before the operation, the third column shows the operation that is performed, and the last column shows the value produced by the operation. The last column shows all values that are affected by the operation—values not shown in the last column are not changed.

In Figure 8.15 examples 2, 3, and 4 show use of the *insert* operation to insert one string in the middle, at the beginning, and at the end of another

	String(s) before the operation	Operation	Returns
1	s1: "1234567890"	length(s1)	10
2	s1: "abcde"	insert (s1, s2, 6)	"12345abcde67890"
	s2: "1234567890"		
3	s1: "abcde"	insert (s1, s2, 1)	"abcde1234567890"
	s2: "1234567890"		
4	s1: "abcde"	insert (s1, s2, 11)	"1234567890abcde"
	s2: "1234567890"		
5	s1: "12345abcde67890"	delete (s1, 6, 5)	"1234567890"
6	s1: "12345abcde67890"	delete (s1, 1, length(s1))	""
7	s1: "12345abcde67890"	substring (s1, 6, 5)	"abcde"
8	s1: "12345"	& (s1, s2)	"12345abcde"
	s2: "abcde"		
9	s1: "12345"	& (s1, s1)	"1234512345"
10	s1: "12345"	& (s1, s2)	"12345"
	s2: ""		

F I G U R E 8.15 Ten examples illustrating use of the string operations in Package 8.1. Additional examples are given in Figure 8.16.

string. Examples 5 and 6 show deletion of a substring from the middle of a string and deletion of an entire string leaving the empty string. Example 7 shows the extraction of a substring from the middle of a string. Finally, examples 8 through 10 show various applications of concatenation.

The operations on strings deal not with the individual characters that make up the string but with substrings. Contrast these operations with the operations on lists in Chapter 4. The *insert* operation for lists, if applied to a string, would insert one character. The *delete* operation for lists, if applied to a string, would delete one character. The string operations actually insert or delete an entire sequence of characters. This difference, operations that act on one object as opposed to operations that act on many objects, is a major difference between data type list and data type string.

We continue with Figure 8.16, which illustrates additional string operations. Examples 1 through 3 illustrate use of *find_char;* examples 4 through

	String(s) before the operation	Operation	Returns
1	s1: "abcdeabcde"	find_char (s1, 'c', 1)	3
2	s1: "abcdeabcde"	find_char (s1, 'c', 5)	8
3	s1: "abcdeabcde"	find_char (s1, 'c', 9)	0
4	s1: "abcdeabcde"	find_string (s1, s2, 1)	3
	s2: "cde"		
5	s1: "abcdeabcde"	find_string (s1, s2, 5)	8
	s2: "cde"		
6	s1: "abcdeabcde"	find_string (s1, s2, 9)	0
	s2: "cde"		

F I G U R E 8.16 Six examples illustrating use of the string operations in Specification 8.1. Additional examples are given in Figure 8.15.

6 show uses of *find_string*. We will discuss implementations of *find_string* in Section 8.3.5.

This ends the discussion of the strings described in Specification 8.1. The next section presents Ada's predefined data type string.

8.3.2 Ada's Predefined Data Type String

The values for Ada's string data type are instances of the unconstrained array of characters shown in Figure 8.17.

type string **is array** (positive **range** <>) **of** character;

FIGURE 8.17 Ada's string data type.

Three instances of type string might be declared as

s1, s2, s3: string (1 . . 20);

One way to assign values to a string is to use string literals as shown in Figure 8.18.

```
--                      1         2
--       12345678901234567890
s1   := "abcde               "
s2   := "abcdefghij          "
s3   := "abcdefghijklmnopqrst"
```

FIGURE 8.18 Assignment of string literals to strings *s1, s2,* and *s3*.

An Ada **string literal** is a sequence of characters enclosed in quotes. As illustrated in Figure 8.18, a literal must be exactly the same length as the string to which it is assigned. The quote character, ", is represented in a string literal by a pair of quotes. The literal for the string of length 1 containing character ' " ' is " " " ". The literal for the string of length 2 that contains two quotation characters is " " " " " ".

An alternate way to initialize *s1* as shown in Figure 8.18 is given in Figure 8.19.

type str20 **is new** string(1 .. 20);
s1, s2 : str20;

s1 := str20'('a', 'b', 'c', 'd', 'e', others => ' ');
s2 := str20'(1 => 'a', 5 => 'e', 4 => 'd', 3 => 'c', 2 => 'b', 6 .. 20 => ' ');

FIGURE 8.19 Two alternate techniques for initializing strings. Compare with Figure 8.18. These initialization schemes apply to any one-dimensional Ada array. Type *str20* is needed in this figure in order to prescribe the meaning of others and the meaning of 6 .. 20.

The usual six relational operators, $=, /=, <, >, <=, >=$, are defined for strings. The result of comparing two strings is as described in the note for function "$<$" in Specification 8.1.

Ada also provides the (con)catenation operator, &, for strings (and one-dimensional arrays). If we declare

```
s1 : string(1 .. 5) := "12345";
s2 : string(1 .. 10) := "1234567890";
s3 : string(1 .. 15);
```

then $s3 := s1 \& s2$ appends $s2$ to the end of $s1$ and assigns the result to $s3$. Thus the value of $s3$ is "123451234567890". Similarly, $s3 := s2 \& s1$ appends $s1$ to the end of $s2$ and assigns the result to $s3$.

Array slices can be used to concatenate substrings. So, $s3(1..6) := s1(1..3) \& s2(8..10)$ assigns the string "123890" to $s3(1..6)$. Note that the size of a string receiving the result of a catenation must exactly equal the sum of the sizes of the strings being catenated. Figure 8.20 summarizes Ada's predefined data type string.

Data type	**String**	
Values	**type** string **is array** (positive **range** $<>$) **of** character;	
Operations		
Assignment	:=	-- *Assign a string to another string of the same length.*
Relational	$=, /=, <, >, <=, >=$	-- *Compare any two strings, the result is of type boolean.*
Slice	S(j .. k)	-- *The substring of S containing characters j through k.*
Concatenation	&	-- *A binary operation that concatenates two strings,*
		-- *or a string and a character, or a character and a string.*
Attributes		
Any Ada type	address, base, size	
Any array type	first, last, length, range	

FIGURE 8.20 A summary of Ada's predefined data type string.

8.3.3 Representation Alternatives for Data Type String

The goal of this section is to discuss representation alternatives for data type string. We begin with Ada's predefined type string. Let $s1$ be declared as

```
s1: string (1 .. 20);
```

We would like to store in $s1$ a character string with any length between 0 and 20. The operations supplied by Ada all treat $s1$ as if its length is exactly 20. So our first concern is to add a notion of length to a particular string.

A common approach—used in programming languages C and Modula-2 for example—is to append the null character, ASCII.nul, to the end of each string. In C (Kernighan, 1988), every string is terminated with the null character. In Modula-2 (King, 1988), a string is terminated with the null character unless it fills the array in which it is stored. Either of these approaches is compatible with Ada's data type string. The disadvantage is that a string must be scanned to determine its length. This affects other operations. For example, to concatenate strings *s1* and *s2* requires determining the length of *s1* in order to know where to position *s2*. Figure 8.21 shows an implementation of function *length* that scans a string until it locates a null character.

```
function length (the_string : string) return natural is
-- Length 4   Complexity 3   Performance O(n)
begin
    for index in the_string'range loop
      if the_string(index) = ASCII.nul then
        return (index - the_string'first);         -- Terminating null character found.
      end if;
    end loop;
    return (the_string'length);                    -- Null character not found.
end length;
```

FIGURE 8.21 An implementation of length if each string is terminated by ASCII.nul—unless the string fills the array in which it is stored. Note that the_string'first can be any positive value.

There are several ways to eliminate scanning a string to determine its length. These techniques all work by storing each string's length with the string. We proceed to discuss several possibilities. Further details are given in Abrahams (1988), Bron (1989), and Boddy (1990).

One approach (Figure 8.22) is to store each string's length as the first byte of the string. This technique is used by, for example, Borland's Turbo Pascal®. Programs that manipulate such strings must provide the logic to treat the first byte in a different way than the remainder of the string. A disadvantage is that such strings are limited to 255 bytes. In many applications, 255 bytes is enough. If longer strings are needed, 2 bytes might be used to store *length*. The maximum string length is then $256^2 - 1$ or 65,535 bytes. If longer strings are needed, more bytes can be used.

4	a	b	c	d			

FIGURE 8.22 A string's length can be stored as the first byte of the string. Such strings are not compatible with programs that expect a character in the first byte.

A second technique is to declare a record type that combines the string with a second field that explicitly stores the string's length. Figures 8.23 and 8.24 show two ways to do this. In Figure 8.23 a record with two fields—length and data—is used. This approach separates the mechanism for storing a string from the mechanism for recording its length—which has the advantage of simplicity. The size of the array that stores the string *max_length* might be supplied as a generic parameter to the strings package. Thus, all strings would

```
type length_field_string is record
    length   : natural;
    data     : string (1 .. max_length);
end record;
```

FIGURE 8.23 Each string is stored as *length_field_string*. This approach separates storage of the string's length from storing the string itself so the representation is simpler. All strings of this type have the same maximum *length—max_length*.

```
type cdr_string (length : positive) is record
    data : string (1 .. length);
end record;
```

FIGURE 8.24 A string declared as a constrained discriminant record type. The strings length is determined without scanning the string, and the representation does not place an upper bound on string length. A cdr_string, once declared, has a fixed length.

have the same maximum length. The data field of *length_field_string* is compatible with Ada's string type, but a *length_field_string* is not.

It is an advantage to have a string representation that is compatible with Ada's data type string because Ada's string operations can then be used to simplify implementation of the operations.

In Figure 8.24 a constrained discriminant record is used to represent the string type *cdr_string*. This approach is efficient in its use of memory because a string fills the array allocated to store it—assuming the underlying implementation allocates instances of discriminant records to minimize the memory used.

A string's length must, however, be specified when the string is declared, and that length cannot be changed. The result of an operation that changes a string's length (e.g., *insert, delete,* or *concatenate*) must be assigned to another string with the correct length—making this approach awkward to use. The need to allocate new record instances to accommodate changes in string length may also be a performance penalty. A *cdr_string* is not compatible with Ada's data type string, but its data field is.

Another approach is based on an unconstrained discriminant record as shown in Figure 8.25. With this representation, the length of a string can be changed dynamically—provided it was declared without a discriminant value and new values are given for both length and data. Thus we have a variable length string that explains using the name *var_string*.

```
subtype string_length is natural range 0 .. max_length;
subtype string_index is natural range 1 .. max_length;

type var_string (length : string_length := 0) is record
    text   : string (1 .. length);
end record;
```

FIGURE 8.25 A string declared as an unconstrained discriminant record type. A *var_string*'s length is changed dynamically.

Logically, there are many similarities between *var_strings* and *length_field_strings* (Figure 8.23). Relative performance depends on how an unconstrained discriminant record is implemented.

If we declare *var1* and *var2* to be of type *var_string*,

var1, var2 : var_string;

then the assignment of initial values can be accomplished as

var1 := (5, "abcde"); var2 := (10, "1234567890");

and the concatenation of these strings can be accomplished using Ada's concatenation operator for arrays as follows:

var1 := (15, var1.text & var2.text);   -- *or*
var1 := (5, var1.text(2 .. 4) & var2.text(5 .. 6));

Another approach (Bron, 1989, and Boddy, 1990) is to append a null character to the end of the string and to store the string's length as the *last* byte of the string—unless the array containing the string is full. Actually, instead of recording the string's length in the last byte, record the distance from the end of the string to the null character that terminates the string. Storing length this way handles the otherwise special case in which the string is one character short of filling its containing array. Several examples of such strings are shown in Figure 8.26.

a	b	c	d	null			3
a	b	c	d	e	f	g	null
a	b	c	d	e	f	g	h

FIGURE 8.26 Storing three example strings. The containing array is of length 8. Each string is (a) terminated by the null character and (b) has the distance from the end of the string to the null character as its last byte—unless the string fills the containing array. The example strings are of length 4, 7, and 8.

A final adjustment is instead of storing an integer in the last byte, store the character whose ordinal position is the desired length. This is necessary since a string is an array of characters—not an array of characters and one integer. So, instead of storing n in the last byte of a string, we would store *char* such that *character'pos(char)* = n. That is, store *character'val(n)*.

This approach is compatible with Ada's predefined type string and with strings stored as arrays of characters with a null terminator. Scanning a string to determine its length is eliminated, and strings may be as long as *character'pos(character'last)* or 128 characters. Other implementations will be discussed, and references to complete implementations that appear in other sources are given.

Boddy (1990) gives details of a compatible scheme to handle longer strings. An Ada adaptation of one version of this scheme stores a string as described in Figure 8.27.

1. Let d be the difference between the length of the containing array and the length of the string. If $d = 0$, the string fills the array and no delimiter is used.
2. If $d \le 127$, the last character in the containing array stores $d - 1$.
3. If $d > 127$ the last character in the array is set to *character'pos(127)*, to mark this case, and the length of the string is stored in the 2 bytes immediately preceding the last character of the array.

FIGURE 8.27 One technique for storing a string as an array of characters.

String representation	Length representation	Comments
Array of characters.	None—the string is assumed to fill the array that contains it.	Ada's predefined string representation.
Array of characters.	Terminate the string with null—unless it fills the array that contains it.	A common technique for representing strings. A string must be scanned to determine its length.
Array of characters.	Use the first byte of the array to record the string's length. Use more bytes for longer strings.	Makes it easy to determine a string's length, but program logic is needed to treat the first character in a different way than the remainder of the string. Long strings require more bytes to store length.
Array of characters.	Terminate the string with null, and record the string's length in the *last* byte of the array. Use more bytes for longer strings.	Has all the advantages of the technique immediately above and eliminates logic to treat the first character as length rather than as part of the string.
A record type with a field to store string length and a field to store an array of characters.	The length is explicitly stored as one field of the record.	Simplifies the storage of length by separating it from storage for the string. The field that stores the string is compatible with Ada's type string. Maximum string length might be set by a generic parameter.
A constrained discriminant record. One field is an array of characters that contains the string.	The record's discriminant value is the string's length.	The field that stores the string is compatible with Ada's type string. When a string's length is changed, a new record instance is needed to store it.
An unconstrained discriminant record. One field is an array of characters that contains the string.	The record's discriminant value is the string's length.	Similar to a constrained discriminant record, but the length of a string can change dynamically.
Pointer to any of the string representations above.	Can be any of the above.	String instances are allocated dynamically. A string must be dereferenced to access its characters. Dynamic allocation may affect performance.

FIGURE 8.28 Summary of string representation possibilities. Discussion of string implementation continues in Sections 8.3.4 and 8.3.5.

Finally, a string can be represented as a pointer to any of the string representations we have discussed so far. This approach has the advantage of using the dynamic allocation capabilities provided by Ada (or any other implementation language) to create and destroy string instances dynamically (an example of this approach appears in Section 2.4.5). Disadvantages include the need to dereference a string to access its characters and the incompatibility with strings represented as arrays of characters. Such incompatibilities can be overcome with appropriate conversion operations, and the object pointed at may be compatible with other string types. Frequent allocation and deallocation of string instances may adversely affect performance.

Figure 8.28 concludes this section with a summary of the representation alternatives we have discussed.

8.3.4 Implementation of a Variable Length Data Type String

This section presents an implementation of Specification 8.1. Other implementations are suggested in the exercises. The implementation does not include procedure *find_string* because this important operation is discussed in detail in Section 8.3.5.

The implementation is based on unconstrained discriminant records— the representation summarized in the seventh row in Figure 8.28 and given in Specification 8.1. The two missing pieces in Specification 8.1 are completed in Figure 8.29.

```
generic
    max_length : in natural := 80;
package string_package is

    subtype string_length is natural range 0 .. max_length;
    subtype string_index is natural range 1 .. max_length;

    type var_string (length : string_length := 0) is private;

    .
    .
    .

private

    type var_string (length : string_length := 0) is record
       text: string (1 .. length);
    end record;

end string_package;
```

FIGURE 8.29 Representation of a variable length string as an unconstrained discriminant record.

The implementation is given below. The complexity of eight of the implementations is 1. Two of the implementations, *delete* and *substring,* contain subtleties in their implementation due to Ada's treatment of array slices. These two implementations are discussed following Package Body 8.1. Implementation of *find_string* is deferred to the next section.

■ **PACKAGE BODY 8.1** **Implementation of Specification 8.1**

package body string_package **is**

```
    function convert_from_ada (ada_string : string) return var_string is
    -- Length 2   Complexity 1   Performance O(n)
        length : string_length := ada_string'last − ada_string'first + 1;
    begin
        return var_string'(length, ada_string(ada_string'first .. ada_string'last));
    end convert_from_ada;

    function convert_to_ada (the_string : var_string) return string is
    -- Length 1   Complexity 1   Performance O(n)
    begin
        return string'(the_string.text(1 .. the_string.text'last));
    end convert_to_ada;

    function length (the_string : var_string) return string_length is
    -- Length 1   Complexity 1   Performance O(1)
    begin
        return the_string.length;
    end length;

    function "&" (the_string : var_string; the_char : character) return var_string is
    -- Length 2   Complexity 1   Performance O(n)
    begin
        return var_string'(the_string.length + 1, (the_string.text & the_char));
    end "&";

    function "&" (left, right : var_string) return var_string is
    -- Length 1   Complexity 1   Performance O(n)
    begin
        return var_string'(left.length + right.length, (left.text & right.text));
    end "&";

    function insert (sub_string : var_string; target_string : var_string; the_place : string_index) return var_string is
    -- Length 4   Complexity 1   Performance O(n)
        sum : string_length := (sub_string.length + target_string.length);
    begin
        return var_string'(sum, (target_string.text(1 .. the_place − 1) &
            sub_string.text & target_string.text(the_place .. target_string.length)));
    end insert;

    function delete (the_string : var_string; the_place : string_index; the_length : string_length) return var_string is
    -- Length 4   Complexity 1   Performance O(n)
        subtype anchor is string(1 .. the_string.length − the_place − the_length + 1);
    begin
        return var_string'(the_string.length − the_length, the_string.text(1 .. the_place − 1) &
            anchor(the_string.text(the_place + the_length .. the_string.length)));
    end delete;
```

(continued)

Package Body 8.1 (continued)

```
function sub_string (the_string : var_string; the_place : string_index; the_length : string_length) return var_string is
-- Length 4   Complexity 1   Performance O(n)
   subtype anchor is string(1 .. the_length);
begin
   return var_string'(the_length,
      anchor(the_string.text(the_place .. the_place + the_length − 1)));
end sub_string;

function "<" (left, right : var_string) return boolean is
-- Length 1   Complexity 1   Performance O(n)
begin
   return (left.text < right.text);
end "<";

function "<=" (left, right : var_string) return boolean is
-- Length 1   Complexity 1   Performance O(n)
begin
   return (left.text <= right.text);
end "<=";

function ">" (left, right : var_string) return boolean is
-- Length 1   Complexity 1   Performance O(n)
begin
   return (left.text > right.text);
end ">";

function ">=" (left, right : var_string) return boolean is
-- Length 1   Complexity 1   Performance O(n)
begin
   return (left.text >= right.text);
end ">=";

function find_char (the_string : var_string; the_char : character; start_search : string_index) return string_length is
-- Length 8   Complexity 3   Performance O(n)
   index : string_index := start_search;
begin
   while index <= the_string.length loop
      if the_char = the_string.text(index) then return index;
      end if;
      index := index + 1;
   end loop;
   return 0;
end find_char;

-- function find_string is discussed and implemented in Section 8.3.5.

end string_package;
```

You might expect the implementation of function *sub_string* to be given as shown in Figure 8.30, instead of as it is actually given in the package body.

```
function sub_string (the_string : var_string; the_place : string_index; the_length : string_length) return var_string is
begin
    return var_string'(the_length, the_string.text(the_place .. the_place + the_length − 1));
end sub_string;
```

FIGURE 8.30 An implementation of *sub_string* that raises CONSTRAINT_ERROR unless *the_place* is 1.

But the implementation in Figure 8.30 causes the exception *CONSTRAINT_ERROR* to be raised unless the value of *the_place* is 1. Before we look at why this is so and ways to take care of the problem, we introduce the informal Ada notion of **sliding semantics**.

Suppose that *s1* and *s2* are Ada strings declared as follows:

s1, s2 : string(1 .. 80);

Then the following assignment is valid:

s1(10 .. 20) := s2(50 .. 60);

The assignment is valid because the number of components is the same for both slices even though the range of index values is not. We can think of the *s2* values in the range 50 .. 60 as sliding into the range 10 .. 20 in *s1*. Hence the term *sliding semantics*. The trouble is that sliding semantics does not always apply.

Sometimes sliding semantics applies as illustrated in the example above. Sometimes matching semantics applies (a function result is one such case), and the range of index values must match exactly. Sometimes the result takes the bounds of the expression. This general issue is discussed in Barnes (1989, pp. 360–361).

Refer again to Figure 8.30. If *the_place* is not 1, the range of index values of the string being returned does not match the range of index values of the result string. To see this, recall (Figure 8.29) that the first index value of any *var_string* is 1. How can we fix the implementation in Figure 8.30?

A first solution attempt might be to use an assignment to force the correct range of index values. This is shown in Figure 8.31.

```
function sub_string (the_string : var_string; the_place : string_index; the_length : string_length) return var_string is
    temp : string(1 .. the_length) := the_string.text(the_place .. the_place + the_length − 1));
begin
    return var_string'(the_length, temp);
end sub_string;
```

FIGURE 8.31 A valid implementation of *sub_string* that contains an unnecessary assignment.

The assignment to *temp* in Figure 8.31 is valid because sliding semantics apply. Since *temp* has the same range of index values as a *var_string* of the same length, the return statement in Figure 8.31 does not raise a constraint error. The shortcoming of the implementation in Figure 8.31 is that it contains a slice assignment that is not needed. Look at the implementation of *sub_string* in the package body to see how that assignment is eliminated.

The only other implementation in Package Body 8.1 for which sliding semantics is an issue is *delete*. Consider the intuitively appealing, but incorrect, implementation of *delete* shown in Figure 8.32.

```
function delete (the_string : var_string; the_place : string_index; the_length : string_length) return var_string is
begin
    return var_string'(the_string.length − the_length, the_string.text(1 .. the_place − 1) &
        the_string.text(the_place + the_length .. the_string.length));
end delete;
```

FIGURE 8.32 An incorrect implementation of *delete*.

The implementation in Figure 8.32 will fail if *the_place* is 1 and *the_length* > 1 but will work in all other cases. If *the_place* > 1, then *the_string.text*(1 .. *the_place* − 1) is a string whose first index value is 1 and matching semantics works for the string that is returned.

If *the_place* is 1, however, *the_string.text*(1 .. *the_place* − 1) is the null string and is disregarded in forming the string to return. Thus, the first index of the returned string is *the_place* + *the_length*, and matching semantics is satisfied only if this sum is 1. Our recommended fix for this problem is given in Package Body 8.1.

It is interesting to consider the instantiation and use of the package for *var_strings*. An example that does that is shown in Figure 8.33.

```
with string_package;

procedure main is

    package string_pak is new string_package (40);

    function "&" (the_string : string_pak.var_string; the_char : character) return var_string
        renames string_pak."&";

    function "&" (left, right : string_pak.var_string) return var_string
        renames string_pak."&";

    function "<" (left, right : string_pak.var_string) return boolean
        renames string_pak."<";
```

FIGURE 8.33 Code to illustrate use of the *var_strings* in Specification 8.1.

(continued)

Figure 8.33 (continued)

```
begin
    declare
        ada_str1, ada_str2    : string(1 .. 20);
        sx1, sx2, sx3         : string_pak.var_string;
    begin
        --                      1               2
        --              12345678901234567890
        ada_str1 := "1234567890            ";
        ada_str2 := "ABCDEFGHIJ            ";

        sx1 := string_pak.convert_from_ada (ada_str1(1 .. 10));
        sx2 := string_pak.convert_from_ada (ada_str2(1 .. 10));

        sx3 := sx1 & '1';
        sx2 := sx1 & sx3;
        sx2 := string_pak.sub_string (sx3, 1, 1);
        sx2 := sx1;
        if sx1 < sx2 then ... ;
        end if;
    end;
end main;
```

F I G U R E 8.33 *(continued)*

The code in Figure 8.33 does not solve a particular problem, but it illustrates the instantiation and use of *string_package*. Note particularly the use of the **renames** clause to avoid awkward expressions involving operators such as "&" and "<". One alternative to these renames clauses is the clause use *string_pak*. Another possibility is, for example, to replace *sx3 := sx1 & 'A'* by *sx3 := string_pak."&" (sx1, 'A')*.

One operation, *find_string*, requires some discussion, which is provided in Section 8.3.5.

8.3.5 Implementation of Procedure *find_string*

We begin this section with an example. Figure 8.34 shows two strings, the first called text and the second called pattern. We want to start at the left end of text and scan to the right looking for an instance of pattern.

```
          1         2         3         4
1234567890123456789012345678901234567890
com comp compu comput compute computer
computer
```

-- Ruler to allow determination
of a character's position.
-- Text to be searched.
-- Pattern to be found.

F I G U R E 8.34 The string to be searched, text, contains 38 characters, and the string to be found, pattern, contains 8. Observe that an instance of pattern exists as the substring including characters 31 .. 38.

Our first algorithm for this search is given in Figure 8.35.

while there is more text to search **loop**
    if pattern equals the substring of text with which it is aligned **then**
      return the position of pattern;
    else slide pattern forward one position;
    end if;
end loop;

FIGURE 8.35 Pseudocode for searching for an instance of pattern in text.

Before discussing this algorithm, let us establish some terminology. A *match* occurs when a substring of text is found that is equal to pattern. A *hit* occurs when a single character of pattern is the same as the corresponding character of text. A *miss* occurs when a character of pattern is different from a corresponding character of text.

Look at Figure 8.34. There are three hits and a miss. The miss involves ' ' in text and 'p' in pattern at position 4. We slide pattern forward one character, Figure 8.36, and begin again. This time there are no hits and the miss involves 'o' in text and 'c' in pattern at position 2.

```
          1         2         3         4
 1234567890123456789012345678901234567890   -- Ruler to allow determination
 com comp compu comput compute computer     -- of a character's position.
  computer                                   -- Text to be searched.
                                             -- Pattern to be found.
```

FIGURE 8.36 After sliding pattern forward one position. A miss occurs at position 2.

Now, Figure 8.37 shows the complete search. Figure 8.37 also records additional information about the search: the text position at which each miss occurs and the cumulative number of character compares that have been made. After moving "computer" to position 5, the first miss occurs at position 9 when ' ' is compared with 'u'. This miss follows hits with characters 'c', 'o', 'm', and 'p'. Pattern is then moved to position 6.

The algorithm illustrated in Figure 8.37 is one that many people would think of when first confronting the implementation of *find_string* and is referred to as the *obvious algorithm*. An Ada implementation of *find_string* that uses the obvious algorithm is given in Figure 8.38.

The **if** statement in Figure 8.38 compares *the_pattern* with the appropriate slice of *the_string*. We cannot be sure how that slice compare will be translated into executable code. It is possible that the left-to-right, character-by-character comparison discussed for the obvious algorithm will not occur. We could replace the **if** statement with a loop that would force the appropriate character compares. We will not bother with that as the important

```
           1         2         3         4
1234567890123456789012345678901234567890
com comp compu comput compute computer     Text to be searched.
computer                                   Miss at  4 after  4 compares
 computer                                  Miss at  2 after  5 compares
  computer                                 Miss at  3 after  6 compares
   computer                                Miss at  4 after  7 compares
    computer                               Miss at  9 after 12 compares
     computer                              Miss at  6 after 13 compares
      computer                             Miss at  7 after 14 compares
       computer                            Miss at  8 after 15 compares
        computer                           Miss at  9 after 16 compares
         computer                          Miss at 15 after 22 compares
          computer                         Miss at 11 after 23 compares
           computer                        Miss at 12 after 24 compares
            computer                       Miss at 13 after 25 compares
             computer                      Miss at 14 after 26 compares
              computer                     Miss at 15 after 27 compares
               computer                    Miss at 22 after 34 compares
                computer                   Miss at 17 after 35 compares
                 computer                  Miss at 18 after 36 compares
                  computer                 Miss at 19 after 37 compares
                   computer                Miss at 20 after 38 compares
                    computer               Miss at 21 after 39 compares
                     computer              Miss at 22 after 40 compares
                      computer             Miss at 30 after 48 compares
                       computer            Miss at 24 after 49 compares
                        computer           Miss at 25 after 50 compares
                         computer          Miss at 26 after 51 compares
                          computer         Miss at 27 after 52 compares
                           computer        Miss at 28 after 53 compares
                            computer       Miss at 29 after 54 compares
                             computer      Miss at 30 after 55 compares
                              computer     Match after 63 compares
com comp compu comput compute computer     Text to be searched.
```

F I G U R E 8.37 Search for an instance of pattern "computer" in a sample text. After each miss the pattern is moved one position to the right. The obvious algorithm.

points about the obvious algorithm have been made. We turn now to a string-matching algorithm, Figure 8.39, that includes the obvious algorithm as a special case.

The main shortcoming of the obvious algorithm is that pattern is compared with a substring of text by scanning from left to right. This means, even with more sophisticated approaches to be mentioned later, that every text character is compared with a pattern character at least once. Using the obvious algorithm (Figure 8.35) means that some text characters are compared with pattern characters more than once. In Boyer and Moore (1977) an algorithm was proposed (the Boyer-Moore algorithm) that was based on scanning the pattern from right to left. We now discuss a simplified version of the Boyer-Moore algorithm beginning with Figure 8.39.

```
function find_string (the_string   : var_string;              -- the_string has length n.
                      the_pattern  : var_string;              -- the_pattern has length m.
                      start_search : string_index) return string_length is
-- Length 8   Complexity 3   Performance O(n)
-- In the worst case, performance is O(mn). Usually, however, we expect a miss when comparing the first
-- character of the_string with the first character of the_pattern. So the number of compares is approximately
-- the number of characters in the_string that are passed before a match is found.
   tk: string_index := start_search;
begin
   while tk <= the_string.length - the_pattern.length + 1 loop
     if the_pattern.text = the_string.text(tk .. tk + the_pattern.length − 1) then
        return tk;
     else tk := tk + 1;
     end if;
   end loop;
   return 0;
end find_string;
```

FIGURE 8.38 An Ada implementation of *find_string* using the obvious algorithm.

```
while there is more text to search loop
    if pattern equals the substring of text with which it is aligned[1] then
        return the position of pattern
    else slide pattern forward as far as possible[2]
    end if
end loop
```

FIGURE 8.39 Pseudocode for the algorithm to be discussed next—Simplified Boyer-Moore. Differences with Figure 8.30 are emphasized by underlining. (1) In the obvious algorithm this is determined by scanning left to right. In the Boyer-Moore algorithm the scan is from right to left. (2) In the obvious algorithm the pattern is moved one position.

The discussion of Simplified Boyer-Moore will be based on the example to which the obvious algorithm was applied in Figure 8.37. Applying Simplified Boyer-Moore to that example produces Figure 8.40. Compare Figures 8.37 and 8.40.

```
         1         2         3         4
1234567890123456789012345678901234567890
com comp compu comput compute computer        Text to be searched.
computer                                      Miss at  8 after  1 compares
    computer                                  Miss at 12 after  2 compares
        computer                              Miss at 17 after  3 compares
             computer                         Miss at 23 after  4 compares
                   computer                   Miss at 30 after  5 compares
                         computer             Match at 31 after 13 compares
com comp compu comput compute computer        Text to be searched.
```

FIGURE 8.40 Simplified Boyer-Moore applied to the example in Figure 8.37.

To begin, "computer" is aligned with the left end of the text. The first compare is at position 8, where 'p' is compared with 'r'. The result is a miss.

Note that the text characters in positions 1 .. 7 are never considered. A miss involving the last character of pattern means there is no point in considering previous text characters. The question now is, How far can "computer" be slid to the right? The answer is, Until there is a 'p' in "computer" to align with the 'p' at position 8 in text. So "computer" is moved four positions to the right. The result is shown in Figure 8.40.

Moving "computer" four positions is based on (1) the text character in position 8 is 'p' and (2) the first occurrence of 'p' in "computer" is four positions from the right end. Can you see that this is the farthest "computer" can be moved without the possibility of passing a match?

Next, compare 'r' with the 'm' at position 12 in text. Since this is a miss we slide "computer" to the right until the 'm' in "computer" aligns with the 'm' at position 12. This moves "computer" five positions and aligns it with the substring of text in positions 10 .. 17.

Next, compare 'r' with the 'o' at position 17 in text. This is a miss, so we slide "computer" to the right until the 'o' in "computer" aligns with the 'o' at position 17. This moves "computer" six positions and aligns it with the substring of text in positions 16 .. 23.

The miss at position 23 ('r' compared with 'c') allows "computer" to be moved seven positions and aligned with substring 23 .. 30 of text. Then the miss at position 30 ('r' compared with ' ') allows "computer" to be moved eight positions and aligned with substring 31 .. 38 of text. Finally, eight compares are needed to determine there is a match with the substring at 31 .. 38.

An algorithm that describes this process is shown in Figure 8.41.

while there is more text to search **loop**
   If pattern equals the substring of text with which it is aligned[1] **then**
     return the position of pattern
   else slide pattern forward as far as possible[2]
   end if
end loop

FIGURE 8.41 A description of a Simplified Boyer-Moore algorithm. (1) In all Boyer-Moore algorithms this is determined by scanning right to left. (2) In the Simplified Boyer-Moore algorithm, pattern is moved to the right until a character in pattern matches the character in text that was originally aligned with the last character of pattern.

The basic premise of the Simplified Boyer-Moore algorithm is illustrated in Figure 8.42. The text characters shown as '?' do not affect how far the pattern is moved. In Figure 8.42 pattern is moved right four positions until the 'p' in computer matches the 'p' aligned originally with the last character in pattern.

```
??????????p??????????     -- Text. '?' indicates an unknown character.
   computer                -- Pattern—before being moved.
       computer            -- Pattern—after being moved.
```

FIGURE 8.42 Simplified Boyer-Moore algorithm. Pattern is moved right four positions until the 'p' in computer matches the 'p' aligned originally with the last character in pattern.

Another example, Figure 8.43, illustrates a partial match. After three hits, a miss occurs when 'a' is compared with 'u'. As before, pattern slides right until an 'r' in pattern aligns with the 'r' in text. Since pattern does not contain a second 'r', the entire pattern is moved one position to the right of the 'r' in text.

```
??????ater??????????     -- Text. '?' indicates an unknown character.
     computer                       -- Pattern—before being moved.
             computer                -- Pattern—after being moved.
```

FIGURE 8.43 Simplified Boyer-Moore algorithm. Text characters 'a', 't', and 'e' do not affect how far pattern moves to the right. Since pattern does not contain a second 'r', the entire pattern is moved one position to the right of the 'r' in text.

A final example, Figure 8.44, is provided for self-study.

```
          1         2         3         4
 12345678901234567890123456789012345678901234567890
 xxxxxter xxxxuter xxxputer xx computer
 computer                                  Miss at  5 after  4 compares
         computer                          Miss at 16 after  5 compares
          computer                         Miss at 13 after 10 compares
              computer                     Miss at 25 after 11 compares
               computer                    Miss at 21 after 17 compares
                    computer               Miss at 34 after 18 compares
                     computer              Match at 31 after 26 compares
```

FIGURE 8.44 Study this figure to verify your understanding of the Simplified Boyer-Moore algorithm.

Figure 8.45 gives an Ada implementation of the Simplified Boyer-Moore algorithm.

An important part of the code in Figure 8.45 is array *advance*. Array *advance*'s values are obtained by preprocessing *the_pattern* and specifying how far *the_pattern* is moved to the right after a miss. Array *advance* contains a value of type *positive* for each character (128 values for the ASCII character set).

Suppose that *the_pattern* is "computer"—a string of length 8. The values in array *advance* in this case are shown in Figure 8.46. Character 'Ω' stands for any character not explicitly shown.

Figure 8.46 shows that the value assigned to each character in *the_pattern* is the number of positions from that character to the right end of *the_pattern*. Thus, for the example at hand, if 'm' is the text character aligned with 'r' when a miss occurs, we know to advance *the_pattern* five positions to the right to align the 'm' in computer with the 'm' in text. If 'A' is the text character aligned with 'r' when a miss occurs, we know to advance *the_pattern* eight positions to the right because no character in *the_pattern* matches 'A'.

What happens if *the_pattern* contains several occurrences of the same letter? The answer is demonstrated in Figure 8.47, where the content of array *advance* is given for the pattern "scintillating", whose length is 13.

function find_string (the_string : var_string; the_pattern : var_string; start_search : string_index) **return** string_length **is**
-- *Length 18   Complexity 3   Performance* (O(n/m))
-- *In the worst case, like the obvious algorithm, performance is* O(mn). *Frequently we expect a miss when a*
-- *character from the_string is compared with the last character of the_pattern. If the character of the_string*
-- *where the miss occurs rarely matches any other character in the_pattern, then the_pattern usually advances*
-- m *characters. Performance is then* O(n/m).
    t0 : string_index := start_search + the_pattern.length − 1;   -- *t0 stores the starting position of each right-to-left scan.*
    tk : string_length := start_search + the_pattern.length − 1;   -- *Index for the text character to compare.*
    pk : string_length := the_pattern.length;   -- *Index for the pattern character to compare.*
    -- advance *stores the distance to advance the_pattern after a miss; all entries are initialized to the length of the_pattern.*
    advance : **array** (natural **range** 0 .. 127) **of** natural := (0 .. 127 => the_pattern.length);
begin
    for k **in** 1 .. the_pattern.length − 1 **loop**   -- *Set the value of advance for all characters in the_pattern, except the last.*
        advance(character'pos(the_pattern.text(k))) := the_pattern.length − k;
    end loop;
    while tk <= the_string.length **loop**

        while (pk > 0) **and then** (the_pattern.text(pk) = the_string.text(tk)) **loop**
            pk := pk − 1; tk := tk − 1;   -- *Compare the_pattern and the_string using a right-to-left scan.*
        end loop;

        if pk = 0 **then return** (t0 − the_pattern.length + 1);   -- *If the_pattern is found return its position;*
        else t0 := t0 + advance(character'pos(the_string.text(t0)));   -- *otherwise slide the_pattern to the right based*
            tk := t0;   -- *on the character in the_string aligned with*
            pk := the_pattern.length;   -- *the last character of the_pattern.*
        end if;
    end loop;
    return 0;
end find_string;

FIGURE 8.45 An implementation of *find_string* using the Simplified Boyer-Moore algorithm.

Ω	c	o	m	p	u	t	e	r
8	7	6	5	4	3	2	1	8

FIGURE 8.46 Entries in array *advance* if the pattern is "computer". The entry for Ω is the value for all characters other than those shown explicitly. Thus, the entry for 'a' is 8, the entry for 'b' is 8, the entry for 'Q' is 8, the entry for '!' is 8, and so on.

Ω	s	c	i	n	t	i	l	l	a	t	i	n	g
13	12	11	2	1	3	2	5	5	4	3	2	1	13

FIGURE 8.47 Entries in array *advance* if pattern is "scintillating". The entry for Ω is the value for all characters other than those shown explicitly. The value for a repeated character is the value determined by its closest position to the right end of pattern. The value for 'i', for example, is determined by its position two characters from the end of the string.

Our introduction to the *find_string* algorithm is complete. The discussion in this section is, in the next section, related to the published algorithms from which these simplified procedures were extracted.

8.3.6 Pattern-Matching Algorithms—A Survey

An often referenced article about pattern matching (Knuth, 1977) describes an algorithm and gives a detailed analysis of its performance. The algorithm is referred to as the Knuth-Morris-Pratt (KMP) algorithm, and we will briefly describe how it works. Consider the example in Figure 8.37 and repeated here in Figure 8.48.

```
         1         2         3         4
12345678901234567890123456789012345678901        -- Ruler to allow determination of a character's position.
com comp compu comput compute computer           -- Text to be searched.
computer        3 hits before a miss.            -- Pattern to be found.
```

FIGURE 8.48 The string to be searched, text, contains 38 characters; the string to be found, pattern, contains 8. An instance of pattern is the substring including characters 31 .. 38.

The KMP algorithm scans both text and pattern from left to right, but an attempt is made to advance the pattern as far as possible following a miss. In Figure 8.48 a miss occurs at position 4 after three hits. The KMP algorithm advances the pattern as far as possible based on the fact that the character in position 4 is *not* a 'p' and the first three characters of text are 'c', 'o', and 'm'.

Knowing that the text character in position 4 is not a 'p' does not help because it could be an 'm', 'o', or 'c' and thus match any of the preceding characters in pattern. But we do know that the 'c' in pattern cannot match either the 'o' or 'm' at positions 2 and 3 of the text. So pattern can advance three positions to align 'c' with ' '. The result is shown in Figure 8.49.

```
         1         2         3         4
12345678901234567890123456789012345678901
com comp compu comput compute computer
   computer                                      -- Zero hits and a miss.
```

FIGURE 8.49 After sliding pattern three positions to the right.

Now (Figure 8.49) a miss occurs when 'c' is compared with ' ', and the best we can do is advance the pattern forward one position—as shown in Figure 8.50.

Now (Figure 8.50) four hits occur before the miss at position 9. The pattern will be slid as far as possible to the right based on the following information: (1) The text character at position 9 is not a 'u', and (2) the four characters of text at positions 5 through 8 are 'c', 'o', 'm', and 'p'. We can advance pattern four positions with no danger of passing a match.

An important question is, Why consider what a text character is *not* when it can be easily read and its exact value known? The reason is that the KMP algorithm decides how far to move pattern based on a prior analysis of the

```
        1         2         3         4
1234567890123456789012345678901234567890
com comp compu comput compute computer
    computer                               -- Four hits before a miss.
```

FIGURE 8.50 After sliding pattern one position to the right.

pattern alone—and the results of that analysis must hold for *any* text string. The prior analysis assigns an integer to each position of the pattern, and that integer tells how far to move pattern based on a miss at that position—independent of the text being searched. Figure 8.51 shows the result of that analysis for our example pattern, "computer".

c	o	m	p	u	t	e	r
1	1	2	3	4	5	6	7

FIGURE 8.51 Preprocessing pattern "computer" for the KMP algorithm gives the results shown. Four hits followed by a miss at pattern character 'u' results in the pattern being slid four positions to the right.

Applying the results in Figure 8.51 we show the complete search using the KMP algorithm applied to the example in Figure 8.48. The result is shown in Figure 8.52.

```
        1         2         3         4
1234567890123456789012345678901234567890
com comp compu comput compute computer        -- Text to be searched.
computer                                      -- Miss at 4 after 4 compares.
    computer                                  -- Miss at 4 after 5 compares.
     computer                                 -- Miss at 9 after 10 compares.
         computer                             -- Miss at 9 after 11 compares.
          computer                            -- Miss at 15 after 17 compares.
             computer                         -- Miss at 15 after 18 compares.
              computer                        -- Miss at 15 after 25 compares.
                 computer                     -- Miss at 22 after 26 compares.
                  computer                    -- Miss at 30 after 34 compares.
                      computer                -- Miss at 30 after 35 compares.
                       computer               -- Match at 31 after 43 compares.
com comp compu comput compute computer        -- Text to be searched.
```

FIGURE 8.52 The KMP algorithm applied to the example in Figure 8.49.

We will not discuss algorithms for preprocessing a pattern for the KMP algorithm. Details are given in Knuth (1977), Smit (1982), Sedgewick (1988), and Sedgewick (1990).

We discussed a simplified version of the Boyer-Moore algorithm (Boyer, 1977), in Section 8.3.5. Let us consider it in more detail. Figure 8.53 shows a portion of text aligned with the pattern "computer". It shows a substring of text aligned with the pattern "computer". After four compares—three hits and a miss—the values of four text characters are known. The remaining text

```
????cter??? ···                                          -- A substring of the text.
computer                                                  -- The original position of pattern.
            computer    -- 1. Advance the pattern 8 positions based on text character 'r'.
        computer        -- 2. Advance the pattern 4 positions based on text character 'c'.
            computer    -- 3. Advance the pattern 8 positions based on text substring 'ter'.
????cter??? ···                                          -- A substring of the text.
```

FIGURE 8.53 The pattern "computer" is aligned with a substring of text. After three hits and a miss, this figure shows three independent techniques for deciding how far to move the pattern.

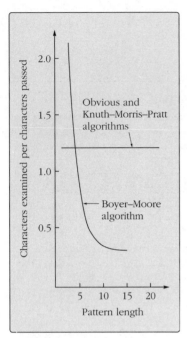

FIGURE 8.54 Characters examined per character passed for the three algorithms we discussed. (See Smit, 1982.)

characters, indicated by ?, are not known. Three independent ways to decide how far to advance pattern are illustrated.

The first is based on the text character aligned with the last character of pattern, an 'r' in the example. Since pattern contains no other 'r', the pattern can be moved eight positions.

The second is based on the text character where the miss occurs—'c' in this case. The pattern can advance to the right four positions, until the 'c' in pattern aligns with the 'c' in the text.

The third is based on attempting to align a substring "ter" in pattern with the substring "ter" discovered in text by the three hits. Since no such substring exists in pattern, it can be slid eight positions. The preprocessing needed to implement this third technique is considerably more complex than that required for the first two techniques.

The simplified algorithm in Section 8.3.5 used only the first technique shown in Figure 8.54 to decide how far to advance a string. A more sophisticated algorithm would use the maximum value generated by all three techniques. As discussed next, however, in many cases of practical interest, the first technique alone gives essentially the same performance as combining all three approaches.

Figure 8.54, based on data in Smit (1982) shows the number of characters examined divided by the number of characters passed for the three algorithms we have been discussing. The point is clear. Neither the obvious nor the KMP algorithm can do better than one character examined per character passed. The performance of these algorithms is approximately the same, since it is rare, for the data considered, to find several hits before a miss. Most of the time is spent looking for the first hit.

The Boyer-Moore algorithm, because it starts on the right of the pattern, has the ability to pass many more characters than it examines. For the data considered in Smit (1982) and for sufficiently long patterns, this is clearly the case. Other implementation issues, such as using fast machine level scan instructions, are discussed in Horesepool (1980). The conclusion is the same as indicated by Figure 8.54: The Boyer-Moore algorithm may be much faster if the pattern length is sufficiently large. Pascal implementations of all the pattern-matching algorithms are given in Sedgewick (1988, pp. 277–291).

Hume (1991) reviews algorithms for pattern matching and develops a framework for comparing and discussing such algorithms. Further, extensive test results that compare the running times for a broad cross section of algorithms and computer architectures are reported. Key portions of the code (in C) used to produce the results are given in the article, and instructions for electronically retrieving all the code are given.

EXERCISES 8.3

1. Let three variable length strings have the text values: s1 = "hot", s2 = "fudge", s3 = "sundae". Find the value of each of the strings after each of the following operations. The effect of the operations is cumulative.

    s1 := s1& s2; s1 := s1& s3; s1 := delete (s1, 1, 4);
    s1 := insert (s1, s2, 6); s1 := s1 & s1;

2. A possible representation for strings is the generic package

    generic
        max_length : **in** positive := 80;
    package string_package **is**
        type var_string **is private**;

    -- *Specification of exceptions, functions, and procedures.*

    private
        type var_string **is array** (positive **range**
        1 .. max_length) **of** character;
    end string_package;

    With this representation, each string, no matter how many characters it actually contains, is stored in an array containing *max_length* characters. The length of a string may be encoded in the array using any of the techniques discussed in this section. To be concrete, suppose the last array component is reserved to store the length of the string. Thus, the maximum string length is 128 (because there are only 128 distinct ASCII characters).

    a. Complete the specification and implementation of *string_package*.

    b. Propose modifications to *string_package* that will allow longer strings to be stored.

3. Determine the number of character comparisons required to find the pattern "compare" in this sentence.

    a. Use the obvious algorithm.

    b. Use the Simplified Boyer-Moore algorithm.

    c. Use the KMP algorithm.

4. Write the specifications for and implement a procedure or function that finds all occurrences of a pattern in a string. Put the positions at which the pattern is found in a queue. Use an instantiation of a queue described in Chapter 3.

5. Determine the values corresponding to those in Figure 8.46 for the patterns (a) "orange" and (b) "cancan".

6. Using implementations of the obvious and Boyer-Moore algorithms and sample text of your choice, construct a graph similar to the one in Figure 8.55.

7. A palindrome is a character string that reads the same backwards as it does forwards. For example, "bob", "abcddcba", and the string of length 0. Specify and implement a function to determine if an input string is a palindrome.

8. In the implementation of *find_string* in Figure 8.45 *the_pattern* is advanced following a miss using the expression

    t0 := t0 + advance(character'pos(the_string.text(t0)));

    Thus, the distance that *the_pattern* is moved to the right depends on the value of *the_string*(t0).

    a. Replace the implementation in Figure 8.45 with an implementation that determines the distance *the_pattern* is moved to the right according to the value of *the_string*(t0 + 1).

    b. Replace the implementation in Figure 8.45 with an implementation that determines the distance that *the_pattern* is moved to the right according to both the value of *the_string*(t0) and the value of *the_string*(t0 + 1).

    Refer to Smith (1991) for experimental results for the implementations described in (a) and (b).

9. A measure of the efficiency of function *find_string* is the number of character compares divided by the number of text characters searched. This measure is taken only among the characters that precede the position at which the pattern is found. Consider the example in Figure 8.37. The efficiency of the obvious

algorithm is 55/30 or 1.83. The efficiency of the Simplified Boyer-Moore algorithm (refer to Figure 8.44) is 5/30 or 0.16, and the efficiency of the KMP algorithm (refer to Figure 8.53) is 35/30 or 1.16.

For a pattern with m characters find lower bounds on the efficiencies of the three algorithms implemented above: the obvious algorithm, the KMP algorithm, and the Simplified Boyer-Moore algorithm. The lower bound is obtained by assuming the most advantageous combination of text and pattern for the algorithm considered.

10. Implement each of the three algorithms: the obvious algorithm, the KMP algorithm, and the Simplified Boyer-Moore algorithm so that they find all occurrences of a target pattern in a given text string. Write code that will determine the speed of these algorithms measured in millions of bytes of text examined per second. Compare the speeds of your implementations using text strings that are readily available to you. For published results of such speed comparisons refer to Hume (1991).

■ 8.4 Summary

In this chapter we discussed characters and strings. We considered Ada's string type and alternative schemes used to allow characters to be displayed in a wide variety of formats. Since Ada's string data type only supports fixed length strings, we described a variety of representations of variable length strings.

Both the specification and implementation of variable length strings (based on one of the representation alternatives—an unconstrained discriminant record) were given in Section 8.3. One of the most interesting string operations, finding a short string or pattern that is embedded in a much longer string, was discussed in more detail.

9

Graphs

■ 9.1 Introduction

The structure of a graph is the most general structure considered in this text. A graph is a generalization of a tree, which, in turn, generalizes a list. The essence of a list structure is that each component, except for the first and last, has a unique predecessor and a unique successor. The essence of a tree is that each component, except for the root and the leaves, has a unique predecessor and a bounded number of successors. In a graph, each component may be related to any other component. We will see how to restrict a graph so that it is a tree or a list.

As an example, consider the 14 states in the partial U.S. map in Figure 9.1 as components of a graph. Two states are related if they share a common boundary. So, for example, Ohio is related to both Pennsylvania and West Virginia. We can illustrate these relationships by artistically arranging the states on a page then drawing an arc between each related pair of states. The graph of those results is shown in Figure 9.2. Note that no state is related to itself.

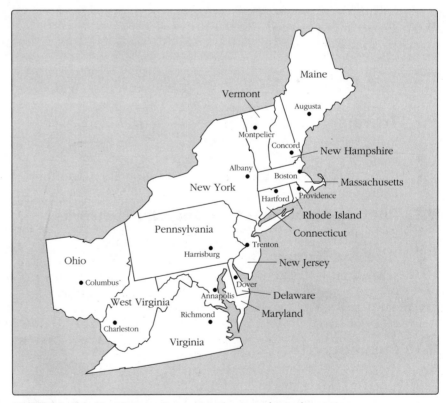

FIGURE 9.1 The 14 states discussed in the examples in this section.

You can easily think of many other examples of graphs. A network of computers with the computers as the nodes and the links between them as the edges is a graph. Graph algorithms called routing algorithms are used to decide how to route messages in such networks. Routing algorithms are dis-

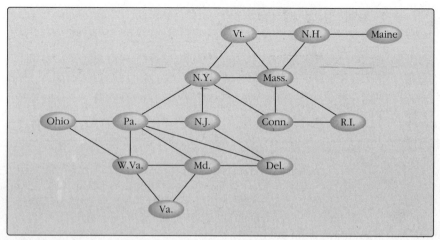

FIGURE 9.2 Example of a graph showing states related if they share a common boundary.

cussed in Section 9.8. Printed circuit boards with the chips as the nodes and the connections between them as the edges is another graph. Graph algorithms are used to decide how the chip connections should be placed on a printed circuit board. A highway system with cities as nodes and the highways between them as the edges is one of many examples of graphs outside computer science. As these examples indicate, graphs are pervasive in our world.

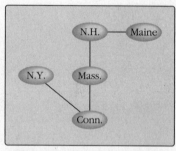

FIGURE 9.3 A subgraph of the graph in Figure 9.2. Also a simple path from Maine to N.Y.

■ 9.2 Terminology

A *graph* consists of nodes and edges. A *node* is a basic component and normally contains some information. An *edge* connects two distinct nodes. In fact, a node can be connected to itself—but we will exclude that case for simplicity. We will illustrate nodes by drawing an ellipse or circle around a node identifier. We will illustrate edges by using arcs or line segments. Figure 9.2 shows an example in which the information in each node is the name of a state. Two states are related if they share a common boundary (Figure 9.1). We will use Figure 9.2 to illustrate the terminology we are introducing.

A *subgraph* is a graph that contains a subset of a graph's nodes and edges (Figure 9.3). A *path* is a sequence of nodes such that each successive pair is connected by an edge. A path is a *simple path* if each of its nodes occurs once in the sequence. A simple path from Maine to N.Y. in Figure 9.2 is Maine, N.H., Mass., Conn., N.Y. (Figure 9.3).

A graph is a *connected graph* if there is a path between every pair of its nodes. A *cycle* is a simple path except that its first and last nodes are the same. In Figure 9.2 a cycle is N.H., Mass., N.Y., Vt., N.H. (Figure 9.4).

Two nodes are *adjacent nodes* if there is an edge that connects them. The *neighbors* of a node are all nodes that are adjacent to it. Figure 9.5 shows N.Y. and its neighbors.

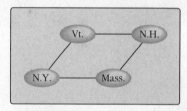

FIGURE 9.4 A cycle.

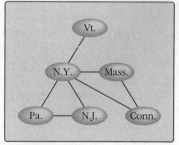

FIGURE 9.5 N.Y. and its neighbors.

What are the main differences between graphs and other structures studied earlier? A graph has no notion of either a first or root node. Given a node in a graph, there is no notion of a prior or parent node and no notion of a next or child node. There is no notion of a last or leaf node. The basic relationship in a graph is simply that any node can be related to any other node (except that we will not allow a node to be connected to itself—although some graphs allow self-connection).

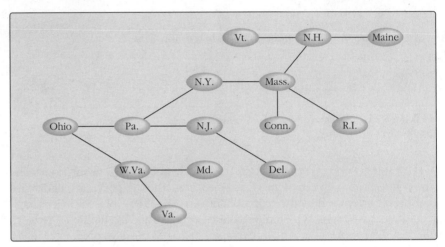

FIGURE 9.6 A spanning tree for the graph in Figure 9.2.

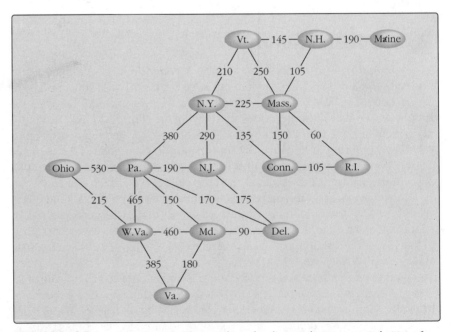

FIGURE 9.7 A weighted graph. The weight is the distance between capital cities of adjacent states.

A tree is a special case of a graph, in which the graph is connected and has no cycles. If a connected graph has n nodes and $n - 1$ edges, it cannot have any cycles and is therefore a tree. Starting with any connected graph, we can remove edges (in order to eliminate cycles) until we get a tree. Such a tree is called a *spanning tree* for the original graph. Figure 9.6 shows a spanning tree for the graph of Figure 9.2.

An *oriented tree* is a tree in which one node has been designated the root node. Choosing any node as the root node in Figure 9.6 makes that graph an oriented tree.

A *directed graph* (or *digraph*) is a graph in which each edge has an associated direction. A *weighted graph* is a graph in which each edge has an associated value. Figure 9.7 shows the graph in Figure 9.2 weighted with the distances, in kilometers, between the capital cities of adjacent states.

EXERCISES 9.2

1. Define each of the following terms.

   graph   simple path   connected graph
   directed graph   cycle   weighted graph
   path   neighbor   spanning tree

2. List five distinct paths from Maine to Ohio in Figure 9.2.

3. Start with the graph in Figure 9.2 and remove edges until a spanning tree is constructed. Repeat this process several times in order to construct several distinct spanning trees.

4. Under what circumstances is a graph a tree? An oriented tree? A list?

5. If a graph with n nodes has all possible edges then it has $\frac{1}{2} n(n - 1)$ edges. How many edges must be removed from a graph with all possible edges to construct a tree? How many edges must be removed from a graph with all possible edges to construct a list?

■ 9.3 Four-Color Problem—An Application

An interesting application of computers, and graphs, is to a mathematics problem originally proposed in 1852. The problem, known as the *four-color problem,* is as follows: If a map of a collection of regions drawn on a sheet of paper, called a planar map, is to be colored so that no adjacent regions are the same color, how many colors are needed? Figure 9.8 shows a simple example.

Analysis of the four-color problem is based on a graph, called the dual graph, formed by replacing each region by a graph node and adding an arc between the nodes that represent regions that share a boundary. Figure 9.8 shows a planar map and its corresponding dual graph.

It is relatively easy to prove that five colors are sufficient to color any map, and in 1852 it was conjectured that four colors are also sufficient—the four-color problem. Figure 9.8 demonstrates that three colors are not sufficient.

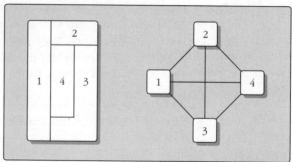

FIGURE 9.8 A map and its associated dual graph. This map shows that at least four colors are needed to avoid using the same color for adjacent regions.

Between 1852 and 1976 many proofs of the four-color problem were presented, and each was eventually shown to contain an error. As a partial result, computer analysis was used to show that four colors were sufficient for any map with up to 96 regions. This established that five colors would only be needed in very complex situations.

Finally, in 1976, Appel, Haken, and Koch (1977) proved the four-color conjecture. Their proof included the use of computer programs to generate an "unavoidable set of 1482 reducible configurations" that would arise if five colors were necessary. A discussion of such difficult proof techniques is given in Haken (1977).

EXERCISES 9.3

1. Draw several examples of maps that can be colored with two colors. For each example map, draw the corresponding dual graph.

2. Draw several examples of maps that require three, but not four, colors. For each example map draw the corresponding dual graph.

3. Is it possible to draw a planar map with five regions such that each region shares a boundary with every other region? If so, give an example. If not, explain why not.

■ 9.4 Graph Representation

This section describes several graph representations, then concludes with specifications based on two of these representations.

9.4.1 Representation

We will consider two approaches to representing graphs: adjacency matrixes and adjacency lists. We begin by showing these two representations for the graph in Figure 9.9.

An *adjacency matrix* representation of the graph in Figure 9.9 is shown in Figure 9.10. It is essentially a two-dimensional array where the indexes correspond to nodes and the array values represent edges. An edge between two nodes is represented by the value 1 (or true), and the absence of an edge is represented by 0 (or false). The neighbors of A, for example, are B, D, and E.

In Figure 9.10 each edge is represented twice—once above the diagonal of the array and once below. Memory could be saved by using only the portion of the array above the diagonal (an upper triangular array) or using only the portion of the array below the main diagonal (a lower triangular array). For a very large graph, it might be worthwhile to use only half the array. But this is awkward in many programming languages, and, as we shall see, the entire array is needed for directed graphs. Using the entire array simplifies the implementation of some operations but extracts a performance penalty because some operations will require updating the redundant array elements. Alternatively, an upper or lower triangular matrix (as discussed in Chapter 2) could be used.

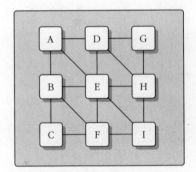

FIGURE 9.9 A graph with 9 nodes and 16 edges.

	A	B	C	D	E	F	G	H	I
A	—	1	0	1	1	0	0	0	0
B	1	—	1	0	1	1	0	0	0
C	0	1	—	0	0	1	0	0	0
D	1	0	0	—	1	0	1	1	0
E	1	1	0	1	—	1	0	1	1
F	0	1	1	0	1	—	0	0	1
G	0	0	0	1	0	0	—	1	0
H	0	0	0	1	1	0	1	—	1
I	0	0	0	0	1	1	0	1	—

FIGURE 9.10 An adjacency matrix representation of the graph in Figure 9.9. The diagonal entries are shown as "—." We do not consider the case in which a node can be connected to itself, so 0 diagonal entries might be appropriate, but using "—" in this figure emphasizes the position of the diagonal.

An adjacency matrix representation makes sense if many nodes are connected so that most array values are 1 (true). If not, then many array values are 0 (false) and record the absence of an edge.

This not only wastes memory, but algorithms that process the graph must look at all array entries in order to find the few that actually represent edges.

For a weighted graph we use an array component of type *integer* or *float* (or a subtype of *integer* or *float*) instead of *boolean*. For a weighted graph each array value indicates if an edge is present and, if so, the edge's weight.

The second approach to graph representation, ***adjacency lists,*** can be viewed conceptually as a list of lists. One list contains an entry for each node in the graph and is called the ***node list.*** Each entry in the node list is associated with another list called the ***edge list.*** Each node in an edge list represents an edge in the graph. Figures 9.11, 9.12, and 9.13 show possible adjacency list representations.

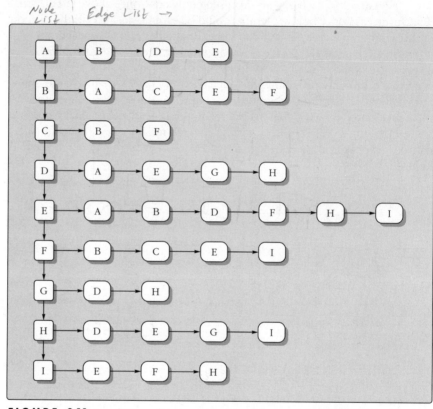

FIGURE 9.11 An adjacency list representation of the graph in Figure 9.9.

The adjacency list in Figure 9.11 is simple—each graph node has an edge node list that identifies all of its neighbors. Each edge in the graph is represented by two edge nodes in the graph's representation. All of a graph node's neighbors can be found by scanning one edge node list. To delete a node, and all its edges, however, is complex. Look at Figure 9.11. When a node is deleted each of its edges must be removed from *two* edge node lists. To make this operation efficient would require a pointer from each edge node to its twin and doubly linked edge node lists.

Another possible representation is shown in Figure 9.12. Each edge in the graph is represented by one edge node in the graph's representation. This representation contains a minimum number of edge nodes. To find all of a graph node's neighbors requires scanning all the edge nodes in the graph's representation—making this representation of little practical interest. But the

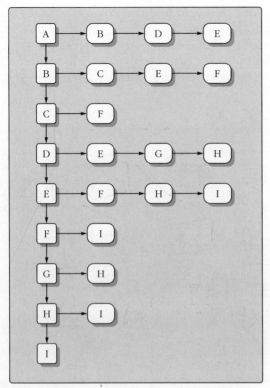

FIGURE 9.12 A second adjacency list representation of the graph in Figure 9.9.

approach in Figure 9.12 can be modified as shown in Figure 9.13 to provide a useful representation in which each edge in the graph is represented by exactly one edge node.

The essential difference between Figures 9.12 and 9.13 is that in Figure 9.12 each edge node occurs once and is a member of one edge list, whereas in Figure 9.13 each edge node occurs once but is a member of two edge node lists.

In Figure 9.13 each graph node has two edge node lists. The first edge node list is shown with solid lines and the second with dashed lines. All of a graph node's neighbors can be found by scanning the two edge node lists associated with that graph node. Deleting a graph node, and thus all of its edges, is complicated.

To simplify the algorithms that operate on this representation, a simple convention is used. The graph node identifiers are placed in edge nodes in sorted order. Note that every edge node in Figure 9.13 contains graph node identifiers in sorted order.

Let N be a graph node's identifier. Then N's first edge list contains only edges (N, X) such that $N < X$. Similarly, N's second edge list contains only edges (Y, N) such that $Y < N$. For example, consider graph node B in Figure 9.13. Graph node B's first edge list contains (B, C), (B, E), and (B, F) and

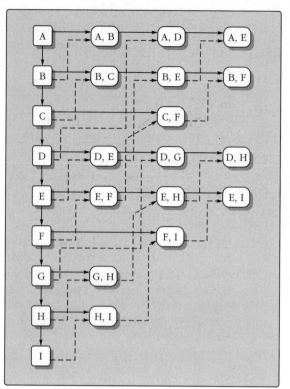

FIGURE 9.13 A third adjacency list representation of the graph in Figure 9.8.

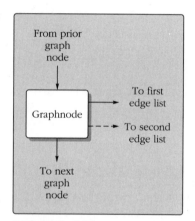

FIGURE 9.14 Details of the graph node representation in Figure 9.13.

alphabetically B < C, B < E, and B < F. Also, graph node B's second edge list contains (A, B) and A < B. Figures 9.14 and 9.15 review the representation scheme in Figure 9.13.

Remember that these conventions about placement and ordering of edge nodes and node identifiers are not essential—they are used to help keep the diagrams and explanations simple.

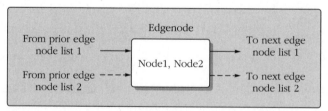

FIGURE 9.15 Details of the edge node representation in Figure 9.13.

In Figures 9.13 and 9.15 each edge node represents an edge between Node1 and Node2, where Node1 < Node2. If N is a graph node, then N's first edge list contains only edges (N, X), where $N < X$. N's second edge list contains only edges (Y, N), where $Y < N$. Node identifiers are placed in edge nodes in sorted order to simplify operations on the graph.

Now, with several possible representations for graphs, we consider how such representations can be realized in Ada. The remainder of this section includes specifications for both adjacency matrix and adjacency list representations.

9.4.2 Graph Specification— Adjacency Matrix Representation

Specification 9.1 is for an adjacency matrix representation of a graph. The graph package is generic and each node contains a value of type *object_type*. Each object has a key value of type *key_type* that is obtained by applying function *key_of* to an object. We will require that the key values in a graph be unique. The maximum number of nodes in a graph is *max_size*—the discriminant value for type *graph*.

The operations in Specification 9.1 include basic operations to insert and delete nodes and edges, search for nodes and edges, update and retrieve a node's content, and return the size of the graph. Implementation of these basic operations is given in Section 9.5. The graph operations that constitute the major topic of this chapter are specified here but described, implemented, and applied in subsequent sections as follows: Discussion and implementation of basic traversal operations is given in Section 9.6, application of traversal algorithms to basic connectivity questions is provided in Section 9.7, and application of traversal algorithms to the problem of routing messages in computer networks is discussed in Section 9.8.

In the **private** clause for Specification 9.1 you will see that graph edges are represented as a two-dimensional unconstrained array of components of type *edge_weight*. One-dimensional Ada arrays support slice assignment, but two-dimensional arrays do not. Thus, the representation in Specification 9.1 restricts the implementation to operations on individual edge components rather than on slices.

An alternative representation of graph edges is an array whose components are arrays. For example, we might have type *rows* be a one-dimensional array of *edge_weights,* then represent edges as an array of rows. Slice assignments can then be used for rows—although columns must still be operated upon component by component.

Note that if graph edges are represented as an array of rows then rows must be a *constrained* array type. That is, in Ada the component type in an array declaration must be constrained. Specification 9.1 follows.

■ **SPECIFICATION 9.1** **Adjacency Matrix Graph Specification**

-- *Structure:*   *A graph consists of nodes and edges. An edge relates (or connects) two distinct nodes and has an*
--   *associated integer value or weight. Each node contains an object of type object_type and each object has*
--   *an associated key value of type key_type. The key value associated with an object is obtained by applying*
--   *function key_of.*
--   *Graph nodes are unique in the sense that a graph cannot contain two equal key values.*

-- *Constraints:*   *The number of nodes in a graph is bounded by max_size.*

(continued)

Specification 9.1 (continued)

generic
    type object_type **is private**;
    type key_type **is private**;
    type edge_weight **is range** <>;   *-- edge_weight must be an integer type.*
    with function key_of (the_object : object_type) **return** key_type;
    *-- **results:** Returns the key value associated with the_object.*

package matrix_graph_package **is**

    type graph (max_size : natural) **is limited private**;

    graph_full   : **exception**;
    graph_empty   : **exception**;
    duplicate_node : **exception**;
    duplicate_edge : **exception**;
    missing_node   : **exception**;
    missing_edge   : **exception**;

    procedure insert_node (the_graph : **in out** graph; the_object : object_type);
    *-- **results:** Insert a node containing the_object into the_graph.*
    *-- **exceptions:** graph_full is raised if the_graph contains max_size nodes. duplicate_node is raised if the_graph*
    --   contains a node whose key value is key_of(the_object).

    procedure insert_edge(the_graph : **in out** graph; key1, key2 : key_type; the_weight : edge_weight);
    *-- **results:** Add an edge to the_graph that connects the nodes whose key values are key1 and key2 and whose*
    --   weight is the_weight.
    *-- **exceptions:** missing_node is raised if the_graph does not contain nodes whose key values are key1 and key2. duplicate_edge is*
    --   raised if the_graph contains an edge between the nodes whose key values are key1 and key2.

    procedure delete_node (the_graph : **in out** graph; the_key : key_type);
    *-- **results:** Delete from the_graph the node whose key value is the_key.*
    *-- **exceptions:** missing_node is raised if the_graph does not contain a node whose key value is the_key.*
    *-- **notes:** If the node whose key value is the_key has edges connecting it to other nodes in the_graph, then those*
    --   edges are also deleted.

    procedure delete_edge (the_graph : **in out** graph; key1, key2 : key_type);
    *-- **results:** Delete from the_graph the edge that connects nodes whose key values are key1 and key2.*
    *-- **exceptions:** missing_node is raised if the_graph does not contain nodes whose key values are key1 and*
    --   key2. missing_edge is raised if the_graph contains nodes whose key values are key1 and key2, but does
    --   not contain an edge connecting those nodes.

    function find_node (the_graph : graph; target_key : key_type) **return** boolean;
    *-- **results:** Returns true if the_graph contains a node whose key value is target_key; otherwise returns false.*

    function find_edge (the_graph : graph; key1, key2 : key_type) **return** boolean;
    *-- **results:** Returns true if the_graph contains an edge between nodes whose key values are key1 and key2;*
    --   otherwise returns false.

(continued)

Specification 9.1 (continued)

function number_of_nodes (the_graph : graph) **return** natural;
-- *results:* *Returns the number of nodes in the_graph.*

function number_of_edges (the_graph : graph) **return** natural;
-- *results:* *Returns the number of edges in the_graph.*

generic
   with procedure proc_node (the_key : key_type);
   with procedure proc_edge (the_edge : edge_weight);
procedure display_graph (the_graph : graph);
-- *results:* *Displays the_graph using the format shown in Figure 9.10.*

generic
   with procedure process (the_object : object_type);
procedure breadth_first_search (the_graph : **in out** graph);
-- *results:* *Applies procedure process to each object in the_graph in an order determined by breadth first search.*

generic
   with procedure process (the_object : object_type);
procedure depth_first_search (the_graph : **in out** graph);
-- *results:* *Applies procedure process to each object in the_graph in an order determined by depth first search.*

generic
   with procedure process (the_object : object_type);
procedure priority_first_search (the_graph : **in out** graph);
-- *results:* *Applies procedure process to each object in the_graph in an order determined by priority first search.*

private
   type node_status **is** (waiting, ready, processed);

   type graph_node **is record**
     object   : object_type;
     status   : node_status;   -- *Status field for traversal.*
     weight : edge_weight;   -- *Used by priority first search algorithms.*
   end record;

   type array_of_nodes **is array** (positive **range** <>) **of** graph_node;
   type array_of_edges **is array** (positive **range** <>, positive **range** <>) **of** edge_weight;

   type graph (max_size : natural) **is record**
     size   : natural := 0;
     nodes : array_of_nodes (1 .. max_size);
     edges : array_of_edges (1 .. max_size, 1 .. max_size) := (1 .. max_size => (1 .. max_size => 0));
   end record;

end matrix_graph_package;

9.4.3 Graph Specification— Adjacency List Representation

It would be preferable if both graph representations—adjacency matrix and adjacency list—had the same specification. At a high enough level of abstraction they do. As presented here, however, they differ as follows.

The number of nodes in an adjacency matrix representation (Specification 9.1) is bounded by the value declared for the discriminant parameter *max_size*. The adjacency list representation places no bound on the number of graph nodes other than that determined by available memory.

The adjacency list representation also requires function "<" so that key values can be ordered. Note that there is nothing inherently necessary about function "<" in the adjacency list representation of a graph. It is added to the generic clauses purely as an aid to implementation, as illustrated in Figures 9.13, 9.14, and 9.15. Although we have emphasized throughout this text that it is a sin to deal with implementation issues in a specification—and though we could force the implementor to get along without function "<"—in violation of principles we normally hold sacred, we include it here as an aid to the implementor. Specification 9.2 follows.

■ **SPECIFICATION 9.2**   **Adjacency List Graph Specification**

-- *Structure:* *A graph consists of nodes and edges. An edge relates (or connects) two distinct nodes and has an*
-- *associated integer value or weight. Each node contains an object of type object_type, and each object has*
-- *an associated key value of type key_type. The key value associated with an object is obtained by applying*
-- *function key_of.*
-- *Graph nodes are unique in the sense that a graph cannot contain two equal key values.*
-- *Constraints:* *The number of nodes in a graph has an unknown upper bound.*
-- *Notes:* *The size of a graph can grow and shrink dynamically and, at its maximum, uses all available memory on the computer system*
-- *running the program. The implication is that dynamic allocation/deallocation is used.*

```
generic
    type object_type is private;
    type key_type is private;
    type edge_weight is range <>;                              -- edge_weight must be an integer type.
    with function key_of (the_object : object_type) return key_type;
    -- results:  Returns the key value associated with the_object.
    with function "<" (key1, key2 : key_type) return boolean;
    -- results:  Returns true if the value of key1 is less than the value of key2; returns false otherwise.
    -- notes:  function "<" is supplied for convenience—it is not an essential part of the adjacency list
    --         representation.

package list_graph_package is

type graph is limited private;

    graph_full       : exception;
    graph_empty      : exception;
    duplicate_node   : exception;
```

(continued)

Specification 9.2 (continued)

>   duplicate_edge   : **exception**;
>   missing_node   : **exception**;
>   missing_edge   : **exception**;

procedure insert_node (the_graph : **in out** graph; the_object : object_type);
  -- **results:** *Insert a node containing the_object into the_graph.*
  -- **exceptions:** *duplicate_node is raised if the_graph contains a node whose key value is key_of(the_object).*
  --   *graph_full is raised if a node containing the_object cannot be added to the_graph.*

procedure insert_edge (the_graph : **in out** graph; key1, key2 : key_type; the_weight : edge_weight);
  -- **results:** *Add an edge to the_graph that connects the nodes whose key values are key1 and*
  --   *key2 and whose weight is the_weight.*
  -- **exceptions:** *missing_node is raised if the_graph does not contain nodes whose key values*
  --   *are key1 and key2. duplicate_edge is raised if the_graph contains an edge between the*
  --   *nodes whose key values are key1 and key2. graph_full is raised if a new edge cannot be*
  --   *added to the_graph.*

  -- *The remaining operations have specifications similar to those in Specification 9.1.*

procedure delete_node (the_graph : **in out** graph; the_key : key_type);
procedure delete_edge (the_graph : **in out** graph; key1, key2 : key_type);
function find_node (the_graph : graph; target_key : key_type) **return** boolean;
function find_edge (the_graph : graph; key1, key2 : key_type) **return** boolean;
function number_of_nodes (the_graph : graph) **return** natural;
function number_of_edges (the_graph : graph) **return** natural;

generic
   with procedure proc_node (the_key : key_type);
   with procedure proc_edge (the_edge : edge_weight);
procedure display_graph (the_graph : graph);

generic
   with procedure process (the_object : object_type);
procedure breadth_first_search (the_graph : **in out** graph);

generic
   with procedure process (the_object : object_type);
procedure depth_first_search (the_graph : **in out** graph);

generic
   with procedure process (the_object : object_type);
procedure priority_first_search (the_graph : **in out** graph);

private
   type node_status **is** (waiting, ready, processed);   -- *Node status for graph traversal.*
   type graph_node;
   type graph_edge;
   type node_pointer **is access** graph_node;
   type edge_pointer **is access** graph_edge;
   type two_edge_lists **is array** (1 .. 2) **of** edge_pointer;

(continued)

Specification 9.2 (continued)

```
type graph_node is record
    object          : object_type;
    edge_list       : two_edge_lists;        -- Pointers to the two edge lists.
    next_node       : node_pointer;          -- Pointer to the next graph node.
    status          : node_status;           -- Status field, needed during graph traversal.
    weight          : edge_weight;           -- Available for priority first search.
end record;

type edge_node is record
    key1, key2      : key_type;              -- Key values of the nodes connected by this edge—in sorted order.
    node1, node2    : node_pointer;          -- Pointers to the nodes connected by this edge.
    next_edge       : two_edge_lists;
end record;

type graph is record
    size            : natural := 0;
    head, tail      : node_pointer;          -- Automatically initialized to null.
end record;
end list_graph_package;
```

EXERCISES 9.4

1. a. What are the advantages and disadvantages of an adjacency matrix representation of a graph?
b. What are the advantages and disadvantages of an adjacency list representation of a graph?
c. Show how to modify the graph representation in Specification 9.1 so that graph edges are represented as an array of arrays rather than as a two-dimensional array.
d. What are the implementation tradeoffs for these two representations?

2. Suppose we consider graphs in which an edge is permitted to connect a graph node to itself. Discuss how such edges might be represented for both adjacency matrix and adjacency list representations.

3. In adjacency list representations of a graph it may be advantageous for each edge node to contain pointers to the two graph nodes the edge connects. Discuss the advantages of these pointers with respect to the *insert* and *delete* operations in Specification 9.2.

4. In adjacency list representations of a graph it may be advantageous for the edge lists to be doubly linked. Discuss the advantages and disadvantages of doubly linked edge lists with respect to the *insert* and *delete* operations in Specification 9.2.

5. The *delete edge* operation is given the key values of graph nodes connected by the edge to be deleted. Describe an adjacency list representation of a graph that makes this operation efficient. Provide, using order-of-magnitude notation, the work required to execute this operation. Is this representation efficient for edge insertion? Why?

6. The *delete node* operation is given the key value of the graph node to be deleted. This operation is complex because all of the edges that connect the target graph node to other graph nodes must also be deleted. Describe an adjacency list representation of a graph that makes this operation efficient. Provide, using order-of-magnitude notation, the work required to execute this operation. Is this representation efficient for node insertion?

7. Modify Specification 9.1 so the graph nodes are stored in a binary search tree. The graph edges are still stored in a two-dimensional array. Do the same for Specification 9.2 (where the edges are still stored in linked lists).

8. Instantiate both Specifications 9.1 and 9.2 for each of the following types for *object_type*: (a) integer, (b) a record type with at least three components.

9. Instantiate Specification 9.1 if *object_type* is one of the lists specified in Chapter 4.
10. Write the specification for a function that returns true if a graph is connected and false otherwise.
11. Write the specification for a function that returns true if a graph is regular and false otherwise. A graph is *regular* if every graph node has the same number of neighbors.

12. **a.** Write the specification for a procedure that deletes from a graph all nodes that satisfy a user-specified condition on the object in each node.
    b. Write the specification for a procedure that deletes from a graph all edges that satisfy a user-specified condition on the objects in the nodes connected by that edge.

■ 9.5 Implementation of Basic Graph Operations

This section presents implementations of the basic operations specified in Section 9.4. Implementation of graph traversal operations is deferred to Section 9.6. Before reporting the actual code we will discuss several performance issues. Look at the code, however, whenever you feel the need.

Figure 9.16 shows the time to insert one graph node into a graph. Results are shown for both adjacency matrix and adjacency list representations. Also shown, for comparison, are the times to add an element to a list stored as an array or a singly linked list. In all cases, insertion includes first scanning all elements in the list to ensure that a duplicate key value is not added, then adding the new graph node to the end of the list. Thus, except for an adjacency matrix representation of a graph, the times shown are essentially those required to traverse a list looking for duplicates.

The reason inserting a node with an adjacency matrix representation takes so long is that each time a node is added all corresponding edge node entries must be set to false. Therefore, if a graph has 1000 nodes, adding a new graph node requires setting 2000 edge node entries—one row and one column—to false.

For an adjacency list representation, when a graph node is added, it is only necessary to assign null values to two graph node edge list pointers. This adds only a small constant to the time needed to traverse the list checking for a duplicate value.

Figure 9.17 shows the average time needed to add an edge node to a graph. To obtain the times shown, we start with a graph with n nodes and no edges. The time to add $n - 1$ edges is measured and divided by $n - 1$, and the result is plotted. Edges are added so that the graph structure is a binary tree with each level, except possibly the last, full. Most of the time is therefore spent traversing the graph nodes to determine the positions of the nodes to connect. Exercises 9.5, 4, asks you to extend the timing studies to include all possible edges to a graph.

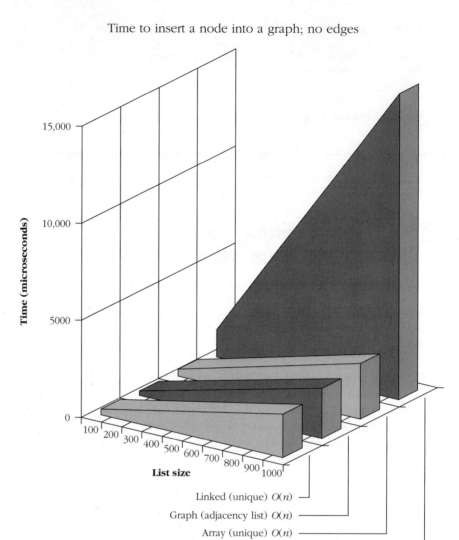

Time to insert a node into a graph; no edges

Linked (unique) $O(n)$

Graph (adjacency list) $O(n)$

Array (unique) $O(n)$

Graph (adjacency matrix) $O(n)$

FIGURE 9.16 Time to insert one node into a graph with duplicates not permitted. For comparison, times to insert an element into a list stored as an array or a singly linked list are also shown.

Insertion using an adjacency matrix representation takes significantly longer because one row and one column of edge representation values must be initialized. This initialization can be avoided by requiring that the delete operation leave unused rows filled with 0 values. Exercises 9.5, 12, asks that this change be made to the implementation.

Figure 9.18 summarizes the performance of basic graph operations. Each performance measure is annotated with a brief description of the required operations. In each case, n is the number of nodes in the graph and e is the

Average time to add one edge when
$n - 1$ edges are added to form a tree

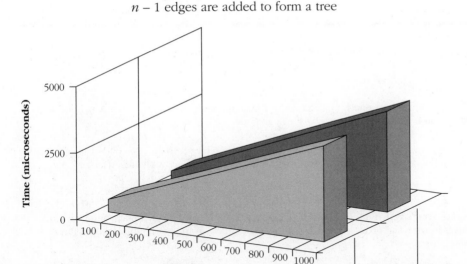

FIGURE 9.17 Time to add an edge to an adjacency matrix or an adjacency list representation of a graph. The times shown are the average for adding $n - 1$ edges to a graph that initially has no edges.

number of edges. The performance measures for an adjacency list represen-tation assume that the e edges are evenly distributed among graph nodes so each graph node has (e/n) edges.

In several cases detail that is not absolutely necessary is provided to clarify the result shown. For example, since $O(e/n)$ is at most $O(n)$, it follows that $O[n + (e/n)] = O(n)$. Reporting $O[n + (e/n)]$ is, however, a better descrip-tion of the algorithm.

The intent of this section is for you to compare the timing results in Figures 9.16, and 9.17 with Figure 9.18 and with the Ada code in Package Body 9.1. Exercises 9.5, 2, asks you to modify Figure 9.18, assuming the graph nodes are stored in either a binary search tree or a hash table. This exercise will require you to review graphs, binary trees, and hash tables.

As indicated in Figure 9.18, the most complex basic operation is *delete*. The complexity occurs because deleting a graph node also requires deleting its edges.

Consider deletion for an adjacency matrix. Figure 9.19 shows the effect of deleting node E from the graph shown. The technique is to re-place the deleted node with the last node. In the example, node I replaces node E. The work required is $O(n)$—find the target node then move one row and one column. The complexity of this algorithm is $O(n + n + n) = O(n)$.

Algorithm	Adjacency matrix	Adjacency list Graph nodes in a linked list
Insert graph node	$O(n + n + n) = O(n)$ Search for a duplicate graph node, and initialize one row and one column to false.	$O(n)$ Search for a duplicate graph node.
Insert edge node	$O(n)$ Search for the graph nodes to connect. The edge node position is calculated.	$O[n + (e/n)] = O(n)$ Search for the graph nodes to connect, then search for a duplicate edge node.
Delete graph node	$O(n)$ Search for the graph node to delete. Replace the deleted node with the last node in the array.	$O[n + (e/n)] = O(n)$ Find the graph node. Traverse both edge node lists and delete the edge nodes. Edge lists are doubly linked.
	$O(n^2)$ A two-dimensional array of edge node representations is moved. The order of the graph nodes is preserved.	$O\{n + (e/n)[n + (e/n)]\} \le O(n^2)$ Find the graph node. Traverse both edge node lists and delete the edge nodes. Edge lists are singly linked, and edge nodes do not include pointers to the graph nodes they connect.
		$O[n + (e/n)^2] \le O(n^2)$ Find the graph node. Traverse both edge node lists and delete the edge nodes. Each edge node contains pointers to the graph nodes it connects. Edge lists are singly linked.
Delete edge node	$O(n)$ Search for the connected graph nodes. The edge node positions are calculated.	$O(n)$ Search for the connected graph nodes. Find and delete the edge node from both lists. Use any of the representations from the row above.

FIGURE 9.18 Performance of basic graph algorithms. The graph contains n nodes and e edges. The edges are assumed to be distributed uniformly among the graph nodes so that each node has (e/n) edges. The graph representations are shown in Figures 9.10 and 9.13.

	A	B	C	D	E	F	G	H	I
A	—	1	0	1	#1	0	0	0	0
B	1	—	1	0	#1	1	0	0	0
C	0	1	—	0	#0	1	0	0	0
D	1	0	0	—	#1	0	1	1	0
E	#1	#1	#0	#1	—	#1	#0	#1	#1
F	0	1	1	0	#1	—	0	0	1
G	0	0	0	1	#0	0	—	1	0
H	0	0	0	1	#1	0	1	—	1
I	0	0	0	0	#1	1	0	1	—

(a)

	A	B	C	D	I	F	G	H
A	—	1	0	1	0	0	0	0
B	1	—	1	0	0	1	0	0
C	0	1	—	0	0	1	0	0
D	1	0	0	—	0	0	1	1
I	0	0	0	0	—	1	0	1
F	0	1	1	0	1	—	0	0
G	0	0	0	1	0	0	—	1
H	0	0	0	1	1	0	1	—

(b)

FIGURE 9.19 Delete node E by replacing E with the last node in the graph node list. In (a) the edge representations to delete are highlighted with the # symbol. (a) Before deleting E; (b) after deleting E.

		Shift this subarray one position left.
Position of the deleted graph node.		
Shift this subarray one position up.		Shift this subarray diagonally up and left.

F I G U R E 9.20 Graph edge representations that must be moved during an adjacency matrix graph node deletion that preserves node order.

A second approach preserves the order of graph nodes by sliding nodes following the node deleted ahead one position. As illustrated in Figure 9.20, this requires moving two-dimensional subsets of the array representing the edges. Since there are $O(n^2)$ values in each subset to be moved, the complexity of this algorithm is $O(n^2)$.

This section concludes with Package Body 9.1 for Specification 9.1.

■ PACKAGE BODY 9.1 Implements Specification 9.1

```
with text_io; use text_io;              -- Used by procedure display_graph.
with queue_package;                     -- Used for breadth first search.
with priority_queue_package;            -- Used for priority first search.

package body matrix_graph_package is

function find_posn (the_graph : graph; target_key : key_type; start : natural) return natural is
-- results:  Returns the position in the_graph of the object whose key is target_key. The sequential search
--              begins at position start. Positions in the_graph before start are not searched. If target_key is not found,
--              0 is returned.
-- Length 6   Complexity 3   Performance O(n)
-- Expect to search half the nodes in the graph.
begin
    for k in start .. the_graph.size loop         -- Sequential search.
      if target_key = key_of(the_graph.nodes(k).object) then
        return k;                                 -- Search succeeds.
      end if;
    end loop;
    return 0;                                     -- Search fails.
end find_posn;

function find_node (the_graph : graph; target_key : key_type) return boolean is
-- results:  Returns true if the_graph contains an object whose key is target_key; otherwise returns false.
-- Length 2   Complexity 1   Performance O(n)
-- Expect to search half the nodes in the_graph.
begin
    return (find_posn(the_graph, target_key, 1) > 0);
end find_node;
```

(continued)

Package Body 9.1 (continued)

function find_either_posn (the_graph : graph; key1, key2 : key_type) **return** natural **is**
-- ***results:*** *Returns the position in the_graph of either the object whose key is key1 or the object whose key is*
--   *key2. If neither key is found, 0 is returned.*
-- *Length 7   Complexity 3   Performance* O(n)
   k : natural := 1;
begin   -- *Sequential search for either one of the two key values.*
     while k <= the_graph.size **loop**
       if key1 = key_of(the_graph.nodes(k).object) **or**
          key2 = key_of(the_graph.nodes(k).object) **then**
          return k;   -- *Return the position of the key value that was found.*
       end if;
       k := k + 1;
     end loop;
     return 0;   -- *Neither key value was found.*
end find_either_posn;

procedure find_both_posn (the_graph : graph; key1, key2 : key_type; first_posn, second_posn : **out** natural) **is**
-- ***results:*** *Assigns first_posn and second_posn as the positions in the_graph of the objects whose keys are*
--   *key1 and key2. If either key value is not found, second_posn is 0.*
-- *Length 11   Complexity 3   Performance* O(n)
-- *Expect to search two-thirds of the graph nodes if both key values are in the_graph.*
     posn1, posn2 : natural := 0;
     remaining_key : key_type := key1;
begin   -- *Search for either one of the two key values.*
     posn1 := find_either_posn (the_graph, key1, key2);
     if posn1 > 0 **and** posn1 < the_graph.size **then**
       if key1 = key_of(the_graph.nodes(posn1).object) **then**   -- *Successful search, set remaining_key as key of node not found.*
          remaining_key := key2;
       end if;
       posn2 := find_posn (the_graph, remaining_key, posn1 + 1);   -- *Search for the remaining_key.*
     end if;
     first_posn := posn1; second_posn := posn2;
end find_both_posn;

function find_edge (the_graph : graph; key1, key2 : key_type) **return** boolean **is**
-- *Length 6   Complexity 2   Performance* O(n)
-- *Expect to search two-thirds of the nodes in the_graph.*
     posn1, posn2 : natural;
begin
     find_both_posn (the_graph, key1, key2, posn1, posn2);
     if posn2 > 0 **and then** the_graph.edges(posn1, posn2) > 0 **then return** true;
     else return false;
     end if;
end find_edge;

procedure insert_node (the_graph : **in out** graph; the_object : object_type) **is**
-- *Length 12   Complexity 4   Performance* O(n)
-- *Search all n graph nodes (for a duplicate), and set 2 * n edge weights to 0.*
     posn   : natural;
     the_node : graph_node := (the_object, waiting, 0);

(continued)

Package Body 9.1 (continued)

```
begin
    posn := find_posn (the_graph, key_of(the_object), 1);          -- Search for a duplicate.
    if posn = 0 then                                    -- Raises a constraint_error if the graph is full.
        the_graph.size := the_graph.size + 1;
        the_graph.nodes(the_graph.size) := the_node;
    else raise duplicate_node;
    end if;


    for k in 1 .. the_graph.size loop
        the_graph.edges(the_graph.size, k) := 0;
        the_graph.edges(k, the_graph.size) := 0;
    end loop;

exception
    when constraint_error => raise graph_full;
end insert_node;


procedure insert_edge (the_graph : in out graph; key1, key2 : key_type; the_weight : edge_weight) is
-- Length 9   Complexity 3   Performance O(n)
-- Expect to search two-thirds of the graph nodes in order to find the pair to connect.
    posn1, posn2 : natural;
begin
    find_both_posn (the_graph, key1, key2, posn1, posn2);
    if posn2 = 0 then raise missing_node;
    elsif the_graph.edges(posn1, posn2) > 0 then raise duplicate_edge;
    else the_graph.edges(posn1, posn2) := the_weight;
        the_graph.edges(posn2, posn1) := the_weight;
    end if;
end insert_edge;


function number_of_nodes (the_graph : graph) return natural is
-- Length 1   Complexity 1   Performance O(1)
begin
    return the_graph.size;
end number_of_nodes;


function number_of_edges (the_graph : graph) return natural is
-- Length 6   Complexity 4   Performance O(n²)
-- Count the edges above the diagonal. Have to look at (1/2) n * (n − 1) array components.
    edge_counter : natural := 0;
begin
    for row in 1 .. the_graph.size loop
        for column in row + 1 .. the_graph.size loop
            if the_graph.edges(row, column) > 0 then
                edge_counter := edge_counter + 1;
            end if;
        end loop;
    end loop;
    return edge_counter;
end number_of_edges;
```

(continued)

Package Body 9.1 (continued)

```
procedure delete_node (the_graph : in out graph; the_key : key_type) is
-- Length 13   Complexity 5   Performance O(n)
-- Find the node to delete (expect to search half the nodes), then copy one row and one column of edge
-- values to new positions—which requires 2 * n moves. If, however, the node to delete is last in the node
-- array, no edge values are moved.
    posn : natural;
begin
    posn := find_posn(the_graph, the_key, 1);                          -- Find the node to delete.
    if posn = 0 then raise missing_node;
    elsif posn < the_graph.size then
                             -- The target node is not last—overwrite the target node with the node in the last array position.
        the_graph.nodes(posn) := the_graph.nodes(the_graph.size);
        for k in 1 .. posn − 1 loop                    -- Move the edge weights from row the_graph.size to row posn.
            the_graph.edges(posn, k) := the_graph.edges(the_graph.size, k);
            the_graph.edges(k, posn) := the_graph.edges(k, the_graph.size);
        end loop;
        for k in posn + 1 .. the_graph.size − 1 loop     -- Move the edge weights from column the_graph.size to column posn.
            the_graph.edges(posn,k) := the_graph.edges(the_graph.size,k);
            the_graph.edges(k,posn) := the_graph.edges(k,the_graph.size);
        end loop;
    end if;
    the_graph.size := the_graph.size − 1;
end delete_node;


procedure delete_edge (the_graph : in out graph; key1, key2 : key_type) is
-- Length 8   Complexity 3   Performance O(n)
-- Expect to search two-thirds of the nodes to find key values key1 and key2.
    posn1, posn2 : natural;
begin
    find_both_posn (the_graph, key1, key2, posn1, posn2);
    if posn2 = 0 then raise missing_node;
    elsif the_graph.edges(posn1, posn2) = 0 then raise missing_edge;
    else the_graph.edges(posn1, posn2) := 0;
        the_graph.edges(posn2, posn1) := 0;
    end if;
end delete_edge;


procedure display_graph (the_graph : graph) is
begin
    -- Implementation is left as an exercise.
end display_graph;


procedure set_waiting (the_graph : in out graph) is
-- Length 2   Complexity 2   Performance O(n)
begin
    for k in 1 .. the_graph.size loop
        the_graph.nodes(k).status := waiting;
    end loop;
end set_waiting;
```

(continued)

Package Body 9.1 (continued)

procedure breadth_first_search (the_graph : **in out** graph) **is**
-- *Implementation is given in Section 9.6.1.*

procedure depth_first_search (the_graph : **in out** graph) **is**
-- *Implementation is given in Section 9.6.2.*

procedure priority_first_search (the_graph : **in out** graph) **is**
-- *Implementation is given in Section 9.6.3.*

end matrix_graph_package;

EXERCISES 9.5

1. Implement the operations for the *list_graph_package* specified in Specification 9.2.
2. Modify Figure 9.18 assuming the graph nodes are stored in (a) a binary search tree or (b) a hash table.
3. Run the required timing studies then plot graphs similar to those in Figures 9.16 and 9.17 for the operations *delete_node* and *delete_edge*.
4. It is argued that if a graph contains many edges, it will be most efficient to represent it using an adjacency matrix. But if it contains few edges, it will be most efficient to represent it using an adjacency list representation. Make this argument more concrete by comparing these two representations (using appropriate timing studies) for graphs with a range of numbers of edges. Recall that the number of edges is between 0 and $\frac{1}{2} n(n - 1)$.
5. Implement procedure *display_graph*.
6. Implement the function specified in Exercises 9.4, 10; that is, a function that returns true if a graph is connected and returns false otherwise.
7. Implement the function specified in Exercises 9.4, 11; that is, a function that returns true if a graph is regular and returns false otherwise.
8. a. Implement the procedure specified in Exercises 9.4, 12(a); that is, a procedure that deletes from a graph all nodes that satisfy a user-specified condition on the object in each node.
   b. Implement the procedure specified in Exercises 9.4, 12(b); that is, a procedure that deletes from a

graph all edges that satisfy a user-specified condition on the objects in the nodes connected by that edge.
9. Replace the implementation in Package Body 9.1 by an implementation that stores graph nodes in a binary search tree. Include measures of size, complexity, and performance with each function and procedure.
10. Replace the implementation in Package Body 9.1 by an implementation that stores graph nodes in a hash table. Include measures of size, complexity, and performance with each function and procedure.
11. Replace the implementation in Package Body 9.1 by an implementation that stores graph nodes in either an upper or a lower triangular matrix—thus reducing the amount of memory required to represent a graph. Include measures of size, complexity, and performance with each function and procedure.
12. Figure 9.16 shows that insertion for an adjacency matrix takes a long time because—for the implementation used—one row and one column of the adjacency matrix have their values set to 0. Modify the implementations of *insert* and *delete* so *insert* does not have to set any values in the adjacency matrix. What effect do these changes have on Figure 9.16?
13. Replace the implementation in Package Body 9.1 by an implementation that uses an array of arrays to represent graph edges. Refer to Exercises 9.4, 1(c) for further discussion. Take advantage of slice operations on arrays wherever possible.

▉ 9.6 Graph Traversal

An important graph operation, *traversal,* is actually a generalization of the traversal of lists and binary trees discussed in Chapters 4 and 5. The idea is simple. We want to process, in an organized way, each node in a graph exactly once. For trees, this permitted us to conduct associative searches and to answer questions about global tree characteristics. These same questions can be answered for graphs. Also, there is a class of graph traversals that permits us to answer connectivity questions such as the following: Are two nodes connected? If so, what is the shortest path between them? Is a weighted graph connected? If so, find the edges that connect all nodes so that the sum of the edge weights is a minimum. In Section 9.7 we will see algorithms that answer these questions. Then, Section 9.8 shows how these ideas can be applied to the problem of routing messages in computer networks.

9.6.1 Breadth First Search

Two basic graph traversal algorithms are breadth first search and depth first search. This section describes breadth first search and concludes with its implementation. Section 9.6.2 provides the same information for depth first search. Both breadth and depth first search are special cases of priority first search—which is described and implemented in Section 9.6.3.

In **breadth first search** one graph node, say *first_node,* is chosen to be processed first, then *first_node*'s neighbors are processed, then the neighbors

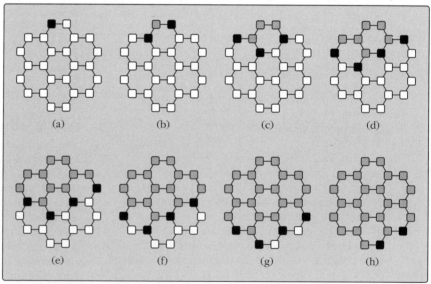

(a) (b) (c) (d)

(e) (f) (g) (h)

F I G U R E 9.21 Breadth first search illustration for a graph with 24 nodes and 30 edges. A gray node was previously processed, a black node is processed at the current step, and a white node will be processed later.

of *first_node*'s neighbors are processed, then the neighbors of the neighbors of *first_node*'s neighbors are processed, and so on. Figure 9.21 shows an example of the order in which nodes are processed during a breadth first search. Eight copies of the graph are shown at various times during the traversal.

Let us discuss Figure 9.21. In (a) the top left node is selected to be processed first. In (b) the two neighbors—of the node processed in (a)—are processed in any order. In (c) the neighbors of the nodes processed in (b) are processed. In (d) the neighbors of the nodes processed in (c) are processed. In (e) the neighbors of the nodes processed in (d) are processed. This method continues until all the nodes are processed as shown in (h).

The purpose of Figure 9.21 is to help you visualize what breadth first search looks like. Note how the nodes currently being processed are equidistant from the starting point. In (b) the nodes processed are all neighbors of the first node processed. In (c) the nodes processed are all distance two from the starting point. In (d) the nodes processed are all distance three from the starting point. Finally, in (h) the two nodes processed are distance seven from the starting point.

Figure 9.21 shows the order in which *groups* of nodes must be processed to constitute a breadth first search. It does not show a specific breadth first search order. It is interesting to determine that the number of distinct paths as the breadth first search progresses in Figure 9.21 is as follows: (a) 1, there is only one processing order for a single node; (b) 2, the two nodes may be processed in any order; (c) 4; (d) 8; (e) 12; (f) 21; (g) 28; and (h) 40.

That is, there are 40 distinct orders in which to visit the nodes during a breadth first search of the graph in Figure 9.21. Can you explain the details of the above computation? The graph nodes are numbered in Figure 9.22 to show two of the breadth first search orders.

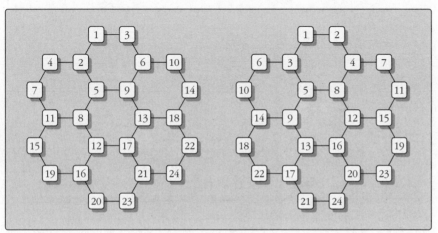

FIGURE 9.22 Two of the 40 breadth first search orders for the graph in Figure 9.21.

Figure 9.23 shows a graph with five nodes that is also a list. There is only one breadth first search order if the first node of the search is A. That one order is shown in the figure.

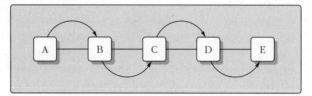

FIGURE 9.23 The only breadth first search order that begins at node A.

Figure 9.24 repeats the graph in Figure 9.23. This time a breadth first search beginning at node C is shown.

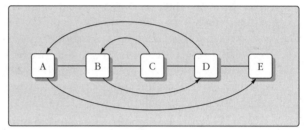

FIGURE 9.24 One of two breadth first search orders that begins at node C. The other order is C, B, D, A, E.

Figure 9.25 presents a graph that is also a tree, along with a breadth first search order that begins at the root. We can characterize the breadth first search of a tree—beginning at the root node—as follows: First the root is processed, then all the nodes at level two are processed, then all the nodes

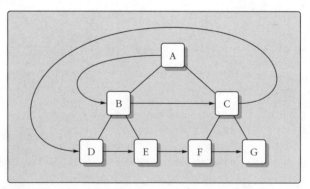

FIGURE 9.25 A graph that is a tree with root at A. (Actually, this graph is a tree if any node is selected as the root node.) Directed arcs show one of the eight possible breadth first search orders.

at level three are processed, and so on. In general, a node at level k is processed after all nodes at level $k - 1$ and before any node at level $k + 1$.

Pause a moment to observe that we have just described a level order traversal of a tree. In general, if a graph is a tree, then a breadth first search of the graph, beginning at the root, is a level order traversal of the tree.

The above discussion is now applied to develop an algorithm for breadth first search. The pseudocode algorithm in Figure 9.26 is intended not only to implement breadth first search but also to be comparable to subsequent graph traversal algorithms. The comparable presentations will help emphasize similarities and differences among the traversal algorithms.

procedure breadth_first_search (the_graph : graph)
    the_queue : queue;

    procedure visit (the_node : graph_node);
    a_node, the_neighbor : graph_node;
    begin
    enqueue the_node in the_queue;   *-- One node is enqueued.*

    while the_queue **is not** empty **loop**
      serve a_node from the_queue;   *-- All nodes are served from the queue, all nodes are processed,*
      process a_node and set a_node's status to *processed*;   *-- and all nodes have their status set to* processed.

      for each neighbor, the_neighbor, of a_node **loop**
        if the_neighbor's status is *waiting* **then**   *-- A node's status is checked twice for each edge.*
        set the_neighbor's status to *ready* and
          enqueue the_neighbor in the_queue;   *-- All nodes, less one, have their status set to* ready *and are enqueued.*
        end if;
      end for;
    end while;

    end visit;

begin
    set the status of each node in the graph to *waiting*;   *-- The status of all nodes is set.*
    for each node, N, in the graph **loop**
      if N's status is *waiting* **then**   *-- The status of all nodes is checked.*
      visit (N);
      end if;
    end for;
end breadth_first_search;

F I G U R E   9.26 Pseudocode for breadth first search. The comments provide operation counts for a connected graph as described in Figure 9.27.

The breadth first search algorithm assigns a status—*waiting, ready,* or *processed*—to each graph node. Initially, each node's status is set as *waiting*. This means that all nodes are waiting to be seen for the first time. The node selected to be processed first is passed to procedure *visit,* where it is placed on the queue used by breadth first search.

The loop in *visit* is the heart of the algorithm. As long as the queue is not empty, a node is served, is processed, has its status set to *processed,* and has all its neighbors (with status *waiting*) added to the queue. Thus, the fundamental mechanism for breadth first search is to process a node then to add all its neighbors to a queue of nodes ready to be processed. Recall (Chapter 5) that this is the basic technique for level order traversal of a tree.

When a node is added to the queue it will be processed before any of its neighbors that are waiting. What happens when a node, say *p,* is processed and one of its neighbors, call it *q,* is already in the queue and therefore has status *ready*? (You might want to construct a simple graph that shows this is possible.) The algorithm in Figure 9.26 simply ignores *q* because *q* is known to already be in the queue. Note that if such nodes were added to the queue, the order in which nodes are processed would not be affected—but nodes served from the queue would have to be checked to see if they had previously been processed. Also, the queue would generally be larger than necessary.

We then see that status must be added to each node because several distinct paths may lead to the same node. A status field was not necessary for list and tree traversals because for these data structures the traversal path to each node is unique.

If a graph is connected, then the first call to procedure *Visit* will process all the graph's nodes. If a graph is not connected, the **for** loop in *breadth_first_search* will guarantee that all nodes are processed.

The comments in Figure 9.26 help you analyze the performance of breadth first search assuming the graph is connected. If a graph contains *n* nodes and *e* edges, you can use the comments to obtain the operation counts in Figure 9.27.

Let us review Figure 9.27. Each node's status is set to three values: *waiting, ready,* and *processed.* One exception occurs when *visit* is called with the first node processed, call it *Q. Q*'s status is *waiting* and the queue is empty. Since *Q* will be enqueued then immediately served and processed, there is no point setting its status to ready in the meantime. This state of affairs will exist anytime

Operation	Total	Comment
Set a node's status	$3n - 1$	Each node (except one) has status *waiting,* then *ready,* then *processed.* The first node processed avoids status *ready.*
Check a node's status	$2e + n$	Each edge connects two nodes. Also, each node's status must be checked in case the graph is not connected.
Enqueue or serve a node	$2n$	Each node is enqueued once and served once.
Process a node	n	Each node is processed once.
Visit an edge	$2e$ or $n^2 - n$	It is $2e$ for an adjacency list representation and $n(n - 1)$ for an adjacency matrix.
Total	$7n + 4e - 1$ or $n^2 + 6n + 2e - 1$	$O(n) + O(e)$ for an adjacency list or $O(n^2) + O(e)$ for an adjacency matrix.

FIGURE 9.27 Node and edge operations during a breadth first search.

Visit is called. If a graph has no edges, then all nodes will skip the *ready* state and the number of status sets will be $2n$. Remember that Figure 9.27 assumes the graph is connected.

Each edge connects two nodes, therefore each edge causes two status checks. In addition, the **for** loop of *breadth_first_search* checks the status of all nodes to assure that all nodes are processed even if the graph is not connected.

Each node is enqueued once, served once, and processed once.

Finally, given a node, say Q, breadth first search needs to determine Q's neighbors. With an adjacency list representation, the neighbors are determined by traversing a list of neighbors (Figure 9.13). Each edge node connects two graph nodes and therefore will be visited twice. The total number of edge visits is thus $2e$.

With an adjacency matrix representation the neighbors are determined by traversing a row of the array (Figure 9.10). Each row contains $n - 1$ entries (excluding the diagonal), and each row is traversed once. The total number of entries traversed is $n(n - 1)$. Even if an adjacency matrix entry is 0 (or false), indicating the absence of an edge, that 0 value must be examined.

The overall effort is seen to be either $O(n) + O(e)$ or $O(n^2) + O(e)$. The maximum value of e is $(\frac{1}{2}) n (n - 1)$ or $O(n^2)$.

For comparison with other data structures Figure 9.28 gives the equivalent of Figure 9.27 for traversal of a list, and Figure 9.29 gives the equivalent of Figure 9.27 for level order traversal of a tree.

Operation	Total	Comment
Process a node	n	Each node is processed.
Find next	n	For a linked list an edge is accessed to find a successor. For an array representation the next array component is accessed.
Total	$2n$	$O(n)$

FIGURE 9.28 Node and "find next" operations during traversal of a list. The overall effort is seen to be $O(n)$.

Operation	Total	Comment
Enqueue or serve a node	$2n$	Each node is enqueued and served once.
Process a node	n	Each node is processed.
Find child	$2n$	Each node has two pointers to possible children. Each pointer must be checked.
Total	$5n$	$O(n)$

FIGURE 9.29 Node and "find child" operations during level order traversal of a binary tree with a linked representation (Figure 5.46). The overall effort is seen to be $O(n)$.

Figure 9.30 now gives the breadth first search implementation that is part of Package Body 9.1.

```
procedure breadth_first_search (the_graph : in out graph) is
-- Length 7   Complexity 3   Performance O(n²)
-- Examine each of the n² entries in the two-dimensional array used to represent graph edges.
    package bfs_queue is new queue_package (natural);
    the_queue   : bfs_queue.queue (the_graph.size);
    object      : object_type;

    procedure visit (k : natural) is
    -- Length 11   Complexity 4
      index : natural;
    begin
      bfs_queue.enqueue(the_queue, k);

      while bfs_queue.number_of_objects(the_queue) > 0 loop
        index := bfs_queue.head(the_queue);
        bfs_queue.dequeue(the_queue);
        process(the_graph.nodes(index).object);
        the_graph.nodes(index).status := processed;

        for neighbor in 1 .. the_graph.size loop
          if the_graph.edges(index, neighbor) > 0 and
             the_graph.nodes(neighbor).status = waiting then
            the_graph.nodes(neighbor).status := ready;
            bfs_queue.enqueue(the_queue, neighbor);
          end if;
        end loop;

      end loop;
    end visit;

begin
    set_waiting (the_graph);
    for k in 1 .. the_graph.size loop
      if the_graph.nodes(k).status = waiting then
        visit (k);
      end if;
    end loop;
end breadth_first_search;
```

FIGURE 9.30 An Ada implementation of breadth first search for the adjacency matrix representation in Specification 9.1. This implementation is part of Package Body 9.1.

9.6.2 Depth First Search

If the queue used to hold nodes that are "ready" in a breadth first search is changed to a stack, the result is a *depth first search*. The change is dramatic. A depth first search processes a node, say *first_node,* then processes one of *first_node*'s neighbors and defers processing the remaining neighbors as long as possible. The deferral occurs because *first_node*'s neighbors are in a stack, and new nodes are continually pushed on the stack on top of them. In Figure 9.31, the example in Figure 9.21 is repeated, this time for a depth first search. The top row shows one depth first search traversal order, and the bottom row shows a second.

Consider Figure 9.31. A black node has been processed. A shaded node has been marked ready and pushed on the stack. A white node has not been seen by the traversal. A depth first search leaves its immediate vicinity and defers processing all but one neighbor of the node last processed. Determine the next three nodes to be processed for each of the two traversals.

Figure 9.31 helps you visualize the depth first search traversal process. We turn now to two examples, then present two depth first search algorithms.

Figure 9.32 shows one of two depth first search orders, beginning at node C, for a graph that is a list. Now consider the depth first search, beginning

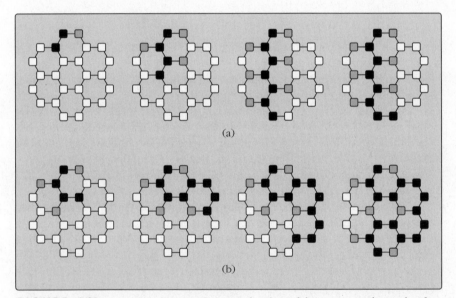

(a)

(b)

FIGURE 9.31 Two depth first search traversal orders of the same sample graph. After a node is processed, one of its neighbors is processed and processing the remaining neighbors is deferred. (a) One possible depth first search traversal order; (b) another possible depth first search traversal order for the same graph and the same initial graph node.

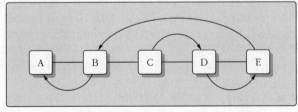

FIGURE 9.32 One of two depth first search orders that begins at node C; the other is C, B, A, D, E.

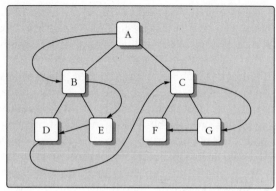

FIGURE 9.33 A graph that is a tree with root at A. (Actually, this graph is a tree if any node is selected as the root node.) Shown using directed arcs is one of the eight possible depth first search orders.

at the root, of a graph that is a tree. Figure 9.33 shows one possible order for a tree with seven nodes.

Figure 9.34 presents a depth first algorithm that is comparable to the algorithm for breadth first search in Figure 9.26.

A table of operation counts, essentially identical to Figure 9.27, can be constructed based on the comments in Figure 9.34. The basic difference between these algorithms is that breadth first search uses a queue whereas depth first search uses a stack. The result is that a depth first search requires $O(n) + O(e)$ operations for an adjacency list representation and $O(n^2) + O(e)$ operations for an adjacency matrix representation.

There is a subtle point regarding depth first search that merits further discussion. In a graph, one node may be encountered several times during a traversal. Putting a node on the queue several times during breadth first search doesn't affect the traversal order—the node put on the queue first will be processed first. It is different for a depth first search. A node on the stack is marked *ready*. If such a node is encountered a second time and is once again pushed on the stack, the traversal order will be changed—the last node pushed on the stack will be the first processed. What do we do? Is a node pushed on the stack every time it is encountered until it is processed? Or once a node is on the stack and marked ready, do we not push it on the stack again?

The algorithm in Figure 9.34 pushes each node on the stack exactly once. Therefore, the order in which a node is processed is determined when that node is pushed on the stack the first time. This issue is complicated by the fact that we can easily write a recursive version of the algorithm in Figure 9.34. It appears in Figure 9.35.

Most people, when discussing depth first search, have in mind the recursive algorithm in Figure 9.35. Note, however, that these two algorithms visit the nodes of most graphs in different orders.

```
procedure depth_first_search (the_graph : graph)                          -- Nonrecursive version.
    the_stack : stack

    procedure visit (the_node : graph_node);
        a_node, the_neighbor : graph_node;
    begin
        push the_node on the_stack;                                       -- One node is pushed on the stack.

        while the_stack is not empty loop
            pop a_node from the_stack;                                    -- All nodes are served from the queue.
            process a_node and set a_node's status to processed;          -- All nodes are processed, and
                                                                          -- all nodes have their status set to processed.

            for each neighbor, the_neighbor, of a_node loop
                if the_neighbor's status is waiting then                  -- A node's status is checked twice for each edge.
                set the_neighbor's status to ready and
                    push the_neighbor on the_stack;                       -- All nodes, less one, have their status set to ready and are enqueued.
                end if;
            end loop;
        end loop;

    end visit;

begin
    set the status of each node in the_graph to waiting;                  -- The status of all nodes is set.
    for each node, N, in the_graph loop
        if N's status is waiting then                                     -- The status of all nodes is checked.
            visit (N);
        end if;
    end loop;
end depth_first_search;
```

FIGURE 9.34 Pseudocode for depth first search. The comments are for operation counts that assume the graph is connected.

During a *nonrecursive* depth first search, after a node is processed, *all* of its neighbors are marked ready and pushed on the stack. Processing these nodes is deferred as long as possible. Thus, the order in which they are processed depends solely on when they are *first* encountered. A second or third encounter of any node during the traversal does not change the order in which the node is processed.

During a recursive depth first search, after a node is processed, one of its neighbors is recursively visited (and hence processed) and the remaining neighbors are not seen by the algorithm. In the recursive algorithm, nodes are never marked ready. The result is that the order in which a node is processed may be determined by its being encountered several times. The exercises provide examples of the different traversal orders produced by recursive and nonrecursive algorithms.

We can use a table like that in Figure 9.27 to calculate the performance of recursive depth first search. It is no surprise that the result is $O(n) + O(e)$

```
procedure depth_first_search (the_graph : graph)                          -- Recursive version.

    procedure visit (the_node : graph_node);
        the_neighbor : graph_node;
    begin
        process the_node and set the_node's status to processed;          -- All nodes are processed and marked processed.

        for each neighbor, the_neighbor, of the_node loop
            if the_neighbor's status is waiting then                      -- A node's status is checked twice for each edge.
                visit (the_neighbor);                                     -- Each node is recursively visited.
            end if;
        end loop;

    end visit;

begin
    set the status of each node in the_graph to waiting;                  -- The status of all nodes is set.
    for each node, N, in the_graph loop
        if N's status is waiting then                                     -- The status of all nodes is checked.
            visit (N);
        end if;
    end loop;
end depth_first_search;
```

FIGURE 9.35 Pseudocode for recursive depth first search. The comments provide operation counts assuming the graph is connected as detailed in Figure 9.36. Compare with Figure 9.26.

Operation	Total	Comment
Set a node's status	$2n$	Each node has status *waiting* and is then processed.
Check a node's status	$2e + n$	Each edge connects two nodes. Also, each node's status must be checked in case the graph is not connected.
Recursively visit a node	n	Each node is recursively visited once.
Process a node	n	Each node is processed once.
Visit an edge	$2e$ or $n^2 - n$	It is $2e$ for an adjacency list representation and $n(n-1)$ for an adjacency matrix.
Total	$5n + 4e$ or $n^2 + 4n + 2e$	$O(n) + O(e)$ for an adjacency list or $O(n^2) + O(e)$ for an adjacency matrix.

FIGURE 9.36 Node and edge operations during a recursive depth first search. The overall effort is seen to be either $O(n) + O(e)$ or $O(n^2) + O(e)$. These results are obtained from the comments in Figure 9.35.

operations for an adjacency list representation and $O(n^2) + O(e)$ operations for an adjacency matrix representation. The specific operations are shown in Figure 9.36.

Figure 9.37 now gives the Ada implementation for recursive depth first search.

```
procedure depth_first_search (the_graph : in out graph) is
-- Length 4   Complexity 3   Performance O(n²)
-- Examine each of the n² entries in the two-dimensional array used to represent graph edges.

    procedure visit (k : natural) is
    -- Length 5   Complexity 3   Recursion 1
    begin
        process (the_graph.nodes(k).object);
        the_graph.nodes(k).status := processed;

        for neighbor in 1 .. the_graph.size loop
            if the_graph.edges(k, neighbor) > 0 and the_graph.nodes(neighbor).status = waiting then
                visit(neighbor);
            end if;
        end loop;

    end visit;

begin
    set_waiting (the_graph);
    for k in 1 .. the_graph.size loop
        if the_graph.nodes(k).status = waiting then
            visit (k);
        end if;
    end loop;
end depth_first_search;
```

FIGURE 9.37 A recursive implementation of depth first search.

9.6.3 Priority First Search

Both depth first and breadth first traversals are special cases of *priority first search*. The major difference among them is that depth first search uses a stack to hold nodes pending processing, breadth first search uses a queue to hold nodes pending processing, and priority first search uses a priority queue to hold nodes pending processing. Important applications of priority first search will be discussed in subsequent sections. In the meantime, an algorithm for priority first search—that is comparable to the algorithms in Figures 9.26 and 9.34—is given next.

Observe that a breadth first search is the special case of a priority first search in which the priorities assigned to nodes as they are added to the priority queue continually decrease. A depth first search is the special case of a priority first search in which the priorities assigned to nodes as they are added to the priority queue continually increase.

Look carefully at the **elsif** statement in the **for** loop of procedure *visit* in Figure 9.38. There is nothing comparable in the algorithms for breadth or depth first search. What is the function of this **elsif** statement?

Recall that in a graph several distinct paths may lead from the first node processed to other nodes in the graph. When a node, call it *N,* is seen by the

```
procedure priority_first_search (the_graph : graph);
    the_priority_queue : priority_queue;

        procedure visit (the_node : graph_node);
        a_node, the_neighbor : graph_node;
    begin
        Assign the_node a priority, set its status to ready,            -- One node has its status set and is enqueued.
            and enqueue the_node in the_priority_queue;

        while the_priority_queue is not empty loop
            serve a_node from the_priority_queue;                       -- All nodes are served from the queue.
            process a_node and change a_node's status to processed;     -- All nodes are processed, and
                                                                        -- all nodes have their status set to processed.

            for each neighbor, the_neighbor, of a_node loop
                Assign the_neighbor a priority;

                if the_neighbor's status is waiting then                -- A node's status is checked twice for each edge.
                    Set the_neighbor's status to ready and
                        enqueue the_neighbor in the_priority_queue;     -- All nodes, less one, have their status
                                                                        -- set to ready and are enqueued.

                elsif the_neighbor's status is ready and the_neighbor's priority is
                    higher than the priority associated with the        -- The number of times a search is made,
                    instance of the_neighbor already in the_priority_queue,  -- and replacement occurs, depends
                    call it old_neighbor, then                          -- on the structure of the graph and
                    replace old_neighbor with the_neighbor;             -- how priorities are determined.
                end if;
            end loop;
        end loop;

    end visit;

begin
    set the status of each node in the_graph to waiting;               -- The status of every node is set.
    for each node, N, in the_graph loop
        if N's status is waiting then                                  -- The status of every node is checked.
            visit (N);
        end if;
    end loop;
end priority_first_search;
```

F I G U R E 9.38 Pseudocode for priority first search. The comments provide operation counts assuming the graph is connected. Compare with Figures 9.26 and 9.34.

traversal algorithm for the first time, it is put in the priority queue along with the priority associated with the path that led to N. If N is seen for a second (or subsequent) time, its associated priority may be different because it is being approached along a different path. Refer to the priority already in the priority queue as N's *old_priority* and the priority associated with the latest path as N's *latest_priority*.

If N's *old_priority* is greater than N's *latest_priority*, the algorithm does nothing—the priority queue already contains N's highest priority. If N's *old_priority* is less than *N*'s *latest_priority,* the algorithm must replace *N*'s priority in the priority queue. It is making a comparison of these priorities and, if necessary, changing *N*'s priority that is the function of the **elsif** statement in Figure 9.38. What would happen if each node with status *ready* is simply added to the priority queue? Figure 9.39 presents an Ada implementation of priority first search.

```
procedure priority_first_search (the_graph : in out graph) is
-- Length 12   Complexity 3   Performance O(n²)
-- Examine each of the n² entries in the two-dimensional array used to represent graph edges.
    type priority_object is record
      node_index   : natural;
      priority      : edge_weight;
    end record;

    function get_weight (the_object : priority_object) return edge_weight;
    function is_equal (left, right : priority_object) return boolean;

    package pfs_priority is new priority_queue_package                    -- Instantiate a priority queue.
      (priority_object, edge_weight, get_weight, "<");
          -- Instantiate the procedure in the priority queue package that replaces an existing entry with an entry that has higher priority.
    procedure new_priority is new pfs_priority.replace (is_equal);

    the_priority_queue : pfs_priority.queue (the_graph.size);

    function get_weight (the_object : priority_object) return edge_weight is
    -- Length 1   Complexity 1
    begin
      return the_object.priority;
    end get_weight;

    function is_equal (left, right : priority_object) return boolean is
    -- Length 1   Complexity 1
    begin
      return (left.node_index = right.node_index);
    end is_equal;

    function get_priority (posn1, posn2 : natural) return edge_weight is
    -- Length 1   Complexity 1
    -- This user-supplied function determines the priority associated with a node and hence the order in which nodes
    -- are processed. In this instantiation the priority is the weight of the edge that attaches a node to one of
    -- the nodes that has already been processed. The priority queue contains all nodes that are neighbors of nodes
    -- already processed. The node that is removed from the priority queue and processed will be the one that is
    -- connected with the highest priority edge.
    begin
      return the_graph.edges(posn1, posn2);
    end get_priority;
```

FIGURE 9.39 An Ada implementation of priority first search.   *(continued)*

Figure 9.39 (continued)

```
procedure visit (k : natural) is
-- Length 14   Complexity 6
   index : natural;
begin
   pfs_priority.enqueue(the_priority_queue, priority_object'(k, 1));

   while pfs_priority.number_of_objects(the_priority_queue) > 0 loop
      index := pfs_priority.head(the_priority_queue).node_index;
      the_graph.nodes(index).weight := get_weight(pfs_priority.head(the_priority_queue));
      process (the_graph.nodes(index).object);
      the_graph.nodes(index).status := processed;
      pfs_priority.dequeue(the_priority_queue);

      for neighbor in 1 .. the_graph.size loop
         if the_graph.edges(index, neighbor) > 0 then
            if the_graph.nodes(neighbor).status = waiting then
               the_graph.nodes(neighbor).status := ready;
               pfs_priority.enqueue(the_priority_queue,
                  priority_object'(neighbor, get_priority (index,neighbor)));
            elsif the_graph.nodes(neighbor).status = ready then
               new_priority (the_priority_queue, priority_object'(neighbor,
                  get_priority (index,neighbor)));
            end if;
         end if;
      end loop;

   end loop;
end visit;

begin
   set_waiting (the_graph);
   for k in 1 .. the_graph.size loop
      if the_graph.nodes(k).status = waiting then
         visit (k);
      end if;
   end loop;
end priority_first_search;
```

FIGURE 9.39 (continued)

What about performance of a priority first search? Consider the two extreme cases—a graph with no edges and a graph with all possible edges.

If the graph has no edges, the maximum depth of the priority queue is 1 so priority queue operations cost $O(1)$. The performance for the adjacency matrix representation is $O(n^2)$ to examine all the array components and $O(n)$ to enqueue, dequeue, and process each object in the graph. With the adjacency list representation the performance is determined by the $O(n)$ cost to enqueue, dequeue, and process each object in the graph.

Suppose the graph has all possible edges. The maximum depth of the priority queue is n so an upper bound on each enqueue, dequeue, and replace

Operation	Graph adjacency matrix	Graph adjacency list
Breadth first search	$O(n^2) + O(e)$	$O(n) + O(e)$
Depth first search	$O(n^2) + O(e)$	$O(n) + O(e)$
Priority first search (graph with no edges)	$O(n^2)$	$O(n)$
Priority first search (graph with all edges)	$O(n^2 \log_2 n)$	$O(n^2 \log_2 n)$
Priority first search (graph with e edges)	$O[n^2 + (n + e) \log_2 n]$	$O[(n + e) \log_2 n]$

FIGURE 9.40 A summary of performance results for graph traversals.

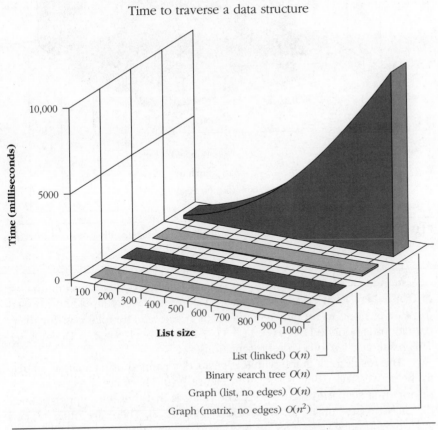

Time to traverse a data structure

List (linked) $O(n)$

Binary search tree $O(n)$

Graph (list, no edges) $O(n)$

Graph (matrix, no edges) $O(n^2)$

FIGURE 9.41 Traversal times for a singly linked list, a binary search tree, and adjacency list and adjacency matrix representations of a graph with no edges. Traversing the adjacency matrix representation of a graph is an $O(n^2)$ operation because each array entry is examined.

Time to traverse a data structure

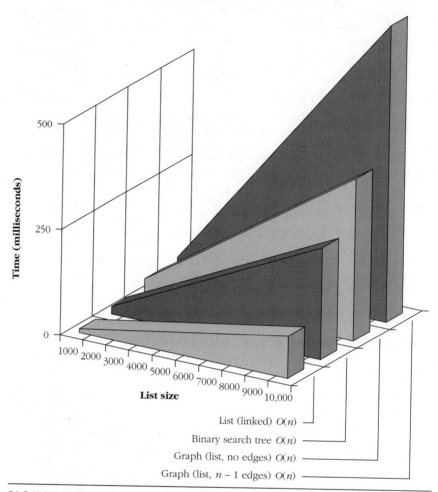

FIGURE 9.42 Comparison of four traversal algorithms that, for the cases considered, require $O(n)$ work.

operation is $O(\log_2 n)$. Each of the n objects is dequeued at a maximum cost of $O(n \log_2 n)$. Each edge that indicates a node that is not already processed causes that node to be either enqueue or replaced. The total cost for these operations is bounded by $[(n-1) + (n-2) + \cdots + 1] \log_2 n = O(n^2 \log_2 n)$. This result applies to both representations.

The result for a graph with e edges is determined using analysis similar to the above. The result is shown in Figure 9.40. There are three results for priority first search in Figure 9.40. The point is that these are upper bounds that may be pessimistic for a particular application. There are other related algorithms (Sedgewick, 1988, pp. 455–467) that should be considered for any particular application.

To conclude this discussion, we provide three figures that compare the

Traverse a graph
Depth first search

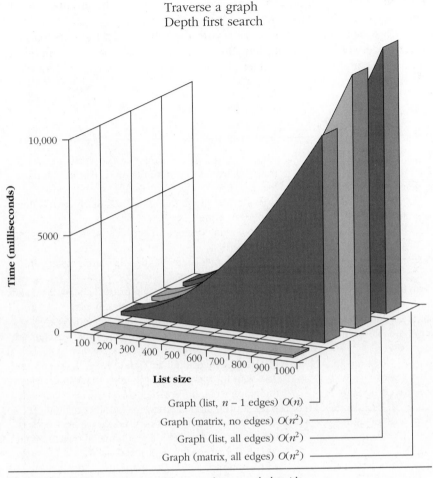

FIGURE 9.43 Comparison of four graph traversal algorithms.

times to traverse a list, a binary tree, and several variations of graphs. Figure 9.41 shows the time to traverse four data structures: a singly linked list, an inorder traversal of a binary search tree, a graph with no edges represented using an adjacency list, and a graph with no edges represented using an adjacency matrix.

Graph traversal includes processing a node then visiting all its neighbors. For an adjacency matrix representation, a row with $n - 1$ entries must be scanned to find the neighbors. Since this is done n times, the algorithm performance is $O(n^2)$. The other three algorithms in Figure 9.41 are $O(n)$.

Figure 9.42 shows traversal times for four data structures with $O(n)$ performance. The graph with $n - 1$ edges is structured like a binary tree. As an exercise explain the relative performances shown in terms of the algorithms used.

Finally, Figure 9.43 shows times for the depth first traversal of four graphs. Observe that three of the four results have $O(n^2)$ performance—including the traversal of an adjacency list representation of a graph. Compare these results with the results in Figures 9.41 and 9.42.

Next, Section 9.7 applies priority first search to extract graphs that minimize edge weights and path lengths. Then, Section 9.8 applies the notion of minimum path lengths to produce algorithms to route messages in a computer network.

EXERCISES 9.6

1. Consider the graph in Figure 9.23.
   Starting at A:
   a. How many distinct breadth first search orders are possible?
   b. How many distinct depth first search orders are possible?
   Starting at C:
   c. How many distinct breadth first search orders are possible?
   d. How many distinct depth first search orders are possible?
   Extend this question to a graph that is list with n nodes. The starting nodes for traversal are (i) an end node and (ii) the middle node.

2. Consider the graph in Figure 9.25.
   Starting at A:
   a. How many distinct breadth first search orders are possible?
   b. How many distinct depth first search orders are possible?
   Starting at D:
   c. How many distinct breadth first search orders are possible?
   d. How many distinct depth first search orders are possible?
   Extend this question to a graph that is a complete binary tree with n nodes where n has the

value $2^k - 1$ for some integer k. The starting nodes for traversal are (i) the root node and (ii) the "left-most" leaf node.

3. Consider the graph in Figure 9.22. Starting with the upper left node:
   a. How many distinct breadth first search orders are possible?
   b. How many distinct depth first search orders are possible?

4. Replace the comments in Figures 9.26, 9.34, 9.35, and 9.38 with your own improved comments.

5. Add comments to Figures 9.30, 9.37, and 9.39.

6. Explain why breadth first and depth first searches are special cases of priority first search.

7. Replace the algorithms in Figures 9.26, 9.34, 9.35, and 9.38 with the simplified algorithms that can be used if the graph to be traversed is known to be connected.

8. Write a program that creates a graph containing n nodes and k edges where the edges connect nodes selected at random. Plot a graph that shows the time required for breadth, depth, and priority first search as a function of n and k. Compare the results with the performance results in Figure 9.40.

9. Implement breadth first, depth first, and priority first traversals for the adjacency list representation of a graph (Specification 9.2).

■ 9.7 Traversal Applications

In this section we modify our graphs by assigning a positive integer or weight to each edge. The weight can be thought of as a cost or a distance, and graphs with such weights are called *weighted graphs* or *networks*.

In Section 9.7.1, given a connected network, we will find a connected subgraph such that the sum of the weights of its edges is minimized. Such a subgraph is called a *minimum spanning tree*. Figure 9.44(a) shows a network and Figure 9.44(b) shows a corresponding minimum spanning tree.

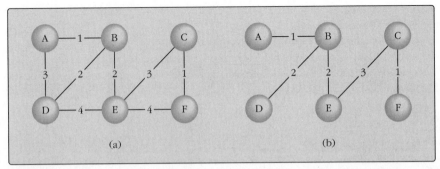

FIGURE 9.44 A connected weighted graph (a), and the corresponding minimum spanning tree (b). For the example in (a) the corresponding minimum spanning tree is unique, although in general it is not. The sum of the edge weights in (b) is 9—the minimum possible sum for edges that connect all six nodes.

In Section 9.7.2, given a connected network and a node, call it N, we will find a connected subgraph such that the path length from N to each other node in the graph is a minimum. Such a subgraph is called a ***shortest path length tree***. Figure 9.45(a) shows a network and Figure 9.45(b) shows a corresponding shortest path length tree.

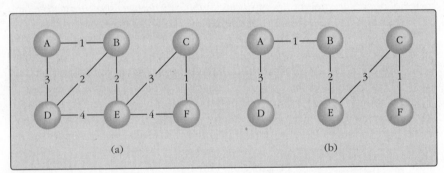

FIGURE 9.45 A connected weighted graph (a) and a corresponding shortest path length tree starting at node A; (b) Note that the solution in (b) is not unique.

The algorithms to solve the two problems discussed in this section are closely related. They are both based on a priority first search and only differ in the method used to assign priorities. Other algorithms for the shortest path length problem, in the case of computer networks, are given in Section 9.8.

Section 9.7.3 discusses an Ada implementation of the minimum spanning tree algorithm.

9.7.1 Minimum Spanning Trees

Let *the_graph* be a connected weighted graph; that is, a network. We will construct a minimum spanning tree, call it *the_minimum_spanning_tree*, corresponding to *the_graph*. An algorithm to do this is given in Figure 9.46.

Initialize the_priority_queue as an empty priority queue;
Initialize the_minimum_spanning_tree as an empty graph;
Add any node in the_graph, say first_node, to the_minimum_spanning_tree;
Add each of first_node's neighbors, and the edge that connects it to first_node, to
    the_priority_queue. The priority for each neighbor is the weight of the edge from the
    neighbor to first_node.

while the_priority_queue is not empty **loop**
    Serve a node, call it the_node, from the_priority_queue.
    if the_node is not in the_minimum_spanning_tree **then**
      Add the_node to the_minimum_spanning_tree;
      for each neighbor, the_neighbor, of the_node **loop**
        Add the_neighbor, and the edge that connects it to the_node, to
        the_priority_queue. The priority for the_neighbor is the weight of the edge
        from the_neighbor to the_node.
      end loop;
    end if;
end loop;

FIGURE 9.46 Algorithm to construct a minimum spanning tree. The element served from the priority queue is the element with the smallest priority. A priority queue entry consists of a node, an edge, and a priority.

Figure 9.46 describes a priority first search in which the nodes in the priority queue are neighbors of nodes in *the_minimum_spanning_tree,* and the priorities are the weights of the edges that connect them to nodes in *the_minimum_spanning_tree.* The node that is added at each step is the node that is closest to *the_minimum_spanning_tree* in the sense that the weighted edge that connects it to *the_minimum_spanning_tree* is smallest.

The algorithm in Figure 9.46 is called a **greedy algorithm** because each node is added on the basis of a locally optimal, or greedy, decision. It must be shown that a sequence of such locally optimal actions leads to a result that is globally optimal. Refer to Graham and Pavol (1985) for a history of the minimum spanning tree problem, several other algorithms for its solution, and further discussion of greedy algorithms.

9.7.2 Shortest Path Length Trees

Let *the_graph* be a connected weighted graph. Let *first_node* and *last_node* be two nodes in *the_graph.* We seek a shortest path between *first_node* and *last_node.* That is, we seek a path between *first_node* and *last_node* such that the sum of the weights of the edges is a minimum. In Figure 9.47(a) there are two shortest paths from A to F. They are A, B, E, F and A, B, E, C, F.

We proceed to solve a generalization of the problem described in the previous paragraph. The new problem is the following: For connected weighted graph, *the_graph,* and node N in *the_graph,* construct the tree that contains the shortest path from N to every other node in *the_graph.* The result is the shortest path length tree for *the_graph* and N.

Figure 9.45 shows a weighted graph and the shortest path length tree for starting node A.

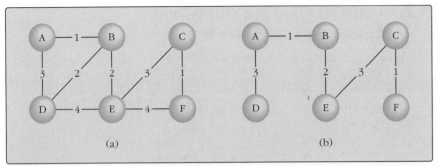

FIGURE 9.47 A connected weighted graph (a) and a corresponding shortest path length tree starting at node A; (b) Note that the solution in (b) is not unique.

Initialize the_priority_queue as an empty priority queue;
Initialize shortest_path_length as an empty graph;
Add *a specified node* in the_graph, say first_node, to shortest_path_length;
Add each of first_node's neighbors, and the edge that connects it to first_node, to
    the_priority_queue. The priority for each neighbor is the weight of the edge from the
    neighbor to first_node.

while the_priority_queue is not empty **loop**
    Serve a node, call it the_node, from the_priority_queue.
    if the_node is not in shortest_path_length **then**
      Add the_node to shortest_path_length;
      for each neighbor, the_neighbor, of the_node **loop**
        Add the_neighbor, and the edge that connects it to the_node, to
        the_priority_queue. The priority for the_neighbor is the weight of the edge from
        the_neighbor to the_node *plus the path length from first_node to the_node.*
      end loop;
    end if;
end loop;

FIGURE 9.48 Algorithm to construct a minimum spanning tree. The element served from the priority queue is the element with the smallest priority. A priority queue entry consists of a node, an edge, and a priority.

    Figure 9.48 provides an algorithm for generating a shortest path length tree that is almost identical to the algorithm in Figure 9.46 for generating a minimum spanning tree. The two places where the algorithms differ are shown in italics in Figure 9.48.

    Compare Figures 9.46 and 9.48. The difference is in the method used to assign priorities. In both algorithms some node, *the_node,* is served from the priority queue and its neighbors are then added to the priority queue. Let *the_neighbor* be such a neighbor of *the_node.* In Figure 9.46 (minimum spanning tree) the priority associated with the_neighbor is the weight of the edge between *the_node* and *the_neighbor.* In Figure 9.48 (shortest path length tree) the priority associated with *the_neighbor* is the weight of the edge between *the_node* and *the_neighbor* plus the path length from *first_node* (the starting node) to *the_node.*

9.7.3 Implementing the Minimum Spanning Tree Algorithm

Implementation of the minimum spanning tree algorithm is based on Specification 9.1. The implementation below in Figure 9.49 does not exactly follow the pseudocode for priority first search in Figure 9.38. Instead, this implementation assumes that *the_graph* is connected and supplies priorities directly as the values of edge weights in the graph.

procedure minimum_spanning_tree (the_graph : **in out** graph; the_tree : **in out** graph) **is**
-- *Length 32   Complexity 9   Performance* O(n²)
    type priority_object **is record**
    node 1 : natural;   -- *Index of the node in the priority queue.*
    node2   : natural;   -- *(node1, node2) is the edge to attach node1 to the_tree.*
    priority : edge_weight;
    end record;

    function get_weight (the_object : priority_object) **return** edge_weight;
    package priority **is new** priority_queue_package (object_type   => priority_object,
                            priority   => edge_weight,
                            priority_of   => get_weight,
                            "<"   => "<");

    the_queue   : priority.queue (the_graph.size);
    pq_object   : priority_object;
    index1, index2 : natural;

    function get_weight (the_object : priority_object) **return** edge_weight **is**
-- *Length 1   Complexity 1*
    begin
        return the_object.priority;
    end get_weight;

begin
    set_waiting (the_graph); the_tree.size := 0;
    if the_graph.size > 0 **then**
        insert_node (the_tree, the_graph.nodes(1).object);   -- *The node with index1 is added to the_tree.*
        the_graph.nodes(1).status := processed;

        for neighbor **in** 2 .. the_graph.size **loop**   -- *The neighbors of the node with index1 are added to the priority queue.*
          if the_graph.edges(1, neighbor) > 0 **then**
            priority.enqueue(the_queue, priority_object'
              (neighbor, 1, the_graph.edges(1, neighbor)));
            the_graph.nodes(neighbor).status := ready;
          end if;
        end loop;

        while priority.number_of_objects(the_queue) > 0 **loop**
          pq_object := priority.head(the_queue);   -- *Get an object from the priority queue.*

FIGURE 9.49 An implementation of the minimum spanning tree algorithm.   *(continued)*

Figure 9.49 (continued)

```
priority.dequeue(the_queue);
index1 := pq_object.node1;
```

if the_graph.nodes(index1).status /= processed **then**   *-- If the object has not been processed,*
```
    index2 := pq_object.node 2;
    insert_node (the_tree, the_graph.nodes(index1).object);    -- add it to the_tree
    insert_edge (the_tree, key_of(the_graph.nodes(index1).object),    -- using the correct edge
        key_of(the_graph.nodes(index2).object), pq_object.priority);
    the_graph.nodes(index1).status := processed;    -- and mark it processed.
```

```
    for neighbor in 1 .. the_graph.size loop    -- For the neighbors of the node just processed that are
      if the_graph.edges(index1, neighbor) > 0 then    -- not already processed, enqueue them using the
        if the_graph.nodes(neighbor).status /= processed then    -- correct edge and priority.
          priority.enqueue(the_queue, priority_object'
              (neighbor, index1, the_graph.edges (index1, neighbor)));
        end if;
      end if;
    end loop;
```

```
  end if;
end loop;
```

```
end if;
end minimum_spanning_tree;
```

FIGURE 9.49 *(continued)*

To convert Figure 9.49 to a shortest path length, implementation requires only minor changes. You are asked to show these changes in the exercises. Then, Section 9.8 presents a distributed implementation of the shortest path length algorithm.

EXERCISES 9.7

1. Consider the connected graph in Figure 9.50. Suppose that every edge has weight 1.

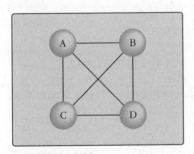

FIGURE 9.50

a. How many distinct minimum spanning trees are there for this graph?

b. How many distinct shortest path length trees are there that begin at A?

2. Suppose that the edge weights for the graph in Figure 9.50 are integers greater than or equal to 1.

a. Assign edge weights so there is only one minimum spanning tree and the sum of the edge weights for all six edges is a minimum.

b. Assign edge weights so that there are at least four shortest path length trees starting at A, and the sum of the edge weights for all six edges is a minimum.

3. Show the changes that must be made in Figure 9.49 to convert the *minimum_spanning_tree* algorithm to an algorithm to return the shortest path length tree.

4. Modify both the specification and implementation of the shortest path length tree algorithm so the user specifies the node used to begin construction of the tree.

5. Write a program that creates a connected graph containing n nodes and k edges where the edges connect nodes selected at random. Plot a graph that shows the time needed to construct the minimum spanning tree and the shortest path length tree as a function of n and k. Compare the results with the results of Exercises 9.6, 8.

6. An Euler path in a connected graph is a path that traverses every edge exactly once. It is known that a connected graph has an Euler path if and only if it contains at most two nodes of odd degree. (A graph node has odd degree if it has an odd number of edges.)

    a. Construct two example graphs—one that contains an Euler path and one that does not.

    b. Specify and implement a function that tests a connected graph to determine if it has an Euler path.

    c. Specify and implement a function that finds an Euler path in a given connected graph.

■ 9.8 Routing Algorithms for Computer Networks

Section 9.7 discussed the construction of shortest path length trees for a weighted graph. In this section a graph node will represent a node in a computer network, and an edge will represent a communications link in that network. An edge's weight usually represents an estimate of the cost or the expected time needed to transmit a packet of information over a link. A typical computer network—GTE Telenet's common carrier network—is shown in Figure 9.51.

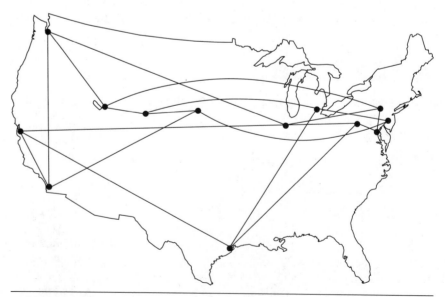

FIGURE   9.51 A typical computer network.

Our discussion will be illustrated by referring to the example network with 6 nodes and 10 edges in Figure 9.52. The edge weights (link costs) are shown as part of the figure.

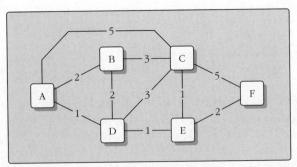

FIGURE 9.52 Example distributed network. Edge weights (link costs) are included.

The algorithm we are going to present is a distributed algorithm. That is, each node in the network carries out its own computations and passes information to each of its neighbors. It is the aggregate of local computations and information sharing among nodes that forms the complete algorithm. We will demonstrate the algorithm by examining it from the point of view of node A. Keep in mind that each other node in the network is simultaneously carrying out the same operations as node A.

Some notation will help describe the algorithm: $link(x, y)$ is the link cost between neighbors x and y. In Figure 9.52 link(A,B) is 2 and link(D,C) is 3.

$cost(s, d)$ is the minimum cost of sending a message from source node s to destination node d. We determine $cost(s, d)$ as follows: Let $cost(s, n, d)$ be the cost of sending a message from source node s to destination node d via s's neighbor n. That is,

$$cost(s, d) = \text{minimum } cost(s, n, d)$$
$$= \text{minimum}\{link(s,n) + cost(n, d)\}$$

where the minimum is determined for all neighbors n of s. For example, the cost of sending a message from A to C, for the data in Figure 9.52, is determined with the following computation:

$$cost(A, C) = \text{minimum } cost(A, n, C)$$
$$= \text{minimum}\{link(A, n) + cost(n, C)\}$$
$$= \text{minimum}\{link(A, B) + cost(B, C), link(A, D) + cost(D, C), link(A, C) + cost(C, C)\}$$
$$= \text{minimum}\{2 + 3, 1 + 2, 5 + 0\}$$
$$= 3$$

Thus, the minimum cost of sending a message from A to C is 3. The path to obtain this minimum is A, D, E, C. Note that all node A needs to know about sending a message to C is that the cheapest route begins by sending the message to D. It can then be left to D to start the message on the remainder of the journey to C.

The algorithm we now describe is based on the principle just illustrated. That is, each node must know, for each destination in the network, which neighbor to send a message to as the first step on the path to that destination. The source node does not know the entire path—only the neighbor that is the first step of the path. When the neighbor receives the message, the neighbor determines the next link on the path and transmits the message accordingly.

To support the routing algorithm each node will store the cost of sending a packet to each destination via each of its neighbors. Each node s in the network keeps two tables. The first table, called the **distance table**, stores cost(s, n, d) for each neighbor n and each destination d. The second table, the **routing table**, stores cost(s, d) along with the neighbor that generates that minimum cost. These two tables are shown in Figure 9.54 for node A for our sample network. Compare Figures 9.53 and 9.54 carefully to verify that the values in Figure 9.54 correctly represent the data in Figure 9.53.

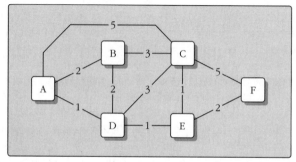

FIGURE 9.53 Sample network. This is the same as Figure 9.52. It is repeated for ease of reference.

	cost(x, n, d) for each neighbor n					
A						
Destination	*B*	*C*	*D*	*Destination*	*next* (n)	*min_cost*(x, d) = *min*{cost(x, n, d)}
B	2	8	3	B	B	2
C	5	5	3	C	D	3
D	4	7	1	D	D	1
E	5	6	2	E	D	2
F	7	8	4	F	D	4
	(a)				(b)	

FIGURE 9.54 The (a) distance table and (b) routing table for node A and the network in Figure 9.53.

Our interest now is—given a set of starting values (e.g., Figure 9.54)—how individual nodes respond to changes in network conditions. In most large networks such changes occur at least every few minutes so adjusting to them is the dominant activity for the distributed shortest path length algorithm.

Given a set of starting values, a shortest path algorithm needs to be able to respond to three types of changes: (1) A new link is added to the network, or a link that had been down is repaired. (2) A link's cost changes, or a link fails or is otherwise removed from the network. (3) A node responds to a routing message received from a neighbor as a result of a change of type (1) or (2) elsewhere in the network. To help state the algorithms for these changes, we repeat the changes using the notation described earlier.

The shortest path algorithm needs to be able to respond to three types of change in the network:

1. A link between s and s's neighbor n^*, with cost link(s, n^*), is added to the network.
2. The link cost between s and s's neighbor n^* changes to link(s, n^*). If a link goes down, its cost becomes infinite.
3. A control message [d, cost(n, d)] is received from neighbor n by node s. This message tells node s that the minimum cost of sending a message from n to d is now cost(n, d).

We will describe the algorithm for each of these three cases in general and in terms of a specific example.

Figure 9.55 shows the example network assuming the link from A to B is down. Figure 9.56 shows the distance and routing tables corresponding to Figure 9.55. Suppose link(A, B), with cost(A, B) = 2, comes up. What does A do?

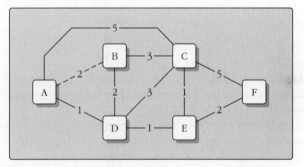

FIGURE 9.55 Example network with the link from A to B down.

The response of node A to link(A, B) coming up is described following this paragraph. As you study the text description of the algorithm, also examine Figure 9.57, where the algorithm's effects on the routing and distance tables are shown. The changes to the tables are annotated to show the step of the algorithm that caused the change.

	cost(s, n, d) for each neighbor n					cost(s, d) =
Destination	B	C	D	Destination	next	min{cost(s, n, d)}
B	—	8	3	B	D	3
C	—	5	3	C	D	3
D	—	7	1	D	D	1
E	—	6	2	E	D	2
F	—	8	4	F	D	4

FIGURE 9.56 Distance and routing tables with link(A, B) down.

	cost(s, n, d) for each neighbor n					cost(s, d) =
Destination	B	C	D	Destination	next	min{cost(s, n, d)}
B	2:[a]	8	3	B	B:[c]	2:[c]
C	—	5	3	C	D	3
D	—	7	1	D	D	1
E	—	6	2	E	D	2
F	—	8	4	F	D	4

FIGURE 9.57 Link(A, B) comes up with cost 2. The distance and routing tables that result are shown. Annotations show the step of the algorithm that produces new values.

Here is the response of node A to link(A, B) coming up:

[a] Set cost(A, B, B) to 2 in the distance table. Note that cost(A, B, B) is equal to link(A, B).

[b] Find the minimum value of cost(A, n, B) and the neighbor that leads to the minimum cost. For our example, the minimum cost is 2 and the neighbor is B.

[c] Since the minimum cost from [b] is less than cost(A, B) in the routing table in Figure 9.56, update the routing table with the values from [b], and send the control message [B, 2] to all of A's neighbors.

[d] Send the control messages [B, 2], [C, 3], [D, 1], [E, 2], [F, 4] to neighbor B.

Observe that node A sends the control message [B, 2] to all of A's neighbors. This informs each neighbor that A has just discovered a cheaper way to send messages to B. Each neighbor must now check to see what effect this will have on its own tables. We will see how shortly.

Node A also sends all the information in its routing table to B. This is because B is a new neighbor of A and before getting these messages has no information about sending messages via A.

The algorithm just described in a particular case is now generalized as shown.

1. A link between s and s's neighbor n^*, with cost link(s, n^*), is added to the network. What does s do?

   [a] Set cost(s, n^*, n^*) to link(s, n^*) in s's distance table.

   [b] Let N be s's neighbor that minimizes cost(x, n, n^*) for all neighbors n. Let C be cost(x, N, n^*). In Figure 9.57, N is B and C is 2.

   [c] If C is less than the value of cost(x, n^*) in the routing table then

      (i) in the row of the routing table with destination n^*, set next to N and cost(s, d) to C.

      (ii) send the control message [n^*, C] to all neighbors.

   [d] Node s sends the control messages [d_1, cost(s, d_1)], [d_2, cost(s,d_2)], ..., [d_n, cost(s, d_n)] for all destination nodes d_k to node n^*.

The next part of the algorithm is needed when a link cost changes. This will be illustrated by increasing the cost of link(A, D) from 1 to 5. What does A do in this case? (Note that D will initiate similar changes.) Figure 9.58 shows the network including two values of the link cost between A and D.

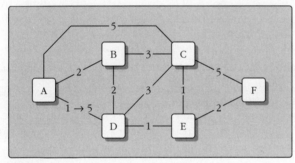

FIGURE 9.58 The cost of link A,D increases from 1 to 5.

The three parts of the algorithm are described below and applied to distance and routing tables in Figure 9.59. Study Figures 9.58 and 9.59 in parallel with the algorithm description. Note that Figure 9.59 shows the tables as they would be with link(A, D) = 1, then gives the changes due to steps [a], [b], and [c] using the symbol =>.

[a] Change the value of cost(A, D, d) for each destination d. In this case add 4 to each cost in the column corresponding to destination D.

[b] For each destination d, find the minimum value of cost(A, n, d) and the corresponding neighbor n. In Figure 9.59, for each row in the destination table, find the minimum cost and the neighbor corresponding to that cost.

[c] For each destination d, if the minimum cost found in [b] is less than cost(A, d) in the routing table, update the routing table with the values from [b], and send control messages to all neighbors. For our example, the control messages sent to all neighbors are [C, 5], [D, 4], [E, 5], [F, 7].

Destination	cost(x, n, d) for each neighbor n			Destination	next (n)	cost(x, d) = min{cost(x, n, d)}
	B	*C*	*D*			
B	2	8	3 => 7	B	B	2
C	5	5	3 => 7	C	D => C	3 => 5
D	4	7	1 => 5	D	D => B	1 => 4
E	5	6	2 => 6	E	D => B	2 => 5
F	7	8	4 => 8	F	D => B	4 => 7

FIGURE 9.59 Changes in the distance and routing tables at node A due to increasing the cost of link (A, D) from 1 to 5. The following control messages are sent to all neighbors: [C, 5], [D, 4], [E, 5], [F, 7].

A general description of the response of a node to cost change for one of its lengths—link—is given next.

2. The value of link(s, n^*) changes. How does s respond?

    [a] All entries in column n^* of s's distance table are modified by an amount equal to the change in the link cost. If the link goes down, these costs are set to infinity.

    [b] For each destination node, compute the minimum of cost(x, n, d). Let N_d be the neighbor that yields the minimum cost for destination d, and let C_d be that minimum cost.

    [c] **for** each destination node d
        if C_d is less than the value of cost(s, d) in the routing table **then**
        enter N_d and C_d in the routing table for destination d, and send the control message [N_d, C_d] to all neighbors of s.

The final piece of the algorithm describes how a node reacts to a control message from a neighbor. To illustrate this case we describe how node A responds to, not a single control message, but all the control messages received due to increasing the cost of link (D, E) from 1 to 5 (Figure 9.60). The advantage of this approach is that the discussion can be related to a change in the graph.

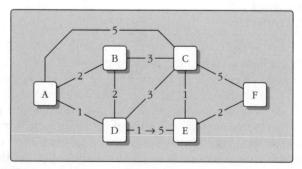

FIGURE 9.60 The cost of link (D, E) is increased from 1 to 5.

Control messages, [C, 3], [E, 4], and [F, 6] are received by node A from neighbor D. These reflect changes in the shortest paths from D to destinations C, E, and F. What does A do?

Consider only the control message [C, 3]. Since this message is from D, it will only affect the value for sending a message to destination C via neighbor D.

[a] In the destination table set cost(A, D, C) = link(A, D) + cost(D, C) = 1 + 3 = 4. This change is shown in the destination table in Figure 9.61.
[b] Find the minimum value of cost(A, n, C), 4 in the example, and the associated neighbor, D in Figure 9.61.

	cost(x, n, d) *for each neighbor* n					
Destination	B	C	D	Destination	*next* (n)	*cost*(x, d) = *min*{cost(x, n, d)}
B	2	8	3	B	B	2
C	5	5	3 =>4	C	D	3 =>4
D	4	7	1	D	D	1
E	5	6	2 =>5	E	D	2 =>5
F	7	8	4 =>7	F	D =>B	4 =>7

FIGURE 9.61 Changes in the distance and routing tables due to node A receiving the control messages [C, 3], [E, 4], and [F, 7]. The following control messages are sent to all neighbors: [C, 4], [E, 5], [F, 7].

[c] Add the new minimum cost and corresponding neighbor to the routing table, and send the control message [D, 4] to all neighbors of A; that is, to B, C, and D.

Figure 9.61 shows the changes for all three control messages. Following Figure 9.61 is a description of the general algorithm for a node's reaction to a control message.

3. A control message [d, cost*(n, d)] is received by node s from neighbor n. How does s respond?
   [a] If $d = s$, do nothing; otherwise, set cost(x, n, d) = link(s, n) + cost*(n, d).
   [b] Compute the minimum value of cost(s, n, d) for destination d. Let N be the neighbor that yields the minimum cost, and let C be that minimum cost.
   [c] **if** C is less than the value of cost(s, d) in the routing table **then** enter N and C in the routing table for destination d, and send the control message [N, C] to all neighbors of s.

The algorithm is complete. A review of its three parts shows that each piece is similar to the other two. In general what happens is the following.

A node, call it s, receives new information about the cost of sending a packet to destination d via neighbor n. The new information is put into s's distance table. The distance table is examined to see if the new value(s) produce change(s) in the entries in the routing table. If so, the new routing table information is sent to all appropriate neighbors.

It is complex, but it can be shown that this distributed algorithm always converges to a correct shortest path length result. The contrast between the centralized shortest path length algorithm in Section 9.7 and this distributed algorithm is striking.

In Section 9.7 we compute the shortest path length from one node, call it S, to all other nodes in a network. Each step of the algorithm adds one node and one edge to an existing graph, call it SPL. At each step SPL is a tree such that the path from S to any node in SPL has minimum path length among those available in the original graph. The edge that is added to SPL is the one that results in the shortest path from S to a node that is not in SPL but is a neighbor of a node that is in SPL. This algorithm can be implemented using a priority queue to store information about nodes that are neighbors of nodes in SPL.

The distributed algorithm described in this section takes a different approach. Each node in the network communicates directly only with its neighbors. Each node depends on its neighbors for information about the path length from that neighbor to each node in the network. Further, a node does not know the shortest path to a destination node—it only knows the neighbor that is on that path. To determine the neighbor on the shortest path to a particular destination, a node must combine the link costs to its neighbors with the information about path lengths the neighbors themselves have supplied. The data structures needed to support this algorithm are tables rather than priority queues, and the main computation is finding the minimum of a row of values in a table.

EXERCISES 9.8

1. Start with the network in Figure 9.52 and delete the edge connecting nodes C and E.
   a. Construct the distance and routing tables for E and its three neighbors.
   b. Show the change in E's distance and routing tables due to adding an edge between nodes C and E with weight 1.
   c. Show the messages sent by node E to each of its neighbors as a result of the addition in (b).
   d. Show the changes in the distance and routing tables for each of E's neighbors due to the messages sent in (c).

2. Write an Ada representation for a simulation of (a) an individual node in a routing network and (b) an entire network.

3. Write specifications for the operations on the nodes in a routing network using the representations in Exercise 2.

■ 9.9 Directed Graphs

As defined in Section 9.2, a directed graph is a graph whose edges have direction. Thus an edge not only relates two nodes, it also specifies a predecessor–successor relationship. A graph can be represented as a directed graph with two edges, one in each direction, between each pair of related graph nodes.

A directed graph, frequently referred to as a digraph, can be illustrated by using arrowheads to show the direction of each edge. An example is shown in Figure 9.62. A directed path is a sequence of nodes $d_1, d_2, \ldots, d_n$, such that there is a directed edge from d_k to d_{k+1} for all appropriate k. In this section a directed path will be referred to as a path. In Figure 9.62 an example path is A, B, D, E.

The representation of a directed graph has similarities to and differences from the representation of an ordinary graph. Let AM be a two-dimensional array used to provide an adjacency matrix representation of a directed graph. If AM(i, j) is true, there is a directed edge from node i to node j. In a directed graph AM is generally not symmetric as it would be if AM were an ordinary graph. Therefore, the full matrix is needed to represent a directed graph. Figure 9.63 shows the adjacency matrix representation of the digraph in Figure 9.62.

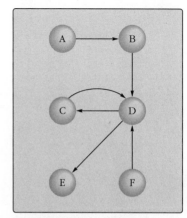

FIGURE 9.62 An example directed graph.

	A	B	C	D	E	F
A	—	true	0	0	0	0
B	0	—	0	true	0	0
C	0	0	—	true	0	0
D	0	0	true	—	true	0
E	0	0	0	0	—	0
F	0	0	0	true	0	—

FIGURE 9.63 Adjacency matrix representation of the digraph in Figure 9.62.

Next, Figure 9.64 shows an adjacency list representation of the digraph in Figure 9.62. The node list is the same as it was for (ordinary) graphs. An edge list entry, which is a single node, represents a directed edge from the node listed in the node list to the node listed in the edge list.

The basic graph operations—*insert_node, insert_edge, delete_node,* and *delete_edge*—are simpler for a digraph because each edge produces only one entry in an adjacency matrix and appears on only one edge list in an adjacency matrix. Exercises 9.9, 1 and 9.9, 2 ask you to modify the specification and implementation of a graph so that they apply to a directed graph.

Traversal of directed graphs is similar to traversal of graphs. Performance improves because traversing a graph requires visiting each edge twice, whereas traversing a digraph requires only one visit of each edge node.

A digraph is more complicated with respect to connectedness. If G is a graph with nodes g_1 and g_2, then the existence of a path from g_1 to g_2 assures us that there is a path from g_2 to g_1. This is not true if G is a directed graph.

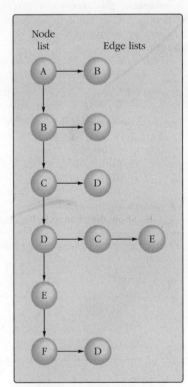

FIGURE 9.64 Adjacency list representation of the digraph in Figure 9.62.

If G is a graph and S_G is a connected subgraph of G, then there is a path between every pair of S_G's nodes. There is no analogous statement for a directed graph.

Let d be a node in a directed graph D. Let $S_D(d)$ be the subgraph of D that includes d and all nodes connected to it. If d_1 and d_2 are nodes in $S_D(d)$ it is not true, in general, that there is a path from d_1 to d_2. The question of which nodes in $S_D(d)$ are connected by a path is answered in the next section.

9.9.1 Transitive Closure

Let D be a directed graph, and let TC_D be the directed graph formed by adding an edge from d_1 to d_2 whenever d_1 and d_2 are nodes in D and there is a path from d_1 to d_2. TC_D is the *transitive closure* of D.

Warshall gives us an elegant algorithm to compute the transitive closure of the adjacency matrix representation of a digraph. It is given in Figure 9.65. To see how Warshall's algorithm works, refer to the directed graph in Figure 9.66 and its adjacency matrix representation in Figure 9.67. A detailed discussion of this example follows Figures 9.65, 9.66, and 9.67.

```
procedure Warshall (the_graph : in out graph) is
-- assumes:   the_graph is a directed graph.
-- results:   the_graph is replaced by its transitive closure.
-- Length 6   Complexity 6
begin
    for i in 1 .. the_graph.size loop              -- Add paths that contain the ith node as an interior node.
        for j in 1 .. the_graph.size loop
        if the_graph.edges(j,i) then               -- If there is a path from j to i, and there is a path from i to k, then
            for k in 1 .. the_graph.size loop       -- record that there is a path from j to k.
            if the_graph.edges(i,k) then
                the_graph.edges(j,k) := true;
            end if;
            end loop;
        end if;
        end loop;
    end loop;
end Warshall;
```

FIGURE 9.65 Warshall's algorithm for computing the transitive closure of a digraph.

The basic idea of Warshall's algorithm is that if there is a path from j to i and another from i to k, then there is a path from j to k. This idea is used to compute the transitive closure with a single pass over the adjacency matrix. To see how, we will use the example in Figures 9.66 and 9.67. We will also use the notion of an interior node. If $d_1, d_2, \ldots, d_n$ is a path, then all the nodes except d_1 and d_n are *interior nodes* of that path.

When i is 1, Warshall's algorithm looks for pairs *edge(j, 1), edge(1, k)*, which are both true. When this occurs there is a path $j, 1, k$ from j to k so *edge(j, k)* is set to true. The effect is to short circuit all paths that contain 1 as an interior node. For the digraph in Figure 9.66, *edge*(3, 2) is set true because of the path 3, 1, 2.

When *i* is 2, Warshall's algorithm adds paths that contain 2 as an interior node. Since paths containing 1 as an interior node are already short circuited, the result is that all paths between nodes involving 1, or 2, or both as interior nodes are short circuited. For the digraph in Figure 9.66, *edge*(1, 4) is set true because of the path 1, 2, 4, and *edge*(3, 4) is set true because of the path 3, 1, 2, 4.

When *i* is 3, Warshall's algorithm adds 3 to the list of possible interior nodes. For the digraph in Figure 9.66, *edge*(4, 1) is set true because of the path 4, 3, 1; *edge*(4, 2) is set true because of the path 4, 3, 1, 2; and *edge*(4, 4) is set true because of the path 4, 3, 1, 2, 4.

In general, processing $i = k$ in Warshall's algorithm produces an adjacency matrix that includes an edge between nodes p and q if there is a path between them that contains nodes 1, 2, ..., k as interior nodes. Figure 9.68 shows the adjacency matrix for the transitive closure of the digraph in Figure 9.66. The validity of Warshall's algorithm is established by induction.

9.9.2 Deadlock Detection

An important problem in computer science is ***deadlock detection***. We start with a simple example to illustrate the concept.

Consider two processes, call them P_1 and P_2, running simultaneously on a computer. Suppose these two processes are accessing two objects called O_1 and O_2. If the objects are bank accounts, then the processes can be programs that transfer funds, make withdrawals and deposits, or perform some other banking function. If the objects contain information about airline flights, the processes can be reserving seats, preparing summary reports, or performing some other business transaction. Whatever the specific case, we assume that two processes are *not* permitted to access one object simultaneously in order to prevent processes from interfering with one another.

For example, suppose P_1 and P_2 both read the balance in one bank account, which is $1,000. Also suppose that P_1 deposits $200 and writes the new balance, $1,200, to the account. P_2 still has the $1,000 balance it originally read. If P_2 processes a $200 withdrawal, it will write a final balance of $800. If the two processes had written their results in the reverse order, the final balance would be $1,200 instead of $800. In either case the result is wrong because the correct final balance is $1,000.

This example illustrates the kind of interference between processes that must be avoided. A common method to control simultaneous access is to allow processes to lock objects so that other processes have either limited or no access to the locked objects. Locks that do not permit any access by other processes are called ***exclusive locks***. We will consider only exclusive locks in this section.

Suppose that P_1 has a lock on O_1 and is waiting for a lock on O_2. Also suppose that P_2 has a lock on O_2 and is waiting for a lock on O_1. A moment's reflection will show you that each process is waiting for the other, and unless

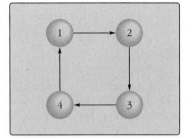

FIGURE 9.66 A directed graph to illustrate the application of Warshall's algorithm.

	1	2	3	4
1	0	true	0	0
2	0	0	true	0
3	0	0	0	true
4	0	0	0	0

FIGURE 9.67 Adjacency matrix representation of the graph in Figure 9.66.

	1	2	3	4
1	true	true	true	true
2	true	true	true	true
3	true	true	true	true
4	true	true	true	true

FIGURE 9.68 Adjacency matrix representation of the transitive closure of the graph in Figure 9.66.

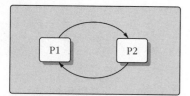

FIGURE 9.69 A waits-for graph that shows that P_1 waits for a lock held by P_2 and that P_2 waits for a lock held by P_1. The two processes are deadlocked.

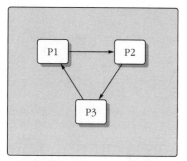

FIGURE 9.70 A waits-for graph that shows a deadlock involving three processes.

one process gives up its lock so that the other can proceed, both processes will wait forever. Such a situation is called *deadlock* or *deadly embrace*.

There is a close relationship between deadlocks and directed graphs. To see this, let the nodes of a graph be the currently executing processes, and let there be a directed edge from node P_1 to P_2 if P_1 is waiting to lock an object on which P_2 holds a lock. The directed graph for the deadlock situation just described is shown in Figure 9.69. Such directed graphs are usually called *waits-for graphs*.

Deadlock can involve more than two processes. Look at Figure 9.70, where P_1 is waiting for a lock held by P_2, P_2 is waiting for a lock held by P_3, and P_3 is waiting for a lock held by P_1. None of these three processes can proceed unless one of them gives up a lock needed by one of the other two.

Some thought will convince you that a deadlock exists among a set of processes if and only if the waits-for graph for those processes contains a cycle. The objective of the remainder of this section is to discuss an algorithm that will detect a cycle in a waits-for graph and hence detect deadlock.

Note in passing that there is a variety of approaches to dealing with deadlocks. For example, it is possible to assume that a process that has been executing longer than some specified time is deadlocked. Such a transaction is aborted, its locks are removed, and it is started over. This policy has risks; a transaction that requires a long time to execute may be started over again and again, using system resources but never finishing. A study of several deadlock resolution techniques and their performance implications is given in Agrawal, Carey, and McVoy (1987). We continue with the examination of a specific technique.

We assume a waits-for graph is maintained for all processes and for the locks for which they are waiting. A process, say P_j, requests a lock on object O_k, and it is discovered that another process, say P_q, already holds a lock on O_k. If the system is not deadlocked, we want to know if allowing P_j to wait for P_q will create a deadlock. Note that this is a simple version of the general deadlock problem. We do not need to search for any conceivable deadlock; we only need to know if allowing P_j to wait for P_q will create a deadlock. If so, either we can not permit P_j to wait or we can take locks away from some other process involved in the deadlock that would result. We will not worry about what to do about an impending deadlock. We will consider only how to discover such a deadlock.

Since checking for a potential deadlock is pure overhead—it accomplishes no real work—we want the deadlock checking algorithm to be fast. The following description is taken from Jiang (1988):

> In this paper a new algorithm for the treatment of deadlock is described. It is not only very efficient . . . but also fairly simple. With this algorithm one can detect all deadlocks as soon as possible and list all participators in the corresponding cycle of the "waits-for" graph.

The algorithm in Figure 9.71 shows the basic process. This algorithm is used for the adjacency matrix representation of a graph discussed throughout this chapter. The only difference is that the elements stored in the edge array

function deadlock (the_graph : graph; k : index) **return** boolean **is**
-- *assumes:* *the_graph is a directed graph.*
-- *results:* *Returns true if the_graph contains a cycle that includes node k; otherwise returns false.*
-- *Length 9   Complexity 6*
    the_copy : graph := the_graph;
begin
    for len **in** 1 .. the_copy.size − 1 **loop**   -- *Construct paths of lengths 1 .. the_graph.size − 1.*
        for i **in** 1 .. the_copy.size **loop**
            if the_copy.edge(k,i) = len **then**   -- *Is there is a path of length len from k to i?*
                for j **in** 1 .. the_copy.size **loop**   -- *If so, is there a path of length len + 1 from k to j?*
                    if (the_copy.edge(i,j) = 1 **and** the_copy.edge(k,j) = 0) **then**
                        the_copy.edge(k,j) := len + 1;   -- *If there is, record it.*
                    end if;
                end loop;
            end if;
        end loop;
    end loop;
    return the_copy.edge(k,k) > 0;
end deadlock;

FIGURE 9.71 An algorithm, Jiang (1988), to check for a cycle containing node k in directed graph G.

are of type *integer* instead of type *boolean*. This algorithm tests to see if process *k* is involved in a deadlock. A study of the algorithm in Figure 9.71 will uncover similarities to Warshall's transitive closure algorithm.

In Jiang (1988) the basic algorithm in Figure 9.71 is extended in two ways. First, a deadlock may be discovered before the procedure terminates. Think of ways to modify procedure deadlock so it will stop as soon as a deadlock is discovered. In this regard, observation of real systems indicates that most deadlocks involve only two processes. How efficient is your improved procedure for determining a deadlock between node *k* and one other node?

A second issue is the determination of all the processes that participate in a discovered deadlock. Discuss how that might be done using the algorithm in Figure 9.71.

9.9.3 Topological Sorting

The concept of *topological sorting* is introduced using the directed graph in Figure 9.72. A topological order for its five nodes is any linear relationship among the nodes that preserves the successor relationship among the graph elements.

Figure 9.73 shows two topological orders for the graph elements in Figure 9.72. Observe that if *Y* is the successor of *X* in Figure 9.72, then *Y* is the successor of *X* in both orders given in Figure 9.73.

One application of topological sorting is to let nodes represent operations to be performed and to let edges represent precedence relationships among the operations. In a construction project the nodes might represent jobs such as electrical wiring, plumbing, and interior wall installation. There are pre-

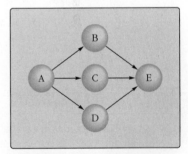

FIGURE 9.72 A directed graph used to illustrate topological sorting.

A B   C   D   E
A C   D   B   E

FIGURE 9.73 Two topological orders for the objects in the directed graph in Figure 10.

cedence relationships such as completing electrical wiring before installing interior walls. A topological ordering of such events in a large construction project helps ensure that conflicting jobs are not performed in the wrong order.

A digraph that contains a cycle does not have a topological order so we can only topologically sort directed acyclic graphs. Such graphs are often called *dags*. There are several approaches to topological sorting; we describe one of them below.

The basic idea of our topological sort algorithm is to find a node with no successor, remove it from the graph, and add it to a list. Repeating this process until the graph is empty produces a list that is the reverse of some topological order. A description of this process is given in Figure 9.74.

Let *the_list* be an empty list.

while the_graph has a node with no successors **loop**
    remove a node with no successors and append it to the tail of the_list;
end loop;

if the loop terminates with the graph empty **then**
    the_list contains the nodes in an order that is the reverse of topological order;
else the graph contains a cycle;
end if;

FIGURE 9.74 An algorithm to sort a directed graph into topological order.

To implement the algorithm in Figure 9.74, start with a depth first search procedure. In a depth first search (of a directed graph) the stack is popped each time a node that has no successors is found. Therefore, instead of processing each node as it is encountered, wait until a node is found with no successors and append it to a list—then pop the stack and continue executing depth first search.

EXERCISES 9.9

1. Modify Specification 9.1 so that it gives the specification of a directed graph.
2. Modify Package Body 9.1 so that it implements the specification of a directed graph.
3. What is the transitive closure of a directed graph that is (a) a list? (b) a binary tree? When is the transitive closure of a directed graph equal to the directed graph?
4. What is the performance (order of magnitude) of Warshall's algorithm (Figure 9.65)?
5. Modify function *deadlock* (Figure 9.71) so that it terminates as soon as a deadlock is detected.
6. Modify function *deadlock* (Figure 9.71) so that it returns a list of all processes that participate in a deadlock. If there is no deadlock, have it return an empty list.
7. What is the performance (order of magnitude) of the deadlock algorithm in Figure 9.71?

■ 9.10 Summary

Considering a graph with n nodes and e edges, in Chapter 9 we looked at a few of the many operations on graphs. Basic operations for constructing a graph, such as *insert_node* and *insert_edge,* require between $O(1)$ and $O(n)$ operations. Operation *delete_node,* which also requires deleting any edges that connect the *target_node* to its neighbors, may require $O(n^2)$ operations.

Traversal operations, breadth and depth first, require $O(n + e)$ operations for an adjacency list representation and $O(n^2)$ for an adjacency matrix representation. If the graph contains most of its edges, then $O(e) = O(n^2)$ and the adjacency matrix representation is preferred. Otherwise, the adjacency list representation is preferred, since it conserves storage and requires less effort for traversal.

A priority first search generalizes the notions of breadth first and depth first searches and is most efficiently implemented using a priority queue as an auxiliary data structure. The performance for a priority first search is bounded by $O[(n + e) \log n]$ for an adjacency list representation and $O[n^2 + (n + e) \log n]$. These bounds are very conservative, since $\log n$ is a very conservative bound for the effort required for one priority queue operation. Priority first searches were applied in Section 9.7 to find minimum spanning trees and the shortest paths between nodes in weighted trees.

In Section 9.8, the shortest path length problem was considered from the point of view of routing messages in computer networks. A distributed algorithm was described and contrasted with the centralized algorithm described in Section 9.7.

Three problems associated with weighted graphs were considered in Section 9.9: finding the transitive closure, topological sorting, and deadlock detection. All of these problems were solved using graph traversal. A good source of additional graph problems and algorithms is Sedgewick (1988, Chapters 29–34).

10

Data Structure Design Notes

◼ 10.1 Introduction

In this chapter we present a discussion of the main issues involved in selecting the package designs in this text. Keep in mind that in addition to representing and implementing data structures using the tools provided by Ada, we also selected techniques that will present basic data structure topics in a way that will be clear to students in a first data structures course.

Section 10.2 reviews the basics of generic formal parameters for packages, then summarizes our use of these parameters. In the simplest case, such as the stacks in Specifications 3.1, 3.2, 3.3, and 3.4, there is a single generic parameter used to declare the type of object that will be placed in an instantiation of the stack package. In a more complex case, for example, the binary search tree in Specification 5.1, one generic parameter describes the objects stored in tree nodes, a second generic parameter describes the key values associated with each object, one generic function extracts a key value from an object, and two generic functions are used to order the objects in the tree.

Section 10.3 discusses two approaches to providing the representation of a data structure. One approach is to provide a *private* type in the specification and place the type's representation in the **private** clause. An alternative is to place the data structures representation in the package body.

Section 10.4 provides an overview of the specifications organized into a single table. The table presents the most important aspects of each data structure in a concise format that allows easy comparison of all the specifications.

Some packages contain operations that require the ability to process the generic objects stored in the data structure. An example is the traverse operation that processes each object in, for example, a list, tree, or graph. Such an operation must itself be generic, and Section 10.5 discusses these generic operations within generic packages.

One of Ada's interesting and useful data types is the *discriminant record*. Section 10.6 discusses this type and some of its uses in representing data structures. Finally, Section 10.7 provides an overview of the representations used for data structures in this text.

◼ 10.2 Generic Types

For the data structures we discuss (stacks, queues, lists, trees, etc.) the logic used to manipulate the structures is independent of the types of the objects encapsulated. Therefore, the packages used to implement the data structures are *generic*.

A formal generic parameter has the following possible types:

type T **is** (<>);	-- *A discrete type.*
type T **is range** <>;	-- *An integer type.*
type T **is digits** <>;	-- *A floating-point type.*
type T **is delta** <>;	-- *A fixed-point type.*
type T **is private**;	-- *Any type with assignment and equality defined.*
type T **is limited private**;	-- *Any type, assignment, and equality not defined.*

The objects manipulated by a stack, for example, are most naturally of generic type **private**. This allows the user to instantiate a stack with any component object type and allows the package body to use the predefined assignment operator. The objects manipulated by other data structures (lists, trees, hash tables, graphs,...) are private for the same reasons.

An object of a **private** type can be

- Passed as a parameter to a procedure or function
- Returned as the result of a function
- Assigned to an object of the same type
- Compared with another object of the same type using the relational operators = and /=

If the data structure objects require an identifier, we include a generic parameter of type *key_type* and a generic function, *key_of,* that extracts a key value from an object. The key value extracted from each object value makes it easy to search for and place objects in any appropriate data structure—such as a sorted list or a binary search tree.

If two values of type *key_type* are to be compared (e.g., during the search of a list or tree), a function is needed to compare two key values. If the default function "=" always returned the correct value, no further provision would be necessary. If *key_type* is actually of type record, or array, or string, or other composite type, however, then the default function "=" may not return the desired result. One way to allow the user to control this is with a generic subprogram parameter such as

with function equal (key1, key2 : key_type) **return** boolean;

This is the approach we have adopted.

Note that formal generic parameters may appear in three nearly identical forms:

with function "<" (item1, item2 : item_type) **return** boolean;   -- *or*
with function "<" (item1, item2 : item_type) **return** boolean **is** <>;   -- *or*
with function "<" (item1, item2 : item_type) **return** boolean **is** less_than;

The difference between these formal generic parameters is that in the first case an actual parameter must be provided for function "<", in the second case the actual parameter may be omitted if a function "<" (with matching profile) is visible at the point of instantiation of the package, and in the third case a default is provided by function *less_than* (with matching profile) that is visible at the point of the formal parameter declaration.

Data structures whose objects are not compared or ordered (stacks, queues, priority queues, etc.) are implemented using a generic package with the following formal generic parameter:

generic
        type object_type **is private**;

Many data structures require that their elements be tested for equality (lists, trees, graphs, etc.). They are implemented using a generic package with the following formal generic parameters:

```
generic
    type object_type is private;
    type key_type is private;
    with function key_of (the_object : object_type) return key_type;
    with function equal (key1, key2 : key_type) return boolean;
```

A default is not allowed for function *equal* primarily because it seems unlikely that a function with identifier *equal* and the correct profile would be available. Not allowing a default does provide some protection against inadvertent use of the wrong function—remote though that possibility may seem in this case.

Some data structures require that their elements be ordered (sorted lists, binary search trees, some types of graphs, etc.). They are implemented using a generic package with the following formal generic parameters:

```
generic
    type object_type is private;
    type key_type is private;
    with function key_of (the_object : object_type) return key_type;
    with function equal (key1, key2 : key_type) return boolean;
    with function "<" (key1, key2 : key_type) return boolean is <>;
```

They are ordered according to their key values. A default is allowed for function "<" because *key_type* is likely to be a subtype of *integer* or *string* or some other type for which function "<" is supplied by the Ada language.

■ 10.3 Private Clause and Data Types Defined in the Package Body

The basic principles of information hiding specify that the data structures used to represent an abstract data type **not** be provided as part of the specification. This prevents the user from manipulating, and perhaps corrupting, values of the type, and it suppresses unnecessary details so that the user's view is simplified.

If a data structure's type is given as part of the specification as, for example,

```
package binary_tree_package is
    type binary_tree is limited private;
```

then details of the type are given in the **private** section of the specification. An advantage of this approach is that instances of the type are declared in exactly the same way as instances of a predefined type. For example,

package trees **is new** binary_tree_package (⋯);

> tree1, tree2 : trees.binary_tree;
> forest : **array** (natural **range** 1 .. 100) **of** trees.binary_tree;

Since there may be many instances of type *binary_tree,* operations on trees must include a parameter of type *binary_tree* so the tree instance that is the target of the operation can be identified. For example, the insert operation for a *binary_tree* is specified as follows:

procedure insert (the_tree : **in out** binary_tree; the_object : object_type);
-- *results: A node containing the_object is added to the_tree.*
-- *exceptions: duplicate_object is raised if the_tree contains a key value equal to*
--   *key_of (the_object).*
                       tree_full is raised if it is not possible to add a node to the_tree.

If the data structure type is not declared in the public portion of its interface, then its representation is placed in the package body rather than in a **private** clause. This is done several times in the text. An example is Specification 3.1 for a stack. The package body that implements Specification 3.1 includes the type statements:

size   : natural **range** 0 .. max_size := 0;   -- *The size of the stack.*
objects   : **array** (1 .. max_size) **of** object_type;   -- *The objects stored in the stack.*

There are advantages and disadvantages to these two approaches. An advantage of placing the representation in the package body is that the data structure type is never a parameter for an operation. This simplifies the interface to the type. For example, the push operation in Specification 3.1 is the following:

procedure push (the_object : object_type);   -- *There is no formal parameter*
-- *results: the_object is appended to the stack as its top object.*   -- *of type stack.*
-- *exceptions: stack_overflow is raised if stack_size = max_size.*

Since this is an introductory text, using a representation that simplifies the interface to a data structure is considered an important objective. Observe that placing the data structure representation in the package body is not an option if any operation is applied to two or more instances of the data structure. For example, specification of the concatenate operation for strings is as follows:

function "&" (left, right : var_string) **return** var_string;
-- *assumes: length (left) + length (right) <= max_length.*
-- *results: Returns the string obtained by appending right to the end of left.*

This operation is not possible if only one instance of a string is provided by the string representation. The inability of a representation to support operations involving two or more instances of a data structure might be regarded as a limitation of this approach. Some data structures—stacks and queues are two examples—however, do not normally include such operations, so it is not normally a limitation for them.

Another limitation of placing a data structure's representation in the package body is that multiple instances of the data structure can only be obtained by multiple instantiations of the data structure's package. For example, obtaining two instances of the stack given in Specification 3.1 requires two instantiations along the lines of the following:

package first_stack **is new** stack(integer, 500);
package second_stack **is new** stack(float, 20);

Also observe that the choice between these representations does not really limit the user's flexibility, since converting from one representation scheme to the other is a minor undertaking.

Another important alternative must be mentioned. Suppose a package specification provides a type as a *limited private* type:

type some_type **is limited private**;

The **private** clause can then declare *some_type* as an access type:

private
    type some_type_representation;
    type some_type **is access** some_type_representation;
end;

The declaration of *some_type_declaration* is an incomplete declaration. Its full declaration can be provided in the package body. But from the user's point of view, this data structure behaves as if the full data structure representation was given in the **private** clause. The user can declare variables of type *some_type,* but the representation details are completely hidden in the package body.

A final important point—we use type **limited private** in the specification of data types in order to guarantee that the only access to a data type instance is via the operations in the specification. User access is therefore limited to the following:

An object of a **limited private** type can be

• Passed as a parameter to a procedure or function
• Returned as the result of a function

■ 10.4 Summary of Data Structure Specifications

A summary of the specifications for a representative sample of data structures in this text is shown in Figure 10.1. The figure abstracts the key aspects of the specifications to provide an overview and make it easy to do a comparison.

Packages	Generic parameters			Specifications	
	Private type(s)	Other parameters	Function(s) and procedures	*Limited* private *type*	Exceptions
stack (3.1)	object_type	max_size			stack_full stack_empty
dynamic stack (3.2)	object_type				stack_full stack_empty
stack (3.3)	object_type			stack (max_size : positive);	stack_full stack_empty
queue (3.4)	object_type			queue (max_size : positive);	queue_full queue_empty
priority_queue (3.5)	object_type priority		**function** priority_of; **function** "<" **is** <>;	priority_queue (max_size : positive);	queue_full queue_empty
list (4.1)	object_type	max_size		list(size : count := 0);	list_full list_empty
linked_list (4.2)	object_type			*linked_list is declared as a record type that can be accessed by the user*	list_full list_empty
indexed_list (4.3)	object_type			indexed_list (max_size : positive);	list_full list_empty faulty_position
sorted_list (4.4)	object_type key_type		**function** key_of; **function** "<" **is** ">"	sorted_list (max_size : positive);	list_full list_empty
ring (4.5)	object_type			ring;	ring_full ring_empty
sequential_io (4.7)	object_type			file_type;	status_error mode_error name_error use_error device_error end_error data_error
binary_tree (5.1)	object_type key_type		**function** key_of; **function** equal; **function** "<" **is** <>;	binary_tree;	tree_full tree_empty duplicate_node missing_node
AVL_tree (5.2)	object_type key_type		**function** key_of; **function** equal; **function** "<" **is** <>;	AVL_tree;	tree_full tree_empty duplicate_node missing_node

FIGURE 10.1 An abstraction of the text specifications. **(continued)**

Figure 10.1 (continued)

Packages	Generic parameters			Specifications	
	Private type(s)	Other parameters	Function(s) and procedures	Limited private type	Exceptions
heap (5.3)	object_type priority		**function** priority_of; **function** "<" **is** <>;	heap is declared as an array type that can be accessed by the user	
B_tree (5.4)	object_type key_type	order	**function** key_of; **function** "<" **is** <>;	B_tree;	tree_full tree_empty duplicate_object missing_object
set (7.1)		object_type **is** (<>);		set;	
hash_table (7.2)	object_type	key_type **is** (<>);	**function** key_of;	hash_table (table_size : natural)	duplicate_key hash_table_full missing_object
string (8.1)		max_length;		var_string (length : string_length := 0)	string_full string_empty
graph (matrix) (9.1)	object_type key_type	edge_weight **is range** <>;	**function** key_of;	graph (max_size : natural);	graph_full graph_empty duplicate_node duplicate_edge missing_node missing_edge
graph (list) (9.2)	object_type key_type	edge_weight **is range** <>;	**function** key_of; **function** "<" **is** <>;	graph;	graph_full graph_empty duplicate_node duplicate_edge missing_node missing_edge

FIGURE 10.1 *(continued)*

Three columns are used to describe the generic formal parameters. In general, as noted above, Ada provides six distinct types for generic parameters. Our data structures use only one of the six, type *private,* and private items are listed in one column.

Additional generic parameters that are neither private nor functions and procedures are, in a few cases, required, and are shown in a second column. In a few cases, the parameters are *discrete* types that are not *private* [type *T* is (<>)] or *integer* types [type *T* is range <>].

The third generic column lists the names of generic procedures and functions of the type. The "is <>" suffix is included to distinguish the cases in which a default that is visible in the scope of the instantiation may be used.

The specification overview contains two columns. If the specification includes a *private* type, that type is shown. If it is a record with discriminant, its discriminant is also shown. It a *limited private* type is not shown, then representation of the data structure is part of the package body. The final column lists the exceptions.

You are encouraged to invest some time looking at Figure 10.1. At the level of abstraction shown, the data structures of this text are all very similar. At any reasonable lower level of abstraction, however, the operations and their specifications appear. The result is that there are significant differences among the data structures.

■ 10.5 Data Structure Traversal

For many data structures a traversal algorithm (or iterator) that applies some user-declared process to each component of the structure is important. The problem is that there are two unknowns—the process to be applied to each object as the traversal progresses and the object to which the process is to be applied. The approach we use is to include a generic traversal procedure for such data structures. For example, a traverse procedure for a binary tree, taken from Specification 5.1, is shown:

```
generic
     with procedure process (object : object_type; level : positive);
procedure traverse (the_tree : binary_tree; traverse_order : order);
```

-- **results:**   *The object in each node in the_tree and the level that node occupies in the_tree are passed to*
--   *procedure process. The order in which nodes are processed is determined by the value of traverse_order*
--   *as follows:*

--   **if** *traverse_order is pre_order* **then**
--   *each node is processed before any node in either of its subtrees.*
--   **elsif** *traverse_order is in_order* **then**
--   *each node is processed after all nodes in its left subtree and before any node in its right subtree*
--   **else** *traverse_order is post_order* **and** *each node is processed after any node in either of its subtrees.*

The details of passing each object in the binary tree to procedure process are handled by the implementation. The user need not be aware of how the tree is implemented. On the other hand, the implementor cannot know what an object is or how the user wants an object processed. The user supplies this information by instantiating *traverse* with an appropriate procedure as a generic parameter for *process*.

An alternative to the approach above is to make *process* a generic parameter for the package instead of a single procedure within the package. The trouble with this approach is that every instantiation of the package would then have to provide a *process* procedure. This would be true even for instantiations that make no use of the *traverse* procedure.

With the approach above only applications that actually use *traverse* need supply procedure *process*. All other users can simply ignore *traverse* and its instantiation.

■ 10.6 Discriminant Records in the Representation of Data Structures

In Ada, if a discriminant record is declared with a default value for the discriminant,

```
type count is natural range 0 .. max_size;
type array_of_objects is array (positive range <>) of object_type;

type list (size : count := 0) is record
     objects : array_of_objects(1 .. size);
end record;
```

and if a variable of that type is declared without a constraint,

```
the_list : list;
```

then *the_list* is unconstrained. That is, the value of the discriminant of *the_list* (*size* in the example) may be changed from time to time as needed. The only requirement is that if the discriminant value is changed, then values must be provided for all components of the discriminant record. For example, assuming that *object_type* is *integer,* we might initialize *the_list* as follows:

```
the_list := (4, (1, 2, 3, 4) );
```

If we declare *list1* and *list2* as

```
list1 : array_of_objects (1 .. 10) := (others => 55);
list 2 : array_of_objects (1 .. 50) := (others => 0)
```

we could, at any time, assign *the_list* the value

```
the_list := (10, list1);
the_list := (50, list2);
```

or, to emphasize the point that *the_list.size* can be changed at will,

```
the_list := (list1'length, list1);
the_list := (list2'length, list2);
```

This approach is advantageous in representing a variety of data structures, and examples are given in Specifications 3.3. and 4.1. In these three examples, the type is *limited private* so the user can only access the data structure through the operations provided in the specification. The user is, however, permitted to assign the discriminant value for each declaration of a data structure instance. The discriminant value fixes the maximum size of the data structure.

In the examples in this text a single discriminant is used in each case. Ada, however, allows any number of discriminants for a single type.

A subtle problem involving *sliding semantics* arises in some cases. Suppose we declare

another_list : array_of_objects (5 .. 15);

so that *the_list* and *another_list* have the same number of components but different index ranges. The assignments

the_list := another_list;
the_list (2 .. 5) := another_list (8 .. 11);

are correct and provide examples of sliding semantics in Ada. That is, the range on the right side of an assignment slides in order to match the range on the left side. The sublety occurs because sliding semantics applies in some instances but not in others. Specifically, sliding semantics occurs in assignment statements (as above), in array object initializations, and during explicit type conversion. Otherwise, sliding semantics does not apply. In particular, sliding semantics does not occur for an aggregate component.

For example, if we attempt

the_list := (length'another_list, another_list);

then *constraint_error* is raised because the index range of *another_list* does not match the index range of *the_list.objects*. One way around this is based on an appropriate subtype conversion. For example,

declare
    subtype anchor **is** array_of_objects (1 .. length'another_list);
begin
    the_list := (length'another_list, anchor (another_list));
end;

Examples of this situation occur in the implementations of functions *delete* and *sub_string* in Package Body 8.1 and in function *tail* in Package Body 4.1 (Lists).

■ 10.7 Private Clause and Representation of Data Structures

The specification of a data structure may also include a **private** clause. The **private** clause provides representation details not available to the user but available to the programming environment. If a specification does not include representation details in a **private** clause, then those details must be provided in the package body.

Figure 10.2 shows the representation details for selected data structures and uses two columns to emphasize whether the representation is supplied in a **private** clause or in the package body. In each case the representation is annotated with a short (and more abstract) description of the representation.

Package	*Private clause*	*Package body*
stack (3.1)	*Implemented as an array of max_size objects.* →	**subtype** count **is** natural **range** 0 .. max_size; **subtype** index **is** positive **range** 1 .. max_size; **type** array_of_objects **is array** (index) **of** object_type latest : count := 0; objects : array_of_objects;

stack (3.2)	*Implemented as a singly linked list of objects.* →	**type** node;
		type node_pointer **is access** node;
		type node **is record**
		    object : object_type;
		    next : node_pointer;
		end record;
		type list_type **is record**
		    head : node_pointer;
		    size : natural := 0;
		end record;

queue (3.4)	**type** array_of_objects **is array** (positive **range** <>) **of** object_type;
	type queue(max_size : positive) **is record**
	    first : natural := 0;
	    last : natural := max_size;
	    size : natural := 0;
	    objects : array_of_objects(1 .. max_size);
	end record;
		← *Implemented as a constrained discriminant record. The queue objects are stored in an array with max_size components. The value of max_size is specified as part of the declaration for each queue instance.*

list (4.1)	**type** array_of_objects **is array** (positive **range** <>) **of** object_type; **type** list (size : count := 0) **is record** objects : array_of_objects(1 .. size); **end record**;	← *Implemented as an <u>unconstrained</u> discriminant record. The list objects are stored in an array with size components. If the value of size is not specified as part of the declaration of a list instance then the array size can be changed dynamically.*

sorted list (4.4)	**type** array_of_objects **is array** (positive **range** <>) **of** object_type;
	type sorted_list (max_size : positive) **is record**
	    size : natural;
	    objects : array_of_objects (1 .. max_size);
	end record;
		← *Implemented as a constrained discriminant record. The list objects are stored in an array with max_size components. The value of max_size is specified as part of the declaration for each list instance.*

FIGURE 10.2   *(continued)*

Figure 10.2 *(continued)*

binary_tree (5.1)	**type** binary_tree_node;
	 type node_pointer **is access** binary_tree_node;
	 type binary_tree_node **is record**
	     object : object_type;
	     left, right : node_pointer;
	 end record;
	 type binary_tree **is record**
	     size : natural := 0;
	     root : node_pointer;
	 end record;
		← *Implemented as a linked binary tree. Each tree node contains an object and two pointers.*

heap (5.3)	*Implemented as an array of objects* → *Type* heap *is given in the package specification (not the* **private** *clause) so it can be directly accessed by the user.*	**type** heap **is array** (natural **range** <>) **of** object_type;
set (7.1)	**type** bit **is new** boolean; **for** bit'size **use** 1; **type** set **is array** (0 .. object_type'pos(object_type'last)) **of** bit; **pragma** pack (set);	← *Implemented as an array of bits.*

hash_table (7.2)	**type** table_object **is record**
	     empty : boolean := true;
	     object : object_type;
	 end record;
	 type array_of_objects **is array** (natural
	   range <>) **of** table_object;
	 type hash_table (table_size : natural) **is record**
	     object_count : natural := 0;
	     probe_count : natural := 0;
	     objects : array_of_objects
	               (0 .. table_size);
	 end record;
		← *Implemented as a constrained discriminant record. The hash table objects are stored in an array with table_size components. The value of table_size is specified as part of the declaration for each hash_table instance.*

string (8.1)	**subtype** string_index **is** natural
	   range 0 .. max_length;
	 subtype string_length **is** natural
	   range 1 .. max_length;
	 type var_string (length : string_length := 0) **is**
	   record
	     text : string (1 .. length);
	 end record;
		← *Implemented as an* <u>*unconstrained*</u> *discriminant record. The string characters are stored in an array with* length *components. If the value of* length *is not specified as part of the declaration of a* var_string *instance then the array size can be changed dynamically.*

F I G U R E 10.2 *(continued)*

APPENDIX

A

Ada
Types
and
Attributes

Figure A.1 is a summary of Ada's predefined types and their attributes and shows nested relationships among these important objects. Figure A.1 shows that all predefined types share attributes *address, base,* and *size.* The predefined type *floating point* is a specialization of types *real* and *scalar* and shares all their attributes.

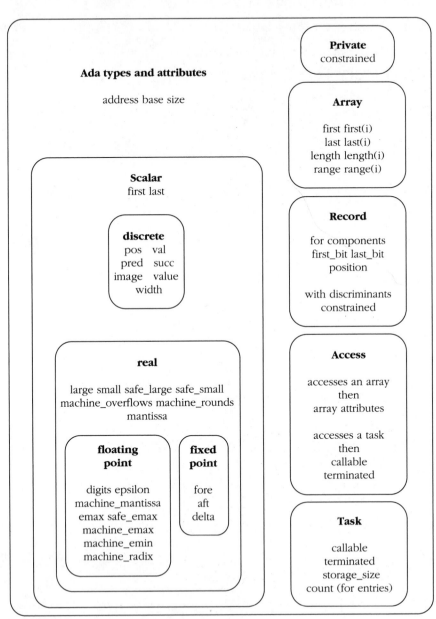

FIGURE A.1 Ada's predefined types and their attributes.

APPENDIX

B

Introduction to Recursion

This appendix provides an introduction to recursion. Section B.1 introduces recursion using several examples. Section B.2 complements Section 4.5 by describing the recursive search of an array using a binary search algorithm. Section B.2 presents a recursive implementation of binary search, whereas Section 4.5 gave an iterative implementation. Section B.3 provides an overview of three important recursive sort algorithms: quicksort, mergesort, and radix sort. The emphasis in Section B.3 is on how recursion is used in these algorithms.

Section B.4 introduces techniques used to implement recursion and is the focal point of this appendix. It provides more detail about how a recursive call (or any procedure or function call for that matter) is actually executed. The main example in B.4 is based on an application of the *quicksort* sorting algorithm. Therefore, you need to understand the *quicksort* algorithm to appreciate this illustration of recursion fully. The advantage is that the example is based on a very important application of recursion.

Section B.5 reviews the important connection between recursion and trees, and Section B.6 does the same for graphs. These sections refer to recursion as one of several ways to execute one segment of code immediately while deferring execution of another segment of code. When recursion is used the deferral is based on a stack. Section B.6 (and Chapter 9) point out that recursion is a special case of a more general mechanism (a priority queue) for such deferrals.

■ B.1 Recursion and Iteration

A function (or procedure) is recursive if it is defined in terms of itself. We begin with a simple example—the specification for function *sum,* which appears in Figure B.1.

function sum (n : natural) **return** natural;
-- ***result:*** *Returns the value of 0 + 1 + 2 + ⋯ + n.*

FIGURE B.1 Specification of sum.

An iterative implementation of function *sum* is given in Figure B.2.

```
function sum (n : natural) return natural is
-- Length 4   Complexity 2   Performance O(n)
    sum_so_far : natural := 0;
begin
    for next in 1 .. n loop
       sum_so_far := sum_so_far + next;
    end loop;
    return sum_so_far;
end sum;
```

FIGURE B.2 An iterative implementation of sum.

A recursive implementation of *sum* begins with the observation that

sum (0) = 0

and

sum (n) = n + sum (n − 1)

This scheme for computing sum is typical of recursive algorithms. It consists of a nonrecursive part (the **basis clause**) and a recursive part (the **inductive clause**). The nonrecursive part is essential because it causes the algorithm to terminate. The recursive part frequently simplifies the function. This simplification is the main reason for the importance of recursion.

Based on the observation above, a recursive implementation of *sum* is given in Figure B.3.

```
function sum (n : natural) return natural is
-- Length 3   Complexity 2   Recursion 1   Performance O(n)
begin
    if n = 0 then return 0;                      -- The basis clause.
    else return (n + sum (n−1));                 -- The inductive clause.
    end if;
end sum;
```

FIGURE B.3 A recursive implementation of sum.

The implementation in Figure B.3 suggests the following computations to evaluate *sum* (5).

sum (5) = (5 + sum (4))   *-- Recursive call to sum (4).*
        = (5 + (4 + sum (3)))   *-- Recursive call to sum (3).*
        = (5 + (4 + (3 + sum (2))))   *-- Recursive call to sum (2).*
        = (5 + (4 + (3 + (2 + sum (1)))))   *-- Recursive call to sum (1).*
        = (5 + (4 + (3 + (2 + (1 + sum (0))))))   *-- Sum (0) returns 0 and the recursive calls terminate.*
        = (5 + (4 + (3 + (2 + (1 + 0)))))   *-- Return (1 + 0).*
        = (5 + (4 + (3 + (2 + 1))))   *-- Return (2 + 1).*
        = (5 + (4 + (3 + 3)))   *-- Return (3 + 3).*
        = (5 + (4 + 6))   *-- Return (4 + 6).*
        = (5 + 10)   *-- Return (5 + 10).*
        = 15

Let us compare the implementations of *sum* in Figures B.2 and B.3. Both have complexity 2 because the loop in the iterative implementation is replaced by an **if** statement in the recursive implementation. Figure B.3 is an example of *tail recursion,* which refers to recursion in the last statement in an algorithm. (In Figure B.3 tail recursion is the only recursion in the algorithm; we will call it *simple tail recursion.*)

The performance of both algorithms is $O(n)$. The iterative implementation executes $O(n)$ additions. The recursive implementation executes $O(n)$ additions and $O(n)$ recursive function calls. At first glance it seems that the recursive implementation suffers from a performance penalty because of the time required by the recursive calls. Remember, however, that the code actually executed is the machine language code generated by the compiler—not the Ada code written by the programmer. It is likely that the executable code generated from the Ada code in both Figures B.2 and B.3 will be identical because most compilers will replace tail recursion by a simple loop. Thus, the executable code, in both cases, would be the machine language equivalent of the loop in Figure B.2. An interesting exercise is to use timing studies to compare the performance of the implementations in Figures B.2 and B.3.

In general a compiler must replace recursive function or procedure calls by machine language instructions. For simple tail recursion (as in Figure B.3) most compilers will generate a simple loop. Convince yourself that it is always possible to replace simple tail recursion by an equivalent loop.

Since it's important to avoid a complicated solution to an easy problem, a much better implementation of function *sum* is the following:

```
function sum (n : natural) return natural is
-- Length 1   Complexity 1   Performance O(1)
begin
    return (n * (n + 1))/2;
end sum;
```

Consider the specification of *factorial* in Figure B.4.

```
function factorial (n : natural) return natural;
-- result:  If n = 0 return 0; otherwise, return 1 * 2 * 3 * ⋯ * n.
```

FIGURE B.4 Specification of factorial.

Write both iterative and recursive implementations (similar to Figures B.2 and B.3) of function *factorial*. There is a third implementation of interest in this case.

The first few values returned by function *factorial* are 0, 1, 2, 6, 24, 120, 720, 5040. These values increase rapidly so only a few such values can be represented on most digital computers. For example, if a computer allocates 32 bits to store integers and uses a two's complement representation, then *integer'last* is 2,147,483,647. The largest factorial that can be computed is then

```
function factorial (the_value : natural) return natural is
-- Length 2   Complexity 1   Performance O(1)
    the_result : constant array (natural range 0 .. 12) of positive :=
        (0, 1, 2, 6, 24, 120, 720, 5_040, 40_320, 362_880, 3_628_800,
        39_916_800, 479_001_600);
begin
    return the_result(the_value);
end factorial;
```

FIGURE B.5 Implementation of factorial by extracting the result from a table.

factorial $(12) = 479{,}001{,}600$. In this case factorial can be implemented using the table lookup process shown in Figure B.5.

There are many other examples of functions that can be implemented recursively, or using a simple loop, or (because the values computed grow rapidly) using a simple table lookup as illustrated in Figure B.5. Two examples are Fibonacci numbers, which are computed for all positive integers by

Fibonacci (1) $= 1$
Fibonacci (2) $= 1$
Fibonacci (n) $=$ Fibonacci $(n - 1) +$ Fibonacci $(n - 2)$ *-- Whenever* n *> 2.*

and Ackermann's numbers, which are computed for all pairs of natural numbers by

Ackermann $(0, n)$ $= n + 1$ *-- For all n ≥ 0.*
Ackermann $(m, 0)$ $=$ Ackermann $(m - 1, 1)$ *-- For all m ≥ 1.*
Ackermann (m, n) $=$ Ackermann $[m - 1,$ Ackermann $(m, n - 1)]$

It is an interesting exercise to implement functions to compute both Fibonacci and Ackermann numbers using as many of the three approaches described above as you can. (It is not easy to write an iterative implementation to compute Ackermann's numbers.)

■ B.2 Recursion and Binary Search

Section 4.5 describes binary search—an algorithm of immense practical importance—that has a natural recursive implementation. The importance of binary search comes from its $O(\log_2 n)$ performance. The description and motivation of binary search is given in Section 4.5, which includes an iterative implementation. We continue with the specification for binary search (Figure B.6) and a recursive implementation (Figure B.7).

```
generic
    type object_type is private;
    type key_type is private;
    with function key_of (the_object : object_type) return key_type;
    type sorted_list is array (integer range <>) of object_type;
    with function ">" (left, right : key_type) return boolean is <>;
function binary_search (the_list : sorted_list; target_key : key_type) return integer;
-- result:    If there is an object in the_list with key_of (object) = target_key, then binary_search returns the
--            index of that object; otherwise, binary_search returns the position that an object with key value
--            target_key would occupy if inserted into the_list.
```

FIGURE B.6 Specification of binary search.

Figure B.7 makes the basis of the binary search algorithm clear. Binary search consists of a sequence of recursive calls—with the length of the target list cut in half for each successive call. The search terminates when either the list size is one or the middle object in the list is the target object.

```
function binary_search (the_list : sorted_list; target_key : key_type) return integer is
-- Length 12   Complexity 5   Recursion 2   Performance O(log₂n)
    low    : integer := the_list'first;
    mid    : integer;
    high   : integer := the_list'last
begin
    if low < high then
      mid := (low + high) / 2;

      if target_key = key_of(the_list(mid)) then return mid;
      elsif target_key > key_of(the_list(mid)) then
         return binary_search(the_list(mid +1 .. high), target_key);
      else return binary_search(the_list(low .. mid), target_key);
      end if;

    elsif target_key > key_of(the_list(high)) then return high + 1;
    else return high;
    end if;
end binary_search;
```

F I G U R E B.7 Recursive implementation of binary search.

We can replace binary search with other algorithms that split the target list at some point other than its midpoint. Interpolation search, for example, estimates the position of the target object assuming list values increase approximately linearly. If the calculation for *mid* in *binary_search* is replaced by

mid := (target_key − key_of(the_list(low))) * (high − low) / (key_of(the_list(high)) − key_of(the_list(low)));

then the result is interpolation search. Care must be taken to make sure the denominator of this new expression for *mid* is not zero. Also, use of the identifier *mid* is no longer appropriate. Because of the complexity of the calculation of the point at which to split the list, interpolation search would only be worthwhile for long lists in which the data values grow in a nearly linear fashion.

Note that binary search is one of a class of algorithms referred to as divide and conquer. At each step of a binary search the size of the list to search is divided in half. The process of dividing the list in half continues until the remaining list has length 1 and the search process is trivial.

B.3 Recursive Sort Algorithms

There are three recursive sorting algorithms in Chapter 6: *quicksort* (Figure 6.56), *mergesort* (Figure 6.65) and *radix sort* (Figure 6.86). In each of these three algorithms the sort process is to divide the list to sort into two sublists then recursively sort each sublist. Each is an excellent example of a divide and conquer algorithm.

The three sort algorithms differ in how a list is divided into the two pieces that are sorted recursively and in how the recursion is terminated. Figures B.8 and B.9 describe these differences.

Algorithm	Process used to divide a list into two lists to be sorted recursively
quicksort	A list object whose value is estimated to be near the median value in the list is selected. The list is divided into one list whose objects are smaller than the selected object and another list whose objects are greater than the selected object.
mergesort	The list is divided in half.
radix sort	The binary representation of each list object is considered, and the algorithm supplies the position of one of the bits to be used to divide the list. The list is divided into one list whose objects have a 0 in the selected bit position and another list whose objects have a 1 in the selected bit position.

FIGURE B.8 The processes used to divide lists into sublists in three sorting algorithms.

Algorithm	How recursion is terminated
quicksort	When the list to sort has less than 15 objects, insertion sort is applied and no further recursive calls are made.
mergesort	When the list to sort has one object (and hence is sorted), no further recursive calls are made.
radix sort	When the list to sort has one object (and hence is sorted), no further recursive calls are made. Also, when all the bit positions in the sort value have been treated, no further recursive calls are made.

FIGURE B.9 How recursion is terminated in three sorting algorithms.

Note that *mergesort,* by dividing the list exactly in half each time, has a worst case performance of $O(n \log_2 n)$. In both *quicksort* and *radix sort* the lists produced by the division process may be far from equal in size. For *quicksort* this may result in a tree of recursive calls (Figure 6.43) of height $O(n)$. The worst case performance of *quicksort* is thus $O(n^2)$. The corresponding tree of recursive calls for *radix sort* is always of height k, where k is the number of bits in the value upon which the list is sorted. The performance of *radix sort* is therefore always $O(k*n)$ no matter how uneven the list divisions may be. As noted in Chapter 6, the value of k is usually at least as large as $\log_2 n$.

Quicksort ends by taking advantage of the efficiency of insertion sort for short lists. A comparable modification would apply some simple sort algorithm to sort small pieces of fixed length before applying *mergesort*. The recursive calls to *mergesort* would then terminate when a list of the size initially sorted was encountered. Refer to Chapter 6 for further details about these sorting algorithms.

■ B.4 Implementing Recursion

When first encountered recursion can seem like magic. How can a procedure call itself? This section gives a simplified explanation of the recursion mechanism.

When any procedure call is made, two execution paths are created. One path follows the procedure call. The second path is execution of the code immediately following the procedure call. The first path is executed immediately while execution of the second path is deferred—until execution of the procedure call is completed.

We need to save, while the procedure call is executed, all information necessary to continue on the second path. The information that must be saved includes the following:

- The address at which execution of the second path is to continue
- The values of all parameters used in the procedure call
- The values of all other variables needed to continue on the second path

This collection of objects is called an ***activation record***. Each time a procedure is called, an activation record is created and initialized with the appropriate values. When the procedure call completes, the space used for the activation record is released to a pool of available space. The idea of an activation record is shown in Figure B.10.

type activation_pointer **is access** activation_record;
type activation_record **is record**
    • The address at which execution of the second path is to continue.
    • The values of all parameters used in the procedure call.
    • The values of all other variables needed to continue on the second path.
end record;

FIGURE B.10 Typical content of an activation record.

The ***run-time system,*** which handles execution of programs, executes a set of procedures (often referred to as the ***prologue***) when a procedure call is made. Among other things, the prologue creates and loads the appropriate values into an activation record.

When execution of the procedure is complete, a set of operations called the ***epilogue*** is executed. The epilogue must, for example, handle the values of formal parameters of modes **out** and **in out**. Finally, the epilogue retrieves the address at which execution of the deferred path is to continue, releases the storage used by the activation record, and causes execution to continue at the specified address.

If several activation records exist simultaneously, they must be managed so that when execution of a procedure completes the correct activation record is retrieved and used to supply the information to continue execution. The correct order is LIFO. That is, when execution of a procedure terminates, the activation record to be retrieved is the one most recently created. The correct data structure for storing activation records is therefore a stack.

Figure B.11 shows a typical slice of memory (a) before, (b) during, and (c) after procedure *main* calls procedure *proc_1*. Note that recursive procedure calls are handled in exactly the same way as ordinary procedure calls.

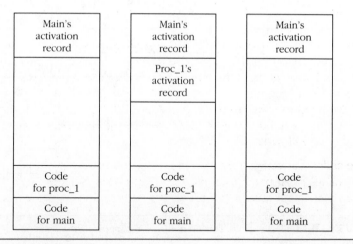

FIGURE B.11 When procedure *main* calls procedure *proc_1* an activation record is pushed on a stack of activation records.

In order to discuss a concrete example, consider the application of *quicksort* to sort a list of 100 objects. The pseudocode for *quicksort* in Figure B.12 is taken from Figure 6.40.

procedure quicksort (the_objects : **in out** objects_to_sort) **is**
     left   : integer := the_objects'first;
     right : integer := the_objects'last;
begin
    if (left < right) **then**
       Rearrange objects the_objects(left), . . . , the_objects(right) to produce a new list such that

       the_objects(left), . . . , the_objects(j − 1) are all smaller than the_objects(j);
       the_objects(j) is in its sorted position;
       the_objects(j + 1), . . . , the_objects(right) are all larger than the_objects(j);

       if (j − left) > 15 **then** quicksort (the_objects(left .. j − 1));
       end if;
       if (right − j) > 15 **then** quicksort (the_objects(j + 1 .. right));
       end if;
    end if;
end quicksort;

FIGURE B.12 Pseudocode for quicksort. Quicksort is discussed in detail in Figure 6.40.

Note the two recursive calls in the *quicksort* algorithm in Figure B.12. The main point of Figure B.13 is to highlight the recursive calls that occur

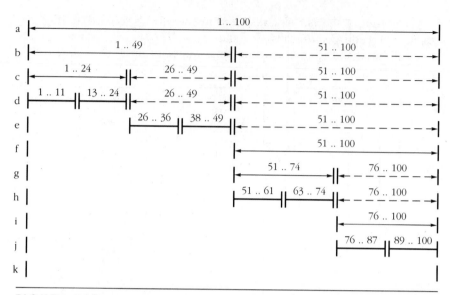

FIGURE B.13 Eleven views, labeled *a, b, . . . , k,* of applying *quicksort* to a list of 100 objects.

during application of *quicksort* to a list of 100 objects. The 11 rows in Figure B.13 (labeled *a, b, . . . , k*) show 11 views of the list as it is sorted.

Each pair of rows in Figure B.13 shows the effect of one execution of the outer **if** statement in Figure B.12. We assume for simplicity that the list is split in half each time it is divided into two parts. A solid line with arrowheads indicates a list to which *quicksort* is (recursively) applied at the current step. A dashed line with arrow heads indicates a list whose processing has been deferred. A solid line without arrowheads indicates a list (of length less than 15) that will be sorted later using a sort algorithm that is efficient for small lists.

Pay particular attention to the lists indicated by dashed lines—these are the lists whose processing has been deferred as a result of the recursive calls of the form *quicksort* [*the_objects(left .. j − 1)*]. Note also that the recursive call in Figure B.12, *quicksort* [*the_objects(j + 1 .. right)*] does *not* cause the execution of any statements to be deferred because it is the last statement in the procedure.

In (a), *quicksort* is applied to the list of 100 objects. In (b), the list has been split: *quicksort* is recursively applied to objects 1 .. 49, the 50th object is sorted, and processing objects 51 .. 100 has been deferred. In (c), the list 1 .. 49 has been split. *quicksort* is applied to objects 1 .. 24, the 25th object is sorted, and processing objects 26 .. 49 has been deferred. In (d), the list 1 .. 24 has been split, but since the two resulting sublists are of length less than 15, they are ignored by *quicksort* and will subsequently be sorted using an algorithm efficient for short lists. Finally, in (k) the *quicksort* process is complete.

Our primary interest is the technique used to defer processing sublists. *quicksort* uses recursion, so the deferred lists are actually placed on a stack.

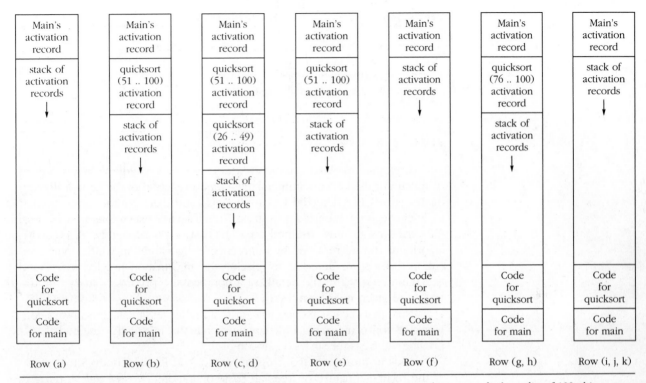

FIGURE B.14 Use of memory for the stack of activation records needed when quicksort is applied to a list of 100 objects as illustrated in Figure B.13. The row references are to the rows in Figure B.13.

Figure B.14 shows a typical use of memory during execution of a procedure *main* that calls procedure *quicksort*. Use the row references in Figure B.14 to relate Figure B.14 to Figure B.13.

■ B.5 Binary Trees and Recursion

Trees are frequently thought of as recursive data structures. In Section 5.3 a binary tree is defined as either empty or a root node together with two binary trees. The two binary trees are disjoint from each other and from the root and are called the left and right subtrees. (Write a recursive definition of a list similar to the recursive definition of a binary tree.)

Note the elegance of the recursive implementation of preorder, inorder, and postorder traversal of a binary tree (Figures 5.38 and Package Body 5.1). During an inorder traversal each node is processed after all nodes in its left subtree and before all nodes in its right subtree. Note how closely the recursive implementation of inorder traversal (Figure B.15) mirrors the description of the traversal process.

The simplicity of the implementation in Figure B.15 occurs because each recursive call traverses an entire subtree. (Write a recursive implementation for list traversal.)

```
procedure inorder (the_node : binary_tree_node) is
begin
    if the_node is not the root of an empty subtree then
        inorder (the_node's left child);
        process (the_node's object);
        inorder (the_node's right child);
    end if;
end inorder;
```

FIGURE B.15 Recursive inorder traversal of a binary tree.

We know that when a recursive call is made, execution of the procedure or function called occurs immediately—and execution of the code following the recursive call is deferred. It is important to note that the information needed to defer execution is placed on a stack. Thus, if several executions are deferred, they are subsequently resumed on a LIFO basis. Consequently, all recursive algorithms can be replaced by nonrecursive algorithms in which some execution threads are deferred by placing the information needed to resume execution on a stack. The details of a nonrecursive preorder binary tree traversal are given in Section 5.6.2.

Note that recursive code written in a high-level language is always converted to nonrecursive machine language code that is actually executed. Stacks provide the basis for such conversions.

Look at the binary tree implementations in Package Body 5.1. Because of the recursive nature of trees all basic operations—*insert, delete, retrieve,* etc.—can be elegantly implemented using recursion.

It is important to observe that there are other ways to defer execution of a code sequence while a procedure call is made. If a queue is used we can craft a simple algorithm for the level order traversal of a tree (Figures 5.6–5.7 and Package Body 5.1).

For the traversal of a list if we "defer" execution using either a stack or a queue, the result is the same. For a binary tree a stack gives us (among others) preorder, inorder, and postorder traversal—while a queue gives us level order traversal.

Chapter 9 and Section B.6 show that algorithms based on deferring execution using stacks and queues are special cases of deferring execution using a priority queue. For graphs, important algorithms are based on this more general deferral mechanism.

Just as recursion is important for binary trees, it is important for *m*-way trees in which each node has from 0 to *m* subtrees. Write a recursive definition of an *m*-way tree, then write pseudocode for basic operations such as *traversal, insert, delete,* and *retrieve.* Then, after referring to Section 5.10, which provides an introduction to B-trees, write similar pseudocode for B-trees.

■ B.6 Graphs and Recursion

There are several important ways to traverse a graph. Each of them, after processing a graph node, stores all the neighbors of that node in some data structure until they are retrieved and processed. The data structure used determines the order in which nodes are processed. Figure B.16 shows three implementation alternatives.

Type of traversal	Data structure used to store graph nodes pending their retrieval and processing	Algorithm references
Breadth first search	Queue	Figure 9.26
		Figure 9.30
		Figure 9.34
Depth first search	Stack	Figure 9.35
		Figure 9.37
Priority first search	Priority queue	Figure 9.38
		Figure 9.39

FIGURE B.16 Data structures used to store graph nodes pending their retrieval and processing during breadth first, depth first, and priority first searches.

When a stack is used, the traversal is depth first and a recursive implementation is possible. Recursive implementations of a depth first search are shown in Figures 9.35 and 9.37. Figure 9.31 gives two illustrations of depth first search for an example graph.

When a queue is used for graph traversal, the traversal algorithm must manage the queue and the traversal is breadth first.

Note that depth and breadth first searches are special cases of priority first search. Chapter 9 gives two important applications of priority first search.

How is recursive (depth first) search a special case of priority first search? During depth first search processing a graph node is deferred by pushing it on a stack. Since a stack is a LIFO data structure, a node pushed on the stack during the first part of the traversal will remain there (unprocessed) until near the end of the traversal.

During a priority first search processing, a node is deferred by placing it (along with its priority) in a priority queue. Each step of the algorithm processes the node with the highest priority. Therefore, if the sequence of priorities assigned to nodes as they are added to the priority queue is strictly increasing, then the priority queue behaves like a stack and priority first search becomes depth first search. Similarly, if the sequence of priorities assigned to nodes is strictly decreasing, then the priority queue acts like a queue and priority first search becomes breadth first search. Refer to Chapter 9 for details about graph traversal.

It is frequently useful to have a good random number generator available to test your implementations. Figure C.1 presents a random number generator that is simple and is described in detail in the reference cited as part of its specification. Figure C.2 presents a unique random number generator.

function random (old : integer) **return** integer **is**
-- *results:* *Starting with a seed value, say the_random_number, a sequence of calls,*
--   *the_random_number := random (the_random_number);*
--   *generates a sequence of pseudo random numbers.*
-- *notes:* *This random number generator is described in Park, S.K., and Miller, K.W.,*
--   *"Random Number Generators: Good Ones Are Hard to Find,"* Communications of
--   the ACM, *October 1988, pp. 1192–1201.*
--   *A test to ensure that this implementation is correct in your environment starts with*
--   *the_random_number = 1 and after 10_000 function calls returns the value*
--   *1_043_618_065. The particular implementation given is for 32-bit integers using*
--   *two's complement representation. The reference above gives other possibilities.*

```
a     : constant integer :=           16_807;
m     : constant integer :=   2_147_483_647;
q     : constant integer :=         127_773;
r     : constant integer :=           2_836;
next  : integer;
```

begin
    next := a*(old **mod** q) − r*(old / q);
    if next > 0
      then return next;
      else return (next + m);
    end if;
end random;

FIGURE C.1 A function to generate random numbers.

-- *Abstract:* *Generates all numbers between 1 and n in random order without repetition,*
--   *one for each call to next_random. After n calls, another random permutation*
--   *of 1 .. n begins and numbers are returned in the subsequent n calls to*
--   *next_random, and so on.*
-- *Limitations:* *The package uses an auxiliary array (1 .. n) of natural. Caution if n is large.*

-- *Package Specification*

generic
    n   : natural;   -- *The size of the set of numbers.*
    seed : integer := 72954;   -- *An arbitrary seed.*
package unique_random **is**
    function next_random **return** natural;
    -- *results:* *Returns the next random integer in the permutation of 1 .. n.*
end unique_random;

FIGURE C.2 A package for generating unique random integers.

(continued)

Figure C.2 *(continued)*

-- *Package Body*

with random, swap;

package body unique_random **is**

    procedure n_swap **is new** swap(natural);
    perm   : **array**(1 .. n) **of** natural;
    size   : natural := n;
    old   : integer := seed;

    function next_random **return** natural **is**
    begin   -- *next_random.*
      if size = 0 **then** size := n; **end if**;
      old := random(old);
      n_swap(perm(old **mod** size + 1), perm(size));
      size := size − 1;
      return perm(size + 1);
end next_random;

begin   -- *Package initialization.*
    for i **in** 1 .. n **loop**
      perm(i) := i;
    end loop;
end unique_random;

F I G U R E   C.2 *(continued)*

D

Implementations to Traverse and Display a B-Tree

This appendix presents code to implement two important B-tree procedures: *traverse* and *put_tree*. These procedures were chosen because they illustrate the similarity between traversal operations for binary trees and the same operations for B-trees and because the availability of an operation to display the content of a B-tree is helpful while testing the implementation of other operations. A challenging exercise is to implement *insert* and *delete* operations for a B-tree.

We begin with code (Figure D.1) to traverse a B-tree (the B-tree representation is given in Specification 5.4). First, compare Figure D.1 with the implementations of preorder, inorder, and postorder traversal of a binary tree given in Package Body 5.4. Note that the code to traverse a B-tree recursively is almost the same as the code to traverse a binary tree recursively. A good exercise at this point is to write the code for a level order traversal of a B-tree and to compare the result with the corresponding traversal implementation for a binary tree.

```
procedure traverse (the_tree : B_tree) is
-- Length 1   Complexity 1   Performance O(n)

    procedure sub_traverse (the_pointer : node_pointer) is
    -- Length 10   Complexity 5
        num_children, half_children : count;
    begin
        if the_pointer /= null then
            num_children := the_pointer.node_size;
            half_children := num_children / 2;

            for k in 0 .. half_children loop          -- Traverse half of the subtrees.
                sub_traverse (the_pointer.pointers(k));
            end loop;

            for q in 1 .. the_pointer.node_size loop  -- Process all objects in one node.
                process(the_pointer.objects(q));
            end loop;

            for k in half_children + 1 .. num_children loop  -- Traverse the remaining subtrees.
                sub_traverse (the_pointer.pointers(k));
            end loop;
        end if;
    end sub_traverse;

begin
    sub_traverse (the_tree.root);
end traverse;
```

FIGURE D.1 An implementation of recursive traversal of a B-tree.

How would Figure D.1 be changed to construct a traversal that corresponds to preorder and postorder traversals of a binary tree?

The next implementation is for procedure *put_tree* that displays the content of a binary tree. Code for a binary tree is given so that it can be compared with the corresponding code for a B-tree. Figure D.2 gives the specification for *put_tree,* Figure D.3 shows the result of applying *put_tree* to an example tree, and Figure D.4 presents the code.

Figure D.3 shows the result of applying *put_tree* to a simple binary tree. The root of the tree appears on the left, and the tree grows from left to right. The last two columns are not part of the output of *put_tree* but have been appended to help explain how *put_tree* works. That explanation follows the implementation.

Look at the traverse procedure in Figure D.4. Processing a node at level

generic
        key_width : positive := 3;
        with procedure put_key (the_key : key_type);
procedure put_tree (the_tree : binary_tree);
-- **assumes:**   *Each key value can be displayed in at most key_width columns. Procedure*
--   *put_key writes the value of key in at most key_width columns—and*
                    does nothing else.
-- **results:**   *the_tree is displayed as shown in the example below. The interesting part is*
--   *writing the vertical lines that connect the children of a common parent!*

FIGURE   D.2 Specification of procedure *put_tree* for a binary tree.

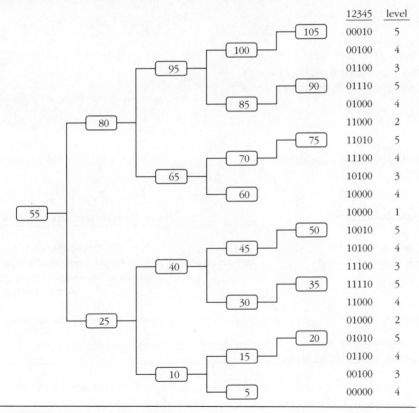

FIGURE   D.3 The result of applying *put_tree* to an example binary tree. Two columns have been appended to help explain how *put_tree* works.

```
procedure put_tree (the_tree : binary_tree) is
-- Length 3   Complexity 1   Performance O(n)
        -- An array of "switches" that records the levels of the tree at which vertical connectors should be displayed.
        -- These switches are turned on and off as the tree is displayed.
        vertical : array (natural range 0 .. 1 + characteristics(the_tree).height) of boolean := (others => false);
        width : constant positive := key_width + 7;

    procedure put_connector (level : natural) is                    -- Write all vertical connectors on one row of the display.
    -- Length 3   Complexity 3
    begin
        for at_this_level in 1 .. level - 2 loop
            if vertical (at_this_level) then
                set_col(count(width*at_this_level)); put ("|");
            end if;
        end loop;
    end put_connector;

    procedure put_node (the_ptr : node_pointer; level : natural) is                    -- Display one node.
    -- Length 12   Complexity 3
    begin
        if level > 1 then
            set_col(count(width*(level-1))); put(" + - - );
        else set_col(3);
        end if;

        put ("["); put_key (key_of(the_ptr.object)); put ("]");

        if the_ptr.left /= null and the_ptr.right /= null then put ("- -|");
        elsif the_ptr.left /= null or the_ptr.right /= null then put ("- - +");
        end if;
        new_line;
    end put_node;

    procedure traverse (the_ptr : node_pointer; level : natural) is
    -- Length 8   Complexity 2   Recursion 2
    begin
        if the_ptr /= null then
            traverse (the_ptr.right, level + 1);                    -- Traverse (and display) the right subtree.

            vertical (level - 1) := not vertical (level - 1);                    -- Flip the switch at level - 1.
            vertical (level) := the_ptr.left /= null;                    -- Turn switch on if there is a left child; otherwise turn it off.
            put_connector (level);                    -- Display all the vertical connectors.
            put_node (the_ptr, level);                    -- Display the node.

            traverse (the_ptr.left, level + 1);                    -- Traverse (and display) the left subtree.
        end if;
    end traverse;

begin
    traverse (the_tree.root, 1);
end put_tree;
```

FIGURE D.4 Implementation of *put_tree*.

q requires setting the switches (which are stored in array *vertical*) at levels $q - 1$ and q, displaying one row of connectors, and displaying the node.

To see how the switches are set, look at Figure D.3. The switch settings for each row displayed, and the level of the node displayed on that row, have been appended for easy reference. For the first row displayed, the node containing 105 is at level 5 in the tree and the switch at level 4 has been turned on. After the node containing 80 is displayed (at level 2), the switches at levels 1 and 2 are on.

If a node is displayed at level q, then *vertical*$(q - 1)$ tells whether the node is a left or right child. If *vertical*$(q - 1)$ is false, then it is a right child and a vertical line is needed to connect the node to its parent—so *vertical*$(q - 1)$ is turned on (set to true). If *vertical*$(q - 1)$ is true, then the node is a left child and *vertical*$(q - 1)$ is turned off.

In addition, if a node is displayed at level q, then *vertical*(q) is turned on if it has a left child and turned off otherwise. Verify this result in Figure D.3.

generic
    with procedure put_key1 (key : key_type);
    with procedure put_key2 (key : key_type);
    key_width : **in** positive;
procedure put_tree (the_tree : B_tree);
-- **assumes:**   *Procedures put_key1 and put_key2 write the value of key in at most key_width columns.*
-- **results:**   *the_tree is displayed as shown in the example below.*
-- **notes:**   *There are two put_key procedures because put_key1 writes a key value left justified and*
                put_key2 writes a key value right justified. This improves the appearance of the displayed tree.

F I G U R E   D.5 Specification of *put_tree* for a B-tree.

We are ready to extend procedure *put_tree* so that it will display a B-tree. Figure D.5 gives the specification.

Figure D.6 shows the result of applying *put_tree* to a sample B-tree. As in Figure D.3, two columns have been appended to the result. The first appended column shows the switch settings (stored in array *vertical*) as the tree is displayed. The second column shows the level of the node just displayed. Recall that if a node is displayed on level q, then only switches in positions $q - 1$ and q may be changed.

Figure D.7 provides the implementation of *put_tree* for a B-tree.

The two versions of *put_tree* given in Figures D.3 and D.7 are sufficient to assist in verifying the validity of other operations on trees. Most important, they also demonstrate the close connection between recursive traversal of binary trees and recursive traversal of multiway trees.

There are some loose ends to tie up in Figure D.7. First, the initialization of array *vertical* calls function *height_of* that returns the height of the B-tree that is the function's argument. Observe that it is particularly easy to determine the height of a B-tree since all leaf nodes are on the same level.

Second, the horizontal width actually needed to display a level in the B-tree may be much less than is actually used by *put_tree*. For example, in Figure

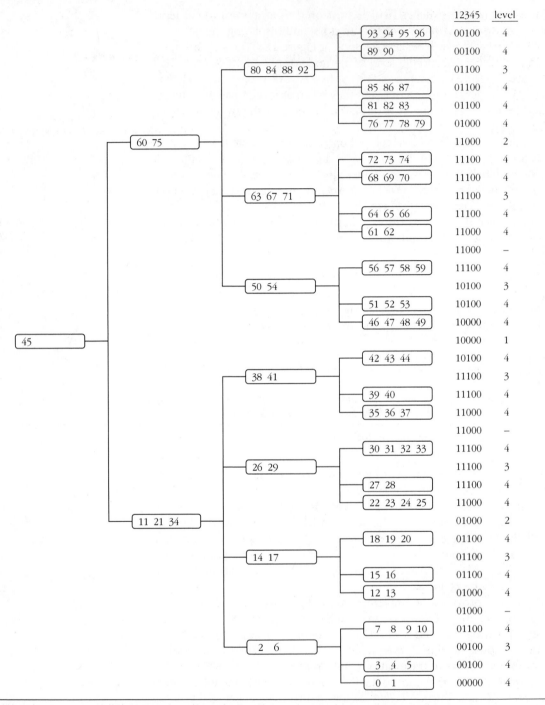

	12345	level
93 94 95 96	00100	4
89 90	00100	4
80 84 88 92	01100	3
85 86 87	01100	4
81 82 83	01100	4
76 77 78 79	01000	4
60 75	11000	2
72 73 74	11100	4
68 69 70	11100	4
63 67 71	11100	3
64 65 66	11100	4
61 62	11000	4
	11000	–
56 57 58 59	11100	4
50 54	10100	3
51 52 53	10100	4
46 47 48 49	10000	4
45	10000	1
42 43 44	10100	4
38 41	11100	3
39 40	11100	4
35 36 37	11000	4
	11000	–
30 31 32 33	11100	4
26 29	11100	3
27 28	11100	4
22 23 24 25	11000	4
11 21 34	01000	2
18 19 20	01100	4
14 17	01100	3
15 16	01100	4
12 13	01000	4
	01000	–
7 8 9 10	01100	4
2 6	00100	3
3 4 5	00100	4
0 1	00000	4

FIGURE D.6 Procedure *put_tree* (Figure D.7) applied to display a sample B-tree.

procedure put_tree (the_tree : B_tree) **is**
-- *Length 6   Complexity 1   Performance* O(n)
    type position **is** (first, middle, last);
    vertical : **array** (natural **range** 0 .. 1 + height_of (the_tree)) **of** boolean := (**others** => false);
    posn : position := first;
    width : **constant** positive := 4*(key_width + 1);
    prior_level : natural := 0;

    procedure put_verticals (depth : natural) **is**   -- *Write all vertical connectors on one row of the display.*
    -- *Length 4   Complexity 3*
    begin
      for at_this_level **in** 1 .. depth − 2 **loop**
        if vertical(at_this_level) **then**
            set_col(positive_count(width*at_this_level)); put("|");
        end if;
      end loop;
    end put_verticals;

    procedure put_prefix (depth : natural; posn : position) **is**
    -- *Length 5   Complexity 2*
    begin
      set_col(positive_count(width*(depth − 1)));
      if posn = first **or** posn = last **then** put(" + − ");
      else put("| − ");
      end if;
    end put_prefix;

    procedure put_node (the_ptr : node_pointer) **is**
    -- *Length 11   Complexity 4*
    begin
      put("[");
      put_key1 (key_of(the_ptr.objects(1)));
      for q **in** 2 .. the_ptr.node_size **loop**
        put_key2 (key_of(the_ptr.objects(q)));
      end loop;
      put("]");
      if the_ptr.pointers(0) /= null **then** put(" − ");
        for q **in** the_ptr.node_size + 1 .. order − 1 **loop**
          put(" − − − ");
        end loop;
        put("|");
      end if;
      new_line;
    end put_node;

    procedure recursive_traverse (the_ptr : node_pointer; level : natural) **is**
    -- *Length 25   Complexity 9*
      num_children, half_children : count;

FIGURE D.7 Implementation of *put_tree* for a B-tree.   **(continued)**

Figure D.7 *(continued)*

```
begin
    if the_ptr /= null then
        num_children := the_ptr.node_size; half_children := num_children /2;

        for k in reverse half_children + 1 .. num_children loop          -- Display half the subtrees.
            recursive_traverse (the_ptr.pointers(k), level + 1);
        end loop;

        if not vertical(level − 1) then
            vertical(level − 1) := true;
            posn := first;                                               -- Is this the first of a sequence of siblings, or
        elsif level > 1 and then the_ptr.parent.pointers(0) = the_ptr then
            posn := last;                                                    -- is it the last, or
        else posn := middle;                                               -- is it neither the first nor the last.
        end if;

        if level > 1 then
            if posn = first and then level = prior_level then            -- Put an extra row between leaf nodes
                put_verticals(level); new_line;                            -- that are not siblings and that would
            end if;                                                  -- otherwise be adjacent. This is purely cosmetic.
            put_verticals(level);                                            -- Write the vertical connectors.
            put_prefix(level, posn);                                      -- Write a horizontal node connector.
        else set_col(2);
        end if;
        prior_level := level;

        put_node (the_ptr);                                                -- Display the node.

        if posn = last then vertical(level − 1) := false;
        end if;

        for k in reverse 0 .. half_children loop                          -- Display half the subtrees.
            recursive_traverse (the_ptr.pointers(k), level + 1);
        end loop;
    end if;
    end recursive_traverse;

begin
    recursive_traverse(the_tree.root, 1);
end put_tree;
```

FIGURE D.7 *(continued)*

D.6 the width used to display the root node is considerably more than is necessary. Also, the width used to display the two nodes on level 2 is more than is required. It is an interesting exercise to modify *put_tree* to use the minimum width needed for each level of the tree.

Operations *insert* and *delete* for B-trees are interesting operations and their implementations are left as exercises.

ABRAHAMS, P. W., "Some Sad Remarks About String Handling in C," *SIGPLAN Notices,* October 1988, pp. 61–68.

AGRAWAL, CAREY, and McVOY, "The Performance of Alternative Strategies for Dealing with Deadlocks in Database Management Systems," *IEEE Transactions on Software Engineering,* December 1987, pp. 1348–1363.

AHO, A. V., and ULLMAN, J. D., *Principles of Compiler Design,* Addison-Wesley, Reading, MA, 1977.

APPEL, K., HAKEN, W., and KOCH, J., "Every Planar Map is Four-Colorable," *Illinois J. Math.,* Vol. 21, 1977.

BARON, R. D., and SHAPIRO, L. G., *Data Structures and Their Implementation,* Van Nostrand Reinhold, NY, 1980.

BAYER, R., and McCREIGHT, C., "Organization and Maintenance of Large Ordered Indexes," *Acta Informatica,* Vol. 1, No. 3, 1972, pp. 173–189.

BELL LABS, *Bell System Technical Journal,* Vol. 57, No. 6 (Issue devoted to UNIX), July–August 1978.

BENTLEY, J., "An Introduction to Algorithm Design," *IEEE Computer,* Vol. 12, No. 2, February 1979.

BENTLEY, J., *Writing Efficient Programs,* Prentice-Hall, Englewood Cliffs, NJ, 1982.

BENTLEY, J., "Programming Pearls," *Communications of the ACM,* Vol. 26, No. 8, August 1983a,b, and No. 12, December 1983c.

BENTLEY, J., "Programming Pearls: Thanks Heaps," *Communications of the ACM,* March 1985, pp. 245–250.

BENTLEY, J. L., and McGEOCH, C. C., *Communications of the ACM,* April 1985, pp. 404–411.

BISHOP, J. M., "Implementing Strings in Pascal," *Software—Practice and Experience,* Vol. 9, 1979, pp. 779–788.

BODDY, D. E., "Fast Strings for Modula-2," *Journal of Pascal, Ada & Modula-2,* March/April 1990, pp. 18–26.

BORLAND INTERNATIONAL, INC., *Turbo Pascal Version 3.0,* Reference Manual, Scotts Valley, CA, 1985.

BORLAND INTERNATIONAL, INC., *Turbo Pascal for the Mac,* User's Guide and Reference Manual, Scotts Valley, CA, 1986.

BOSWELL, F. D., CARMODY, F. J., and GROVE, T. R., "A String Extension for Pascal," Computer Systems Group University of Waterloo, *WATNEWS,* September–October 1982, pp. 22–24.

BOTTENBRUCH, H., "Structure and Use of ALGOL 60," *Journal of the ACM,* Vol. 9, No. 2, 1962, p. 214.

BOYER, R. S., and MOORE, J. S., "A Fast String Searching Algorithm," *Communications of the ACM,* October 1977, pp. 762–772.

BRON C., and DIJKSTRA, E. J., "A Better Way to Combine Efficient String Length Encoding and Zero-Termination," *SIGPLAN Notices,* June 1989, pp. 11–19.

BURKE, R. W., GOLDSTINE, H. H., and von NEUMANN, J., "Preliminary Discussion of the Logical Design of an Electronic Computing Instrument," Report prepared for the U.S. Army Ordinance Department, 1946. Reprinted in Bell, C. G., and Newell, A., *Computer Structures: Readings and Examples,* McGraw-Hill, NY, 1971.

CICHELLI, R. J., "Minimal Perfect Hash Functions Made Simple," *Communications of the ACM,* Vol. 23, No. 1, January 1980.

References and Bibliography

CLARK, R., and KOEHLER, S., *The UCSD Pascal Handbook,* Prentice-Hall, Englewood Cliffs, NJ, 1982.

COFFMAN, E. G., and HOFRI, M., "On Scanning Disks and the Analysis of Their Steady State Behavior," *Proceedings of the Conference on Measuring, Modelling and Evaluating Computer Systems,* North Holland, NY, October 1982.

COMER, D., "The Ubiquitous B-Tree," *ACM Computing Surveys,* June 1979, pp. 121–137.

COMPUTING REVIEWS, *ACM Computing Reviews,* January 1982.

COOPER, D., *Standard Pascal: User Reference Manual,* W. W. Norton, NY, 1983.

FELLER, W., *An Introduction to Probability Theory and Its Applications,* Wiley, NY, 1950.

FORSYTHE, G. E., MALCOLM, M. A., and MOLER, C. B., *Computer Methods for Mathematical Computations,* Prentice-Hall, Englewood Cliffs, NJ, 1977.

GRAHAM, R. L., and PAVOL, H., "On the History of the Minimum Spanning Tree Problem," *Annals of the History of Computing,* January 1985, pp. 43–57.

GRIES, D., "Current Ideas in Programming Methodology," in *Research Directions in Software Technology,* P. Wegener (Ed.), MIT Press, Cambridge, MA, 1979, pp. 254–275.

GUTTAG, J. V., "Abstract Data Types and the Development of Data Structures," *Communications of the ACM,* Vol. 20, No. 6, June 1977.

HAKEN, W., "An Attempt to Understand the Four-Color Problem," *Journal of Graph Theory,* Vol. 1, No. 3, 1977, pp. 193–206.

HALL, A. V. P., and DOWLING, G. P., "Approximate String Matching," *Computing Surveys,* December 1980, pp. 381–402.

HALSTEAD, M., *Elements of Software Science,* Elsevier–North Holland, NY, 1977.

HILL, F. J., and PETERSON, G. R., *Introduction to Switching Theory and Logical Design,* Wiley, NY, 1968.

HOARE, C. A. R., "Quicksort," *Computer Journal,* April 1962, pp. 10–15.

HOFRI, M., "Disk Scheduling: FCFS vs. SSTF Revisited," *Communications of the ACM,* Vol. 23, No. 11, November 1980.

HORSEPOOL, R. N., "Practical Fast Searching in Strings," *Software—Practice and Experience,* Vol. 10, 1980, pp. 501–506.

HU, T. C., *Combinatorial Algorithms,* Addison-Wesley, Reading, MA, 1981.

HUANG, B., and LANGSTON, M. A., "Practical In-place Merging," *Communications of the ACM,* 1988, pp. 348–354.

HUME, A., and SUNDAY, D., "Fast String Searching," *Software—Practice and Experience,* November 1991.

IEEE, Standard Pascal Computer Programming Language, ANSI/IEEE 770 X3.97-1983, The Institute of Electrical and Electronic Engineers, 1983.

JAESCHKE, G., "Reciprocal Hashing—A Method for Generating Minimal Perfect Hashing Functions," *Communications of the ACM,* Vol. 24, No. 12, December 1981.

JENSEN, K., and WIRTH, N., *PASCAL User Manual and Report,* Springer-Verlag, NY, 1974.

JIANG, B., "Deadlock Detection Is Really Cheap," *SIGMOD Record,* June 1988, pp. 2–13.

JONES, T. C., "Programming Quality and Productivity: An Overview of the State of the Art," ITT Programming Technology Center, Stratford, CT, 1981.

KARLGREN, H., "Representation of Text Strings in Binary Computers," *BIT,* 1963, pp. 52–59.

KERNIGHAN, B. W., and RITCHIE, D. M., *The C Programming Language,* 2nd Edition, Prentice–Hall, Englewood Cliffs, NJ, 1988.

KING, K. N., *Modula-2: A Complete Guide,* D. C. Heath and Company, Lexington, MA, 1988.

KNUTH, D. E., *The Art of Computer Programming: Fundamental Algorithms,* Vol. 1, 2nd Edition, Addison-Wesley, Reading, MA, 1973a.

KNUTH, D. E., *The Art of Computer Programming: Sorting and Searching,* Vol. 3, Addison-Wesley, Reading, MA, 1973b.

KNUTH, D. E., MORRIS, J. H., and PRATT, V. R., "Fast Pattern Matching in Strings," *SIAM Journal on Computing,* June 1977, pp. 323–349.

LAKSHMANAN, K. B., JAYAPRAHASH, S., and SINHA, P. K., "Properties of Control-Flow Complexity Measures," *IEEE Transactions on Software Engineering,* Vol. 17, No. 12, December 1991, pp. 1289–1295.

LARSON, P., "Expected Worst-Case Performance of Hash Files," *Computer Journal,* August 1982, pp. 347–352.

LISKOV, B. H., SNYDER, A., ATKINSON, R., and SCHAFFERT, C., "Abstraction Mechanisms in CLU," *Communications of the ACM,* Vol. 20, No. 8, August 1977.

LISKOV, B. H., and ZILLES, S. N., "Specification Techniques for Data Abstractions," *IEEE Transactions on Software Engineering,* Vol. 1, No. 1, 1975.

LUM, V. Y., YUEN, P. S. T., and DODD, M., "Key-to-Address Transform Techniques: A Fundamental Performance Study on Large Existing Formatted Files," *Communications of the ACM,* April 1971, pp. 228–239.

MACLANE, B., and BIRKHOFF, G., *Algebra,* Macmillan, NY, 1967.

MATICK, R. E., *Computer Storage Systems and Technology,* Wiley, NY, 1977.

McCABE, T. J., "A Complexity Measure," *IEEE Transactions on Software Engineering,* Vol. SE-2, No. 4, 1976, pp. 308–320.

McCabe, T. J., and Butler, C. W., "Design Complexity Measurement and Testing," *Communications of the ACM,* Vol. 32, No. 12, December 1989, pp. 1415–1425.

Mitchell, J. G., Maybury, W., and Sweet, R., "Mesa Language Manual," Version 5.0, CSL 79-3, XEROX, Palo Alto Research Center, Systems Development Department, Palo Alto, CA, 1979.

Motzkin, D., "Meansort," *Communications of the ACM,* April 1983, pp. 250–251.

Myers, G. J., *Advances in Computer Architecture,* 2nd Edition, Wiley, NY, 1982.

Nievergelt, J., "Binary Search Trees and File Organization," *Computing Surveys,* September 1974, pp. 195–207.

OMSI Pascal-1 VI.2, *User's Guide,* Oregon Software, 2340 S.W. Canyon Road, Portland, OR, 1980.

Paice, C. D., "Information Retrieval and the Computer," *MacDonald and Jane's Computer Monographs,* London, 1977.

Pascal/MT +, "Language Reference and Applications Guide," Release 5.1.

Pearson, P. K., "Fast Hashing of Variable-Length Text Strings," *Communications of the ACM,* Vol. 33, No. 6, June 1990.

Perlis, A. J., Sayward, F. G., and Shaw, M. (Eds.), *Software Metrics: An Analysis and Evaluation,* MIT Press, Cambridge, MA, 1981.

Radke, C. E., "The Use of Quadratic Residue Research," *Communications of the ACM,* February 1970, pp. 103–105.

Reingold, E. M., and Hansen, W. S., *Data Structures in Pascal,* Little, Brown, 1986.

Rivest, R., "On Self-Organizing Sequential Search Heuristics," *Communications of the ACM,* Vol. 19, No. 2, February 1976.

Sack, J.-R., and Strothotte, T., "An Algorithm for Merging Heaps," *Acta Informatica,* June 1985, pp. 171–186.

Sale, A. H. J., "Strings and the Sequence Abstraction in Pascal," *Software—Practice and Experience,* Vol. 9, 1979, pp. 671–683.

Sedgewick, R., "Implementing Quicksort Programs," *Communications of the ACM,* Vol. 21, No. 10, October 1978, pp. 847–856.

Sedgewick, R., *Algorithms,* 2nd Edition, Addison-Wesley, Reading, MA, 1988.

Sedgewick, R., *Algorithms in C,* Addison-Wesley, Reading, MA, 1990.

Shaw, M., "The Impact of Abstraction Concerns on Modern Programming Languages," Carnegie-Mellon University, Computer Science Technical Report CMU-CS-80-116, 1980.

Shen, V. Y., Conte, S. D., and Dunsmore, H. E., "Software Science Revisited: A Critical Analysis of the Theory and Its Empirical Support," *IEEE Transactions on Software Engineering,* Vol. SE-9, No. 2, March 1983, pp. 155–165.

Signum Newsletter, "The Proposed IEEE Floating-Point Standard," Special Issue of the ACM Special Interest Group on Numerical Mathematics, October 1979.

Sipala, P. "Optimum Cell Size for the Storage of Messages," *IEEE Transactions on Software Engineering,* January 1981, pp. 132–134.

Smit, G. De V., "A Comparison of Three String Matching Algorithms," *Software—Practice and Experience,* Vol. 12, 1982, pp. 57–66.

Smith, P. D., "Experiments with a Very Fast Substring Search Algorithm," *Software—Practice and Experience,* October 1991.

Sprugnoli, R., "A Single Probe Retrieving Method for Static Sets," *Communications of the ACM,* Vol. 20, No. 11, November 1977.

Stanat, D. F., and McAllister, D. F., *Discrete Mathematics in Computer Science,* Prentice-Hall, Englewood Cliffs, NJ, 1977.

Standish, T. A., *Data Structure Techniques,* Addison-Wesley, Reading, MA, 1980.

Stoll, R. R., *Sets, Logic, and Axiomatic Theories,* W. H. Freeman, San Francisco, 1961.

Tanenbaum, A. S., *Structured Computer Organization,* Series in Automatic Computation, Prentice-Hall, Englewood Cliffs, NJ, 1976.

Tanner, M. R., "Minimean Merging and Sorting: An Algorithm," *SIAM J. Computing,* 1978, pp. 18–38.

Tyner, P., *iAPX General Data Processor Architecture Reference Manual,* Order No. 171860-001, Intel Corporation, Santa Clara, CA, 1981.

United States Department of Defense, *Reference Manual for the Ada Programming Language,* ANSI/MIL-STD-1815A-1983, 1983.

Vaucher, J., "Pretty Printing of Trees," *Software—Practice and Experience,* Vol. 10, 1980, pp. 553–561.

Vitter, J. S., "Implementations for Coalesced Hashing," *Communications of the ACM,* December 1982, pp. 911–926.

Vitter, J. S., "Analysis of the Search Performance of Coalesced Hashing," *Journal of the ACM,* April 1983, pp. 231–258.

von Neumann, 1946; see Burke, 1946.

Wainwright, R. L., "A Class of Sorting Algorithms Based on Quicksort," *Communications of the ACM,* April 1985, pp. 396–403.

Wiederhold, G., *Database Design,* 2nd Edition, McGraw-Hill, NY, 1983.

Wirth, *Algorithms + Data Structures = Programs,* Prentice-Hall, Englewood Cliffs, NJ, 1976.

Wirth, N., *MODULA-2,* Report No. 36, Eidgenoessische Technische Hochschule, Institut für Informatik, Zurich, 1980.

Wirth, N., *Algorithms & Data Structures,* Prentice-Hall, Englewood Cliffs, NJ, 1986.

WRIGHT, W. E., "Some Average Performance Measures for the B-Tree," *Acta Informatica,* March 1985, pp. 541–557.

WULF, W. A., LONDON, R. L., and SHAW, M., "An Introduction to the Construction and Verification of Alphard Programs," *IEEE Transactions on Software Engineering,* SE-2, No. 4, December 1976.

YAO, A. C., and YAO, F. F., "The Complexity of Searching an Ordered Random Table," *Proceedings of the Conference on the Foundations of Computer Science,* Houston, TX, October 1976, p. 173.

Index

1. Redesign the linked list specification to hide the *linked_list, node,* and *node_access* types, and provide the operations on the list (Figure 4.6) as functions and procedures.

2. Use the linked list package (Specification 4.2) to build an implementation of the simple list package (Package Body 4.1).

3. Add operations to the linked list abstraction (Specification 4.2 and Package Body 4.2) that

    a. Exchange a node with its predecessor in the list by relinking the nodes.
    b. Exchange a node with its successor in the list by relinking the nodes.

4. Design, implement, and test a doubly linked list data type analogous to Specification 4.2 and Package Body 4.2 for singly linked lists.

4.4 Indexed and Mapped Lists

This section concerns lists whose objects have an associated or embedded value that allows the objects to be accessed efficiently by specifying the value. The objects in indexed lists have associated positions in the list, whereas the objects in mapped lists have embedded keys. Specifying the position or key uniquely determines which object of the list is being referenced. Sections 4.4.1 and 4.4.2 discuss these two list types.

4.4.1 Indexed Lists

A list is an ***indexed list*** if some of its operations allow actions on the list that are based on positions in the list. Recall that one of the aspects of linearity is that we can pair the objects of the list one to one with integers starting with, for example, 1 for the head or first object, and pairing successive integers with successive objects of the list until the last list object is paired with n, the number of objects in the list. We call the integer with which an object is paired the object's ***position***.

Suppose we have an operation

procedure delete (the_list : **in out** indexed_list; at_index : positive);

that removes (deletes) the ith object from a list, where $i = at\_index$. The operation is based on position since that is the way the object to be removed is identified.

Specification 4.3 is the specification of a list that has the property of being indexed. It has operations that are somewhat different from the operations of the basic list given in Specification 4.1. The intent is to show not only the indexing property but also some of the possible variations in operating on linear structures. We'll see even more variety in other types of lists.

One significant operation that was added is the *change* function, which allows changes to specified objects that are in the list. An object is denoted by its position. The same is true with the other operations of the type.

■ SPECIFICATION 4.3   Indexed Lists

-- *Structure:* A set of objects of a user-specified type where the objects are ordered linearly.
--   Each list object is associated with an integer; the first (head) list object is associated
--   with 1. Each other list object is associated with an integer that is one greater than the
--   integer associated with its predecessor in the list.
-- *Constraints:*   0 <= number_of_objects <= max_size.   -- list_size and max_size appear below.

generic

    type object_type **is private**;   -- Type of objects in the list.

package indexed_list_package **is**

    type indexed_list (max_size : positive) **is limited private**;

    list_full   : **exception**;
    list_empty   : **exception**;
    faulty_position   : **exception**;

    procedure insert (the_list   : **in out** indexed_list;
                    at_index   : positive;
                    the_object : object_type);
-- *results:*   The object is inserted into the_list at position at_index; all list objects following the
--   object are at positions one greater than before the insertion.
--*exceptions:*   A faulty_position exception is raised if at_index > number_of_objects(the_list) + 1.
--   A list_full exception is raised if number_of_objects(the_list) = max_size.
-- *notes:*   At_index can be one greater than number_of_objects(the_list) to allow appending new objects to the end of the list.

    function list_object (the_list : indexed_list; at_index : positive) **return** object_type;
-- *results:*   Returns a copy of the object of the list at position at_index.
-- *exceptions:*   A faulty_position exception is raised if at_index > number_of_objects(the_list).

    procedure delete (the_list : **in out** indexed_list; at_index : positive);
-- *results:*   The object at position at_index is deleted from the list; all objects following it
--   take positions one less than before the deletion.
-- *exceptions:*   A faulty_position exception is raised if at_index > number_of_objects(the_list).

    procedure change (the_list   : **in out** indexed_list;
                   at_index   : positive;
                   the_object : object_type);
-- *results:*   The object in the list at position at_index is changed to the new value the_object.
-- *exceptions:*   A faulty_position exception is raised if at_index > number_of_objects(the_list).

    procedure clear (the_list : **in out** indexed_list);
-- *results:*   number_of_objects(the_list) is 0.

    function number_of_objects (the_list : indexed_list) **return** natural;
-- *results:*   Returns the number of objects in the list.

(continued)

Specification 4.3 (continued)

private

    type array_of_objects **is array** (positive **range** <>) **of** object_type;

    type indexed_list (max_size : positive) **is record**
      size   : natural;
      objects   : array_of_objects (1 .. max_size);
    end record;

end indexed_list_package;

Implementation of the specification is straightforward. An array of objects is ideal for storing the list since arrays have the property of being efficiently indexed.

Package Body 4.3 is an implementation of Specification 4.3. It uses discriminent records and arrays.

■ PACKAGE BODY 4.3 Indexed Lists—Implements Specification 4.3

```
package body indexed_list_package is

    procedure insert (the_list     : in out indexed_list;
                      at_index     : positive;
                      the_object   : object_type) is
-- Length 9   Complexity 4   Performance O(n)
    begin
        if      the_list.size = 0              then  the_list.size := 1;
                                                     the_list.objects(1) := the_object;
        elsif   at_index > the_list.size + 1    then raise faulty_position;
        elsif   the_list.size = the_list.max_size  then raise list_full;
        else    the_list.objects(at_index + 1 .. the_list.size + 1)
                            := the_list.objects(at_index .. the_list.size);
                the_list.objects(at_index) := the_object;
                the_list.size := the_list.size + 1;
        end if;
    end insert;

    function list_object (the_list : indexed_list; at_index : positive) return object_type is
-- Length 4   Complexity 2   Perfomance O(1)
    begin
        if at_index > the_list.size
            then raise faulty_position;
            else return the_list.objects(at_index);
        end if;
    end list_object;
```

(continued)

Package Body 4.3 (continued)

```
procedure delete (the_list : in out indexed_list; at_index : positive) is
-- Length 5   Complexity 2   Performance O(n)
begin
  if at_index > the_list.size
    then raise faulty_position;
    else  the_list.objects(at_index .. the_list.size − 1)
                        := the_list.objects(at_index + 1 .. the_list.size);
          the_list.size := the_list.size − 1;
  end if;
end delete;

procedure change (the_list    : in out indexed_list;
                  at_index    : positive;
                  the_object  : object_type) is
-- Length 5   Complexity 2   Performance O(1)
begin
  if at_index > the_list.size
    then raise faulty_position;
    else the_list.objects(at_index) := the_object;
  end if;
end change;

procedure clear (the_list : in out indexed_list) is
-- Length 1   Complexity 1   Performance O(1)
begin
  the_list. size := 0;
end clear;

function number_of_objects (the_list : indexed_list) return natural is
-- Length 1   Complexity 1   Performance O(1)
begin
  return the_list.size;
end number_of_objects;

end indexed_list_package;
```

The list is held in an array *objects* [Figure 4.8(a)]. Figure 4.8 shows the sequence of actions necessary to insert a new object into the interior of the list. If the insertion is at position i, then the list objects in the range $i .. n$ (n = list size) have to be shifted to make room for the new object. The new object is subsequently inserted into the vacated space at position i. Assuming each position is an equally likely target for an insertion, the expected number of objects to be moved is

$$[n + (n − 1) + (n − 2) + \cdots + 1 + 0]/(n + 1) = n/2 \sim O(n)$$

Therefore, we can conclude that the *insert* operation has an expected performance of $O(n)$.